# The Evolution and Everyday Practice of Collective Patient Involvement in Europe

Alexander Haarmann

# The Evolution and Everyday Practice of Collective Patient Involvement in Europe

## An Examination of Policy Processes, Motivations, and Implementations in Four Countries

Springer

Alexander Haarmann
NIVEL
Utrecht
The Netherlands

ISBN 978-3-319-64594-0 ISBN 978-3-319-64595-7 (eBook)
DOI 10.1007/978-3-319-64595-7

Library of Congress Control Number: 2017950210



Printed on acid-free paper

This Springer imprint is published by Springer Nature
The registered company is Springer International Publishing AG
The registered company address is: Gewerbestrasse 11, 6330 Cham, Switzerland

# Summary/ Samenvatting/ Zusammenfassung/ Sammanfattning


## Introduction

This study deals with the development of collective patient involvement in the Netherlands, England, Germany, and Sweden. Starting point for this study is on the one hand the theoretical classification of the Dutch and the English healthcare system as completely different regarding funding, organisation, and governance. On the other hand, this is contrasted by the observation that both countries have legislated a virtually identical form of collective patient involvement at hospitals with identical competences. With discussions on the topic emerging at the same time, the question is, what factors contributed to this development or hampered it in other countries?

## Theory and Methodology

As laws (not only) regarding patient involvement are passed in parliament, this is the arena in focus of this study. The aim of the theoretical part, then, is to some extent to guide the search for factors of influence. It is mainly comprised of two components: First, a variant of the ideational approaches in order to answer the question whether or not the path hitherto pursued still gives satisfactory answers to the perceived problems and where new ideas stem from. The second component is the 'actor-centred institutionalism', which is employed in order to bring in institutional path dependency as well as actors' preferences, interests, powers, and relations between them. Both parts can be understood to contribute to an ideal-typical sequential model of policy processes.

The study has an exploratory, qualitative, and comparative case study design. In order not to fall for any random factor that only appears to have influenced the policy process, two additional countries were sought that match the English and Dutch healthcare system well, namely, Sweden and Germany. Next to academic literature, green and white papers, legal texts and regulations, expert interviews, and parliamentary minutes comprised the main sources. The categories found were based upon single codes, which were derived by selective and open coding.

## Results

In summary, all four countries have developed their own particular ways of patient involvement, which do not converge. The countries can be categorised as having their focus on involvement at the provision level (England and the Netherlands) or at the policy level (Germany and Sweden). Each case has followed its highly individual path with mostly politicians as the main drivers for legislative changes. Their main motives range from more democratisation, through the adaptation of sickness funds to a system of marketised healthcare insurance, and more independence and accountability of hospitals to sticking to self-governance in social insurances as the main mode of involvement. The search for a new leitmotif for the governance of the healthcare sector can be discerned as the common factor for the Netherlands and England. The analysis shows that more attention should be paid to different stances among complex actors—such as political parties—and the actors' perception as a potentially decisive factor in the political process.

Eventually, a new model of the policy process can be derived. The analysis resulted in four abstract factors as the main distinguishing points within this process: (a) the framing of the problem at hand; (b) the constellation, context, relation, etc. in the political realm; (c) the relation and influence of other actors as well as; a (d) the persistence of existing institutions.

# Samenvatting

## Inleiding

Dit boek analyseert de veranderingen van collectieve medezeggenschap in Nederland, Engeland, Duitsland en Zweden. Het uitgangspunt van deze studie is aan de ene kant de totaal verschillende theoretische indeling van Nederland en Engeland ten opzichte van de financiering, de organisatie en het bestuur van het zorgstelsel. Aan de andere kant is er de observatie dat beide landen een wettelijke regeling kennen met bijna identieke vormen en rechten van collectieve medezeggenschap van patiënten in ziekenhuizen. Aangezien de discussie over het thema medezeggenschap gelijkertijd ontstaan is in beide landen is de vraag welke factoren deze ontwikkeling hebben bevordert of – in andere landen – hebben geremd.

## Theorie en Methodologie

Het zijn de politici die wetten aannemen met betrekking tot collectieve medezeggenschap, en daarom plaatst deze studie het parlement in het middelpunt. Het theoretische deel heeft als doel richting te geven aan de zoektocht naar invloedfactoren. Het bestaat uit twee componenten: Ten eerste, een variant van een ideële aanpak om na te gaan of het pad dat tot nu toe is bewandeld nog steeds gewenste oplossingen op waargenomen problemen biedt biedt en hoe nieuwe ideeën ontstaan. De tweede component is 'acteur gecentreerde institutionalisme', wat zowel de institutionele padafhankelijkheid, als ook voorkeuren, belangen, en macht van de acteuren, alsmede de onderlinge relaties omvat. Beide componenten zullen bijdragen aan een ideaaltypisch, stapsgewijs model van het beleidsprocess.

De studie heeft een exploratief, kwalitatief en vergelijkend ontwerp. Om het risico te vermijden onzuivere conclusies te trekken op basis van toevallige factoren, zijn twee aanvullende landen, die vergelijkbaar zijn met het Nederlandse en Engelse zorgstelsel, aan de studie toegevoegd: Duitsland voor de vergelijking met Nederland en Zweden voor de vergelijking met Engeland. Naast wetenschappelijke literatuur vormen parlementaire nota's, teksten van wetten en verordeningen, parlementaire handelingen en interviews met deskundigen de belangrijkste bronnen van deze studie. De afgeleide categorieën zijn gebaseerd op selectief en open coderen.

## Resultaten

De belangrijkste uitkomsten kunnen worden samengevat als dat alle vier de landen hun eigen vorm van medezeggenschap hebben ingevoerd en er geen convergentie plaatsgevonden heeft. De landen kunnen worden ingedeeld in twee groepen: Nederland en Engeland, die de focus leggen op medezeggenschap van zorgverleners, en Duitsland en Zweden, waar de focus op het beleidsniveau rust. Ieders casus heeft daarbij zijn eigen individuele pad gevolgd, waarbij meestal politici de voornamelijkste sturende factor waren voor wetgevende veranderingen. De belangrijkste motivatie varieerde tussen de wens voor meer democratisering in de zorg, aanpassing van patiëntenrechten in verband met de veranderingen van het zorgstelsel, meer onafhankelijkheid en verantwoordelijkheid van ziekenhuizen, en het vasthouden aan het corporatistische zelfbestuur. Het zoeken naar een nieuw leidmotief voor het besturen van de zorgsector is een gezamelijke factor in Nederland en Engeland. De analyse toont aan dat verschillende standpunten binnen complexe acteuren – zoals bijvoorbeeld politieke partijen – en het perspectief van deze acteuren als mogelijk doorslaggevende factoren, meer aandacht zouden moeten krijgen.

Uiteindelijk kan een nieuw beleidsproces worden afgeleid. De analyse resulteert in vier abstracte factoren, die de verschillen tussen de respectieve landen het best weergeven: a) Het kader van actuele problemen, b) de constellatie, de context, de relatie etc. in het politieke domein, c) de relatie en de invloed van andere factoren en d) de standvastigheid van bestaande instellingen.

## Zusammenfassung

## Einleitung

Dieses Buch behandelt die Veränderungen kollektiver Patientenbeteiligung in den Niederlanden, England, Deutschland und Schweden. Ausgangspunkt dieser Studie ist einerseits die theoretische Klassifizierung des niederländischen und des englischen Gesundheitssystems als sehr unterschiedlich im Hinblick auf die Finanzierung, die Organisation und die Governance. Andererseits steht dem die Beobachtung gegenüber, dass beide Länder Gesetze über eine fast identische Form der kollektiven Patientenbeteiligung in Krankenhäusern mit nahezu identischen Rechten erlassen haben. Da zudem die Diskussion über das Thema Patientenbeteiligung zur gleichen Zeit entstand, stellt sich die Frage, welche Faktoren identifiziert werden können, die zu dieser Entwicklung beigetragen – oder, in anderen Ländern, sie behindert – haben.

## Theorie und Methodologie

Es sind Politker, die Gesetze (nicht nur) bezüglich Patientenbeteiligung verabschieden, weshalb die Studie auf diese Arena fokussiert. Das Ziel des theoretischen Teils ist es deshalb, die Suche nach Einflussfaktoren zu einem gewissen Teil zu leiten. Der theoretische Teil besteht aus einer Variante der ideenbasierten Ansätze – um die Frage zu beantworten, ob der Pfad, der bisher beschritten wurde, immer noch zufriedenstellende Antworten auf wahrgenommene Probleme gibt und woher neue Ideen stammen – und dem ‚akteursbasierten Institutionalismus' – um sowohl die institutionelle Pfadabhängigkeit als auch die Präferenzen, Interessen, Macht der Akteure und deren Beziehungen untereinander einzubeziehen. Beide Teile können als Beitrag dazu verstanden werden, zu einem idealtypischen, sequentiellen Modell des Policy-Prozesses beizutragen.

Die Studie ist als exploratives, qualitatives und vergleichendes Fallstudiendesign ausgelegt. Um nicht falschen Schlussfolgerungen aufgrund ausschließlich zufälliger Faktoren aufzusitzen, die Einfluss auf den Gesetzgebungsprozess hatten, wurde nach zwei weiteren Ländern gesucht, die das englische und niederländische Gesundheitssystem spiegeln. Diese wurden aus Gründen der Ähnlichkeit in Schweden und Deutschland gefunden. Neben der wissenschaftlichen Literatur, Grün- und Weißbüchern, Gesetzestexten und Verordnungen, machten Experteninterviews und

Parlamentsprotokolle die Hauptquellen aus. Die gefundenen Kategorien basieren auf den einfachen Codes, die durch selektives und offenes Kodieren gefunden wurden.

## Ergebnisse

Als Hauptergebnisse können zusammengefasst werden, dass alle vier Länder ihre eigene Form der Patientenbeteiligung gefunden haben und in dieser Hinsicht keine Konvergenz stattfindet. Die Länder können in zwei Gruppen kategorisiert werden: England und die Niederlanden, die den Fokus auf Beteiligung auf Leistungserbringerebene legen, und Deutschland und Schweden, die ihn auf die politische Ebene legen. Jeder Fall ist seinem höchst individuellen Pfad gefolgt, auf dem vor allem Politiker die Haupttriebkraft für die Gesetzgebung waren. Die Hauptmotivation reichte dabei von einem Wunsch zur Demokratisierung, ging über die Anpassung des Systems an eine marktliche Krankenversicherung, stärkere Unabhängigkeit und Accountability von Krankenhäusern, bis hin zum Festhalten an der Selbstverwaltung in den Sozialversicherungen als hauptsächliche Beteiligungsform. Die Suche nach einem neuen Leitmotiv kann für die Regierungen in den Niederlanden und England ausgemacht werden. Die Analyse macht deutlich, dass komplexe Akteure – wie z. B. politische Parteien – differenzierter nach unterschiedlichen Standpunkten *innerhalb* betrachtet werden sollten und die Wahrnehmung der Akteure als möglicherweise entscheidender Faktor im politischen Prozess angesehen werden kann.

Letztlich kann ein neues Modell des Policy-Prozesses gewonnen werden. Die Analyse resultiert in vier abstrakten Faktoren, die die Differenzen in den Ländern am besten benennen: a) Die Rahmung des aktuellen Problems, b) die Konstellation, der Kontext, die Beziehung usw. im politischen Bereich, c) die Beziehung und der Einfluss anderer Faktoren sowie d) die Beharrlichkeit bestehender Institutionen.

# Sammanfattning

## Inledning

Denna studie analyserar förändringarna av kollektiv patientmedverkan i Nederländerna, England, Tyskland och Sverige. Utgångspunkt är å ena sidan den teoretiska klassifikationen av den nederländska samt den engelska hälso- och sjukvården som är helt olikartade med hänsyn till finansiering, organisation och styrning. Å andra siden är denna indelning kontrasterad med iakttagelsen att både länderna har lagstiftat nästan identiska former av patientmedverkan vid sjukhus med nästan samma rättigheter. Om man vet att diskussionen om att ge patienterna större inflytande över vården dök upp vid samma tid är frågan, vilka faktorer har bidragit till respektive bromsat denna utveckling i andra länder.

## Teori och metodologi

Det är politiker som lagstadgar lag, varför de står i fokus för denna studie. Ändamålet med den teoretiska delen är, i viss mån, att leda sökandet efter inflytelsefaktorer. Den består främst av en variant av idébaserade ansatser – för att svara på frågan om det hittills gångna spåret (se spårbundenhet/ path dependency) fortfarande ger tillfredställande svar på upplevda problem och var nya idéer härrör. Den andra är 'aktörscentrerad institutionalism' – för att visa såväl institutionell spårbundenhet som aktörers preferenser, intressen, makt samt inbördes relationer. Båda parter kan tänkas bidra till en idealtypisk modell av policyprocessen.

Undersökningen följer en explorativ, kvalitativ och jämförande studiedesign. För att inte undgå att upptäcka slumpartade faktorer, som endast verkar ha påverkat policyprocessen, söktes ytterligare två länder vars hälso- och sjukvårdssystem liknar jämförelseländernas hälso- och sjukvårdssystem. Valet föll på Sverige och Tyskland. Vid sidan om vetenskaplig litteratur, green och white papers, lagtexter och förordningar, utgör expertintervjuer och parlamentsprotokoll huvudkällorna. Kategorierna som arbetades fram under analysprocessen baseras på enstaka koder som vunnits ur selektiv och öppen kodning.

## Resultat

En sammanfattning av huvudresultatet visar att alla fyra länder har utvecklat sin egen form av patientmedverkan som inte konvergerar med varandra. Länderna kan kategoriseras i två olika klasser: De som fokuserar på medverkan i sjukvårdsorganisationer (England och Nederländerna) och de som fokuserar på medverkan i den politiska beslutsprocessen (Sverige och Tyskland). Varje fall har följt sitt högst individuella spår där det oftast var politikerna som utgjorde drivkraften bakom lagförändringar. Deras huvudmotiv utgjordes av allt från att stärka demokratin, anpassning till ett affärsliknande sjukvårdsförsäkringssystem till mer oberoende och lyssnande sjukhus samt en vilja att hålla fast vid självstyrelsen inom de sociala försäkringarna. Sökandet efter ett nytt huvudmotiv för styrningen inom hälso- och sjukvården kan anses vara den gemensamma faktorn för Nederländerna och England. Analysen förtydligar att framtida studier borde ta mer hänsyn till olika opinioner inom 'komplexa aktörer' – såsom t. ex. politiska partier – och att dessa aktörers uppfattning kan vara den avgörande faktorn för förståelsen av policyprocessen.

Så småningom kan en ny modell för den politiska processen erhållas. Analysen resulterade i fyra abstrakta faktorer som utgör den främsta skillnaden inom den politiska processen i respektive länder: a) inramning av problemet i fokus, b) konstellation, kontext samt relationer m. m. inom det politiska fältet, c) relation och inflytande av andra aktörer samt d) den utnyttjade motståndspotentialen hos redan existerande institutioner.

# Acknowledgements: The Jigsaw Puzzle

As with jigsaw puzzles and its pieces, it is with people during a research project. Whether they contribute with an important detail or with an overall idea or whether they provide a seemingly unimportant part, without the help of each of them, a huge number of pieces would be missing—and everyone knows how disturbing the wooden brown gap of a table below can be in an otherwise splendid picture of pure blue sky in a jigsaw puzzle!

In that sense, and even though I bear the full responsibility for any kind of mistakes and errors that may be found in this book, I would first of all like to thank my interviewees without whom a major source of information and a good deal of insight would be missing! It were sometimes affirmative, sometimes eye-opening conversations, which at first sight sometimes did not seem to have too much to do with the topic at hand. However, in the end all of them were interesting and important for the outcome!

Ninni Mäki transcribed the Swedish and Antonia Weinrich the German interviews. Britta Baumgarten and in particular Anne-Katharina Koch cross-checked the coding of interviews. Ninni Mäki, Jolanda van der Noll, and Amy Potappel took a thorough look at the language mistakes to be found in the respective summaries. Ralf Götze, Philine Weyrauch-Herrmann, and Caroline Warfelmann helped with comments and remarks to increase the readability and plausibility of the different chapters as did Konstanze Haarmann, who also thoroughly and patiently checked the bibliography and formatting. Daniel Smith undertook the overall correction of language-related mistakes. Many thanks to all of you!

In the *Dutch* part of my jigsaw puzzle, I got several pieces and help in sorting them from Sandra van Beek, Ilse Haverkamp, Hans Maarse, and Frans van Waarden. *Een bijzonder dank* goes to Peter Groenewegen, who hosted me at Netherlands institute for health services research (NIVEL), always had a good suggestion at hand, who always knew whom to contact or where to look things up!

In the *English* part of my picture, I would like to thank Marian Barnes, Seán Boyle, Colin Campbell, Antonia Kearton, Bernhard Kittel, Stefan Leibfried, Jane Lewis, Ulrich Sedelmeier, Heide Weishaar, and John Wilkes for their part in helping me to make my stay in the UK a successful one by—amongst other things—talking to people, organising administrative things, or simply having an interesting conversation! A warm thanks goes to Joan Costa-i-Font and Waltraud Schelkle at the London School of Economics and Political Sciences (LSE) as well as to Richard Freeman at the University of Edinburgh, who facilitated my field research in the UK. A very special thanks goes to Christine Hogg and Naomi Chambers! Without their advice and help my stay would have been definitively less fruitful than it turned out to be in the end!

For help on the *Swedish* part, I am grateful for various sorts of support from Tone Alm Andreassen, Karsten Vrangbæk, Emil Erdtman, Hanna Fagersjö, Christina Fleetwood, Peter Garpenby, Ann-Charlotte Nedlund, Anne Sjöberg, Caroline Åkerhielm, and Göran Sundqvist. *Ett jättestort tack* goes to Barbro Krevers, who undertook some efforts to host me at the department "*Medicin och hälsa*" at Linköping University, who took her valuable time to discuss things through, and who never got tired to lend me the specs to see Sweden from a Swedish perspective.

And there were the ones who accompanied me right from the start and kept the whole picture together: Heinz Rothgang, who never failed to remind me to focus on the larger picture and the commonalities between the four case studies. In addition, you contributed with ideas and contacts to find suitable interviewees for the German case study and facilitated the contact to the LSE. And Peter Groenewegen, who has always taken his time to read my drafts with an interested eye and to thoroughly discuss my concerns. Marking all suggested improvements and discussed points, be it in content, literature, or on the structural level, would run like a golden thread throughout the book; you have helped me to find my own way through the pile of pieces by not getting tired of providing me with guiding remarks, by pointing at the obvious and somewhat unobvious shortcomings of the several drafts. Next to them, Ralf Götze and Achim Schmidt had all the reason to be bored about the $x^{th}$ half-baked version of a draft but did not get tired to offer positive criticism.

Overall, such a complex project would not have been feasible without the institutional support of various kinds by Bremen International Graduate School of Social Sciences (BIGSSS), for which I would like to exemplarily mention the excellent work of the IT guys around Hartmut Asendorf, Jasmin Schmidt for the administrative part, and Olaf Groh-Samberg, who was field coordinator/ chair for most of my time at BIGSSS.

However, writing a thesis is about much more than just the research part. It is also about being socially embedded, having a good time with others at good times and finding a sympathetic ear in worse, and feeling supported and sustained by others, to simply know that there is someone there. Also in that respect, I would first of all like to thank my sister Konstanze and my mother, who have followed this—as any other—project with an interested eye and a supportive mind for years now. It is probably also to them I owe a good deal of the confidence that as long as there is a spark of reality in a new idea, even something as terribly crazy, tedious, demanding, and exciting as a doctoral dissertation can be done (cf. "*Laß meinen großen Bruder in Ruh'!*"). And, of course, there is a good number of friends and colleagues I would like to mention: Thomas Danell and Cornelia Appel-Walter,

Çetin Çelik, Carmen and Mayank Golpelwar, Philine Weyrauch-Herrmann, Katja Uglanova, Britta Baumgarten, Yvonne Burghardt, Anup S. Ninan, Alexandra and Imke Kaasch with their 'gang', Melanie Ahlemeier, Elma Laguna, Bianca Lehmann, and Caroline Warfelmann. Since this project drew out, there are also a number of colleagues in several projects that I felt supported by in various forms. In this respect, I would like to mention Achim Koch in place for the whole "German General Social Survey (GGSSS/ALLBUS)" team and in place for some colleagues at the Institute of Social Medicine and Health Economics Astrid Eich-Krohm, Wolfram Herrmann, and Bernt-Peter Robra. Anne Pierson and Anna Gallinat from EuroHealthNet and Katarzyna Mletzko for many people within the JA-CHRODIS shall not be missing in this list, with whom it was a pleasure to work with even during the most stressful days and who took a considerable part of the workload off in times I was finalising this manuscript!

For all the (motivating, inspiring, wonderful) conversations and nice time spent together, for being there, for...: Thank you so much for your help and support in whatever way I felt it!

*Hartelijk bedankt voor jullie hulp en steun!*
*Tusen tack för er hjälp och ert stöd!*
*Ganz vielen Dank für Eure Hilfe und Unterstützung!*
Cologne, Germany, March 2017

# Contents

# Abbreviations

| | |
|---|---|
| ÄDEL | Äldredelegationen – Delegation of the Care of the Elderly to the Municipalities |
| AOK | Allgemeine Ortskrankenkasse – General Local Sickness Fund |
| AOV | Dutch Party General Association of the Elderly |
| ARP | Anti-Revolutionaire Partij – Dutch Anti-revolutionary Party |
| ASB | Arbeitersamariterbund – German welfare organisation |
| AWBZ | Algmene Wet Bijzondere Ziektekosten – Exceptional Medical Expenses Act |
| B90/ Grüne | Bündnis 90/ Die Grünen – Germany's Green Party |
| BDA | Bundesvereinigung der Deutschen Arbeitgeberverbände – National Confederation of German Employers' Associations |
| BDI | Bundesverband der Deutschen Industrie – Federal Association of German Industry |
| BIVA | Bundesinteressenvertretung der Nutzerinnen und Nutzer von Wohn- und Betreuungsangeboten im Alter und bei Behinderung – Federal Interest Representation of Users of Housing and Care Facilities at Old Age and Handicap |
| CAMHS | Child and Adolescent Mental Health Services |
| CBS | Centraal Bureau voor de Statistiek – Central Statistical Office |
| CCG | Clinical Commissioning Groups |
| CD | Centrum Democraten – Dutch Centre Democrats |
| CDA | Christen Democratisch Appél – Christian Democratic Appeal |
| CDU/ CSU | Christlich Demokratische/ Soziale Union – Germany's christian democratics |
| CHAI | Commission for Healthcare Audit and Inspection |
| CHC | Community Health Council |
| CHI | Commission for Health Improvement |
| CIZ | Centrum Indicatiestelling Zorg – Centre for Needs Assessment |
| CNV | Christelijk Nationaal Vakverbond – Christian National Union Association |
| CPPIH | Commission for Patient and Public Involvement in Health |

| | |
|---|---|
| CR | Cliëntenraad – Client Council |
| CSCI | Commission for Social Care Inspection |
| CSU | Clinical Support Unit |
| CU | Christen Unie – The Dutch Christian Union Party |
| DGB | Deutscher Gewerkschaftsbund – German Confederation of Trade Unions |
| DH | Department of Health |
| DIHK | Deutscher Industrie- und Handelskammertag – Chamber of Industry and Commerce |
| DKG | Deutschen Krankenhausgesellschaft – German Hospital Society |
| DPWV | Deutscher Paritätischer Wohlfahrtsverband – German umbrella of numerous smaller welfare organisations |
| DTC | NHS Diagnostic and Treatment Centre – minor hospitals at the interface between NHS hospitals & community healthcare |
| FDP | Freie Demokratische Partei – Germany's Liberal Party |
| FNV | Federatie Nederlandse Vakbeweging – Federation Dutch Union Movement |
| FP | Folkpartiet – Swedish Conservative Centre Party |
| FT | NHS Foundation Trust Hospital |
| FTGA | Foundation Trust Governors' Association |
| FTN | Foundation Trust Network |
| G-BA/ GemBA | Gemeinsamer Bundesauschuss – Joint Federal Committee |
| GKV | Gesetzliche Krankenversicherung – Mandatory Sickness Fund |
| GMG | Gesundheitsmodernisierungsgesetz – Health Modernisation Act |
| GP | General Practitioner |
| GPV | Gereformeerd Politiek Verbond – Reformed Political Association |
| HC | Healthcare |
| HeimG | Heimgesetz – Home Act |
| HeimmwV | Heimmitwirkungsverordnung – Federal User Involvement Regulation for Long-term Care |
| HI | Historical Institutionalism |
| HSL | Hälso- och Sjukvårdslagen – Healthcare Act |
| HSO | Handikapporganisationernas Samarbetsorgan – Swedish Umbrella for Disability Organisations |
| ICAS | Independent Complaints Advocacy Service |
| IQWiG | Institut für Qualität und Wirtschaftlichkeit im Gesundheitswesen – Institute for Quality and Economy in Healthcare |
| KBV | Kassenärztliche Bundesvereinigung – Federal Association of Statutory Health Insurance Physicians |
| KD | Kristdemokraterna – Sweden's Christian Democratic Party |
| KL | Kommunallag – Municipality Act |

| | |
|---|---|
| KV | Kassenärztliche Vereinigung – Association of Statutory Health Insurance Physicians |
| KVP | Katholieke Volkspartij – Dutch Catholic Party |
| KZ | Kwaliteitswet Zorginstellingen – Quality Act for Care and Healthcare Institutions |
| KZBV | Kassenzahnärztliche Bundesvereinigung – Federal Association of Statutory Health Insurance Dentists |
| LF | Landstingsförbundet – Association of County Councils (predecessor of SKL) |
| LINks | Local Involvement Networks |
| LO | Landsorganisationen i Sverige – Swedish labour union umbrella for workers |
| LOBB | Landelijke Organisatie Bewonerscommissies Bejaardenhuizen – National Patient and Consumer Platform |
| LOC | Landelijke Organisatie Cliëntenraden – National Organisation of Client Councils – nowadays: LOC zeggenschap in zorg – LOC participation in (health-)care |
| LPF | (Politieke Vereniging) Lijst Pim Fortuyn – (Political Association) List Pim Fortuyn |
| LSR | Landelijke steunpunt (mede)zeggenschap – National Support Point Co-determination/ Involvement |
| LSS | Lag om stöd och service till vissa funktionshindrade – Act on Support and Service for Certain Disabled |
| M | Moderaterna/ Moderata Samlingspartiet – Sweden's Liberal Party |
| MBL | Medbestämmande i Arbeitslivet – Co-determination on the Work Place |
| MHP | Vakcentrale voor middengroepen en hoger personeel – Union centre for the middle class and higher personnel |
| MP | Member of Parliament |
| MP | Miljöpartiet de Gröna – the Swedish Green Party |
| NHS | National Health Service |
| NICE | National Institute for Health and Care Excellence |
| NPCF | Nederlandse Patiënten Consumenten Federatie – Dutch Patients Consumers Federation |
| NPD | Nationaldemokratische Partei Deutschland – German populist right-wing party |
| NPM | New Public Management |
| NRES | National Research Ethics Service |
| NSCS | National Care Standards Commission |
| NSPH | Nationell Samerkan för Psykisk Hälsa – National Collaboration for Mental Health |
| OSC | Overview and Scrutiny Committee |
| PALS | Patient Advice and Liaison Service |

| | |
|---|---|
| PatBeteiligungsV | Patientenbeteiligungsverordnung – Federal Patient Involvement Decree |
| PbR | Payment by Result |
| PCG | Primary Care Group |
| PCT | Primary Care Trust |
| PFI | Private Finance Initiative |
| PKV | Private Krankenversicherung – Private Health Insurance |
| PPI | Public and Patient Involvement |
| PPIF | Patient (and Public Involvement) Forum |
| PPR | Politieke Partij Radikalen – Dutch Political Party Radicals |
| PvdA | Partij van de Arbeid – The Dutch Social Democratic Party |
| PVV | Partij voor de Vrijheid – Dutch Party for Freedom |
| RHA | Regional Health Authority |
| RHS | Regional Health Service |
| RIAGG | Regionale Instelling voor Ambulante Geestelijke Gezondheidszorg – Regional Institution for Ambulatory Mental Care |
| RPF | Reformatorische Politieke Federatie – Reformatory Political Federation |
| RVZ | Raad voor de Volksgezondheid en Zorg – Council for Public Health and (Health-)Care |
| RWI | Raad voor Werk en Inkomen – Council on Work and Income |
| S/SAP | Socialdemokraterna/Sveriges Socialdemokratiska Arbetarpartiet – Sweden's Social-democratic Labour Party |
| SACO | Sveriges akademikers centralorganisation – Swedish labour union umbrella for academics and teachers |
| SBU | Statens beredning för medicinsk utvärdering – State authority of medical assessment |
| SD | Sverigedemokraterna – populist right-wing pary |
| SER | Sociaal-Economische Raad – Social-economic Council |
| SFS | Svensk Författningssammling – Swedish Constitutional Collection |
| SGB | Sozialgesetzbuch – Social Law |
| SGP | Staatskundig Gereformeerde Partij – Christian Reformed Party |
| SHA | Strategic Health Authority |
| SJ | Statens Järnvägar – Swedish Railsways |
| SKL | Sveriges kommuner och landsting – Swedish Association of Local Authorities and Regions (successor of LF) |
| SNS | Studieförbundet Näringsliv och Samhälle – Studies Network Economy and Society |
| SoL | Socialtjänstlagen – Social Services Act |
| SoS | Socialstyrelsen – The National Board of Health and Welfare |
| SoU | Socialutskott – Swedish Government's Social Committee |
| SOU | Statens offentliga utredningar – Reports of the Swedish Government Commissions |
| SP | Socialistische Partij – Dutch Socialist Party |

| | |
|---|---|
| SPD | Sozialdemokratische Partei Deutschlands – Germany's Social-democratic Party |
| SpiBu | Spitzenverband Bund der Krankenkassen – Central Federal Association of (Mandatory) Health Insurance Funds |
| TCO | Tjänstemännen Centralorganisation – Swedish labour union umbrella for civil servants |
| UPD | Unabhängige Patientenberatung Deutschland – Independent Patient Consultation |
| VGN | Vereniging Gehandicaptenzorg Nederland – Association of Mental Care Netherlands |
| VVD | Volkspartij voor Vrijheid en Democratie – The Dutch Liberal Party |
| VWS | Ministerie van Volksgezondheid, Welzijn en Sport – Ministry for Public Health, Well-being, and Sports |
| WBO | Wet op de Bejaarden-Oorden – Nursing Home Act |
| WCK | Wet Cliënt en Kwaliteit – Client and Quality Act |
| WDFI | Wetsontwerp Democratisch Functioneren van gesubsidieerde Instellingen – Bill on the Democratic Functioning of Subsidised Healthcare Institutions |
| WDFZ | Wetsvoorstel Democratisch Functioneren van Zorginstellingen – Bill on the Democratic Functioning of (Health-)Care Institutions |
| WGBO | Wet Geneeskundige Behandelingsovereenkomst – Medical Treatment Agreement Act |
| WHO | World Health Organisation |
| WKCZ | Wet Klachtrecht Cliënten Zorgsector – (Health-)Care Sector Complaints Act |
| Wlz | Wet langudrige zorg – Long-term Care Act |
| WMCZ | Wet medezeggenschap cliënten zorginstellingen – Client Participation Act |
| WMF | World Monetary Fund |
| WMO | Wet Maatschappelijke Ondersteuning – Societal Support Act |
| WOR | Wet op Ondernemingsraden – Working Councils Act |
| WTG | Wet Tarieven Gezondheidszorg – Healthcare Charges Act |
| WZV | Wet Ziekenhuisvoorzieningen – Act Hospital Supply |
| ZDH | Zentralverband des Deutschen Handwerks – Central Association of German Trades |
| ZFW | Ziekenfondswet – Sickness Fund Act |
| ZVW | Zorgverzekeringswet – Health Insurance Act |

# List of Figures

# List of Tables

# Part I
# Introduction

# Chapter 1
# Introduction

## 1.1 The Underlying Puzzle of the Book

The underlying puzzle of the book becomes apparent by combining two different threads: one is derived from a theoretical perspective on the field of health care while the other is the empirical observation of changes in patient involvement, that contradicts the theoretical postulation. Let us turn to the first part of the puzzle.

### *1.1.1 Health Care System Types: The First Element*

> Thus, healthcare is a kind of topography which looks different depending on which hill you stand on, so to speak. (interview 42; author's translation)

After the creation and extension of health care systems in many European countries after the Second World War, by the 1960s many societies felt the need to address the question of how to contain ever growing expenditure. Likewise, the decades up to now have left their imprint and changes. Though under permanent change, some parameters have remained constant. It is these constant characteristics that typologies try to summarise. Despite some shortcomings such typologies do offer a good overview of their respective field. In line with Weber's concept ideal types and 'elective affinities' (1968, 1991 (1904), p. 73), one of the major advantages of more refined typologies is that they link the health care type with the mode of funding, the type of benefits, the main actors, the way it is organised, and how services are managed (Bonoli & Palier 1998, p. 322). In consequence, existing typologies not only point out differences, but suggest that each type of welfare/health care state has its specific set of funding, organisation, provision, and governance (Ebbinghaus & Kittel 2006, pp. 227 et seq.) that is not interchangeable. Research conducted by Böhm, Schmid, Götze, Landwehr and Rothgang (2013)



A. Haarmann, *The Evolution and Everyday Practice of Collective Patient Involvement in Europe*, DOI 10.1007/978-3-319-64595-7_1

supports this reasoning to the degree that all of the classified 29 OECD countries are not only grouped in six out of 27 theoretically possible health care system types but also in a way that could be expected according to common health care state typologies.

One of the most influential welfare state typologies is Esping-Andersen's 'Three Worlds of Welfare Capitalism' (Esping-Andersen 1990) finding broadly the same differences as Marshall (1992 (1949)) and Titmuss (1974) as important conceptual precursors: focussing on work relations and the relation between welfare state and its citizens he derives the 'liberal', the 'conservative/Bismarckian/paternalistic' and 'social-democratic' welfare state type. As much as Esping-Andersen sparked a scientific discussion about the welfare state he also received criticism. The most relevant point of criticism in the context of this book relates to the flipside of a general typology: They are rather a general approximation and do not fit all particularities (for a general criticism on typologies cf., e.g., Crouch 2005).[1] While the United States are portrayed as a strong representative of the liberal welfare state type its pension system has, for instance, often been called Bismarckian–lite (cf., e.g., Hinrichs 2007; Schludi 2005) as it follows an approach that is claimed to belong to the conservative type of welfare states. The same holds true for the Swedish pension system, while the country in general is claimed to represent the social democratic type. Great Britain, in contrast, even though categorised as belonging to the liberal welfare type, maintains a National Health Service, which much more resembles the 'social-democratic' welfare states than a privatised system.

To avoid these inconsistencies, sector-specific typologies have been developed over the years. One of the most comprehensive starting points for typologies on the health care system has been provided by Neubauer and Birkner (1984), who distinguish several types of what might be called 'Types of Healthcare States'. In rough terms they can be classified into systems…

- in which patients PAY for health care services ON THEIR OWN (*Eigensicherung*),
- in which health care is organised as a CHARITY (*Fürsorge*),
- in which health care PROVISION is granted as a citizen's social right (*Versorgung*), and
- in which health care benefits are based on CONTRIBUTIONS TO HEALTH INSURANCES—be they mandatory social or private ones (*Versicherung*).

Meanwhile, several different, more refined typologies concerning the health care system have been published (for an overview of several variants of classifications cf. Böhm et al. 2013, Sect. 2). Despite (slight) differences in the underlying concepts employed and the considered aspects, which result in only a limited overlap of

[1]The other two main points of criticism can be regarded that, first, his typology covers only a small number of 'western' countries, that even excludes southern European countries and other highly developed ones such as Japan or South Korea. Second, though departing from the traditional male-breadwinner model he does not include the even then obvious diversification in families, occupational life, and life designs and disregards the systematic discrimination against women at work (for an overview cf. Lewis 1997).

**Table 1.1** Different typologies of health care and welfare states

| Typology according to... | | | |
|---|---|---|---|
| Neubauer and Birkner (1984) | Wendt and Rothgang (2007) | Moran (2000) | Esping-Andersen (1990) |
| • Pay on your own<br>• Charity | (Predominantly Characterised by) Private Health Care | • Supply | Liberal |
| Provision | (Predominantly) State-run/National Health Care System | Entrenched/ Command & control | Social-democratic |
| Insurance | (Predominant) Logic of Social Insurance | Corporatist | Conservative |

the different approaches, all of them can be traced back to a basic guiding thread and roughly 'translated' into the respective terminology of other approaches (see Table 1.1).

The kind of patient involvement the Netherlands and England introduced is tightly interwoven into the health care system's governance. In that sense, we can consider it as a key element of the health care system. Depending to different typologies, they are aligned along funding, provision, organisation, and governance. This constitutes the first element in the puzzle of this study.

### 1.1.2 *Changed Roles in Health Care and Involvement: The Second Element*

> When I was educated as a physician in the late 1950s only two things were expected from patients, namely obedience and gratitude, and beyond that they had to keep silent for the rest. (Els Borst (D66); Tweede Kamer der Staten-Generaal (1994); author's translation)
>
> Medical and economic logic would be adequately represented by the healing professions, in order to achieve viable compromises in the interest of patients and beneficiaries [...], in order to achieve a reasonable balance between medical necessity, on the one hand, and economic provision, on the other [— the naive view might suggest]. If that were the case, patient involvement would not have been required. (Etgeton 2009, p. 222; author's translation)

Having taken a closer look at typologies of welfare and health care states, the second element of the puzzle is derived from the empirical observation of changes in the roles of patients and citizens. Health Care systems have changed substantially over the last decades in most western countries. Four major lines of development can be identified: First, a sometimes dramatic DEMOGRAPHIC CHANGE (cf., e.g., Fendrich & Hoffmann 2007; Ried 2006; Henke & Reimers 2006), which virtually everywhere results in a higher utilisation of provision owing to more ailments and higher morbidity in later life. Second, in combination with changed lifestyle, eating, and drinking habits the so-called EPIDEMIOLOGICAL TRANSITION with its change of morbidity patterns resulting in a relative decline of acute sicknesses in exchange for the relative rise of chronic illnesses (cf. amongst others Omran 1971; National Institute on Aging 2007, 2011; Caselli, Mesle & Vallin 2002; He, Muenchrath & Kowal 2012). Third, NEW TECHNOLOGIES have been developed, which facilitate treatment options that did not exist only a short while ago (cf., e.g., Henke & Reimers 2006). And, finally, the fourth line can be found in POLICY REFORMS that try to give an answer to the first three developments and that lead to parametric changes in funding, taxes/contributions, the perceived achievable optimum of provision and quality as well as in the governance of the health care field that cannot be ignored when looking at developments over time.

In turn, all the mentioned changes have their implications for both society at large and the health care system in particular and are mirrored in both of them. One of most relevant implications in the context of this book is the altered relation between patients and the medical profession: Somewhat pointedly, the introductory quotes above catch the relation between patient and physician in a view that held true without being contested for about three decades after the Second World War without being contested. Nowadays, 'shared decision making' has become one of the most mentioned concepts in describing treatment decisions. Though its factual impact on everyday practice might be questioned, the hierarchical difference, the god-like admiration, and obedience have diminished. This has in combination with other societal transformations led to a new relation between the actors involved in the health care system and either redefined the roles or even shaped completely new roles for patients (Rega 2007, pp. 60 et seq.; Chap. 5; Egmond, Heerings & Munnichs 2014). To these societal transformations we can amongst other things add higher average levels of education, individualisation, higher personal responsibility regarding the self-management of chronic illnesses, and new leitmotifs concerning how to curtail ever increasing spending levels as well as raising quality levels (Badura 2000; Fleetwood 2005, pp. 5–6). Originating in the late 1960s, growing self-confidence of patients and relatives to voice criticism gave patient organisations as part of the patient movement an upswing. In consequence, patients now become more involved in the field of health care provision and/or policies. They no longer remain a 'topic', but become actors in their own right (cf. also Fleetwood 2005, pp. 5–6). Although steering and governance of the health care system at large and (health-)care providers in particular had been undergoing change anyway (Jakubowski & Saltman 2013), the new role of patients has influenced this change.

The new patient' roles can be identified at two distinct levels:

- The first one is closer at hand and applies to the INDIVIDUAL RELATION BETWEEN PHYSICIAN AND PATIENT. Typical rights associated with this level are, e.g., the choice of provider and 'shared decision making' on treatment. There has been an increasing body of literature about individual involvement in recent years, and quite often the understanding of participation/involvement is linked solely to this individual level (cf., e.g., Isfort, Redaèlli & Butzlaff 2007; International Alliance of Patients' Organizations 2007; Leenen, Gevers & Pinet 1993; Eldh 2006; Thompson 2007; Nanz & Fritsche 2012).

- The second level is that of COLLECTIVE PATIENT INVOLVEMENT. This usually touches issues that concern the majority or at least a larger group of patients and mostly aims at improving provision and services.

These two strata give rise to corresponding new roles and encompass a wide array of opportunities to become involved in one's own issues within the context of health care. In turn, if the opportunity to be involved is used, it also entails new responsibilities.[2]

Collective involvement, however, is far from new and is often tightly interconnected with the question about the legitimacy of services, which, again, is tightly interwoven with the accountability of those in charge (Abromeit & Stoiber 2007; Thomas 2002). It has, in addition, undergone significant changes in some places as it has been adapted to new needs, but to some degree also according to new concepts surrounding the relation between state and citizens.

### *1.1.3 Bringing Two Elements of the Puzzle Together*

The focus of this book lies on *collective patient and/or citizen involvement in hospitals* as a particular type of involvement. The Netherlands and England will serve as case studies, illustrating one path of development that health care might take. Though it may not belong to the most visible policy fields, as compared to the politics surrounding pension or health care expenditure, which draw a lot more public attention, involvement has played a significant role in the health care system of most modern democratic states. This is exemplified in the early involvement of lay-people in sickness funds in the conservative welfare states, many health insurances modelled after them, and lay commissioners in the history of the NHS in Great Britain. Over the last three to four decades, the topic has received growing attention—and sometimes interest—among patient associations, providers, and politicians alike: patients and their kin want to be involved, while providers either view it as a waste of time or as a means to remain competitive by receiving valuable input in order to react to criticism, satisfy patients, and improve processes and quality. For politicians it is a good field to either ignore or meet the demand of patients without compromising interests of other actors.

In this context and in front of a backdrop of coherence of organisation, funding, and provision within the health care system type described above, two empirical observations call for attention (see Table 1.2 on page 9 for a summary): Only a few years after corporatism began to decline in the Netherlands the country introduced collective patient involvement in nursing homes, old people's homes,

[2](Vienonen 2000, p. 61) arrives at three different possibilities to be involved and distinguishes between self-governance, the choice of provider, and involvement via patient/consumer organisations, which touches a slightly different layer. Overall, which forms of involvement are highlighted depends on the focus of the topic in question and is rarely right or wrong in absolute terms.

and hospitals via with the so-called Client Participation Act (*Wet medezeggenschap cliënten zorginstellingen*, WMCZ), which came into force in 1996. So called Client Councils (*cliëntenraden*) are formed by and comprised of those residing or being cared for in the institution or being treated as patients. They have regular meetings with the management of the institution about whatever topic the council deems to be of interest to the residents or patients as a collective. The act includes several stipulated rights, which mainly concern the annual report, plans to extend, decrease, or close wards, mergers with other institutions, changes to the interior fittings, or the future strategy of the institution to name the most essential ones. At about the same time the bill was under discussion in the Dutch parliament, the first ideas emerged to give citizens in the catchment area of English hospitals a greater say in how they are run while at the same time giving hospital management greater financial and managerial freedoms. Owing to an ever increasing distance between citizens and politicians, hospitals were felt to be too tightly governed by Whitehall and lacking legitimacy. This was aggravated not least by an increasing number of intermediate agencies and the thick layer of consultants that accumulated within the NHS over time. It took another decade before in 2004 a similar concept was implemented through the establishment of Foundation Trust Hospitals (FTs) in 2004 ('Health and Social Care (Community Health and Standards) Act 2003') as involvement in the Netherlands. Comparing the setup and rights of involvement between the legislation of the two countries reveals surprising similarities while the list of stipulated rights is virtually identical.

Now, bringing the two elements of the puzzle together, we can conclude that, on the one hand, we have the theoretical hypothesis that health care systems of the same type follow the same logic in funding, organising, providing, and governing health-care. In line with this argumentation, it follows that England and other countries with national health systems should have arrived at a similar method of funding, providing, and governing their services, while for their part the Netherlands and other conservative welfare states would choose another path.

On the other hand, we can empirically observe that both countries have found an almost identical solution to involve their patients in-patient care, which is deeply interwoven with the sector's governance. Furthermore, England's and the Netherland's empirical solutions not only strengthen patient involvement but in some sense establish an additional board of lay-people that management has to engage with. Thereby, legislation in the Netherlands and England deeply alters the relation between the involved actors and potentially weakens the traditional chains of legitimacy.

This contradiction between theoretical hypothesis (countries should be different in governance if other key elements suggest this; see Table 1.2) and empirical deviation from it (countries are almost identical regarding patient involvement) begs explanation: Why do these two countries deviate? Is it an exception? Is the typology not precise enough to capture these outliers? And if so: why and under what circumstances? Are these two countries special cases or a new trend?

**Table 1.2** Main characteristics of differences between the Netherlands' and England's hospital sector

| The Netherlands | UK |
|---|---|
| Funded by contributions to health insurances | Tax-funded |
| Provision mainly by privately run not-for-profit hospitals | Provision by public hospitals |
| Governed by private management | Governed by consultants and agencies |
| Legitimacy via involvement in health insurances | Legitimacy via general elections |
| Client council | Council of governors |

Source: Own compilation

## 1.2 Aim and Question of the Book

> Amid a growing consensus that representative democracy without participative democracy is insufficient (e.g. Burns, Hambleton & Hoggett 1994; Pratchett 2000), citizen involvement in governance is based on the view that 'ordinary people' should have more of a say in shaping the public services that play a major role in their lives. (Simmons, Birchall, Doheny & Powell 2007, p. 461)

As shown in the previous chapter, the contradiction of the theoretical claim by health care system typologies and the empirical observation of deviation from this claim is where the puzzle of this study starts. This chapter will elaborate on the question and aim of the book

Much has been written about both countries' respective reform of involvement: Positive things have been emphasised by those in favour of the new organisation (cf., e.g., LeGrand 2006, 2007), critics have highlighted (potential) problems (cf., e.g., Moore 2003; Klein 2003, 2004; Kmietowicz 2004; Wilmot 2004; O'Dowd 2008a,b), some have assessed the financial achievements that came with greater managerial independence in England (cf., e.g., O'Dowd 2006; Monitor—Independent Regulator of NHS Foundation Trusts 2007, 2008), whilst yet others embarked on a partial evaluation of the implementation process with regard to the extended say of patients in the Netherlands (cf., e.g., Savornin Lohman 2000; Laterveer, Teerink & Peter 2004; van der Voet 2005; Boer, Hendriks, Damman, Spreeuwenberg & Rademakers 2007; Nederlandse Zorgautoriteit 2007). What all these publications have in common is that they cover a very specific area in either country. What is lacking are comprehensive studies about underlying reasons, motives, and a detailed analysis of the (intended) outcomes. Furthermore, both countries are treated separately only, cross-national comparisons do—to my knowledge—not exist.

In general, approaches that have been employed to explain other reforms in welfare states might be employed to answer the question at hand. A cautious look shall check whether or not the most common of them are capable of explaining the phenomenon we are confronted with. One attempt, floated particularly amongst economists, is the assumption of external ruptures—for instance, the oil crises of the 1970s—that, in turn, put welfare states under strain.

One often maintained option is that the financial strain in itself causes welfare states to act. Another string of action postulates that welfare states under pressure compete with each other for well-trained employees, resources, and markets, which makes welfare states' benefits a costly endeavour that is under permanent scrutiny. A third alternative for explanation is often seen in a unification of norms and legal frameworks caused by globalisation and Europeanisation, which causes states to react.

Interestingly, in all of the mentioned scenarios welfare states are claimed to react more or less uniformly: As economic pressure affects all countries (relatively) equally, the assumption is that it is eventually 'solved' by a *common* policy trend. One of the most commonly asked questions is whether this results in the continuation of separate developments or the 'convergence of healthcare systems' (cf., e.g., Schmid, Cacace, Götze & Rothgang 2010, pp. 456–457; Rothgang, Schmid & Schneider 2012). Another development postulates a 'race to the bottom', which means that welfare states cut their benefit levels in order to stay competitive. In the end, only residual welfare states remain according to the reasoning (Swank 2005; Genschel 2004). In the case of globalisation, the closest explanation at hand is that the European Union assumes increasingly more competences in the field of welfare policies (Hagen 2001, cf., e.g.,), which results in legislation and regulation at a minimum level being adopted by the member states.

If the assumption of external pressure as reason for reaction holds true and is as uniform as maintained, this would imply that we have to do with a widespread international phenomenon towards the introduction of patient involvement at least. However, a common trend towards changes in the governance of health care systems in the wake of crises, market competition, and Europeanisation cannot be spotted. In favour of the argument outlined it might be argued that not all countries are affected by a particular crisis to the same extent and at exactly the same point in time, so that variations might occur (cf., e.g., Hemerijck, Unger & Visser 2001). It might also be that fields not directly underlying economic pressures develop distinctly (Tritter, Koivusalo, Ollila & Dorfman 2010, p. 75).

Nevertheless, the question needs to be posed why we can observe changes of governance and patient involvement in the Netherlands and England while other countries maintain their policies or pursue different pathways. In conclusion it must be said that though without doubt serious events like wars, financial crises, natural disasters, and other external ruptures as well as tightening competition can have their impact on societies and policies, it remains unclear why and under which conditions countries are affected very differently despite the universality of these external ruptures. Regarding increased international competition, we might wonder why a 'race to the bottom' should encourage states to introduce patient involvement, which, at least in the beginning, requires additional funding. In consequence, even if this argument would eventually prove true, more refined mechanisms must be sought in order to arrive at better theoretical underpinning.

Another explanatory approach is the economisation and marketisation of health care systems. Are, thus, different pathways and degrees of patient involvement just a matter of different degrees of marketisation so that maybe we are dealing with time-lags, that in the long run will converge anyway? Even though undeniably we have to do with a decreasing role of some traditional forms of involvement, for instance, the self-governance in social insurances, whereas state hierarchy and marketal elements are on the rise (Schmid et al. 2010, p. 470; Haarmann, Klenk & Weyrauch 2010), this has hitherto not led to any more homogeneous pattern in patient involvement. Similar doubts might arise regarding the argument that internationalisation (or Europeanisation) is the driving force behind convergence (regarding that argument cf., e.g., Schulte 1998; Tritter et al. 2010, Chap. 4; on the misperception of uniform development and change cf., e.g., Rothgang et al. 2012).

In consequence, this study is an exploratory one. Despite the limitations that come with exploratory studies, the aim is to identify the decisive factors of influence which eventually led to the legislation on this new type of patient involvement. These factors might, for instance, comprise economic context factors, actors, tangible necessities or interests, or societal changes. It might result in a completely new explanation or—which is more likely—in modifications of existing literature. Therefore, this book's main question is:

***What factors can be identified to have contributed to or hampered the implementation of collective patient involvement in hospitals?***

In order not to be misled by any random factors that only appear to have influenced the policy process, it was decided to contrast the Netherlands and England as the two main countries to the counter-cases Germany and Sweden (for more detailed information on this see Sect. 4.2.1 on page 58). As they belong to the same health care type, this theoretically not only keeps the number of factors somewhat smaller, but allows also for better contrasting empirical observation with theoretical description.

The core question is interlinked to numerous others, some of which *need* to be addressed in order to arrive at an answer to the main questions, others are rather optional. One of the more important spin-off questions in this context is whether it is conversion or hypothesised convergence of European welfare states that occurs. First thought to be facilitated in particular by policy learning (cf., e.g., Bennett 1991; Schmid & Götze 2009), other mechanisms have been found. While some authors doubt that convergence occurs or question the specific relevance of any converging developments (cf., e.g., Smith, Mossialos & Papanicolas 2012; Howlett, Ramesh & Per 2009) empirical research points out that convergence does occur in specific areas—as, for instance, the mode of funding (cf., e.g., Bennett 1991; Schmid et al. 2010; Alber & Standing 2000; Rothgang et al. 2012; Götze, Cacace & Rothgang 2009). Be that as it may, the question in this context is whether, for instance, the Dutch departure from a corporatist governance model in its social insurances is a first indicator for its general decline? Are the Netherlands and England, in that understanding, maybe the pioneers for a new general form of patient involvement with other countries to follow soon?

As legal and regulatory texts can cause the illusion of a well-functioning reality—and, in a functionalist perspective, solved problems—knowing only the stipulations about how things *should* be does not necessarily mirror real life. As we know from the literature, the implementation of patient and public involvement is not free from friction and problems (Dalton et al. 2016, 3; Groenewegen, Kroneman, van Erp, Broeren & van Birgelen 2016; Pollard et al. 2014, 4; Sanders, van Weeghel, Verheul, Pieters & Wit et al. 2013, 4; Martin 2008, 1; Hogg 2008; Ashton, Mays & Devlin 2005; Baggott, Allsop & Jones 2004; Contandriopoulos 2004; Hogg 1999; Rodwin 1997). This includes amongst other issues the imbalance of knowledge and skills between patient representatives and care providers, which sometimes results in strategically taking advantage of the imbalance, sometimes rather in the provision of information than involvement in decisions, the difficulty that often there is an overrepresentation of the highly educated, the autochthon, the elderly, and women in the patient representation, and that various interest groups try to interfere in order to keep the influence of public and patient involvement low. Thus, in order to capture the whole picture, a somewhat less important secondary issue of this study—which, however, is of vital importance for an accurate assessment—is to take a cursory glance at the accordant implementation in the respective countries. This part of the question can be summarised as follows:

***Have the main goals pursued by respective legislation been achieved according to key actors in the field?***

## 1.3 Structure of the Book

This book is subdivided into four broad parts. The FIRST PART, the introduction, has hitherto included the development of the puzzle. The SECOND PART consists of three chapters: Chap. 2 'Patient Involvement: Who, What for, and in What Way?' on page 19 will attempt a description of patient involvement, and clarify terminology. It will set the focus of this book as patient *involvement* (in contrast to participation) in hospitals. The theoretical framework in Chap. 3 'A Theoretical Framework for the Study' on page 31 integrates ideational approaches and 'actor-centred institutionalism' into a joint framework of the ideal-typical policy process. The chosen approaches allow to answer the questions where new ideas stem from, when they are exchanged against older ones, considers preferences, strategies, interests, power of actors as well as the relation between them, and looks at the hampering influence of existing institutions. Chapter 4 'Methodology and Study Design' on page 55 will go into the methodological details and the study design, which will be defined as an explorative, comparative, qualitative study, which, besides the literature, predominantly draws on legal texts, parliamentary minutes, and expert interviews as sources. The Netherlands and England as the main countries will be compared to Germany and Sweden, which belong to the same health care state types, respectively, and keeps the number of varying factors somewhat lower.

Thereafter, the THIRD, THE EMPIRICAL PART will take a closer look at case studies in the Netherlands (Chap. 5 on page 75), England (Chap. 6 on page 131), Germany (Chap. 7 on page 187), and Sweden (Chap. 8 on page 221). The structure of these chapters is to some degree standardised: after a cursory overview of the respective country and its health care system, potential equivalents to collective patient involvement at the level of providers are looked at as well as at the more general development of patient involvement. After discussing some country specific aspects, the development of the two legal acts introducing collective patient involvement in hospitals is traced for the two main countries, i.e., the Netherlands and England. The chapters are completed with an attempt to roughly assess the form of involvement found in the four countries with its strengths and weaknesses.

The FOURTH AND LAST PART attempts to condense and more systematically compare the results. Whereas the focus in the empirical part lies in the thick description of the development, it is now in the comparative chapter 'Comparison: Bringing Four Cases Together', 9 on page 275 that more abstract conclusions are drawn and an attempt at a cautious generalisation is made. Each country has its own way of involvement, even though the respective factors of influence and paths are highly individual. After arriving at a number of commonalities, a revised model of the policy process will be presented. In light of the commonalities and the factors that proved to be of theoretical importance, the main 'story' of each country will be given. Finally, two types of countries can be discerned: One, that implemented involvement at the level of (health-)care providers and one where involvement takes place at the policy level.

## References


Abromeit, H., & Stoiber, M. (2007). Criteria of democratic legitimacy. In A. Hurrelmann, S. Schneider & J. Steffek (Eds.), *Legitimacy in an age of global politics* (Chap. 3, pp. 35–56). Basingstoke/New York: Palgrave Macmillan.

Alber, J., & Standing, G. (2000). Social dumping, catch-up, or convergence? Europe in a comparative global context. *Journal of European Social Policy, 10*(2), 99–119.

Ashton, T., Mays, N., & Devlin, N. (2005). Continuity through change: The rhetoric and reality of health reform in New Zealand. *Social Science and Medicine, 61*(2), 253–262.

Badura, B. (2000). Reform des Gesundheitswesens durch Aktivierung der Bürger Versicherten und Patienten—eine Einführung. In H. Ettischer & K. Salice-Stephan (Eds.), *Bürgerbeteiligung im Gesundheitswesen—eine länderäbergreifende Herausforderung—Ideen, Ansätze und internationale Erfahrungen*. Forschung und Praxis der Gesundheitsförderung (Chap. 2.1, 10, pp. 34–39). Köln: Bundeszentrale für gesundheitliche Aufklärung (BZgA).

Baggott, R., Allsop, J., & Jones, K. (2004). Representing the repressed? Health consumer groups and the national policy process. *Policy and Politics, 32*(3), 317–331.

Bennett, C. J. (1991). What is policy convergence and what causes it? *British Journal of Political Science, 21*, 215–233.

Boer, D. de., Hendriks, M., Damman, O., Spreeuwenberg, P., & Rademakers, J. (2007). *Ervaringen van verzekerden met de zorg en de zorgverzekerars*. Utrecht: NIVEL.

Böhm, K., Schmid, A., Götze, R., Landwehr C., & Rothgang, H. (2013). Five types of OECD healthcare systems: Empirical results of a deductive classification. *Health Policy, 113*(3), 258–269.

Bonoli, G., & Palier, B. (1998). Changing the politics of social programmes: Innovative change in British and French Welfare Reforms. *Journal of European Social Policy, 8*, 317–330.

Burns, D., Hambleton, R., & Hoggett, P. (1994). *The politics of decentralisation*. Basingstoke: MacMillan.

Caselli, G., Mesle, F., & Vallin, J. (2002). Epidemiologic transition theory exceptions. *Journal of Population Sciences, 9*, 9–51. Retrieved January 20, 2017, from http://wwwdemogr.mpg.de/Papers/workshops/020619paper40.pdf.

Contandriopoulos, D. (2004). A sociological perspective on public participation in health care. *Social Science and Medicine, 58*, 321–330.

Crouch, C. (2005). Die Bedeutung von Governance für Vielfalt und Wandel im modernen Kapitalismus. In M. Miller (Ed.), *Welten des Kapitalismus* (pp. 101–126). Frankfurt/New York: Campus Verlag.

Dalton, J., Chambers, D., Harden, M., Street, A., Partker G., & Eastwood, A. (2016). Service user engagement in health service reconfiguration: A rapid evidence synthesis. *Journal of Health Services Research and Policy, 21*, 195–205.

Ebbinghaus, B., & Kittel, B. (2006). Europäische Sozialmodelle à la carte: Gibt es institutionelle Wahlverwandtschaften zwischen Wohlfahrtsstaat und Arbeitsbeziehungen? In J. Beckert, B. Ebbinghaus, A. Hassel & P. Manow (Eds.), *Transformationen des Kapitalismus*. Schriften aus dem Max-Planck-Institut für Gesellschaftsforschung (Vol. 57). Frankfurt: Campus.

Eldh, A. C. (2006). *Patient participation—what it is and what it is not*. Örebro Studies in Caring Sciences. Örebro: Universitetsbiblioteket, Örebro University.

Esping-Andersen, G. (1990). *The three worlds of welfare capitalism*. Princton: University Press.

Etgeton, S. (2009). Patientenbeteiligung im gemeinsamen bundesausschuss. In W. Schroeder & R. Paquet (Eds.), *Gesundheitsreform 2007. Nach der Reform ist vor der Reform* (pp. 222–228). Wiesbaden: VS Verlag.

Fendrich, K., & Hoffmann, W. (2007). More than just aging societies: The demographic change has an impact on actual numbers of patients. *Journal of Public Health, 15*(5), 345–351.

Fleetwood, C. (2005). *Brukarsamverkan inom hälso- och sjukvård i Sverige och Storbritannien—Handikapporganisationernas delaktighet i planering och utveckling av vård* (Master of Public Health—MPH 2005:41, Nordiska högskolan för folkhälsovetenskap, Göteborg).

Genschel, P. (2004). Globalization and the Welfare State: A retrospective. *Journal of European Public Policy, 11*(4), 613–636.

Götze, R., Cacace, M., & Rothgang, H. (2009). Von der Risiko- zur Anbieterselektion—Eigendynamiken wettbewerblicher Reformen in Gesundheitssystemen des Sozialversicherungstyps. *Zeitschrift für Sozialreform, 2*, 149–175.

Groenewegen, P., Kroneman, M., Erp, K. van, Broeren, R., & Birgelen, C. van. (2016). *Kennissynthese: Patiëntenparticipatie in de eerste lijn*. Utrecht: NIVEL and Zorgbelang Brabant.

Haarmann, A., Klenk, T., & Weyrauch, P. (2010, March). Exit, choice—and what about voice? Public involvement in corporatist healthcare states. *Public Management Review—'Special Issue on Welfare Governance Reforms and Effects in the Post-Golden Age', 12*(2), 213–231. Retrieved January 20, 2017, from http://wwwinformaworldcom/smpp/title~db=all~content=g919646875.

Hagen, K. (2001). Towards a europeanisation of social policies? *Politique Europe'enne, 1*(2), 67–86.

He, W., Muenchrath, M. N., & Kowal, P. (2012, May). *Shades of Gray: A Cross-Country Study of Health and Well-Being of the Older Populations in SAGE Countries, 2007–2010*. United States Census Bureau. Washington: U.S. Government Printing Office.

Hemerijck, A., Unger, B., & Visser, J. (2001). How small countries negotiate change—twenty-five years of policy adjustment in Austria, the Netherlands and Belgium. In F. W. Scharpf & V. A. Schmidt (Eds.), *Welfare and Work in the Open Economy Volume II: Diverse Responses to Common Challenges in Twelve Countries* (Chap. 5, Vol. 2, pp. 175–263). Oxford: Oxford University Press.

Henke, K. D., & Reimers, L. (2006, August). *Zum Einfluss von Demographie und medizinischtechnischem Fortschritt auf die Gesundheitsausgaben*, Zentrum für innovative Gesundheitstechnologie (ZiG). Berlin. Retrieved January 20, 2017, from http://www.igetuberlinde/fileadmin/fg176/IGEPrintreihe/200601.pd.

Hinrichs, K. (2007). Enlarging freedom of choice: Pension reforms in the nordic countries and Germany. In B. Hvinden & H. Johansson (Eds.), *Citizenship in Nordic Welfare States: Dynamics of Choice Duties and Participation in a Changing Europe* (Chap. 14, pp. 200–215). Milton Park, Abingdon: Routledge Chapman and Hall.

Hogg, C. (1999). *Patients, power and politics—from patients to citzens*. London/Seven Oaks/New Delhi: SAGE.

Hogg, C. (2008). *Citizens, consumers and the NHS: Capturing voices*. London: Palgrave Macmillan.

Howlett, M., Ramesh, M., & Per, A. (2009). *Studying public policy: Policy cycles and policy subsystems*. Cary/New York: Oxford University Press.

International Alliance of Patients' Organizations. (2007). *What is Patient-Centred Healthcare? A Review of Definitions and Principles*. London.

Isfort, J., Redaèlli, M., & Butzlaff, M. E. (2007). Die Entwicklung der partizipativen Entscheidungsfindung: Die Sicht der Versicherten und der Ärzte. In J. Böcken, B. Braun & R. Amhof (Eds.), *Gesundheitsmonitor 2007—Gesundheitsversorung und Gestaltungsoptionen aus der Perspektive von Bevölkerung und Ärzten* (pp. 76–94). Gütersloh: Bertelsmann.

Jakubowski, E., & Saltman, R. B. (Eds.). (2013). *The changing national role in health system governance—A case-based study of 11 European countries and Australia*. Observatory Studies Series. Copenhagen: WHO Regional Office for Europe on behalf of the European Observatory on Health Systems and Policies.

Klein, R. (2003). Governance for NHS foundation trusts. *British Medical Journal, 326*, 175–176.

Klein, R. (2004). The first wave of NHS foundation trusts. *British Medical Journal, 328*, 1332.

Kmietowicz, Z. (2004). UK Health Commission downgrades four foundation trusts. *British Medical Journal, 329*, 187.

Laterveer, M. J., Teerink, F., & Peter, N. A. (2004). *De Cliëntenraad Centraal; de meerwaarde van medezeggenschap voor directeuren en bestuurders in de zorgsector*. Utrecht: Vereniging Directies zorgsector Nederland in samenwerking met LOC.

Leenen, H. J. J., Gevers, J. K. M., & Pinet, G. (1993). *The rights of patients in Europe*. Deventer/Boston: Published on behalf of the World Health Organization, Regional Office for Europe—Kluwer Law and Taxation Publishers.

LeGrand, J. (2006). *Motivation, agency, and public policy: of knights and knaves, pawns and queens, revised*. Oxford: University Press.

LeGrand, J. (2007). The politics of choice and competition in public services. *The Political Quarterly, 78*(2), 207–213.

Lewis, J. (1997). Gender and Welfare Regimes: Further toughts. *Social Politics, 4*, 160–177.

Marshall, T. H. (1992 (1949)). Citizenship and social class. In T. H. Marshall & T. Bottomore (Eds.), *Citizenship and social class* (Vol. 1, pp. 3–51). London/Concord, MA: Pluto Press.

Martin, R. G. (2008). 'Ordinary people only': Knowledge, representativeness, and the publics of public participation in healthcare. *Sociology of Health and Illness, 30*, 35–54.

Monitor—Independent Regulator of NHS Foundation Trusts. (2007). *Annual reports and accounts—1 April 2006–31 March 2007*. London: The Stationery Office.

Monitor—Independent Regulator of NHS Foundation Trusts. (2008). *Annual report and accounts – 1 April 2007–31 March 2008*. London: The Stationery Office.

Moore, W. (2003). Plans for foundation trusts could spark pay spiral. *British Medical Journal, 326*, 256.

Moran, M. (2000, June). Understanding the welfare state: The case of health care. *British Journal of Politics and International Relations, 2*(2), 135–160.

Nanz, P., & Fritsche, M. (2012). *Handbuch Bürgerbeteiligung—Verfahren und Akteure Chancen und Grenzen*. Schriftenreihe. Bonn: Bundeszentrale für politische Bildung.

National Institute on Aging. (2007, March). *Why population aging matters: A global perspective*. Washington: U.S. Department of State.

National Institute on Aging. (2011, October). *Global health and aging*. Geneva: World Health Organization.

Nederlandse Zorgautoriteit. (2007). *Verzekerdeninvloed Zorgverzekeringswet*. Utrecht: Nederlandse Zorgautoriteit.

Neubauer, G., & Birkner, B. (1984). Alternativen der organisation und steuerung des gesundheitswesens. In G. Neubauer (Ed.), *Alternativen der Steuerung des Gesundheitswesens im Rahmen einer Sozialen Marktwirtschaft* (pp. 13–70). Gerlingen: Robert Bosch Stiftung.

O'Dowd, A. (2006). Foundation trusts turn in strong financial performance. *British Medical Journal, 332*, 686.

O'Dowd, A. (2008a, August). Foundation trusts still do not enjoy full autonomy, MPs hear. *British Medical Journal, 337*, a691

O'Dowd, A. (2008b, February). Foundation trusts still have to prove their worth, MPs say. *British Medical Journal, 337*, a2188

Omran, A. R. (1971). The epidemiologic transition: A theory of the epidemiology of population change. *The Milbank Memorial Fund Quarterly, 49*(4), 509–538.

Pollard, L., Agarwal, S., Harrad, F., Lester L., Cross, A., & Wray, P. E. A. (2014). The impact of patient participation direct enhanced service on patient reference groups in primary care: a qualitative study. *Quality in Primary Care, 22*, 189–199.

Pratchett, L. (2000). *Renewing local democracy*. London: Frank Cass.

Rega, I. M. (2007). *Patienten- und Bürgerbeteiligung im Gesundheitswesen Deutschlands, Finnlands und Polens*. Göttingen: Universitätsdrucke Göttingen.

Ried, W. (2006). *Demographischer Wandel, medizinischer Fortschritt und Ausgaben für Gesundheitsleistungen: eine theoretische Analyse*. Wirtschaftswissenschaftliche Diskussionspapiere. Greifswald: Ernst-Moritz-Arndt-Universität, ECONSTOR. Retrieved January 20, 2017, from https://www.econstor.eu/dspace/bitstream/10419/32351/1/523673787.pdf.

Rodwin, M. (1997). The neglected remedy: Strengthening consumer voice in managed care. *American Prospect, 34*, 45–50.

Rothgang, H., Schmid, A., & Schneider, S. (2012). Transformationen des Interventionsstaates und ihre Erklärung: Das Beispiel nationaler Gesundheitssysteme. In M. Bach (Ed.), *Der entmachtete Leviathan: Löst sich der souveräne Staat auf?* (Vol. Sonderband 5, pp. 175–196). Baden-Baden: Nomos.

Sanders, A. R., Weeghel, I. van, Verheul, W., Pieters, R. H., & Wit, et al., N. J. de. (2013). Effects of improved patient participation in primary care on health-related outcomes: A systematic review. *Family Practice, 30*, 365–378.

Savornin Lohman, J. de. (2000). Evaluatie—Wet medezeggenschap cliënten zorgsector. In J. de. Savornin Lohman (Ed.), *Evaluatie Wet medezeggenschap cliënten zorginstellingen*. Utrecht: Verwey-Jonker Instituut.

Schludi, M. (2005). *The Reform of Bismarckian Pension Systems: A Comparison of Pension Politics in Austria, France Germany Italy and Sweden*. Amsterdam: Amsterdam University Press.

Schmid, A., Cacace, M., Götze, R., & Rothgang, H. (2010, August). Explaining health care system change: Problem pressure and the emergence of "Hybrid" health care systems. *Journal of Health Politics, Policy and Law, 35*(4), 455–486.

Schmid, A., & Götze, R. (2009). Cross-national policy learning in health system reform: The case of diagnosis related groups. *International Social Security Review, 62*(4), 21–40.

Schulte, B. (1998). Wohlfahrtsregime im Prozess der europäischen Integration. In S. Lessenich & I. Ostner (Eds.), *Welten des Wohlfahrtskapitalismus. Der Sozialstaat in vergleichender Perspektive* (pp. 255–270). Frankfurt/Main: Campus.

Simmons, R., Birchall, J., Doheny S., & Powell, M. (2007). 'Citizen governance': opportunities for inclusivity in policy and policy making? *Policy and Politics, 35*(3), 457–478.

Smith, P., Mossialos, E., & Papanicolas, I. (2012). Performance measurement for health system improvement: Experiences, challenges and prospects. In J. Figueras & M. McKee (Eds.), *Health systems, health, wealth and societal well-being*. Maidenhead: Open University Press.

Swank, D. (2005). Globalisation, domestic politics, and Welfare State Retrenchment in capitalist democracies. *Social Policy and Society, 4*(2), 183–195.

The Stationery Office. (2003, November 20). *Health and social care (Community Health and Standards) Act 2003*. London: The Stationery Office Limited.

Thomas, P. G. (2002). Accountability. In B. G. Peters & J. Pierre (Eds.), *Handbook of public administration* (pp. 549–556). London/Thousand Oaks/New Delhi: SAGE.

Thompson, A. G. H. (2007). The meaning of patient involvement and participation in health care consultations: A taxonomy. *Social Science and Medicine, 64*, 1297–1310.

Titmuss, R. M. (1974). What is social policy? In B. Abel-Smith & K. Titmuss (Eds.), *Social policy: An introduction* (Chap. 2, pp. 23–32). New York: Pantheon Books.

Tritter, J., Koivusalo, M., Ollila, E., & Dorfman, P. (2010). *Globalisation, Markets and Healthcare Policy—Redrawing the Patient as Consumer*. Critical Studies in Health and Society Abingdon. New York: Routledge.

Tweede Kamer der Staten-Generaal. (1994, September 7). *Notulen Tweede Kamer der Staten-Generaal—89ste vergadering, 7 september 1994, Aanvang 13.00 uur*. 's Gravenhage.

van Egmond, S., Heerings, M., & Munnichs, G. (2014, March 26). *Sterke verhalen uit het ziekenhuis: Leren van patiëntenervaringen voor goede zorg*. Den Haag: Rathenau Instituut.

Vienonen, M. A. (2000). Von einer Ethik der Ignoranz hin zur Bürgerbeteiligung. In H. Ettischer & K. Salice-Stephan (Eds.), *Bürgerbeteiligung im Gesundheitswesen—eine länderübergreifende Herausforderung—Ideen, Ansätze und internationale Erfahrungen* (Chap. 3.1, 10, pp. 58–64). Forschung und Praxis der Gesundheitsförderung. Köln: Bundeszentrale für gesundheitliche Aufklärung (BZgA).

Voet, G. W. van der. (2005). *De kwaliteit van de WMCZ als medezeggenschapswet* (Doctoral dissertation, Rotterdam, PhD-Thesis).

Weber, M. (1991 (1904)). Die Objektivität sozialwissenschaftlicher und sozialpolitischer Erkenntnis. In *Schriften zur Wissenschaftslehre* (pp. 21–101). Stuttgart: Reclam.

Weber, M. (1968). *Die Protestantische Ethik II. Kritiken und Antikritiken*. Hamburg: Siebenstern.

Wendt, C., & Rothgang, H. (2007). *Gesundheitssystemtypen im Vergleich—Konzeptionelle Überlegungen zur vergleichenden Analyse von Gesundheitssystemen* (Vol. 61). Universität Bremen, Sonderforschungsbereich 597 (Staatlichkeit im Wandel).

Wilmot, S. (2004). Foundation trusts and the problem of legitimacy. *HealthCare Analysis (HCA), 12*(2), 157–170.

# Chapter 2
# Patient Involvement: Who, What for, and in What Way?

> *IV The people have the right and duty to participate individually and collectively in the planning and implementation of their health care. 'Declaration of Alma-Ata' (WHO 1978)*

Before heading on to the theoretical and methodological part of the study, it is necessary to take a somewhat closer look at patient involvement and its definition. There is a wide variety of reasons why patient involvement is to be desired. Hirschman's famous '*Exit, Voice and Loyalty*' (1970) has contributed theoretically to the topic. It entailed much scholarly discussion, inspired many contributions to the theme, and is used by actors from diverse backgrounds (for a small selection cf. Barry 1974; Bundeszentrale für gesundheitliche Aufklärung (BZgA) 2000; Dowding, John, Mergoupis & van Vugt 2000; Forster & Gabe 2008; Greß, Delnoij & Groenewegen 2003; Greß, Höppner, Marstedt, Rothgang & Thamm 2008; Greß & Rothgang 2008; Grit & Bal 2009; LeGrand 2006, 2007; Rodwin 1997; Young 1974). Somewhat exaggerated it might be said that while free-market liberals tend to rather support the idea of *exit*—or, in its later alternative framing, *choice*—and *voice* should get no 'louder' than in customer/patient surveys, it is the latter that is highlighted by many involved in the self-governance of social insurances or in patient organisations.

However, developments over the past decade have increasingly shown that voice and exit are neither exclusive nor conflicting instruments, and which should be prioritised over the other is difficult to decide upon (Saltman & von Otter 1989; cf. also Chinitz 2000, pp. 64–65). Already in 1978, the World Health Organisation in its famous 'Declaration of Alma-Ata' (WHO 1978) formulated the desideratum that patients should be 'individually and collectively' involved in health care, a demand that was reiterated with the 'Declaration on the Promotion of Patients' Rights in Europe' some 15 years later (WHO 1994). This, amongst other reasons, has also led politicians, policy advisers, and researchers to become involved in a slow-moving discourse about involvement and governance (cf., e.g., Berwick 2002; Department of Health 2012; Eurohealth 2013).



A. Haarmann, *The Evolution and Everyday Practice of Collective Patient Involvement in Europe*, DOI 10.1007/978-3-319-64595-7_2

Rega (2007, chap. 2) discerns several aims of patient involvement: There are normative and utilitarian arguments for involvement such as self-determination and the dignity of the individual, democratisation of health care, or transparency (cf. also Potvin 2007; Tritter, Koivusalo, Ollila & Dorfman 2010). There are functional reasons including patient safety, the optimisation of health care services, capacity planning, and, more generally, the goal attainment of (social) policy aims that grant a patient the status of an expert (cf. Badura 2000; Barnes, Newman & Sullivan 2007, pp. 34–37; Coulter 2000; Tritter & McCallum 2006; WHO 1978, 1996; WHO Regional Office for Europe 2006). And lastly there are psychological reasons—that might in some cases be translated into functional ones—which include higher patient satisfaction, 'greater confidence, reduction in anxiety', 'better relationships with professionals', as well as the feeling to be involved—to which numerous additional reasons might be added (Farrell 2004, pp. 2–3; cf. also Potvin 2007; Thompson 2007).

In the following sections, we will take a look at different kinds of involvement the question in what way to involve whom.

## 2.1 Forms of Involvement and Legitimacy

> [I]nvolvement means: You do not stay sitting behind your geraniums, but you make yourself heard, you make yourself seen, while co-determination, in my experience, [is] a somewhat more formal spot. (interview 6; author's translation)
>
> The underlying issues are essentially the same—'nobodies' in several arenas are trying to become 'somebodies' with enough power to make the target institutions responsive to their views, aspirations, and needs. (Arnstein 1969, p. 216)

In practical terms, involvement takes different shapes depending on the respective tradition of the health care system in a country. Nevertheless, it can be argued that most, if not all of them are linked to what may be called a *chain of legitimacy*, which—even though other reasons play in—is essential in the context of this book.[1]

While for MARKET-LIKE SOLUTIONS in health care legitimacy basically is created through a contract between patient—or, in more contractual terminology: purchaser of services—and physician—provider of services—this is more complicated in countries with solidary funding. In COUNTRIES WITH SELF-GOVERNANCE in social insurances the predominant form of involvement is traditionally targeted at the insured, who in a modernised form might be called users or clients, which,

[1]This is not the place to go into details about the wide field of studies on legitimacy and accountability (for an overview of different types of legitimacy cf., e.g., Nedlund 2012, chap. 2). In this context it shall suffice that democratic states need to legitimise their expenditures—in particular those funded by taxes or solidary contributions. This can be done in several ways and affects different facets of legitimacy. Of most importance for this study are input legitimacy—in short: what have citizens to say about policies—and output legitimacy—i.e. basically the question 'who gets what, when, how' (Nedlund 2012, pp. 34–44).

in turn, creates a mixed form of legitimacy. In COUNTRIES WITH SOME TYPE OF NATIONAL HEALTH SYSTEM (NHS) legitimacy has traditionally been created via general elections of MPs in charge of health care policies, be it on the national or regional level, who then on behalf of the citizens direct or order health care services. They are, in turn, accountable to the population.

These different forms might be the expression of differences in focus, purpose, (ideological) preference, and quality of involvement. One of the first attempts to systematise several types of involvement and get definitions straight was Arnstein's 'ladder of citizen participation' (Arnstein 1969). Its basic idea is that there are different degrees of being involved, with only the three uppermost categories comprising real citizen power. According to this view, citizen control and, thereby, full insight and self-determination of citizens is the main goal in an ideal world. Arnstein discerns eight different, hierarchical steps:

(a) Citizen Control
(b) Delegated Power
(c) Partnership
(d) Placation
(e) Consultation
(f) Informing
(g) Therapy
(h) Manipulation

The fact that several scholars followed up on her research (to name just a few: Rocha 1997; Thompson 2007, for an overview cf. Tritter & McCallum 2006) shows the relevance of and the interest in such a classification.

However, as much as being a starting point, Arnstein's typology was also subject to considerable criticism. Main reasons mentioned are that it is too hierarchical and oversimplified an approach, that it lacked specifications of the (potential) methods and means of involvement, and that it failed to reflect about different capabilities of those to be involved. It has also been said that it underestimates the complexity of decision making and that it might end up in misallocating resources by a too lop-sided consideration of interests (for an overview cf. Tritter & McCallum 2006). In my opinion much more important in this context, however, is the fact that there is not the one and only ideal form of involvement, but that there can and should be several forms/levels of involvement that can be adapted to the specific geographical, organisational, or individual need (cf. also Tritter & McCallum 2006, chap. 7). However, most often there is a focus solely on one or two forms of involvement, while other forms are not as explicated in the literature.

Collective involvement can be organised differently. It might, for instance, occur under the aegis of general consumer organisations, be represented via patient organisations, be included in a larger corporatist system, formed as a committee, constitute a council, or be incorporated into decision-making bodies that exist anyway—with all their respective advantages and disadvantages (cf. also Simmons, Birchall, Doheny & Powell 2007). Tightly interwoven is the question about the constitution of the respective form of involvement for which, amongst other ways, elections, appointment, access via membership, or the acceptance of volunteers can be thought of. Both the different variants of forms of involvement as well as their constitution are accompanied by different degrees of legitimacy. Usually, elections are seen as the most democratic means of constituting boards and committees, while appointment is often rather seen as a second class solution (cf., e.g., House of Commons 2010; Simmons et al. 2007, pp. 462 et seq., 470–471). Literature on patient involvement shows at the same time that pensioners and individuals with a higher educational background are the two groups whose share in most forms of voluntary involvement is higher than their share in the general population (cf., e.g., de Savornin Lohman 2000), which might play its part in decreasing legitimacy. It is also known that a short residence time, varying mental capabilities, and frailty affects the possibilities of involvement in nursing homes, so that the decision about its form and constitution is often a delicate balancing act. This shows that what holds true for individual involvement in treatment decisions holds even more so true for collective involvement: It is not only due to preferences, but also other critical factors, for instance, time, educational resources, and various constraints that not everyone easily can compensate for (cf. van de Bovenkamp 2010, pp. 155 et seq.). If, now, only is striven for what Arnstein calls 'citizen power', this would automatically exclude larger societal groups from being involved. Moreover, there are voices claiming that real influence requires participation in decision-making. Others maintain that participating and co-deciding in health care would rather give rise to interest conflicts among patients and the risk to be worn down between professional, more powerful actors, for instance, the pharmaceutical industry, health insurances, and multi-national hospital corporations. To conclude, it is safe to say that it is difficult terrain for which no ready-made recipe is available.

Next to this difference in focus there is nowadays talk of citizen, patient, beneficiary/insured, member, user, consumer, or client involvement depending on the respective country and perspective. The different terminology partly reflects different traditions, partly different target groups, but does not necessarily describe different forms of involvement, let alone different rights or qualities of involvement. While, for instance, the terminology used in the Netherlands is one of the user and client involvements, the term 'public and patient involvement' (PPI) is the common one in England describing by and large the same. While the terminology of the respective country will be applied with regard to this country, the term PPI will be used in a more general context as a wider, more encompassing term that also reflects the interest of net tax/contribution payers as well as potential patients.

On the other hand, while the target group is not necessarily a good indicator to characterise involvement, there are in particular vast differences in what is actually meant by the specific label: Sometimes there is talk of involvement, sometimes participation, co-decision making, or empowerment to just mention a few. As they denote completely different concepts, the following questions need to be posed: How much involvement is necessary and how much involvement is possible? Is it really necessary and desirable that patients decide about every little thing in the everyday practice of a health care organisation? There are good reasons to ask for a seriously intended involvement in a sincere discussion about key issues that affect the group in question, as early on as possible, that take considerations from each side as seriously as the other and without preconceived opinion; taking control of the everyday business, however, would question the advantages of professional specialisation in general. An assessment of these questions, however, might differ from case to case, so that no global answer can be given.

Yet, one underlying question of Arnstein's ladder still waits to be answered: What aim is pursued with patient involvement, what function should it have? Even though not identical in organisation and aims, a look at patient organisations might be useful, the more so since they in some cases considerably influenced the early ideas of patient involvement. On a very abstract level, the aim of patient organisations can be summarised as helping to stop the passive reception of medical treatment (Oudenampsen 1999, p. 58). On a more concrete level Trappenburg (2008, pp. 40, 42, 46, 68–70) identifies six different functions of patient organisations (cf. also Coulter 2000, p. 141):

(a) Raising awareness for the problems experienced
(b) Representing and lobbying towards greater society and the state
(c) Representing, lobbying against, and co-operating with the medical profession
(d) Taking things in own hands
(e) Making contact between fellow sufferers
(f) Helping each other.

In particular the points (a) and (c), depending on the type of involvement (b), too, are of equal importance to patient involvement, even though the medical profession as the addressee is exchanged for the management of a nursing home or hospital or for politicians. Transverse to these functions runs the potential tension of the two aims of solely representing co-patients and co-residents, on the one hand, and to rather steer health care providers and/or politicians on the other (Simmons et al. 2007, pp. 459–461).

Against that backdrop, the definitional, somewhat crude differentiation between three different ways of involvement—which can exist parallel to each other—is made in order to elucidate what kind of involvement this book is primarily dealing with. It is a rather pragmatic approach to delimit terms that are of importance in this study, which includes the awareness and necessity of other definitions, of which, again, given different context factors all and none are right or wrong (cf. also Simmons et al. 2007).

PATIENT PARTICIPATION will be used in the sense of co-decision making, in a formally or de facto equal position of management and patient side. In a somewhat lengthy definition Potvin describes participation very aptly as

> "[...] a generic term to encompass: those practices that involve collaborative relationships in the form of exchanges of opinion, knowledge or other resources between various groups of actors concerned by, and willing to, devote time and resources to issues of relevance to health in order to participate in decision making regarding priorities, planning, implementation or evaluation of public health programs." (Potvin 2007, p. 111)

Distinct from patient participation is PATIENT INVOLVEMENT, which gives patients the opportunity to have their say in suggesting topics to be discussed with the management, complaining about deficiencies, and consulting the management on intended developments, strategies, investments, etc. The abovementioned definition can be altered for patient involvement, if 'participate in decision making' is interchanged with 'consult in the process of decision making'.

As collective involvement most often necessarily involves only a smaller fraction of patients, large scale ONE-WAY FORMS OF COMMUNICATION, for instance, patient satisfaction surveys can complement collective patient involvement. Though the possibility to engage in discussions is naturally limited, it can create a larger image of what is going on.

Having said that and following the two acts in question here, what is in the focus of this book is patient/resident *involvement*. The definitional distinction points out that collective patient *involvement* is not about (co-)decision making, but about being given a serious possibility to have a say, to have a voice, and discuss things with decision makers. In front of this backdrop, although patient involvement may be interwoven into the organisational structure of a health care provider and a state or subordinate authority, it is still (formally) not part of the decision-making process in its narrower sense, since the final say is left to the professional decision-makers. In that sense, it has less competency than governance but at the same time reaches well beyond it. Moreover, as mentioned above, this study focuses on the hospital as the institution to be involved in. As the following chapter will show, this does not preclude that other forms of involvement will be dealt with.

## 2.2 Equivalents to Patient Involvement

As could be shown in the previous chapters, the question concerning the categorisation of patient/citizen participation/involvement incorporates a multitude of facets, which is one of the reasons why Arnstein's hierarchical, one-dimensional model is rather unsuitable for many purposes. Many of the underlying dimensions of patient/citizen participation/involvement have already been dealt with above, which can be reformulated into questions to help to describe what actually is meant when terms like participation, involvement, or empowerment are employed: What is the overall purpose of participation/involvement? Is it about individual or collective involvement? Which group is targeted? Is it a one-off event or a standing institution? What *competencies* do lay actors hold (summarised in Fig. 2.1 on the facing page).

In the context of this study it is therefore essential to regard potential equivalents to patient involvement. Many other attempts to involve people in health care and receive input from them bear the traits of patient involvement. They might constitute reasons in other countries not to perceive the necessity to implement collective

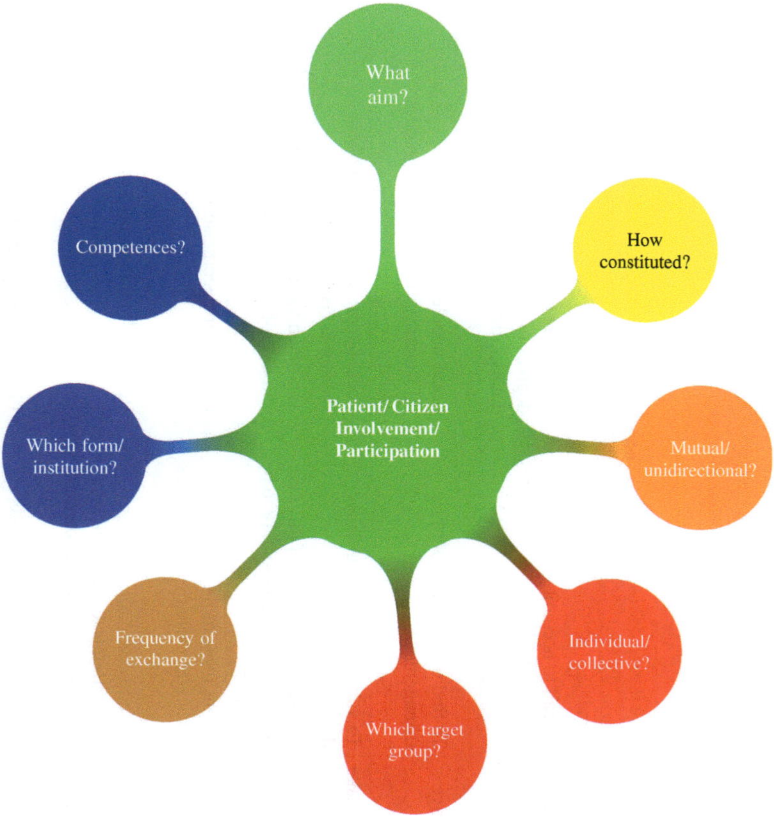


**Fig. 2.1** Dimensions of involvement. Source: Own depiction

patient involvement in hospitals. Table 2.1 on the next page is a first attempt to compile options that potentially serve an equivalent function of involvement. It not only consists of legitimatory structures such as democratic accountability or the patient/customer physician/provider relationship, but also includes other attempts to somehow involve people at some point or another. As it is difficult to gain a good overview and deeper insight into involvement in other countries, the list by no means intends to be exhaustive and needs to be complemented by other options that can be found in the respective country.

**Table 2.1** Approaches and equivalents to community involvement

| | Values and assumptions | Aims | Downsides |
|---|---|---|---|
| Democratic accountability | People who make decisions on behalf of others should be accountable, requiring open decision making | To call to account | Depending on arrangements varying degrees of direct and close democratic accountability at local level |
| Research | Research methods are more objective and can identify needs and obtain feedback from local people | To find the facts to inform management | Local people as source of information might lack the broader picture |
| Consultation exercises | Managers need to manage but also take account of local people's views | To validate and/or legitimate decision making | Local people as advisers, without sharing decisions |
| Community health councils, LINks, Patients Forums[a], *HealthWatch*[a] | Local people need a channel to keep them informed and help them express their views to the NHS | To enable the views of different sections of the community to be heard | Too much variation in effectiveness and lack of accountability |
| User groups and voluntary organisations | Voluntary organisations have knowledge and experience of services and can contribute to planning and management | To put forward the views of particular users or communities | Focuses on specific services and interests |
| Empowering communities | Local people, particularly from disadvantaged communities, need assistance to articulate their needs and act to achieve them | To 'empower' disadvantaged communities to influence local services and their environment | Requires long-term investment |
| Corporatist self-governance[a] | Representatives of unions and employers are working for the common interest of patients and net-payers | Disburden the state and give members of sickness-funds a say in their own affairs | Low legitimacy owed to decreasing organisation rates and less uniform employment biographies |

| | | | |
|---|---|---|---|
| Ombudsman system[b] | Practical implementation of rights and help patients with their complaint procedures | Representing patients towards providers and politics | Most often only retroactive once damage/ malpractice is done |
| Patient as complainant[a,c] | Patient complains about experienced low quality in health care | To improve health care services for others & prevent them from making the same bad experience | Depending on arrangements unsystematic approach dependent on the willingness of individuals with a varying welcoming attitude towards criticism |
| Patient as customer[a] | Patient is the informed customer who actively chooses for providers and services | Achieving lower prices, higher quality, and customer-oriented services | Diverse capabilities of citizens to put their interests through |

Source: top section of table is adopted from Hogg (1999, p. 109)
[a]Added by author
[b]Based on Fallberg (2003)
[c]Following the results of Bouwman, Bomhoff and Friele (2014)

## References


Arnstein, S. R. (1969, July). A ladder of citizen participation. *Journal of the American Institute of Planners, 35*(4), 216–224.

Badura, B. (2000). Reform des Gesundheitswesens durch Aktivierung der Bürger, Versicherten und Patienten—eine Einführung. In H. Ettischer & K. Salice-Stephan (Eds.), *Bürgerbeteiligung im Gesundheitswesen—eine länderübergreifende Herausforderung—Ideen, Ansätze und internationale Erfahrungen* (Chap. 2.1, 10, pp. 34–39). Forschung und Praxis der Gesundheitsförderung. Köln: Bundeszentrale für gesundheitliche Aufklärung (BZgA).

Barnes, M., Newman, J., & Sullivan, H. C. (2007). *Power, participation and political renewal—case studies in public participation*. Bristol: The Policy Press.

Barry, B. (1974). Exit, voice, and loyalty: Responses to decline in firms, organization, and states by Albert O. Hirschman. *British Journal of Political Science, 4*(1), 79–107.

Berwick, D. M. (2002). A user's manual for the IOM's 'Quality Chasm' report: Patients' experiences should be the fundamental source of the definition of "quality". *Health Affairs, 21*(3), 80–90.

Bouwman, R., Bomhoff, M., & Friele, R. (2014). *Burgers die melden bij de Inspectie voor de Gezondheidszorg (IGZ): Verwachtingen en ervaringen van burgers die een klacht over de gezondheidszorg melden bij de IGZ*. Utrecht: NIVEL.

Bundeszentrale für gesundheitliche Aufklärung (BZgA). (2000). *Bürgerbeteiligung im Gesundheitswesen: Eine länderübergreifende Herausforderung Ideen, Ansätze und internationale Erfahrungen*. Köln: Bundeszentrale für gesundheitliche Aufklärung (BZgA).

Chinitz, D. (2000). Regulierter Wettbewerb und Bürgerbeteiligung—Lektionen aus Israel. In H. Ettischer & K. Salice-Stephan (Eds.), *Bürgerbeteiligung im Gesundheitswesen—eine länderübergreifende Herausforderung—Ideen, Ansätze und internationale Erfahrungen*. Forschung und Praxis der Gesundheitsförderung (Chap. 3.2, 10, pp. 64–72). Köln: Bundeszentrale für gesundheitliche Aufklärung (BZgA).

Coulter, A. (2000, May). Stärkung des Einflusses von Patienten, Verbrauchern und Bürgern—Die Effektivität politischer Instrumente. In H. Ettischer & K. Salice-Stephan (Eds.), *Bürger beteiligung im Gesundheitswesen—eine länderübergreifende Herausforderung—Ideen, Ansätze und internationale Erfahrungen*. Forschung und Praxis der Gesundheitsförderung (Chap. 5.1, 10, pp. 138–151). Köln: Bundeszentrale für gesundheitliche Aufklärung (BZgA).

Department of Health. (2012, April 30). *Greater voice for patients—the Health and Social Care Act 2012*. London: Department of Health

Dowding, K., John, P., Mergoupis, T., & van Vugt, M. (2000). Exit, voice and loyalty: Analytic and empirical developments. *European Journal of Political Research, 37*(4), 469–495.

Eurohealth (2013). Governing public hospitals, 19.1

Fallberg, L. (2003). Patients ombudsmen—a different approach to improve quality in health services. *European Journal of Health Law, 10* 339–342.

Farrell, C. (2004, May). *Patient and public involvement in health: The evidence for policy implementation*. London: Department of Health.

Forster, R., & Gabe, J. (2008). Voice or choice? Patient and public involvement in the national health service in England under new labour. *International Journal of Health Services, 38*(2), 333–356.

Greß, S., Delnoij, D., & Groenewegen, P. P. (2003). Exit and voice in Dutch social health insurance. *CESifo Dice Report*, 3 47–53.

Greß, S., Höppner K., Marstedt G., Rothgang, H., & Thamm, M. (2008). Durchsetzung von Versicherteninteressen. In S. Greß, K. Höppner, G. Marstedt, H. Rothgang, & M. Thamm (Eds.), *Einflussnehmen oder Aussteigen? Theorie und Praxis von Selbstverwaltung und Kassenwechsel in der GKV* (pp. 19–89). Berlin: edition sigma.

Greß, S., & Rothgang, H. (2008). Hirschmanns Konzept: Exit, voice and loyalty in der GKV. In B. Braun, S. Greß, H. Rothgang, & J. Wasem (Eds.), *Einflussnehmen oder Aussteigen? Theorie und Praxis von Selbstverwaltung und Kassenwechsel in der GKV* (pp. 11–17). Berlin: edition sigma.

Grit, K., & Bal, R. (2009, April). *Creating health care consumers—the performative effects of voice and choice options*. Paper prepared for workshop 15 'Voice and Choice in Health Politics'.
Hirschman, A. O. (1970). *Exit, voice, and loyalty: Responses to decline in firms, organizations, and states*. Cambridge, MA: Harvard University Press.
Hogg, C. (1999). *Patients, power & politics—from patients to citizens*. London: SAGE.
House of Commons. (2010, May 11). House of lords reform: The 2009 White Paper and developments to April 2010.
LeGrand, J. (2006). *Motivation, agency and public policy: Of knights and knaves, pawns and queens, Revised*. Oxford: Oxford University Press.
LeGrand, J. (2007). The politics of choice and competition in public services. *The Political Quarterly, 78*(2) 207–213.
Nedlund, A.-C. (2012, June). *Designing for legitimacy—policy work and the art of juggling when setting limits in health care* (Doctoral dissertation, Linköping University Linköping).
Oudenampsen, D. G. (1999). *De patiënt als burger de burger als patiënt* (Doctoral dissertation, Universiteit Utrecht, Utrecht: Verwey-Jonker Instituut).
Potvin, L. (2007). Managing uncertainty through participation. *Health and Modernity, 10* 103–128.
Rega, I. M. (2007). *Patienten- und Bürgerbeteiligung im Gesundheitswesen Deutschlands, Finnlands und Polens*. Göttingen: Universitätsdrucke Göttingen.
Rocha, E. M. (1997). A ladder of empowerment. *Journal of Planning Education and Research, 17*(1), 31–44.
Rodwin, M. (1997). The neglected remedy: Strengthening consumer voice in managed care. *American Prospect*, September/October, 45–50.
Saltman, R. B., & von Otter, C. (1989). Voice, choice and the question of civil democracy in the Swedish welfare state. *Economic and Industrial Democracy, 10*, 195–209.
de Savornin Lohman, J. (2000). Evaluatie—Wet medezeggenschap cliënten zorgsector. In J. de. Savornin Lohman (Ed.), *Evaluatie Wet medezeggenschap cliënten zorginstellingen*. Utrecht: Verwey-Jonker Instituut.
Simmons, R., Birchall, J., Doheny S., & Powell, M. (2007). 'Citizen governance': Opportunities for inclusivity in policy and policy making? *Policy & Politics, 35*(3), 457–478.
Thompson, A. G. H. (2007). The meaning of patient involvement and participation in health care consultations: A taxonomy. *Social Science & Medicine, 64*, 1297–1310.
Trappenburg, M. (2008). *Genoeg is genoeg*. Amsterdam: Amsterdam University Press.
Tritter, J. Q., & McCallum, A. (2006). The snakes and ladders of user involvement: Moving beyond Arnstein. *Health Policy, 76* 156–168.
Tritter J., Koivusalo, M., Ollila, E., & Dorfman, P. (2010). *Globalisation, markets and health care policy—redrawing the patient as consumer*. Critical studies in health and society. Abingdon: Routledge.
van de Bovenkamp, H. M. (2010). *The limits of patient power* (Doctoral dissertation, Erasmus Universiteit Rotterdam, Rotterdam).
WHO. (1978). *Declaration of Alma-Ata*. Copenhagen: WHO.
WHO. (1994, March 28). *A declaration on the promotion of patients' rights in Europe*. Amsterdam: WHO.
WHO. (1996). *Ljubljana charter on reforming health care in Europe*. Copenhagen: WHO.
WHO Regional Office for Europe. (2006). *Ninth futures forum on health systems governance and public participation*. Copenhagen: WHO.
Young, D. R. (1974). Exit and voice in the organization of public services. *Social Science Information, 13* 49–65.

# Chapter 3
# A Theoretical Framework for the Study

*[A] student [of sociology] who has difficulty thinking of at least three sensible explanations for any correlation that he is really interested in should probably choose another profession (Stinchcombe 1968, p. 13)*

*On the Day of Judgement, when all laws are known, these may suffice to explain all phenomena. But in the meantime we do give explanations; and it is the job of science to tell us what kinds of explanations are admissible. (Cartwright 1983, pp. 51–52)*

Given the complexity of comparing four countries, the complexity and flexibility of any theory that needs to incorporate four pathways in the evolution as a welfare state, is not an easy endeavour (cf., e.g., Rothgang, Schmid & Schneider 2012). The main aim is to explain the course of policy development in countries with overall pretty similar economic and broader political circumstances. Given the field's complexity and interconnectedness, a single or narrow theory is likely to prove unsuitable regarding the complexity of the policy field of health care. Which theories and approaches can match and possibly explain the empirical findings? Since the phenomenon we are dealing with is apparently not caused by some international, external one-off cause, affecting all countries alike, we need to seek the explanation in the four countries themselves. To that end, some requirements for the theoretical framework need to be set up.

FLEXIBILITY—First, a framework is needed that is sufficiently flexible to explain what elsewhere has been labelled 'supervenience' (Maier 2003, p. 59; Wendt 1999, pp. 155 et seq.), i.e. why different pathways lead to the same result in England and the Netherlands, on the one hand, and (similar?) pathways to a dissimilar result in Germany and Sweden on the other (cf. Maier 2003, p. 59; Steinmo 2008, pp. 123, 124). Even though it does not seem to apply at first sight, this flexibility should include the possibility of selective policy learning (cf. Bennett 1991; Hall 1993; Sabatier 1993a,b).

INSTITUTIONAL LEGACY—A second precondition is that the framework should take the institutional legacy—in the form of democratic legitimacy or self-

 
A. Haarmann, *The Evolution and Everyday Practice of Collective Patient Involvement in Europe*, DOI 10.1007/978-3-319-64595-7_3

governance, for instance—into account while at the same time it should be capable to explain change and its underlying reasons and motivations.

ACTORS—Since we are dealing with different kinds of institutions, groups, and organisations—in brief: actors—the framework should take the respective actors as well as their perceptions, opinions, norms and values, motivations, and strategies into consideration. This is much in line with Boudon's (1981) understanding of social processes—which, in turn, can be regarded to be based on Katz and Lazarsfeld's *Personal Influence* (1955). An essential difference to his view, however, is that the behaviour and actions of individual and collective actors can differ. Furthermore, methodological individualism does not take structural hindrances into account in the way this study does (see Sect. 3.1 on page 34).[1]

COMPATIBILITY WITH METHODS—A third precondition is that the theory should be compatible with methods and available sources. That means that employing approaches that epistemologically draw on discourses is futile, since in the case of England the time frame of the legislation process was hardly sufficient to form such a discourse. This applies also to a theory that does not take into consideration the *collective* character of the main actors, namely politicians and patients.

COVERING THE COMPLETE PROCESS—And finally, it should ideally be able to explain how the policy process is shaped from cradle to the enactment of the bill in order to not leave out any factor of explanatory value.

To some extent, this study shares the view authors like Elster (1998) and Hedström and Swedberg (1998) hold, returning to the basic ideas of (social) mechanisms in social science. In this understanding, social mechanisms are no laws in the sense of the 'laws of physics', but a striving to detect patterns and regularities between phenomena or actions and observable effects (Elster 1998; Hedström & Swedberg 1998). The term 'effect' is to some extent used interchangeably here with 'resulting phenomenon' or colloquially 'something striking' in this study and not, as Gerring (2007, pp. 43–44) suggests in a rather statistical sense as 'magnitude of a causal effect'. A simple definition is proposed by Elster: 'Roughly speaking, mechanisms are *frequently occurring and easily recognizable causal patterns that are triggered under generally unknown conditions or with indeterminate consequence.* They allow us to explain but not to predict.' (Elster 1998, p. 45; emphasis in original) An alternative definition could read as follows: 'A social mechanism is a plausible hypothesis, or set of hypotheses, that could be the explanation of some social

[1]This holds in particular true for what he calls 'cumulative processes' (Boudon 1981, chap. 6), which can be paraphrased as a 'mutually conditional sequence of actions in a long(er)-term development process'. At the same time, his understanding can be perceived a forerunner of Coleman's (1990) famous 'bathtub model', sometimes also called 'boat model': Effects on an aggregated level can very often be traced back to individual processes based on single (individual or collective) actors (for the application on the relation between health care provider and patients between macro- and micro-level cf. Groenewegen 1995, Symposium: 'Medische sociologie: empirisch-theoretisch onderzoek' te Utrecht). In sum, they shape macro processes. In addition, it bears, in part, reminiscence of Kuhn's 'scientific revolutions' (Boudon 1981, p. 89; Kuhn 1976).

phenomena'. (Schelling 1998, chap. 2) The inability to predict in a lawlike sense does, of course, not exclude the possibility to make an educated guess on other cases that have not been studied. Understanding 'short-range generalisation' in *that* sense is, in contrast, possible, allowed, and desired. Wanting to contribute something beyond the scope of only these four countries and owing to the fact that there is usually more than one possible explanation, I agree with Elster that 'some kind of story must be told for the explanation to be convincing, whereby with 'story' I mean 'lawlike generalization at a lower level of aggregation' ' (Elster 1998, p. 48). This attempt, of course, has its clear limitations of generalisability, as the mechanisms found are deeply rooted in the cases under research (on the generalisability of case studies cf. Gerring 2007, pp. 178–180, 182).[2]

In line with the approach taken here, hardly any case study is suited to conceptualising grand theories of social sciences even though it may contribute parts and depper understanding to it. This is definitively not the place to discuss the theoretical development in the social and political sciences at large, either. In concreto, however, the understanding of theory is much closer to Merton's (1967) criticism on Parsons' and others grand-scale theory-building, who rather advocated to stay close to social mechanisms, i.e. short(er)-range approaches in theory-building (on this topic cf. also Hedström & Swedberg 1998, p. 6). In this sense, this study aims at the 'explanations specifically tailored to a limited range of phenomena' (Hedström & Swedberg 1998, p. 24).[3]

As the primary aim is to answer the question *why these* two countries have introduced formal patient involvement, general theories on governance, corporatism, and their development might support some arguments, their perspective, however, is too narrow for answering the question of this study. The same applies to approaches understanding policies as the sole result of a negotiation of actors, for which the actor network theory might apply (for an application and overview cf. Potvin 2007), since more potential factors need to be considered.

The role of theory in this book is a 'tentatively guiding one', claiming neither to be 'true' nor 'complete'. Thus, given the explorative character of the study, no theory will be tested in the classical sense. The theories and approaches used here will rather offer some broader guideline to what aspects attention should be paid, which ones offer potential mechanisms that have been found of value in other case studies. Nevertheless, the mechanisms that have been active in *these* four cases need to be explored going beyond these guiding theories: maybe the same mechanisms will be found, maybe others are of more relevance, maybe

[2]'Case studies may uncover or refine a theory about a particular causal mechanism—such as collective action dynamics—that is applicable to vast populations of cases, but usually the effects of such mechanisms differ from one case or context to another'. (George & Bennett 2005, p. 31).

[3]Beyond this consensus, Hedström and Swedberg and Elster are in disagreement on the actual goal. Whereas Elster states laws to be the goal ('Although it is difficult to establish laws in the social sciences, that goal will always, for better or for worse, continue to guide scholars'. (Elster 1998, p. 62)), Hedström and Swedberg view laws in the social sciences as rather impossible, a stance, I would endorse.

the combination and intermeshing of several mechanisms proves to be the best approach. In the following, a number of theories and concepts will be presented that fulfil several or most of abovementioned criteria. As will be shown, all of them have their strengths and shortcomings. This, in turn, makes it difficult to lean on a single type of theory, but makes it necessary to draw on a mixture of them.

## 3.1 Institutionalism

Institutional analysis has undergone some considerable change over time. Had institutions been 'the vessel in which politics took place' within the social sciences during the first decades of the twentieth century, one of the most important achievements of historical institutionalism in later years was to have shown that the leeway of politicians within this 'vessel' is very much constrained by existing institutions (Steinmo 2008, pp. 199, 123 et seq.). Institution can thereby be defined as 'an established order comprising rule-bound and standardized behaviour patterns' (Jary & Jary 2000; cf. also Fuchs-Heinritz et al. 1995, p. 302) and might be social (such as marriage), economic, power-regulating, or political in kind. As this leaves room for a whole array of questions and perspectives, historical institutionalism forms only a part of a wider interest in institutions, subsumed under the label 'new institutionalism' or 'neo-institutionalism' (Kaiser 1999, pp. 196–204). New institutionalism differs from the traditional view in political sciences insofar as it broadens the perspective beyond political, constitutional structures, and focuses—in contrast to sociology—only on formal institutions (cf. Kaiser 1999, p. 191; for a brief discussion of the definition of the term 'institution' cf. Mayntz & Scharpf 1995, pp. 40–43; to delimit the boundaries of institutionalism cf. also Hall & Taylor 1996).

### *3.1.1 Historical Institutionalism*

In contrast to other fields of institutional studies, historical institutionalism is—as the name suggests—specifically inclined to analyse the impact of institutions on institutions themselves and decision-making and thereby, in a way, seizes upon the age-old question what is more decisive: the structurally imposed general framework or the freedom to decide. Historical institutionalism has undergone some considerable development, both with regard to the basic questions as also to the degree of detail. Skocpol's (1979) study on some of the great revolutions in history can be perceived as one of the first and still well-known books within what nowadays is called historical institutionalism. This perspective can be summarised as the first question of historical institutionalism: Do institutions matter, and what role do they play?

An example for the second phase of historical institutionalism can, e.g., be seen in Immergut's (1992) study on health care policy in European countries. At that time, the importance of institutions was already taken for granted, while the focus was shifted towards the analysis of the impact of institutions on decision-making processes, e.g., within the welfare state. In doing so, scholars not only recognised the hampering impact of institutions but also the structuring quality of the choices at hand (cf. Steinmo 2008, p. 124), for which Dowding (1995, p. 44) coined the telling term 'structural suggestions' (cf. also Kaiser 1999, p. 191). March and Olsen (1984, 1989) have tried to summarise the state of historical institutionalism in the mid 1980s as 'heuristics'. Even though the diverse branches of historical institutionalism probably do not agree to *all* points March and Olson mention in their summary, it can be seen as a first basis most authors would agree on and upon which future scholars build. Overall, the perception that institutions are restricting is predominant (cf., e.g., Windhoff-Héritier 1988). What, in contrast, can be learned from sociological institutionalism is that it also highlights the enabling component of institutions as Münnich (2011, p. 492) amongst others rightly points out (cf. also DiMaggio & Powell [1983] 1991, pp. 69–70).

Amongst others, the discovery of two major mechanisms, which are also recognised in more general theory, can be attributed to historical institutionalism: The *first* is that the number of veto-players/points matters considerably (Immergut 1990, 1992; Tsebelis 2002). A veto-player can be understood as any powerful actor who challenges plans and bills of in particular political actors. The power and/or the number of veto-players can be perceived as one of the standard aspects in qualitative as well as quantitative policy analysis. Typical examples would be strong trade unions, a strong constitutional court, or strong bicameralism often in combination with federalism, but also multi-party government can assume the role of a veto-player. It can be assumed that this mechanism is of some importance with regard to our sample of countries: in Germany, the competency for the hospital infrastructure rests with the federal states, whereas the organisation of funding of primary care falls within the competency of the Federal Government. Moreover, the Federal Constitutional Court has played some role in the shaping of structures within the health care insurance sector (Busse & Riesberg 2005; Ismayr 2009; Rothgang et al. 2012). In Sweden it is the county councils' task to commission or provide health care (Glenngård, Hjalte, Svensson, Anell & Bankauskaite 2005; Jahn 2009).

The number of veto-players/points alone, however, is irrelevant in itself. First the interplay between an actor, who wants to change something—often: the government—and other actors—be it collaborating or the abovementioned vetoing ones—is of crucial importance. However, other mechanisms that might be subsumed under the concept of veto-points in its wider sense cannot be ruled out right from the start, either. In the Netherlands, one hampering factor for a quick political solution is definitively that governments are usually comprised of a number of diverse parties (Haarmann 2012; Lepszy & Wilp 2009, p. 372). Béland (2005, p. 14) suggests that countries with multi-actor systems like the Netherlands favour 'coordinative discourse' over 'communicative discourse' which might be part of the explanation why legislation processes are rather lengthy, but are not dealt with for any longish period of time in parliament. However, this would be contradicted by Sweden, where coming to an agreement with at best all actors was one characteristic of the political system, a characteristic which is wearing off, lately.

In this book the *second* major mechanism, the concept of 'path dependence' (e.g. Ebbinghaus 2006; Immergut 2006; Pierson 2000; cf. also the 'structural suggestions' by Dowding 1995, p. 44) plays an at least equally important role. Path dependence is, simply speaking, just another expression for the discovery that previous policies and institutions play a restricting role with regard to policies and changes of institutions of the future: A health care system based on sickness funds is unlikely to be changed into a national health system in a short amount of time, as pay-as-you-go pension schemes might not that easily be converted into fully funded ones. In the same line of argument they are at first glance rather unlikely to change the chain of legitimacy: translated into the field of patient participation, this would mean that any move away from the strong institution of self-governance in Germany as well as the weaker one in the Netherlands would be inhibited or hampered by the existing institutions. However, we should bear in mind that it is *unlikely*, though not *impossible*, as the process of Italy and Spain to a well-performing regional health system and the departure of corporatism as the ruling concept in the Netherlands illustrate.

At the same time, the expectation towards the state—in its broad sense and with respect to the relation between government, subordinate, supervisory authorities (Rothgang et al. 2012, pp. 185–186)—is that it remedies problems no matter whether it was involved in their emergence or not. One example for this can be seen in the recent economic crisis when the state, long declared dead, came to the banks' rescue (cf. Rothgang et al. 2012, pp. 175–176; cf. also Sejersted 2011, pp. 431 et seq.). This implies a shift in the role of the state from being a monopolist of authority (*'Herrschaftsmonopolist'*) to a manager of authority (*'Herrschaftsmanager'*) (Rothgang et al. 2012, p. 178).

However, historical institutionalism also received a good deal of criticism, too. Two major concerns are of relevance for this study: The first main concern is that the approach is good at describing the impact of institutions on society and the policy making process, but that it fails to address and explain their change (e.g. Steinmo 2008, p. 129), let alone their emergence.[4] Another variant of this critique states that the approach's view is too deterministic (Crouch & Farrell 2002; Ebbinghaus 2006, p. 1). Second—and related to the first—the question arose, how change can be possible in an environment that is restricting and static? The most common explanation for change—if this possibility was accepted at all—had been external ruptures, external shocks, or critical junctures (Immergut 2006, p. 4; Steinmo 2008). The occupation of the Netherlands by Nazi Germany during the Second World War

[4]This holds true for any functionalist approach, too, as Rothgang et al. (2012, pp. 187–188) amongst many others rightly argue: Whereas functional deficits are sufficient for a description of change for many authors, they fail to address the mechanisms and time variable that can be of crucial value to the explanation of changes.

and the imposed introduction of a health insurance after the German model is one example of such a rupture. The oil-price shocks during the 1970s with the far-reaching implications in many societal areas in the western world are another. Both situations urged actors to react. Beyond these external sources, action in historical institutionalism can be perceived as a theoretical problem: who should initiate change if (political) actors, according to historical institutionalism, are degenerated into *re*-actors, if they are unable to set their own agenda, let alone their own imprint beyond the limits of already existing institutions and can rather be interpreted as 'simple hostages of the institutions that they inhabit' (Steinmo 2008, p. 133)?

Authors contributing to the *third* phase of historical institutionalism have, therefore, tried to address these conceptual problems: The focus has shifted from a mapping of institutions in the welfare states to the change of them triggered by reforms (Palier & Martin 2007, p. 535; cf. also Rothstein 1998; for example, cf., Bonoli & Palier 2007; Clegg 2007; Guillén & Palier 2004; Hemerijck & Schludi 2000; Hemerijck, Unger & Visser 2001; Mayntz 1990; Palier 2001, 2006, 2010; Rhodes 2000). In addition—and that is of more importance in this context—they have tried to apply a more dynamic perspective to historical institutionalism. The general view here is that 'incremental change' is another option for development to occur, which could be translated into 'extensive change over time by many small steps' or 'gradual reinterpretation of institutions' (Ebbinghaus 2006, p. 3; cf., e.g., Hacker 2004, p. 9; Mahoney & Thelen 2009; Streeck & Thelen 2005). Despite their differences, both external ruptures and incremental change can lead to the same result.

Exceptions from the general rule that most publications within the framework of historical institutionalism do not contribute to its theoretical development, include the often cited attempt to explain the evolution of institutions by Thelen (2003) and Ebbinghaus (2006, p. 3) and the attempt to get closer to the change of institutions and policies by Streeck and Thelen (2005). Streeck and Thelen (2005, p. 19) focus on the potential of institutions themselves by stating that 'change is often endogenous and in some cases is produced by the very behavior an institution itself generates'. This changed view made even concepts like policy learning (cf., e.g., Bennett 1991; Sabatier 1993b; Steinmo 2008; Palier 2001) possible, which previously would not have made any sense at all within historical institutionalism.

Unravelling what most often is summarised under either 'path stability' or 'breaking the path', 'path departure', or the more radical change 'path switching' (cf. Ebbinghaus 2006, p. 3), Streeck and Thelen mention five types of transformation of how change can occur. As these different processes can tell important things about the quality of change and its potential implications, they shall briefly be summarised (for an overview cf. Streeck & Thelen 2005, p. 31):

DISPLACEMENT describes change that is mostly fostered by overwhelmingly powerful or rather powerful actors that are willing to take the risk of failure. They implement or support an element or institution foreign, outdated, or 'unsuitable' to the environment in question. At some point in time this element becomes important in relation to the hitherto dominant one specifically in those instances that have been shown incoherent and prone to unreliability. They may have the chance to become the new standard (Streeck & Thelen 2005, pp. 19–22). As examples might be regarded the turn from public provision of health care services in Sweden to a purchaser–provider split including some form of competition.

LAYERING describes a kind of change by adding a parallel or functionally equivalent layer of institution, which over time devaluates the original institution in place (Streeck & Thelen 2005, pp. 22–24). One of the most cited examples for this type of change is the inauguration of a privately and fully funded pension tier, whereby the pay-as-you-go pension schemes lost in importance.

DRIFT can be intended or simply evolving. It describes the seemingly untouched continuation of institutions which no longer match the actual need (Streeck & Thelen 2005, pp. 24–26). An example for a policy change by drift would be to keep spending for the vaccination against tuberculosis at a high level, whereas the majority of deaths are caused by different sicknesses. Or keeping the so-called widows annuity in existence although measures for training and integration into the labour market specific to women would be much more needed.

CONVERSION redirects existing institutions 'to new goals, functions, or purposes' (Streeck & Thelen 2005, p. 26), be it intentional, unintentional, or as a result of compromise (Streeck & Thelen 2005, pp. 26–29). Ebbinghaus' 'functional transformation' is an alternative label for the same process (Ebbinghaus 2006, p. 3). As one example for conversion we can mention the depletion of the public German pension scheme from the preservation of standard of living to a mere minimum pension.

EXHAUSTION does not describe change of an institution in its narrower sense, but its gradual breakdown (Streeck & Thelen 2005, pp. 29–30). The abolition of early retirement in several European countries is one of the mentioned examples.

Concerning the actor in all these types of transformation, it becomes clear that whether or not an actor is powerful, again, depends on the framing institutions and the one for which she acts. Streeck and Thelen's (2005) transformations can therefore rather be regarded to build on top of the existing literature on historical institutionalism, an important add-on, which, however, should not be regarded as a stand-alone. Furthermore, though Streeck and Thelen (2005) provide a good description of different pathways of change, even this faces three main problems: For the *first*, the suggested pathways are not distinct so that the application to specific institutional changes becomes blurry and thereby difficult to apply. Considering self-governance in sickness funds in Germany as an example, we can see that its importance has gradually worn off while the Joint Federal Committee (*Gemeinsamer Bundesausschuss*, G-BA) as a self-administered institution equipped with further reaching competences is installed. It is difficult to say whether it is an instance of layering, drift, or exhaustion.

*Second*, even this attempt at categorisation remains a description of how change progresses, which only in some instances leaves some leeway for actors to deliberately initiate change. *Third*, how change specifically occurs and what the motivation for actors to take action is still coming out of nowhere. So far, no convincing answer could be provided for why, at the one end of the scale, incremental change occurs, even less why it is created, or why, on the other end, 'displacement' is shaped.

### 3.1.2 The Basic Idea About Actor-Centred Institutionalism

The approach of actor-centred institutionalism stays within the framework of institutional analysis, but tries to overcome some of the aforementioned shortcomings of historical institutionalism. One of the major contributors to actor-centred institutionalism stated that '[t]he primary business of interaction-oriented policy research within the framework of actor-centred institutionalism is to explain past policy choices' (Scharpf 1997, p. 43), which makes the approach an ideal choice as a theoretical foundation. With historical institutionalism it shares the view that 'institutions, not assumptions, reduce empirical variance' (Scharpf 1997, p. 38; cf. also Mayntz & Scharpf 1995, p. 49; Scharpf 1997, pp. 40, 47). Institutions are here understood as 'systems of rules that structure the courses of actions that a set of actors may choose' (Scharpf 1997, p. 38), which comes close to a rather broad sociological definition (cf. Scott 1995, p. 48). Moreover, institutions not only restrict but also enable new options, perceptions, and preferences upon which decisions are built (Scharpf 1997, pp. 39–42). The hampering influence of the number of veto players found in historical institutionalism is translated into higher costs of negotiation and the difficulties reaching an agreed decision between a growing number of actors, whereas majoritarian decision making comes at a lower price (Mayntz & Scharpf 1995, p. 58; Scharpf 1997, p. 59).

Unlike historical institutionalism, however, institutions are only one part of the focus providing the framework within which actors operate. In contrast to many sociological approaches, actor-centred institutionalism treats collective actors—in the terminology of actor-centred institutionalism 'corporate' or 'composite actors'—analytically as an entity, allowing to include trade unions, governments, political parties, interest groups etc. (Coleman 1974; Mayntz & Scharpf 1995, pp. 48–51; Scharpf 1997, pp. 39, 54 et seq.; Touraine 1977). Essential, furthermore, is the underlying assumption of overall rationally acting actors: taking into consideration the potential asymmetry between the, often conflicting, interests and expectations of actors and considering what rational ways there are to pursue them (cf. Groenewegen 1995, Symposium: 'Medische sociologie: empirisch-theoretisch onderzoek' te Utrecht) actor-centred institutionalism is much more able to make assumptions about the potential course of action taken by them. This, of course, can be refined much more than the example given by Scharpf who concludes that in order '[...] to reduce the danger of losing office, democratically accountable governments must attempt to adopt public-interest-oriented policies'. (Scharpf 1997, p. 40).

In a typology Scharpf (1997, pp. 55, 57) subdivides actors into different classes. According to this typology, politicians and patient organisations as the two major actors can be characterised as antagonistic actors of the same type, which he labels 'association'. Even though this characterises governments and associations somewhat unfittingly, what is important in this respect is that both actors are comparable in type and basically follow the same rules. This eases the task of analysis to some degree where patient organisations are involved.

### 3.1.3 Strategic Actors

Whereas institutions frame the environment of actors, the actors themselves are, as the name suggests, at the core of actor-centred institutionalism. After first having identified the set of interactions within a given policy field, actors can be identified in a second step (Mayntz & Scharpf 1995, p. 52; Scharpf 1997, p. 43). Scharpf continues to explain that the first step is not only needed to gain an overview of what actors there are in a specific field but also to understand the relation between them: 'Since the choices are interdependent, it is likely that no single actor will be able to determine the outcome unilaterally. What matters is the actor constellation'. (Scharpf 1997, p. 69; cf. also Mayntz & Scharpf 1995, p. 53). Upon this, third, they can be 'characterized by capabilities, specific perceptions, and specific preferences', which also includes all kinds of perceptions and evaluation of the problems at hand (Scharpf 1997, p. 43), for instance, perceptions on the relations between goals and instruments. This fits Kingdon's (2003, pp. 111–112) observation of how important it is, how a problem is framed, and what categories are used to describe it.

Since many European countries, irrespective of the type of welfare/health care state, face similar problems, the last point is particularly important to this study. It should, accordingly, be made much stronger than its mentioning en passant by Scharpf: the (slightly) different perception of the same problem may lead to similarly diverse solutions as a consequence of the heritage of different institutional traditions. Perceptions may, in that sense, be roughly interpreted as a point on a continuum between the following two extremes: (a) as 'objective assessments' of problems—to the extent that is possible at all—; or (b) like a somewhat distorted view of reality, be it owing to lack of information, based on certain underlying values, or strategic decision. This problem of limited rationality and limited availability and transparency of information is taken into consideration:

> The major difficulty with actor-centred approaches is that they must, at bottom, rely on intentional explanations that are inevitably based on subjectivities (Dennet 1981; Rosenberg 1988). It is not in the real world but in the actor's mental image of the world that the attribution of causes and expected effects must be located (Scharpf 1997, p. 60)

It can be argued, however, that the actors' explanations and perceptions is just what we want to get at. How else could we understand and explain why they decided for certain options and acted as they did? Seen from this perspective Scharpf's postulation does not pose a problem, as long as the employed sources for the analysis reflect the true considerations and motives of the actors at the time of their action. The only requirement arising from this observation is that the researcher needs to crosscheck with other sources in order to find out to what extent the stated version comes close to 'objective' measures or developments or to what extent it is distorted or misunderstood. In this line, the type of argumentation is also of less importance: whether it is functionalist, constructivist, or anything else is irrelevant (cf., e.g., Schmid, Cacace, Götze & Rothgang 2010, pp. 460, 468; cf. also Rothgang, Schmid & Schneider 2011). This keeps actor-centred institutionalism highly adaptable as does the very broad formulation that any action is triggered by a 'problem', be it external or internal, caused back in time or coming up recently, objective and measurable or in the actors' perception (Scharpf 1997, p. 43). Furthermore, Scharpf (2000, p. 86; 1997, p. 54) points out that even seemingly minor or unimportant actions should not be disregarded as they can be the decisive piece of information that influences, changes, or even facilitates a whole chain of actions. Moreover, the approach comes with relatively few presuppositions as the actors' orientations can both be relatively stable or changeable.

Overall the analyst faces the problem that often we are dealing with individual actors speaking for a party or an association for which it cannot be taken for granted that convictions and opinions concur with the party's or association's official position. Scharpf's solution is to extrapolate the presented view on the larger institution whereby the individual actor of a larger institution is taken as its representative:

> For policy research, this implies that we need to relate individual behavior—which is all that we are able to observe empirically—to the appropriate (individual or social) unit of reference on whose behalf action is taken and from whose perspective intentional choices can be explained. (Scharpf 1997, p. 61)

This, however, can be contested on reasonable grounds. We only need to take a look at how any spokesperson's presentation of a party contrasts the image that is given by any deviant party member or backbencher to see that the limitations of methodological individualism have been reached.

It is self-evident that with introduction of perception a constructivist element has been put into the theoretical toolbox which, in turn, raises the question why actors frame a problem as they do. In general it can be said that actors try to satisfy their own self-interest and use their ability to strategic action (Mayntz & Scharpf 1995, p. 57; Scharpf 1997, pp. 64, 58; cf. also Boudon 1981). This entails two things: first, this self-interest needs to be taken into account if the intention is to make assumptions about the underlying motives for policy reforms. Second, Scharpf's example of strategic action basically argues that it is about a better bargaining position (Scharpf 1997, p. 64). Yet, since it is the respective government that can enact legislation on patient participation it is, without taking other actors less seriously or disregarding their orientations and aims, *the* decisive collective actor in the field. This makes it necessary to specifically focus on their intentions, which can vary extremely.

This is where we might encounter difficulties for two reasons. First, it might be difficult to discern between strategy and real intention since we, at least tò some extent, often need to rely on how actors present themselves and what they publicly relate. This problem is universal, is probably to be experienced no matter what theoretical approach is chosen (on different forms of strategy cf. also Sect. 3.2.1 on page 45) and as intricate as the question raised above whether any 'objective' perception is possible at all. Second, therefore, '[f]or our explanations it is of utmost empirical interest whether and how perceptions deviate from the best knowledge possible (that often is only recognised in retrospective)'. (Scharpf 2000, p. 115) However, it is not an easy task to ascertain on what informational grounds actors base their decisions. In contrast to most scholars subscribing to the economic stream of rational choice, actor-centred institutionalism assumes that actors are neither unlimitedly rational nor omniscient (Mayntz & Scharpf 1995, p. 41; Scharpf 1997, pp. 62–63), while at the same time, the suggested assumption '[. . . ] that the specific combinations of knowledge and ignorance tend to be shared among actors in institutionalized interactions—and that, for the same reason, they will be accessible to researchers as well' (Scharpf 1997, p. 62) might hold true in an ideal world, but might prove as difficult as the assumption of omniscience in rational choice approaches. In consequence, we need to content ourselves with crosschecking with the evidence we can draw from other sources and the course of action taken.[5]

## 3.2 On Agendas, Ideas, and Paradigms

### *3.2.1 Ideas*

> I can trace the paths of ideas. But my personal theory is that people plant seeds every day. There are a lot of ideas around, and there is no lacking of ideas. The real questions is, which of these ideas will catch hold? When you plant a seed, you need rain, soil, and luck. (interviewee interviewed and cited by Kingdon (2003, p. 77))

Even from a rather empirical angle, at least some, instances suggest that an 'incremental or gradualism model' does not describe agenda change particularly well, since the interest in a topic does not (always) build up gradually (Kingdon 2003, p. 80). This is where ideas become vital, more so for radical paradigm shifts but they might even play a decisive role for gradual changes. In that, ideas can provide an answer to the question concerning what the underlying assumptions are based on. As described by Hall (1993) and Münnich (2011, p. 491), ideas can fill newly discovered or long known gaps and shortcomings to supersede an old paradigm. Authors like Hall (1993, pp. 288–289) or Kingdon (2003, p. 125) even argue that it is less the influence of pressure groups is the driving cause which makes politicians rethink policies but new ideas.

Gaining an overview of the ideational approach is not an easy endeavour: as Maier (2003, pp. 26, 62–64) rightly points out it would do more justice to speak of *several* approaches under one umbrella, since even the terminology varies across different authors. Nevertheless, he shows, too, that the majority can be united under a loose framework (to gain an overview of the different streams cf. Münnich 2011 and Maier 2003). Despite its relative newness, the approach has experienced a rapid development, which has led to a number of diverse branches in a pretty short amount

[5]While Mayntz and Scharpf (1995, pp. 60–65) argue for a number of more analytical options—abstraction from reality, network analysis, and game theory—a later version only deals with the lastmentioned (Scharpf 1997, pp. 69 et seq.). Due to the quality and kind of data, however, the structure of actor-centred institutionalism described so far needs to suffice, as the game theoretical reflections undertaken by Scharpf (1997) are impossible to conduct in *this* study.

of time, which otherwise is only known from more traditional theories. It has taken a similar road as institutionalism, in that the focus has shifted from '*Do* ideas matter?' to '*How* do ideas matter?' or in '*how far* do ideas matter?' (Münnich 2011, p. 497; cf. also Maier 2003, p. 25). Though it can be used as an independent piece of theoretical framework, it has been shown to work very well if combined with institutional approaches, too (cf., e.g., Béland 2005; Hall 1993; Schmid, Cacace, Götze & Rothgang 2010).

As Münnich (2011, p. 489) points out, not taking the underlying ideas—or the rhetoric used, as an expression of the underlying ideas (Maier 2003, p. 46)—into consideration does not necessarily distort results. However, ideas can serve as a strengthening and/or 'testing' of the findings:

> The empirical proof of certain institutions or interests 'in the form of ideas' in the orientation of the actor means that ideas play a role for the actor. The explanation does not automatically get wrong because it is based on objective institutions or interests. First where doubts arise whether the objective structures and the subjective motivations drawn upon for explanation point into the same direction ideas become interesting for causal explanations, too. [. . . ] A similar reasoning is applicable which aim is not to find out about the origin of action of *individual* actors, but about the overall structure of the political discourse. (Münnich 2011, p. 489; emphasis in original)

Besides this point an ideational approach has more to offer. The most crucial contribution is that it can deliver a better explanation for underlying motives, as institutionalism is ill-suited to explain change (Béland 2005, p. 4). While the key message of historical institutionalism can be read as 'existing institutions restrict the scope of action in actors' actor-centred institutionalism rather highlights the relation between different actors within a given restricting and enabling framework of institutions. Both approaches only give some insufficient insight into where institutions, actors, and in particular their issues originate. This is where ideas come into play, which can be thought of as the origin of policy processes. In this sense, we can not only infer on the actors' interrelations, abilities, power resources, preferences, and perceptions but we can conceptually go back to their 'origin'.

The most common reading is that ideas are born all the time and form a reservoir of mostly unused ideas. At certain points in time, some of them become relevant, whereas others remain insignificant. Even though their origin is difficult to locate, Kingdon (2003, pp. 116 et seq.) describes them to root in the 'primeval soup' of ideas.

More important, however, is the question of *when* an idea is becoming dominant over others, which seems to be tightly interwoven with the question *how* they become dominant. Summarising Kingdon's line of argumentation the policy community produces a shortlist of ideas, which in the process of discussion is consecutively 'softened up' to make them more acceptable, agreeable, or appealing (Kingdon 2003, pp. 117 et seq., 127 et seq., 139), before 'policy entrepreneurs' choose an idea and take the lead in propagating it (Kingdon 2003, p. 179). The process of 'softening up' continues throughout the process of finding and choosing among alternatives. This process, how ideas become effective, consists of several steps:

> Though a drastic oversimplification, public policy making can be considered to be a set of processes, including at least (1) the setting of the agenda, (2) the specification of alternatives from which a choice is to be made, (3) an authoritative choice among those specified alternatives, as in a legislative vote or decision, and (4) the implementation of the decision. [...; Thereby, t]he *agenda*, as I conceive of it, is the list of subjects or problems to which governmental officials, and people outside of government closely associated with those officials, are playing some serious attention at any given time [...; or, to put it differently, the most] pressing problems of the moment (Kingdon 2003, pp. 3–4).

The term ' 'policy idea' refers to specific policy alternatives [...] as well as the organized principles and causal beliefs in which these proposals are embedded' (Béland 2005, p. 2). In order to be successfully picked, however, the alternatives at hand need to be 'real policy choices' in the sense that they are perceived to contribute to the solution of the problem, though it is sometimes sufficient to provide an acceptable and desirable policy alternative (Béland 2005, pp. 9, 12). And sometimes it does not even seem to be clear, why a specific alternative is chosen as Kingdon (2003, p. 110) admits. To put it differently: 'Ideas are out there and they have an impact on politics only when seized upon by political actors and through this process find an entry point into politics'. (Hansen & King 2001, p. 259) As Kingdon points out, choosing between alternatives is like

> [...] a garbage can into which various kinds of problems and solutions are dumped by participants as they are generated. The mix of garbage in a single can depends on the mix of cans available, on the labels attached to the alternative cans, on what garbage is currently being produced, and on the speed with which garbage is collected and removed from the scene. (Cohen, March & Olsen 1972, p. 2)

However, as this quotation points out, ideas do not stand alone, but are embedded into the world where they are born, with its institutions, its actors, and their preferences, perceptions, and values (Schmid, Cacace, Götze & Rothgang 2010, p. 461): 'Ideas have real power in the real world, however [...] they do not acquire political force independently of the constellation of institutions and interests already present there'. (Hall 1989, p. 390) The obvious conceptual difficulty that this poses is that it is difficult at times to discern, whether ideas play a causal or mediating role and what the real impact of ideas actually is, if all other factors are counted in (Münnich 2011, pp. 495, 490). How, for instance, can we differentiate between interests and ideas, between ideas and values, between ideas and ideology? Kingdon's results suggest that, quite naturally, ideology limits the scope of what 'may be thought', what is desirable and what undesirable. Ideology might even suggest solutions, which were not even asked for by a country's citizens (Kingdon 2003, pp. 108, 133). The same holds most probably true for values, depending on which many ideas remain unthought or are not taken up (cf. also Kingdon 2003, pp. 110–111). Moreover, if you cannot decide whether ideas are genuine or interestled, is there not the danger that ideas are absorbed entirely (Münnich 2011, p. 494)? Furthermore, we might even say that, once an idea is born or once an idea is accepted, circumstances have changed immediately as actors and institutions relate to it (cf. Groenewegen 1994, 1998). Béland (2005, p. 8) argues that,

> [a]gainst the impression that policy ideas have little consistency, it must be stressed that most alternatives are grounded in a policy paradigm, which constitutes the structured intellectual background of policy decisions. These paradigms serve as 'road maps' to experts and policy-makers by providing them with a relatively coherent set of assumptions about the functioning of economic, political and social institutions.

The consequence thereof leads, according to the author, to politicians who tread beaten paths, stay within the same paradigm and make similar choices. Regarding this parallel between institutionalism and ideational approaches, we can not only speak of compatibility (Béland 2005, pp. 2, 13; Hall 1993; Schmid et al. 2010, p. 461), but can claim that ideas shape the perception of problems and suitable solutions (Schmid et al. 2010, p. 460).[6] Furthermore, ideational approaches can provide the missing link in the chain of institutionalist and actor-centred approaches: the start or early stages of the legislation process.

Beyond similar concepts of institutionalism and ideational approaches, there are three devices that would be subsumed under 'strategic actors' in actor-centred institutionalism that might be worth a closer in this study, since to me they seem formulated much more pointed under the ideational approach: The term 'IDEAS AS HOOKS' describes the selling of ideas by means of different reasoning or decisions, in order to make the original idea more appealing or more acceptable (Maier 2003, pp. 47, 48). Whether actors actually believe in their hooks or whether it is simply used as a strategy, is difficult to discern, as we can only observe what is rhetorically uttered (Maier 2003, pp. 50, 54). However, as Maier (2003, p. 47) points out, this strategy would at least need a sufficiently large group that (potentially) 'buys' the hooks as realistic options.

The concept of 'COUPLING', in contrast, describes the use of help in argumentation by another topic, wrapped to a package that is sold as one piece. The additional topic can, thereby, be a practical necessity or a strategic helper: 'Thus solutions come to be coupled with problems, proposals linked with political exigencies, and alternatives introduced when the agenda changed'. (Kingdon 2003, p. 173) This can, for instance, be done by referring to commonly employed symbols,

[6]This also becomes apparent in the concepts used: The ideational approach knows its equivalent for 'path dependency', too, in that new ideas are still associated with higher costs and 'need to prove its adequacy and suitability' and that institutions help to form and change ideas (Hirschman 1991; Münnich 2011, pp. 490–491; Sikkink 1993, p. 26), is described as 'incrementalism' (Kingdon 2003, p. 79); or in that actors are described to be 'rhetorically entrapped' (Schmidt 2008, p. 312). 'Path break' or 'path departure' can be translated into 'paradigm shift'. The 'window of opportunity', one of the standard concepts in institutional analysis, is called 'policy window' or substituted by highlighting the importance of timing (Kingdon 2003, pp. 166–169). Further similarities are that it is sometimes explicitly referred to the line of erratic, pragmatic, rationalistic, and institutional argumentation (Kingdon 2003, pp. 14–15). This includes a subjective perception, using arguments to the actors' advantage, taking strategic considerations into account. The underlying claim, here, is that, similar to the rational choice reasoning, actors are goal-conscious about what they want to achieve (Maier 2003, p. 29). As will be shown in the subsequent section, the assumption, however, that the perception of actors and objective givens coincide will be challenged in this book (on that assumption cf. Maier 2003, p. 46).

introducing new policies in disguise: 'Policy entrepreneurs succeed in imposing certain policy ideas partly because they appeal to the public through the mobilization of political symbols ever-present in the shared ideological repertoires available in their society'. (Béland 2005, pp. 10–11). One example mentioned by Cox (2004) is when the conservative, 'bourgeois' government of Sweden explicitly referred to social democracy and its values in order to foster acceptance for and legitimise its welfare state reforms (cf. also Cox 2001, 2009).

The last explicated issue to mention here are 'SPILL-OVER EFFECTS' that in the institutionalist interpretation have generally been treated as side-effects or were subsumed under certain forms of change (Kingdon 2003, pp. 190 et seq.). Looking at them from an ideational perspective, spill-over effects may come unintended but may be calculated in or accepted against the perceived advantages, too. A spill-over effect of strengthening the second pillar of the German pension-system, for instance, is the meanwhile projected emerging old-age poverty.

### *3.2.2 Policy Paradigms*

Policy paradigms can be understood as a general guiding principle or philosophy along which policies are formed based upon specific normative ideas. Whereas their boundaries can at times become blurred with ideologies (cf. socialism vs. capitalism as paradigm on a very abstract level), they can take very specific forms. Depending on their arrangement and legislation, they can barely have any immediate or very decisive implications for the population.

Paradigms can, of course, shift similarly as institutions can change. Kuhn's (1976) work with its postulation of paradigm shifts within science received wide reception from the field of Science and Technology Studies but also international relations (for very vivid and impressive examples of this reception cf. Shapin & Schaffer 1985; cf. also Checkel 1997; McNamara 1998; Skogstad 1998). Though not taken up to the same extent, it can also be applied to the study of policy making as Hall (1993) convincingly demonstrates: based on Kuhn's '*Structure of Scientific Revolutions*' (1976), Hall (1993) sets off from an existing policy paradigm, which though it can be changed is basically not challenged by first and second order changes. A first order change is reversible and described as a readjustment of the levels or settings of policy instruments, whereas the overall goal remains the same (Hall 1993, pp. 280–281; Kuhn 1976), which can be translated into 'incremental change'. Change of the second order occurs when policy instruments as well as their settings are altered; the overall goal, again, remains the same (Kuhn 1976; cf. also Hall 1993, pp. 280–283). Even though the description 'incremental change' matches, too, changes are said to be irreversible. These two types describe policy adaptation to new circumstances and/or conditions like parametric reforms, including new groups into the system of social security and the like.

This means that for most of the time no change occurs. Going around in circles while sticking to a certain paradigm, however, does not preclude pragmatic and deviating solutions (Béland 2005, p. 8) or that most of the abovementioned mechanisms of the institutional approach lose their effect:

> Politics can also be pragmatic: It is conceivable that a certain *policy* gains acceptance, while regulators do not necessarily share the underlying philosophy. Therefore, a standard to assess the degree of influence of certain ideas needs to be found which is not dependent on the *result*. (Münnich 2011, p. 490; cf. also Maier 2003, p. 58; on the problem to distinguish the real impact of ideas cf. also Béland 2005, pp. 8–9; emphasis in original)

In contrast, third order change results in a reorientation of goals. This is where shifts in policy paradigms—or, to keep the Kuhnian analogy, 'policy revolutions'—occur: existing policies are challenged in such a way that smaller changes no longer pose a convincing answer any longer, the beaten track does not lead to any feasible solution (Hall 1993, p. 284; cf. Kuhn 1976), or trespass certain thresholds (cf. also Rothgang, Schmid & Schneider 2012, p. 179). Moreover, phenomena appear that cannot be explained by the theoretical background hitherto used for the policies in question (Hall 1993, p. 285; cf. Kuhn 1976). In this sense, an example of the change of policy paradigms within the realm of health care is the transition from poverty relief to health care and health care insurance/provision.[7]

The question might now be posed of what value are policy paradigms when there are equivalents for most parts in either ideational or institutionalist approaches.[8] The main contribution for this study arises from the combination of ideational approaches with those surrounding paradigm shifts: the latter can complete the set of theories and approaches by giving a general answer to the question concerning when ideas are chosen and used as a new paradigm. Thus, the likelihood that new

[7]The solution hitherto applied—poor houses or poor relief to tackle poverty—was no longer perceived to be convincing, as sickness and illness were finally understood as one major cause of poverty. In consequence, the policy goal, instruments, and the self-image of the state changed: The state took the role of a regulator (as an early measure, for instance, set minimum quotas for physicians), an enabler, in some countries even as a provider of health care. This step from the state as the mere administrator of citizens and, specifically in times of war, user of citizens as a resource to a state that also takes care of its citizens occurred in various points in time for different countries and with slightly different reasons (cf. Cohn 1992:2, pp. 37, 89 et seq.; Immergut 1990, p. 394; Kuhnle 2000; Mathisen 1993, pp. 76, 129; Qvarsell 1991, p. 209; Ritter 1983, 1998; WHO 1996, p. 3).

[8]This is the more valid, since there are many issues that are left unclear regarding the change of policy paradigms: We do not get to know any hypotheses about the length of period of the process (is it a short event? can it stretch over several years?), the group of people (which group(s) of actors need to accept a shift of policy paradigms?), nor about their relative share that is needed to speak of a shift of paradigms (is it the acceptance by one key group or is a relative majority of groups or citizens needed?). A working suggestion is that similar to path dependency and path breaks the process of shifts might take a longer period of time, so that it is the final result that counts. As we are dealing with legislation processes, I would suggest that winning over the majority of decision makers is what counts, who, in turn, might be influenced by other actors. It might, however, be just as well argued that it is the societal reality which counts, which would imply that a bad implementation of involvement rights might not bring about a new paradigm in societal life or provoke a change in policy paradigms, when larger parts have shifted without a shift in the legal basis. It is, thus, a matter of what level and what group in society is focused on.

paradigms are chosen by politicians is higher when a new guiding principle is sought, be it that the one hitherto used is no longer convincing or that a new one is overwhelmingly better.

## 3.3 Conclusions

As could be shown, the complexity of the field makes it difficult for single theoretical approaches to cover the width of factors that might potentially explain this question. Therefore, this chapter presented two major approaches complemented by a detail of a third. As actors are the key to understanding in these cases, actor-centred institutionalism will be used as the baseline to which elements of the other approaches are added. These approaches have not only been shown to be useful in the literature on welfare state reform and policy change, they are also able to fill each other's shortcomings and integrate the width of conceivable factors. Moreover, looking at an idealised policy process from cradle to implementation, there is some temporal sequence in which these approaches can be logically ordered. To summarise the model, the illustration in Fig. 3.1 with its corresponding numbers could read as follows:

(1) According to the ideational approach, ideas are born any time in the public realm.
(2) A first step for them is to enter the discourse, where they get the chance to become tested against the existing solutions/institutions. Though the discourse step exists, the abovementioned restrictions of the study prevent the use of this method.
(3) This is where historical and actor-centred institutionalism comes into play: Which, if any of the ideas are considered to be a serious alternative to the already existing, depends on the status quo, the perceived quality of the alternative in terms of problem solving capacity as well as its practicality in everyday life. For the institutional part, the backing, strength, and importance

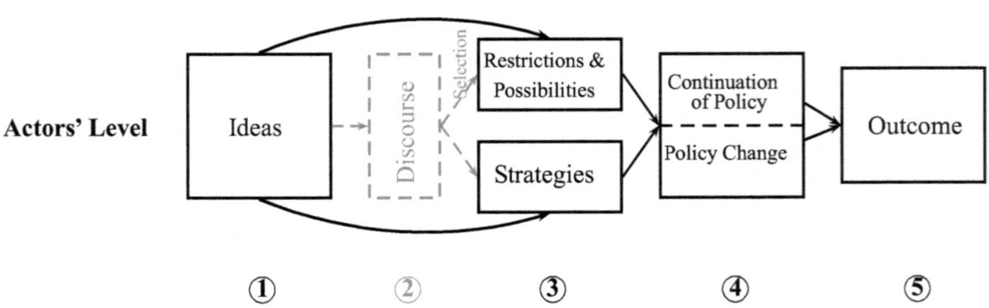


**Fig. 3.1** Model of simplistic policy processes & the different theoretical approaches employed. Source: own depiction

of institutions play in. On the part of the (important) actors involved, strategies and interests as well as their relative power can be added as decisive factors…

(4) …for the decision, whether or not an existing policy is continued or changed. As we saw above, this can take various forms: from slight modifications to the abolition and/or replacement of institutions.

(5) All these steps finally manifest in the outcome, which can be everything from status quo to a completely different solution.

This does not necessarily mean that they actually need to occur in that order, but it seems rather logical that, e.g., ideas in their wider meaning often precede the restrictions and perceptions, even though of course it might be argued that even the kind of ideas is restricted by institutional limitations or actors' values. In that sense, the depiction of the policy process should rather be viewed as an ideal-typical one.

## References


Béland, D. (2005). Ideas and social policy: An institutionalist perspective. *Social Policy and Administration, 39*(1), 1–18.

Bennett, C. J. (1991). What is policy convergence and what causes it? *British Journal of Political Science, 21*, 215–233.

Bonoli, G., & Palier B. (2007, December). When past reforms open new opportunities: Comparing old-age insurance reforms in Bismarckian Welfare systems. *Social Policy & Administration, 41*(6), 555–573.

Boudon, R. (1981). *The logic of social action—an introduction to sociological analysis*. London: Routledge & Kegan Paul.

Busse, R., & Riesberg, A. (2005). *Gesundheitssysteme im Wandel: Deutschland*. Kopenhagen: WHO Regionalbüro im Auftrag des Europäischen Oberservatoriums für Gesundheitssysteme und Gesundheitspolitik.

Cartwright, N. (1983). *How the laws of physics lie*. New York: Oxford University Press.

Checkel, J. T. (1997). *Ideas and international political change Soviet/Russian behavior and the end of the cold war*. New Haven: Yale University Press.

Clegg, D. (2007, December). Continental drift: On unemployment policy change in Bismarckian welfare states. *Social Policy & Administration, 41*(6), 597–617.

Cohen, M., March, J., & Olsen, J. (1972). A garbage can model of organizational choice. *Administrative Science Quarterly, 17*, 1–25.

Cohn, D. (1992:2). *Reforming health care in Canada and Sweden*. Stockholm: University of Stockholm, International Graduate School of International Studies.

Coleman, J. S. (1974). *Power and the structure of society*. New York: Norton.

Coleman, J. S. (1990). *Foundations of social theory*. Cambridge, MA: Belknap Press of Harvard University Press.

Cox, R. H. (2001, April). The social construction of an imperative: Why welfare reform happened in Denmark and the Netherlands but not in Germany. *World Politics, 53*(3), 436–498.

Cox, R. H. (2004, April). The path dependence of an idea: Why Scandinavian welfare states remain distinct. *Social Policy & Administration, 38*(2), 204–219.

Cox, R. H. (2009). Ideas and the politics of labour market reforms. In I. Dingeldey & H. Rothgang (Eds.), *Governance of welfare state reform—a cross national and cross sectoral comparison of policy and politics* (Chap. 9, pp. 200–218). Cheltenham: Edward Elgar.

Crouch, C., & Farrell, H. (2002, June). *Breaking the path of institutional development? Alternatives to the new determinism*. Max-Planck-Institut für Gesellschaftsforschung—Discussion Paper 02/5. Köln.

Dennet, D. C. (1981). International systems. In *Brainstorms: Philosophical essays on mind and psychology* (pp. 3–22). Cambridge: MIT Press.

DiMaggio, P. J., & Powell, W. W. ([1983] 1991). The iron cage revisited: Institutional isomorphism and collective rationality in organizational fields. In W. W. Powell & P. J. DiMaggio (Eds.), *The New Institutionalism in Organizational Analysis* (pp. 63–82). Chicago: University of Chicago Press.

Dowding, K. (1995). Interpreting formal theory. In K. Dowding & D. King (Eds.), *Preferences, institutions, and rational choice* (pp. 43–59). Oxford: Clarendon Press.

Ebbinghaus, B. (2006). From path dependence to path departure in welfare reform analysis. *APSA—European Politics & Society Newsletter. 5*(2), 1–4.

Elster, J. (1998). A plea for mechanisms. In P. Hedström & R. Swedberg (Eds.), *Social mechanisms: An analytical approach to social theory* (Chap. 3). Cambridge: Cambridge University Press.

Fuchs-Heinritz, W., Lautmann, R., Rammstedt, O., & Wienold, H. (Eds.). (1995). *Lexikon zur Soziologie* (3. Auflage). Opladen: Westdeutscher Verlag.

George, A. L., & Bennett, A. (2005). *Case studies and theory development in the social sciences*. Cambridge, MA: MIT Press.

Gerring, J. (2007). *Case study research—principles and practices*. Cambridge: Cambridge University Press.

Glenngård, A., Hjalte, F., Svensson, M., Anell, A., & Bankauskaite, V. (2005). *Sweden: Health system review*. In V. Bankauskaite (Ed.), Health systems in transition. Copenhagen: WHO Regional Office for Europe on behalf of the European Observatory on Health Systems and Policies.

Groenewegen, P. P. (1994). The shadow of the future: Institutional change in health care. *Health Affairs, 13*(5), 137–148. Winter.

Groenewegen, P. P. (1995, October 6). Het gedrag van hulpverleners en patiënten: Toepassingen van de methode van de sociologische modelbouw. *Tijdschrift voor Sociale Gezondheidszorg*, 4–9.

Groenewegen, P. P. (1998). Besluitvorming in de gezondheidszorg op macroniveau. In C. W. Aakster & J. W. Groothoff (Eds.), *Medische sociologie—Sociologische perpectieven op ziekte en zorg* (5th ed., Chap. 2, pp. 295–302). Groningen: Wolters-Noordhoff.

Guillén, A. M., & Palier, B. (2004). Introduction: Does Europe matter? Accession to EU and social policy developments in recent and new member states. *Journal of European Social Policy, 14*(3), 203–209.

Haarmann, A. (2012). Niederlande: Soziale Sicherung zwischen staatlicher Grundsicherung und For-Profit-Versicherern. In T. Klenk, P. Weyrauch, A. Haarmann, & F. Nullmeier (Eds.), *Abkehr vom Korporatismus?* (pp. 367–438). Frankfurt a.M.: Campus.

Hacker, J. S. (2004). Privatizing risk without privatizing the welfare state: The hidden politics of social policy retrenchment in the United States. *American Political Science Review, 98*, 361–391.

Hall, P. A. (1989). Conclusion: The politics of Keynesian ideas. In P. A. Hall (Ed.), *The political power of economic ideas. Keynesianism across nations* (pp. 361–391). Princeton: Princeton University Press.

Hall, P. A. (1993, April). Policy paradigms, social learning, and the state—the case of economic policymaking in Britain. *Comparative Politics, 25*(3), 275–296.

Hall, P. A., & Taylor, R. C. R. (1996). Political science and the three new institutionalisms. *Political Studies, 44*(5), 936–957.

Hansen, R., & King, D. (2001, January). Eugenic ideas, political interests, and policy variance: Immigration and sterilization policy in Britain and the US. *World Politics, 53*(2), 237–263.

Hedström, P., & Swedberg, R. (1998). Social mechanisms: An introductory essay. In P. Hedström & R. Swedberg (Eds.), *Social mechanisms: An analytical approach to social theory* (Chap. 1). Cambridge: Cambridge University Press.

Hemerijck, A., & Schludi, M. (2000). Sequences of policy failures and effective policy responses. In F. W. Scharpf & V. A. Schmidt (Eds.), *Welfare and work in the open economy* (Chap. 3, Vol. 1, pp. 125–228). Oxford: Oxford University Press.

Hemerijck, A., Unger, B., & Visser, J. (2001). How small countries negotiate change—twenty-five years of policy adjustment in Austria, the Netherlands and Belgium. In F. W. Scharpf & V. A. Schmidt (Eds.), *Welfare and work in the open economy volume II: Diverse responses to common challenges in twelve countries* (Chap. 5, Vol. 2, pp. 175–263). Oxford: Oxford University Press.

Hirschman, A. O. (1991). *The rhetoric of reaction*. Cambridge: Belknap Press.

Immergut, E. M. (1990). Institutions, veto points and policy results: A comparative analysis of health care. *Journal of Public Policy, 10*(4), 391–416. 10–12.

Immergut, E. M. (1992). *Health politics: Interests and institutions in Western Europe*. Cambridge: Cambridge University Press.

Immergut, E. M. (2006). From constraints to change. *APSA—European Politics & Society Newsletter, 5*(2), 4–6.

Ismayr, W. (2009). Das politische System Deutschlands. In W. Ismayr, S. Richter, & M. Söldner (Eds.), *Die politischen Systeme Westeuropas* (4th ed., pp. 515–566). Wiesbaden: VS, Verlag für Sozialwiss.

Jahn, D. (2009). Das politische System Schwedens. In W. Ismayr, S. Richter, & M. Söldner (Eds.), *Die politischen Systeme Westeuropas* (4th ed., pp. 107–150). Wiesbaden: VS, Verlag für Sozialwiss.

Jary, D., & Jary, J. (Eds.). (2000). *Collins dictionary sociology* (3rd ed.). Glasgow: HarperCollins.

Kaiser, A. (1999). Die politische Theorie des Neo-Institutionalismus: James March und Johan Olsen. In A. Brodocz & G. S. Schaal (Eds.), *Politische Theorien der Gegenwart* (Chap. 8, pp. 190–211). Opladen: Leske + Budrich.

Katz, E., & Lazarsfeld, P. (1955). *Personal influence*. Chicago: Free Press.

Kingdon, J. W. (2003). *Agendas, alternatives, and public policies* (2nd ed.). New York: Longman.

Kuhn, T. S. (1976). *Die Struktur wissenschaftlicher Revolutionen* (2nd ed.). Frankfurt a.M.: Suhrkamp.

Kuhnle, S. (2000). The Scandinavian welfare state in the 1990s: Challenged but viable. In M. Ferrara & M. Rhodes (Eds.), *Recasting European welfare states* (pp. 209–228). London: Frank Cass.

Lepszy N., & Wilp, M. (2009). Das politische System der Niederlande. In W. Ismayr, S. Richter, & M. öldner (Eds.), *Die politischen Systeme Westeuropas* (4th ed., pp. 405–450). Wiesbaden: VS, Verlag für Sozialwissenschaft.

Mahoney, J., & Thelen, K. (2009). A theory of gradual institutional change. In J. Mahoney & K. Thelen (Eds.), *Explaining institutional change: Ambiguity, agency, and power* (Chap. 1, pp. 1–37). Cambridge: Cambridge University Press.

Maier, M. L. (2003). Wissens- und ideenorientierte Anätze in der Politikwissenschaft: Versuch einer systematischen Übersicht. In M. L. Maier, F. Nullmeier, T. Pritzlaff, & A. Wiesner (Eds.), *Politik als Lernprozess—Wissenszentrierte Ansätze der Politikanalyse* (pp. 25–77). Opladen: Leske + Budrich.

March, J. G., & Olsen, J. P. (1984). Organizational factors in political life. *American Political Science Review, 78*, 734–749.

March, J. G., & Olsen, J. P. (1989). *Rediscovering institutions. The organizational basis of politics*. New York: Free Press.

Mathisen, J. (1993). *Sykepleiehistorie*. Oslo: Universitetsforlaget.

Mayntz, R. (1990). Politische Steuerbarkeit und Reformblockaden: Überlegungen am Beispiel des Gesundheitswesens. *Staatswissenschaften und Staatspraxis, 3*(1), 283–307.

Mayntz, R., & Scharpf, F. W. (1995). Der Ansatz des akteurzentrierten Institutionalismus. In R. Mayntz & F. W. Scharpf (Eds.), *Gesellschaftliche Selbstregelung und politische Steuerung* (Chap. 2, pp. 39–72). Frankfurt am Main: Campus.

McNamara, K. R. (1998). *The currency of ideas. Monetary politics in the European Union*. Ithaca: Cornell University Press.

Merton, R. K. (1967). On sociological theories of the middle range. In R. K. Merton (Ed.), *On theoretical sociology: Five essays, old and new* (pp. 39–72). New York: Free Press.

Münnich, S. (2011). Wie weit reicht der Einfluß von Ideen?—Herausforderungen und Grenzen ideen- und diskursorientierter Wohlfahrtsforschung. *Zeitschrift für Sozialreform, 57*(4), 487–498.

Palier, B. (2001, June). *Beyond retrenchment*. Working Paper Series. Center for European Studies.

Palier, B. (2006, June). *Farewell to Bismarckianism? Welfare reforms in France*. Prepared for the Conference 'A Long Goodbye to Bismarck? The Politics of Welfare Reforms in Continental Europe'.

Palier, B. (2010). Ordering change: Understanding the 'Bismarckian' welfare reform trajectory. In B. Palier (Ed.), *A long goodbye to Bismarck?* (Chap. 1, pp. 19–44). Amsterdam: Amsterdam University Press.

Palier, B., & Martin, C. (2007, December). From "a frozen landscape" to structural reforms: The sequential transformation of Bismarckian welfare systems. *Social Policy & Administration, 41*(6), 535–554.

Pierson, P. (2000, June). Increasing returns, path dependence, and the study of politics. *American Political Science Review, 94*(2), 251–267.

Potvin, L. (2007). Managing uncertainty through participation. *Health and Modernity, 10*, 103–128.

Qvarsell, R. (1991). *Vårdens idéhistoria*. Stockholm: Carlsson bokförlag.

Rhodes, M. (2000). Restructuring the British welfare state: Between domestic constraints and global imperatives. In F. W. Scharpf & V. A. Schmidt (Eds.), *Welfare and work in the open economy volume II: Diverse responses to common challenges in twelve countries* (Chap. 2, Vol. 2, pp. 19–68). Oxford: Oxford University Press.

Ritter, G. A. (1983). *Sozialversicherungen in Deutschland und England: Entstehung und Grundzüge im Vergleich*. München: C. H. Beck'sche Verlagsbuchhandlung.

Ritter, G. A. (1998). Bismarck und die Grundlegung des deutschen Sozialstaates. In F. Ruland, B. B. Maydell, & H.-J. Papier (Eds.), *Verfassung Theorie und Praxis des Sozialstaats* (pp. 789–820). Karlsruhe: C. F. Müller Verlag.

Rosenberg, A. (1988). *Philosophy of social science*. Boulder: Westview.

Rothgang, H., Schmid, A., & Schneider, S. (2011). *Transformationen des Interventionsstaates und ihre Erklärung: Das Beispiel nationaler Gesundheitssysteme*.

Rothgang, H., Schmid, A., & Schneider, S. (2012). Transformationen des Interventionsstaates und ihre Erklärung: Das Beispiel nationaler Gesundheitssysteme. In M. Bach (Ed.), *Der entmachtete Leviathan: Löst sich der souveräne Staat auf?* (Vol. Sonderband 5, pp. 175–196). Baden-Baden: Nomos.

Rothstein, B. (1998). The political and moral logic of the universal welfare state. In *Just institutions matter: The moral and political logic of the universal welfare state* (Chap. 6, pp. 144–170). Cambridge: Cambridge University Press.

Sabatier, P. A. (1993a). Advocacy-Koalitionen, Policy-Wandel und Policy-Lernen. Eine Alternative zur Phasenheuristik. In A. Héritier (Ed.), *Policy-Analyse Kritik und Neuorientierung. Politische Vierteljahresschrift* (Vols. Sonderheft 24, pp. 116–148). Opladen: Westdeutscher Verlag.

Sabatier, P. A. (1993b). Policy change over a decade or more. In P. A. Sabatier & H. C. Jenkins-Smith (Eds.), *Policy change and learning an advocacy coalition approach* (pp. 13–39). Boulder, CO: Westview Press.

Scharpf, F. W. (1997). *Games real actors play—actor-centered institutionalism in policy research*. Boulder, CO: Westview Press.

Scharpf, F. W. (2000). *Interaktionsformen. Akteurzentrierter Institutionalismus in der Politikforschung*. Wiesbaden: VS Verlag für Sozialwissenschaften.
Schelling, T. C. (1998). Social mechanisms and social dynamics. In P. Hedström & R. Swedberg (Eds.), *Social mechanisms: An analytical approach to social theory* (Chap. 2). Cambridge: Cambridge University Press.
Schmid, A., Cacace, M., Götze, R., & Rothgang, H. (2010, August). Explaining health care system change: Problem pressure and the emergence of "hybrid" health care systems. *Journal of Health Politics, Policy and Law, 35*(4), 455–486.
Schmidt, V. A. (2008). Discursive institutionalism: The explanatory power of ideas and discourse. *Annual Review of Political Science, 11*, 303–326.
Scott, W. R. (1995). *Institutions and organizations*. Thousand Oaks, CA: SAGE.
Sejersted, F. (2011). *The age of social democracy—Norway and Sweden in the twentieth century*. Princeton: Princeton University Press.
Shapin, S., & Schaffer, S. (1985). *Leviathan and the air-pump: Hobbes, Boyle and the experimental life—including a translation of Thomas Hobbes, Dialogus physic...* Princeton, NJ: Princeton University Press.
Sikkink, K. (1993). The power of principled ideas: Human rights policies in the United States and Western Europe. In J. Goldstein & R. O. Keohane (Eds.), *Ideas and foreign policy beliefs, institutions, and political change* (Chap. 6, pp. 139–172). Ithaca: Cornell University Press.
Skocpol, T. (1979). *States and social revolutions: A comparative analysis of France, Russia and China*. Cambridge: Cambridge University Press.
Skogstad, G. (1998). Ideas, paradigms and institutions. Agricultural exceptionalism in the European Union and the United States. *Governance, 11*(4), 463–490.
Steinmo, S. (2008). What is historical institutionalism? In D. Della Porta & M. Keating (Eds.), *Approaches in the social sciences* (Chap. 7, pp. 118–138). Cambridge: Cambridge University Press.
Stinchcombe, A. L. (1968). *Constructing social theories*. Chicago: University of Chicago Press.
Streeck, W., & Thelen, K. (2005). Introduction: Institutional change in advanced political economies. In W. Streek & K. Thelen (Eds.), *Institutional change in advanced political economies* (pp. 3–39). New York: Oxford University Press.
Thelen, K. (2003). How institutions evolve. In J. Mahoney & D. Rueschemeyer (Eds.), *Comparative historical analysis in the social sciences* (Chap. 6, pp. 208–240). Cambridge: Cambridge University Press.
Touraine, A. (1977). *The self-production of society*. Chicago: University of Chicago Press.
Tsebelis, G. (2002). *Veto players: How political institutions work*. New York/Princeton: SAGE Foundation/Princeton University Press.
Wendt, A. (1999). *Social theory of international politics*. Cambridge: Cambridge University Press.
WHO. (1996). *Health care systems in transition: Sweden: Preliminary version*. Copenhagen: World Health Organization, Regional Office for Europe.
Windhoff-Héritier A. (1988). Institutionelle Interessenvermittlung im Sozialsektor Strukturmuster verbandlicher Beteiligung und deren Folgen. In H.-H. Hartwich (Ed.), *Macht und Ohnmacht politischer Institutionen* (pp. 158–176). Opladen: Westdeutscher Verlag.

# Chapter 4
# Methodology and Study Design

After the overarching question of the book has been defined and the theoretical framework set, it remains to be decided upon the methodological framework of the book. What method is best suited to answer the main question? This chapter will address this issue.

## 4.1 To Begin With: What Methodology Suits Question and Theory?

The understanding of methods in this study is that of tools. In this case, they shall help to reconstruct a historical process of policy making (cf. Bohnsack 2010; Eckstein 1973; Fenno 1986; Roberts 1996). Picking suitable methods means to choose from a vast range off the methods' shelf. The well-established and often used approach in welfare state research to combine quantitative datasets from various sources does not seem expedient regarding this type of research question. Given the small number of countries, the exploratory character of the study, and the focus on the policy process the means of choice are qualitative methods.[1]

Despite some differences between quantitative and qualitative research the task of methods as tools is in general to enable good and sound science. This includes conducting objective, reliable, and valid research that contributes to refining theory,

[1] It is impossible to name the sheer endless multitude of literature on qualitative methods, which beyond classic approaches (as, e.g., for an arbitrary mention, Glaser and Strauss 1967 and Jahoda, Lazarsfeld and Zeisel (1933)) has been considerably growing in interest and literature over the last decade with a number of interesting cross- or multi-method approaches (cf. Creswell & Plano Clark 2007; Denzin 1989; Denzin & Lincoln 2003; Tashakkori & Teddlie 1998). As representatives of the great number of handbooks and articles Bohnsack (2010), Coffey and Atkinson (1996), Denzin (1989), Denzin and Lincoln (2003), Flick (2009), Kelle and Kluge (1999), Lamnek and Krell (2010), Marshall and Rossman (2006), Yin (2009) shall be mentioned.



A. Haarmann, *The Evolution and Everyday Practice of Collective Patient Involvement in Europe*, DOI 10.1007/978-3-319-64595-7_4

theory building, and testing of hypotheses (cf., e.g., Diekmann 1996; Flick 2007, 2009; George & Bennett 2005; Ragin 1994). The latter requires at least a certain amount of generalisability.

## 4.2 Case Study Design

> The case study [...] should not be defined by a distinctive method [...] but rather by the goals of the research relative to the scope of the research terrain. (Gerring 2007, p. 68)
>
> Regretfully, the term 'case study' is a definitional morass. (Gerring 2004, pp. 341–342)

Even if the range is confined to qualitative methodologies and methods the choice is still great. Not least in similar studies, some of which have become a classic, a case study design has been proven fruitful in several ways (in order to name a few Allison 1971; Hinrichs 2001; Jahoda, Lazarsfeld and Zeisel 1933; Lijphart 1968; Park, Burgess & McKenzie 1925; Skocpol 1979): not only have their results been insightful and in some cases pioneering the case studies approach is also sufficiently flexible as it is not coupled with a specific method (George & Bennett 2005, pp. 67–83; Gerring 2007, pp. 37–85). The observant reader will have noticed that most of the examples mentioned date several decades back. It is in this line that Lieberson (1991, p. 307) reminds us that the

> [a]pplication of this method to a small number of cases is not new to sociology, being in one form or another a variant of the method of analytic induction, described by Znaniecki (1934) and analyzed succinctly by Robinson (1951) and Turner (1953). The conclusions rely, on a formalized internal logic derived from Mill's (1872) method of agreement and his method of difference.

There are a number of points, 'good' case studies have in common: They give the reader detailed, yet (theoretically) guided and context sensitive information on the case. This is no end in itself, it rather bears the potential for better explanations, as '[u]nderstanding the details of the story reduces the risk of spurious explanations' (Elster 1998, p. 49; cf. also Elster 1998, pp. 69–70; Mooney Marini & Singer 1988) and, in addition, ideally enables the reader to form his or her own view on the case. This is the more important as the researcher of case studies runs the risk of selection bias in cases and/or sources, overinterpretation of events, overgeneralisations of the results to name a few (cf., e.g., George & Bennett 2005, pp. 22–25, 32; George & McKeown 1985; Gerring 2007 p. 73; Mahoney 2003, p. 362). More generally, the case study approach has received criticism in particular from rather quantitatively oriented researchers (for a short overview cf. Ebbinghaus 2006; Gerring 2004, p. 341). Lieberson (1991, 1994) goes as far as to maintain that qualitative case study research cannot draw the conclusions usually drawn: Apart from unidentified variables, measurement errors, and the dubious quality of data, deterministic conclusions are drawn based on case study research where only probabilistic assertions are possible.

In my opinion, the lesson to be learned from Lieberson's criticism is that in want of better methods in many areas we would lack a considerable scientific contribution in the absence of case studies. Therefore, we should strive to make case studies and their interpretation better and lower the aims set: where possible, known and avoidable issues should be avoided and a transparent report on the procedures during the research process given, in order to ensure replicability. The story told—as in a deterministic sense the result may be phrased—is in this sense the most plausible/likely hypothesis of causality that ideally could be tested with different methods in consecutive studies. Even though, theoretically, case studies can serve both confirmatory purposes as hypotheses generating ones, compared to other types of studies '[t]heory testing is not the case study's strong suit." (Gerring 2007, pp. 38–43, in particular p. 42; Gerring 2004). As the main aim of this book lays much more in generating hypotheses (cf. Lijphart 1971) than testing any preconceived theoretical presuppositions or hypotheses this is absolutely essential.

Gerring (2004, p. 342; for alternative definitions cf. George and Bennett 2005, pp. 18–17; Lieberson 1991, pp. 308) refers to a rather fuzzy definition of the term 'case study' and argues,

> [...] that for methodological purposes a case study is best defined as an in-depth study of a single unit (a relatively bounded phenomenon) where the scholar's aim is to elucidate features of a larger class of similar phenomena. It is demonstrated that case studies rely on the same sort of covariational evidence utilized in non-case study research. Thus, the case study method is correctly understood as a particular way of defining cases, not a way of analyzing cases or a way of modeling causal relations. (Gerring 2004, p. 341)

However, it is in particular the comparative analysis that is of interest here, because single case studies may result in a deep insight into *one* specific case but might not converge into more general conclusions since generalising from one case is next to impossible. Moreover, the abovementioned criterion of generalisability would either require to opt for a policy or country that is 'typical' or 'representative' for most others—which neither applies to the Netherlands and England nor to the policy field of patient involvement. However, the potential limitations such as selection bias and untested and wrong assumptions and conclusions cannot be talked away and should constantly be born in mind.

A way to improve case studies is to compare them along predefined topical lines. One of the main advantages is that the comparison allows for keeping a detailed overview of each of a small number of cases while drawing conclusions from it at a more abstract level. Each country can be understood as a single case of several units. Table 4.1 breaks down the comparative and temporal component of covariation into different types of study design. Since we are eventually interested in the comparison of events in countries that (a) sometimes evolve over a considerable period of time and (b) occur at different points in time in different countries so that the influence of a covariation of time cannot be ruled out the option of choice is what Gerring calls 'comparative-historical'.

**Table 4.1** 'Research designs: a covariational typology'

| | | Temporal variation | |
|---|---|---|---|
| | | No | Yes |
| Spatial Variation | None (1 unit) | [Logically impossible] | Single unit, temporal variation study |
| | Within-unit | Subunits study, synchronically | Subunits study, diachronically |
| | Across-unit | Cross-sectional | Time-series cross-sectional |
| | Across- and within-unit | Hierarchical | **Comparative-historical** |

Source: adapted from Gerring 2004, p. 343 (emphasis by the author)

### *4.2.1 Choice of Countries and 'Plausibility Probing'*

Drawing conclusions from what has been said about case studies, we will attempt what George (1979) and George and Smoke (1974) have called 'structured, focused comparison' (cf. also George & McKeown 1985). By this can be understood a comparison of a small number of cases/countries that is 'structured' in that it is partly guided by 'theoretically relevant general questions' and 'focused' in that it—at least in a second step—'deals selectively with only those aspects of each case that are believed to be relevant' (George & McKeown 1985, p. 41). The assumed relevance might stem from two different sources. Of course it should prove to empirically contribute to answer the question at hand. Nevertheless, relevance might as well stem from theoretical aspects, which ideally go hand in hand.

Though the comparison cannot be about 'testing' a theory or an approach in the sense of a quantitative test (cf., e.g., Gerring 2007, p. 172; Lamnek 2005, pp. 298 et seq.), the byproduct of this contrast/comparison can be a 'test', or to phrase it differently: 'probing', of plausibility. It can best be viewed as a mixture of what George and Bennett (2005, pp. 75, 32) describe as 'heuristic' and 'plausibility probing' case studies, thereby increasing the validity of the study as a whole.

When it comes to criteria for choosing the counter countries of comparison, the most important characteristic is here that they do not have any formal patient involvement at the level of hospitals. Beyond that, since we assume a shift or an expansion of governance to new actors, the potential countries for comparison should share a similar heritage in terms of governance in order have a similar point of departure. In short: What we need, are cases that are as dissimilar as possible in the manifestation of patient involvement and as similar as possible in terms of health care organisation, institutional heritage, and responsibilities, all in order to keep the number of influential key factors low, which can otherwise be thought to distort our findings (George & McKeown 1985, p. 25; Lijphart 1971).

This is where we can recur to the revised classification of health care systems —not for the sake of typologies or in the belief that they depict the world in all its facets, but in order to choose two countries to compare the Netherlands and England that are claimed to be similar. In order to arrive at a pairwise comparison with THE NETHERLANDS we need a country with sickness funds at best with a history of self-governance; a country with hospitals run by municipalities, charity organisations, or not-for-profit entrepreneurs. These hospitals, however, should not fall under state administration, but be responsible as stand-alone entities. Preferably, the country also has a strong tradition in corporatism. In an ideal country to be compared to ENGLAND the responsibility for the health care system should lie in the hands of the state or a subordinate entity. This applies to both provision, in particular in the hospital sector, as well as to governance. The main form of patient representation should at least once have occurred via elected members of parliament or councils.

Since the criteria for a match to the Netherlands apply to several countries—to Austria, Belgium, and Germany, to just mention a few (Busse & Blümel 2014; Gerkens & Merkur 2010; Hofmarcher 2013)—, the choice of a counter country was rather easy. As the health insurance system in the Netherlands including its governance was imposed by Germany and both countries share a larger number of similarities this seemed a natural choice and the best match (cf. also Götze 2016). As the Netherlands is a unitary state we do not need to select a subsidiary entity. In contrast, we need to do so for the case study on Germany, because equivalents could be found at this political and administrative layer. Reflecting on the recent changes in involvement rights in the care sector we opted for the federal states Hamburg and Sachsen (Saxony). A detailed explanation for the choice can be found in the chapter on Germany (see Sect. 7.2 on page 192).

Finding a match for England was not as easy a task. As for the Netherlands, a number of countries were qualified for comparison: Denmark, Finland, Italy, Norway, Spain, and Sweden more or less meet the criteria (Barros, Machado & de Almeida Simões 2011; Glenngård, Hjalte, Svensson, Anell & Bankauskaite 2005; Olejaz et al. 2012; Ringard, Sagan, Sperre Saunes & Lindahl 2013; Scalzo et al. 2009; Vuorenkoski 2008).[2] The responsibility for hospitals lies with the national government in Norway since its health care reform in 2002 (Christensen & Lægrid 2010; Johnsen 2006; Lægrid, Opedal & Stigen 2005; Ringard et al. 2013; Stigen 2010), which would make it the perfect match. It took some time to find out that actually the health care reform of 2002 brought a formalised right to involve patients in each health care region as well. Overall, the practice as well as the legal grounds were too similar to the English case to choose the country for comparison (Andreassen 2005; Bakke & de Vibe 2009; 2009; Thorsen 2010; Trondheim Kommune 2005).

Of the countries left, only Finland stands out with its municipal, sometimes regional responsibility for health care, while the responsibility in the other four

[2]A warm thanks goes to Tone Alm Andreassen at the Oslo and Akershus University College of Applied Sciences for some discussion on the Norwegian health care system and its reforms, who at that time worked for the Norsk institutt for forskning om oppvekst, velferd og aldring (NOVA). A special thanks goes to Karsten Vrangbæk at the University of Copenhagen, who patiently answered a number of questions on Denmark's health care system.

**Table 4.2** Choice of countries for this study

| | Main cases | Counter-cases |
|---|---|---|
| Insurance based,<br>legitimacy via corporatist governance | The Netherlands | Germany<br>• Hamburg<br>• Sachsen |
| NHS-system,<br>legitimacy via democratic elections | England (for the UK) | Sweden<br>• Östra Götaland<br>• Skåne<br>• Västerbotten |

Source: own compilation

countries generally falls to larger political and administrative regions. As the provincial level comes closer to the national one this is to be preferred. After some enquiries, it became clear that even in Denmark a similar arrangement as in England and Norway is in place. In the end, Sweden was chosen out of a mixture of theoretical reflections and pragmatic reasons. It might be argued that comparing the matured welfare state Sweden entails fewer potential external factors of influence compared to relative late-comers Italy and Spain, which, furthermore, are under enormous financial strain. Next to this, the author's good knowledge of the country made the research process and access easier. Responsibility for the health care system is devolved to the county councils, so that sub-national entities needed to be chosen. A detailed explanation for the choice of Östra Götaland, Skåne, and Västerbotten as county councils within Sweden is provided in the respective chapter on Sweden (see Sect. 8.2 on page 230).

The final study design is, hence, a fourfold comparative one: Sweden is matched to England while Germany will be compared with the Netherlands. Table 4.2 gives an overview of the choice of countries.

### 4.2.2 *Pitfalls on the Way—Or: What to Learn From Previous Case Studies*

After having decided upon which countries to compare, we should consider where we want to position the cases in the wider array of this study, and what pitfalls can be avoided. Irrespective of the differences between the various ways to conduct a case study, several conclusions can be drawn from many of them (cf. for instance Anderson 2006; Bönker 2005; Hinrichs 2001; Immergut 1992, 1990; Pierson 2003). Establishing a connection between two macro-phenomena does not suffice to result in a convincing case study. Here, the ties to other factors and different levels need to be highlighted in the process and an explanation attempted by a detour via meso- and/or micro-level (cf. also the bathtub model by Coleman 1990). In want of the convincing power of statistical analysis, a coherent line of argument, a stringent 'storyline', and a convincing analysis becomes all the more important, because case studies must bridge complexity and depth in order to arrive at a more abstract level of conclusion (Gerring 2007, p. 66). Moreover, ideally, case studies should exclude alternative explanations. Where this is not possible, the next best solution is to point out alternative, mutually exclusive hypotheses that can be tested in future research. Therefore, case study research quite often explicitly calls for theoretical guidance (cf. George & Bennett 2005, p. 8), where this is possible.

Another question refers to the relation between theory and methods. As Campbell notes,

> [i]n a case study done by an alert social scientist who has thorough local acquaintance, the theory he uses to explain the focal difference also generates predictions or expectations on dozens of other aspects of the culture. (Campbell 1975, p. 179)

Even though I would stress that it does not harm to take existing theoretical assumptions into consideration when choosing comparative cases and I would in this case not advise to go to such lengths as to disregard all previous knowledge, the researcher must be aware of the potential push in one or another direction this previous knowledge and the chosen theories exert on the analysis. The same holds true for ad-hoc theories emerging under the process of research. Even though this should be done with utmost consideration and reflected in a transparent manner, one should be cautious when taking over theories that prove to be ill-fitting to the results.

As a last lesson, it is hard to impossible to conclude from a perspective based solely on the present. The mentioned studies have convincingly shown that (political) decisions are rooted in a longer process that takes much more factors into consideration than can be detected in a short-term view on a specific topic. Therefore, another key characteristic in most 'good' case study research is the emphasis on processes rather than snapshots in time. This necessitates a historic perspective into the past development of the topic leading eventually to the decision in question, which, in this sense, makes many studies historical studies (cf. Büthe 2002).

## 4.3 Historical Processes

> The process-tracing method attempts to identify the intervening causal process—the causal chain and causal mechanism—between an independent variable (or variables) and the outcome of the dependent variable. (George & Bennett 2005, p. 206)

It is precisely the historical aspect mentioned in the previous section that underlies this study. Or, to phrase it differently: many interesting things of 'Now' lie in the past. The difficulty that arises is from what point in time to start the analysis of the process to neither waste time with unnecessary details nor to set the starting point too late and thereby miss out potentially important factors. For this study it was decided to start the analysis when either different forms of involvement than hitherto employed are mentioned by one of the sources, a discussion on the topic enters the parliamentary realm, or major changes in involvement occur. As will be explained in the chapters on the respective countries this point in time varies from one country to another.

It has also been mentioned already that it is not about single decisions, but that rather the encompassing process is of major importance. One approach in vogue helping to analyse complex and longer-term processes is 'process tracing' (cf., e.g., Checkel 2005; George & Bennett 2005, pp. 13, 205 et seq.; Gerring 2007, 172 et seq.; Mahoney 2003; Tansey 2007; Vennesson 2008; cf. also Fenno 1986). The idea behind process tracing is far from new. Roberts (1996), for instance, names several authors who set off for a similar undertaking, while in a narrower sense, process tracing can be viewed to be a specific subform of Campbell's (1975) 'pattern matching' (George & Bennett 2005, chap. 1 & 10; Gerring 2007, pp. 41–42). Overall, it can roughly be equated to what in 'colloquial scientific language' is often called 'thick description', sharing the detailed description of a situation and a process as a first step on the way to analysis. As Checkel (2005, pp. 3–4) describes the approach, using process tracing for analysing processes has the advantage to learn more about the underlying reasons for a decision than only by looking at the outcome. Reading other authors, the idea about process tracing remains abstract and fuzzy. If it were no more than that, the main message could, thus, be summarised by saying: Try not to overlook any important information or fact that might be relevant! Basically, however, '[f]ollowing George and McKeown (1985), the effort to infer causality through the identification of causal mechanisms can be called 'process tracing' ' (Mahoney 2003, p. 363), which makes the approach somewhat less abstract and more rooted in what researchers are seeking anyway. Taking as much information into the analysis as possible harbours the risk of distraction. Its basic purpose, however, is the permanent cross-check between (a) the empirical data, (b) what might be called provisional, ad-hoc 'theories' of mechanisms during the research process, and (c) the existing theoretical literature. Even though the aim is to draw some rather mechanistic conclusions, which in some respect are crude simplifications of 'real life', thorough knowledge of each step in the process is needed, in order to decide what details need to be considered and which can be bypassed (cf. Checkel 2005; George & Bennett 2005, chap. 10; Gerring 2007, chap. 7; Tansey 2007).

This cross-check is the essential benefit of process tracing, which leads Gerring (2007, chap. 7) to describe it under the headline 'internal validity'. The following quotation makes the point even clearer:

> [W]e would distinguish retaining a theory that has general utility in many cases from retaining a historical explanation of a particular case. *A satisfactory historical explanation of a particular case needs to address and explain each of the significant steps in the sequence that led to the outcome of that case.* If even one step in the hypothesized causal process in a particular case is not as predicted, then the historical explanation of the case needs to be modified, perhaps in a trivial way that is consistent with the original theory, or perhaps in a crucial way that calls into question the theory's general utility and its applicability to other cases. *It is this insistence on providing a continuous and theoretically based historical explanation of a case, in which each significant step toward the outcome is explained by reference to a theory, that makes process-tracing a powerful method of inference.* (George and Bennett 2005, pp. 29–30; emphasis added by the author)

Regretfully, it remains unclear and fuzzy how a 'theory's general utility' is defined by George and Bennett, and what its relation is to the theory's 'applicability'. It might be *guessed* that it includes typical criteria to assess a theory such as range, truth, and information content. However, this is not made explicit.

## 4.4 Methods, Sources, and Analysis

### *4.4.1 Methods and Sources*

Though some authors view process tracing as a method in its own right (cf., e.g., George & Bennett 2005), or at least a suitable and worthy surrogate, I would argue that it definitively needs to be combined with other methods wherever this is possible. As much as a case study is rather a framework of research, to the same extent process tracing is a tool. However, it does not say anything about the specific methods to be used, which depends on the availability of sources, the topic and its specific requirements, and, not least, the suitability for the study in question. Having said this, it needs to be decided what kind of methods, sources, and methods of analysis that are at our disposal.

We need to realise that it is politicians that transform ideas and suggestions into legals acts that, ideally, tackle the felt concerns and perceived problems. In consequence, they are the cornerstone around which we can weave our analysis: as we are dealing with legal acts in the Netherlands and England anyway, they are the starting points. They can be captured by parliamentary minutes which document the argumentation during the parliamentary readings leading to them. They do not occur in empty space, but are deeply embedded in the field of policy making in the respective countries, in their society, and their discourses, which we need to take into consideration in our analysis. Since green and white papers are often the ground on which parliamentary action is based green and white papers, reports by parliamentary commissions as well as scientific reports referred to during the legislation process will be employed as further sources.

Not all questions and context factors will be covered by these source. Consequently, we need to complement the information in objective as well as subjective terms. The latter is the more important if we want to understand politicians' ground for decision-making. One possibility to capture the information needed would be to draw on societal or political discourses (cf., e.g., Hepburn & Potter 2004; Nullmeier 2001; van Dyk 2008). However, patient participation did not receive any wider societal reception beyond the more restricted circles of patient associations and health care professionals. Furthermore, the legislation process in England was extremely short and witnessed only very few parliamentary readings. This results in the situation that there is hardly any documented discourse available for analysis, which goes beyond the parliamentary minutes. If we want to employ the same methods in our main countries—and to the extent that is possible also for our countries of comparison—then this restriction rules out discourse analysis.

The next best type of source are expert interviews (for a sample of the literature on expert interviews cf. Bogner, Littig & Menz 2009; Büthe 2002; Charmaz 2006; Christmann 2009; Dunn 2011; Froschauer & Lueger 2003; George & Bennett 2005; Gerring 2007; Mayring 2000b; Meuser & Nagel 2009; Roberts 1996; Wolff 2000). Interviewing experts has the advantage that they experienced the field in question first hand that they have witnessed the process we are interested in, and that they explicitly and implicitly have something to say about the motivation and their assessment.

To the advantages can be counted that even though some informational asymmetry exists, both interviewee and interviewer can be assumed as interested in the topic and expert in the field (Pfadenhauer 2009), the interview can be conducted in a more natural way. Furthermore, the researcher's explanation and framing of the topic can be relatively short (Gläser & Laudel 2010, pp. 167, 182, Meuser & Nagel 2009), which, in turn, results to a greater extent the interviewee filling in. This affects also the way to conduct and analyse the interviews. Questions can be posed relatively directly, as we can assume that most issues have been reflected by the interviewee. As we are usually interested in the information given during the interview as well as in the way facts are presented and explained, we do not need to pay as much attention to *how* they are said (cf. Meuser & Nagel 2009, 1989) While the choice of words can be essential in the course of analysis, the length of breaks in the interview, the stressing of specific vowels, or other salient pronunciation are of less importance. On the other hand expert interviews in this area are trickier than other types of interviews: Be it politicians or patient organisations, they are used to 'selling' their policy and 'marketing' their message. This can lead to a polarised depiction of the situation, facts, and action of themselves and other actors as well as disguise the 'true' rationale.

In order not to fall for drawing any conclusions that are biased by these subjective and/or interest-led answers, the choice of experts as a source of information requires two measures: *First*, the categories of experts need to be balanced. It was therefore decided to not only include politicians belonging to the government at the time of enactment but also representatives of the major opposition party. They should have been involved in the legislation process at some point in time (Glaser & Laudel 2009, pp. 113–116; Meuser & Nagel 2009). Ideal candidates would be former ministers, undersecretaries, members of (sub-)committees on health, or high-ranking administrative staff at the time of the legislation process. These experts are complemented by patient representatives of the most relevant type in the respective country and a selected number of patient representatives in various hospitals in the Netherlands and England. They shall at best have dealt with the subject during the legislation process and have a good overview of the current development of implementation into everyday practice. The overall aim was to cover the 'whole story', to realise commonalities and discrepancies in the stories told by different types of experts. The category of researchers was added in order to mirror the findings with their understanding of the process and to complement the literature and list of interviewees if anything of interest or importance had been missed. The different categories of groups for expert interviews are subsequently summarised:

- Representatives of Politicians in Government
- Representatives of Politicians in Opposition
- Representatives of Patients
- Researchers

*Second*, the analysis needs to consider that statements of experts are necessarily subjective, which requires an apt theoretical background. Potential interviewees might propose an interview on the phone, which might be the only chance to talk to them. Weighing the disadvantages of mixed modes of interviews and the sometimes tricky pitfalls of telephone interviews (cf. Christmann 2009) against the benefits of talking to the interviewee who was targeted as the best choice, it was decided in this study that the disadvantages do not outweigh the advantages.

Next to these particularities, basically the same rules of good conduct apply (cf. amongst others Bogner, Littig & Menz 2002; Bogner et al. 2009; Bogner & Menz 2009; Froschauer & Lueger 2003; Meuser & Nagel 1989, 2009; Pfadenhauer 2009; Tansey 2007). Even here the golden rule of posing well-informed, yet not overly informed questions in a neutral, unchallenging, understanding manner apply. In contrast to many other forms of interview, in later phases of the interview some indirectly provoking questions and/or statements are allowed as well as stating the interviewer's own opinion, if this helps to elicit the interviewee's authentic opinion (chap. 4 Gläser & Laudel 2010).

All interviews were conducted in the language of the respective country. My previous experience suggests that the availability of information and the choice of interviewees is the greater the more natural the encounter between interviewee and researcher is and the more comfortable the situation for the interviewee. Moreover, the interviewee's capability to portray in part complex contextual situations in the own language is generally higher, which increases the interviewee's willingness to agree to an interview as does the amount of information given. This applies to both oral and printed information. All interviews were based on the same semi-structured core interview guideline in order to cover the complete range but still come as close as possible to a normal conversation. It was then translated to the various languages (see Appendices A.1 on page 333, A.2 on page 335, A.3 on page 337, and A.4 on page 339 in the appendix). This core guideline was consecutively adopted according to the country, the terminology used locally, and the type of interviewee. Since 'patient involvement' bears completely different connotations in every country and is, therefore, understood in one way or another the most essential advantage of this procedure was the possibility to be able to better explain what is meant in this study and 'pick interviewees up' where they were. Another advantage was that no systematic effects arose as a result of a different command of English. It was usually offered to send the guidelines to the interviewee in advance, as they often wanted to be prepared. After the interview it was offered to send the transcript, in case this had been agreed after the interview and in order to give the interviewee the opportunity to correct any statements that they would not support any longer. Interviewees made use of this opportunity in only few cases and with more annotations than actual changes. At the same time, they were informed about how the interview would be processed and that excerpts might be used as quotations. In that context they were given three options they could choose from: to be mentioned by (a) full name, position, and organisation, (b) only position and organisation, or (c) give a rough description of the organisation. Answers varied, which is reflected in the lists of experts finally interviewed in the 'Sources' chapters of the respective case studies (cf. Tables 5.1 on page 82, 6.1 on page 137, 8.2 on page 232, and 7.2 on page 194). The interviews were transcribed and analysed in the original language in order to retain the original information untouched as long as possible. The translation for quotations in this book has been translated as close to the original as possible, and inner contradictions and language mistakes have not been eradicated.

### *4.4.2 Analysis*

> The respondent never lies—accurate interpretation of what he says depends on the skill of the analyst. (Manning 1967, p. 315)

Now that we have described the sources and methods of data acquisition, it still needs to be decided about the methods of data analysis. Given that the one major part of sources is comprised of interviews and speech during parliamentary debates techniques are required that are specifically suited for interview and text analysis. In order to get the most out of these sources and comply to good scientific practice, it uses the relevant procedures of different established methods of analysis.

Before continuing to the explicit methods of analysis, some thought should be dedicated on the relation between theory and empirical data. In contrast to the procedure described by Gläser and Laudel (2010, chap. 5) for qualitative content analysis, the coding of the material in this study does not commence from theoretically derived categories. Though the theoretical framework helps to look for and highlight certain aspects and in that sense offers some first broad categories, the majority of codes is immediately derived from the data material itself and, where applicable, condensed into categories. Likewise, the very approach towards the data differs from the one described by grounded theory in that the study explicitly draws on existing theoretical approaches, i. e. does not go into the field or approach the material with 'blank mind' (cf. Glaser & Strauss 1967; Charmaz 2006). However, the task of theory in this study is not to tell what reality looks like but to offer frames to describe it that might need to be changed in the course of the study. In that sense, the procedure followed here is less open as it does not start from scratch, but shares the idea of grounded theory that interviews and texts shall speak for themselves without a preconceived assumption, unladen with a 'theory' in mind.

In that understanding, what Mayring (2000a, p. 3–4) describes as 'inductive category development' in combination with 'open coding' (cf. also Hsieh & Shannon 2005; Mayring 2000b, pp. 74–76) comes closest to describing the approach used here. Another point of departure is what Strauss and Corbin call 'open' and 'selective' coding (Flick 2009, pp. 306–313) while also 'axial coding' were a substantial part of the analysis. Both described procedures allow to keep codes rather descriptive and at a low level of abstraction in a first step. The transcribed interviews, the legal texts as well as the parliamentary minutes were coded according to meaningful units of meaning, which could be comprised of a simple clause to the length of a paragraph. As common, sections could be labelled with several codes where applicable. In a second and third step codes were harmonised and aggregated on a higher level of abstraction, upon which the aggregation to categories was based (Kuckartz 2005; Mayring 2000b, pp. 102–108). For coding, the software RQDA was used (Huang 2011).[3] The allocation and revision of codes and the pooling to form categories was an iterative process until no further codes needed to be added or merged. In general, it was attempted to use the same code-names for each country in order to maintain comparability. However, since the development, topics, and emphasis in the respective countries differed, each country has its own additional set of codes and categories next to the ones applying to all countries alike. The attempt was to code as much text as possible, resulting in only few gaps. In consequence, not all codes are really relevant to answer this study's question, so that only a selected number of them is used to make an argument in the respective chapters (highlighted blue in the list).

The overall character of the analysis could be described to lie somewhere between the notion of 'in-depth analysis' on the one hand and a summary of content as Mayring's (2000b) content analysis would yield on the other, clearly tending towards the first. The pursued analysis allows reading between the lines and for an additional order of reflection on the content.

Roughly speaking, the analysis of the sources itself follows a two-step approach. The first stage orients itself on what elsewhere has been called 'formulating interpretation' (Bohnsack 2010, pp. 134–135) and is primarily used in the chapters on the respective countries. In order to give the reader the possibility to form an opinion about the reasons for patient involvement given by the interviewees, the suggested reasons are mentioned rather unfiltered at this stage.

The second stage attempts to get beyond the viewpoint of the legal texts and interviewees and arrive at a 'reflecting interpretation' (Bohnsack 2010, pp. 135–141). The approach followed here is similar to 'classifying structuring' (Mayring 2000b, pp. 90–91), though deviating in some important respects: structuring is not

---

[3]The only exemption are the Swedish interviews, for which the software OpenCode (ICT Services and System Development and Division of Epidemiology and Global Health and Department of Public Health and Clinical Medicine, Umeå University, Sweden 2009) was used.

In this context I would like to take the opportunity to give credit to the developers of the free and very helpful software I have been using during my research: The reference manager JabRef (JabRef Development Team 2003–2016), the powerful text editor TeXnicCenter (Weinkauf & Wiegand 2012–2014), and the underlying MikTeX (Schenk 2009–2013) as well as various other contributors building upon this LaTeX-distribution. Concerning technical support, a special thanks goes to Ulrike Fischer, and the users cgnieder, Malipivo, and Stefan Kottwitz in different LaTeX-fora. The same holds true for the excellent (online) dictionaries I used (Cowie, Crowther, Ramsaran, Hardcastel, Howarth, Wehmeier, & Woods et al. 1992; Hemetsberger 2002–2013; 'Oxford Advanced Learner's Dictionary' 2011; Paul 2004–2009; Slot Webcommerce b.v. 2012).

necessarily conducted in a chronological order of the interview, but rather means grouping similar lines of arguments within one interview and across interviews. Similar to the criteria mentioned by Mayring (2000b, p. 90), attention was particularly paid to codes that…

- are of theoretical interest,
- occur frequently or across several interviews, and
- stand out in that they find an underpinned plausible or convincing alternative explanation for the study's question that is worth following.

No matter how formalised these steps and criteria may sound, naturally a good portion of (subjective) interpretation remains. Ideally, however, the amount of subjectivity is reduced to such an extent that not only the reader but also another researcher conducting the study under similar conditions would draw the same or at least similar conclusions. Even though no full-grown cross-check was feasible in this study, excerpts of one interview each from the English and German case study were coded anew by a second person in order to get an idea about the quality of coding. The overall result proved satisfactory.

## References

Allison, G. T. (1971). *Essence of decision: Explaining the Cuban missile crisis*. Boston: Little Brown.

Anderson, K. M. (2006). Sweden: After social democratic hegemony. In E. M. Immergut, K. M. Anderson, & I. Schulze (Eds.), *The handbook of West European pension politics* (Chap. 8, pp. 349–395). Oxford: Oxford University Press.

Andreassen, T. A. (2005). *Brukermedvirkning i helsetjenesten: arbeid med brukerutvalg og andre medvirkningsprosesser* (1st ed.). Oslo: Gyldendal akademisk.

Bakke, T., & de Vibe, M. (2009). …med pasientens øyne... —Brukermedvirkning—et gjennombrudd for ledere, medarbeidere og pasienter. In T. Konsmo (Ed.), *Rapport fra kvalitetsprosjektet—Norsk sykepleierfobund*. Oslo: kunskapssenteret.

Barros, P. P., Machado, S. R., & de Almeida Simões, J. (2011). Spain: Health system review. *Health systems in transition*. Copenhagen: WHO Regional Office for Europe on behalf of the European Observatory on Health Systems and Policies.

Bogner A., Littig, B., & Menz, W. (Eds.). (2009). *Interviewing experts*. Research methods series. New York: Palgrave McMillan.

Bogner, A., Littig, B., & Menz, W. (Eds.). (2002). *Das Experteninterview. Theorie, Methode, Anwendung*. Opladen: Leske + Budrich.

Bogner, A., & Menz, W. (2009). The theory-generating expert interview: Epistemological interest, forms of knowledge, interaction. In A. Bogner, B. Littig, & W. Menz (Eds.), *Interviewing experts*. ECPR research methods series (Chap. 2, pp. 43–80). London: Palgrave.

Bohnsack, R. (2010). *Rekonstruktive Sozialforschung: Einführung in qualitative Methoden* (8th ed.). Opladen & Farmington Hills: Barbara Budrich.

Bönker, F. (2005). Changing ideas on pensions: Accounting for differences in the spread of the multipillar paradigm in five EU social insurance countries. In P. Taylor-Gooby (Ed.), *Ideas and welfare state reform in Western Europe* (Chap. 5, pp. 81–99). Basingstoke: Palgrave Macmillan.

Busse, R., & Blümel, M. (2014). Germany—Health system review (Vols. 16). *Health systems in transition*. Copenhagen: WHO Regional Office for Europe.

Büthe, T. (2002). Taking temporality seriously: Modelling history and the use of narratives as evidence. *American Political Science Review, 96*(3), 481–493.

Campbell, D. T. (1975). 'Degrees of Freedom' and the case study. *Comparative Political Studies, 8*(2), 178–193.

Charmaz, K. (2006). *Constructing grounded theory—A practical guide through qualitative analysis*. London: SAGE.

Checkel, J. T. (2005, October). *It's the process stupid! Process tracing in the study of European and international politics*. Arena Working Paper No. 26. Oslo.

Christensen, T., & Lægrid, P. (2010). *Reforming Norway's welfare administration*. Stockholms: Statskontoret.

Christmann, G. B. (2009). Expert interviews on the telephone: A difficult undertaking. In A. Bogner, B. Littig, & W. Menz (Eds.), *Interviewing experts*. ECPR research methods series (Chap. 7, pp. 157–183). London: Palgrave.

Coffey, A., & Atkinson, P. (1996). *Making sense of qualitative data*. Thousand Oaks: SAGE.

Coleman, J. S. (1990). *Foundations of social theory*. Cambridge, MA: Belknap Press of Harvard University Press.

Cowie, A., Crowther, J., Ramsaran, S., Hardcastel, M., Howarth, P., Wehmeier, S., & Woods, M. et al. (Eds.). (1992). *Oxford advanced learner's dictionary of current english*. Bielefeld: Cornelsen.

Creswell, J., & Plano Clark, V. (2007). *Designing and conducting mixed methods research*. London: SAGE.

Denzin, N. K. (1989). *The research act: A theoretical introduction to sociological methods* (3rd ed.). Englewood Cliffs: Prentice-Hall.

Denzin, N. K., & Lincoln, Y. S. (Eds.). (2003). *Handbook of qualitative research* (2nd ed.). Thousand Oaks: SAGE.

Diekmann, A. (1996). *Empirische Sozialforschung: Grundlagen, Methoden, Anwendungen*. Reinbek bei Hamburg: rowohlts enzyklopädie.

Dunn, W. N. (2011). *Public policy analysis* (5th ed.). Boston: Pearson.

Ebbinghaus, B. (2006). When less is more: Selection problems in large-N and small-N cross-national comparisons. In K. -S. Rehber (Ed.), *Soziale Ungleichheit, kulturelle Unterschiede: Verhandlungen des 32. Kongresses der Deutschen Gesellschaft für Soziologie*. DGS (Vol. 1–2, pp. 4013–4021). München: Campus.

Eckstein, H. (1973). Case study and theory in political science. In F. I. Greenstein & N. W. Polsby (Eds.), *Handbook of political science* (Vol. 7, pp. 79–138). Reading, MA: Addison-Wesley Press.

Elster, J. (1998). A plea for mechanisms. In P. Hedström & R. Swedberg (Eds.), *Social mechanisms: An analytical approach to social theory* (Chap. 3). Cambridge: Cambridge University Press.

Fenno, R. F. (1986, March). Observation, context, and sequence in the study of politics. *The American Political Science Review, 80*(1), 3–15.

Flick, U. (2007). *Managing quality in qualitative research*. SAGE qualitative research kit (4th ed.). London: SAGE.

Flick, U. (2009). *An introduction to qualitative research* (4th ed.). London: SAGE.

Froschauer, U., & Lueger, M. (2003). *Das qualitative Interview: Zur Praxis interpretativer Analyse sozialer Systeme*. UTB, Facultas, WUV.

George, A. L. (1979). Case studies and theory development: The method of structured focused comparison. In P. G. Lauren (Ed.), *Diplomatic history: New approaches*. New York: The Free Press.

George, A. L., & Bennett, A. (2005). *Case studies and theory development in the social sciences*. Cambridge, MA: MIT Press.

George, A.L., & McKeown, T. J. (1985). Case studies and theories of organizational decision making. *Advances in Information Processing in Organizations, 2*, 21–58.

Gerkens, S., & Merkur, S. (2010). Belgium. *Health systems in transition*. WHO Regional Office for Europe on behalf of the European Observatory on Health Systems and Policies.

George, A. L., & Smoke, R. (1974). *Deterrence in American foreign policy: Theory and practice*. New York: Columbia University Press.
Gerring, J. (2004). What is a case study and what is it good for? *American Political Science Review, 98*(2), 341–354.
Gerring, J. (2007). *Case study research—principles and practices*. Cambridge: Cambridge University Press.
Gläser, J., & Laudel, G. (2009). On interviewing "good" and "bad" experts. In A. Bogner, B. Littig, & W. Menz (Eds.), *Interviewing experts*. ECPR research methods series (Chap. 5, pp. 117–137). London: Palgrave.
Gläser, J., & Laudel, G. (2010). *Experteninterviews und qualitative Inhaltsanalyse als Instrumente rekonstruierender Untersuchungen*. Wiesbaden: VS Verlag.
Glaser, B. G., & Strauss, A. L. (1967). *The discovery of grounded theory strategies for qualitative research*. Chicago: Aldine.
Glenngård, A., Hjalte, F., Svensson, M., Anell, A., & Bankauskaite, V. (2005). Sweden: Health system review. In V. Bankauskaite (Ed.), *Health systems in transition*. Copenhagen: WHO Regional Office for Europe on behalf of the European Observatory on Health Systems and Policies.
Götze, R. (2016, August 18). *Ende der Dualität? Krankenversicherungsreformen in Deutschland und den Niederlanden*. Frankfurt: Campus.
Hemetsberger, P. (2002–2013). Deutsch-Englisches Wörterbuch. Retrieved from www.dict.cc
Hepburn, A., & Potter, J. (2004). Discourse analytic practice. In C. Seale, G. Gobo, J. F. Gubrium, & D. Silverman (Eds.), *Qualitative research practice* (Chap. 12, pp. 180–196). London: SAGE
Hinrichs, K. (2001). Elephants on the move—patterns of public pension reform in OECD countries. In S. Leibfried (Ed.), *Welfare state futures* (pp. 77–102). Cambridge: Cambridge University Press.
Hofmarcher M. M. (2013). Austria. In W. Quentin (Ed.), *Health systems in transition*. WHO Regional Office for Europe on behalf of the European Observatory on Health Systems and Policies.
Hsieh, H.-F., & Shannon, S. E. (2005). Three approaches to qualitative content analysis. *Qualitative Health Research, 15*(9), 1277–1288.
Huang, R. (2011). RQDA: R-based Qualitative Data Analysis. Retrieved January 20, 2017, from http://rqda.rforge.rproject.org/
ICT Services and System Development and Division of Epidemiology and Global Health and Department of Public Health and Clinical Medicine, Umeå University Sweden. (2009). OpenCode 3.6. Retrieved from http://www.phmed.umu.se/enheter/epidemiologi/forskning/opencode/
Immergut, E. M. (1990). Institutions, veto points, and policy results: A comparative analysis of health care. *Journal of Public Policy, 10*(4), 391–416. 10–12.
Immergut, E. M. (1992). *Health politics: Interests and institutions in Western Europe*. Cambridge: Cambridge University Press.
JabRef Development Team. (2003–2016). *JabRef*. JabRef Development Team. Retrieved from http://jabref.sourceforge.net
Jahoda, M., Lazarsfeld, P. F., & Zeisel, H. (1933). *Die Arbeitslosen von Marienthal. Ein soziographischer Versuch über die Wirkungen langandauernder Arbeitslosigkeit*. Leipzig: Hirzel.
Johnsen, J. R. (2006). *Health systems in transition: Norway*. In V. Bankauskaite (Ed.), Copenhagen: WHO Regional Office for Europe on behalf of the European Observatory on Health Systems and Policies.
Kelle, U., & Kluge, S. (1999). *Vom Einzelfall zum Typus—Fallvergleich und Fallkontrastierung in der qualitativen Sozialforschung*. Qualitative Sozialforschung. Opladen: Leske + Budrich.
Kuckartz, U. (2005). *Einführung in die computergestützte Analyse qualitativer Daten*. Wiesbaden: VS Verlag für Sozialwissenschaften.
Lægrid, P., Opedal, S., & Stigen, I. (2005). The Norwegian hospital reform: Balancing political control and enterprise autonomy. *Journal of Health Politics, Policy and Law, 30*(6), 1027–1064.
Lamnek, S. (2005). *Qualitative Sozialforschung*. München: Psychologie Verlags Union.
Lamnek, S., & Krell, C. (2010). *Qualitative Sozialforschung: Lehrbuch* (5th ed.). Weinheim: Beltz.

Lieberson, S. (1991, December). Small N's and big conclusions: An examination of the reasoning in comparative studies based on small number of cases. *Social Forces, 70*(2), 307–320.
Lieberson, S. (1994). More on the uneasy case for using mill-type methods in small-N comparative studies. *Social Forces, 72*(4), 1225–1237.
Lijphart, A. (1968). *The politics of accommodation: Pluralism and democracy in the Netherlands*. Berkeley: University of California Press.
Lijphart, A. (1971, September). Comparative politics and the comparative method. *American Political Science Review, 65*(3), 682–693.
Mahoney, J. (2003). Strategies of causal assessment in comparative historical analysis. In J. Mahoney & D. Rueschemeyer (Eds.), *Comparative historical analysis in the social sciences* (Chap. 10, pp. 337–372). Cambridge: Cambridge University Press.
Manning, P. K. (1967). Problems in interpreting interview data. *Sociology and Social Research, 51*, 302–316.
Marshall, C., & Rossman, G. B. (2006). *Designing qualitative research* (Chap. 5, pp. 151–176). Thousand Oaks: Sage.
Mayring, P. (2000a). Qualitative content analysis. *Forum Qualitative Sozialforschung, 1* (2, Art. 20).
Mayring, P. (2000b). *Qualitative Inhaltsanalyse—Grundlagen und Techniken*. Weinheim: Deutscher Studienverlag.
Meuser, M., & Nagel, U. (1989). *Experteninterviews—vielfach erprobt, wenig bedacht* (No. 6). Vorstand des SfB 186. Arbeitspapier. Bremen.
Meuser, M., & Nagel, U. (2009). The expert interview and changes in knowledge production. In A. Bogner, B. Littig, & W. Menz (Eds.), *Interviewing experts*. ECPR research methods series (Chap. 1, pp. 17–42). London: Palgrave.
Mill, J. S. (1872). *A system of logic* (8th ed., Vols. 2). London: Longmans, Green, Reader & Dyer.
Mooney Marini, M., & Singer, B. (1988). Causality in the social sciences. *Sociological Methodology, 18*, 347–409.
Nullmeier, F. (2001). Politikwissenschaft auf dem Weg zur Diskursanalyse? Theorien und Methoden. In R. Keller, A. Hirseland, W. Schneider, & W. Viehöver (Eds.), *Handbuch Sozialwissenschaftliche Diskursanalyse—Theorien und Methoden* (pp. 285–313). Opladen: Leske + Budrich.
Olejaz, M., Juul Nielsen, A., Rudkjøbing, A., Okkels Birs, H., Krasnik, A., & Hernández-Quevedo, C. (2012). Denmark: Health system review. *Health systems in transition*. Copenhagen: WHO Regional Office for Europe on behalf of the European Oberservatory on Health Systems and Policies.
Oxford Advanced Learner's Dictionary. (2011). Retrieved from http://oald8.oxfordlearnersdictionaries.com/
Park, R. E., Burgess, E. W., & McKenzie, R. D. (1925). *The city*. In M. Janowitz (Ed.), The heritage of sociology. London: University of Chicago Press.
Paul, T. (2004–2009). uitmuntend—Hier leer je Nederlands. Retrieved from www.uitmuntend.de
Pfadenhauer, M. (2009). At eye level: The expert interview—a talk between expert and quasi-expert. In A. Bogner, B. Littig, & W. Menz (Eds.), *Interviewing experts*. ECPR research methods series (Chap. 3, pp. 81–97). London: Palgrave.
Pierson, P. (2003). Big, slow-moving, and... invisible—macrosocial processes in the study of comparative politics. In J. Mahoney & D. Rueschemeyer (Eds.), *Comparative historical analysis in the social sciences* (Chap. 5, pp. 177–207). Cambridge: Cambridge University Press.
Ragin, C. R. (1994). The goals of social reasearch. In *Constructing social research* (Chap. 2, pp. 31–53). Thousand Oaks, CA: Pine Forge Press.
Ringard, Å., Sagan, A., Sperre Saunes, I., & Lindahl, A. K. (2013). Norway: Health system review. *Health systems in transition*. Copenhagen: WHO Regional Office for Europe on behalf of the European Observatory on Health Systems and Policies.
Roberts, C. (1996). *The logic of historical explanation*. University Park: Pennsylvania State University Press.

Robinson, W. S. (1951). The logical structure of analytic induction. *American Sociological Review, 16*, 812–818.

Scalzo, A. L., Donatini, A., Orzella, L., Cicchetti, A., Profili, S., & Maresso, A. (2009). Italy: Health system review. *Health systems in transition*. Copenhagen: WHO Regional Office for Europe on behalf of the European Oberservatory on Health Systems and Policies.

Schenk, C. (2009–2013). MikT$_E$X. Retrieved from http://miktex.org/

Skocpol, T. (1979). *States and social revolutions: A comparative analysis of France, Russia and China*. Cambridge: Cambridge University Press.

Slot Webcommerce B.V. (2012). mijnwoordenboek. Retrieved from http://www.mijnwoordenboek.nl

Stigen, I. M. (2010). *The structural anatomy of hospital government systems in Norway Denmark and the United Kingdom—A comparison*. NIBR Report. Oslo: Norsk institutt for by- og regionforskning.

Strauss, A. L., & Corbin, J. (1990). *Basics of qualitative research*. London: SAGE.

Tansey, O. (2007). *Process tracing and elite interviewing: A case for non-probability sampling*. Oxford: Nuffield College.

Tashakkori, A., & Teddlie, C. (1998). *Mixed methodology: Combining qualitative and quantitative approaches*. London: SAGE.

Thorsen, L. (2010). Brukermedvirkning—hva innebærer det? Sykehuset Innlandet HF. Brumunddal.

Trondheim Kommune. (2005). *Brukerråd, hva da?*

Turner, R. H. (1953). The quest for universals in sociological research. *American Sociological Review, 18* 604–611.

van Dyk, S. (2008). Best practices under construction—Ein 'discursive turn' in der vergleichenden Wohlfahrtsstaatenforschung? *Zeitschrift für Sozialreform, 54*(4), 363–389.

Vennesson, P. (2008). Case studies and process tracing: Theories and practices. In D. Porta & M. Keating (Eds.), *Approaches and methodologies in the social sciences* (Chap. 12, pp. 223–239). Cambridge: Cambridge University Press.

Vuorenkoski, L. (2008). *Finland: Health system review*. In P. Mladovsky & E. Mossialos (Eds.), *Health systems in transition*. Copenhagen: WHO Regional Office for Europe on behalf of the European Oberservatory on Health Systems and Policies.

Weinkauf, T., & Wiegand, S. (2012–2014). T$_E$XnicCenter. Retrieved from http://texniccenter.org/

Wolff, S. (2000). Dokumenten- und Aktenanalyse. In U. Flick, E. von Kardorff, & I. Steinke (Eds.), *Qualitative Forschung Ein Handbuch* (pp. 502–513). Reinbek: Rowohlt.

Yin, R. K. (2009). *Case study research: Design and methods*. Thousand Oaks: SAGE.

Znaniecki, F. (1934). *The method of sociology*. New York: Holt, Rinehart & Winston.

# Part II
# Case Studies

# Chapter 5
# The Netherlands

*cli - 'ën - ten - raad (m) Iedere zorginstelling is volgens de Wet Medezeggenschap Cliënten Zorginstellingen (WMCZ) verplicht een cliëntenraad in te stellen. Deze behartigt uw algemene belangen zoals de voeding, de hygiëne en de klachtenregeling binnen een zorginstelling.*[1]

*'me - de - zeg - gen - schap of me - de - 'zeg - gen - schap (f of n) 1 het recht mee te doen in besprekingen en bij de besluitvorming over zaken die betrekking hebben op het werk in bedrijven;* m. *houdt in dat de werkgever luistert naar de wensen van de werknemers.; in 1950 was er al een Wet op de Ondernemingsraden, die grote bedrijven verplichtte werknemers via formeel overleg te horen over het (personeels)beleid; vanaf 1970 werd het recht op inspraak ook in andere sectoren vastgelegd, bijvoorbeeld van studenten en ouders in het onderwijs; 2 de modieuze managementterm van het begin van de jaren negentig; in organisaties wordt dit meestal opgevat als meer participatie van medewerkers in de onderneming waarvoor zij werken, met als een van de bedoelingen het stimuleren van initiatief en ondernemingsgeest; het heeft bijzondere implicaties voor vrouwen waar het gaat om geleidelijk afbreken; 3* m. door cliënten bij zorginstellingen in Nederland is sinds *1996* geregeld in de Wet medezeggenschap cliënten zorginstellingen *(WMCZ)*[2]

## 5.1 Introduction

The Netherlands, with a population of approximately 16.78 million and an average of 498 citizens per square kilometre is one of the most densely populated countries of Europe (as of 13 October 2013; Centraal Bureau voor de Statistiek 2013a). This holds in particular true for the province of Zuid-Holland (more than 1200 citizens/km$^2$) and the so-called Randstad, the imaginary rectangle between the

[1]http://www.encyclo.nl/begrip/Clientenraad; accessed on 22 August 2016.

[2]www.encyclo.nl/begrip/Medezeggenschap; accessed on 22 August 2016.



A. Haarmann, *The Evolution and Everyday Practice of Collective Patient Involvement in Europe*, DOI 10.1007/978-3-319-64595-7_5

four largest cities Amsterdam, The Hague, Rotterdam, and Utrecht. In contrast, especially the northeastern (Groningen, Friesland/Fryslân, Drenthe) and southwestern provinces (Zeeland) are at or below half of the national average and, thus, comparatively sparsely populated (Centraal Bureau voor de Statistiek 2004). As a founding member of the 'European Coal and Steel Community' in 1951, the predecessor of European Union, the small open economy has kept this economical outward orientation up to this day.

### *5.1.1 The Dutch Welfare State: A Unique Case*

The Netherlands is a generous and comprehensive welfare state which, over time, has found some remarkable solutions for its problems. Even more than its larger neighbours Germany and Great Britain, it is to be seen as a collection of different sub-systems of the welfare state rather than a unitary system. The main reason for this lies in its peculiarity: No matter which of the prominent welfare state typologies of the last 30 years is applied, none fits in entirety (cf., e.g., Esping-Andersen 1990; Hicks, Misra, & Nah Ng 1995; Schmid 2002; Schmidt 2005; Neubauer & Birkner 1984; Goodin & Smitsman 2000; Arts & Gelissen 2002). Its main source of funding are social contributions for the respective social insurances, which are based on the principle of solidarity. This would make it what most often is called a 'conservative' welfare state. However, besides tax-funded subsidies for some social insurances, which can be found elsewhere as well, there are two basic coverage systems which are not linked to the logic of insurance or the individual employment history, for which all residents are entitled to receive benefits under certain preconditions. According to the 'General Old Age Act' ('*Algemene Ouderdomswet*', 1956) each year of residence in the Netherlands entitles to some 2% of a state pension that after 50 years amounts to 90% of the minimum wage. The 'Long-term Care Act' ['*Wet langdurige zorg*', 2014 (Wlz)] is the second health-related system, which secures citizens from "uninsurable costs of illnesses". Being in force since 1 January 2015, it replaces the 'Exceptional Medical Expenses Act' ('Algemene wet bijzondere ziektekosten—AWBZ' 1967). While the field of home services (*huishoudelijke verzorging*) was transferred to the 'Societal Support Act' ('Wet maatschappelijke ondersteuning (WMO)', 2006; 'Wet maatschappelijke ondersteuning 2015', 2014; cf. also Schäfer et al. 2010, pp. 159–160; Centraal Bureau voor de Statistiek 2009, pp. 62–63) in 2007 the 'Long-term Care Act' has retained long-term treatments and/or care. Hence, the Netherlands combines elements of conservative welfare states—with their contribution-based protection through social insurances—with those which usually are associated with social democratic welfare states (cf. Esping-Andersen 1990).

Even the health care system is an exception: Since 2006 it is the first European social insurance to be based on private insurances. While the larger part of the contribution is income-related, the previous branch of private health insurances based on insurance risks was abolished.

### 5.1.2 Care and Health Care Provision: An Overview

One of the main characteristics for the Netherlands is the strong gatekeeping function of GPs in primary care (Schäfer et al. 2010, pp. 19, 23). Another is that many institutions of in-patient care are owned by foundations, parishes, or municipalities, while recently a concentration of providers has set in. The government has delegated the task of needs testing with regard to long-term care (Wld) benefits to the 'Centre for Indication Assessment in Healthcare' (*Centrum Indicatiestelling Zorg*, CIZ) and the 'Office of Youth Care' (*Bureau Jeugdzorg*, BJZ). If they reach a positive decision, patients or their immediate relatives receive care that is funded by the national Wld fund and administered by the 'Council of Health Insurances' (*College voor zorgverzekeringen*, CVZ), the 'Central Administration Office' (*Centraal Administratie Kantoor*, CAK), and finally the regional 'Care Offices' (*Zorgkantoren*) (Schäfer et al. 2010, pp. 14, 159–160). Primary and secondary care is provided by approximately 9418 (GPs as of 2013 Hassel, Kastelijn, & Kenens 2015) and for a number of years the relatively stable number of around 130 hospitals (as of 2016 Nederlandse Vereniging van Ziekenhuizen 2016, p. 14). Old age care was provided by '479 nursing homes, 1131 residential homes and 290 combined institutions' (as of 2009; Deuning 2013b), which can be considered as a substantial growth (cf. Schäfer et al. 2010, p. 160). To this some "248 home care services and 255 nursing homes with home care" can be added (as of 2007; Deuning 2007). Health Care for the handicapped is delivered in about 100 psychiatric care units funded by the health insurance and the Long-term Care Act (Wld), 140 units for care of physically handicapped people, and 454 old people's homes and nursing services (Centraal Bureau voor de Statistiek 2012a). On the recipients side were 505,190 individuals who received benefits according to the 'Societal Support Act' [*Wet maatschappelijke ondersteuning* (WMO)] (Giesbers 2011) and 802,060 who received benefits according to the AWBZ in 2013 (Giesbers 2013), i.e., approximately 7.8% of the total population. Of the latter, there were approximately 63,600 in disability care and 25,350 in mental health care in 2009 (Centraal Bureau voor de Statistiek 2010a).

### 5.1.3 A Long History of Involvement

> Dutch scholars argue that corporatism in their country is not based on the absence of political conflict. Rather, the institution hide conflict from public discussion.
> (Cox 1993, p. 49)

Formalised participation of citizens has not emerged all of a sudden in the Netherlands: The country has had strong means of participation in virtually all areas of societal life for many decades. It described itself as what in English comes closest to a 'consultational democracy' (*overlegdemocratie*; cf., e.g., Lewe, Reef, & Hartmann 2002, p. 162). As in many European countries this consultation culture has declined over the last two or three decades. Despite the deterioration with respect to the multitude and quality of participation, a distinct concern regarding participation compared to many other countries can still be found. Within its range everything from advisory bodies of relevant actors in the respective field or commissions of inquiry, who can express their stance during the legislation process on the national level, to hearings on regional and local level can be found. Furthermore, and in particular with regard to the labour market, the Netherlands can be regarded as one of the classical corporatist states of Europe (cf. Wintle 2000; Cox 1993; Woldendorp & Keman 2007; Ebbinghaus 2010). Here, the term '*poldermodel*' and the 'Wassenaar Agreement' are known in the literature, politics, and industrial relations far beyond the Dutch borders and are symbols for the power of joint problem solving (Visser & Hemerijck 1998; Hemerijck, Unger, & Visser 2001; Eichhorst & Hemerijck 2008; van Paridon 2004, pp. 401–402; Stichting van de Arbeid 1982; cf. also van Paridon 2004, pp. 388–396).

Besides industrial relations, the sphere of social insurances is the second main field of activity for corporatism (cf. also Pressel 2010, p. 349). Traditionally, all social insurance branches were in one way or another self-administered by the social partners with only the partly tax-funded state-run pension fund with its tripartite administrative board constituting an exemption. Nowadays, most insurances are governed by expert boards, a professional management, or responsibility has been devolved to municipalities, the only exception being the administration of unemployment benefits, which still is left to the social partners. Deprived of the former importance of classical corporatism, competences were partly individualised and shifted to citizens who often still have a say via an advisory board or as the highest formal decision-making body in many health insurances (cf. Haarmann 2012, pp. 403–405, 413–423).[3]

In conclusion, it might be said that involvement in the form of corporatism in the Netherlands has, as in many other European countries, been on the decline, participation was not abolished altogether, but—as will be shown below—rather remodelled to fit a new demand and zeitgeist.

[3]Benefits which are subject to bilateral negotiations between the social partners [like the mandatory occupational pension funds (cf., e.g., Anderson 2006, pp. 727–728; Trampusch 2000; Roebroek & Hertogh 1998, p. 298)] are exempted from this trend. Of the several institutionalised councils the *Raad van State* (Council of State), founded in 1531, is probably the oldest advisory council in the Netherlands. It comprises appointed experts from all kinds of societal sectors. It not only advises on a large number of legislative processes it is at the same time the highest administrative court of the Netherlands (Raad van State 2010). The competences of the tripartite *Sociaal-Economische Raad* (SER; Social Economic Council), which advises since 1950 and consists of representatives of employers, employees, and *kroonleden* (Members of the Crown; appointed experts), are more specific: for all kinds of legislation regarding socio-economic consequences—be it pensions or maximum permissible values of pollutants—advice can be requested by the cabinet and/or parliament. However, the council can advise proactively as well. The second main task is the supervision of organisations governed by public law (*Publiek-rechtelijke bedrijfsorganisaties* (PBO); Sociaal-Economische Raad 2010a,b). The rather recent *Raad voor Werk en Inkomen* (Council for Work and Income) consists of members of employers, employees, and municipalities, It advises on possibilities for a better functioning of the labour market and the reintegration of unemployed or incapacitated persons (Raad voor Werk en Inkomen (RWI) 2010).

### 5.1.4 *The Political System, Parties, and Trade Unions*

The Netherlands is a constitutional monarchy with the king or queen as the head of state, who since 2013 is king Willem-Alexander. Despite its centralistic orientation, the country holds some elements which resemble federal structures as, for example, the provinces have some leeway for their own administration. This is rather limited in nature and concerns mainly topics like regional development, public transport, and to some extent supervisory functions towards municipalities and the 'water boards' (*waterschappen*) and their task to maintain dikes and regulate water levels. These 'federal' elements also find their expression in the *Staten-Generaal*, the overarching term for both houses of parliament: the 150 seats of the House of Representatives, the Second Chamber of the Staten-Generaal (*Tweede Kamer der Staten-Generaal*), are assigned according to the election results that determine proportional representation in each constituency every 4 years. It is the *Tweede Kamer* where most everyday politics happens, here is where the right of initiative lies. In contrast, the 75 members of the Upper House, the *Eerste Kamer*, sometimes also called *Senaat*, are elected by the respective provincial councils every 4 years and have the task to check the bills of the *Tweede Kamer* for their feasibility. Though it does not possess the right of legislative proposal and cannot demand changes of a bill, it can accept or reject a bill (cf. amongst others Anderson 2006, pp. 717 et seq.; Lepszy & Wilp 2009; Berndt 2010).

Since there is no election threshold in the Netherlands, smaller parties have a higher chance to be voted into the *Tweede Kamer*. With regard to building a government, this means that a coalition government consisting of three or four parties is rather a common than a rare phenomenon. One consequence is that over the course of the last 20 years 18 different parties have been represented in the House of Representatives. In the same period, six different parties have belonged to coalition governments. The higher number of coalition partners in a government, in turn, rather often leads to early elections. The specific constellation requires the Dutch skill of negotiation and consensus as well as persistence.

Traditionally, there are three major parties: The social democratic *Partij van de Arbeid* (PvdA) is a post-world war merger of three parties with roots dating back to the nineteenth century, including a leftist denominational party. There is the conservative, market liberal party *Volkspartij voor Vrijheid and Demokratie* (VVD) and the moderately conservative 'Christian-democratic Appeal' (*Christen-Democratisch Appèl*; CDA) as the third of the three traditionally strongest parties. Founded in 1980 as a merger of other denominational parties it has lost considerable support over the last years. The CDA is the party which formed most governments in the post-war period, which also is owed to a number of cabinet reshuffles. For a couple of years, the right-wing populist 'Party for the Freedom' (*Partij voor de Vrijheid*; PVV), which often is said to consist solely of its party chairman Geert Wilders, caught up and became the third strongest party in the 2012 elections. Even though most parties reject collaboration with the PVV, the last minority government formed by VVD and CDA was tolerated by the PVV, which lent it credibility and made it more acceptable. Besides these parties the 'Socialist Party' (*Socialistische Partij*; SP); the 'Democrats 66' (*Democraten 66*; D66), a social-liberal party founded in 1966; 'GreenLeft' (*GroenLinks*; GL), which originated from the environmental movement, christian parties as well as former pacifist-socialist and communist parties; the 'Christian Union' (*Christen Unie*; CU); the 'Politically Reformed Party' (*Staatskundig Gereformeerde Partij*; SGP); the 'Party for the Animals' (*Partij voor de Dieren*; PvdD); and the party '50 plus' are members of the House of Representatives after the general elections in 2012.

Dutch trade unions are very heterogeneous and lack strong umbrella organisations like Germany or Austria, for instance. Nowadays, there are around 50 unions and three larger umbrella organisations with between 1.21 million and 129,000 members (Visser 2009; Fulton 2011; for more detailed information on unions cf. van Cruchten & Kuijpers 2007; Visser 2009). When it comes to involvement outside industrial relations, however, trade unions no longer play a significant role. However, they played a role as representatives of the beneficiaries of some sickness funds and they are still of importance when it comes to demands put forward by staff in nursing homes, hospitals, etc.

Compared to other European countries, consumer organisations are relatively strong. Depending on the point of view, patient organisations are also seen as consumer organisations. Most often, this is also expressed using a standard term, the 'patient and client organisation' (*patiënten- en cliëntenorganisaties*). One of the two largest umbrella organisations, the 'Dutch Patients Consumers Federation' (*Nederlandse Patiënten Consumenten Federatie*, NPCF), illustrates this.

In the following chapters, first, the sources employed in the Dutch case study will be presented. Thereafter, we briefly examine pillarisation and de-pillarisation, which have to be understood in order to fully comprehend the younger history of the country. Followed by a description of the development within the health care system in general, we will analyse the transition from a corporatist welfare state to one in which many regulated private actors constitute the cornerstones of patient involvement. This entailed the legislation of individual patient rights, which are dealt with subsequently before turning to the 'Client Participation Act' as the main part of this chapter. Finally, a thorough look will be taken at the implementation of patient involvement in the Netherlands.

## 5.2 Sources

This case study bases on a wide variety of different sources, which can broadly be classified into six different types:

- scientific literature,
- grey literature,
- Green and White Papers by the government or government commissions,
- draft proposals, bills, and acts,

- parliamentary minutes, and
- expert interviews.

The choice of interview partners was guided by the attempt to look at participation at the level of (health-)care provision from as many different angles as possible, trying to cover even the issues which are at the edge of the topic but might help to arrive at an answer to the questions why patient involvement was enacted and how it is implemented.[4] In order to achieve this, the study was not limited in scope to hospitals but was rather enlarged to also encompass different kinds of long-term care as well, for which the law applies. Furthermore, owing to the unitary structure of the country it was less important to see implementation in different parts of the country but rather the implementation in different (health-)care sectors. Therefore, it was sought to cover a variety of actors so that in the end politicians, representatives of patient organisations, researchers, and members of the 'Client Councils' across different (health-)care sectors were interviewed.

Regarding politics, the aim was to gain access to those people who were involved in the national legislation process. Interview requests were almost exclusively answered positively and people were surprisingly willing to take part in the study. The only problem was that at the time of the study the enactment of the main act in question, the 'Client Participation Act' (*Wet medezeggenschap cliënten zorginstellingen*, WMCZ), was decided upon more than 15 years ago, accordant preparations had begun even another 15 years earlier. This made it somewhat more difficult for politicians and administrators to recall the happenings of the lengthy legislation process. The advantage, however, was that looking back they could oversee and evaluate the match between what they had intended and how the act has actually been implemented. Table 5.1 provides an overview of the finally conducted interviews for the Dutch case study.

## 5.3 Pillarisation and Depillarisation as Societal Preconditions for Involvement

> In one pillar you had everything for everyday life, from cradle to grave, with schools, newspapers, TV stations, consultation offices, GPs, home care. That has changed. [...; But still:] That sits well in our culture, of course, that we like it when everything fits into its small, little corner. We like that. (interview 2; author's translation)

The story of patient involvement in the Netherlands would be more difficult to understand if there had not been the experience of both pillarisation and depillarisation. The many smaller parties mentioned in the introduction were as

[4]Given the more encompassing nature of the Dutch word *zorg*, which can denote long-term care, forms of social care, as well as health care, it will be translated as (health-)care where indistinguishable.

**Table 5.1** Overview of conducted interviews in the Netherlands

| No. of interview | Category of interview partner | Organisation and/or Name | Date |
|---|---|---|---|
| 1 | Patient Platforms | 1 Representative, client/customer organisation, national umbrella | March 2008 |
| 2 | | 1 Representative, client/customer organisation (the same as '1'), national umbrella | May 2010 |
| 3 | | 1 Representative, Landelijk steunpunt (mede)zeggenschap (LSR), national umbrella | March 2008 |
| 4 | | Jasper Boele, director of Landelijk steunpunt (mede)zeggenschap (LSR) | May 2010 |
| 5 | Other Organisations | 1 Representative, Nederlandse vereniging van ziekenhuizen (NVZ) | November 2010 |
| 6 | Members of *Cliëntenraden* | 1 Representative, Antonius Hospital Nieuwegein | October 2010 |
| 7 | | 1 Representative, Mental Care Altrecht | October 2010 |
| 8 | | All members of the Client Council, Humanitas Akropolis Nursing Home Rotterdam | November 2010 |
| 9 | Politicians | Member of Government (VVD) 2003–2007 | February 2008 |
| 10 | | Els Borst (D66), Minister of Health, Welfare, and Sports 1994–2002, formerly hospital director | October 2010 |
| 11 | | Hans Simons (PvdA), Undersecretary of Public Health, Welfare, and Sports 1989–1994, hospital director for 5 years afterwards | November 2010 |
| 12 | Researchers | Dick Oudenampsen, Verwey-Jonker Instituut | May 2010 |
| 13 | | Margo Trappenburg, Universiteit van Amsterdam | November 2010 |
| Total length of recorded interviews: 11 h 24 min | | | |

much an expression for the fragmentation of societal life in the Netherlands as their comparatively late foundation in the present form. The small-scale structures of parties advance the development of coordinated interest groups and result in the strong need for consensus orientation as an integral part of politics between these groups (Katzenstein 1984). This, in turn, is characteristic for what has been called 'consociational democracy' (van Waarden 2002a; Wintle 2000; Lijphart 1968a; Wielenga 2004). One of the downsides is a frequently slowed down legislation process: initiatives might take one or two decades before the respective bill is finally enacted (cf. also Hemerijck et al. 2001). On the upside, however, this also means that all political parties and, owing to a system of reconcilement, most relevant societal actors, back legal acts for a longer time compared to many other countries.

Even though the overarching term for these phenomena of fragmentation, *verzuiling*, pillarisation, was used earlier on by different scholars (cf., e.g., van Doorn 1956; Ponsioen & Veldkamp 1956; Schöffer 1956), it was Lijphart (1968b, 1984) who coined the notion and used it in a more comprehensive way (cf. Hupe 1993, p. 365; for a good summary of various scholarly positions in a comparative perspective cf. Wintle 2000). The reasons for pillarisation (*verzuiling*) can, according to some scholars, be traced back in history to some extent: Over centuries the Dutch nation state was a weak state, the initiative lay by private actors and societal groups. Even after the national state gained more power it remained common to solve problems within your own circle.[5] A second reason for pillarisation was the need for pacification between the two major denominations in the Netherlands. The majority of citizens belonged to protestant churches, which in a way still had the status of a state religion. However, giving equal rights to all religious communities made it possible for everyone to live in any province—quite in contrast, e.g., to the German *Länder*, in which all citizens needed to change their faith. At the same time, however, this facilitated a nationwide development of parallel societies (van Waarden 1992, p. 143; van Waarden 1993, p. 203; cf. also van Kersbergen 2009; Stuurman 1983). Both reasons can be seen as the foundation for pillarisation, which, to some lesser extent could be found in many other western European countries with a mixed denominational population.

Pillarisation, in its modern sense, began to develop during the time of industrialisation. It originates in the controversy surrounding the distribution of political rights among the main denominational groups. Large parts of cultural, political, and everyday life took place in a person's own circle whilst contact to other groups happened rather solely between the respective elites of these groups. The dividing line basically ran between denominational and ideological groups (Lijphart 1968b; Stuurman 1983; van der Grinten & Kasdorp 1999; Anderson 2006, pp. 714, 718). Each group had its subdivisions, with manifold consequences for (almost) every sphere of everyday life: children attended schools belonging to their 'own' group (Lijphart 1968b, pp. 56 et seq.; Stuurman 1983, p. 59; cf. also de Swaan 1989,

[5]Although it was mainly monasteries, parishes, and guilds that were the first entities providing charities, the growing and increasingly wealthy towns took over some social responsibilities for those living outside their own parish (Roebroek & Hertogh 1998, p. 109), which might be described as an urbanisation—instead of nationalisation—of social policy. For several centuries the Netherlands can be characterised as a loose union of rather powerful city states with only few competences on the central level (cf. Lehmbruch 1996, pp. 163 et seq.; van Waarden 1992, p. 144), which left even the defence of its external borders to private organisations (van Waarden 1992, p. 148; van Waarden 2002b, p. 40). Consequently, the political coordination of the up to 1200 representatives of the respective towns in the Staten-Generaal was a tedious endeavour (van Waarden 1992, p. 144) in such a weak state (cf. Atkinson & Coleman 1989). It was not until the influence of the French revolution that a more powerful central state was established and competences enhanced (van Waarden 1992, p. 42; Roebroek & Hertogh 1998, p. 47; cf. also Haarmann 2012, p. 366).

p. 216); you helped the people in need of your own group and clubs and associations were organised accordingly; and you read your 'own' newspaper (Lijphart 1968b, pp. 46 et seq.). This small-scale way of dissociation also affected the organisation of labour in that employees could choose between social-democratic/socialist, communist, catholic, and united-protestant labour unions or those around different vocations (Lijphart 1968b, pp. 41 et seq.). Similarly, and closer to the topic concerned here, you sought care in a catholic, protestant, or municipal hospital or nursing home respectively.

By the end of the 1960s, pillarisation was on its decline. With the onset of depillarisation (*ontzuiling*), it was no longer only at the level of the elites that interaction occurred: These boundaries disappeared and, hence, the concept of pillarisation has lost its relevance in contemporary Dutch society since the beginning of the 1990s (Lijphart 1968b, p. 109; van Waarden 1992, p. 154; van der Grinten & Kasdorp 1999). This, in turn, brought about new constellations and coalitions of groups, unions, and parties. These new coalitions and collaborations, however, did not occur along new lines of groups. Rather, they paved the way for a much more individualised society, which was an essential part of individualisation.[6]

It can be argued that the experience of belonging to a larger society, i.e., not separated by denominational boundaries, was an essential precondition for the 'Client Participation Act' (WMCZ). Without depillarisation patients would have stayed in nursing homes and old people's home of their respective denomination so that problem solving would have been perceived less needed and/or would have remained within the own group again. In that sense, it was a necessary, yet not sufficient condition for the enactment of the WMCZ. This assumption received some support from interview partners. One of the interviewed researchers linked the process of depillarisation with the question of legitimacy and ownership on the one hand, and the emergence of patient organisations on the other hand:

> As a result of depillarisation the question naturally is: Who is actually the owner [of (health-)care facilities]? And that is, I would think, an important question, which institutions are still struggling with. The principal question, then, is: Is a facility the property of clients? [...] Or is it the property of a foundation, which includes (health-)care provision, but is financed by the authorities to an important degree? [...]
>
> At the same time the private initiative was hollowed out because pillarisation was in its final state. And that made the question really prominent: What is the legitimacy of the professionals [...] and the management? Why are they the boss? Actually, a movement arose at a certain point in time in order to clearly give clients and family members much more influence. [...]

[6]One of the most apparent examples for depillarisation is the composition of a number of political parties. As has been shown in section 'The Political System, Parties, and Trade Unions', 5.1.4 on page 79, a number of them were founded rather late in comparison with other European countries and are sometimes composed of rather surprising predecessors, which can be attributed to depillarisation setting in. To give the most illustrative example: The CDA ('*Christen Democratisch Appèl*'), was founded first in 1980 and seeks to unite all voters who want to see policies guided by Christian values. Its precursors were several parties, which represented their electorate in part with highly divergent programmes: The *Katholieke Volkspartij* (KVP) ran for Catholic votes while the *Anti-Revolutionaire Partij* (ARP) and the *Christelijk-Historische Unie* (CHU) campaigned for different strata of Protestants (cf. also Haarmann 2012, p. 367).

> I think that depillarisation actually implied that more attention had to be paid to the individual, thus, that in effect the whole idea of 'your own pillar answers for your needs' was swept away. At a certain time you see that organisations of patients and relatives emerge everywhere, which mainly put the position of the chronically ill, the chronically ill patient on the agenda since there often was not enough attention to specific illnesses. (interview 12; author's translation)

Needless to say, this can only be a necessary condition for a specific change. However, as was shown, pillarisation had its share in developing civil commitment, as the state guaranteed the independence of societal groups and, in earlier years, rather took the role of a facilitator. The 'necessity' to become involved was much lower within each single pillar. Upon this basis, depillarisation allowed for involvement in the society as a whole.

## 5.4 Developments in Health Insurance: A History of Attempted Cost Containment

Another precondition for the emergence of a new form of patient involvement was the development within health care and care. The times when the state solely assumed the role of a passive facilitator of rights long since gone, the question as to what recipes are most suitable to arrive at a more effective governance is constantly changing. Over time, the state has chosen different pathways. In what follows, we will take a closer look at the development in the health care sector. This is not only an area which illustrates the competing and changing governance strategies but, more importantly, it shows the context in which involvement in the sense of this study emerged (cf. Schee, Delnoij, Hutten, Verwij, & Kerssens 2000).

### *5.4.1 Growth Control by Legislative Regulation*

The early and mid-1960s were an expansive phase of the welfare state in the Netherlands (for more information cf. Roebroek & Hertogh 1998; Companje 2008; Hartmann 2000; Haarmann 2012, pp. 393–397). With regard to health care, the Exceptional Medical Expenses Act (AWBZ) saw the light of day. Even the 'Sickness Fund Act' (*Ziekenfondswet*)) was enacted in 1964, replacing the old unbeloved *Ziekenfondsbesluit* (Sickness Fund Decree) as it came into force under strong pressure from Nazi-Germany (cf., e.g., Commissie over 'de toekomstige ontwikkeling der sociale verzekering in Nederland' (Commissie van Rhijn), 1945, p. 37; Roebroek & Hertogh 1998, p. 192; Kappelhof 2004; Companje 2008, pp. 486 et seq.). Beginning in the late 1960s politicians became concerned about the "wild and skewed growth" of especially hospital and specialist care in a "patchwork" health care system and, in turn, the growing costs (van der Grinten & Kasdorp 1999, p. 13 Lieverdink 2001, p. 1185), which was subsequently accentuated with the beginning of the oil crises

(Companje 2008, pp. 578 et seq.; Green-Pedersen 2002, pp. 94, 96). Today we know that contrary to the perception then, the exceptional rise in expenditures can for the greatest part be traced back to the extended coverage of in-patient care from 70 to 365 days in the context of the transfer of particular rights from the Sickness Fund Act to the then recently adopted AWBZ (Companje 2008, p. 581). Back then, however, the political answer to attain the aim of growth control was regulation. The 'Hospital Supply Act' (*Wet Ziekenhuisvoorzieningen* (WZV)) was one of the first instruments and regulated the capacities of hospitals from 1971 onwards, while the green paper 'Structuring Healthcare' (*Structuurnota Gezondheidszorg*) framed the preconditions for a coordinated and compelling (health-)care and a strengthened primary care (Hartmann 2000, p. 134; van der Grinten & Kasdorp 1999, pp. 13 et seq.; Exter, Hermans, Dosljak, & Busse 2004; Companje 2008, pp. 581 et seq.; Schäfer et al. 2010, p. 20). In addition, the 'Tariffs in the Healthcare Sector Act' [*Wet Tarieven Gezondheidszorg* (WTG)] set the contribution rate for sickness funds as well as remunerations for doctors and hospitals from 1979 onwards (Hartmann 2000, pp. 133 et seq.; Companje 2008, p. 584). The last main measures, which had been proven successful in other countries for quite some time, were structural changes, for instance, a forced reduction of bed capacities and substitution of medicines by generics (Hartmann 2000, p. 139). Another measure was the attempt to raise people's cost-awareness and work towards a responsible utilisation of health care (Trappenburg 2008, pp. 74–78).

However detailed and comprehensive these regulations were, they did not live up to the expectations of politicians. Unintended consequences arose such as long waiting lists in in-patient care, which were particularly pronounced in the mid and late 1990s. All of these approaches proved, at least in some respects, unsuccessful in the long run and the belief in cost control by classical regulation began to wane in the political sphere (cf., e.g., Oudenampsen 1999, p. 62; Lieverdink 2001; van der Grinten & Kasdorp 1999).

### 5.4.2 From Sickness Funds to Private Health Insurances

Vis-à-vis the experience that regulation does not necessarily deliver the politically intended outcome, a new solution was sought. This was found in the liberalisation/marketisation of many formerly public tasks in almost all societal areas, including the health care sector (van der Grinten & Kasdorp 1999). The commission 'Structure and Funding of Healthcare' (*Structuur en Financiering Gezondheidszorg*) with its chairman Dekker, a former manager in the private sector, was appointed the task to evaluate the health care system and to suggest measures to make it more effective. Its final report 'Willingness to Change' (*Bereidheid tot verandering*; Commissie 'Structuur en Financiering Gezondheidszorg' (Dekker) 1987) was published in 1987 and proposed the abolition of the distinction between private and statutory health insurances. Instead, a uniform type of competing and more effective health insurance should be introduced that negotiated prices with health care providers.

This strikingly resembles the privatised health insurance market of today (cf., e.g., Oudenampsen 1999, p. 27; on the plan and the criticism of it Groenewegen 1994; cf. also Bartholomée & Maarse 2006). Besides that, the commission not only demanded that patients should take greater responsibility for their own health, as propagated by the green paper 'Patient policy' (*Nota patiëntenbeleid*) of 1981 but also for the first time raised the idea to give patients a greater say in health care matters. This was completely in line with the individualisation taking place in society at the time.

However, it also mirrored the development of the governance of sickness funds. In contrast to many other societal groups, patients were not overly represented in any advice councils at the regional or national level for a long time. In the case of two important councils consulting the political sphere about (health-) care issues, the 'Health Council' and the 'Council for Public Health and Care' (*Gezondheidsraad* and *Raad voor de Volksgezondheid en Zorg*), this still holds true today (cf. Trappenburg 2008, p. 51). The national 'Sickness Fund Council' (*ziekenfondsraad*) with its representatives drawn from sickness funds, employers, employees, (health-)care providers, and ministerial staff was an exception between 1949 and 1996, when lay involvement made way for a professionalised governance (Zorginstituut Nederland 2011). Beyond this, for a very long time there were mainly two possibilities for citizens to participate in health care matters: they could either become active in the Red Cross and patient organisations, an involvement which remained at a very general level. The other option was to become involved in the administration of a sickness fund (Oudenampsen 1999, pp. 53, 55, 59).

Originally modelled after the German health insurance, patients' stakeholders governed the sickness funds by occupying the highest decision-making body, which according to the logic of the early sickness funds was the main means of involvement. The insured would indirectly benefit from influencing strategy, the amount of contributions, and the benefits of a fund.[7] Over time, this model was adopted by most insurances. The individual beneficiaries are thought to represent the interest of the insurance's members in general. With an ever increasing density of regulation by the state since the beginning of the 1970s and the introduction of a professionalised management in the funds from 1992 onwards (NPCF 2003, p. 4) the decisional latitude for lay-people was considerably watered down (Haarmann 2012, p. 402): "The focus of self-regulation is relocated from national to regional level. The pillarised and closed governance system in health care was broken under

[7]The composition of the board varied according to the type of fund. For example, although the board of the '(Royal) Dutch Medical Society' [*(Koninklijke) Nederlandse Maatschappij tot bevordering der Geneeskunst* (KNMG), literally: '(Royal) Society for the Promotion of the Art of Healing'] did include beneficiaries and employees of the fund, it was mainly composed of physicians. In contrast, the social partners could be found on the boards of sickness funds established by companies (cf. Companje 2008, pp. 494, 495, 498, 565, 570; Haarmann 2012, pp. 396–397). The boards of the Friendly Societies (*Onderlinge Waarborgmaatschappij*, even called *Onderlinge Verzekeringen* or shortly *Onderlingen*) were usually solely comprised representatives of the insured (de Swaan 1989, pp. 150 et seq.).

the influence of the state and the market" (Oudenampsen 1999, p. 222; author's translation). Since then, relevant influence by patients on the health care system at large could only issue from the broad agenda of the SER.

This tendency of de-corporatisation and of rather individual composition of the collective bodies was strengthened by the decline of support for corporatism in the early 1990: The lay-members of the Boards of Members were perceived to be unable to restrain costs, which furthered the decline of corporatism and, subsequently, the turn to the market.[8] Though it took about 20 years of incremental change and a number of additional commissions, most of the main recommendations by the Dekker Commission were implemented in the profound health care reform of 2006, except for the integration of the AWBZ into a general health insurance (*Zorgverzekeringswet*, (ZVW); 'Zorgverzekeringswet' 2005). Besides cost containment there were additional reasons for the enactment of the *Zorgverzekeringswet*. Of major importance was the deliberate ending of what was perceived a two-tier system of health insurances (Götze 2016; Haarmann 2012, p. 415). Another was a changed view on the role of the state, which resulted in the policy to let societal actors take over as much governance as possible and leave the state's tasks limited to tasks of coordination and supervision (Tweede Kamer der Staten-Generaal 1991). Even the aim to have no-one uninsured and let everyone contribute to a solidary funding of health care was one of the motives (cf. also Centraal Bureau voor de Statistiek 2007; Haarmann 2012, pp. 33, 34; Greß, Delnoij, & Groenewegen 2003, p. 48; Rijksoverheid 2009; Centraal Bureau voor de Statistiek 2010b, 2012b; for more details on the reform and its implications cf. Schäfer et al. 2010; Bartholomée & Maarse 2006; Friele 2009; Schut & van de Ven 2005; Schut & Bruijn 2007; Enthoven 2008; Haarmann 2012; Götze 2010).

[8]In the early 1990s, a broad parliamentary majority was in favour of a (re-)corporatisation of the so-called employee-insurances (insurance against the risks of unemployment, accidents, and illness) by devolving more administrative competences to the social partners (Roebroek & Hertogh 1998, p. 418). Before the Buurmeijer commission—a parliamentary commission with the objective to come up with a proposal for the organisational future of the Dutch social insurances—published its report, an alternative concept was designed according to which the social partners would have to play a considerably less prominent role. Corporatism was heavily contested for having caused the so-called Dutch Disease: Trade unions and employers had supported a labour market policy which had led to high wages after the demise of regulated wage policy and a high share of people being on paid sick leave, which deeply affected the Netherlands in the crisis of the late 1980s (Trampusch 2000, pp. 263–265; cf. also van Paridon 2004, pp. 388–396). While on its decrease in the health care sector anyway, it affected in particular the other branches of social insurances.

In 1992, the alternative proposal was accepted in parliament. In a nutshell, the commission supported the decision, drawing the conclusion that payments of benefits had run smoothly under the governance of social partners (*bedrijfsvereniging*), the legislator's demand to cut costs, however, had not received sufficient attention. Without means testing and the motivation to re-integrate the unemployed or those on sick pay, it was maintained the social partner had rather acted out of self-interest. The report stated two reasons which were found to be responsible for this misconduct: First, the social partners were administering and controlling the funds. Second, the government was found to have dealt too considerately with the social partners, resulting in a mutual blockade (Roebroek & Hertogh 1998, pp. 421 et seq.; Visser & Hemerijck 1998, pp. 198 et seq.; Borghi & van Berkel 2007, pp. 89, 95; Trampusch 2000, p. 311; footnote is based on: Haarmann 2012, pp. 383–384).

For an interpretation of privatisation as decentralisation cf. Atun 2007.

A first step on the long road to the ZVW was the splitting of contributions for sickness funds in an earnings-related part and a flat rate in 1989 (Greß, Manouguian, & Wasem 2006, p. 8 Companje 2008, p. 589) and the suspension of the obligation to contract ambulatory care providers in 1991, which most funds did not make any use of (Okma 2008, p. 8). This was followed by the 'Reform Act Health Insurance System, second phase' (*Wet stelselwijziging ziektekostenverzekering tweede fase*), that abolished geographically defined boundaries for sickness funds in 1992. The idea was that equipping sickness funds with proper means of competition and giving citizens the choice of sickness funds, competition between sickness funds would foster more effective health care provision, cheaper premiums, and higher quality of care (Companje 2008, p. 590; den Exter et al. 2004; van der Kraan 2006).

The major health care reform of 2006 is the attempt to privatise all health care insurances without losing the character of a social insurance based on solidarity by retaining an income-related part of the contributions. Notwithstanding, competition was increased by raising the flat-rate part of the contribution (Greß et al. 2006, p. 17; Agasi 2008, 282 et seq.). One consequence of the reforms is the concentration on just a few insurers: were there almost 120 sickness funds in the early 1990s and still 57 in 2005 there were only 22 insurances with 35 different labels left by 2014 (Independer 2014). These insurances, however, are to a large extent brands of only nine insurance groups. In consequence, 90% of all Dutch citizens are insured with the four largest groups (Aartse et al. 2008, pp. 9, 18; Nederlandse Zorgautoriteit (NZa) 2012). It remains to be seen whether or not competition with this level of market concentration will work in the longer run (cf. also Friele 2009, pp. 30–47) and what the consequences for involvement in sickness funds will be.

### 5.4.3 Patient Rights

Though patient rights were enacted long before a decision was finally reached concerning the privatisation of Dutch health insurances, legislation is tightly linked to the development described above and can be understood as prescient action directed at the planned changes. Though researchers are divided about the reforms' impact on lay-people's influence on health care insurances (e.g. NPCF 2003; Haarmann 2012), it is safe to say that it became increasingly confined to the own health insurance, while patients, and especially recipients of care, became increasingly aware of their weak position. At the same time, the green paper 'Policy on Patients' (*Nota Patiëntenbeleid*) called for more individual responsibility and less involvement by the state (Tweede Kamer der Staten-Generaal 1980–1981), without, however, providing the necessary tools.

In order to remedy the problem, the idea emerged to empower patients by individual patient rights. A very specific reason for finally taking action besides rather general considerations was the call by the abovementioned Dekker commission to strengthen the position of patients (Commissie 'Structuur en Financiering Gezondheidszorg' (Dekker) 1987, cf., e.g., 102). Under the impression of the report the following newly introduced acts clearly had the character of consumer rights. To the most important of these rights (cf. also den Exter et al. 2004, p. 143) can be counted the...

- 'Medical Treatment Agreement Act' [*Wet op geneeskundige behandelingsovereenkomst* (WGBO)] of 1994, which grants patients the right of comprehensive information about their condition and the requirements for the treating physician to ask for the consent of the patient about the suggested therapy.
- 'Care and Healthcare Complaints Act' [*Wet klachtrecht cliënten zorgsector* (WKCZ)] enacted in 1995, which stipulates that there have to be guidelines on how complaints are dealt with in each care or health care unit and gives patients the right to bring a legal action against the care provider in case they cannot solve the problem on their own.
- 'Quality for Care and Healthcare Units Act' [*Kwaliteitswet Zorginstellingen* (KZ)] of 1996 which grants enforcible quality measures.

Though this line of description might give rise to the impression of a linear story of patient involvement politicians and experts were divided. Following in the footsteps of the Dekker commission the Commission 'Choosing and sharing' (*Commissie Keuzen in de zorg—kiezen en delen*) led by its chairman, the cardiologist Dunning sought to reform the Dutch health insurance system. Its report states that health care should be dedicated to the individual seeking care. The only tasks for patient organisations mentioned, though, are contributions to enduring solutions for cost containment. In other instances patients are perceived only as a potential threat to containing costs (Commissie 'Keuzen in de zorg' (Dunning) 1981).

In the end, the acts on *individual* patient rights were passed during the term of the first 'purple coalition' in the Netherlands, which consisted of the social democratic party (PvdA), the liberal party (VVD), and the social-liberal party (D66) while the 'Medical Treatment Agreement Act' was already arranged by the previous coalition of Christian-Democrats (CDA) and Social Democrats already.

### 5.4.4 Emergence and Origins of the Patient Movement

First patient organisations date back to the turn from the nineteenth to the twentieth century when associations sought to better the situation for deaf and blind people (Oudenampsen 1999, p. 89; Trappenburg 2008, pp. 18, 39). Much more relevant in the context of this work, however, is the patient movement of the late 1960s and 1970s (Oudenampsen 1999, p. 90; Trappenburg 2006, p. 48; Trappenburg 2008, p. 18). Most often to be found in psychiatric care, the groups originated in parents' and relatives' endeavour to improve conditions for their in-patient children and relatives and strive for their (relatives') rights for a higher quality of (health-)care provision and life. This motivation for setting up these associations originated in that...

> The critical forces in the psychiatric care were of the opinion that psychiatric patients were the victim of societal structures causing sickness, and that, therefore, it had to be tried to alter these structures, instead of totally betting on the medical model for treatment of the patient. (Trappenburg 2008, pp. 39–40; author's translation)

To put it differently: patients were fighting against the power to define a condition, its social implications, and thereby the fate of a whole social person solely lying in the hands of the medical profession. The issue was to receive comprehensive information on a patient's condition and, in turn, a say in the choice about how they should be treated (Rijkschroeff 1989, p. 2; Oudenampsen 1999, p. 41). At that stage the patient movement might be characterised as a scattered grassroots movement. Nevertheless, patient organisations were successful in a number of prominent examples and paved the way for more involvement by managing to negotiate agreements with providers. These successes were later often taken up by national patient rights legislation in the years to come (Trappenburg 2008, pp. 68, 86).

### 5.4.5 Patient Organisations and Involvement on the Rise

> Organisations of citizens and particularly patient/consumer organisations are in this perspective [of a positive and active term of citizenship] bearers of democratisation processes in healthcare, for which [...] also the relationship between experts and lay-people and the democratic governance of the development in medical sciences and technique is on the agenda. [...] The patient is thereby not only a citizen who is entitled to social rights but also someone who campaigns for good healthcare.
> (Oudenampsen 1999, p. 42; author's translation)

The positive development of the patient movement led to a different mutual perception of the actors involved. This was taking place at two different levels.

On the national level, the government looked favourably on the patient movement almost right from the start. From the late 1980s onwards, the government has viewed patient organisations as a full-grown dialogue partner or as the '3$^{rd}$ party in healthcare' (Tweede Kamer der Staten-Generaal 1987–1988; cf. also Oudenampsen 1999, p. 105; Trappenburg 2008, p. 85). Nowadays, patient organisations are incorporated in the 'Council on Societal Development' (*Raad voor Maatschappelijke Ontwikkeling*) and the 'Health Council' (*Gezondheidsraad*), both advising the government (Trappenburg 2008, p. 107).

Similarly, at the level of (health-)care provision, which in this context is more in focus, matters have been developing for several decades. The first establishment of what today is called patient/user involvement was a so-called ward council (*zaalraad*) in psychiatric care in 1952 (Trappenburg 2008, p. 92; de Savornin Lohman 2000, p. 33). Though there is not much known about the development of this institution in the 1950s and 1960s, by the second half of the 1970s so-called Patient, Client, Resident, or Family Boards/Councils could be found in a growing number of residential mental care homes throughout the country. Patients, their relatives, and/or volunteers acted as partners for the provider's management in establishing an atmosphere of permanent dialogue (Oudenampsen 1999, pp. 80, 105, 124; Trappenburg 2008, p. 81; cf. also Rijkschroeff 1989). Over time this model spread to other sectors, so that at the beginning of the 1990s, for example, 80% of all nursing homes for people with physical impairments had a Residents' Council (Trappenburg 2008, p. 92). All these initiatives were on a voluntary basis and came into existence without any legal framework.

This also entailed a change in the ascription of roles: A pointed description could read that the medical profession and care providers changed in the eyes of patient organisation from being hostile institutions to becoming another actor you can argue, discuss, or cooperate with in order to improve the treatment in general and your condition in particular (Trappenburg 2008, p. 190; cf. also Oudenampsen 1999, p. 93; van de Bovenkamp 2010, p. 81). The other way around, patients are no longer necessarily seen as passive recipients and subordinate in a patient–doctor relationship. Physicians have reacted to criticism and subsequently see most patients as responsible partners (cf. Oudenampsen 1999, p. 58). In contrast, sickness funds saw their position as the sole representative of patients undermined by the patient initiatives (Trappenburg 2008, pp. 68, 191). This has again changed their mind sets and urges them to fight for the favour of their members, clients, and contribution payers. Interestingly, in the context of the health care reform of 2006 the insurances' task is not only to fund (health-)care provision but also to ensure—at least to some extent—the quality of provision. In that respect it is reasoned that (potential) patients rather align with the financier than with the provider of services (on this assumption cf. also Kjær 2004), a point of view that is debatable (see Section 'Client Councils as a Countervailing Power?', 5.6.4).

After the first wave of foundations of new patient organisations in the 1970s and 1980s, decreasing the geographical distance between the once scattered initiatives, network-building and cooperation began on a regional level, too. This was partly due to the success of local initiatives, partly to the new tasks which came along with it. The 'Clients' association' (*Cliëntenbond*), which brings together most patient organisations in mental care, was the first national network/umbrella organisation. Among the most important members are the 'National Patient and Resident Councils' [*Landelijke Patiënten- en Bewonersraden* (LPR)] founded in 1980 and the foundation of the 'National Platform in Mental Care Association' (*Vereniging Landelijk Platform GGz*) founded in 2005. Founded in the same year were also the 'National Patient and Consumer Federation' [*Nederlandse Patiënten Consumenten Federatie* (NPCD)] and the 'Network for challenged persons or chronically ill' [*Netwerk voor mensen met een beperking of chronische ziekte* (ieder(in))] (Oudenampsen 1999, pp. 67, 90; Oudenampsen & Steketee 2000; cf. also Nederland & Duyvendak 2004; van de Bovenkamp 2010, pp. 60–61).[9] These so-called patient

[9]ieder(in) [lit.: everyone (in)] originated from a merger between *Platform VG* and the 'Dutch council of chronically ill and handicapped persons' [*Chronisch zieken en Gehandicapten Raad Nederland* (*CG-Raad*)] in 2014; the NPCD emerged from the 'National Organisation for Resident

platforms are unique and differ from ordinary patient organisations in that they are non-sectoral, i.e., they neither represent a specific group of chronically ill patients nor are they an umbrella organisation of sectoral patient organisations. In contrast, they ideally represent the entirety of all recipients of (health-)care. The development was heavily supported by the Dutch government, which found it wrong to let sectoral, thus partial patient organisations, take care of the client councils with the very diverse health issues of their grassroots or represent them towards the state. Some authors also found that the government wanted them to be critical towards the medical profession right from the start (van de Bovenkamp 2010, p. 64), a finding that, however, is left to interpretation.

Nowadays, there are two major umbrella organisations, that support client councils with brochures, training, legal help and lobbying activities (cf. LSR 2004; LSR et al. 2006; Laterveer, Teerink, & Peter 2004. While the 'National Organisation of Client Councils' [*Landelijke Organisatie Cliëntenraden* (LOC)] is active for councils in mental care, social care, home care, nursing homes, old-age homes, care for addicts, and youth, the 'National Support Point Co-determination/Involvement' [*Landelijke steunpunt (mede)zeggenschap* (LSR)] works for physically handicapped and the hospital sector.

Whereas raising societal and professional awareness of problems of the ill as well as protesting against the conditions in mental care were the main focus of action points in the past, these tasks have since made room for a huge variety of societal tasks. Nowadays, patient organisations have risen to be important actors which, amongst other things, evaluate new structures and treatments in health care, advise political institutions, advise their members and people seeking help, cooperate with the medical profession and care providers in order to find new ways of treatment, initiate and fund (medical) studies, and in some matters assume supervisory functions (Trappenburg 2008, pp. 42, 46, 62, 68–70, 102–104, 154–158, cf. also Oudenampsen 1999, p. 93).

### 5.4.6 The Rise of Popularity of Involvement in the Political Sphere

Given the change of representation in sickness funds, more so, however, owing to the introduction of market elements into the health care sector it was the declared aim of the Dutch Government to grant more rights to patients in order to empower them to balance potential disadvantages of the market. The green paper 'Structuring Healthcare' (*Structuurnota Gezondheidszorg*) of 1974 (Tweede Kamer der Staten-Generaal 1974; cf. Trappenburg 2008, p. 81) was the first official paper to mention

---

Councils in Retirement Homes' [*Landelijke Organisatie Bewonerscommissies Bejaardenhuizen* (LOBB)] and the 'National Patient and Consumer Platform' [*Landelijk Patiënten/Consumenten Platform* (LP/CP)] in 1992.

patients as an independent group that should be involved speaking of a process of "socialisation" and "democratisation of healthcare" (Tweede Kamer der Staten-Generaal 1974, p. 21). In that context,

> [d]emocratisation in organisations and administrative situations takes place at every level of healthcare.
>
> Inside the organisations of social services this implies an adequate participation of workers in the decision making process and the possibility for control by (potential) patients. By striving for involvement of workers and possibly also (potential) patients in the administration of the organisation of social services it is the intention to add a contribution to this form of democracy. (Tweede Kamer der Staten-Generaal 1974, pp. 21–22; author's translation)

While it can be noted that it is clearly influenced by the concept of traditional neo-corporatism, the green paper 'Policy on Patients' (*Nota patiëntenbeleid*) of 1981 took the idea a step ahead and advised legislation on collective involvement (Tweede Kamer der Staten-Generaal 1980–1981; cf. Oudenampsen 1999, p. 96; Trappenburg 2008, pp. 81–82):

> The relevance of the state in these [trends of a changed position of patients in (health-) care] is varied; in some respects [it is] marginal, in others essential when it comes to the underpinning of the legal position of the patient and to the creation of conditions for a healthcare which is adapted to the needs and requirements of the individual patient. [...]
>
> An elaboration of the idea of participation of patients and users on the level of the (health-) care unit will take place in cooperation with the involved organisations. [...] In order to strengthen the position of the patient councils, a comprehensive, legal regulation is necessary. [...]
>
> [For hospitals, a]dequate forms of democratisation and the participation of users shall be developed in cooperation with (health-)care units, social services, and users to that end. (Tweede Kamer der Staten-Generaal 1980–1981, pp. 12, 23, 25; author's translation)

## 5.5 The Legislative Process to Collective Patient Involvement

> I took [the draft bill] into the Senator—I was an eager young fellow at the time—and we engaged in pleasantries. After about twenty minutes, he indicated that I should leave. I said to him, 'But Senator, don't you want to ask me any questions about this, discuss the policy implications or anything?' 'No,' he said, 'I'll just introduce it tomorrow.' 'But Senator,' I said, 'aren't you even going to read the bill?' 'No,' he said, 'I'll just introduce it tomorrow.' Then he said, 'Let me tell you something. We'll introduce this tomorrow, but it will take twenty to twenty-five years for it to be brought into being. If it takes that long, there's not much point in my looking at the bill now, is there?' (Kingdon 2003, p. 116)

Despite the turn to market elements as the assumed most effective steering-mechanism for cost containment and despite patient rights legislation, institutions were sought to enable recipients of long-term care have a say in their everyday affairs. The main difference to ordinary patient rights is that they do not aim at the individual level, but specifically address matters that are of general interest to the recipient of care or residents in a nursing home. Thereby, the overall concept of quality is broadened to encompass more than the official quality definitions and also include the views of those concerned. Clients' preferences are thereby understood as a deliberate means to raise and safeguard quality in care.

The 'Client Participation Act' (WMCZ), that is in focus here, had two predecessors, broadly mirroring the process in society at large as well as the organisational context factors. In order to understand the changes over time, the key points of the bills will be presented before continuing to the legislation in force today.

### *5.5.1 WDFI: Bill on the Democratic Functioning of Subsidised Health Care Institutions (1984)*

> Because the 1970s were the years of democratisation, of involvement, participation in the Netherlands. That grew strong. [. . .] And, thus, that was the idea, that parents of a child must have a say in the policy of the school as [much as] someone, who is sitting in a nursing home, must have a say in the policy of the nursing home. Thus, a complete wave of democracy and involvement. And that is ultimately the background of the act. (interview 10; author's translation)

With its background in times of strong democratic and social movements, the political intention of the 'Bill on the Democratic Functioning of Subsidised Healthcare Institutions' [*Wetsontwerp Democratisch Functioneren van gesubsidieerde Instellingen* (WDFI)] was to democratise care by giving patients a say (van der Voet 2005, p. 8). One of the more general reasons given by the 'Commission Democratic and Appropriate Functioning of Subsidised Healthcare Institutions' was that care, which is funded in solidarity in a democratic state, should also be accordingly democratically distributed (Commissie van advies inzake het democratisch en doelmatig functioneren van gesubsidieerde instellingen 1977; Commissie van der Burg 1979). Based on the reports of two commissions on the topic and the coalition agreement of the previous government (government van Agt III), the bill was initiated in 1984 (van der Voet 2005, pp. 21–25; for an overview of the different governments and the most important key developments in the field see Table 5.2). It proposed that client councils of all subsidised/publicly funded institutions with long-term relations to citizens like schools, social housing, or health care should be given advisory competences. The councils were envisaged to be elected by all clients having an affiliation to the institution for longer than three months. Furthermore, it was proposed that in case the likewise included internal complaint procedure proved to be unsuccessful there would be a possibility to bring issues against the provider of these services to court. Besides the aim of democratisation, one of the main goals was to harmonise the characteristics found throughout the various forms of already existing patient involvement in the field (van der Voet 2005, pp. 21–26).

The bill was criticised for lack of clarity, for measuring all the different branches of residential care home with one yardstick, and for the perceived subsequent costs. Moreover, it was maintained that other measures in democratisation, which were in their implementation phase, made the bill unnecessary. Furthermore, it was doubted that the inflexible measure of launching a law would achieve what it supposedly aimed at (van der Voet 2005, pp. 21–25).

**Table 5.2** Overview and composition of Dutch Government 1977–1998

| Period | Cabinet | Coalition parties | Annotation |
|---|---|---|---|
| 05/1973–12/1977 | den Uyl | PvdA, KVP, ARP, PPR, and D66 | Commission van der Burg is constituted |
| 12/1977–09/1981 | van Agt I | CDA and VVD | Final report commission van der Burg is released |
| 09/1981–05/1982 | van Agt II | CDA, PvdA, and D66 | |
| 05/1982–11/1982 | van Agt III | CDA and D66 | Coalition agreement on democratisation of (health-)care |
| 11/1982–07/1986 | Lubbers I | CDA and VVD | WDFI is initiated; 'Decree on Regulations of Democratisation in Retirement Homes' is introduced |
| 07/1986–11/1989 | Lubbers II | CDA and VVD | WDFZ is initiated; report of Dekker commission is published |
| 11/1989–08/1994 | Lubbers III | CDA and PvdA | WMCZ was initiated and negotiated |
| 08/1994–08/1998 | Kok I | PvdA, VVD, and D66 | WMCZ, WGBO, WKCZ, and KZ were enacted and implemented |

Source: own compilation

In the end, in 1986 the bill was withdrawn by the minister in charge as no sufficient parliamentary backing could be achieved.

### 5.5.2 WDFZ: Bill on the Democratic Functioning of (Health)Care Institutions (1988)

Despite the failure of the WDFI in parliament, the topic outlived the bill: In the context of a reform of the 'Retirement Homes Act' [*Wet op de Bejaardenoorden* (WBO)] in 1985 it was decided that the provinces should further democratisation via their regulations. In the same year, the parliament introduced the draft of the 'Decree on Regulations of Democratisation in Retirement Homes' (*Besluit Democratiseringsregelen Bejaardenorden*). Though published in the *Staatscourant* already, it was never enacted. According to de Savornin Lohman (2000, p. 33), many provinces had already incorporated the key pillars of the decree in their policies, anyway.

One of the reasons why the decree was never enacted was to give way for a universal solution for all kinds of (health-)care. To that aim, the 'Bill on the Democratic Functioning of (Health-)Care Institutions' [*Wetsvoorstel Democratisch Functioneren van Zorginstellingen* (WDFZ)] was introduced into parliament in 1988 under the coalition government of the Christian Democrats (CDA) and liberal party (VVD). In contrast to its predecessor, the new bill was restricted to the field of in-patient health care and care and proposed a mandatory council of clients, which was to be elected by the residents (van der Voet 2005, pp. 30–35). It contained very extensive rights to give advice and complain about decisions the care recipients would not agree to.

The following parliamentary debate proved difficult. It lingered around questions like the following: Should hospitals be included or not? How could the goal of deregulation be achieved by passing very detailed laws? Would the act be necessary and enhance the influence of dependent care recipients (van der Voet 2005, pp. 37–40)? The scientific literature dealt with detailed questions such as whether the limits of democratisation had been exceeded, whether works councils would be merged with the client council, expressing concern about privacy since all minutes of meetings should be made public, and speculating on the stance residents with world views different from their care home were supposed to take (van der Voet 2005, pp. 42–48).

In the end, this bill was also withdrawn by undersecretary Simons in 1991.

### *5.5.3 WMCZ: Client Participation Act*

> Hence, in the council of patients and clients it is never about getting the wrong pharmaceuticals or something like that, but it is primarily about the well-being, Are the patients being well cared for [. . .]. And that can be traced back in history that the act is above all written for institutions where you stay for years or for the rest of your life. (interview 10; author's translation)

When the third attempt was launched, clients/residents councils had become even more common. At the same time, individual patient rights legislation was underway. Moreover, it was decided to split the scope of the failed WDFZ into a part on having a say, the 'Client Participation Act' [literally: Act on Participation in (Health-) Care Institutions; *Wet Medezeggenschap Cliënten Zorginstellingen* (WMCZ)], and a part which regulates legal complaint procedures on an individual basis, the '(Health-)Care Sector Complaints Act' [*Wet Klachtrecht Cliënten Zorgsector* (WKCZ)]. In doing so, the WMCZ became completely separated from any individual patient–provider relation, which can be viewed as smoothing the way for greater parliamentary acceptance (cf. van der Voet 2005, pp. 42–48). Originally, both bills were introduced contemporaneously by the coalition consisting of the Christian Democrats and the Social Democrats (CDA and PvdA) in 1992. Over the run of the parliamentary debate the general elections brought forth the first 'purple coalition' consisting of Social Democrats and the liberal parties VVD and D66. The bill, however, continued to be subject of debate and the parliament eventually passed the law in 1994 with effect from 1 January 1996 onwards (Tweede Kamer der Staten-Generaal 1994c).

This is not the place to either discuss all the intricacies and peculiarities of the act nor the competences and relations between the actors involved; this has been done in greater detail elsewhere (cf., e.g., van der Voet 2005; Trappenburg 2008; van de Bovenkamp 2010). Here, an overview shall suffice. The act applies to *all* publicly funded in-patient health care or care institutions, be they long- or short-term, residents' care homes, or acute care hospitals (Tweede Kamer der Staten-Generaal 1992–1993b; Tweede Kamer der Staten-Generaal 1992–1993a; van der Voet 2005, pp. 50–51). In all these individual institutions a Client Council (*Cliëntenraad*) needs to be established. The act distinguishes between the 'normal' right of involvement (*gewoone adviesrecht*) and an extended say—which might also be called right of consent (*verzwaard adviesrecht*; see Section "Extended Right of Consent in the WMCZ" in Appendix B)—which concerns all daily issues like food, spare time activities, furnishings in the residents' rooms, the annual report, etc. While the advice proffered in the former case *should* merely be heard, it *has to be followed* by the care provider in the latter. If the (health-)care provider wants to deviate from the advice given by the client council, the management and council of clients need to jointly discuss the topic at least once, before the provider may take a deviant decision. This has to be substantiated towards the council of clients and the authorities. In case the client council disagrees, the decision can be negotiated in a local mediating commission. Residents/patients have the right to be informed of any decision and planning of the management in advance in order to be able to formulate subsequent advice.

In some sense, the inhabitants/patients become the third tier in the governance of a (health-)care institution: They can appoint one member of the supervisory board, advise for one member of the board of directors, and thereby additionally influence some of the governance in their institution. The client council meets the board of directors as well as the supervisory board—usually to a lesser extent—on a regular basis to discuss topics that are of concern to either or both parties. Members of the council are usually recruited by approaching potential candidates, candidates coming forward to volunteer, or by advertisements. Usually, they are voted in by the present members of the council. Figure 5.1 gives an overview of a typical organisation of a (health-)care provider.

#### 5.5.3.1 The Legislation Process of the WMCZ (1992–1994)

> [W]e realised that it is about a compromise bill that our former coalition partner—I will try to put it as nuanced as possible—was not really waiting for. According to some, there even seemed to be talk of a longstanding guerilla war by the CDA against enactment and regulation on this point. (Middel, PvdA; Tweede Kamer der Staten-Generaal (1994a); author's translation)

The main argument in favour of the bill was to guarantee a minimum level of patient involvement, which, at the same time, should facilitate further initiatives adapted to the local circumstances (van der Voet 2005, pp. 51–55). Reference was explicitly made to the introduction of marketal elements, which, according to the minister in charge, Mrs. d'Ancona, her successor, Mrs. Borst, and undersecretary Mr. Simons made patient involvement even more important for the

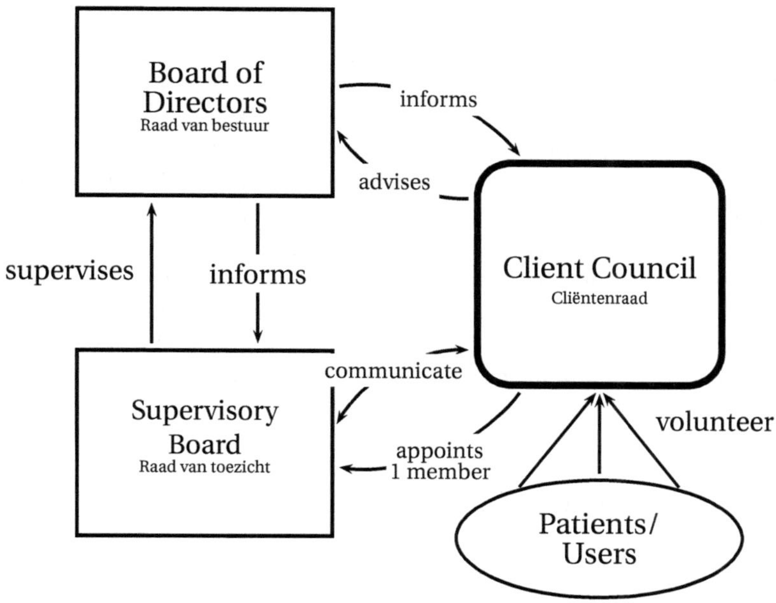


**Fig. 5.1** Schematic overview of relations between the local actors according to the WMCZ. Source: own depiction

smooth functioning of the health care sector. The act clearly bore the character of a minimum compromise, which seems to have been reached only after much individual commitment on the part of the three politicians involved.

This is not the place to go into the huge variety of arguments, concerns, and severe party political differences. This has been done elsewhere in great detail (cf. van der Voet 2005). The more relevant points in this context were amongst others the feared additional costs, doubts about the necessity of legislation on involvement in the light of a broad spread of voluntary solutions, and whether hospitals should be included or not. (A summary of the main discussion points in the legislation process can be found at Section "Topics Under Discussion During the Legislation Process of the WMCZ" in the Appendix B.) Interestingly, the management of the concerned institutions often adopted the stance of the opposition parties during the legislation process, if they had no previous experience of involvement. Their main concern was whether the act would limit their scope of action and give away too many competences to lay-people who do not know anything about business, but have excessive demands. This included also fears, that can be explained by the aftermath of pillarisation. One of the scenarios mentioned in the parliamentary debates was that atheist clients or those of a different belief 'hijacked' an institution of a specific denomination, thereby imposing their view onto it.[10] Institutions having the experience with resident involvement were much more positive.

The situation in parliament was specifically delicate as the former coalition partners PvdA and CDA had negotiated the bill and had achieved a compromise when forming the government. Now after the general election parts of the CDA tried to undermine the compromise since they no longer felt bound to it. After intense debates in parliament, a majority of all parties consisting of AOV (*Algemene Ouderen Verbond*), CD (*Centrumdemocraten*), CDA, D66, GroenLinks, PvdA, SP, and VVD (Tweede Kamer der Staten-Generaal 1994c) finally voted in favour of the act in 1994. Thus, despite almost 15 years of a somewhat interrupted legislation process, general doubts, and detailed criticism of different political fractions, the law was supported almost unanimously. The WMCZ became effective on 1 January 1996.

#### 5.5.3.2 The Character of the WMCZ

> But mainly [it was] also the question: Don't you give too much influence to people, who are in a phase of their lives in which they absolutely cannot master this influence, because you also give influence to people with mental constraints. And you give influence to people, who are mentally ill, and you also give influence to people who are physically ill or demented. (interview 10; author's translation)

Whereas the enactment of individual patient rights fits smoothly into the wider image of introducing market elements, the coming of the WMCZ with its *hybrid* character is not so obvious: In a sense, it bridges the *individual* 'consumer' of (health-)care with the *collective* role of patients in (health-)care, which is to advise and, in part, to decide about (health-)care related issues on a more general layer.

Important to note here is that in contrast to the first wave of 'New Public Management' (NPM), when participation simply meant that patients were renamed consumers and involvement merely meant that patients could fill in surveys that resembled market research (for a more general critical argumentation cf., e.g., Borins & Grüning 1998), involvement is established on a collective basis with a more immediate consequence for everyday life. In contrast to the strong focus on efficiency of NPM and concerned with the quality of care, patients and residents were thought to be complementary to the newly invented quality indicators. Following the logic that at least the chronically ill are experts on their treatment and much better in assessing the quality of health care provision than any supervisory

[10] '[I]f you actually do not get Catholics on the council of clients in a Catholic house and they pretty soon say that we are no longer allowed to celebrate the mass... You know that still tremendously lives on in the Netherlands as does the thinking in a Catholic house or a Protestant or who knows what. You are someone or you are a nobody, but you belong to some group. And, therefore, they were afraid at that point that you get many, many people from a different background into a house that this would affect the culture of the house. [...] And what is interesting, is that [...] a part of the Dutch patient movement is still very much pillarised.' (interview 2; author's translation)

authority, they had to be involved, at best as close as possible to where services are generated. A number of scandals in (health-)care added to this perception.

> That was a period, when the administrative burdens for institutions should be constrained, and client councils were also viewed that they were an administrative burden. However, various scandals in care occurred at that time, where residents had been maltreated or where care was organised very badly. And then, the first who then complained about it were the client councils. [. . . ] Thus, there was such a council of clients and family members, they got into the picture as the ones who named and shamed that. And that has led to a turnaround. And what you see right now, is that councils of clients [. . . ]—especially in the long term care have a legitimate position. (interview 12; author's translation)

This view of the patient as expert was the third main factor, which worked in combination with the mentioned wish to democratise (health-)care. It is also in line with the changed view on the role of the state: its task, as politicians see it, is to serve as a network manager (Oudenampsen 1999, p. 81; Trappenburg 2008, pp. 78–89), who refrains from tight regulation and supervision of actors but provides the legal and supportive framework. Thereby, so the idea, the state has enough power and competences to prevent a stalemate between the parties involved, but simultaneously leaves enough leeway for them to build up sustainable constellations. In that sense, the WMCZ has rightfully been labelled as 'legally conditioned self-regulation' (*wettelijk geconditioneerde zelfregulering*).

#### 5.5.3.3 The Underlying Idea Is Subject to Change

Of all of these reasons, the one being closest at hand is that it finally codified an existing practice rooted in the desire to better the situation for recipients of care. It should end the practice of provincial regulation that was found to be conflicting with the constitution. The interviewees mentioned expectation that the longer hospitalisation period was decisive at the time of enactment, is—though true—not really convincing.

Taking a more abstract look at it, however, it can be observed that though democratisation is the golden threat that permeates the whole time-span from the first discussions in the early 1980s until the final enactment, the emphasis changed over time. The first emphasis was clearly solely on democratising society, of which health care was only a subpart. A good summary of this could read as follows:

> The bill that we are dealing with today and tomorrow is the final result of what once was started as a very ambitious legislation project in the area of democratisation of subsidised institutions.[11] It has its ideological roots in the 1960s and 1970s, when managements and authorities were mistrusted, and the power of the grassroots needed to be enhanced.
>
> van Middelkoop (GPV; Tweede Kamer der Staten-Generaal 1994a; author's translation)

[11]The word as it is used here refers to what elsewhere would be called 'public funding', i.e., the flow of taxes and/or—in countries with social insurances—health insurance contributions of whatever provenance. In the debate surrounding health care issues, the term marked the difference between solely privately funded providers and those funded by public money and contributions.

This perspective of mistrust also found its expression in the original proposal to exempt provincial and municipal institutions from the WMCZ. In contrast to private actors, municipalities and provinces are democratically elected and, thereby, controlled and legitimised so that in conclusion "there is no reason to regulate" management and institutions run by them (Tweede Kamer der Staten-Generaal 1994b, p. 24).

It becomes clear that the aim is not the inherent wish of a democratisation of patients *per se*, but rather about a formal democratisation which exerts the function of control. From a grand purpose of democratisation of society at large the focus shifted and grew more pragmatic while at the same time it was narrowed down. Though at its core you might still name it democratisation, you might as well call it 'reshaping the roles of actors in the field of in-patient care' (see Section 'Summary', 5.5.4). More pragmatism, however, does not necessarily mean less ideological, since what has changed is that the emphasis on democratisation as a means of exerting control has been exchanged for control through and over the market. The delicate balance between referring to the initial undertaking and the more pragmatic reasoning at the time of enactment can also be traced back in the minutes of the parliamentary debate:

> Democratisation is always advocated by us, not as an aim, but primarily as a means, as an instrument to an end. And then, to what end? To openness, to publicity, transparency of policies, influence on the management, being involved in the policies of the institution by clients or their representatives, so that the policies are adjusted to what clients need. [...] Thus, not the organisational interest of the institutions itself or of the managers prevails, but the interest of the client. Middel (PvdA; Tweede Kamer der Staten-Generaal 1994a; author's translation)
>
> The extent to which individual clients are concerned at a specific institution, however, is in our mind of less importance than the fact that citizens, provided they are in need of certain (health-)care, need to rely on certain institutions and, thus, are dependent. [...] The illustrated obstructing factors are equally present in all (health-)care institutions funded by collective resources. Therefore, there is the possibility in all institutions that clients are confronted with (health-)care provision that is not optimally coordinated according to the needs and wishes of clients once they need (health-)care. We hold it important that it is ensured in all (health-)care institutions that an institutionalised client representation can advocate the interests of the clients in that institution. [...] In contrast to the Council [of the State; *Raad van State*] do we think that this dependency relation also exists owing to the limitation with voting by feet [...]." (Tweede Kamer der Staten-Generaal 1992–1993a, pp. 3, 21; cf. also Raad van State 1992; author's translation)

Thus, the emphasis changed from pure democratisation of, amongst other things, (health-)care to enabling and protecting a watchdog in the interest of the collective of care recipients. This holds in particular true in light that marketal mechanisms such as simply choosing a different provider fail for several reason since the 'healthcare market' is very specific in kind. The underlying idea of democratisation was, however, never relinquished.

#### 5.5.3.4 Further Developments

The positive political stance can also be seen in the attitude towards patients in the years following the enactment. While the main line of reasoning has not changed, the government strove to develop patient rights. This included extending of them and pooling the different acts into one. A first draft, which was started under the initiative of the ministry, was discussed with patient and consumer organisations as well as the umbrella organisations of providers. Both agreed for the same reasons that the draft was not so much desirable in practice (cf. also interview 2). This joint view can be regarded as a token for the good collaboration between recipients of care and patients on the one and (health-)care providers on the other hand. In consequence, the ministry withdrew the proposal altogether. A new bill was worked out in close cooperation with and a strong say from patient and consumer organisations as well as the umbrella organisations of providers (cf. interview 2 and 4). In 2010, the 'Client and Quality Act' [*Wet Cliënt en Kwaliteit* (WCK)] was introduced by the coalition government consisting of CDA, PvdA, and CU (cf. de Groot 2006; Raad voor de Volksgezondheid en Zorg 2006; Nederlandse Patiënten Consumenten Federatie (NPCF) 2007). Beside the WMCZ it was also to supersede the WGBO, WKCZ, KZ, and three additional patient rights (Klink & Bussemaker 2008; LSR 2008). With regard to the WMCZ, one of the most severe changes would have been that for service-providers with several hospitals and nursing homes an additional 'central council' for all branches combined would be needed beside the local 'client council'. Furthermore, in cases of planned mergers the council should have had an extended right of counselling ('Wet cliëntenrechten zorg' 2010). Though scheduled to be effective as of 1 January 2011, the bill for what now was called '(Health-)Care Consumer Act' (*zorgconsumentenwet*) was declared 'controversial' after the change in government in mid-2012 (Rijksoverheid 2010), so that the legislation process was halted.

In spring 2015, the parties PvdA and VVD started a joint campaign to strengthen the position of client councils by giving them their own budget. One of the suggestions was to make the sum dependent on the provider's turnover and allocate a fixed percentage share as the client council's budget. This could, for instance, be used for schooling or the expertise of external consulting without the need to ask for approval from the provider in order to make councils more independent (LOC 2015; Bouwmeester 2016).

This is in line with the government's efforts to strengthen clients' say in order to raise the quality of care (NOS 2015). On 29 May 2015 a meeting took place between one of the umbrella organisations and some of its members of the client councils and politicians of the Social Democrats. On the agenda was the question, how the WMCZ can be developed for the future (Heuts 2015). By late 2016 first the Minister of Public Health, Wellbeing, and Sports has published a draft bill for consultation with relevant stakeholders. It seizes upon the idea of a client council's own budget, suggests the adjustment of fields for the right of consent in order to match everyday practice and focus more on the quality of care than formal governance, and suggests to extend the possibilities to employ external expertise ('Wetsvoorstel Wet tot wijziging van de Wet medezeggenschap cliënten zorginstellingen' 2016). Politicians seem inclined to follow this topic.

### 5.5.4 Summary

Overall, in this chapter we were able to identify a number of preconditions, actor-constellations, and motives that eventually led to the enactment of patient involvement and recipients of care in the Netherlands. And we observe that the whole process towards a new health care policy consists of several steps: planning phase, preparatory, accompanying measures of the individual, then collective layer, and, finally, the health care reform of 2006. This stepwise approach could be observed in other earlier contexts (cf. Groenewegen 1998, p. 301).

As the most important precondition can be regarded the depillarisation of the Dutch society. It was necessary to create individuals and a society, where common interests bonded people across lines of their denomination or world view.

The main underlying factor was and still is the idea to democratise (health-) care, which calls for recipients having a greater say in (health-)care impacting their own everyday lives. In combination with a changed view on the state that rather coordinates than intermingles, the aim is to maintain and, where necessary, raise the quality of services. As a third factor, the WMCZ follows the logic that actual recipients of care know best what should be changed in order to raise quality—be it of care or living conditions. In that sense, it is also empowering recipients of care while the state pulled out. Residents are intended to take the same role as out-patients, namely a countervailing power against the provider (e.g. RVZ—Raad voor de Volksgezondheid & Zorg 2010, pp. 33 et seq.). The change of emphasis towards the logic of competition can also be discerned in the change of language, when patients and residents became clients while physicians and nursing homes became competing providers in the terms of legislation.

Another factor was the conversion of the health insurance. Even though patient involvement would probably have been enacted either way, it shifted the focus and shaped involvement to make patients and recipients of care the co-custodians of good quality. Both individual patient rights for health care and the collective right WMCZ for in-patient (health-)care were preparatory steps for the introduction of competition and private insurances. In contrast to individual patient rights, however, the WMCZ required the insight that for long-term in-patient care individual patient rights according to the logic of the market do not suffice. Usually, exit as a strategy is not an option (on other presumptions of a health care market cf. Cohn 1992). This is because most people in need of care are either fragile, mentally or physically impaired so that moving house can have a considerably negative effect on their lives, or they would need to travel long distances as not each and every hospital is specialised in all treatments. The WMCZ is intended as an instrument to strengthen the role of the new-found 'clients'. This line becomes the more evident, when looking at different government documents, which stress the necessity for patient organisations to professionalise in order to become sparring partners on equal terms with providers (Tweede Kamer der Staten-Generaal 1987–1988, 2000–2001, 2005). This also reshaped the relationships between the actors in the field.

Decisive for its acceptance in parliament was that it yielded a good compromise between actors that viewed the act as too far-reaching and those, who rather saw it as a toothless step backwards. The in comparison with its two predecessors less specific content was another point, which made it more acceptable (cf. also interview 12). Furthermore, it supports, in a way, the solution of problems between the actors involved and leaves the role of an impartial spectator to the state (cf. Tweede Kamer der Staten-Generaal 1991; van der Voet 2005, pp. 30–32, 170). Politicians were divided about this endeavour up to the very enactment. They supported, however, the basic idea and were adamant to find a solution in the end. Despite general doubts and detailed criticism of a political fraction, it is noteworthy that from the first more specific green paper in 1980 up to the enactment of the WMCZ seven different governments supported the general idea of patient/user involvement. At least on the political side patients are accepted as the 'third party' between insurers and providers and their input highly valued (van de Bovenkamp 2010, p. 65).

Relatives, recipients of care, and pensioners were the driving force behind the project in a double sense until politicians took the parliamentary lead: They were, first, the ones who, in collaboration with the providers, brought about change on the institutional level. And they were, second, the ones who pushed politics via their associations and organisations to codify the existing practice (interviews 4 and 12). The establishment of non-sectoral patient umbrella organisations eased the collaboration and networking between the councils considerably.

## 5.6 Appraisal of Implementation

> The WMCZ is a rose that still needs to get some more colour.
> (de Savornin Lohman 2000, p. 62; author's translation)

This chapter will deal with the appraisals and perceptions of the implementation of the WMCZ. It will thereby draw on official evaluations commissioned by patients' umbrella organisations and the state, scientific literature, and the interviews for this study. While the first deliver a good overview on a more abstract level, the interviews give deeper insight into the everyday business of client councils, patient organisations, and the interplay between providers and the boards. The overall impression is that it took ten to 15 years for providers and recipients of care to get used to a new way of communication. Despite vast differences between sectors and individual houses, involvement seems to be on the right path even though some points work out differently than the legislator intended.

### 5.6.1 Change Over Time: An Overview

There is a whole series of publications trying to evaluate the implementation, the impact, and the functioning of the WMCZ (for the most important of them cf., e.g., de Savornin Lohman 2000; Raad voor de Volksgezondheid en Zorg 2003; Hoogerwerf, Nievers, & Scholten 2004; de Groot 2006; LSR 2007; Oudenampsen, Kamphuis, Lammerts, Homberg, & Kromontono 2008; Dongen, Bulsink, Homberg, & Kamphuis 2008; Trappenburg 2008). Even though it needs to be borne in mind that the latest reports date from almost a decade back, the reports show that patient involvement in the Netherlands is on the right path, but that there is much room for improvement left.

Going into more detail, a change can be discerned over time. Overall, the hope that the WMCZ would be perceived as a minimum law and that providers and clients would negotiate about additional rights did not bear fruits. In other instances, however, the formalisation was able to provide new impulses for further development. As could be expected, the first—as the consecutive—evaluation was in general much more positive for sectors which had already been used to client involvement prior to the enactment of the WMCZ (de Savornin Lohman 2000).

According to information provided by nearly all of my interviewees the situation can no longer be compared to what it was in the late 1990s and has changed for the positive since then. This is also reflected in the more recent evaluations: even though there is room for improvement, things have become more settled in many areas. In particular patient organisations have become sought after partners for discussion. This leads some voices even to state that some of the developments have gone too far: patients would assume too many supervisory functions which they are not capable of while the advice of physicians would be of less value, because lay-people try to contest it with their superficial knowledge (Trappenburg 2006).

### 5.6.2 One Law to Unite Them All…

> [It is all about t]hinking from a clients' perspective! And that is no more or less than: What does it mean for the client? [...] I always tell the councils: you do not need to pose more questions to yourself as the council. That is what it [the clients' perspective] is about. (interview 3; author's translation)

Though the legal text leaves a great amount of individual freedom for implementation, it needs to be borne in mind that preconditions and context variables vary substantially for the different sectors, which makes an unitary evaluation an intricate undertaking. One of the reasons for the different reception can also be seen in the different ways of emergence: Whereas 83% of all nursing homes for people with physical impairments had a resident board by 1989 (Spaan 1989; cf. also Trappenburg 2008, p. 92), and the figure even grew to an estimated 98% by 1999 (de Savornin Lohman 2000, p. 34), in the hospital sector it was hardly existing at all. To some extent, this prehistory of the law can still be read in the figures as a representative survey among client councils commissioned by the LSR in 2007 shows: For the larger part councils have existed for some time in the field of mental care (43% longer than 11, thereof 19% longer than 15 years), while they were not established in other areas until the time around and after the WMCZ became effective (for home care, for instance: 3% longer than 15 years, 40% even less than 6 years ago, i.e., even long after the legal requirement; Lammerts et al. 2008c, p. 10; Lammerts et al. 2008b, p. 10; Lammerts et al. 2008a, p. 10).

Even the background of the members on the councils varies considerably, with a higher share of patient organisations' representatives and relatives in home care and relatively more volunteers in hospitals and home care (Lammerts et al. 2008a, p. 11; Lammerts et al. 2008b, p. 13; Lammerts et al. 2008c, p. 10; Lammerts et al. 2008d, p. 11).

### 5.6.3 The Way of Working Together

> Thus, what we do is to attempt to place the client councils on the right chair, because you are not the management, you are a member of the council. You won't sit in the management's chair, either. (interview 3; author's translation)

Working together and compromising on controversial topics is certainly not an easy endeavour. Providers, who usually think in rather technically abstract terms of amongst other things personnel, funding, expenses, and efficiency need to understand concepts of taste of food, sociability of an institution, convenience of services, and comfort afforded by the house. Recipients of care, who often have difficulties understanding their tax demands or telephone bill need to get used to think in terms of annual accounts, strategy concepts, or planning for mergers and a building constructions (cf. also Baur 2010), in particular since we often speak of old and demented people and those in mental care. It is more than natural that a larger share of the target population has difficulty understanding a matter that even graduates outside of economics might find challenging to understand.

Moreover, one common confusion was that 'co-determination' (*medezeggenschap*), as the legal text puts it, was understood as 'co-decision' instead of 'involvement in a decision-making process', while the final decision is left to the provider. It takes some effort and a learning curve of approximately 15 years to internalise the new roles, know the rules, and make yourself understood to your counterpart (interviews 1–4, 6–8).

In the stage of finding their role coaching and support by patient platforms were important for many to get some orientation (cf. also Binkhorst, Weerts, & Schipaanboord 2005; LSR 2004; LSR et al. 2006). According to research, the overwhelmingly accepted self-perceived role of the client councils is advising and collaborating with the management (Lammerts et al. 2008a, p. 21; Lammerts et al. 2008b, p. 21; Lammerts et al. 2008c, p. 21; Lammerts et al. 2008d, p. 20).

#### 5.6.3.1 Filling the Legal Framework with Content

> Thus, they have actually very much influence on the policies, in case they claim it and do not let the management do what they like with them. (interview 10; author's translation)

It is quite natural that as many recipients of long-term and elderly care are dependent on their providers, they fear the consequences of 'inappropriate' or 'demanding' behaviour, which can make them rather passive and accepting. In addition, a higher share of candidates for and members of the client councils belong to a generation where respect towards any kind of authority is much more deeply rooted than in later generations.[12] So, what do members of the client councils perceive as the right approach to deal with the management?

Collaboration is seen as the best approach as long as one of the parties involved does not feel superior, since the contrary approach of protest has proven not to lead to constructive results.[13] Too brisk a behaviour could in any case create opponents instead of partners. Thus, the overall conclusion drawn by one of my interviewees is as follows:

> The problem is always that the client council needs to collaborate with the executive board. However, if it comes to a controversy with each other it does not get better for anyone! And if you [say]: Well, we'll take it to court—since that can be done—then that is no type of collaboration any longer. Therefore, it is a question of give and take. [...] It is difficult to [say]: We demand this and we demand that, since then such an executive board says: There is no money for that! You may demand whatever you want! [...] That will not happen! (interview 7; author's translation)

Thus, as in politics, compromise needs to be found on the controversial topics. Finding the right balance of being self-conscious but not too demanding and uncompromising regarding the most important topics without being uncooperative was a difficult lesson to learn.

Enacted as a minimum framework only mentioning the most important rights of involvement, the legal text led to much uncertainty regarding what the position of the client council should be. For a long time, client councils stuck to the list of the extended right of consent (see Appendix B.1.2), but did not fill the framework with their own content (cf. also de Savornin Lohman 2000, p. 75). On the patients' side

---

[12]This also leads to the misapprehension of having a certain obligation and/or gratitude towards a provider once you take an official position on the board (cf. also Trappenburg 2008, p. 170): " 'Well, once you are chairperson we can never do anything bad against the [...; hospital].' Really? Why not? [...] I do my work as the chairperson of the 'clients consulting' from the clients' perspective. [...] Hence, I am funded by all kinds of [sources], but that does not mean that my opinion is bought by that. The opinions they buy that is the client perspective." (interview 6; author's translation)

[13]"Originally, we had something of a unionist approach that if we did not like something then we pounded our fist on the table. And meanwhile, in the course of time it has changed to: We want to be partners and a party for patients, organisations. Thus, we have arrived at another level. And also from the scientific [point of view] that we thereby will achieve more results than the fist on the table. The Netherlands is after all a *polder* and the polder model is deeply rooted in politics and the collaboration between trade unions and employers. And that, I think, is also in the field of healthcare a great way of working." (interview 6; author's translation)

learning their role primarily implied setting their own priorities, finding their own agenda, accepting advance knowledge of the management, and getting external help where necessary. It does not make sense, so the interviewees' conclusion, to put too much effort into understanding each and every figure contained in the annual accounts when at the same time, for example, public transport is miserable, food lacks taste, and there are deficiencies in housing (interviews 1–4, 6–7). Despite some progress in this direction, the legislator's intention to provide a framework, that could individually be adapted and voluntarily filled with additional rights, did not materialise.

#### 5.6.3.2 Management or the Clash of Two Lifeworlds

> The [client] council often serves rather as the louse in the fur than being seen as a board of advice which quite naturally is consulted. (Hoogerwerf et al. 2004, p. 23; author's translation)
>
> Look, such a client council, they do not want to talk a full hour about the temperature of the tea. However, if it feels it is not heard—that keeps coming back. And the member of the executive board keeps thinking: 'Why do I sit here?' and tries to suck the client council with him into his world of the system, of control, of long-term perspective, whereas the client council has the focus on the short-term. (interview 1; author's translation)

For a comprehensive evaluation, the management's side should not be left out, as their changed role was probably as difficult. In my interviews, the collaboration with the management is usually assessed positively by members of the client councils (interviews 6–8), while patient platforms are much more critical and view the management in a number of institutions as having been a major impediment to the councils' development. The most common reproach is that the management keeps their client councils busy with complicated and technical matters, thereby steering it to whatever topic they want or simply keeping it busy in order to prevent it from being active on its own:

> How do you deal with the flow of information from the board of directors? They dump it, let the council of clients keep busy. [...] You can flood the councils with information. And boards of directors have a knack for it. (interview 3; author's translation)[14]

[14]A longer version of this reasoning reads: "And what I get to hear is [...] that they [the client councils] muddle along, since the agenda is very much dictated by the executive board. Thus, it is very much like: You get such a pile of terribly complicated documents: the annual account and the budget and the policy plans. And all of the hospitals and all the old people's homes are busy with planning enormous new constructions and negotiations on mergers. Everything is terribly complicated. [...; T]hen, I think, you do not do anything beyond that. [...] And what you hope a client councils [will do] are all the things which are not listed there. And that is what they want to do. However, at the moment when you have an agenda like: we need to [talk about] the budget, the annual account, the policy plans, and this and that—as these are all things which are legally codified as the things we need to advise about—then the rest you contribute is a very small point on the agenda, in case there is some time left. Thus, that is, I think, the major problem client councils have. Like: How do you protect your own priorities? (interview 13; author's translation; cf. also interview 4)

However, even management needed time to get accustomed to the new situation and to overcome two common misconceptions: In the beginning

> [e]veryone says: 'Yes, but we do it after all for the patient, we intend after all the best for the patient.' Thus, in everyone's perception it was also something of: 'We do it for them. Why would you doubt that? And why would you set another body on top in order to test that even more? After all, we do it well!' (interview 3; author's translation)
>
> That was primarily the fear that the client council would sit on the management's chair that there, thus, would be two captains on one boat the management and the council of clients. That was the strongest fear that it would become ungovernable. (interview 1; author's translation)

The abovementioned allusion of strategic action by the management is in part owing to the codification of certain rights in the legal text, in part to prevent too much involvement, and in part to create its own room of manoeuvre:

> The management finds it difficult to share power, or influence, or whatsoever, because this is what you do. [...] And it can actually be really tedious: It is difficult if you have a 'club' [client council] that asks critical questions, and that asks: Why do you do this now and not something different? And we think it is important that a different choice is made. Yes, that is tiresome. [...] In this sense institutions were definitively not happy in 1996. [...] (interview 2; author's translation; cf. also interview 3)

Management is, however, also thinking in new terms and ways: in one of the studies on the WMCZ a member of an executive board was quoted, who indirectly complained about the client council complaining about such small things as the temperature of the tea instead of thinking in terms of budget, a vision, and important planning for the months ahead (van Bloemendaal 2008 cited in: Trappenburg 2008; cf. also van Egmond, Heerings, & Munnichs 2014). Thus, getting things across the border between the two lifeworlds is not an easy endeavour, and it takes time.[15] Most interview partners on the patients' side ensured me that those times were long gone. However, the tea in the narrative being the symbol for the quality of everyday life—as for recipients of care, not seldom unable to brew the tea on their own, the difference between lukewarm and hot tea can mean the world—it is also a matter of taking the members of the council seriously.

[15]The following somewhat lengthy quotation very vividly illustrates the separate worlds client councils and management live in: "However, the weirdest thing is, when you tell it to such a management team in a normal way, they absolutely get something like: 'Ah, but that was not the intention! Have absolutely not realised that.' [...] And then, usually it often happens that a member of the executive board often comes late or has less time than noted down on the agenda. Thus, there comes such a member of the executive board to a meeting, who rushed in in his jacket, and then he said, 'Yes, I know it is..., but I only have ten minutes time, because then I need to [talk to] the city councillor.' And you see such a council of clients absolutely... Whereupon I said, 'It is of course interesting, such a councillor.' I say, 'But thereby you basically show that the deputy is more interesting than your own client council.' I say, 'Is that so?'—'No, that is not the case!' I say, 'But have you thought through that it gets across that way?'—'No, I had not realised!' I say, 'Well, then it is quite negligent that you, in addition, arrive five minutes late when you only have ten minutes!' [...] A client council would not do this easily. There are a lot of councils which do not immediately realise where they get that feeling from. And if you know it already, that you tell it. [...] And no legal act will remedy this." (interview 2; author's translation)

Nowadays, there are less problems of that kind. As an overall assessment from the patients' side it was said that in half of the instances it works well, while there is still much room for improvement for the other half. Somewhat pointedly, the client council has changed in the eyes of many providers from being a 'club of naggers', who are aiming to take over management and claim more resources, to be another body that is still subordinate, for which not all wishes can and need to be fulfilled, that has the advantage of receiving immediate feedback and proposals for improvements, that often do not cost too much, but result in more content clients. At the same time, however, I came across a (growing) perception among management that client councils are outdated (in particular interview 11). In that view, they belong to the old type of corporatism, which is superseded by much more efficient instruments like (web-)surveys, complaint boxes, or customer relation managers, who/which, in turn, are more modern, more efficient, and, thus, superior to the old instruments, as one interviewee put it:

> The whole [development] of new information technology, where people can react after they have been admitted, how they liked it, what improvements are possible etc. Well, that is a much more immediate consumer influence than a meeting five times a year of such a council of clients. [...] It is a bit like it is rather the solution of the 70s. (interview 11; author's translation)

#### 5.6.3.3 Influence, Competences, and Professionalisation of Client Councils

> If the Board of Directors really does not want [to let the council of clients be involved], just forget about it. (Hoogerwerf et al. 2004, p. 20; author's translation)

Among the three client councils that were interviewed, the institution for mental care stood out as having achieved the most tangible outcomes. Three examples might serve to give the reader an impression of what kind of topics were taken up. The first one is that the client council has managed to bring in a new and different caterer than management originally intended and that they have put a rating system into place in order to prevent that taste and quality wanes over time. They are proud of having taken the initiative and gotten the caterer of the national airline while at the same time they are working for more individualised solutions such as cooking food on their own if patients wish so. The second example is that they have convinced management and physicians that the electronic patient file is not only fed with cryptic abbreviations, but that a print-out in comprehensible language is handed out to the patient including the weekly goals that were agreed on. The third example is maybe the most far-reaching: The client councils and the executive board have agreed to phase out rooms for isolation under the course of 5 years. A number of different processes have led to 5–10% less separations immediately (interview 7).

These examples illustrate four things:

1. Clients can have considerable influence on everyday life, surroundings, policies of the provider, and treatment, provided it concerns a larger number of clients,
2. councils are capable to take the initiative with improvements for clients in mind,

3. to follow things up, and
4. to propose realistic and realisable changes.

As all cases in this study show, success does not set in automatically, but relies substantially on the effort put into the work of the client council (cf. also Hoogerwerf et al. 2004, p. 23), something that has not changed over the years. This is usually dependent on the enthusiasm of a small number of patients/users, which makes success somewhat vulnerable. Furthermore—and that seems to be of at least equal importance—the goodwill to discuss things and the appreciation of the client councils by the management is crucial for success. The relative success of client councils and the consensus found in many cases, however, is owed to the development of both patients/clients and providers alike.

The development that has occurred on the side of client councils bears all the characteristics of professionalisation, as members have often become experts in the field. This has had the ambivalent effect that it has frequently led to a new profile for potential members of the councils, which begins with some minimum criteria for recruitment such as that potential candidates need to be capable to think in somewhat more abstract terms and ends with looking for candidates with very specific skills, for instance, in business administration or advertisement (interviews 2, 4, 6, 7, and 13; cf. also Trappenburg 2008, pp. 150–154).

Taking a look at the overall work done under the headline of client councils, there is a price tag attached to it, which for the majority of councils is likely to exceed the low five digit range. They usually comprise costs of stationery, schooling fees, a membership fee for the umbrella organisations, and most often a proportional share of staff for supporting the administrative work of the council. There are even instances where a better flow of organisation brought some saving in institutions. However, other cases do also exist: the budget for the work of the client council in one of the institutions for long-term care in this study including the costs resulting from its suggestions were declared to amount to 200,000 € p. a. In light of these figures, it can be said that those politicians who during the parliamentary debates proclaimed that client councils would hardly imply any additional expenditure lacked the creativity to imagine the length and intensity of change that the councils' proposals can bring about. This relates to the general question of how much we are willing to pay for good quality of (healt-)care. Depending on the size of the institution it really needs considerable commitment and resources from the provider's side to spend such amounts. In conclusion, as important the involvement of recipients of care is, in the end it is not only the provider's right to decide on whether or not the client council's proposals can be implemented, it is also the provider's duty to economise and make ends meet.[16]

[16]Considering the relation between management and clients, there is one observation that can be regarded as not specifically confined to any particular country. Visiting one of my interviewees, I was given the chance to be present during one of the regular meetings of the council of clients after the very interview. The interview by and large gave the same impression as most other interviews, i.e., the collaboration between council and provider worked well, the director had a sympathetic ear

### 5.6.4 *Client Councils as a Countervailing Power?*

> Countervailing power is also such a thing: is it a good, the right term? [...] in fact you need to make sure that the client perspective is taken into account as much as possible. [...] Thus, you need to create a position, but if you need to create a countervailing power... That implies that actually there is no power! (interview 4; author's translation)
>
> That is democratic ideology, thus to some extent it is honestly meant. But for some part, I think, for sure it has also been a case of divide and rule. (interview 13; author's translation)

Patients as the 'countervailing power' against providers is a Dutch peculiarity. In the context of the new health insurance system, a balance of the market is what is sought. Now that the role of the state has turned to an enabling one while staying out of immediate issues, patients/users need a mighty ally in order to be able to encounter the mighty provider, so the underlying idea. In that line of argumentation, health insurances are the natural ally for patients to keep costs low. Together they are thought to form a countervailing power against excessive demands for resources by providers. It is far from natural that this assumption materialises. Appealing to the assumed ally against a provider of long-term care could rebound on clients, since even though health care insurances are obliged to ensure good quality of provision, it is still an actor that also aims to limit the budget of institutions in order to keep expenditure low to compete on the market. This, in turn, can impact on the living conditions of those who incautiously complained:

> If now a client council full-throatedly exclaims: With Altrecht it is a gem, because there is a closed unit, which does not perform [...; at all]. What they do then is the following: 'Oh, fine. Mister and Missus Altrecht, you will receive 90% of what you applied for. For the remaining 10% you need to prove first. Improve the points we have heard about. And we want to measure what you have improved'. In such a situation the salaries of the employees will continue to be paid. The buildings will continue to be maintained. If then 10% need to be cut, who, then, has been deceived? (interview 7; author's translation; see also interview 13)

---

for them, and they could achieve a lot to the advantage of their grassroots. The impression during the following meeting of the board was different: The members complained that once again the organisational support for the provision of information to their co-residents was not satisfactorily given and that papers to be discussed with the management came in rather too late to be able to be well-prepared. A tour through the institution yielded similar differences: When some individuals were asked whether they would like to join the council of clients, they refused with the explanation that it would require too much commitment and that the board would not achieve too much anyway.

This reminds us once again of the subjectivity of answers which is in line with the methodological framework's attempt to capture actors' subjective view as well. The validity of the data seems safeguarded in this case, since more or less *all* involved actors consistently report about the same image and draw the same conclusions. Nevertheless, one promising starting point for future research interested in the assessment of policy processes and their implementation seems to me to complement any quantitative or qualitative data by participant observation in meetings of the council of clients as well as in joint meetings of the council and the institution's management. Studies such as by Aalbersberg (2008) and van Bloemendaal (2008) might serve as a good example for further research.

Some researchers view the concept of allying clients and insurers as a deliberate act of politicians. In that view, patients and residents of care are used as instruments to reduce the power of the medical profession Trappenburg (2006) and van de Bovenkamp (2010, p. 64). My impression is that in the beginning it was a sincere concern of politicians to democratise (health-)care and to give recipients of care a say in everyday matters. Though this was mixed with ideas of decentralisation and deregulation—including some devolution of supervisory competencies—the main aim remained to support a stronger say. The interviews underlined that the focus was much more on finding a solution to govern and rather than on using patients as a tool to achieve something:

> How do you govern institutions, since the state actually had very little control over things? [. . . ] It happened, but they were [deficient] instruments. And in that the aspiration was that a council of clients or family councils or clients should play a greater role in that, should play a corrective role." (interview 12; author's translation)

As a matter of fact—and following the logic that patients and recipients of care are closer to the provider—they are actually deployed as an instrument in the sense that the state entrusts a tiny bit of governance and supervision to them, which previously had solely been undertaken by supervisory authorities. As it is about a rearrangement of roles and relations in the field, it is quite natural that the medical profession is also affected.

## 5.6.5 *Problems*

However, next to a positive development of patient involvement there are also a number of problems, to which some attention should be paid. In addition to a very basic difficulty concerning representativity, the sectoral differences are particularly apparent in the hospital sector. And finally it is about funding and the relation between patients' umbrella organisations and client councils.

### 5.6.5.1 Representativity and Legitimacy

> Elections by and of the clients are by far—though not exclusively—the manner to guarantee representativity. (Tweede Kamer der Staten-Generaal 1994b, p. 5; author's translation)

If the councils are to have legitimacy on their own, as a basic precondition they need to be perceived as representative. In one evaluation study the question is posed as to whether the average council actually does conform to this precondition. Though somewhat older, the strength of this survey lies in the feature that both the client council and the executive board were asked. Interestingly, the statements of both groups overlap to a very high degree, so that even studies conducted among patients/residents can only cautiously be assumed to be of wider generalisability. Most councils have a rather professional organisation with a chairman and treasurer, and many are supported by a secretary for some hours a week. The average council of clients has some five to nine members (LSR 2007, p. 38) and does not show any disproportion between sexes or age groups so that at first glance the typical image of a group dominated by pensioners does not seem to be confirmed (LSR 2007, p. 39). This might, however, be owing to the very broad age categories. In contrast to these figures sounding very balanced, we can see a higher share of members with higher education. Furthermore, there is the strikingly low percentage of around eight percent of members with migrant background (LSR 2007, pp. 38–39), though the figure for the Netherlands in general is 20.6% (as of 1 January 2011; Centraal Bureau voor de Statistiek 2013b). This, however, might be attributed to a different structure of recipients of care compared to the general population to a larger extent, particularly regarding old-age or long-term care: many first-generation migrants either move back to their country of origin or are more often cared for by their relatives.

However, none of my interviewees complained about difficulty in recruiting new members for the councils, except for the group of allochthonous (interview 6). The overwhelmingly dominant way of recruiting new members is by approaching people who are considered suitable by present members (LSR 2007, p. 11; interviews 2 and 4). Most often, these candidates are then elected by the existing members of the council. With around 90% of the respondents answering that the representativity of the council is very good, good, or satisfactory representativity does not seem to be an issue among both the client councils and the executive boards. Thus, this is not an issue among the actors in the Netherlands (LSR 2007, pp. 31, 39; cf. also Trappenburg 2008, p. 175; interviews 2 and 4).

However, not only the representativity and work of the council of clients is decisive for living up to expectations, but also the frequency and quality of contact to their grassroots. Results from assessment research suggest again that the kind of institution is decisive for the type of contact and the mode of providing information that is preferred on average (Lammerts et al. 2008a, pp. 29–30; Lammerts et al. 2008b, p. 29; Lammerts et al. 2008c, pp. 26–27; Lammerts et al. 2008d, pp. 28–29). Furthermore, valuation result suggests that client councils have contact much more frequently with their co-patients as compared to institutions of home care and hospitals where patients/recipients of care are either widely spread over the countryside or are most often not that much attached to a specific institution (Lammerts et al. 2008a, p. 28; Lammerts et al. 2008b, pp. 28–29; Lammerts et al. 2008c, pp. 26–27; Lammerts et al. 2008d, p. 28).

Of course, these are self-reported information and at least show the self-understanding of councils and a clear tendency. The most specific and maybe most ambitious example from my interviews for the contact to grassroots is that next to having regular office hours and being approachable on the phone, members of the client council usually visit all wards once a quarter and at least once every half year. The advantage of this practice is that even users who do not dare to or are not capable of getting to the office hours are visited and that the council's members, who for the greatest part are (former) patients themselves, get to see how things are on site at first hand.

### 5.6.5.2 Sticking Point Hospitals

> The wrong instrument for a good aim. (interview 11; author's translation)

As could be shown above, a huge variation can be found between different (health-)care sectors. Even though a very positive development can be noted in many instances, this seems less clear in the case of the hospital sector. Given the short-term nature of contacts, the extension to the hospital sector was debated right from the start of the legislation process. In the end, for most hospitals these apprehensions must be acknowledged to hold true. In 1998, i.e., 4 years after the law had passed parliament and 2 years after it had become effective, a representative survey in hospitals revealed the following figures: In 18% of the responding hospitals a council of clients was in place, 19% stated that one would be instituted 'soon', 52% responded that management was consulting with patient organisation about setting up a council, and 11% frankly admitted that there was none in place (Wael 1998). The reasoning by hospitals was that the turnover of patients is too great for patients to feel any bond towards the hospital. In addition, there is a loophole in the legal text, which states that instead of a client council the cooperation with patient organisations might fulfil the same task in specific cases ('Wet medezeggenschap cliënten zorginstellingen' 1996, p. 10), which was invoked by hospitals. Evaluation reports draw the same picture of a difficult landscape for patient involvement:

> In the sectors, where the tradition of involvement was absent, the introduction of the WMCZ has functioned as a 'jemmy' to bring forth changes. The effect of the introduction of the law is dependent on the approach and the commitment of the different actors towards involvement. Where there is talk of resistance against the formal, more obliging character of the WMCZ, as is in hospitals, the client councils have barely made any progress." (LSR 2007; author's translation; cf. also Tweede Kamer der Staten-Generaal 2000–2001, p. 8)

With approximately 130 hospitals in the Netherlands (as of 2013); van Hassel, Kastelijn, & Kenens 2013; Deuning 2013a), the number of hospitals without a client council was according to information provided by my interviewees down to approximately five in 2006 (interview 3) and three in May 2010 (interviews 2 and 4) while all of them have some kind of council meanwhile. Despite this formal progress and despite the assurance that the results of the older evaluations do not hold true any longer, there seem to be good reasons for the relatively meagre outcome in the sector. This seems on the one hand to be grounded on patients' lack of willingness to become active in institutions of short-term treatment, on the other hand on a rather negative attitude of providers (interview 11).

One of the questions during my interviews was, why hospitals were included in the first place, though they had not been included in the WMCZ's two predecessors. Answers from all parties involved were rather similar: Even though no specific reason was mentioned, it was assumed that probably it was owing to the fact that hospital stays were considerably longer in former days. Even though this sounds somewhat unconvincing, because according to that reasoning you would not even need patient involvement for a period of two weeks, it was mentioned by most interviewees. All of them were critical about establishing client councils in the hospital sector from today's point of view—politicians, (former) providers, as well as patient platforms as the following three, rather lengthy answers to the question from the patients', politicians', and providers' side show:

> To be honest, I do not know, either. And I have to say that I really wonder whether we really want it for hospitals, because I also see, regarding hospitals that I think: How long are you represented in a hospital? Two days, three days if everything goes well? I do not know whether I really think that it should be legally mandatory for hospitals. I can very well imagine to exclude them. [...] [W]here people receive long-term care, live in an institution or receive home care on a long-term basis by the same provider, there it is important that people have the influence on what is going on, since that really determines your life. Thus, I think it is really different there. (interview 2; author's translation)
>
> People are in hospital for a week. Well, what do you need participation for, then? Back then, we found that we could not disregard hospitals. And at the time the law was made, people were still hospitalised sometimes for weeks or months. At that time we did not find it so odd. [...] In a hospital [...] I find it difficult to have such a client council, unless that hospital is specialised in long-term care such as the Cancer Institute. Retrospectively, the law can be perceived suitable for nursing homes, old-people's homes, disability care, mental care institutions, where people need to stay for years, because they simply cannot live on their own. It is a very good model for such institutions. [In] a hospital, where people are for a week it does not make so much sense. If you want to know whether they are very satisfied, you can better do a survey. (interview 10; author's translation)
>
> I think that [...] they [the client councils] do not have a strong position in hospitals [...]. [S]uch a council of clients is for most people a reality that is far away.[...] And I think, to be honest, if I were responsible in the Hague as minister nowadays I would rethink the role of the client councils. The function is taken over by others. [...] I think, for some part it is the zeitgeist. It is: We would like to oppose clients having influence. Hence, I think that is the most honest explanation, we have basically very few reasons to oppose them. Just the opposite, but that has blocked our view on what the effective role of such a client council could be. Thus, something has been introduced which you should think about a bit more for the hospital sector. That is something different for an old-age home or a nursing home, or for a mental care institution that is substantially different. Even for a primary care institution in a village or a city with a dentist and a GP, and social work etc. (interview 11; author's translation)

Despite the critical view of all actors, patient organisations issued several complaints to urge hospitals remaining without a council of clients to establish them. In order to finally meet the legal requirements, hospitals have made use of the individual flexibility the law grants to providers: Next to the majority of hospitals with a 'classical' client council there are two noteworthy alternatives. One is employed by the country's eight university hospitals. Next to a close collaboration with patient organisations, in 1998 they established a larger, joint council of clients of about 50 members, which is intended to specifically represent their long-term patients such as those undergoing treatment for cancer (Nederlandse Federatie van Universitair Medische Centra (NFU) 2012; Nederlandse Federatie van Universitair Medische Centra (NFU) 2016; interviews 5 and 4). A second alternative is the so-called clients consulting (*cliëntenberaad*; interview 6). It is based on a scientific report by van der Kraan & Meurs (2008) and attempts to fulfil the advising function while being more flexible for providers at the same time (cf. also van Bodegraven-van der Maas & Ras 2010). The council is constituted by approximately 50 alternating members, who are asked to participate according to the topics in question (interview 6). That way, one group suffering from and/or specialised in one specific illness can have its say on issues that concern it, while another does not need to be present and can give its advice more competently on 'its' specific topic. Collaboration with several patient organisations ensures that representatives for the topic in question are easily found (van Bodegraven-van der Maas & Ras 2010).

#### 5.6.5.3 The Relation to Patient Platforms and Related Difficulties

As interesting as the relation between the provider and the client council is, the relation between the councils and patient organisations and patient platforms (on the platforms see Sect. 5.4.5) is probably worth a thesis in its own right. Though the focus is on councils of clients here, four points shall nevertheless be raised here, as they are directly interrelated to and/or effect the work of client councils. Though the respective platform's composition differs, what they have in common is that most often the two main pillars of funding are membership contributions by the respective client councils and state subsidies (van de Bovenkamp 2010, p. 65). Finding the 'right' balance of funding and in the relation to the councils is not always an easy endeavour.

Though, of course, patient platforms are partial and have a contextual and ideological closeness to the patients' side, this by no mean necessarily implies that they understand each other automatically. van Bloemendaal (2008) finds in her work that far from all client councils value and understand the patient platforms. In light of titles like the following it seems that between patient platforms' work and the core clientele of mental care institutions, nursing homes, and old-age homes it seems that also here lifeworlds differ considerably: "Assessment framework for responsible care. An operationalisation of the vision document 'On the way to norms of responsible care' in a set of indicators and a governance model for the N & C sector or *Client councils and improvement process*" (italics in the original text already; author's translation; cited in Trappenburg 2008, p. 168).

Client councils can become member of the patient platform and receive schooling, support, evaluation, and follow-up of their work, as well as legal and practical advice from patient platforms. They can participate in numerous events organised by the respective patient platforms. According to the information received the usual membership fee came to lie somewhere between 20,000 € and 32,000 € in 2010 (interviews 7 and 8). The amount is paid by the respective client council, whose budget, in turn, is paid by the provider.

Not everyone is satisfied with the platforms' work. The assessment of one interviewee's client council was that the feedback during the first year of their membership in the patient platform was not worthwhile. The reasoning was that instead of the membership fee of roughly 20,000 € a project employee could be hired, whose work can be more targeted and whose feedback is much more immediate than the platform's (interview 7). In fact, the council is involved in the relatively recently established 'support point mental care' (*steunpunt GGZ*), a local, independent organisation in several parts of the Netherlands, which supports patients suffering from mental ailments and illnesses and collaborates with patient organisations and providers. This can be viewed as an indicator for the perception that patient platforms have become too professional and too remote from their grassroots. In that context we may speak of the representation of patients by 'professionals of patients', but no longer themselves (cf. also van de Bovenkamp 2010, p. 70). Thus, also being a service provider to client councils they are dependent on conforming with the needs of all of them, which they are aware of: "But meanwhile [...] we are approximately 10% dependent on subsidies, and the rest we get from contributions, from products. If we are not client targeted [...] we have no money, then it stops automatically." (interview 4; author's translation)

What client councils and patient organisations and platforms have in common is—depending on the perspective—shortage of time or a chronic shortage of volunteers. Consistent with the literature (cf., e.g., van de Bovenkamp 2010, p. 88; Trappenburg 2008, pp. 115–138), interviewees mentioned that they do not have enough volunteers to do all the work that could be done (interviews 1–4). This difficulty roots in two circumstances: First, in that the huge majority of staff are volunteers, and it is difficult to recruit new ones (cf. also Trappenburg 2008, p. 70), whilst, second, members of patient organisations and platforms have to attend two or three appointments each day, because they are invited to give their opinion and advice. This can result in the feeling of being overrun or overburdened by the sheer amount of activities.

Speaking of 'lopsidedness' and power-imbalance, patient platforms were—and to some extent still are—financially supported by the government, since very much to the liking of the government, they are perceived to represent the general interest (Oudenampsen 1999, p. 68; Trappenburg 2008, pp. 82, 85). Many organisations have overcome dependency on the state by not only levying contributions from their members but also offering services, courses, and consultation and have thereby created their own financial foundation. Moreover, the system of subsidising patient platforms was reformed in 2008, the base amount substantially cut to approximately 7500 € per year and organisation (as of 2008) and made dependent on certain requirements, while the main form of funding shifted to be project based (Tweede Kamer der Staten-Generaal 2008a,b,c). As with other projects, funding was bound to specific conditions, which were to further the government's interest. This made the situation intricate: even though the literature addresses the problem that organisations soften their criticism when dependent on subsidies (cf. van de Bovenkamp 2010, p. 70) and although it is more than reasonable to impose certain requirements on the flow of tax money, it needs to be seen rather critically if the government is able to steer any organisation's orientation. Moreover, the basic problem of dependency is not solved this way. The interviewees in the patient platforms, for which the following quotation is representative, agreed in their discontent over the reform: "How does the province [...] want to use us for their policy? Or may we, since we have both feet on the ground, decide for ourselves what we do?" (interview

6; author's translation)[17] In 2012 the Dutch government announced to change the system of subsidies anew (Tweede Kamer der Staten-Generaal 2012). The new system gives a higher proportion of project-independent subsidies once again and is intended to give patient organisations more independence to do the things they think are of importance.

### *5.6.6 Conclusion*

> Thus, in that sense it is, in my opinion, still absolutely not so much about what is actually regulated in the law, since that is no more and no less than a kind of bottom-line. However, it is of course much about: How do you deal with each other, and do you take each other somewhat seriously? If you do not take each other seriously then such a law does not change anything at all. (interview 2; author's translation)

Patient involvement at provider level has come a long way in the Netherlands. Recipients of care can achieve a lot—provided enough time and effort is put into the task and providers cooperate. However, these two strong preconditions are not always met. It is a landscape with a huge variety: from client councils which present their management with long list of their rights to patient organisations who fight to improve their everyday living conditions; from providers who deeply inside still perceive their client council as a group of naggers for whom any engagement is just a waste of time to those who want to contribute to change that little something in their institution. And the broad majority of everything in between.

Patient organisations and platforms are accepted as a 'third party' by the state, while critics claim that they are either too unprofessional, not able to think in abstract terms, or too professional to represent the ordinary patient.

Despite a number of successes and advantages, even the limits have become clear. Whereas involvement works fairly well in long-term care, just hospitals stick out as the sector where councils of clients have least gained a foothold—if at all. Disregarding the few examples of specialised hospitals for longer treatments in cases of, e.g., cancer, burns, transplantations, AIDS, etc., where again long-term relationships are established, the instrument of a client council in each institution is not the means of choice. Solutions such as found in the so-called clients consulting (*cliëntenberaad*) might be an alternative to the classic council. Nevertheless, it should be borne in mind that even they will probably never play the same role nor have the same importance as their counterparts in long-term care.

---

[17]Other interviewees agreed: "But the project are rewarded only if they execute government policy, if they contribute to the execution of government policy. And *that* is well a problem, because by this the government determines for a large part what you do as an organisation, and that must principally not be. Yes, you are a kind of extension [of the government]." (interview 2; author's translation)

"In fact, our government may give [. . . ; us] money as a client movement, but it must also leave the freedom to choose. And maybe to think about concepts, which can become reality first in ten years. [. . . ]—And the support is also really clever, because then they can say: Well, the clients also think that way. Yes, of course they think that way, because they are also dependent on [. . . ] money." (interview 4; author's translation).

Overall, whether the WMCZ can be seen as a success depends on the purpose and the expectation it is linked with. If it was the intention to democratise all provision of care and to level out hierarchy between providers and recipients of care to the greatest extent it has clearly failed. If it was the intention to create preconditions for recipients of care to have a greater say, to give them a tool to be able to improve their living conditions, to sensitise, and sometimes even create a mutual understanding for each other, it is a success story to some greater extent. Breaking down a submissive, pretentious, or antagonistic conduct and to gather providers as well as recipients of care around the same table in order to talk with instead of talk about each other is probably the greatest achievement of the WMCZ and more valuable than might be thought in the first place.

## References

Aalbersberg, S. (2008). *Medezeggenschap in een cliëntenraad: realisme of een utopie? Een onderzoek naar de medezeggenschap van individuele cliënten met een verstandelijke handicap in de organisatie triAde*. Master Thesis, Erasmus universiteit Rotterdam.

Aartse, J., Graat, E., Gramser, T., et al. (2008). *Zorgmonitor—Jaarboek 2008*. Zeist: Vektis.

Agasi, S. (2008). Die Krankenversicherung in den Niederlanden zwei Jahre nach der Reform—Finanzentwicklung und Markttrends. *Zeitschrift für Sozialreform, 54*(3), 279–303.

Anderson, K. M. (2006). The Netherlands: Political competition in a proportional system. In E. M. Immergut, K. M. Anderson, & I. Schulze (Eds.), *The handbook of West European pension politics* (Chap. 15, pp. 713–757). Oxford: Oxford University Press.

Arts, W., & Gelissen, J. (2002). Three worlds of welfare capitalism or more? A state-of-the-art report. *Journal of European Social Policy, 12*(2), 137–158.

Atkinson, M. M., & Coleman, W. D. (1989). Strong states and weak states: Sectoral policy networks in advanced capitalist economies. *British Journal of Political Science, 19*(1), 47–67.

Atun, R. (2007). Privatization as decentralization strategy. In R. B. Saltman, V. Bankauskaite & K. Vrangbæk (Eds.), *Decentralization in health care—Strategies and outcomes* (Chap. 14, pp. 246–271). New York: McGraw Hill; Maidenhead: Open University Press.

Bartholomée, Y., & Maarse, H. (2006). Health insurance reform in the Netherlands. *Euro Health, 12*(2), 7–9.

Baur, V. E. (2010). Relationeel empowerment door dialoog: cliënten en managers in de ouderenzorg. In T. Abma, M. Visse, B. Molewijk, & G. Widdershoven (Eds.), *Reflectie en participatie in zorg* (Chap. 12, pp. 209–224). Den Haag: Boom Lemma.

Berndt, U. (2010). Zwischen Selbstbeschränkung und Parteipolitik: die "Erste Kammer" der Niederlande. In G. Riescher, S. Ruß, & C. M. Haas (Eds.), *Zweite Kammern* (pp. 389–405). München: Oldenbourg.

Binkhorst, T., Weerts, M., & Schipaanboord, A. (2005, April). *Patiënten betrekken bij de zorg in het ziekenhuis—Een Handboek*. CBO, PP/CP & NPCF.

Borghi, V., & van Berkel, R. (2007). New modes of governance in Italy and the Netherlands. The case of activation policies. *Public Administration, 85*(1), 83–101.

Borins, S., & Grüning, G. (1998). New public management—Theoretische Grundlagen und problematische Aspekte der Kritik. In D. Budäus, P. Conrad, & G. Schreyögg (Eds.), *Managementforschung 8* (pp. 11–53). Berlin/New York: deGruyter

Bouwmeester, L. (2016, August 23). Vergroot inspraak cliënten en patiënten. Retrieved January 20, 2017, from http://wwwpvda.nl/berichten/2015/4/Vergroot+inspraak+clienten+en+patienten.

Centraal Bureau voor de Statistiek. (2004). Toen en nu—bevolkingsdichtheid. Retrieved January 20, 2017, from wwwcbs.nl/NR/rdonlyres/B3C3AA9F-507E-46F6-B13F-3DB408870D9C/0/2004k4b15p010art.pdf.

Centraal Bureau voor de Statistiek. (2007, May 2). *Persbericht—Ongeveer 241 duizend mensen onverzekerd tegen ziektekosten*

Centraal Bureau voor de Statistiek. (2009). *Gezondheid en zorg in cijfers 2009*. Den Haag/Heerlen.

Centraal Bureau voor de Statistiek. (2010a, December 2). AWBZ-zorg met verblijf; leeftijd en geslacht. Retrieved January 20, 2017, from http://statline.cbs.nl/StatWeb/publication/?VW=T&DM=SLNL&PA=71568ned&LA=NL.

Centraal Bureau voor de Statistiek. (2010b, March 31). Statistiek Wanbetalers. Retrieved April 22, 2010, from http://www.cbs.nl/nlNL/menu/themas/gezondheidwelzijn/cijfers/incidenteel/maatwerk/2010wanbetalerszorgverzekering20062009mw.htm.

Centraal Bureau voor de Statistiek. (2012a, October 29). Zorginstellingen; financiën, personeel, productie, capaciteit, SBI 2008. Retrieved January 20, 2017, from http://statline.cbsnl/StatWeb/publication/?VW=T&DM=SLNL&PA=81732NED&LA=NL.

Centraal Bureau voor de Statistiek. (2012b, November 20). Zorgverzekeringswet; wanbetalers overige kenmerken per 31 december. Retrieved January 20, 2017, from http://statline.cbs.nl/StatWeb/publication/?VW=T&DM=SLNL&PA=81066NED&LA=NL.

Centraal Bureau voor de Statistiek. (2013a, October 21). Bevolking; kerncijfers. Retrieved January 20, 2017, from http://statline.cbs.nl/StatWeb/publication/?VW=T&DM=SLNL&PA=37296ned&D1=a&D2=0,10,20,30,40,50,60,%2811%291&HD=1306050924&HDR=G1&STB=T.

Centraal Bureau voor de Statistiek. (2013b, March 15). Bevolking; kerncijfers. Retrieved January 20, 2017, from http://statline.cbsnl/StatWeb/publication/?VW=T&DM=SLNL&PA=37296ned&D1=a&D2=0,10,20,30,4050,%2811%291&HD=1303151251&HDR=G1&STB=T.

Cohn, D. (1992). *Reforming health care in Canada and Sweden*. Stockholm: University of Stockholm, International Graduate School: International Studies.

Commissie 'Keuzen in de zorg' (Dunning). (1981). *kiezen en delen—Advies in hoofdzaken*.

Commissie over "de toekomstige ontwikkeling der sociale verzekering in Nederland" (Commissie van Rhijn). (1945). *De toekomstige ontwikkeling der sociale verzekering in Nederland*. 's Gravenhage: Algemeene Landsdrukkerij.

Commissie 'Structuur en Financiering Gezondheidszorg' (Dekker). (1987). *Bereidheid tot verandering*. 's Gravenhage: Distributiecentrum Overheidspublikaties (DOP).

Commissie van advies inzake het democratisch en doelmatig functioneren van gesubsidieerde instellingen. (1977). *Rapport van de commissie van advies inzake het democratisch en doelmatig functioneren van gesubsidieerde instellingen*. Staatsuitgeverij. 's Gravenhage.

Commissie van der Burg. (1979). *Advies inzake het rapport van de Commissie van Advies betreffende het democratisch en doelmatig functioneren van gesubsidieerde instellingen (Rapport Commissie van der Burg*. Staatsuitgeverij. 's Gravenhage.

Companje, K.-P. H. (2008). *Tussen volksverzekering en vrije markt*. Amsterdam: aksant.

Cox, R. H. (1993). *The development of the Dutch Welfare State—From workers' insurance to universal entitlement*. Pittsburgh: University of Pittsburgh Press.

de Groot, G. R. J. (2006, November). *Beter verzekerd?—Onderzoek naar aanknopingspunten voor een Zorgconsumentenwet met het oog op de verhouding consument-verzekeraar*. Den Haag: Raad voor de Volksgezondheid en Zorg.

den Exter, A., Hermans, H., Dosljak, M., & Busse, R. (2004). *Health care systems in transition—Netherlands*. Copenhagen: WHO Regional Office for Europe on behalf of the European Observatory on Health Systems and Policies.

de Savornin Lohman, J. (2000). Evaluatie—Wet medezeggenschap cliënten zorgsector. In J. de. Savornin Lohman (Ed.), *Evaluatie Wet medezeggenschap cliënten zorginstellingen*. Utrecht: Verwey-Jonker Instituut.

de Schut, F. T., & Bruijn, D. (2007). *Collectieve zorgverzekeringen en risicoselectie - Onderzoek uitgevoerd in opdracht van de Nederlandse Patiënten Consumenten Federatie (NPCF)*. Rotterdam.

de Swaan, A. (1989). *Zorg en de staat*. Amsterdam: Uitgeverij Bert Bakker.

Deuning, C. (2007). Thuiszorginstellingen 2007. In RIVM (Ed.), *Volksgezondheid Toekomst Verkenning, Nationale Atlas Volksgezondheid*. Bilthoven. Retrieved August 23, 2016, from http://www.rivm.nl/vtv/object_map/o2137n21300.html.

Deuning, C. (2013a). Locaties algemene en academische ziekenhuizen 2013. In RIVM (Ed.), *Volksgezondheid Toekomst Verkenning: Nationale Atlas Volksgezondheid*. Bilthoven: RIVM. Retrieved May 9, 2014, from http://zorgatlas.nl/zorg/ziekenhuiszorg/algemene-en-academische-ziekenhuizen/aanbod/locaties-algemene-en-academische-ziekenhuizen-2013/#breadcrumb.

Deuning, C. (2013b). Verpleeg- en verzorgingshuizen per gemeente 2009. In RIVM (Ed.), *Volksgezondheid Toekomst Verkenning: Nationale Atlas Volksgezondheid*. Bilthoven: RIVM. Retrieved August 23, 2016, from http://zorgatlas.nl/zorg/langdurige-zorg/verpleging-en-verzorging/verpleegenverzorgingshuizen-per-gemeente2009/#breadcrumb.

de Wael, V. N. (1998). *Cliëntenraden Algemene Ziekenhuizen—Eindverslag Inventarisatieonderzoek*. Utrecht: Nederlandse Patiënten/Consumenten Federatie.

Ebbinghaus, B. (2010). Reforming Bismarckian corporatism: The changing role of social partnership in Continental Europe. In B. Palier (Ed.), *A long goodbye to Bismarck—The politics of welfare reforms in Continental Europe* (Chap. 10, pp. 255–278). Amsterdam: Amsterdam University Press.

Eichhorst, W., & Hemerijck, A. (2008, December). *Welfare and employment: A European dilemma?* Bonn: Forschungsinstitut zur Zukunft der Arbeit (IZA).

Enthoven, A. (2008, April 8). A living model of managed competition: A conversation with Dutch health minister Ab Klink. *Health Affairs, 27*(3), W196–W203.

Esping-Andersen, G. (1990). *The three worlds of welfare capitalism*. Princeton: Princeton University Press.

Friele, R. D. (2009, September). *Evaluatie Wet marktwerking gezondheidszorg*. Programma evaluatie regelgeving: deel 28. Den Haag: ZonMw.

Fulton, L. (2011). Arbeitnehmerbeteiligung in Europa—Niederlande. Retrieved January 20, 2017, from http://de.worker-participation-eu/Nationale-Arbeitsbeziehungen/Laender/Niederlande/Gewerkschaften.

Giesbers, H. (2011, March). Personen met huishoudelijke hulp (Wmo) 2009. In RIVM (Ed.), *Volksgezondheid Toekomst Verkenning, Nationale Atlas Volksgezondheid*. Retrieved August 23, 2016, from http://wwwzorgatlas.nl/zorg/langdurige-zorg/personen-met-huishuidelijke-hulpwmo2007.

Giesbers, H. (2013, March). Totaal aanspraak op AWBZ-zorg per gemeente 1 januari 2013. In RIVM (Ed.), *Volksgezondheid Toekomst Verkenning, Nationale Atlas Volksgezondheid*. Retrieved August 23, 2016, from http://zorgatlas.nl/zorg/langdurige-zorg/totaal-aanspraak-opawbzzorg/.

Goodin, R. E., & Smitsman, A. (2000). Placing welfare states: The Netherlands as a crucial test case. *Journal of Comparative Policy Analysis: Research and Practice, 2*(1), 39–64.

Götze, R. (2010). *The changing role of the state in the Dutch healthcare system*. TranState Working Papers.

Götze, R. (2016, August 18). *Ende der Dualität? Krankenversicherungsreformen in Deutschland und den Niederlanden*. Frankfurt: Campus.

Green-Pedersen, C. (2002). *The politics of justification—Party competition and welfare-state retrenchment in Denmark and the Netherlands from 1982 to 1998*. Amsterdam: Amsterdam University Press.

Greß, S., Delnoij, D., & Groenewegen, P. P. (2003). Exit and voice in Dutch social health insurance. *CESifo Dice Report, 3*, 47–53.

Greß, S., Manouguian, M., & Wasem, J. (2006). *Krankenversicherungsreform in den Niederlanden— Vorbild für einen Kompromiss zwischen Bürgerversicherung und Pauschalprämie in Deutschland?*
Groenewegen, P. P. (1994, Winter). The shadow of the future: Institutional change in health care. *Health Affairs, 13*(5), 137–148
Groenewegen, P. P. (1998). Besluitvorming in de gezondheidszorg op macroniveau. In C. W. Aakster & J. W. Groothoff (Eds.), *Medische sociologie—Sociologische perpectieven op ziekte en zorg* (5th ed., Chap. 2, pp. 295–302). Groningen: Wolters-Noordhoff.
Haarmann, A. (2012). Niederlande: Soziale Sicherung zwischen staatlicher Grundsicherung und For-Profit-Versicherern. In T. Klenk, P. Weyrauch, A. Haarmann, & F. Nullmeier (Eds.), *Abkehr vom Korporatismus?* (pp. 367–438). Frankfurt a.M.: Campus.
Hartmann, A. K. (2000). *Zwischen Differenzierung und Bürgerbeteiligung Bestand und Perspektiven*. Doctoral Dissertation, Ruhr-Universität Bochum.
Hemerijck, A., Unger, B., & Visser, J. (2001). How small countries negotiate change—Twenty-five years of policy adjustment in Austria, the Netherlands and Belgium. In F. W. Scharpf & V. A. Schmidt (Eds.), *Welfare and work in the open economy Volume II: Diverse responses to common challenges in twelve countries* (Chap. 5, Vol. 2, pp. 175–263). Oxford: Oxford University Press.
Heuts, P. (2015, June). "Wat hebben jullie nodig?" Cliëntenraden & LOC in Tweede Kamer. *Zorg & Zeggenschap*.
Hicks, A., Misra, J., & Nah Ng, T. (1995, June). The programmatic emergence of the social security state. *American Sociological Review, 60*, 329–349.
Hoogerwerf, R., Nievers, E., & Scholten, C. (2004, July). *De invloed van cliëntenraden—Het verzwaard adviesrecht in de dagelijkse praktijk vanuit cliëntenraadperspectief.* Research voor beleid bv. Leiden.
Hupe, P. L. (1993). Beyond pillarization—The (post-) Welfare State in the Netherlands. *European Journal of Political Research, 23*(4), 359–386.
Independer. (2014). Marktoverzicht: aantal zorgverzekeraars. Retrieved August 23, 2016, from https://wwwindepender.nl/zorgverzekering/info/marktcijfers/aantal-zorgverzekeraars.aspx.
Kappelhof, T. (2004). Omdat het historisch gegroeid is. *Tijdschrift voor Sociale en Economische Geschiedenis, 2*, 71–91.
Katzenstein, P. J. (1984). *Corporatism and change: Austria, Switzerland, and the politics of industry*. Ithaca, N.Y.: Cornell University Press.
Kingdon, J. W. (2003). *Agendas, alternatives, and public policies* (2nd ed.). New York/San Francisco/Boston: Longman.
Kjær, A. M. (2004). *Governance*. Oxford: Oxford University Press.
Klink, A., & Bussemaker, J. (2008, May). Brief aan de Vorzitter van de Tweede Kamer der Staten-Generaal: Programma "Zeven rechten voor de cliënt in de zorg: Investeren in de zorgrelatie".
Lammerts, R., Verwijs, L. M., Homberg, J., Hekkert, K. D., de Kroon, S. J. W., & Kamphuis, H. C. M. (2008a). *Patiënten-, gehandicapten- en ouderenorganisaties in Nederland— Cliëntenraden in beeld—Cliëntenraden van GGz-instellingen in 2008*. Utrecht: LSR.
Lammerts, R., Verwijs, L. M., Homberg, J., Hekkert, K. D., de Kroon, S. J. W., & Kamphuis, H. C. M. (2008b). *Patiënten-, gehandicapten- en ouderenorganisaties in Nederland— Cliëntenraden in beeld—Cliëntenraden van revalidatiecentra in 2008*. Utrecht: LSR.
Lammerts, R., Verwijs, L. M., Homberg, J., Hekkert, K. D., de Kroon, S. J. W., & Kamphuis, H. C. M. (2008c). *Patiënten-, gehandicapten- en ouderenorganisaties in Nederland— Cliëntenraden in beeld—Cliëntenraden van thuiszorgorganisaties in 2008*. Utrecht: LSR.
Lammerts, R., Verwijs, L. M., Homberg, J., Hekkert, K. D., de Kroon, S. J. W., & Kamphuis, H. C. M. (2008d). *Patiënten-, gehandicapten- en ouderenorganisaties in Nederland— Cliëntenraden in beeld—Cliëntenraden van ziekenhuizen in 2008*. Utrecht: LSR.
Laterveer, M. J., Teerink, F., & Peter, N. A. (2004). *De Cliëntenraad Centraal; de meerwaarde van medezeggenschap voor directeuren en bestuurders in de zorgsector*. Utrecht: Vereniging Directies zorgsector Nederland in samenwerking met LOC.

Lehmbruch, G. (1996). Die korporative Verhandlungsdemokratie in Westmitteleuropa. *Swiss Political Science Review, 2*(4), 1–41.

Lepszy, N., & Wilp, M. (2009). Das politische System der Niederlande. In W. Ismayr, S. Richter, & M. Söldner (Eds.), *Die politischen Systeme Westeuropas* (4th ed., pp. 405–450). Wiesbaden: VS, Verlag für Sozialwissenschaft.

Lewe, A., Reef, J., & Hartmann, H. (2002). Arbeitsmarktpolitik in den Niederlanden. In F. Frick (Ed.), *Arbeitsmarktverwaltung im Wandel—Erfahrungen aus 15 Ländern im Vergleich* (pp. 151–170). Gütersloh: Verlag Bertelsmann Stiftung.

Lieverdink, H. (2001). The marginal success of regulated competition policy in the Netherlands. *Social Science & Medicine, 52*, 1183–1194.

Lijphart, A. (1968a). Typologies of democratic systems. *Comparative Political Studies*, 1 3–44.

Lijphart, A. (1968b). *Verzuiling pacificatie en kentering in de Nederlandse politiek*. Academische Paperbacks. Amsterdam: J. H. de Bussy.

Lijphart, A. (1984). Time politics of accomodation: reflections — Fifteen years later. *Acta Politica, 19*(1), 9–18.

LOC. (2015, April 13). Politiek vraagt om eigen budget voor cliëntenraden. Retrieved April 13, 2015, from www.loc.us3.list-manage.com/track/click?u=2982793de6c3238b690a06f6d&id=a088f0c375&e=9538cf0095.

LSR. (2004). *handboek medezeggenschap—een handreiking voor cliëntraden uit de curatieve sector*. Utrecht: LSR.

LSR. (2007, March). *een onderzoek naar de praktijk van de wmcz in ziekenhuizen en revalidatie-instellingen*, Utrecht: LSR.

LSR. (2008, September). Ontwikkelingen wet 'Cliënt en Kwaliteit'.

LSR et al. (2006, November). *Cliëntenraden, gedoemd te (mis)lukken—Tien tips voor het effectief benutten van cliëntenraden in ziekenhuizen*.

Nederland, T., & Duyvendak, J. W. (2004). *De kunst van effectieve belangenbehartiging door de patiënten- en cliëntenbeweging—De praktijk*. Utrecht: Verwey-Jonker Instituut.

Nederlandse Federatie van Universitair Medische Centra (NFU). (2012). Cliëntenraad. Retrieved January 22, 2015, from http://www.nfu.nl/patientenzorg/clientenraad.

Nederlandse Federatie van Universitair Medische Centra (NFU). (2016). Platform CRAZ. Retrieved January 20, 2017, from http://www.nfu.nl/patientenzorg/craz.

Nederlandse Patiënten Consumenten Federatie (NPCF). (2007, March). *De Zorgconsumentenwet—Wat er in moet staan*. Utrecht: NPCF.

Nederlandse Vereniging van Ziekenhuizen. (2016). *Voorpublicatie: Brancherapport algemene ziekenhuizen 2016*.

Nederlandse Zorgautoriteit (NZa). (2012, June). *Marktscan—Zorgverzekeringsmarkt—Weergave van de markt 2008–2012*. Utrecht: NZa

Neubauer, G., & Birkner, B. (1984). Alternativen der Organisation und Steuerung des Gesundheitswesens. In G. Neubauer (Ed.), *Alternativen der Steuerung des Gesundheitswesens im Rahmen einer Sozialen Marktwirtschaft* (pp. 13–70). Gerlingen: Robert Bosch Stiftung.

NOS. (2015, April 4). VVD, PvdA willen cliëntenraden versterken. Retrieved January 20, 2017, from http://nos.nl/artikel/2028484-vvd-pvda-willen-clientenraad-versterken.html.

NPCF. (2003, June). *Invloed van verzekerden op het functioneren van zorgverzekeraars*. Werkdocument. Utrecht: NPCF.

Okma, K. (2008, January). Recent changes in Dutch health insurance: Individual mandate or social insurance? Paper Commissioned by the National Academy of Social Insurance.

Oudenampsen, D. G. (1999). *De patiënt als burger de burger als patiënt*. Doctoral Dissertation, Universiteit Utrecht, Utrecht: Verwey-Jonker Instituut.

Oudenampsen, D., Kamphuis, H., Lammerts, R., Homberg, J., & Kromontono, E. (2008, December). *Patiënten- en Consumentenbeweging in Beeld*. Utrecht: Nederlandse Patiënten Consumenten Federatie (NPCF).

Oudenampsen, D., & Steketee, M. (2000). De patiëntbeweging: van afhankelijkheid naar eigen regie. In *Emancipatie en subcultuur—Sociale bewegingen in België en Nederland*. Amsterdam: Instituut voor Publiek en Politiek.

Ponsioen, J., & Veldkamp, G. M. J. (1956). *Vraagstukken der hedendaagse samenleving*. Bussum.
Pressel, H. (2010). Die Veränderung des Organisationsrechts der gesetzlichen Krankenkassen und ihrer Verbände durch die Große Koalition: Entstehung, Bestandsaufnahme und Ausblick. *Zeitschrift für Sozialreform, 56*(3), 347–372.
Raad van State. (1992, November 12). *Regels ter bevordering van medezeggenschap van cliënten van uit collectieve middelen gefinancierde zorgaanbieders op het terrein van de maatschappelijke zorg en gezondheidszog (Wet medezeggenschap cliënten zorginstellingen)—Advies Raad van State* 's Gravenhage.
Raad van State. (2010). De Raad van State in het kort. Retrieved January 20, 2017, from www.raadvanstate.nl/over_de_raad_van_state/raadvanstateinhet_kort/.
Raad voor de Volksgezondheid en Zorg. (2003). *Van patiënt tot klant*. Raad voor de Volksgezondheid. Zoetermeer: Raad voor de Volksgezondheid en Zorg.
Raad voor de Volksgezondheid en Zorg. (2006). De patiënt beter aan zet met een Zorgconsumentenwet? Den Haag: Raad voor de Volksgezondheid en Zorg.
Raad voor Werk en Inkomen (RWI). (2010). Over de RWI. Retrieved January 22, 2015, from www.rwi.nl/nlNL/Over_de_RWI.
Rijkschroeff, R. A. I. (1989). *Ondersteuning van participatie in de geestelijke gezondheidszorg*. Doctoral Dissertation, Universiteit Amsterdam, Amsterdam.
Rijksoverheid (Ed.). (2009). Persbericht—Wanbetalers.
Rijksoverheid. (2010, June). Samenvatting Wet cliëntenrechten zorg. Retrieved January 20, 2017, from www.rijksoverheid.nl/documenten-en-publicaties/brochures/2010/04/23/samenvatting-wet-clientenrechten-zorg.html.
Roebroek, J. M., & Hertogh, M. (1998). *De beschavende invloed des tijds*. 's Gravenhage: VUGA Uitgeverij.
RVZ—Raad voor de Volksgezondheid, & Zorg (Ed.). (2010). *De patiënt als sturende kracht*. RVZ—Raad voor de Volksgezondheid & Zorg.
Schäfer, W., Kroneman, M., Boerma, W., van den Berg, M., Westert, G., Devillé, W., & van Ginneken, E. (2010). The Netherlands: health system review In E. van Ginneken & R. Busse (Eds.), *Health systems in transition*. Copenhagen: WHO Regional Office for Europe on behalf of the European Observatory on Health Systems and Policies.
Schmid, J. (2002). *Wohlfahrtsstaaten im Vergleich* Opladen: Leske + Budrich.
Schmidt, M. G. (2005). *Sozialpolitik in Deutschland*. Wiesbaden: VS Verlag.
Schöffer, I. (1956). Verzuiling, een specifiek Nederlands probleem. *Sociologische Gids*, (7), 121–127.
Schut, F. T., & van de Ven, W. P. M. M. (2005). Rationing and competition in the Dutch health-care system. *Health Economics, 14*, S59–S74.
Sociaal-Economische Raad. (2010a). Raad, Vergoedingen. Retrieved January 20, 2017, from www.ser.nl/nl/raad.aspx.
Sociaal-Economische Raad. (2010b). Taken. Retrieved January 20, 2017, from www.ser.nl/nl/taken.aspx.
Spaan, J. M. (1989). *Verpleeghuizen in cijfers*. Utrecht: NZI.
Stichting van de Arbeid. (1982, November 24). *Centrale aanbevelingen inzake aspecten van een werkgelegenheidsbeleid (Accord van Wassenaar)* . 's Gravenhage.
Stuurman, S. (1983). *Verzuiling kapitalisme en partriarchaat*. Nijmegen: SUN Socialistiese Uitgeverij Nijmegen.
Trampusch, C. (2000). *Arbeitsmarktpolitik, Gewerkschaften und Arbeitgeber Ein Vergleich der Entstehung und Transformation der öffentlichen Arbeitsverwaltungen in Deutschland, Großbritannien und den Niederlanden zwischen 1909 und 1999*. Göttingen: Georg-August-Universität.
Trappenburg, M. (2006). Societal Neurosis in Health Care. In J. W. Duyvendak, T. Knijn & M. Kremer (Eds.), *Policiy People and the New Professionalisation* (pp. 48–63). Amsterdam: Amsterdam University Press.
Trappenburg, M. (2008). *Genoeg is genoeg*. Amsterdam: Amsterdam University Press.
Tweede Kamer der Staten-Generaal. (1974). *Structuurnota Gezondheidszorg*.

Tweede Kamer der Staten-Generaal. (1980–1981). *Nota Patiëntenbeleid.*

Tweede Kamer der Staten-Generaal. (1987–1988). *2:e Voortgangsnota Patiëntenbeleid.*

Tweede Kamer der Staten-Generaal. (1991). *Nota—Zicht op wetgeving.* 's Gravenhage: SDU uitgeverij.

Tweede Kamer der Staten-Generaal. (1992–1993a). *Memorie van toelichting—Regels ter bevordering van de medezeggenschap van de cliënten van uit collectieve middelen gefinancierde zorgaanbieders op het terrein van de maatschappelijke zorg en gezondheidszorg (Wet medezeggenschap cliënten zorginstellingen)* (H. Ancona & H. Simons, Eds.).

Tweede Kamer der Staten-Generaal. (1992–1993b). *Wetsvoorstel van Regels ter bevordering van de medezeggenschap van de cliënten van uit collectieve middelen gefinancierde instellingen op het terrein van de maatschappelijke zorg en gezondheidszorg (Wet medezeggenschap cliënten zorginstellingen)—Oorspronkelijke tekst van het voorstel van wet en van de memorie van toelichting zoals voorgelegd aan de Raad van Staate en voor zover nadien gewijzigd* (H. Ancona & H. Simons, Eds.).

Tweede Kamer der Staten-Generaal. (1994a, September 6). *Notulen Tweede Kamer der Staten-Generaal—88ste vergadering 6 september 1994, Aanvang 14.00 uur.* 's Gravenhage.

Tweede Kamer der Staten-Generaal. (1994b, January 6). *Regels ter bevordering van de medezeggenschap van cliënten vanuit collectieve middelen gefinancierde zorgaanbieders op het terrein van de maatschappelijke zorg en gezondheidszorg (Wet medezeggenschap cliënten zorginstellingen)—Memorie van antwoord* (H. Ancona & H. Simons, Eds.). 's Gravenhage.

Tweede Kamer der Staten-Generaal. (1994c, September 27). *Stemmingen in verband met het wetsvoorstel Regels ter bevordering van de medezeggenschap van de cliënten van uit collectieve middelen gefinancierde zorgaanbieders op het terrein van de maatschappelijke zorg en gezondheidszorg (Wet medezeggenschap cliënten zorginstellingen)*

Tweede Kamer der Staten-Generaal. (2000–2001). *Structuurnota Patiënten/consumentenbeleid—Nota Met zorg kiezen.*

Tweede Kamer der Staten-Generaal. (2005, December 23). Patie¨nten/consumentenbeleid—Brief van de Staatssecretaris van Volksgezondheid, Welzijn en Sport. Voortgangsnota patiëntenbeleid. Den Haag.

Tweede Kamer der Staten-Generaal. (2008a, July 30). Subsidiebeleid VWS—Brief van de Minister en Staatssecretaris van Volksgezondheid, Welzijn en Sport. Den Haag.

Tweede Kamer der Staten-Generaal. (2008b, September 24). Subsidiebeleid VWS—Brief van de Minister van Volksgezondheid, Welzijn en Sport. Den Haag.

Tweede Kamer der Staten-Generaal. (2008c, March 6). Subsidiebeleid—Brief van de Minister en Staatssecretaris van Volksgezondheid, Welzijn en Sport. Den Haag.

Tweede Kamer der Staten-Generaal. (2012, June 18). Subsidiebeleid VWS—Brief van de Minister van Volksgezondheid, Welzijn en Sport. Den Haag.

van Bloemendaal, H. (2008). *Medezeggenschap in cliëntenraden: 'an art of voice'.* Universitet Utrecht. Master thesis universiteit Utrecht.

van Bodegraven-van der Maas, L., & Ras, L. (2010, June). *Evaluatieverslag—Cliëntenberaad St. Antonius Ziekenhuis te Nieuwegein.* Utrecht: Hogeschool Utrecht

van Cruchten, J., & Kuijpers, R. (2007). Vakbeweging en organisatiegraad van werknemers. *Sociaaleconomische trends, 1*, 7–17.

van de Bovenkamp, H. M. (2010). *The Limits of Patient Power.* Doctoral Dissertation, Erasmus Universiteit Rotterdam, Rotterdam.

van der Grinten, T., & Kasdorp, J. (1999). *25 jaar sturing in de gezondheidszorg: van verstatelijking naar ondernemerschap.* Den Haag: SCP.

van der Kraan, W. G. M. (2006). *Vraag naar vraagsturing.* Doctoral Dissertation, Erasmus Universiteit Rotterdam, Rotterdam.

van der Kraan, W. G. M., & Meurs, P. (2008). *Effectieve medezeggenschap—Een verkennend onderzoek naar effectieve vormgeving van medezeggenschap van cliënten in algemene ziekenhuizen.* Rotterdam: Erasmus Medisch Centrum Rotterdam—Instituut Beleid en Management Gezondheidszorg.

van der Schee, E., Delnoij, D., Hutten, J. B. F., Verwij, J. A., & Kerssens, J. J. (2000). *De invloed van verzekerden op het bestuur van ziekenfondsen*. Utrecht: NIVEL.

van der Voet, G. W. (2005). *De kwaliteit van de WMCZ als medezeggenschapswet*. Doctoral Dissertation, Ph.D. Thesis, Rotterdam.

van Dongen, M. C. A. M., Bulsink, D., Homberg, D. J., & Kamphuis, H. C. M. (2008). *Patiënten-, gehandicapten- en ouderenorganisaties in Nederland—Cliëntenraden in beeld—Patiënten- en gehandicaptenorganisaties in 2008* (CG-raad, LPGGz, NPCF & Platvorm VG, Eds.). Utrecht: CG-raad et al.

van Doorn, J. A. A. (1956). Verzuiling: een eigentijds probleem van sociale controle. In *Sociologische Gids* (Vol. 3, pp. 41–49).

van Egmond, S., Heerings, M., & Munnichs, G. (2014, March 26). *Sterke verhalen uit het ziekenhuis: Leren van patiëntenervaringen voor goede zorg*. Den Haag: Rathenau Instituut.

van Hassel, D. T. P., Kastelijn, A., & Kenens, R. J. (2013, December). *Cijfers uit de registratie van huisartsen—Peiling 2013*. Utrecht: NIVEL.

van Hassel, D. T. P., Kastelijn, A., & Kenens, R. J. (2015, March). *Cijfers uit de registratie van huisartsen—Peiling 2015*. Utrecht: NIVEL.

van Kersbergen, K. (2009). Religion and the Welfare State in the Netherlands. In K. Kersbergen & P. Manow (Eds.), *Religion, class coalitions, and welfare states* (Chap. 5, pp. 119–145). Cambridge/New York/Melbourne: Cambridge University Press.

van Paridon, K. (2004). Wiederaufbau—Krise—Erholung: Die niederländische Wirtschaft seit 1945. In F. Wielenga & I. Taute (Eds.), *Länderbericht Niederlande* (399, pp. 363–422). Schriftenreihe. Bonn: Bundeszentrale für politische Bildung.

van Waarden, F. (1992). The historical institutionalization of typical national patterns in policy networks between state and industry. *European Journal of Political Research, 21*(1–2), 131–162.

van Waarden, F. (1993). Über die Beständigkeit nationaler Politikstile und Politiknetzwerke. Eine Studie zur Genese ihrer institutionellen Verankerung. In R. Czada & M. G. Schmidt (Eds.), *Verhandlungsdemokratie, Interessenvermittlung, Regierbarkeit* (pp. 191–212). Opladen: Westdeutscher Verlag.

van Waarden, F. (2002a). Dutch consociationalism and corporatism: A case of institutional persistence. *Acta politica—International Journal of Political Science, 37*(1–2), 44–67.

van Waarden, F. (2002b). Privatisering: Macht, Cultuur en Rationaliteit. In H. J. de Ru & J. Peters (Eds.), *Verzelfstandiging en Marktwerking Stand van Zaken en Perspectieven* (pp. 33–55). Den Haag: SDU.

Visser, J. (2009, January). Die ICTWSS-Datenbank: Datensammlung über institutionelle Besonderheiten von Gewerkschaften, Lohnfestsetzung, staatliche Intervention und Sozialpakte. Retrieved August 23, 2016, from http://www.uvaaias.net/208.

Visser, J., & Hemerijck, A. (1998). *Ein holländisches Wunder?* Frankfurt/New York: Campus.

*Wet cliëntenrechten zorg* (2010, April 23). Ministerie van Welzijn, Volksgezondheid en Sport (VWS). Retrieved August 23, 2016, from http://www.rijksoverheid.nl/bestanden/documenten-en-publicaties/brochures/2010/04/23/samenvatting-wet-clientenrechten-zorg/publiekssamenvatting-wcz.pdf.

*Wet inzake een algemene ouderdomsverzekering (Algemene Ouderdomswet (AOW))* (1956, June). Ministerie van Justitie. 's Gravenhage.

*Wet houdende algemene verzekering bijzondere ziektekosten (Algemene wet bijzondere ziektekosten (AWBZ))*. (1967). Ministerie van Justitie. 's Gravenhage.

*Wet maatschappelijke ondersteuning 2015 (WMO)*. (2014, July 18). Ministerie van Volksgezondheid, Welzijn en Sport. 's Gravenhage.

*Wet maatschappelijke ondersteuning (WMO)* (2006, June 29). Ministerie van Volksgezondheid, Welzijn en Sport. 's Gravenhage.

*Wet van 16 juni 2005, houdende regeling van een sociale verzekering voor geneeskundige zor ten behoeve van de gehele bevolking (Zorgverzekeringswet)* (2005, July 14). Ministerie van Volksgezondheid, Welzijn en Sport en Ministerie van Justitie.

*Wet van 29 februari 1996, houdende regels ter bevordering van de medezeggenschap van de cliënten van uit collectieve middelen gefinancierde zorgaanbieders op het terrein van de maatschappelijke zorg en gezondheidszorg (Wet medezeggenschap cliënten zorginstelling- en)* (1996). 's Gravenhage.

*Wet van 3 december 2014, houdende regels inzake de verzekering van zorg aan mensen die zijn aangewezen op langdurige zorg (Wet langdurige zorg)* (2014, December 3). Ministerie van Veiligheid en Justitie. Ministerie van Veiligheid en Justitie.

*Wetsvoorstel Wet tot wijziging van de Wet medezeggenschap cliënten zorginstellingen.* (2016, September).

Wielenga, F. (2004). Konsens im Polder? Die politische Kultur in den Niederlanden nach 1945. In F. Wielenga & I. Taute (Eds.), *Länderbericht Niederlande* (399, pp. 13–129). Schriftenreihe. Bonn: Bundeszentrale für Politische Bildung.

Wintle, M. (2000). Pillarisation, consociation and vertical pluralism in the Netherlands revisited: A European view. *West European Politics, 23*(3), 139–152.

Woldendorp, J., & Keman, H. (2007). The polder model reviewed: Dutch corporatism 1965–2000. *Economic and Industrial Democracy, 28*(3), 317–347.

Zorginstituut Nederland. (2011). Historie. Retrieved August 23, 2016, from www.zorginstituutnederland.nl/organisatie/historie.

# Chapter 6
# England

> *ˈgʌvənə(r) **1** a person who governs; esp.,* 1) *a person appointed to govern a dependency, province, town, fort, etc.;* 2) *the elected head of any state of the U.S.; 3)* any of the group of persons who direct an organization or institution: the board of governors of a hospital; 4) `Chiefly Brit.` *the person in charge of an organization or institution, as a prison; **2** a mechanical device for automatically controlling the speed of an engine or motor as by regulating the intake of fuel, steam, etc.; **3*** `Brit., Informal` *a person having authority; esp., one's father or employer: as a term of address, somewhat old-fashioned*[1]
> *ɪnˈvɒlvmənt* **1** [uncountable] `i.` (in/with something) the act of taking part in something; *US involvement in European wars* [synonym: participation]; ***2*** *[uncountable, countable]* `i.` *(in/with something) the act of giving a lot of time and attention to something you care about;* her growing involvement with contemporary music; ***3*** *[countable, uncountable]* `i.` *(with somebody) a romantic or sexual relationship with somebody that you are not married to;* He spoke openly about his involvement with the singer.[2]

## 6.1 Introduction

With some 54 % of the area and approximately 84 % of the population (as of : 8 August 2013; Office for National Statistics 2013a) of the United Kingdom, England is the largest country of both Great Britain and the United Kingdom. The 53.9 million inhabitants (Office for National Statistics 2013b) in 2013 are geographically and socio-economically unequally distributed at an average of 397 citizens per square kilometre. It has a prosperous South-East including London and less well-off regions in the North and East of the country, heavily populated areas—like

[1]www.yourdictionary.com/governor; accessed on 12 February 2017.

[2]http://www.oxfordadvancedlearnersdictionary.com/dictionary/involvement; accessed on 12 February 2017.



A. Haarmann, *The Evolution and Everyday Practice of Collective Patient Involvement in Europe*, DOI 10.1007/978-3-319-64595-7_6

Greater-London, the West Midlands, Merseyside, and Tyne and Wear—and sparsely populated ones—for instance, along the Welsh and Scottish borders (cf. also Baggott 2004, pp. 93–94). Being one of the first industrialised countries of the world it has suffered from structural changes in the labour market and undergone severe changes in its economic structure. The restructuring process has amongst other things resulted in London becoming Europe's major financial market place.

As England, Northern Ireland, Scotland, and Wales comprise different legislative sovereignties over some areas of legislation including health care, the choice of England was in part a necessity, and in part owing to practical reasons: The 'Health and Social Care (Community Health and Standards) Act 2003' in focus in this chapter applies to England only.

This chapter focuses on public involvement in NHS Foundation Trust Hospitals in England. After a general cursory glance at some key characteristics of England, its political system, and the NHS, we are going to take a closer look at public and patient involvement (PPI) throughout the history of the NHS in chapter 'Patient and Public Involvement Within the NHS', 6.3 on page 136. Chapter 'NHS Foundation Trusts', 6.4 on page 149 deals with the health care reform which introduced NHS Foundation Trust Hospitals and analyses the underlying reasons for its enactment. In want of any reliable and encompassing evaluation of involvement in Foundation Trusts, Sect. 6.5 on page 167 is finally going to attempt a first, very rough appraisal of the implementation of PPI in everyday life. As known from other studies, patient involvement needs time to leak into an organisation's culture. However, a number of basic conceptual shortcomings exert an impeding influence on the implementation.

### *6.1.1 The NHS*

This is my truth, now tell me yours. (Nye Bevan, architect of the NHS)

The United Kingdom is categorised as a residual, lib-lab, or liberal welfare state by the vast majority of scholars (cf. e. g. Esping-Andersen 1990; Hicks, Misra & Nah Ng 1995; Schmid 2002; Schmidt 2005), relying on either low flat rate or means tested benefits. With the pension and labour market reforms over the last few years (cf. Clasen & Clegg 2006; Dingeldey 2007; Immergut, Anderson & Schulze 2006) the country has moved into this direction even more, leaving the NHS as the only comprehensive service. As described to some greater detail in chapter 'Health Care System Types: The First Element', 1.1.1 on page 3, the NHS sticks out in this general assessment and does not fit the typology at all: it is the prototype of a health care system providing tax-funded, close-to-universal health care, which is to a great extent free of cost at the point of provision.

Nowadays, England has around 380 hospitals (thereof 222 NHS hospitals), ranging from small community hospitals of five beds for basic treatment up to university and teaching hospitals of more than 2,000 beds (including specific hospitals for learning disabilities, mental care, and maternity services; National

Registry 2013. Among them, and as of 28 November 2016, there are 156 Foundation Trust Hospitals for acute health care, of which 41 provide mental health care (Monitor 2015; NHS Improvement 2016b). Overall, this makes 3.9 hospital beds per 1,000 citizens (average for the years 2000 to 2009; WHO 2010, 122–123), which is at the very low end in European terms. Taking the general and acute beds available for overnight stays in England in the NHS solely, the ratio drops to merely 1.94 beds per 1,000 inhabitants (National Health Service 2014).

This is not the place to go into the details of the development of the NHS, which has been done better by many others (cf. e. g. Baggott 2004; Bartlett 1994; Baur, Heimer & Wieseler 2003; Boyle 2011; European Observatory on Health Care Systems 1999; Klein 1999; Lamping & Tamm 1994; Lowe 1993; Ogu 1981; Oliver 2005; Staender 2007; Vienonen 2000); here, some basic facts shall suffice. The origin of England as a welfare state is actually similar to the history of the medical profession and health care in the Netherlands, Sweden, and Germany: the medical profession was only developing in the late 19th century, struggling to establish itself as a profession and to secure a livelihood (Garpenby 1989, pp. 34–36; Ogu 1981, pp. 334–340). Friendly societies, sick clubs, and charities were the main sources of health care funding (Baggott 2004, pp. 79–83;Garpenby 1989, pp. 36–38;White 1933).

The NHS was founded in 1948 to tackle the problem of low quality of health care provision for a major number of citizens and against the backdrop of the occurrences and deprivation during the Second World War (Baggott 2004; Bartlett 1994; European Observatory on Health Care Systems 1999; Klein 1999; Ogu 1981; Oliver 2005). It can be perceived as one of the country's most important modernisation projects after the Second World War. British citizens show a strong identification with the NHS, an accomplishment they are proud of to the present day (cf. e. g. Clarke & Newman 2005). After the first two decades of establishing, consolidating, and extending services, the NHS is nowadays in a state of constant reform. Numerous governance, organisational, and parametric reforms have been imposed (cf. e. g. Greener & Powell 2008; Klein 1979; Rowe & Shepherd 2002). Having always been centralised, the shift of power from physicians to consultants heralded the start of the attempt at a more centralised governance, for which the main reason was the wish to make health care provision more efficient and raise—or at least maintain—quality. However, after three decades of attempted centralisation and tighter regulation, it must be realised that the implementation of these rules is as varied in the communities as ever before (Oliver 2005). What is more, since the Thatcher-era the NHS had to deal with declining resources and massive underfunding for many years with a share of between 5.5 % and 6 % of the GDP (cf. e. g. Boyle 2011, pp. 72, 170, 379,194–200; European Observatory on Health Care Systems 1999, pp. 36, 70, 79). Next to that, there were serious problems with the length of waiting lists, problems within the management, steering, evaluation, and accountability of the NHS at latest from the 1980s onwards.

### 6.1.2 The Political System, Parties, and Interest Groups

The country is, as the Netherlands and Sweden, a parliamentary monarchy with Queen Elizabeth II as the monarch since 1952. The parliament, which in its present form, dates back to 1688 (UK Parliament 2011d) with predecessors going back to the eighth century (UK Parliament 2011b), consists of two chambers: The *House of Lords* has 740 life-long members. Since the legislative reforms of 1911, 1949, and 1999, it possesses decreasing competences, which nowadays in effect are confined to a suspensive veto right of up to one year. Its members carry the hereditary title of a Lord or Lady or are appointed to the title for life (UK Parliament 2011c,a). As they are not bound to party compliance, one of the advantages of the House of Lords can be seen in a stance that is rather unbiased by party-politics towards the issues in question. Compared to most other European parliamentary systems the institution appears a bit dated, as members are either appointed for life or are members due to birth, i. e. in neither case democratically elected.

The main legislative work, however, is done in the *House of Commons* with its 650 members. They are democratically elected every fifth year to represent their respective constituency in parliament. As a consequence of the British election rules, according to which the 'First-Past-the-Post' (also known as a 'The-Winner-Takes-it-All' system) principle applies there have been strong one-party governments for many decades. As a matter of fact, the UK experienced its first coalition government since 1922 after the general elections in 2010, when the Conservative Party and the Liberal Democrats formed the present government (Rallings & Thrasher 2000, pp. 67–68). Since the general elections in May 2015 the Conservatives hold a thin majority of 50.8 % of the seats.

The party landscape is comprised of many, often regional parties among which four main parties can be identified. The Labour Party is what in most other countries would be called a social-democratic party, though it understood itself as a 'socialist party' for many years and as late as 1983, while the association with socialist groups can be observed up to the present day (cf. e. g. Labour Party 1945, 1979, 1983; Wilson 1974). The Conservative Party has roots dating back to the early 19th century, and its members—after its predecessor—are still frequently referred to as 'The Tories'. Sir Winston Churchill is probably one of the most recognised politicians from the Conservatives' ranks, while Margaret Thatcher was probably the most controversial one. The third player among the top three is the party of Liberal Democrats, which originated from a merger between the former Liberal Party and the Social Democratic Party in 1988 (Liberal Democrat History Group 2011). Neither too successful nor at the losing end, it played a decisive role after the general elections in 2010 becoming the junior partner of the Conservatives. Since the elections in May 2015 the Scottish National Party (SNP) has taken over the third place in parliament. Though founded back in the 1930s, it only recently has entered public reception in many respects with the referendum about Scottish independence, which was heavily favoured and propagated by the party.

### 6.1.3 Decentralisation

Over the course of the last two decades attempts have been started to decentralise some of the competences. In contrast to many other countries, this meant less the devolution of responsibilities to regions, counties, or municipalities, but giving the different countries of the United Kingdom limited autonomy over a number of policy areas. This is why amongst other things the educational and the health care system looks different in Northern Ireland, Scotland, and Wales compared to England, while foreign policy, internal security, and defence remained in the sphere of the UK's parliament in London (for a comparison of the different health care systems cf. e. g. Bevan et al. 2014; Longley, Riley, Davies & Hernández-Quevedo 2012; National Audit Office 2012; O'Neill, McGregor & Merkur 2012; Steel & Cylus 2012).

Within the countries of the UK, there are only few topics that are the municipalities' tasks: housing, childcare as well as some treatments of long-term and care of the elderly are typical municipal responsibilities. In contrast to many other European countries, the vast majority of tasks are centralised in Belfast, Edinburgh, Cardiff, and London, respectively, as other intermediary political or governance levels are missing by and large (Sturm 2009, 2006).

The following sections have a similar structure to the one on the Netherlands. It will first take a look at the choice of sources for this case study. After an overview of different means of (historic) involvement in the NHS, the case study will continue to the concept of Foundation Trust Hospitals and its predecessor. Here, the factors leading to the introduction of patient and public involvement in hospitals are portrayed, before, finally, an attempt based upon the conducted interviews will be made at assessment of the implementation.

## 6.2 Sources

Conducting interviews in England was considerably more difficult than in any other of the four countries. There were basically three reasons for this. The *first* was that apparently what is to be considered research in the regulatory sense and what not it is ill-defined. The 'National Research Ethics Service' (NRES) was established to review applications and grant approval for research conducted on the NHS, which is a rather lengthy procedure. Four and a half months into the application, I relinquished it, when I learned that applying for permission was unnecessary because my type of research falls within the category of 'service review'.

A *second* factor for a lower interview turnout was the rather low willingness of administrative staff who execute tasks related to the topic to participate. In a system of continuous change and ever new directives it is not surprising that people do not see participation in the research of a foreign researcher as their first priority.

The *third* obstacle was the willingness of (former) MPs to participate. In the end, two were willing to take part, with one of them actually keeping the appointment (see Table 6.1).[3] Though far from ideal, the low number of interviews with MPs is to some extent compensated by the fact that much more Green and White Papers have been published by the British Department of Health compared to its counterpart in the Netherlands. Thanks to this fact, it is less of a necessity to derive additional information from interviews.

Owing to the aforementioned difficulties in getting the ethics commission's approval and the categorising of my research as 'service review', there were some restrictions regarding the participation of lay-people—i. e. governors—in the study. Therefore, it was chosen to target those people at the interface between Board of Directors, the Council of Governors, and the administration. Though not directly comparable to the interviews in the Netherlands, with the downside that the portrayed views might deviate from those taken by the governors themselves, it nevertheless has some strong sides: the people interviewed have a much broader overview of what is going on in the hospital, of what the entirety of the hospital's governors do, all the more so when it comes to the side of the Board of Directors. All of the interviewees showed strong sympathy for the work of the governors. Some seemed to completely identify with the governors' work, whereas others were more critical about either the way participation is designed in general or actually implemented in everyday life. Overall, interviews seemed sufficiently comparable to the Dutch case study in that they portrayed the broad picture of problems, advantages, fears, and successes. Unfortunately, my request to conduct an interview with the supervisory authority, Monitor, was, again, denied.

## 6.3 Patient and Public Involvement Within the NHS

> Services are not necessarily made responsive to the public simply by giving citizens a democratic voice, and a distant one at that, in their make up. (Powell 1997, pp. 79–80)

Involvement of citizens in the NHS has been an issue in the discussion around and within the NHS since long. In the pre-NHS era there were broadly three types of hospital within what became the newly founded acute sector (cf. e. g. Baggott 2004, p. 85; Staender 2007, p. 26):

[3]Despite an intensive follow-up, most of the 19 MPs contacted repeatedly in writing and additionally on the phone refused to participate in the study with a few not responding at all. Reasons given for not being willing to take part in the study were manifold. The most common were lack of time, the author not being a member of their constituency, and lack of interest in health care policy—even expressed by high-ranking former chairmen of important health care committees.

**Table 6.1** Overview of conducted interviews & talks in England

| No. of interview | Category of interview partner | Organisation and/ or name | Date |
|---|---|---|---|
| 14 | 1 Chairperson, governors' umbrella organisation | Foundation trust governors' association (FTGA) | March 2011[a] |
| 15 | Governors | 1 Public governor at an acute FT in the south of England | March 2011[a] |
| 16 | | 1 Membership manager, mid-sized acute FT in the East Midlands | March 2011 |
| 17 | | 1 Membership manager, foundation trust in the north east of London, mental care | March 2011 |
| 18 | | 1 Membership manager, large foundation trust providing acute, community and adult services in the North-East of England | April 2011 |
| 19 | MPs | MP (Labour) 1997 – 2010 & member of health commission; voted 'moderately against' FTs[b] | March 2011 |
| 20 | Authorities | Joan Saddler, national director for patient and public affairs | March 2011[c] |
| 21 | Researchers | Marian Barnes, University of Brighton | November 2009 |
| 22 | | Seán Boyle, London school of economics | April 2011[d] |
| 23 | | Naomi Chambers, University of Manchester | November 2009 & August 2014[d] |
| 24 | | Ian Greener, Durham University | November 2009[d] |
| 25 | | Christine Hogg, London Metropolitan University | March 2011[d] |
| Total length of recorded finterviews: 4 hrs 54 min | | | |

[a]Interviews were conducted on the phone and not audiotaped
[b]cf. TheyWorkForYou (2012)
[c]Interviewee asked to not audiotape the interview
[d]Interview was not audiotaped

a) private for-profit hospitals, which needed to be paid for by patients at the point of service,
b) hospitals run by charity foundations, and
c) hospitals run by the municipality.

In general, the latter two were to be paid for, too. However, drawing back on the poor law, their initial aim was to provide treatment for poor people virtually for free,[4] which remained so for those who could not afford other treatment. More important in this context, however, the two latter were directly accountable to the local citizenship (Hogg 1999, pp. 84–86).

When the NHS was founded in 1948, dividing lines ran, broadly speaking, between the following divisions, each following its distinct line of accountability (cf. also Klein 1999; Ogu 1981):

ACUTE AND HOSPITAL CARE was and still is the core of the NHS Whitehall can exert the most direct influence on.

MENTAL CARE as ambulatory or short-term care is provided by the centrally led NHS as well. In comparison, mental care has never caught the same attention as has acute or later on primary care for some time.

PRIMARY CARE is provided by GPs who are associated with the NHS through contracts. Through this arrangement, they have retained a rather wide scope of decision-making and are ultimately only very indirectly accountable for their work.

COMMUNITY or SOCIAL CARE lies in the responsibility of the respective municipality. Though it provides all kinds of long-term care—for instance, care for the elderly and care for the physically or mentally challenged—it is often not perceived as an integral part of the core NHS.

Interestingly, Bevan proposed a locally driven hospital system with the municipalities responsible for their hospital in order to give health care provision a coherent structure and safeguard uniform quality standards (Hogg 1999, p. 85). The communities being worried about being overburdened with financial and organisational tasks, opposed this proposal (Baggott 2004, pp. 85–86; Hogg 1999, p. 85). In terms of democratic accountability, this would have been much closer to the citizens and in a way anticipated what Foundation Trust Hospitals are supposed to accomplish.

In consequence and despite several reorganisations, which—at least at the top level—integrated the different services somewhat better, the main source of legitimacy within the NHS remained in the democratic election of politicians, and to some extent still remains (cf. also Boyle 2011, p. 22):

---

[4]This attitude appears to have been partly taken over into the NHS as Julian Tudor Hart noted (cited in: Hogg (1999, p. 38)): 'Doctors traditionally recognized two kinds of patient. Paying patients, like other customers, were always right and therefore had to be humoured. Non-paying, public service patients, were supposed to earn their right to care by having serious or at least interesting diseases, and to be grateful for getting any care at all; beggars can't be choosers'.

Great Britain based its welfare policy much longer on the 'poor law', even though the distinction between 'deserving' and 'undeserving poor' was watered down. While the idea to establish a national health system, consequently, was in line with the tradition of public provision of poor relief and, thus, came up very early, social insurances attracted in particular liberal forces. Consequently, the National Insurance Act of 1911 included a compulsory health insurance for employees. As family members were not covered, the friendly societies as well as the municipal hospitals providing health care services for the poor continued to play an important role in the fragmented health care system (Boyle 2011, p. 25; Ogu 1981, pp. 315–316, 337–339, 351–353).

> Democratic accountability within the NHS comes through the Secretary of State to Parliament. The public, as citizens, elect an MP as their representative to make decisions on their behalf. This means that in health policy the only representation for citizens is at national level, which is far removed from where the decisions that affect them are made. (Hogg 1999, p. 84)

Interestingly enough, the fact that the democratically 'elected local governments and the various boards and committees' as well as charities (Ministry of Health 1959; Staender 2007, p. 169) 'ran' parts of the NHS services between 1948 and 1973 was viewed—at least by *some* researchers—as a sufficient representation of the public (cf. Milewa, Harrison, Ahmad & Tovey 2002, p. 40). As Klein (1979, p. 78), however, pointed out in 1979 already, the common MP's feasibility to influence local matters as general health care let alone control or actively change policies was limited with a rather circumscribed accountability (cf. also Milewa, Harrison, Ahmad & Tovey 2002, p. 40): they could enquire about certain facts and deficiencies, but they did not possess the capacity to oversee policy implementation and rarely had the opportunity to directly influence government politics. In consequence, upon being elected, politicians turn the citizens' will into policies targeted at health authorities and aimed at improving the service by transferring some responsibility to *health authorities* which, in turn, contract *GPs* and run *hospitals* (cf. also European Observatory on Health Care Systems 1999, pp. 14, 16, 20, 107–108). This whole chain of legitimacy is very indirect and pretty remote form ordinary citizens.

Active shaping of health care policies was more or less reserved for the Secretary of State for Health. And yet, Bevan's famous bedpan analogy, according to which Whitehall is to be held accountable for every bedpan dropped in any of the NHS hospitals, and the impact it has on political decision makers is one side, the increasing power of medical professionals in general and consultants in particular is quite another (Staender 2007, pp. 143, 145–150). Was the original aim in part to achieve better performance (Baggott 2004, pp. 89–90; Oliver 2005, pp. S76–S78; Staender 2007, pp. 36–38) it did not make hospitals independent from central influence and directives, whereas surely a local culture of implementation of and/ or resistance to these directives was added. Though officially perceived as a system of 'command and control', it can in fact rather be described as one of 'exhort and hope' as Klein put it later on (cited in Oliver 2005, p. S76). The introduction of *GP commissioning groups* in order to 'purchase' health care for their patients on large scale exacerbates the problem for primary care. Particularly in the context of the choice and market rhetoric commencing in the 1990s (Baggott 2004; Baggott, Allsop & Jones 2004; European Observatory on Health Care Systems 1999; Hogg 2008) we can state that there were severe problems of legitimacy:

> Health ministers had full responsibility for health policy, but had little direct control over the activities of the NHS. It was well-known that power over service developments was concentrated at local level; in the hands of doctors who were not accountable to ministers for their actions or for the resources they used. (Baggott 2004, p. 91)

### *6.3.1 Equivalents to Patient Involvement Within the NHS and Its Legitimacy*

In order to understand the full picture of patient and public involvement (PPI) we take a short detour via the equivalents of involvement within the NHS. In contrast to the following chapter, the two options below are frequently mentioned as examples of involvement in the UK. However, a closer analysis reveals that no equivalent worth the name can actually be spotted.

#### 6.3.1.1 Patient Organisations

One of the most important actors in the British context are patient organisations. Many of them organised as charity organisations or foundations, they mainly collect funding in order to provide information, fund research, sometimes even treatment. Compared to their Dutch counterparts, however, patient organisations as political actors remain rather pale on the national, public agenda (cf. Wood 2000, pp. 57, 108). This might be due to the politicians' perception that doctors and—later on—managers were the professionals who, according to national politics, knew better how to utilise the scarce resources than lay-people. This development might, however, also be the response to an NHS constantly operating on the brink of breakdown over several decades (cf. e. g. Boyle 2011, pp. 170, 379,194–200;European Observatory on Health Care Systems 1999, pp. 36, 70, 79), where patient organisations took the role of the NHS' stopgap.

Overall, patient organisations fulfil an important task in society. Strictly speaking, however, single, illness-specific organisations cannot be counted as being equivalent to PPI as although their aims might be the same, the people involved and their employed means differ considerably.

#### 6.3.1.2 Ombudsman

Far from being new, the idea to establish an intermediary to mediate between the state and/ or its authorities, on the one hand, and individuals, on the other, was put into practice with the 'National Health Service Reorganisation Act 1973'.[5] The office of a Health Service Commissioner was installed (Baggott 2004, pp. 308 et seq.; Fallberg and MacKenny 2003; Hogg 1999, pp. 42–44; 'National Health Service Reorganisation Act 1973', p. 345) and strengthened by the 'Health

[5]Originating in the old Norse word *umboð* for 'mandate' or 'authorisation', the term ombudsman used to name someone who is authorised to speak on behalf of someone in court in early 18th century's Sweden (Fallberg & MacKenny 2003, pp. 344-345). It developed into a term for an office which is to advocate citizens in any kind of complaint procedure against state bureaucracy in the modern welfare state at an as inofficial and local level as possible.

Service Commissioners Act 1993' (Boyle 2011, pp. 55–57; European Observatory on Health Care Systems 1999, p. 37; cf. also Parliamentary and Health Service Ombudsman 2010; The Stationery Office 1993). Ideally, the office of the Health Service Commissioner safeguards the practical implementation of patient rights by reacting upon complaints and taking the role of a proactive agent to improve the situation for the common good. However, in a country which for a long time only granted patients a charter with a list of fuzzy 'rights' that *should* be followed but cannot be guaranteed in practice, let alone legally enforced ( Baggott 2004, p. 316; Baggott, Allsop & Jones 2005, pp. 24–25; Coulter 2000; Tritter, Koivusalo, Ollila & Dorfman 2010, p. 102; Staender 2007, pp. 187–189) this becomes a difficult, if not impossible, yet, the more important task. The office of the Health Service Commissioner does not replace any existing complaints procedure or any one added later on, but rather supplements them by providing guidance and help in filing a complaint (cf. Fallberg & MacKenny 2003, p. 349). Thereby, paradoxically, the independent, 'informal' character of a highly official office listening to and helping those individuals seeking help is contrasted to the 'poor administration'—in the sense of bad administration—that they have suffered from (cf. Parliamentary and Health Service Ombudsman 2010, p. 7; cf. also Fallberg & MacKenny 2003, p. 344). Furthermore, despite all kinds of formalised complaint procedures, due to the protest of the medical profession there is no complaint procedure that includes the *medical treatment* itself (Hogg 1999, pp. 32–33). In conclusion it can be said that even though the service can be perceived to be a *voice* it is rather a kind of post-care voice, a complainant voice, rather than an active voice improving services and, thus, no proper equivalent for patient involvement in England.

### 6.3.2 Formal Means of Public Involvement—A Continuous Story of Discontinuity

> We trained very hard, but it seemed that every time we were beginning to form up into teams, we would be reorganized. I was to learn later in life that we tend to meet any new situation by reorganizing, and a wonderful method it can be for creating the illusion of progress, while producing confusion, inefficiency, and demoralization.
>
> (Gaius Petronius (66))
>
> The Government always argue that the next reform in the health service will do the trick, but then a few months later another set of reforms is announced, often contradictory to the previous ones, and followed by a new—guess what?—health service reform Bill.
>
> (Lord Clement-Jones; House of Lords 2003)

The following chapters will provide an overview of equivalents and predecessors of citizen involvement in Foundation Trust hospitals in its narrower sense. In this context, only the more direct means of involvement are mentioned that can be regarded in line with or as equivalents to involvement in Foundation Trust hospitals. Other forms, such as citizen juries or user panels, are therefore not regarded. Given the quick pace of reforms, it is difficult to keep up with the developments unfolding.

Therefore, the developments since 2012 are outlined only, without going into the details where they are not immediately linked to patient involvement in the hospital sector.

The first newer attempts at the local level date back to 1972, which factually means that England was at an early stage out to promote alternative ways of representation—i. e. beyond the traditional representation by elected MPs and authorities within the municipalities—like the Netherlands. To put things into context and to give justice to other countries, however, it must be admitted that the gap between policy rhetoric and practice has seldom been wider than in the UK. Nevertheless, the last ten to fifteen years showed some progress in closing this gap, at the same time, however, a somewhat contradicting emphasis on individual choice, too.

Depending on how much detail is gone into when looking at the history of involvement and which aspect and/ or level of the health care system is highlighted, authors arrive at somewhat different categories when discerning different phases of direct patient/ citizen involvement. Milewa et al. (2002) identify four different periods to which one might add a fifth, whereas Tritter et al. (2010) suggests three somewhat wider ones.[6]

[6]Interestingly, the Department of Health (2005) not only views the means of involvement in the sense of this book as PPI but subsumes even services and bodies to level criticism and issue complaints as a form of involvement. In 2005 the Department of Health summarised the existing ways of involvement as follows:

- 'Patient Advice and Liaison Service (PALS)—NHS provision of accessible support, advice and information to patients and carers
- Overview and Scrutiny Committees (OSCs)—local authority councillors have the powers to review and scrutinise the planning, provision and operation of the health service and to make recommendations for improvement
- section 11 of the 'Health and Social Care 2001a', which places a duty on the NHS to consult and involve patients and the public in the planning and development of health services and in making decisions affecting the way those services operate
- patient forums [also called: Patient and Public Involvement Forum (PPIF)] – independent bodies made up of volunteers and set up to monitor the quality of the NHS from the patient perspective; PPIFs do not exist at FTs [Foundation Trust Hospitals]
- complaints investigations by the NHS, with the Health Care Commission managing the independent review stage of the complaints procedure
- Independent Complaints Advocacy Service (ICAS)—the provision of independent support to patients wishing to complain about the NHS
- NHS Foundation Trust Boards." (Department of Health 2005, pp. 11–12)

In this context, Milewa, Harrison, Ahmad & Tovey 2002 point at the very broad meaning in which the term 'public involvement' is used in the first place. While 'healthcare manager might thus think of "involvement" in terms of consulting citizens about plans that have already been prepared' advocacy organisations might rather think of being included in the very planning process itself (Milewa et al. 2002, pp. 49–50). By this vagueness the term suits many purposes and becomes pretty meaningless.

**Table 6.2** Overview of British governments 1970–2015

| Commencing | Head of government | Government party/parties |
|---|---|---|
| June 1970 | Edward Heath | Conservatives/ Tories |
| March 1974 | Harold Wilson | Labour |
| April 1976 | James Callaghan | |
| May 1979 | Margaret Thatcher | Conservatives/ Tories |
| November 1990 | John Major | |
| May 1997 | Tony Blair | Labour |
| June 2007 | Gordon Brown | |
| June 2010 | David Cameron | Conservatives & Liberal Democrats |
| since July 2016 | Theresa May | Conservatives & Liberal Democrats |

Source: own compilation

#### 6.3.2.1 The Outset of Patient Involvement—Community Health Councils

Community Health Councils (CHCs) were one of the well-known institutions of PPI. Concerning direct representation of 'consumers' in ambulatory care—a term that was employed fairly early in the UK compared to the other three countries of this study—elected councillors were responsible for representing consumers and accountable to the local health authority (Black 1986). The proposed extension of the model to hospitals did not come off since the newly elected Labour government of 1997 believed that the independence of the Health Authority and the intermingling of management tasks and consumer representation would lead to a clash of interests (Black 1986) (Table 6.2).

In the hospital sector, citizen representation was traditionally done via 'Hospital Management Committees' to which a share of 'lay-people' were appointed by the municipality (Staender 2007, p. 169). Usually, however, these were not ordinary lay-people from the street, but quite often experts who were only 'lay' in the sense that they did not have any other professional affiliation with the hospital. That led Hogg (1999, p. 85) to the conclusion that the medical profession in the NHS after 1948 was for the first time left without any control from lay-people.[7]

[7] The upcoming of PPI needs to be seen in the context of an emerging civil rights movement in the 1960s. A first 'Patient Participation Group' was founded in Berinsfield, South Oxford in 1972 as a voluntary instrument to involve patients in a more extensive way than before (Tritter, Koivusalo, Ollila & Dorfman 2010, p. 98), which later on served as a model for the so-called Community Health Councils (CHCs) established in 1974 on a national basis (Baggott 2004, pp. 306 et seq.; Baur, Heimer & Wieseler 2003, p. 72; Boyle 2011, p. 62; Dabbs 2000; European Observatory on Health Care Systems 1999, p. 22; Hogg 2008, pp. 21 et seq.; Klein 1979, p. 75; Klein & Lewis 1976; Milewa et al. 2002, p. 40; Mullen, Murray-Sykes & Kearns 1984; Staender 2007, p. 37; The Stationery Office 1973; Tritter et al. 2010, p. 99). The main reason on the isle was that experiencing the aftermath of the Second World War Britain, which ended the rationing of essential food first in 1954, was struck by a severe economic crisis for long, and had struggled for sufficient living and housing standards for decades. Amongst other things, this led to high infant and maternal mortality rates until well into the 1970s, which can be perceived as a much stronger driver than the situation

CHCs served the purpose of three target groups, namely to represent the patients, the staff, and the state/ municipality of the district in matters of hospital care and to deal with grievances by any of the involved groups (Staender 2007, p. 169). Half of the members of CHCs were appointed by local authorities, a sixth by the Secretary of State for Health, and a third by local organisations (like charity and patient organisations, for instance). CHCs were funded by the Health Authority with which they were to meet once a year and meant to be a link between the traditionally hierarchical and central NHS administration and the local providers in all NHS divisions. In effect this meant that citizens could try to influence decisions on the local level via patient organisations, which, in turn, could possibly get on a third of the number of seats in the CHC, which in turn was rather loosely linked to the NHS structure and held an only advisory function. It is important to emphasise that they, everything together taken, were not thought of as representatives in the typical sense but as directly accountable to the Secretary of State for Health (Klein 1979, p. 73). Nevertheless, CHCs were a huge step ahead in terms of involvement and still resemble the key characteristics of today's PPI.

In hindsight, the Department of Health motivates the establishment of CHCs as follows:

> In 1974, the then Government tried to give greater prominence to the views of patients by creating community health councils. They attempted to combine three distinct functions: supporting individual patients and complainants; monitoring local hospital and community (but not primary care) services; and providing a citizen's perspective on service changes. (Department of Health 2000, p. 93)

In addition, Community Health Councils were intended to be distinct from the 'production side', which in practice proved to be a doubtful construction, because the medical profession was heavily overrepresented. However, this overrepresentation, provided with only limited powers in combination with ill-defined tasks and targets in its very heterogeneous composition weakened CHCs in contrast to other actors in the field (Baggott, Allsop & Jones 2004; Black 1986; Hallas 1976; Hogg 2008, 87–105; Klein & Lewis 1976). With a low budget, threatening their independence when it came to unpopular decisions for authorities, and provided with insufficient information it does not come as a surprise that they were criticised for being ineffective (Baggott 2004, p. 308; on strengths and weaknesses cf. also Dabbs 2000, p. 159). Moreover, Hogg (2008) discerns different political approaches, which, in turn, reflect the practice of the mid 1990s:

> The original Conservative vision was of the CHC as a local consumer group, who would make representations to health authorities on behalf of local residents about detailed aspects of the local delivery of services. They did not want CHCs to become involved in policy or be in any way political. The Labour vision was more ambitious. They wanted CHCs to strengthen democracy in the health service, and to take on professionals and help implement national policies at local level. (Hogg 2008, p. 34)

---

in mental care in the other three countries (Barnes, Harrison, Mort, Shardlow & Wistow 1999, pp. 12–15, 42, 45; Hogg 1999, interview 25; cf. also Beresford and Holden 2000, interview 20), which often was the starting point for patient involvement.

After some time, the political focus shifted towards establishing quality controls, fostering accountability, and strengthening the managerial influence within the NHS (Boyle 2011, p. 27; European Observatory on Health Care Systems 1999, p. 8; Milewa, Harrison, Ahmad & Tovey 2002, p. 40; Tritter, Koivusalo, Ollila & Dorfman 2010, p. 100), marking the beginning of a bifurcated process with an emphasis on first managerialism, then market and choice, on the one hand, and—for the most part rhetorical—emphasis on 'patient and public involvement' (PPI) all the way down to date.

#### 6.3.2.2 Lack of Accountability and Legitimacy

Nevertheless, the accountability and democratic legitimation of the NHS were increasingly perceived as an issue that needed to be tackled. The paper 'Local Voices' finally tried to bridge this gap. The 'Calman and Hine Report' (Expert Advisory Group on Cancer to the Chief Medical Officers of England and Wales 1995) on providing cancer services urged for the stronger incorporation of patients' views and needs in the planning and delivery of health care. Though the bifurcating line of argumentation between more market and more involvement continued, all subsequent governments put greater emphasis on PPI. Succeeding with none of these emphases, Paton's conclusion regarding this time 2000 is in line with what Tritter et al. conclude:

> Through the translation of patient into consumer, neo-liberal political economy emphasises exit rather than voice, and replaces political relationships with market forces (Marquand 2004). The shift from a patient-centred NHS model to a market-oriented one was achieved via a linguistic turn which transformed the patient into a consumer; the rhetoric of civil society is subsumed by one of individual choice.

Regarding the paper *Local Voices: The Views of Local People in Purchasing for Health* 1992 (NHS Management Executive 1992), however, he concludes that it 'was more about communication of the inevitable to the public than about participatory purchasing'. (Paton 2000, p. 13)

#### 6.3.2.3 From Unwanted Interference to Valued Input

An overall evaluation of the period just described could read that despite the political rhetoric of promoting PPI, the driving force behind the first wave of reforms was rather cost containment through a different organisational structure and the provision of incentives to cut waiting lists (cf. also Appleby, Harrison & Devlin 2003). After Labour was elected into government in 1997, they tried to drive forward more consistent policies with regard to public involvement. This did, however, not end the ambivalence between the rhetoric of market and participation, which were seen to be compatible with one another. The White Paper 'The new NHS Modern and Dependable: A National Framework for Assessing Performance' proposed changes, which emphasised the link between local implementation—mostly by experts—and national guidelines (Department of Health 1998), while 'Saving Lives: Our Healthier Nation White Paper *and* Reducing Health Inequalities: an Action Report' (Department of Health 1999) stressed the importance of a 'three way partnership' between local NHS bodies, the local governments, and individuals who are to take 'informed decisions' on their treatments (Department of Health 1999, p. 5). The most tangible outcomes were a focus on a stronger sensitivity of medical staff towards the needs of patients as well as giving staff and local authorities a larger say in health care matters (cf. Department of Health 1998; Tritter et al. 2010, p. 105).

The way chosen to implement this stronger local rooting was to abolish GP fundholders and convert them into Primary Care Groups (PCGs) in 1999. These PCGs consisted of several GP practices, which, in turn, given a record of good performance, could apply to receive Primary Care Trust (PCT) status from 2000 onwards (Milewa et al. 2002, p. 41; Tritter et al. 2010, p. 104). According to the paper 'The new NHS Modern and Dependable: A National Framework for Assessing Performance' (Department of Health 1998), the original plan was that each PCG was to be governed by a board consisting of several local stakeholders, including a member from the community. Comparing the assessment and application procedure to become a PCG and PCT, respectively, to the one chosen for the application and governance of Foundation Trusts later on, we can discern a concept that is strikingly similar (Milewa et al. 2002, p. 41; Tritter et al. 2010, p. 104). Perceived to be superior, PCGs were to be phased out after the reform in 2001.[8] Lobbying by the British Medical Association and the General Medical Services Committee showed effect and secured a composition of the board with less lay-people (Tritter, Koivusalo, Ollila & Dorfman 2010, p. 104).

One of the reasons for a stronger emphasis on involvement of the public and patients was that they were seen to be able to monitor and thereby improve the quality of services (cf. Hogg 2008; Tritter et al. 2010, p. 105). The papers 'Involving Patients and the Public in Healthcare—A Discussion Document' (Involving Patients and the Public in Healthcare—A Discussion Document 2001b) and 'The NHS plan—A plan for investment—A plan for reform' (The NHS plan—A plan for investment—A plan for reform 2000) continued the line of argumentation of the aforementioned white papers, but explicitly added involvement of patients in decision-making processes by stating:

> The relationship between central government and the NHS has veered between command-and-control and market fragmentation. Neither model works. The NHS cannot be run from

---

[8]The advantage of PCTs over PCGs was that usually they formed larger entities, they incorporated primary and social/community care and held a larger budget, commissioning a major part of services. Given the broader approach certain financial freedoms were linked to this type of commissioning. PCTs were abolished with the 'Health and Social Care Act 2012' in 2012 (Department of Health 2012). Their tasks were allocated to the newly established 'Clinical Commissioning Groups' (CCG), 'Commissioning Support Units' (CSU), and the municipalities.

> Whitehall. Standards cannot simply be set locally either. [...] The relationship between service and patient is too hierarchical and paternalistic. [...]
>
> The patient's voice does not sufficiently influence the provision of services. Local communities are poorly represented within NHS decision-making structures. Despite many local and national initiatives to alter the relationship between the NHS and the patient, the whole culture is more of the last century than of this. Giving patients new powers in the NHS is one of the keys to unlocking patient-centred services. [...]
>
> Patients and citizens have had too little influence at every level of the NHS. [...] Patients are the most important people in the health service. It doesn't always appear that way. Too many patients feel talked at, rather than listened to. This has to change. [...] To bring this about, patients must have more say in their own treatment and more influence over the way the NHS works. (The NHS plan—A plan for investment—A plan for reform 2000, pp. 30, 94, 88)

The measures taken in the wake of the paper were:

a) Community Health Councils were completely abolished (Department of Health 2000, p. 95; Milewa et al. 2002, p. 42; Tritter et al. 2010, p. 106) and
b) replaced by a 'Patient Advocacy and Liaison Service' (PALS) (Involving Patients and the Public in Healthcare—A Discussion Document 2001b; Milewa et al. 2002, p. 42) based at each NHS Trust. It took over most roles of the former CHCs, but serves rather as a complaint board, on the one hand, and an entity linking management with the public's concerns, on the other (Boyle 2011, p. 57; Department of Health 2000, pp. 20, 91, 94, 95, 122; Department of Health 2001b, p. 18).
c) Another task was to support the newly established 'Patients' Forums', also called 'local advisory forums'. Half of its members were constituted by patient groups and representatives of voluntary organisations, whereas the rest was to be randomly drawn from the trust's annual patient survey. Taking over another of CHC's tasks Patients' Forums shall 'monitor standards and use unannounced inspections', except for in Foundation Trust Hospitals (FTs), where they were unprovided (Department of Health 2000, pp. 47, 94; Department of Health 2001b, pp. 9–12; Hogg 2008, pp. 144–145; Health Committee 2003, p. 31).

Besides these steps, other measures were taken to better involve citizens and coordinate PPI.[9] Scholars arrive at the conclusion that the approach by early New Labour did not depart too much from the ideas of implementing NPM by the Conservatives (Tritter et al. 2010, p. 107), which finds its expression in subsequent reports, like the so-called Kennedy Report (Department of Health 2001b), highlighting the importance of patient involvement but stressing managerialism as a remedy to improve the quality and patient safety of services at the very same time (Tritter et al. 2010, p. 107).

---

[9]This included a closer monitoring of patients' assessment of the services providers, publishing an annual report on it (Department of Health 2000, p. 93), including patients as one third of the members of the 'Modernisation Board', patients representation on the 'Independent Reconfiguration Panel' as well as the 'Commission for Health Improvement' (Department of Health 2000, pp. 94–95; Department of Health 2001b, p. 19), and a stronger coordination of PPI activities by the 'Commission for Patient and Public Involvement in Health' (CPPIH) (Hogg 2008, pp. 125, 131 et seq.).

The year 2003 can be regarded the starting point for the heyday of the discussion surrounding choice as the focus shifted from 'market' to 'choice'. Some fragments, however, survived and were rephrased as competition, whereas the potential of cooperation within limited competition appears to have been realised.

The 'Commission for Patient and Public Involvement in Health' (CPPIH) officially started operation in January 2003, whereas Patients' Forums started their work in December that year (Hogg 2008, p. 126). During the readings for the "Health and Social Care (Community Health and Standards) Act 2003", which mainly took place between April and September, it was announced to close down Patients' Forums. Though they were kept alive until April 2008, the fact that the same government attempted to abolish a vehicle for a policy that was not yet even implemented testifies a certain lack of concepts and clear vision. As the main reasons for the abolishment of Patients' Forums can be regarded the lack of national political support and the fact that the boards within the trusts began to act like CHCs, namely by being completely diverse in terms of decision-making processes and composition, by renouncing democratic elections and favouring uncontested elections of the public representatives as well as an increased exertion of control by the CPPIH (Table "6.3").

Apparently, five years later in 2007 it was time for yet another round of reorganisation, when the 'Local Government and Public Involvement in Health Act 2007' was passed and came up with the latest invention: LINks, **L**ocal **I**nvolvement **N**etwor**ks**. Looking at their predecessors, namely the CHCs, the resemblance regarding the number of members, the tasks of LINks, and their competences is striking. Thus, regarding PPI, it has despite many a reorganisation basically arrived at its point of departure. The government has once again chosen an authority to set up and support LINks, which, this time, is called 'host organisation' and organised by the local community (Hogg 2008, pp. 158 et seq.; cf. also Boyle 2011, p. 63).

### *6.3.3 Summary—'Reorganisation as an Obsession'*

Ever tried. Ever failed. No matter. Try again. Fail again. Fail better. (Molloy, Samuel Beckett (1951))

Overall, it can be concluded that compared to many other countries, England was quite early to strengthen some form of PPI in health care planning. The recent emphasis may mirror the general trend to involve citizens in state services and society at large (interview 16), but appears for a long time to have been at least unsystematic if not completely confined to the sphere of rhetoric. The countless reorganisations within the NHS (for an overview regarding PPI cf. e. g. Bartlett 1994; Boyle 2011; European Observatory on Health Care Systems 1999; Klein 1999; Ogu 1981; Oliver 2005) not only affected its organisational structure, but have at the same time for the most part changed the ways citizens could exert influence on health care matters, thereby hardly permitting the new processes to settle in.

**Table 6.3** Overview of (historical) possibilities & layers of involvement

| | | 1948 | 1974 | 2001 | 2004 | 2012 & onwards |
|---|---|---|---|---|---|---|
| Hospital management boards | GPs | | | | | |
| | Hospital sector | | | | | |
| | Community care | | | | | |
| CHCs | GPs | | | | | |
| | Hospital sector | | | | | |
| | Community care | | | | | |
| Patients' forums | GPs | | | | | |
| | Hospital sector | | | | | |
| | Community care | | | | | |
| LINks | GPs | | | | | |
| | Hospital sector | | | | | |
| | Community care | | | | | |
| PALS | GPs | | | | | |
| | Hospital sector | | | | | |
| | Community care | | | | | |
| FTs | GPs | | | | | |
| | Hospital sector | | | | | |
| | Community care | | | | | |
| HealthWatch | GPs | | | | | |
| | Hospital sector | | | | | |
| | Community care | | | | | |

Source: own depiction

McLachlan (1990) speaks in this context even of 'reorganisation as an obsession' during the 1980s and 1990s. In addition, primary care, acute care, and community services have received very different political attention over the decades: whereas hospital care generally was the holy cow of the NHS during general election times, there were some attempts to strengthen primary care, and to improve community services. Against the backdrop of this fragmentation of services—with each their respective chain of accountability and own body of PPI—the impression left is less one of a thought-through structure, but rather of a confusing multiplicity that has emerged by sometimes well-willing and/ or well-wishing intentions that were, however, badly implemented and politically exploited.

## 6.4 NHS Foundation Trusts

Has the focus so far been on PPI, the organisation of hospitals plays into the answer why Foundation Trust Hospitals were initiated. Traditionally, most hospitals were run as local infirmaries or community hospitals, underlining the close ties to either the municipality or a local charity organisation. Most of them were transformed into 'NHS Trusts' in one of the four major conversion waves after this corporate form was introduced in 1990 (Bartlett 1994, pp. 151, 154–155, 157 et seq.; Hogg 1999, p. 86; Robinson 2002; cf. also Greener 2004, p. 665; Oliver 2005, S77), practically a non-profit enterprise (Bartlett 1994, p. 159) sometimes also called 'NHS Hospital Trusts'.

### *6.4.1 The NHS Trust as Precursor—'Foundation Trust Light'*

The 'National Health Service and Community Care Act 1990' laid the basis for NHS Trusts and was enacted with the majority of the Conservatives, which at the same time introduced the nowadays rhetorically widely avoided 'internal market". The community hospitals that exist nowadays are either the few remaining ones that were not transformed to NHS Trusts or—oddly enough—those which were added very recently as a 'new' form of local, basic hospital. Nevertheless, essential parts of the underlying logic remain.

When it comes to financial and governmental freedoms, NHS Trusts can be viewed as the precursor of Foundation Trust hospitals, which in the initial proposal were envisaged to hold a number of extensive rights. NHS Trusts were initially part of the broader approach 'citizen governance' (Simmons, Birchall, Doheny & Powell 2007): notwithstanding the fact that 'Self-Governed Schools'[10] and NHS Trusts were envisaged at the very same time, only the first mentioned were introduced in England and Wales ('Education Act 1986'; 'Education Reform Act 1988a') as well as in Scotland ('School Boards (Scotland) Act 1998b,'Self-Governing Schools etc. (Scotland) Act 1989'). Like today's Foundation Trust hospitals, these schools have a local 'school board' comprised of parents, representatives of the school authority, the community, and stakeholders in the area.

In 1989, in particular hospital managers and the medical profession had hoped for more managerial and financial leeway from Whitehall, at least to the same amount it was given to teachers and parents. However, in these days the concern arose among politicians, how to control independently governed hospitals, so that giving it completely 'out of hands' was too hot an issue at that time (Bartlett 1994, p. 154). Nevertheless, compared to their predecessors, NHS Trusts enjoy some independence (cf. European Observatory on Health Care Systems 1999, pp. 16, 18, 30; Boyle 2011, pp. 27–28, 43, 109–110, 136, 175, 179): even though deficits have to be balanced in the same year they arise while excesses have to be paid over to the Department of Health and larger investments can only be made through the superior Health Authority local managers have at least to some leeway. NHS Trusts

[10]Sometimes even called 'Foundation Schools' or 'School Trusts'. In 2010 a new discussion on 'Foundation Schools', modelled after Foundation Trust Hospitals emerged, but did not lead to enactment.

are assessed with what is referred to as '3* rating' of NHS Trusts (Boyle 2011, p. 364; cf. also Oliver 2005, S78), a simplified instrument to assess and supervise NHS Trusts and an attempt to transparently show the quality of provision to citizens.

### 6.4.2 *Foundation Trusts—Concept, Structure, and Supervision*

> An NHS foundation trust is a public benefit corporation which is authorised under this part to provide goods and services for the purposes of the health service in England. ('Health and Social Care (Community Health and Standards) Act 2003' part 1, sec. 1, 1)
>
> NHS foundation trusts embody a new form of social ownership that provides a much stronger means whereby health services can become more responsive to local needs. (John Hutton, member of the House of Commons for Barrow and Furness (Labour), 8 May 2003; House of Commons 2003e)

Technically, Foundation Trusts (FTs) are just another form of enterprise and governance model to run hospitals. Applicants to FT status have continuously been accepted since 1 April 2004 so that 156 FT hospitals exist as of 28 November 2016 (NHS Improvement 2016b).

The originally proposed plan of annual authorisation waves, which should give the opportunity to evaluate the concept of FTs (Health Committee 2003, p. 33), was never actually pursued. Whilst it was initially promised that '[b]y 2008 all hospital trusts will be in a position to apply for NHS foundation trust status' (Department of Health 2004b, pp. 51, 52; cf. also Health Committee 2003, p. 47), there were still 61 acute care and 15 mental NHS Trusts left as of 21 March 2014 (NHS Choices 2014a,b). Though again the promise by Cameron's conservative-liberal coalition government was to transform *all* hospitals into FTs by 2014 (Public and Patient Experience and Engagement Team 2011, pp. 12, 20; Secretary of State for Health 2010, pp. 13, 128–130), this number had hardly changed by the finishing of this book. The concept of 'earned autonomy' originally introduced for NHS Trusts in the year 2000 but likewise applied to FTs (Bojke & Goddard 2010, p. 10; Department of Health 2002a; Department of Health 2004b, pp. 73, 75; Health Committee 2003, pp. 59 et seq.; Health Committee 2003, p. 27; Robinson 2002, p. 506; Secretary of State for Health 2010, 5, 72, 159; Staender 2007, p. 157) exchanges good performance for autonomy: According to the legislator's will, only NHS Trusts with a three star rating are eligible to apply for FT status in order to prevent economic failure (Department of Health 2004b, pp. 73, 75; Health Committee 2003, pp. 24, 27–29; cf. also Foundation Trust Network 2006, p. 4; Tuffs 2006), which can be a futile consideration (cf. 6.5.1 on page 169; on the linkage between rating and performance cf. also Bojke and Goddard 2010, p. 3). In the beginning, mainly acute care and mental hospitals applied for FT status (cf. Monitor 2010b), whilst in the meantime, several different types of FTs have emerged: Next to the initial type of acute and elective care hospital mental care FTs were soon to follow. A later development are FTs operating ambulance and/ or community services.

Looking at the rhetoric of announcements and propositions initially made when Foundation Trust hospitals were proposed it is striking how similar it is compared to that employed when NHS Trusts were established: Both highlight the revolutionary step of becoming independent from Whitehall, the only slight difference being the emphasis on managerial leeway in the first and local accountability in the latter case (cf. also Robinson 2002, p. 507). In that light, Foundation Trusts simply seem to be yet another attempt to get things right this round.

FTs are—according to their logic—membership based. In line with British tradition and in contrast to the Netherlands, the focus is on *public* and patient involvement, so that not only those treated in the hospital but also those who are linked to it in one way or another can become members, most often through residency, working in the catchment area, or being a member of staff. Going through the information provided by the respective FT hospitals on their membership, it becomes clear, however, that there is no homogeneous definition beyond a very airy concept of what the base for membership is: Some FTs have chosen for an opt-in model, in which people register who are interested in the work of the hospital, whereas others have decided to implement an opt-out strategy in which all people having contact with, living in the catchment area, or being treated in the hospital are automatically enrolled. Some include all their staff in their membership figures, others apply the opt-in procedure also for this group.

The requirements for the Council of Governors are—particularly in contrast to the Netherlands and the membership criteria—subject to very specific national regulations, as e. g. Sect. 6 and 37 of the 'Health and Social Care (Community Health and Standards) Act 2003' and its explanatory notes reveal (Department of Health 2002a, 2003; Monitor—Independent Regulator of NHS Foundation Trusts 2008a; NHS 2005). They specify amongst other things that NHS Trusts seeking FT status as well as FTs themselves must take measures to ensure that the membership is representative for the hospital's constituencies and how elections for governors are to take place. Other regulations are much more open to discretionary provision and neglect coordination and collaboration such as e. g. incorporating key local actors into the council.

FTs have a one-tier board which usually is comprised of executive and non-executive directors to which medical and other directors might be added (Department of Health 2004a, cf. Fig. 6.1; cf. e. g. Monitor—Independent Regulator of NHS Foundation Trusts 2010). It is here that the ultimate decisive power on operational as well as strategic decision-making lies. Linked to this board is what most often is called a 'Board of Governors', 'Council of Governors', or 'Membership Council', different terms for the same body.[11] In order to prevent the confusion between

[11]Looking at the usage of the different names it seems that in later time there has been a shift away from the first mentioned to the latter two (cf. also Ipsos MORI 2008, p. 15).

One reason for this might be the following experience: 'If you use the word "board", they think of themselves like a board of directors, which is what they're not. So you've got to be very careful to make sure that there is a distinction between the role of Governors and the role of the board of directors in running the organisation'. Chair, Foundation Trust (Ipsos MORI 2008, p. 15)

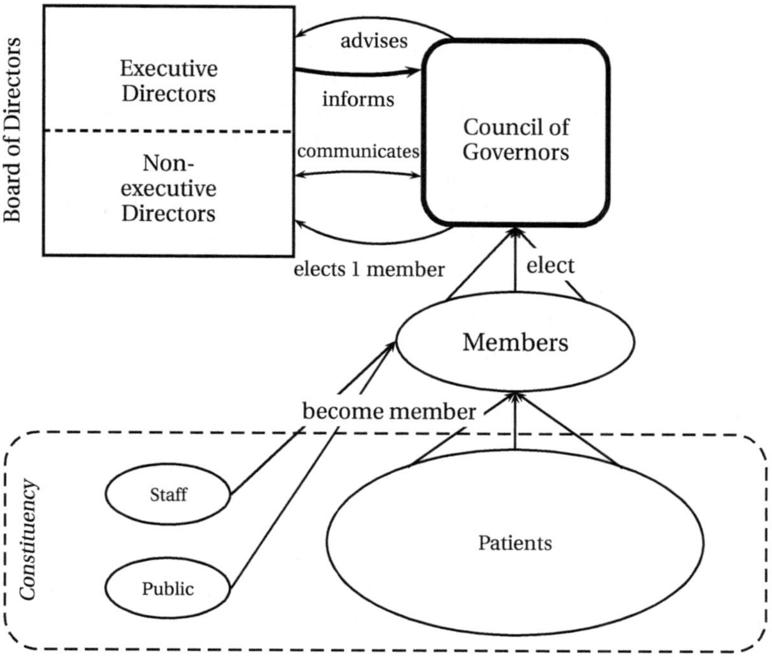


**Fig. 6.1** Overview of official levels of involvement in foundation trusts. Source: own depiction

Directors' and Governors' Board and to prevent the impression that the council consists of a wider membership, I will use the term 'Council of Governors' henceforth, which is one of the most commonly used terms.

The council's size can be determined by the FT's management, though a minimum number of seats applies. It is usually also dependent on the size of the membership and consists of several groups of people:

- The majority of seats should be reserved for who most often are called 'PUBLIC GOVERNORS' or 'ELECTED GOVERNORS', i. e. patients or residents in the catchment area representing 'Joe Bloggs' (Department of Health 2002a; Monitor—Independent Regulator of NHS Foundation Trusts 2008b, p. 3).
- The second most usual part is constituted by 'STAFF GOVERNORS'. As staff form part of the membership they can elect their own governors (Department of Health 2002a; Monitor—Independent Regulator of NHS Foundation Trusts 2008b, p. 3).
- In addition to these groups, the majority of FTs invite KEY ACTORS AND PARTNERS from the area—e. g. a mental hospital, the social services board, Clinical Commissioning Group and Commissioning Support Group, the community council, teaching hospitals, or medical universities, etc.—to send a representative most often called 'public governors' or 'appointed governors' ('Health and Social Care (Community Health and Standards) Act 2003').

The latter group may in some instances be fully eligible to vote while in other cases they are not. In contrast to being appointed by a sending institution, the governors of the first two groups, in contrast, are elected every three years ('Health and Social Care (Community Health and Standards) Act 2003'). As best practice, it has—at least in some hospitals—been established that more frequent elections which only exchange a part of the Governors are a good choice in terms of continuity within the council. The different electorates and constituencies form one common Council of Governors. The most powerful competences held are

- the right of regular meetings with the Board of Directors,
- the right to approve the annual report, and
- to (re-)elect the Chief Executive and at least one non-executive member of the Board of Directors (Department of Health 2002a, p. 21; 'Health and Social Care (Community Health and Standards) Act 2003')

Interestingly, these are exactly the same minimum competences that its Dutch counterpart hold. Here as there, they are quite often complemented locally, so that the council e. g. may agree to the appointment of a new head of a ward.

There have been several reforms of the supervisory authority, which amongst other things has the tasks to advises applicant hospitals, grants FT status, regulates as well as evaluates and supervises FTs (for more on the supervisory authority see 6.5.1 on page 168).

There are two umbrella organisations linking Foundation Trusts. One is the member-based 'Foundation Trust Governors' Association', which also offers several training courses for its members. The other is the 'Foundation Trust Network', a network to foster the exchange of information between FT hospitals and outer representation.

### *6.4.3 The Legislation Process—Legislation on the Fast-track*

> Instead [of hearing an interesting debate], rather oddly, we have heard a Labour party with a centre of gravity that is rather out of sympathy with the principle that underlies the Bill argue for the Bill, while the Liberal Democrats and the Conservative party have argued against it, although their centres of gravity support its direction. (Francis Maude, member of the House of Commons for Horsham (Conservatives), 7 May 2003 The Stationery Office (2003))

Interestingly, Foundation Trusts as a new type of hospital and form of governance were neither mentioned when a number of white papers on the NHS were published in 2000 and 2001 (cf. Department of Health 2000, 2001b,c,d) nor in Labour's party manifesto (Labour Party 2001), though the latter went into some details of how Labour envisaged an improved health care service, and though "Involving Patients and the Public in Healthcare—A Discussion Document 2001b" (Department of Health 2001b) was explicitly on PPI. Basically, only one year passed between the first public mentioning of Foundation Trust Hospitals and passing the act that legislated them (Boyle 2005, p. 6–7; House of Lords 2003). As a consequence, the usual practice of publishing a Green and then a White Paper so that the comments on them can be integrated in the final bill was not observed. The first specification could be found in the bill, which is why the following analysis builds mainly on the parliamentary readings. Such hurried policy making was also commented on during the legislation process:

> I am concerned that the policy is part of a growing trend of policy making on the hoof. [...] The policy has not been properly thought through and there has been no proper consultation. [...] I was not elected on the basis of foundation trusts; I was elected to get rid of the ethos that is behind foundation trusts. [...] Where is the Green Paper? Where is the White Paper? (David Hinchliff, member for the House of Commons for Wakefield (Labour), 8 May 2003 (House of Commons 2003e))

The act was not solely on the introduction of FTs, which can be viewed as one of the major reasons for its acceptance. It included a number of various other improvements. As a nice instance of 'coupling' (Kingdon 2003, p. 173), the bill on the "Health and Social Care (Community Health and Standards) Act 2003" was presented as a natural, inseparable unity, despite its very heterogeneous points.[12] In order to fully understand its potential perception we need to recall the state of the NHS in the early 2000s: There were calls for better dental and paediatric care as well as higher funding, while hospitals had been asking for more scope of decision making for decades. In order to arrive at a more efficient health care provision primary health care would need to be developed more strongly than in the past. With these points in mind, looking somewhat closer at the various parts of the bill reveals its potential for approval. The bill suggested:

- Increase in spending levels
- Measures to improve dental care
- Measures to improve paediatric care
- Measures to strengthen primary care
- Establishment of the two supervisory authorities 'Commission for Healthcare Audit and Inspection' (CHAI) & 'Commission for Social Care Inspection' (CSCI)
- New competences for the Welsh assembly regarding health care
- NHS charges
- Complaint procedures
- Foundation Trusts:
  - Decentralisation and greater freedom for FTs
  - Establishment of a new regulator for FTs
  - Private Borrowing
  - Democratisation of health care provision

[12] When asked what MPs would lose if support for Foundation Trust hospitals were denied, Alan Milburn, the then Secretary of State for Health (Labour; October 1999 – June 2003) replied: 'They would lose the whole Bill'. (House of Commons 2003a).

Taking a closer look at the parliamentary readings, they reveal two things: Whereas most parts were fairly uniformly accepted and welcomed with only minor concerns by a cross-party majority of MPs.[13] The section on FTs took about two thirds of speaking time during the parliamentary readings. Despite a comfortable Labour majority of 167 MPs only a tiny Labour majority of 17 to 50 MPs voted in favour of the different sections (House of Commons 2003a).[14] This underlines the fact that Labour MPs were as critical as Conservatives during the parliamentary reading, even though sometimes for different reasons. Moreover, the government received harsh criticism from the opposition, because the small majority was only achieved with the help of the Labour MPs from Wales and Scotland, who are not affected by the act anyway and were, thus, voting on solely English issues. Furthermore, the legislation process is also questionable from a constitutional perspective: The constitutional right of the House of Lords to amend a bill was disregarded by the Labour government, arguing that 'the other house' were not entitled to these amendments, because its members are not elected.

However, even more important in a comparison of countries, it also shows that this kind of legislation would almost have been impossible in countries which apply an electoral system according to proportional representation (as e. g. the Netherlands but also many other countries including Germany and Sweden), and those which have decentralised responsibilities to subordinate territorial units (such as e. g. Germany and Sweden). In these countries it seems unlikely that a government would find itself in a situation, in which it is able to override the vast opposition of its own party ranks let alone territorial entities or constitutional institutions. Furthermore, it requires a strong vision to push a bill through despite strong inner-party opposition. All evidence speaks for the small circle around Tony Blair and Alan Milburn as the driving force behind the project.[15]

[13]'Even if agreement cannot be reached on those two points [regarding FTs; the author], I confirm that the Opposition will be happy to let the rest of the Bill, apart from part 1 [on FTs; the author], go straight into law'. Tim Yeo, member of the House of Commons for South Suffolk (Conservatives), 19 November 2003 (House of Commons 2003a).

[14]Voting is on each section of a bill.

[15]This assumption is supported by the interviews: 'That is one of your questions: that was one of the great people pushing it. And the Secretary of State at the time was Alan Milburn. And I think it is quite important that our first Secretary of State after 1997 was Frank Dobson, who is very much of the old style, and I am sure he resisted these kind of things, which explains why Alan Milburn, who was one of Tony Blair's sort of people, he was brought in the sort of: Do it! And a lot of it has got to do with Tony Blair, feeling that he was getting a lot of hassle when he was going around Europe and people were telling him that European nations were much better in providing health care. And he was going around, saying, "We have got the best health service in the world!" Which in some ways it is, but it is not. You cannot make statements like that. And he was getting a lot of hassle there, so there is evidence that he wanted to improve the NHS. And he did by putting lots of more money into it, not necessarily by improving productivity'. (interview 19).

#### 6.4.3.1 Quality of Care and Performance—the Main Target

> I do not think [...; public involvement] was the real driver of it at all.
> (interview 19)

As described in the chapters 'Patient and Public Involvement Within the NHS', 6.3 on page 136 and 'The NHS Trust as Precursor—'Foundation Trust Light'', 6.4.1 on page 150 above, it becomes clear that neither the idea of PPI is new nor the perception of continuous reforms as an appropriate answer to the structural weaknesses of the NHS. Although the rhetoric might raise the impression that one of the aims of Foundation Trusts was the strengthening of PPI and accountability, they were actually completely unrelated in the first place. Basically, they were viewed as the new remedy to a number of problems within the NHS—namely problems of access, the quality of care, perceived inefficiencies in service provision, and the comparatively low funding of health care (cf. e. g. Boyle 2011, p. 353; European Observatory on Health Care Systems 1999, pp. 18–19, 24–25, 36, 38, 46, 102, 107). Returning from a visit to Spain, Alan Milburn, the then Secretary of State (Labour; October 1999 – June 2003), seemed to have been impressed by Spanish FTs (cf. also Durán, Lara & van Waveren 2006, pp. xviii, 77, 149, 154)[16]: Visiting a hospital in Madrid

> I was struck by the fact that the greater independence it enjoyed from the rest of the state run health system had given patients there faster waiting times and improved outcomes despite dealing with a more severe case mix than comparable state run hospitals. (Alan Milburn, Secretary of State for Health, 7 May 2003 (House of Commons 2003b))

Subsequently, a seminar was held to learn more about the experiences with the FT model in other countries, delivering the rather promising evidence that Spanish FTs' 'experience is centred around quality and patient satisfaction' yielding 'very good quality', while Swedish representatives maintained that 'there had been a dramatic reduction in hospital waiting times' since the introduction of FTs (Department of Health 200b).

Having said that, the story of FTs is also a story of 'selective' policy learning—or, to be more precise, 'institution learning', or 'ideational learning' (cf. also Leiber, Greß & Manouguian 2010)—as politicians were interested in the organisational form of FT hospitals in the first instance, not in any encompassing policy. The selectiveness can be seen in several points: While trials in Germany, Portugal and Sweden are reported to have been 'more positive', the negative and devastating experiences in several other countries like Spain and Australia were ignored. The most drastic step was taken by New Zealand: This country had its policy even reversed and drawn back from a model similar to foundation trusts only a few years

[16]Spain began to transform all public hospitals into public foundations in 1999 (García-Armesto, Abadía-Taira, Durán, Hernández-Quevedo & Bernal-Delgado 2010, p. 48). 'Spain has presented an interesting experience of innovative hospital management (foundations) since 1997, when relevant legislation was adopted. Public hospitals with foundation status are self-governing units with less external bureaucratic control and emphasis on outcomes'. (Durán et al. 2006, p. xviii).

earlier.[17] Experiences were not really convincing in the US, either, and professionals as well as politicians were rather unhappy in Australia, too (Edwards & Lewis 2008, p. 55; House of Commons 2003b,d; Lewis & Hinton 2008; Mohan 2003). Despite these rather negative reports, Labour continued pursuing its plan. Furthermore, it is selective, since although Denmark and Sweden were referred to in the preparation of the bill, Boyle (2005, p. 46) mentions that reference was no longer made to them during the legislation process. And, third, it was selective, as there was no mention at all of the Netherlands or Norway[18] and their model of patient involvement. The fact that particularly Spain was more prominent in the political debate could be read as lack of knowledge. However, some of my Dutch interviewees mentioned that British authorities had made some visits to the Netherlands in order to find out more about how things were done on the other side of the channel. Therefore, a conclusion that comes closer to reality is that, at the point when the concept of FTs was discussed for the very first time, the idea of PPI formed no prominent part of it.

Seeing the potential of Spanish FTs in other countries, New Labour appears to have enthusiastically adopted them as a positive template for this new form of hospital. Only later on were they adapted to the English needs. Regarded from that angle, decentralisation as well as democratisation are merely vehicles to arrive at the intrinsic goal of the reform: Freedom for hospital governance in order to improve access, quality, and efficiency in health care. Confronting one interviewee with my impression that these reasons were the main triggers for the introduction of FTs rather than strengthening PPI (cf. interview 19 and 20; House of Commons 2003b,e,d,a; House of Lords 2003; The Stationery Office 2003) , the reply was: 'That is what I am saying that the patient involvement was not initially the important thing' (interview 19). This is also is nicely summarised in the following quotation:

> [...] Tony Blair was anxious to bring the NHS up to what they talked about in those days was European standards, because the amount of money spent on our NHS was way below the average for Europe. Places like Holland, and Germany, and France were spending much more per head. And there was a feeling that we were not spending enough on the NHS. And if we spent more, plus tried to make it more productive, then we would get much better results [incomprehensible; without having to spend huge amounts of more money]. But it did not work out like that. That was one of the driving forces. (interview 19)

#### 6.4.3.2 Decentralisation and Independence—The Tool

As aforementioned, a number of different measures were taken in order to achieve the main goal of the reform (see Sect. 6.4.3 on page 154), namely raising the quality of services and performance of the NHS. For the hospital sector, the most important and most discussed measure was the decentralisation from the Department of Health to the independent Foundation Trusts. This should be undertaken in order to make

[17] so-called Crown Health Enterprises (Ashton, Mays & Devlin 2005)

[18] For further information cf. Bakke and de Vibe (2009); Christensen and Lægrid (2010); Johnsen (2006); Lægrid, Opedal and Stigen (2005); Trondheim Kommune (2005).

services more locally rooted and, thus, more responsive and accountable to local citizens' needs:

> By empowering individual NHS trusts [sic!] to run services in response to local demand and need, it becomes possible for all to have high standards of access to services wherever they are. This is critical in tackling the health inequalities which permeate many of our most deprived areas. Part 1 of the Bill will, therefore, establish NHS foundation trusts as a new type of NHS organisation, based on a new corporate form—the public benefit corporation. (Lord Warner member of the House of Lords (Labour), 8 September 2003 (House of Lords 2003))

However, if these freedoms had been promised to NHS Trusts already (cf. Sect. 6.4.1 on page 150), what had become of them if this promise needed to be repeated now? Alan Milburn's assessment of this piece of Conservative legislation was in any case highly negative: He reflects that

> NHS trusts were supposed to guarantee self-governing status. In fact they were at best a half way house and at worst a sham. Trust status promised independence but in practice didn't guarantee it. In reality their legal status–with direct accountability to Ministers–meant that Whitehall continued to hold on to the purse strings... (Alan Milburn, Secretary of State for Health, 7 May 2003 (House of Commons 2003b))

Of course, even here, party politics play in: Whereas this statement could be attributed to the wish to make a point in favour of the introduction of FTs, Francis Maude (Conservative), who had been strongly in favour of NHS Trusts when they were introduced, was disillusioned, too. However, his contribution was intended as a pledge against going into the same direction again:

> I was struck by how little difference the creation of supposedly self-governing trusts under Conservative reforms in the 1990s made to accountability in reality. People continued to feel that the system was centrally planned and bureaucratically driven. (Francis Maude, member of the Houses of Commons for Horsham (Conservative), 7 May 2003 (House of Commons 2003b))

In conclusion, during the legislation process this is what everyone could agree to: NHS Trusts had not lived up to the initial expectations, and the current situation was far from what it should be. In that respect, Alan Milburn's speech during the first reading can be perceived a good summary to which most MPs as well researchers (cf. e. g. Bartlett 1994; Day 2006; Robinson 2002, p. 507) would have agreed:

> Today, however, the NHS is controlled from the top down. If it is to be more responsive, it needs to be run from the bottom up. It cannot be right that while Whitehall is free to direct every hospital to do everything from how to cook turkeys to how to wash the bed linen [...] hospitals are not free even to appoint their own doctors or nurse consultants. (Alan Milburn, Secretary of State for Health (Labour), 7 May 2003 (House of Commons 2003b))

In that view, hospitals possess much more potential, which to a large extent is not released owing to interference from Whitehall. In the context of citizen involvement, the talk of 'giving power into local hands' might at first sight seem like another phrase for democratisation.[19] However, analytically it simply adds to 'liberating the NHS', which refers to decentralisation and managerial freedom. Likewise, one might be confused whether or not decentralisation and independence are two sides of the same coin, which indeed they are to some extent. Freeing hospitals from Whitehall in this context, however, is an intertwined act not only of decentralising power to some local authority but also giving more freedom to hospitals, which are to be run like a private enterprise with much more consideration for local people's needs. Seen from the government's viewpoint, the two measures that were supposed to yield the greatest impact was, first, that FTs can decide which wards should be strengthened, which services acquired, which units maybe scaled down or even closed down. The second concerns the possibility to borrow on the private capital market ('Health and Social Care (Community Health and Standards) Act 2003'), which was thought to result in a better overall funding of health care.

#### 6.4.3.3 Democracy and Accountability—a Nice Add-on

> A model of governance and representation that involves people being appointed to NHS trusts is no longer acceptable [. . . ]. Let us have some democracy. (John Hutton, member of the House of Commons for Barrow and Furness (Labour), 8 May 2003 (House of Commons 2003e))
>
> In my view, the Bill has no credibility. It has no real support within the national health service or in the country. [. . . ] No one in my constituency accepts the need for that kind of artificial democracy, as the hospitals already offer patients forums. [. . . ] There is no need for this supposed democracy, which will not make the slightest difference, because the money is held by the PCTs, which are undemocratic. The whole thing is therefore nonsense. (Kate Hoey, member of the House of Commons for Vauxhall (Labour), 8 July 2003; House of Commons (2003d))

So far, the story focused on the main driver to establish Foundation Trusts—raising service quality—and decentralisation and independence as the instruments to achieve it. However, Public and Patient Involvement on the level of health care

[19] And indeed, there is much to it. In the context of 'Local Voices', an initiative for more accountability in the early 1990s, the NHS Management stated that 'to give people an effective voice in the shaping of health services locally will call for a radically different approach from that employed in the past. In particular, there needs to be a move away from one-off consultations towards ongoing involvement of local people in purchasing activities (NHS Management Executive 1992)' (cited in Hogg 1999, p. 94).

In that context, however, Paton (2000, p. 13) concludes that '[. . . ] the language of consumerism was used to justify an increasing stress upon market. [. . . ] *Local Voices* was more about communication of the inevitable to the public than about participatory purchasing' (cited in Tritter, Koivusalo, Ollila & Dorfman 2010, p. 102). Concluding from this, we can draw two interesting parallels. One is that this is for the $x^{th}$ time a serious and durable approach on raising accountability by involving locals is announced (cf. amongst others: CHCs, Local Voices, NHS Trusts, Foundation Trusts). The second is that every time well-worded statements including well-sounding buzz-words are employed they remain content-free to some degree, since otherwise no further campaigns only a few years later would be needed. It can, therefore, be assumed that they serve a strategic purpose to secure the support by the public and MPs.

provision, the actual topic of this book, has not been mentioned as a reason for inventing FT so far. So, why did the Labour government deviate from their Spanish role model?

As mentioned in Sect. 6.3 on page 136, the lack of democracy and accountability had lingered on in the NHS for years, which was criticised by a huge cross-party majority (cf. e. g. European Observatory on Health Care Systems 1999, p. 19; Health Committee 2003, p. 16; Tuohy 2003). In that context, one of my interviewees draw the conclusion that the attempt to higher accountability 'was partly rhetoric, but partly it was a genuine feeling' (interview 19).

In the context of FTs, democracy was spoken of as value *per se*, but it was also viewed as a vehicle to improve accountability to the communities. Both citizens and staff as an integral part of 'the public' (cf. e. g. Department of Health 2001c, p. 12) were seen to be able to monitor services and improve quality (see Sect. 6.3.2.3 on page 146; Department of Health 2001b, 2000, p. 105; Hogg 2008; Tritter, Koivusalo, Ollila & Dorfman 2010). Thus, interlinking the originally completely unrelated ideas of managerial leeway with giving patients and locals a say in how the hospitals are run seemed to many in the government's ranks a good way to resolve issues of both quality and accountability (Tritter et al. 2010, p. 98; cf. also interview 22). Consequently, the 'Health and Social Care (Community Health and Standards) Act 2003' was advertised as putting '[...] power and resources in the hands of local staff and local communities by strengthening primary care trusts and creating NHS foundation trusts' (Alan Milburn, Secretary of State for Health (Labour), 7 May 2003, House of Commons 2003b); cf. also Forster and Gabe 2008; Lewis and Hinton 2005; Robinson 2002, p. 507).[20] The arguments of the proponents of the bill ran accordingly along the same line:

> [P]atients will have for the first time a way to direct and shape the organisations and really to influence how they are run. Together with local management flexibility, this will mean that local decisions can be taken which will be more responsive to the needs of local patients. [...; The public] will have a say in how that hospital is run. Local people will have the opportunity to become involved in the running of their NHS foundation trust, with rights to elect or become governors. (Lord Warner, member of the House of Lords (Labour), 8 September 2003 (House of Lords 2003))

[20]A potential additional reason for taking in citizens was brought up by one interviewee, which unfortunately I could not confirm by any other sources so that it should be treated with caution:

'It has also to be said that it was a strong feeling [...] that the unions had too much say in the running of hospitals. [...] There was the feeling that this was a force which dragged down innovations and doing things differently and doing things in different ways. Like with most of these things there is probably a bit of truth on either side'. (interview 19)

Giving patients a say was in that sense also a vehicle to curtail the power of a certain actor in the field, in this case the trade unions. Supposing that this actually had been an issue at hand, the outcome, however, is ambiguous: On the one hand, staff do not really lose influence as staff most often forms part of the Governors' Council. On the other hand, decentralising negotiations to the local level takes somewhat from the union power. It might also be weakened by the increase of managerial competences and by amalgamating staff and other Governors into one council.

Though all parties and scholars welcomed the attempt to bring in a better reflection of local needs, perceiving public involvement as a democratic right (Lewis & Hinton 2008, p. 19) in principle, the government attracted heavy criticism in a number of respects. Next to worrying about the complexity and cost of maintaining registers of electors and elections (e. g. Frank Dobson, member for Holborn and St. Pancras (Labour); House of Commons 2003d), one very prominent point was that the NHS was going into the wrong direction and actually took a step back regarding accountability: Since Primary Care Trusts (PCT) had been established in 1999 by the Labour Government (cf. Sect. 6.3.2.3 on page 146; European Observatory on Health Care Systems 1999, p. 92) they purchased secondary care from hospitals for their patients. With the same act as FTs were established the commissioning rights of PCTs were extended. Another reform of extending this right was implemented from 2005 onwards, so that PCTs were the main commissioner of hospital services in the UK until the reform in 2012 (Boyle 2011, pp. xxiii, 23, 37; on 'payment by results' (PbR) cf. Department of Health Payment by Results team 2010; Foundation Trust Network 2009). Instead of giving the public a say in how and what services are commissioned and thereby following the adopted route of strengthening primary care, so ran the argument across *all* parties, hospital care was once again prioritised (cf. also Anderson, Florin, Gilliam & Mountford 2002; Callaghan & Wistow 2006; Lewis 2008; Milewa, Harrison, Ahmad & Tovey 2002; North and Werkö 2002; Callaghan & Wistow 2006):

> Where is the logic in applying any democratic leverage in the system not to the commissioners of health care, but to the providers? If there is a place for local democracy to be involved in the determination of the spending of health funds, it would have been far more logical to bring in election at the level of primary care trusts, where decisions about the commissioning of services, and therefore the spending of funds, will be taken. What is the point of introducing a democratic element into the providers—the hospitals? (Dr. Liam Fox, member of the House of Commons for Woodspring (Conservative), 8 May 2003, (House of Commons 2003e))[21]

Even though the emphasis is slightly different, the arguments running in both the Labour Party (cf. e. g. Kate Hoey, member of the House of Commons for Vauxhall (Labour), 7 May 2003 (House of Commons 2003b)) and among the Liberal Democrats were pretty similar:

> The best way of protecting and promoting the interests of patients is to give more power to those who are responsible for planning and buying services on their behalf, rather than to those who provide care. [...] The Government propose a sham democracy for foundation hospital trusts. (Dr. Evan Harris, member of the House of Commons for Oxford West and Abingdon (Liberal Democrats), 8 May 2003 (House of Commons 2003e))

[21] The question—like its answer—could have been posed in the Netherlands as well—but was not. This has to do with two fundamental factors inherent in the health care system: For one, the state and its subordinate authorities are the actual purchasers—and in many cases providers—of health care. While in this view, it is the task of the authority-like NHS as a whole, it is rather the individual user (or, depending on the view, GP) who asks for primary care services in the Netherlands. Second, the Dutch government view involvement in primary care as sufficient: Individual patient rights secure the possibility to meet GPs on more equal terms and enable patients to take further steps if they are not satisfied. Moreover, beneficiaries can often get involved in their health care insurance's governance, which is perceived to be a strong ally of patients towards health care providers.

The government's argument against this was as follows:

> As I have said to my hon. Friend in the past, I have no objection in principle to that. However, the issue is one of timing. She knows that in her area as well as mine, the primary care trusts are just up and running. They are new organisations and many of them are embryonic. [...] Frankly, they are not at a suitable stage of development to allow them to do that. Down the line, I have no objection whatever to the idea of applying the democratic or foundation principle to primary care trusts. (Secretary of State for Health Alan Milburn (House of Commons 2003c))

Interestingly, this did not prevent the government from implementing PPI in another new organisation.

### 6.4.4 The Legislation Process—Cross-Party Concerns

From a thorough analysis of the parliamentary minutes in both Houses of Parliament, a number of concerns can be derived which will be discussed in the following sections.

#### Two-Tier NHS

It was feared that the proposed freedoms would disadvantage NHS Trusts and other hospital types. This was based on two concerns: First, by creating much more attractive workplaces attracting more and better qualified staff, in particular nurses. Some even feared that FTs could afford higher pay so that they could 'poach staff' from other hospitals (George Howarth (member of the House of Commons for Knowsley, North and Sefton, East) 7 May 2003; House of Commons 2003b; Moore cf. also 2003). Whereas the first concern could not be ruled out during the debates, the second could be refuted by the fact that FTs are bound to paying the national wages so that no inequality would emerge in that respect (interview 19; House of Commons (2003b,e,d)).

Along the same line, it was, second, feared that FTs would cream-skim NHS resources. If they can borrow money from government and private financiers there would be no resources left for other hospitals so that, in turn, the uneven distribution of money would reinforce the inequality in hospital performance. At the same time, patients' preferences could drag resources away from poorer-performing hospitals (Health Committee 2003, p. 41). Both points would lead to a two-tiered health care system, it was argued. To some extent these apprehensions were unfounded, as the total amount of borrowing per hospital is capped no matter where the money stems from. This regulation makes sense in order to not overburden hospitals with debt. On the other hand it contradicts the act, since hospitals have no incentives to seek private capital beyond what is given by the government. This led others to maintain that '[t]he Government seem to have missed the point of the system in Spain and Sweden'. (Dr. Liam Fox, member of the House of Commons for Woodspring (Conservative), 8 May 2003 House of Commons (2003e)).

The government's main response to these concerns was threefold:

- FTs would become independent, but not without supervision, so that the system could not get out of control.
- A two-tierism could not evolve as all NHS Trusts would become FTs within five years.
- Pouring money into the system (and making the private financial market another source of borrowing) would cushion the costs of reorganisation and remedy the general shortage of money (Department of Health 2004b, p. 52).

### Implementation of Freedoms

A second field of conflict was about how much the announced freedom actually would be worth. To many, the independence of FTs was not safeguarded and therefore a bit of window-dressing:

> The freedoms that come with this Bill—they are not many, and some of them are illusory when the Bill is studied closely—are earned at a price. It is a high price: it is about hitting Whitehall targets, achieving the star rating, and going through the hoops that Ministers set. There is still control, but it is slightly less clear where that control exists. In truth, freedom is granted at the pleasure of the Secretary of State. (Siobhain McDonagh, member of the House of Commons for Mitcham and Morden (Labour), 19 November 2003 (House of Commons 2003a))

Other MPs were more specific and identified the relation between the Secretary of State for Health and the regulatory authority Monitor as a potential problem. In that context, FTs were depicted by the grace of the Secretary of State:

> The term 'independence' was not used in a sense that any of us would recognise. The regulator is appointed by the Secretary of State, he can be dismissed by the Secretary of State, his pay and conditions and pension are determined by the Secretary of State, he has to report to the Secretary of State on anything the Secretary of State deems fit, and he cannot grant foundation status except with the prior agreement of the Secretary of State. The system is to be run by the Secretary of State in all but name. (Dr. Liam Fox, member of the House of Commons for Woodspring (Conservative), 8 May 2003 (House of Commons 2003e))

To give justice to the Department of Health's intentions, we should, however, put this comment into context: Though control is definitively tight and definitively tighter than on the continent, which even made Bill Moyes, the chairman of Monitor, plead for less government interference (Cole 2005), every supervisory authority is in some sense controlled by politics. It is definitively not as independent as the rhetoric suggests, in British terms; however, the regulatory agency is relatively independent compared to the time prior to Foundation Trusts (cf. also the chapter 'Supervisory Authority—Assessments and Reform', 6.5.1 on page 168).

#### 6.4.4.1 Party Politics and Strategic Reasoning

> I am sorry, Mr. Deputy Speaker. It is always nice to look into the eyes of my hon. Friends when trying to be reassuring and tell them how it is. My only other choice is to look at that lot over there. *[Interruption.]* Well, one or two of them are not too bad, but some of them really do suck. (John Hutton, Minister of State for Health, 8 July 2003; House of Commons (2003d))

As mentioned above, criticism on the bill was not reserved to the opposition (see Sect. 6.4.3 on page 156). Accordingly, strategies to convince the own party ranks were applied.[22] Interestingly, this was an almost exclusive endeavour undertaken by the Labour party, which tried to build on past experience and portray the Conservative Party's intention as always wanting to smash the NHS. Against that threat, Labour MPs should unite, no matter how divided they might be over the details, making it a question of political ideology, not objective arguments:

> Friends who have concerns about certain aspects of the Bill that the Conservatives want it to be opposed for three simple reasons. First, so that they can claim that Labour could not reform the NHS; secondly, the NHS itself is therefore unreformable; thirdly, as a result, the very first principle of the NHS–care for free–must now go. Whatever they say, the Conservatives do not want NHS reform to happen–they want it to fail. That is their strategy for this Bill, but ours is about strengthening the national health service. (Alan Milburn, Secretary of State for Health, 7 May 2003 (House of Commons 2003b))

This sketchy stereotypical advertising prooved only partly successful, as there still was a larger number of Labour MPs who did not simply swallow it but rather continued to argue against their own government's and party's plans. One of the most prominent opponents was the former Secretary of State for Health:

> Unlike the Conservatives and the Liberal Democrats, many Labour Members have been against the foundation hospital proposal from the outset. We believe that it will be damaging and divisive, not just for the NHS, but for the Labour party as well. (Frank Dobson, member of the House of Commons for Holborn and St. Pancras (Labour) and former Secretary of State for Health (May 1997–October 1999), 19 November 2003 (House of Commons 2003a))

In contrast to many other occasions, this does not seem to have been mere rhetoric. The Minister of State for Health was reminded that the direction portrayed by him was not according to the Labour agenda as there had been no talk of FTs only half a year before:

[22]Though unrelated, I do not want to withhold the following repoartee: 'Mr. [Robert] Jackson: The Government are going in the right direction, but there is some poetic justice here, in that the Secretary of State is being attacked in the same terms as the Labour party used to attack us when we were trying to free up the system. On reflection, does he not think that we should take that into account when we conduct our debates on this matter in the House? He is facing exactly the same charges about privatisation and two-tierism as we did. Member of the House of Commons for Wantage (Conservative)

Mr. [Alan] Milburn: Support from the hon. Gentleman is about as welcome as myxomatosis in a rabbit hutch—although I hope that it does not have the same deadly consequences'. 7 May 2003 (House of Commons 2003b).

> May I remind my hon. Friend that there is also a very clear Labour agenda on the national health service? It was expressed by our party conference, and it is not foundation hospitals. (Dr. Desmond Turner, member of the House of Commons for Brighton, Kemptown (Labour), 19 November 2003 (House of Commons 2003a))

In addition to the aforementioned ‘coupling’, the legislation process also offered a nice example of ‘ideas as hooks’ (Maier 2003, pp. 47, 48): FTs as cooperatives or mutual organisations, after which also the FTs’ governance was claimed to have been modelled (Department of Health 2002a, pp. 10, 17–19). Judging from the parliamentary minutes and other sources, this attempt never received too much attention (cf. also Boyle 2005, p. 7; Health Committee 2003, p. 14; Klein 2003, p. 174). However, it seems to have been an idea that many found appealing among the Labour MPs:

> There was a lot of talk at the time about Foundation Trusts could become mutual organisations, not like limited companies, but they could model themselves on cooperatives and mutual organisations. And that was a deliberate attempt—because there was a lot of resistance in the House of Commons on the Labour side to setting up these FTs, but there were quite a few—almost all Labour MPs were members of cooperative societies, coops [...]. I do not think there was a serious attempt to turn these things into mutuals. I think that was a kind of politic of gloss that was put on to try to confuse some of my colleagues. (interview 19)

#### 6.4.4.2 Reception Outside Parliament

> If I receive, as Chairman of the Health Committee, one clear message from national health service staff, it is that the Government have delivered record, massive levels of funding, to their great credit. The message to me is: now let us get on with the job; the last thing that we need is more restructuring. (David Hinchliff, member for Wakefield 1987– 2005 (Labour); (House of Commons 2003c))

As shown, the proposal of Foundation Trusts was highly controversial within both Houses of Parliament, but also outside of parliament the reception was divided: The King’s Fund called for a new, independent type of hospital at about the same time when the Labour government threw in its proposal (Pook 2002). The most positive group were consultants, but even they were somewhat ambivalent. While they were keen to get some more managerial freedoms, hearings in the Health Commission revealed that even they were not asking for FTs (Health Committee 2003, 24; interviews 19 and 22). Nurses were not opposed, but not too happy about it, either (Royal College of Nursing—Policy Unit 2005). The overall impression left is that the NHS was weary of reforms and reorganisations, aiming at political goals, but not changing anything for the workforce. In that context, the involvement of citizens was sometimes also seen as an additional burden in the ‘super hospital’ to come (Boyle 2005, p. 7). Another point among staff and patient organisations alike was that with ‘patient forums’ once again an accepted and an apparently working concept of PPI was eliminated.

Even the academic circle was divided: As in the political realm, some of them highlighted the potential benefits, while others were sceptical about the implementation as well as the promised independence and feared tierism of the NHS and too much competition, a repeated disaster of the 'internal market' (cf. e. g. Allsop & Baggott 2004; Clarke & Newman 2005; Dewar 2003; Dixon, LeGrand & Smith 2003; Florin & Dixon 2004; Gosling 2009; Klein 2003, 2004; LeGrand, Mays & Mulligan 1998; Lewis & Hinton 2008; McGauran 2002; Mohan 2003; Morone & Kilbreth 2003; Moore 2003; Morrell 2006; O'Dowd 2006, 2008; Palmer 2005a,b; Robinson 2002; Palmer 2005b, 4–6).

Beyond the professional public, the discourse hardly got out to the common public, which in part is owing to the fact that it was one reform among many and other parts of the bill received more attention.

## 6.5 Appraisal of Involvement in Foundation Trusts

Now, having touched upon the steps on the way to and the most important reasons for the introduction of Foundation Trust hospitals, the remaining chapters shall be dedicated to an attempted appraisal of the PPI in FTs.

In general, looking at the performance of FTs, the government's goal of a managerially more independent and financially sound health care seems to have been achieved (Bojke & Goddard 2010; House of Commons Health Committee 2008a,b; cf. also Àlvarez & Durán 2013; Monitor 2014c). Some of the FT hospitals even fare so well that they have been planning to establish branches abroad (Bojke & Goddard 2010, pp. i, 3; Clover 2011; Moorfields Eye Hospital NHS Foundation Trust 2010). This, however, might for better or worse also be the result of Monitor's selection and needs to be closely watched. It remains also to be seen how performance develops after the recent cuts on the NHS budget. As more attention has been paid to finances of FTs and less to quality issues, evidence is rather thin. However, the existing data suggest that, according to the quality indicators, FTs perform better than non-FTs (Bojke & Goddard 2010, pp. 6–7; cf. also Day 2006), while patient surveys usually show high satisfaction with services. The average FT hospital scored 3.05 on Monitor's four-point 'continuity of service' rating, whereas the 'governance rating' is between the categories 'no evident concerns' and one that basically is investigating somewhat deeper into potential concerns (date of reference 19 December 2014; own calculations based on Monitor 2015).[23] There were 17 FTs in which the continuity of services were under 'significant' or 'material risk' and 26 for which Monitor takes 'enforcement action in special measures' (date of reference 19 December 2014; own calculations based on Monitor 2015).

Before turning to FTs themselves, however, some attention will be paid to the authorisation and regulation authority.

[23]The category is labelled 'Monitor is requesting further information following multiple breaches of the A&E target and a continuity of services risk rating of 2, before deciding next steps'.

### 6.5.1 Supervisory Authority—Assessments and Reform

> Well, it is at arm's length, but the British system has a tradition of having these semi-independent bodies where they know what the government wants. They are not going to go off for a completely different direction. So, if they stick to the initial brief, they can be fairly independent within that brief. And what happens as if there is a big falling out then the chairman and/ or the chief executive resign and they get somebody else in. But it was by the standard of many British government institutions pretty independent. (interview 19)

Monitor—or in its original full title: Monitor—Independent Regulator of NHS Foundation Trusts—became the newly founded supervisory authority specifically for FTs. Initially, the term 'Monitor—the independent regulator of Foundation Trusts' was almost used as a brand's name and mentioned several times in full length in every public document as if to beseech its factual independence. After a reform a reform of Monitor in 2012, the term was exchanged for 'Monitor—Making the health sector work for patients' putting greater emphasis on control again. With the reform of 2012 Monitor became also the supervisory authority for NHS Trusts, got new tasks, and a changed role as supervising authority. On 1 April 2016 Monitor was incorporated into 'NHS Improvement' (NHS Improvement 2016a,c). This changed the emphasis from control to support for improvement. NHS Improvement is addressing the overall NHS again. Just like Monitor tasks of NHS Improvement are to advise applicant hospitals, grant FT status, regulate as well as evaluate and supervise FTs. If it deems the performance of an FT below a specific threshold, it can eventually take over everyday business until the problem is resolved (Department of Health 2002a, p. 29). This could be observed in numerous examples over the last couple of years (cf. e.g. Monitor 2013b,c, 2014b; Bojke & Goddard 2010, pp. 11–12; cf. also Monitor 2008, 2014a). This leads to the situation that 'putting hospitals in[to] local hands' and furthering local accountability only works as long as the hospitals are well performing.

However, parallel to the organisational changes monitoring and assessment procedures developed. While in its very early days an adapted version of the overall three star rating of NHS Trusts was employed this was replaced by a five-point scale for economic risk rating and a four-point scale for governance ratings. With the reform of 2012 the system changed to a four-point compound assessment scale for economic risk rating and a three-point rating for the assessment of the FT's governance (for more information on the ratings of FTs cf. Monitor 2013d, 2008, 2010c; cf. Kmietowicz 2004; Williams 2011). After being incorporated into NHS Improvement in 2016 the completely new 'Single Oversight Framework' was introduced, the fourth assessment tool in the by then 12 years history of FTs, which, yet again, cannot be compared to its predecessor (NHS Improvement 2016c). This makes comparisons difficult and obscures quality shortages for citizens.

Though more than a decade has passed since the establishment of FTs, it is still subject of debate as to what exactly should happen with a hospital that is technically bankrupt (cf. Monitor 2010a). In general, the issue of assessing FTs even led Monitor's chairman early on to state in 2005 that 'determining whether a trust was failing was "gloriously ill defined" (cited in Cole 2005). Early on already, scholars like e. g. Palmer (2005a) and Edwards and Lewis (2008) called attention to the paradoxical situation that emerges when a FT continuously fails the set standards and is about to go bankrupt (cf. also Wilmot 2004): Being a 'corporation' they should go out of business, being an integral part and tax-funded property of the NHS, however, government cannot allow to simply close down hospitals. Hence, though the likelihood is assessed to be rather small (Oliver 2005, S77) what is going to happen in such a case and who is going to pay for the loss?

These are merely a few of the reasons why regulations are under constant revision in an attempt to adapt to emerging problems. Next to an overhaul of the regulatory framework, section 15 of the 'Health Act 2009' newly introduced the possibility of de-authorisation of FTs (cf. also 'National Health Service Act 2006' section 52b–52e; Secretary of State for Health 2010). So far, however, these cases have been mostly solved by mergers by economically stronger FTs (cf. e. g. Monitor 2013a; Co-operation and Competition Panel 2013; ELFS Shared Services 2014), once again a development similar to the school sector (interview 19). The government's point of view seems to be as follows: The economic success of an FT is to a large part owing to good management. A prospering FT, in turn, has proven its managerial superiority by success, which then will spill over to the hospitals taken over.

Basically, one of the main reasons for the change of Monitor's role in 2012 was in particular the revelation of unacceptable practices and intolerable circumstances at the foundation trust hospital Mid Staffordshire (often abbreviated to Mid Staffs). The hospital had been granted FT status only several months beforehand, and Monitor's assessment of governance and performance attested good to best marks. They gave little indication for the dreadful state of affairs the hospital was in, with a sheer neglect of patients and high death-rates (cf. Francis 2010a,b; Gosling 2009, p. 6), which leads one of my interviewees to conclude that obviously finance rating was given much more weight than quality of care and governance (interview 19). After an accumulation of incidents, complaints, and inexplicable deaths, the developments were first covered by the local, soon by the national press and caused a national as well as public uproar and led to demands to take action. Being a *national* health system it also reminded the collective consciousness of similar cases in the past amongst which as two of the most severe can be counted the case of Ely hospital with 'cruel ill-treatment' as common practice (Howe 1969) and the case of the Bristol Royal Infirmary where ethically questionable practices such as the removal of an estimated 16,000 organs of late persons without (full) consent occurred over several decades (Department of Health, Department for Education and Employment, Home Office 2001). The occurrences at Mid Staffs caused an investigation to take a closer look at the documentation and incidences. The report concluded that the underlying figures to apply for FT status had in part been falsified without Monitor realising it. Overall, the 'acceptance of poor standards' of quality or even lack of care, food, hygiene, and other services led to misdiagnosis, delays, injuries, indignant behaviour, and premature death (Francis 2010a,b).

The case, in turn, also illustrated very impressively that Monitor's tools, namely reliance on process data provided by the organisation itself, were relatively inapt to provide the necessary information for a proper assessment of the performance of hospitals. As a practical consequence, Monitor's assessment became more cautious. Overall, the average rating decreased, which probably is not solely owing to a worse result, but also caused by a changed way of assessing FTs. It seems that inquiries and investigations are started already at an earlier phase, too. This applies to both developing plans to improve local policies and finances in collaboration with FTs at risk of failing as well as taking over their governance in more severe cases. Another concrete consequence of the occurrences at Mid Staffordshire was the claim to involve the staff more closely in the governance of FTs. So, from having a rather formal part in involvement while the focus was on patient and citizen involvement their role was strengthened. However, according to one of my interviewees it is still a bit of an interpretation and therefore not difficult to somewhat smarten statistics and reports in order to trigger a good rating (interview 17; for an evaluation of the impact of Monitor cf. frontier economics (2009) and Williams (2011).).[24]

## 6.5.2 *Implementation at the Foundation Trusts*

After this look at the supervising authority, the following chapters turn to an appraisal of the implementation of PPI in FTs. A number of aspects are worth taking a closer look at. To the best of my knowledge, no encompassing evaluation has been conducted so far. The studies published so far are fragmented, highlight only specific aspects, and rely on process data, Monitor's rating criteria, and a handful of case studies with rather anecdotal evidence. This makes the interviews of this study counting half the number of interviews of the latest official report in FTs alone all the more important. Despite the small grounds upon which to base an assessment, they suffice to say that some problems stand out.

### 6.5.2.1 The Interplay Between Monitor and Foundation Trusts

While most researchers and interviewees seemed to agree to the role and independence of Monitor, their assessment of the independence of FTs varies more considerably. Overall, different expectations about and different dimensions of

[24]'So I think, again, we talk about strong accountability, but I do not actually think we have this. [...] Are they actually looking at the right things? Because you have to ask yourself: Mid Staffordshire they were doing their quarterly reports in, their figures were fine, their governance was fine, and what is actually happening on the ground? [...] How can ever a receptionist making clinical decisions on an accident emergency patient. [...] Because you have got all these lists of indicators. But it is very easy for a trust to manipulate figures and to say: Right, we have got to reach green on these indicators and this is what we are going to hit it. It is again all about ticking boxes, making sure you are meeting targets but actually not looking what is on the neck'. (interview 17).

independence can be discerned as the following quotations show. The first refers to regulation regarding the documentation of every action, the membership figures as well as the obligation to provide certain services, which overall is experienced as far too tight to be called independent. In addition, it juxtaposes three different states of (in-)dependence: One prior to becoming an FT with only little managerial freedom, one with the relatively most independence during the first time after becoming an FT, and one after the Mid Staffordshire scandal when managerial independence was curtailed once again:

> As how independent do you experience... (laughter) [...] They [Monitor; the author] have been burnt. So, what is actually happening now is that it is going back. [...] It all comes full circle: Foundation Trusts were kind of left at arm's length but now they have to be pulled back. (interview 17)

Others, in contrast, rather emphasised the comparatively large scope of discretion, financially as regarding own priority settings:

> FTs can make their own decisions. They are free of government control... We built new hospitals here in the north-east in our trust. Even before we became a FT there were plans in place to approve our hospital. [...; I]t has taken 20 years to plan a hospital at one time [...]—and we built [...; name of a purpose built hospital branch] in two years. [...] So, I think that is that local focus. (interview 18)
>
> They introduced more financial freedom. In fact they have not made use of them all that much, but they have a lot more freedom to borrow and to invest. And that is why it is talked about relaxation of central control by the Department of Health. (interview 19)

Similar to the assessment of Monitor, an overall summary could read that FT hospitals enjoy considerably more managerial and financial freedoms compared to other types of NHS hospitals, but that they are by no means free to do whatever they want. Instead they are still tightly monitored and increasingly regulated. This is in line with the few reports existing on the topic (Bojke & Goddard 2010; O'Dowd 2008; Ham & Hunt 2008; Ipsos MORI 2008; Day 2005).

#### 6.5.2.2 Membership Numbers, Governors, and Representativity

> Most people are only really interested in the hospital when they've got a reason to use it or a relative has. I think people only really get involved when they see it affecting them. I'm not sure how far people do want a voice in what happens in the hospital. I'm not sure that the need to have a voice or the wish to have a voice is all that strong. (Ipsos MORI 2008, p. 34)

Now, at least in the context of this book, managerial freedom is only of importance if citizens can exert influence on the management. There are a number of points referring to this question. Monitor stipulated representativity of the membership. According to the legal text, the membership ought to be representative for the served public and staff constituencies ('Health and Social Care (Community Health and Standards) Act 2003' section 6, 37). However, questions remain what the constituency of a university hospital serving patients from all over the country, of a hospital in a larger city with several FTs, or a hospital close to the Scottish or Welsh border is? Even if the catchment area is geographically confined: How would you deal with a situation where the Council of Governors cannot agree on topics due to noncohesive needs of the population in the served area as e. g. in the metropolitan areas (cf. Health Committee 2003, pp. 19–20; House of Commons 2003b,e,d,a; House of Lords 2003)? Hence, sometimes it simply seems impossible to achieve the goal of representativity, as responses from the interviews reveal:

> [W]hen we are discussing about the differences in demographic you see immediately how our recruitment campaign in a white, affluent area is not going to be the same as a recruitment campaign in a deprived area with high ethnic minorities. [...] For example, the gender split across both boroughs is about equal: 49 : 51 male-female, roughly half and half. And yet, our membership, I would say, is probably about 65 % female. [...] And also, you have to look at it: What is the actual benefit of being a member? Well, at the moment you get a newsletter and you can elect governors [...]. (interview 17)

Nevertheless, no matter how adverse circumstances are, the representativity of the council of governors is required:

> This is one of the key things that the regulator cares about that the membership is representative. The problem with making the council representative is we have no say in who is elected. So if they want to elect four white people in [...; one of the boroughs], even though it is 65 % Asian, there is not a lot we can do about it. (interview 17)

In order to tackle this problem, one trend set in around the year 2010, when Monitor required FTs to increase their membership targets. Targets are set separately for each different membership group, in order to prevent a mismatch in the respective proportions. However, both reports and my interviewees spoke of considerable difficulties attracting a larger number of people to become members as they do not see advantages making the effort worthwhile (Ham and Hunt 2008, p. 16;Ipsos MORI 2008, p. 34; interviews 16–18). Against that background some targets seem to be a bit out of proportion. One of the FTs in which I conducted an interview agreed to a membership number of 30,000 by late March 2011. Only shortly after the negotiations for this target, Monitor decided to more than triple the target to 100,000 for 2011 (interview 18), something that even with the then implemented opt-out membership is extremely difficult to achieve.

#### 6.5.2.3 Governors and Their Role in Foundation Trusts

> When I talked to them they wanted to have garden parties and in the countryside picnics together. [...] And they all agreed that it was a good idea to go to flower shows in the summer. (interview 16)

The difficulties with regard to a fuzzy definition of what constitutes the membership continue when it comes to the election and role of governors. The examples mentioned vary extremely, work seems to depend on few individuals and range from very active and successful instances of councils to those that are only held together by the local membership manager (interviews 14–18; Ham and Hunt 2008, p. 14). Reservations some interviewees in FTs shared were that governors had no idea of what their tasks should be and that it is difficult to make them focus on the broader image and strategy instead of specific figures (interviews 16–18; Bojke and Goddard 2010, p. 3). Moreover, though most governors seem to be very committed, at the same time, they seem to have difficulties to connect back to their constituency and sometimes do not get active beyond the narrowly-defined formal rights—an all too close parallel to the Netherlands. As there, the boards also fulfil a social role for their members. On either side of the channel, a varying lack of understanding between managers and governors can be observed: The main thing for management is to focus on figures and strategy, while for governors it is apparently important to also have the social component, which makes the office more attractive and the bond to their hospital tighter.

One essential point for a successful organisation is a clear role definition of functionaries. It is quite telling in this context that the 'Health and Social Care (Community Health and Standards) Act 2003' meticulously describes how the council is to be elected and what conditions have to be met; it also mentions some formal competences of the Governors. In contrast, however, it leaves the role of Governors paradoxically vague (cf. also Bojke & Goddard 2010, p. 2; Lewis 2005; Mills 2007; Abbott, Smith, Procter & Iacovou 2008; Ipsos MORI 2008; Lewis & Hinton 2008; Monitor—Independent Regulator of NHS Foundation Trusts 2008b). This leads to the contradiction that

> [o]n the one hand, as the Secretary of State argued, 'you cannot have the Board of Governors interfering in the day to day decisions of the hospital otherwise the thing will never run'. On the other hand, the Board of Governors is ultimately accountable to the membership for the stewardship of the Trust and must be able to make an objective and meaningful contribution to the way in which it is run. (Health Committee 2003, p. 20)

The reaction from official side in order to better define their role came rather late (cf. Monitor—Independent Regulator of NHS Foundation Trusts 2008b; Monitor 2009; Central Manchester University Hospitals, NHS Foundation Trust 2010; Monitor 2010c; cf. also Mills 2007; Chambers, Harvey, Mannion, Bond & Marshal 2013; Morrell 2006, p. 374). Beyond very general brochures, the impression left is that finding out about their roles is an interdependent process between the members of the management, the governors, and potentially the input from their constituencies (cf. interviews 14–18), especially as the official Foundation Trust Network (FTN) is felt not to provide help (interview 16). Getting there is, as in the Netherlands, no easy task (cf. Gregory 2012) since, as my interviews suggest, an organisation needs time to adapt to new structures and improving involvement (interviews 16–18; Bojke and Goddard 2010, p. i). Therefore, the early reports, conducted only about one year after the introduction of FTs (Lewis 2005; Healthcare Commission 2005; Foundation Trust Network 2006; Gosling 2009) might be misleading.

In accordance with other research (Ham & Hunt 2008, p. 10) the size of the council of governors in the hospitals researched here varies between roughly 20 and 70 (cf. also interview 15–18). Right now, there seem to be two opposite movements: One part of FTs attempts to increase the size of their Governors Council in order to raise variety and representativity, while another reduces the size in order to be able to discuss topics in more depth and to more easily reach a consensus. The reported election turnout varies between 15 % and 55 % (Ham & Hunt 2008, p. 18; interviews 15, 16, and 18; cf. also Bojke & Goddard 2010, p. 2), while results between 20 % and 35 % seem to be common. Overall, it is to be wondered whether we should speak of PPI and general democracy in the sense of the law or whether it makes more sense to speak of user involvement as in the Netherlands. Some of the interviewees supported the idea to rather opt to be representative for the membership and their service users instead of the constituency (especially interview 18).

In the meantime, many elections are uncontested (cf. e. g. South Tyneside Council on behalf of South Tyneside Foundation Trust 2010; cf. also Cornforth 2003; Klein 2003; Wilmot 2004; Greener & Powell 2008; Kuhlmann, Allsop & Saks 2009). Furthermore, sometimes not all seats in the council of governors can be filled (interview 18), a problem that is likely to exacerbate over the next years to come, because as in the Netherlands a professionalisation of governors is setting in England, too (interviews 16–18). In particular in the field of mental care two distinct factors seem to be at work: The long-term nature of treatment, as opposed to acute care, works in favour of more involvement (interviews 16–19). At the same time, no one wants to be associated with mental care, which is a major impediment (interview 17).

#### 6.5.2.4 Interplay Between Governors and Boards and Governors' Involvement

> It is very hard to get a director of finance, who has worked in the NHS for 20 years, to write something that a governor can understand. (interview 17)

Even though all these points are important and the problems associated with them need to be addressed, the main question in the context of this study, however, remains: How much influence can the council of governors exert? This includes the cooperation between the board of directors and the council of governors. This is all the more interesting in view of the price tag, which is considerably higher than its counterpart in the Netherlands. It is clear that citizen involvement does not come for free, but in view of the estimated additional costs for the administration of membership and election registers, additional posts as membership managers and governance of approximately £ 200,000 on average per year and FT (appr. 266,650 €; £ 1 ≈ 1.333 € (1 February 2015), £ 1 ≈ 1.119 € (23 February 2017); House of Commons Health Committee 2008b, p. 21), it should be ensured that involvement is more than mere rhetoric. Levying a membership fee of e. g. £1 per member as many FTs do might help FTs financially but probably is the wrong symbol in this context.

Next to the economic success, one of the more encompassing reports draws the conclusion that... '[t]he notion that FTs are more democratic in nature and are more accountable to local people has not really been supported by the research evidence. However, some FTs appear to be taking seriously the challenge of involving local communities in local health issues' (Bojke & Goddard 2010, p. 3). This is in accordance with the overall evaluation by one of my interviewees. According to him, the will to really involve citizens is lacking, while the focus on finances and professionalisation results in less involvement:

> Well, actually nobody really wants to give the public proper involvement in the NHS. There is a lot of lip-service paid. But what happens with foundation trusts now: When there are vacancies on foundation trust boards they tend to put businessmen and -women on the board, people who understand finances and understand some business management rather than people who have an interest in the community. There are very few new appointments in the last two years—probably even more than that—to foundation trust boards of people who have got involvement in the community, because they really focus on their financial matters.
>
> And these membership schemes on foundation trusts, most of them do not really work. [...] They are supposed to have elections amongst the membership, but some of them have a quite small membership, some of them have a quite large membership that is scattered over a huge area. So there is no real cohesion in the elections. And they elect one person to the board. I know quite a few, one or two of them that say that they make their voice heard, but most of them admit that they do not have much effect on the running of the hospital. (interview 19)

The narratives of the interviewees in the FTs somewhat complement but also contrast this view. Beyond the aforementioned problems of role definition (cf. Sect. 6.5.2.3 on page 172), they also mention problems in the adaptation to the new roles of the management and an increased workload owing to the necessary processes of communication and coordination between governors and management (interviews 15–18). They also all agree in that the public/appointed governors hardly attend any meetings, which impedes the collective work and lets them describe the cooperation with other institutions as rather poor.

Boyle (2005) reminds us that membership organisations do not deliver good services *per se*, but that their outcome requires a common understanding of the problems at hand and a common goal about what should be achieved. Overall, however, despite the problems the collaboration between the board of directors and the governors body is described as '[...] a good relationship. And on the whole they set out from the outset to welcome the governors to be inclusive' (interview 18). The conclusion drawn resembles exactly the one drawn in the Netherlands: There are some problems to be tackled, but FTs are undergoing a learning curve with things turning to the better. Most of the interviewees state that of course there are limitations to which extent the management can implement all demands made by the governors, but that in general the management takes governors seriously, is willing to discuss matters with the governors, and to follow their vote. Though there is some variation in activity, all of them mentioned the work in several subcommittees, a gathering frequency of between six times per year to twice a month, and a meeting frequency of the governors and the management of six times a year to monthly (interviews 15–18), whereby the non-executive directors are naturally slightly less involved. Overall, they portray the governors' work as highly influential. Reading between the lines, this is not only accredited to the governors' active proposals, but also to the very fact that management is confronted with 'real people'—in contrast to the professional board of non-executives: 'I think it is good for our directors to meet what are actually normal people and these normal people in the form of our elected governors. And they have the chance to challenge' (interview 16).

Taking these accounts together, they yield a not only mixed, but contrasting picture. A preliminary appraisal of PPI could, therefore, read that in terms of accountability and influence on decisions in health care, it is a step forward compared to previous arrangements. However, whether it is an improvement compared to the arrangements in place some 20 years ago or in absolute terms new wine in old wineskins still needs to manifest itself.

## 6.6 Summary: Involvement—a Long-Grown Idea Pursued

> One of the main criticisms is fragmentation; the patient or citizen is faced with a bewildering array of institutions whose roles are poorly understood, even by experts. Indeed, the area is now full of confusing acronyms—PALS, ICAS, PPIFs, CPPIH—adding to public incomprehension. Even ministers appeared confused about the various responsibilities of these bodies. (Baggott 2004, pp. 330-331)

This chapter has shown that 'public and patient involvement' (PPI) in England is no new phenomenon, but has existed for the greatest part of the 20$^{th}$ century. However, in order to show that they care about the NHS and that their policies are more feasible than those of the political opposition, politicians seem to be tempted to permanent reform and reorganisations, which according to Walshe (2003, pp. 106, 108) not only miss their set aims but are costly and 'commonly circular', too. In an impressive chronology he lists 18 health care reforms during the period from 1982 to 2003 and shows 'that there has been some kind of organizational upheaval in some part of the NHS almost every year for the past twenty years, and that the pace of change seems to grow ever faster' (Walshe 2003, p. 106). This trend reached the peak of absurdity, when 'health forums' were abolished by the same government before they were implemented in order to make room for Foundation Trust hospitals (FTs). Overall, the development has been path changing in several ways: With FTs, Labour introduced a new form of hospitals, that does not follow the path beaten so far, which also have a number of wider implications. Furthermore, despite the repeated promise to convert all hospitals to FTs within a reasonable period of time, meanwhile a two-tier system of hospitals has emerged—something that Labour always claimed to prevent.

Having said that, the reform in question ('Health and Social Care (Community Health and Standards) Act 2003') brought a larger number of changes such as improved dental and paediatric services, an huge intermediate boost of funding, and a change in the remuneration of GP services. Foundation Trusts (FTs) were only one aspect of the whole reform. Combining both improvement and the creation of FTs at the same time is a good empirical example for strategic 'coupling'. This chapter could show that basically raising efficiency and the quality of services was the main driver of the reform—not PPI. To accomplish this aim, decentralisation to single hospitals—in contrast to regional or local authorities as attempted before—and increasing the scope of financial and managerial decision making was chosen as the instrument of choice.

The unusually quick legislation process without green and white papers was definitely extremely controversial, not only regarding the usual rights of the House of Lords and considerations within the ranks of the opposition parties or the NHS, but also within the Labour party's banks: Despite a comfortable majority of the government, the bill was enacted only with a tiny majority based on the Scottish and Welsh MPs, whose constituencies are not affected by the act. Concerning the theoretical framework, the case is a nice example of 'institution' or 'ideational learning' from Spanish hospitals which were adapted to British needs. Furthermore, besides 'coupling' of highly demanded improvements we can detect 'ideas as hooks' with the popular comparison of FTs as mutuals. While even the former Labour secretary of health opposed the bill, Tony Blair and Alan Milburn can be viewed as the driving forces of the project. Despite their rhetorical renunciation of market-like solutions and their accusing the Tories as the gravediggers of the NHS, an integral part of their reforms is formed by financial freedom and competition, which lets the difference between an improved internal market and the present forms grow rather thin. Looking at the peculiarities of the British political system, it seems very unlikely that the reform would have been enacted in any other of the four countries in this study: Even when having a strong cross-party opposition, the 'first past the post' election system and the unitary and largely centrally administered state strengthens the position of the government and leaves it with few veto-points.

Given the complexity of the reform and owing to the very heterogeneous local implementation an overall assessment is difficult. While many good arguments can be made for a relative success of FTs in terms of finances and performance, their function as membership organisations can be seen critically: The interviews confirmed that time is needed to get everyone accustomed to the new structures and roles, but described FTs as being on the right track. However, they also revealed concerns and problems, which overall match with the picture drawn by the few anecdotal official assessments. This is in line with Bojke's (2010, p. 3) conclusion that FTs, though often concerned with local involvement, are not more democratic than other types of hospitals.

Given the unsystematic approach to PPI, it comes as no surprise that only shortly after the introduction of FTs 'choice' became a new hobby horse in politics, leading to the half-hearted pursuance of voice and exit as two parallel agendas (Tritter, Koivusalo, Ollila & Dorfman 2010, pp. 99, 110, 112; cf. also LeGrand 1997, 2007). In addition, only a few years after the reform funding was substantially curtailed again, many positive outcomes owing to increased personnel were removed.

## References


Abbott, S., Smith, R., Procter S. & Iacovou, N. (2008). Primary Care Trusts: What is the role of boards? *Public Policy and Administration 23*, 43–59.

Allsop, J., & Baggott, R. (2004). NHS in England from modernisation to marketisation. In N. Ellison, L. Bauld, & M. Powell (Eds.), *Social Policy Review* (pp. 29–44). Beverly Hills: Sage.

Àlvarez, A., & Durán, A. (2013). Muddling Through the economic crisis. In D. McDaid, S. Merkur, & A. Maresso (Eds.), *Eurohealth—Governing Public Hospitals* (Vol. 19, 1st ed., pp. 8–11). Quarterly of the European Observatory on Health Systems and Policies. London: LSE Health.

Anderson, W., Florin, D., Gilliam, S., & Mountford, L. (2002, February). *Every Voice Counts: Primary Care Organisations and Public Involvement*. London: King's Fund.

Appleby, J., Harrison, A., & Devlin, N. (2003). *What is the Real Cost of More Patient Choice?* London: Kings Fund.

Ashton, T., Mays, N., & Devlin, N. (2005). Continuity through change: The rhetoric and reality of health reform in New Zealand. *Social Science & Medicine, 61*(2), 253–262.

Baggott, R. (2004). *Health and Health Care in Britain* (3rd ed.). Houndsmill, Basingstoke/ New York: Palgrave.

Baggott, R., Allsop, J., & Jones, K. (2004). Representing the repressed? Health consumer groups and the national policy process. *Policy & Politics, 32*(3), 317–331.

Baggott, R., Allsop, J., & Jones, K. (2005). *Speaking for Patients and Carers*. Houndsmill/ New York: Palgrave.

Bakke, T., & de Vibe, M. (2009). *...med pasientens øyne...—Brukermedvirkning—et gjennombrudd for ledere, medarbeidere og pasienter* (T. Konsmo, Ed.). Rapport fra kvalitetsprosjektet— Norsk sykepleierfobund. Oslo: kunskapssenteret.

Barnes, M., Harrison, S. H., Mort, M., Shardlow, P., & Wistow G. (1999). The new management of community care: User groups, citizenship and co-production. In G. Stoker (Ed.), *The New Management of British Local Governance*. London: Macmillan Press.

Bartlett, W. (1994). Die Reform des britischen Gesundheitssystems von 1990—Privatisierung, non-profit-Trusts und Käufer-Anbieter-Verträge. In B. Blanke (Ed.), *Krankheit und Gemeinwohl. Gesundheitspolitik zwischen Staat, Sozialversicherung und Medizin*. Opladen: Leske + Budrich.

Baur, R., Heimer, A., & Wieseler S. (2003). *Reformen im Gesundheitswesen* (J. Böcken, M. Butzlaff, & A. Esche, Eds.). Gütersloh: Verlag Bertelsmann Stiftung.

Beresford, P., & Holden, C. (2000). We have choices: Globalisation and welfare user movements. *Disability & Society, 15*(7), 973–989.

Bevan, G., Karanikolos, M., Exley J., Nolte, E., Connolly S., & May N. (2014, April). *The Four Health Systems of the United Kingdom: How Do They Compare?*. London: Nuffield Trust.

Black, N. (1986, October). Consumer representation in the NHS. *British Medical Journal, 293*, 976.

Bojke, C., & Goddard, M. (2010, September). *Foundation Trusts: A Retrospective Review*. York: Centre for Health Economics, University of York.

Boyle, S. (2005, June). *What Foundation Trusts Mean for the NHS*. LSE Health and Social Care Discussion Paper No. 18. London.

Boyle, S. (2011). *United Kingdom (England): Health System Review*. Health Systems in Transition. Copenhagen: WHO Regional Office for Europe on behalf of the European Observatory on Health Systems and Policies.

Callaghan, G. D., & Wistow G. (2006). Publics, patients, citizens, consumers? Power and decision making in primary health care. *Public Administration, 84*(3), 583–601.

Central Manchester University Hospitals, NHS Foundation Trust. (2010, July). *Foundation Trust Governor Role Information Pack*. Manchester.

Chambers, N., Harvey, G., Mannion, R., Bond, J., & Marshal, J. (2013, October). *Towards a Framework for Enhancing the Performance of NHS Boards: A Synthesis of the Evidence About Board Governance, Board Effectiveness and Board Development* (Vols. 1). Health Services and Delivery Research. London: National Institute for Health Research.

Christensen, T., & Lægrid, P. (2010). *Reforming Norway's Welfare Administration*. Stockholms: Statskontoret.

Clarke, J., & Newman, J. (2005). What's in a name? New Labour's citizen-consumers and the remaking of public services. Manchester.

Clasen, J., & Clegg, D. (2006). Beyond activation reforming European unemploment—Protection systems in post-industrial labour markets. *European Societies, 8*(4), 527–553.

Clover B. (2011, March 10). Moorfields abandons Abu Dhabi expansion plan. *Health Service Journal*. https://www.hsj.co.uk/moorfields-eye-hospital-nhs-foundation-trust/moorfields-abandons-abu-dhabi-expansion-plan/5026675.article

Cole, A. (2005, October). Foundation trust regulator calls for less government interference. *British Medical Journal, 331*(7523), 985.

Co-operation and Competition Panel. (2013, September 20). *Merger of parts of University Hospitals Bristol NHS foundation trust and north bristol NHS trust*. London: Monitor.

Cornforth, C. (Ed.). (2003). *The Governance of Public and Non-Profit Organizations: What Do Boards Do?* London: Routledge.

Coulter, A. (2000, May). Stärkung des Einflusses von Patienten, Verbrauchern und Bürgern—Die Effektivität politischer Instrumente. In H. Ettischer & K. Salice-Stephan (Eds.), *Bürger beteiligung im Gesundheitswesen—eine länderübergreifende Herausforderung—Ideen, Ansätze und internationale Erfahrungen* (Chap. 5.1, 10, pp. 138–151). Forschung und Praxis der Gesundheitsförderung. Köln: Bundeszentrale für gesundheitliche Aufklärung (BZgA).

Dabbs, C. (2000, May). Eine staatliche innovation: Community health councils in England und Wales. In H. Ettischer & K. Salice-Stephan (Eds.), *Bürgerbeteiligung im Gesundheitswesen—eine länderübergreifende Herausforderung—Ideen, Ansätze und internationale Erfahrungen* (Chap. 5.3. 10, pp. 157–165). Forschung und Praxis der Gesundheitsförderung. Köln: Bundeszentrale für gesundheitliche Aufklärung (BZgA).

Day, M. (2005). Foundation hospitals are not accountable to their communities. *British Medical Journal, 331*, 926.

Day, M. (2006, July 15). Three in five NHS trusts in England fail on basic care. *British Medical Journal, 333*, 114.

Department of Health. (1998, January). *The new NHS Modern and Dependable: A National Framework for Assessing Performance*. The Stationery Office. London.

Department of Health. (1999, July). *Saving Lives: Our Healthier Nation White Paper and Reducing Health Inequalities: An Action Report*. London.

Department of Health. (2000, July). *The NHS Plan—A Plan for Investment—A Plan for Reform*. The Stationery Office. London.

Department of Health. (2001a). *Health and social care act 2001*. London: Department of Health.

Department of Health. (2001b, September). *Involving Patients and the Public in Healthcare—A Discussion Document*. The Stationery Office. London.

Department of Health. (2001c, July). *Shifting the Balance of Power Within the NHS*. London.

Department of Health. (2001d, September). *The Expert Patient: A New Approach to Chronic Disease Management for the 21st Century*. London.

Department of Health. (2002a). *A Guide to NHS Foundation Trusts*. London.

Department of Health. (2002b). *Seminar on Foundation Trust: Learning from European Organisations: Summary of Messages*. The Stationery Office. London.

Department of Health. (2003, November 20). *Health and Social Care (Community Health and Standards) Act 2003—Explanatory Notes*. The Stationery Office Limited. London.

Department of Health. (2004a). *NHS Foundation Trusts: A Guide to Developing Governance Arrangements*. London.

Department of Health. (2004b, June). *The NHS Improvement Plan*. Stationery Office. London.

Department of Health. (2005). *Creating a Patient-Led NHS—Delivering the NHS Plan*. London: Department of Health.

Department of Health. (2007). *Local Government and Public Involvement in Health Act 2007*. Department of Health. London.

Department of Health. (2012). *Health and Social Care Act 2012*. Department of Health.

Department of Health, Department for Education and Employment, Home Office. (2001, January). *The Removal, Retention and use of Human Organs and Tissue from Post-mortem Examination—Advice from the Chief Medical Officer*. The Stationery Office. London.

Department of Health Payment by Results Team. (2010, September 30). *A Simple Guide to Payment by Results*. Department of Health. London.

Dewar, S. (2003, October). *Government and the NHS—Time for a New Relationship*. shaping the new NHS. London: King's Fund.

Dingeldey, I. (2007). Between workfare and enablement—The different paths to transformation of the welfare state: A comparative analysis of activating labour market policies. *European Journal of Political Research, 46*, 823–851.

Dixon, J., LeGrand, J., & Smith, P. (2003, May). *Can Market Forces Be Used for Good?* shaping the new NHS. London: King's Fund.

Durán, A., Lara, J. L., & van Waveren, M. (2006). *Spain: Health System Review*, (V. Bankauskaite, Ed.). Health Systems in Transition. Copenhagen: European Observatory on Health Systems and Policies.

Edwards, N., & Lewis, R. (2008). Who owns and operates healthcare providers and does it matter? *Journal of the Royal Society of Medicine, 101*(2), 54–58.

ELFS Shared Services. (2014). Norfolk and Suffolk NHS Foundation Trust Merger Case Study. Retrieved January 20, 2017, from www.elfsnhs.co.uk/moreinfo.asp?currentid=139

Esping-Andersen, G. (1990). *The Three Worlds of Welfare Capitalism*. Princton: University Press.

European Observatory on Health Care Systems. (1999). *Health Care Systems in Transition: United Kingdom*. Copenhagen: Regional Office for Europe on behalf of the European Observatory on Health Systems and Policies.

Fallberg, L., & MacKenny, S. (2003). Patient Ombudsmen in Seven European Countries: An Effective Way to Implement Patients' Rights? *European Journal of Health Law, 10*, 343–357.

Florin, D., & Dixon, J. (2004, January). Public involvement in health care—The NHS needs to be clear about the aims and how to achieve them. *British Medical Journal, 328*, 159–161.

Forster, R., & Gabe, J. (2008). Voice or choice? Patient and public involvement in the national health service in England under new labour. *International Journal of Health Services, 38(2)*, 333–356.

Foundation Trust Network. (2006). *Foundation Trusts: Two Years on*. London.

Foundation Trust Network. (2009, August). Payment by results update. *briefing*. London

Francis, R. (Ed.). (2010a, February). *Independent Inquiry into care provided by Mid Staffordshire NHS Foundation Trust January 2005—March 2009*. London: The Stationery Office.

Francis, R. (Ed.). (2010b, February). *Independent Inquiry Into Care Provided by Mid Staffordshire NHS Foundation Trust January 2005—March 2009*. London: The Stationery Office.

Frontier Economics. (2009). *Measuring Monitor's Impact*. London.

García-Armesto, S., Abadía-Taira, M. B., Durán, A., Hernández-Quevedo, C., & Bernal-Delgado, E. (2010). *Spain: Health System Review*. Health Systems in Transition. Copenhagen: WHO Regional Office for Europe on behalf of the European Observatory on Health Systems and Policies.

Garpenby, P. (1989). *The State and the Medical Profession—A Cross-National Comparison of the Health Policy Arena in the United Kingdom and Sweden 1945–1985* (Doctoral dissertation, TEMA, Linköpings universitet, Linköping/Kungälv).

Gosling, P. (2009, June). Foundation trusts: Five years on. *Health Service Review*, 5–7.

Greener, I. (2004). Health service organization in the UK: A political economy approach. *Public Administration, 82*(3), 657–676.

Greener, I., & Powell, M. (2008). The changing governance of the NHS: Reform in a post-Keynesian health service. *Human Relations, 61*(5), 617–636.

Gregory, W. (2012, June 30). *Developing the Role of Governors in NHS Foundation Trusts* (Doctoral dissertation, The University of Manchester Manchester Business School). MA-thesis.

Hallas, J. (1976). *CHCs in Action*. London: Nuffield Provincial Hospitals Trust.

Ham, C., & Hunt, P. (2008, July). *Members governance in NHS foundation trusts: A review for the department of health*. University of Birmingham.

Health Committee (Ed.). (2003, May). Foundation Trusts—Second Report of Session 2002–03, Volume I: Report and Proceedings of the Committee.

Healthcare Commission. (2005). *The Healthcare Commission's Review of NHS Foundation Trusts*. London: Healthcare Audit & Inspection.

Her Majesty's Stationery Office. (1988a). *Education Reform Act 1988*. Her Majesty's Stationery Office. London.

Her Majesty's Stationery Office. (1988b). *School Boards (Scotland) Act 1988*. Her Majesty's Stationery Office. London.

Her Majesty's Stationery Office. (1989). *Self-Governing Schools etc. (Scotland) Act 1989*. Her Majesty's Stationery Office. London.

Hicks, A., Misra, J., & Nah Ng, T. (1995, June). The programmatic emergence of the social security state. *American Sociological Review, 60*, 329–349.

Hogg, C. (1999). *Patients, Power & Politics—From Patients to Citzens*. London, Seven Oaks, New Delhi: SAGE.

Hogg, C. (2008). *Citizens, Consumers and the NHS: Capturing Voices*. London: Palgrave Macmillan.

House of Commons. (2003a, November). House of Commons Hansard Debates on the Health and Social Care (Community Health and Standards) Act 2003, 19 November, London.

House of Commons. (2003b, May). House of Commons Hansard Debates on the Health and Social Care (Community Health and Standards) Act 2003, 7 May, London.

House of Commons. (2003c, May). House of Commons Hansard Debates on the Health and Social Care (Community Health and Standards) Act 2003, 7 May, London.

House of Commons. (2003d, July). House of Commons Hansard Debates on the Health and Social Care (Community Health and Standards) Act 2003, 8 July, London.

House of Commons. (2003e, May). House of Commons Hansard Debates on the Health and Social Care (Community Health and Standards) Act 2003, 8 May, London.

House of Commons Health Committee (Ed.). (2008a, October 17). Foundation trusts and Monitor, Volume II: Oral and written evidence.

House of Commons Health Committee (Ed.). (2008b, October 17). Foundation trusts and Monitor, Volume I: Report, together with formal minutes.

House of Lords (Ed.). (2003). House of Lords Hansard Debates on the Health and Social Care (Community Health and Standards) Bill 8 September, London.

Howe, G. (1969). *Report of the Committee of Enquiry into Allegations of Ill-treatment of Patients and Other Irregularities at the Ely Hospital, Cardiff (Howe Report)*, (Department of Health and Social Security, Ed.). London: HMSO.

Immergut, E. M., Anderson, K. M., & Schulze, I. (Eds.). (2006). *The Handbook of West European Pension Politics*. Oxford: Oxford University Press.

Ipsos MORI. (2008, January). *Survey of Foundation Trust Governors—Research Study Conducted for Monitor—Independent Regulator of NHS Foundation Trusts*. London.

Johnsen, J. R. (2006). *Health Systems in Transition: Norway* (V. Bankauskaite, Ed.). Copenhagen: WHO Regional Office for Europe on behalf of the European Observatory on Health Systems and Policies.

Kingdon, J. W. (2003). *Agendas, Alternatives, and Public Policies* (2nd ed.). New York/ San Francisco/ Boston et al.: Longman.

Klein, R. (1979). Control, participation, and the British national health service. *Milbank Memorial Fund Quarterly: Health and Society, 57*, 70–94.

Klein, R. (1999). *The New Politics of the National Health Service*. London & New York: Longman.

Klein, R. (2003). Governance for NHS foundation trusts. *British Medical Journal, 326*, 175–176.

Klein, R. (2004). The first wave of NHS foundation trusts. *British Medical Journal, 328*, 1332.

Klein, R., & Lewis, J. (1976). *The Politics of Consumer Representation*. London: Centre for Studies in Social Policy.

Kmietowicz, Z. (2004). UK health commission downgrades four foundation trusts. *British Medical Journal, 329*, 187.

Kuhlmann, E., Allsop, J., & Saks, M. (2009). Professional governance and public control: A comparison of healthcare in the United Kingdom and Germany *Current Sociology, 57*(4), 511–528.

Lægrid, P., Opedal, S., & Stigen, I. (2005). The Norwegian hospital reform: Balancing political control and enterprise autonomy. *Journal of Health Politics, Policy and Law, 30*(6), 1027–1064.

Lamping, W., & Tamm, I. (1994). Die Grundlegung der Krankenversicherung in Deutschland und England: Analyse ihrer Genese, Funktion und politischen Ausgestaltung. In B. Blanke (Ed.), *Krankheit und Gemeinwohl. Gesundheitspolitik zwischen Staat, Sozialversicherung und Medizin* (pp. 111–148). Opladen: Leske + Budrich.

LeGrand, J. (1997). Knights, knaves or pawns? human behaviour and social policy. *Journal of Social Policy, 26*(2), 149–169.

LeGrand, J. (2007). The politics of choice and competition in public services. *The Political Quarterly, 78 (2)*, 207–213.

LeGrand, J., Mays, N., & Mulligan, J.-A. (1998). *Learning from the NHS Internal Market*. London: King's Fund.

Leiber S., Greß, S., & Manouguian, M.-S. (2010, August). Healthcare system change and the cross-border transfer of ideas: Influence of the Dutch model on the German health reform 2007. *Journal of Health Politics, Policy and Law, 35*(4), 539–568.

Lewis, R. (2005, May). *Governing Foundation Trusts—A New era for Public Accountability*. London: King's Fund.

Lewis, R. (2008, June). Power to the patients. *Public Finance*. http://www.publicfinance.co.uk/2008/06/power-patients-richard-lewis

Lewis, R. Q. (2005). NHS foundation trusts. *British Medical Journal, 331*, 59–60.

Lewis, R., & Hinton, L. (2005, October). *Putting Health in Local Hands*. London: King's Fund Publication.

Lewis, R., & Hinton, L. (2008). Citizen and staff involvement in health service decision-making: Have national health service foundation trusts in England given stakeholders a louder voice? *Journal of Health Services Research & Policy, 13*(1), 19–25.

Longley, M., Riley, N., Davies, P., & Hernández-Quevedo, C. (2012). *United Kingdom (Wales): Health System Review*. Health Systems in Transition. Copenhagen: WHO Regional Office for Europe on behalf of the European Oberservatory on Health Systems and Policies.

Lowe, R. (1993). *The Welfare State Britian Since 1945*. Houndsmills/ Basingstoke/ London: The Macmillan Press.

Maier, M. L. (2003). Wissens- und ideenorientierte Anätze in der Politikwissenschaft: Versuch einer systematischen Übersicht. In M. L. Maier, F. Nullmeier, T. Pritzlaff, & A. Wiesner (Eds.), *Politik als Lernprozess—Wissenszentrierte Ansätze der Politikanalyse* (pp. 25–77). Opladen: Leske + Budrich.

Marquand, D. (2004). *Decline of the Public: The Hollowing Out of Citizenship*. Cambridge/ Malden: Polity Press.

McGauran, A. (2002). Foundation Hospitals freeing the best or dividing the NHS? *British Medical Journal, 324*, 1298.

McLachlan, G. (1990). *What Price Quality? The NHS in Review*. London: Nuffield Provincial Hospitals Trust.

Milewa, T., Harrison, S., Ahmad, W., & Tovey, P. (2002). Citizen's participation in primary health-care planning: Innovative citizenship practice in empirical perspective. *Critical Public Health, 12*(1), 39–53.

Mills, C. (2007, February). *What is the Role of the Governors of an NHS Foundation Trust?*. London: mutuo.

Ministry of Health. (1959, December 24). *Elections for the Hospital Management Committee Regulations*. London.

Mohan, J. (2003). *Reconciling Equity and Choice? Foundation Hospitals and the future of the NHS*. London: Catalyst.

Monitor. (2008, April). *Identifying Risk, Taking Action: Monitor's Approach to Service Performance in NHS Foundation Trusts*. London: Monitor.

Monitor. (2009, October). *Your Statutory Duties—A Reference Guide for NHS Foundation Trust Governors*. London.

Monitor. (2010a, March). *Consultation on the De-Authorisation of NHS Foundation Trusts*. London.

Monitor. (2010b, December 1). *NHS foundation trusts 1 December 2010 – NHS foundation trusts by authorisation date*. London: Monitor

Monitor. (2010c). *The NHS Foundation Trust—Code of Governance*. London.

Monitor. (2013a). Foundation trust merger cases. Retrieved August 24, 2016, from http://www.monitornhsft.gov.uk/monitors-new-role/cooperation-and-competition/casework/foundation-trust-merger-cases

Monitor. (2013b, July 16). Health sector regulator puts six foundation trusts in special measures. Retrieved January 20, 2017, from http://webarchive.nationalarchives.gov.uk/20140106173514/http://www.monitor.gov.uk/home/news-events-publications/latest-pressre-leases/health-sector-regulator-puts-six-foundation-trus

Monitor. (2013c, October 25). Monitor places King's Lynn into special measures and appoints new leadership. Retrieved January 20, 2017, from http://webarchive.nationalarchives.govuk/20140106173514/http://www.monitor.gov.uk/home/news-events-publications/latest-press-releases/monitor-places-king%E2%8%99s-lynn-special-measures-and-appoints-new-leadership

Monitor. (2013d, August). *Risk Assessment Framework*. London: Monitor.

Monitor. (2014a, May 2). *A Guide to Special Measures*. Monitor. London.

Monitor. (2014b, May 1). Heatherwood and Wexham Park NHS Foundation Trust put in special measures. Retrieved August 24, 2016, from http://www.monitor.gov.uk/home/news-events-publications/latest-press-releases-24

Monitor. (2014c). Historic Foundation Trust urplus/deficit data with summary.

Monitor. (2015). NHS foundation trusts by authorisation date. Retrieved January 22, 2015, from https://www.gov.uk/government/uploads/system/uploads/attachment_data/file/369544/List_of_FTbyauthorisationdatesANDmentalhealthFTs1_Nov2014.pdf

Monitor—Independent Regulator of NHS Foundation Trusts. (2008a, December). *Applying for NHS Foundation Trusts Status - Guide for Applicants—Overview of Changes*. Monitor. London.

Monitor—Independent Regulator of NHS Foundation Trusts. (2008b, May). *Developing the Role of NHS Foundation Trust Governors*. London.

Monitor—Independent Regulator of NHS Foundation Trusts. (2010, June). *The role of boards in improving patient safety*. London: Monitor – Independent Regulator of NHS Foundation Trusts.

Moore, W. (2003). Plans for foundation trusts could spark pay spiral. *British Medical Journal, 326*, 256.

Moorfields Eye Hospital NHS Foundation Trust. (2010, January). Minutes of the Public meeting of the Board of Directors held on 28th January 2010 at Moorfields, Ebenezer Street.

Morone, J. A., & Kilbreth, E. H. (2003). Power to people? Restoring citizen participation. *Journal of Health Politics, 28*(2–3), 271–288.

Morrell, K. (2006). Policy as narrative: New Labour's reform of the national health service. *Public Administration, 84*(2), 367–385.

Mullen, P., Murray-Sykes, K., & Kearns, W. E. (1984). Community health council representation on planning teams: A question of politics? *Public Health, 98*(3), 143–151.

National Audit Office. (2012, June 29). *Healthcare Across the UK: A Comparison of the NHS in England, Scotland, Wales and Northern Ireland* [Report by the comptroller and auditor general]. London.

National Health Service. (2014, November 20). Average daily number of available and occupied beds open overnight by sector: July to September 2014.

National Registry. (2013). Total number of hospitals and treatment centres in England and Wales able to participate in the NJR and the proportion actually participating in 2012.

NHS. (2005). *A Short Guide to NHS Foundation Trusts*. London.

NHS Choices. (2014a). All acute trusts. Retrieved January 20, 2017, from http://www.nhs.uk/ServiceDirectories/Pages/AcuteTrustListing.aspx

NHS Choices. (2014b, March 21). All mental health trusts. Retrieved January 20, 2017, from http://www.nhs.uk/ServiceDirectories/Pages/MentalHealthTrustListing.aspx

NHS Improvement. (2016a, April 1). Monitor is now part of NHS Improvement. Retrieved January 23, 2017, from https://www.gov.uk/government/news/monitor-is-now-part-of-nhs-improvement

NHS Improvement. (2016b, November 28). NHS foundation trust directory. Retrieved January 23, 2017, from https://www.gov.uk/government/publications/nhs-foundation-trust-directory/nhs-foundation-trust-directory#a-list-of-all-nhs-foundation-trusts

NHS Improvement. (2016c, September 30). Single Oversight Framework. Retrieved January 23, 2017, from https://improvement.nhs.uk/resources/single-oversight-framework/

NHS Management Executive. (1992). *Local Voices: The Views of Local People in Purchasing for Health*. Department of Health. London.

North, N., & Werkö, S. (2002). Widening the debate? Consultation and participation in local health care planning in the english and Swedish health services. *International Journal of Health Services, 32*(4), 781–798.

O'Dowd, A. (2006). Foundation trusts turn in strong financial performance. *British Medical Journal, 332*, 686.

O'Dowd, A. (2008, August). Foundation trusts still do not enjoy full autonomy MPs hear. *British Medical Journal, 337*, a691.

Office for National Statistics. (2013a, August 8). Population Estimates for UK, England and Wales, Scotland and Northern Ireland, Mid-2011 and Mid-2012. Retrieved August 24, 2016, from http://www.onsgov.uk/ons/rel/pop-estimate/population-estimates-foruk--englandandwales--scotland-and-northern-ireland/mid-2011-and-mid-2012/index.html

Office for National Statistics. (2013b). Population Estimates Summary for the UK. Retrieved August 24, 2016, from http://www.ons.gov.uk/ons/rel/popestimate/population-estimates-for-uk--englandandwales--scotland-and-northern-ireland/2013/rft--mid-2013-uk-population-estimates.zip

Ogu, A. I. (1981). Landesbericht Großbritannien. In P. A. Köhler & H. F. Zacher (Eds.), *Ein Jahrhundert Sozialversicherung* (pp. 269–443). Berlin: Duncker & Humblot.

Oliver, A. (2005). The english national health service: 1979–2005. *Health Economics, 14*, S75–S99.

O'Neill, C., McGregor, P., & Merkur, S. (2012). *United Kingdom (Northern Ireland): Health System Review*. Health Systems in Transition. Copenhagen: WHO Regional Office for Europe on behalf of the European Oberservatory on Health Systems and Policies.

Palmer, K. (2005a). *How Should We Deal with Hospital Failure? Facing the Challenges of the New NHS Market*. London: King's Fund Publication.

Palmer, K. (2005b, April). *NHS reform: Will it deliver the desired health outcomes?* presented at Kings Fund seminar.

Parliamentary and Health Service Ombudsman. (2010, July). *Making an Impact—Annual Report 2009–10*. The Stationery Office. London.

Paton, C. (2000). New Labour new health policy? In A. Hann (Ed.), *Analysing Health Policy* (Chap. 2, pp. 10–31). Aldershot/ Burlington/ Singapore/ Sydney: Ashgate Publishing.

Pook, C. (Ed.). (2002, January). *The Future of the NHS: A Framework for Debate*. London: King's Fund.

Powell, M. (1997). *Evaluating the NHS*. Buckingham: Open University Press.

Public and Patient Experience and Engagement Team. (2011, March). *HealthWatch Transition Plan*. Department of Health. London.

Rallings, C., & Thrasher, M. (2000). *British Electoral Facts, 1832–1999*. Aldershot & Burlington: Ashgate.

Robinson, R. (2002). NHS foundation trusts. *British Medical Journal, 325*, 506–507.

Rowe, R., & Shepherd, M. (2002, June). Public participation in the new NHS: No closer to citizen control? *Social Policy & Administration, 36*(3), 275–290.

Royal College of Nursing—Policy Unit. (2005, April). *Royal College of Nursing Survey of First Wave NHS Foundation Trusts*. London.

Schmid, J. (2002). *Wohlfahrtsstaaten im Vergleich*. Opladen: Leske + Budrich.

Schmidt, M. G. (2005). *Sozialpolitik in Deutschland*. Wiesbaden: VS Verlag.

Secretary of State for Health. (2010, December). *Liberating the NHS: Legislative Framework and Next Steps*. The Stationery Office. London.

Simmons, R., Birchall, J., Doheny, S., & Powell, M. (2007). 'Citizen governance': opportunities for inclusivity in policy and policy making? *Policy & Politics, 35*(3), 457–478.

South Tyneside Council on behalf of South Tyneside Foundation Trust. (2010, December). Notice of Uncontested Election. Retrieved August 24, 2016, from https://admin.stft.nhs.uk/documents/files/for-trust-members/elections2010/Notice-of-Uncontested-Election-Hebburn-Public-Constituency.pdf

Staender, J. (2007, October). *Krankenhauspolitik in England*, (Doctoral dissertation, Universität Bielefeld).

Steel, D., & Cylus, J. (2012). *United Kingdom (Scotland): Health System Review*. Health Systems in Transition. Copenhagen: WHO Regional Office for Europe on behalf of the European Observatory on Health Systems and Policies.

Sturm, R. (2006). Staatsaufbau und politische Institutionen. In H. Kastendiek & R. Sturm (Eds.), *Länderbericht Großbritannien* (3rd ed., 543, pp. 14–52). Schriftenreihe. Bonn: Bundeszentrale für politische Bildung.

Sturm, R. (2009). Das politische System Großbritanniens. In W. Ismayr, S. Richter, & M. Söldner (Eds.), *Die Politischen Systeme Westeuropas* (4th ed., pp. 265–306). Wiesbaden: VS, Verlag für Sozialwiss.

The Expert Advisory Group on Cancer to the Chief Medical Officers of England and Wales. (1995, April). *A policy framework for commissioning cancer services: A report by the expert advisory group on cancer to the chief medical officers of England and Wales*. London: Department of Health, Welsh Office.

The Labour Party. (1945). *1945 Labour party election manifesto—let us face the future: A declaration of labour policy for the consideration of the nation—victory in war must be followed by a prosperous peace*. Labour Party.

The Labour Party. (1979). *1979 Labour party manifesto—the labour way is the better way—foreward*. Labour Party.

The Labour Party. (1983). *Foreward*. London: Labour Party.

The Labour Party. (2001). *Ambitions for Britain—Labour's Manifesto 2001*. London.

The Liberal Democrat History Group. (2011). A concise history of the Liberal Party, SDP and Liberal Democrats. Retrieved March 8, 2011, from http://wwwliberalhistoryorguk/itemsingle.php?itemid=4&item=history.

The Stationery Office. (1973). *National Health Service Reorganisation Act 1973*. The Stationery Office. London.

The Stationery Office. (1986). *Education Act 1986*. Her Majesty's Stationery Office. London.

The Stationery Office. (1990, June 29). National Health Service and Community Care Act 1990. The Stationery Office. London.

The Stationery Office. (1993). *Health Service Commissioners Act 1993*. The Stationery Office. London.

The Stationery Office. (2003, November 20). *Health and Social Care (Community Health and Standards) Act 2003*. The Stationery Office Limited. London.

The Stationery Office. (2006). *National Health Service Act 2006*. The Stationery Office. London.

The Stationery Office. (2009). *Health Act 2009*. The Stationery Office. London.

TheyWorkForYou. (2012). MPs. Retrieved January 20, 2017, from http://www.theyworkforyou.com/mps/?date=1997-05-01

Tritter, J., Koivusalo, M., Ollila, E., & Dorfman, P. (2010). *Globalisation, Markets and Health-care Policy—Redrawing the Patient as Consumer*. Critical Studies in Health and Society Abingdon: Routledge.

Trondheim Kommune. (2005). *Brukerråd, hva da?* Trondheim: Trondheim Kommune.

Tuffs, A. (2006, March). Foundation trusts turn in strong financial performance. *British Medical Journal, 332* 686.

Tuohy, C. H. (2003). Agency Contract, and governance: Shifting shapes of accountability in the health care arena. *Journal of Health Politics, 28*(2–3), 195–215.

UK Parliament. (2011a). A changing house—The life peerages act 1958. Retrieved January 20, 2017, from http://collection.seuroparchive.org/ukparliament/20090625150547/lifepeeragesact.parliament.uk/lifepeeragesact/

UK Parliament. (2011b). Living heritage—Birth of the English Parliament. Retrieved January 20, 2017, from http://www.parliament.uk/about/living-heritage/evolutionofparliament/originsofparliament/birthofparliament/overview/origins

UK Parliament. (2011c). Living heritage—Parliament Bill 1949. Retrieved January 20, 2017, from http://www.parliament.uk/about/living-heritage/evolutionofparliament/houseoflords/parliamentacts/overview/parliamentbill1949

UK Parliament. (2011d). Living heritage—The glorious revolution. Retrieved January 20, 2017, from http://www.parliamentuk/about/livingheritage/evolutionofparliament/parliamentaryauthority/revolution/keydates/keydates166088

Vienonen, M. A. (2000). Von einer Ethik der Ignoranz hin zur Bürgerbeteiligung. In H. Ettischer & K. Salice-Stephan (Eds.), *Bürgerbeteiligung im Gesundheitswesen—eine länderübergreifende Herausforderung—Ideen, Ansätze und internationale Erfahrungen* (Chap. 3.1, 10, pp. 58–64). Forschung und Praxis der Gesundheitsförderung. Köln: Bundeszentrale für gesundheitliche Aufklärung (BZgA).

Walshe, K. (2003). Foundation hospitals: A new direction for NHS reform? *Journal of the Royal Society of Medicine, 96*, 106–110.

White, A. B. (1933). *Self-Government at the King's command. A study in the beginnings of English Democracy*. Westport Conneticut: Greenwood Press.

WHO. (2010). *World Health Statistics*. Geneva.

Williams, D. (2011, January). Monitor prepares for new role as economic regulator. *Public Finance, 1*, 8–9.

Wilmot, S. (2004). Foundation trusts and the problem of legitimacy. *HealthCare Analysis (HCA), 12*(2), 157–170.

Wilson, H. (1974, October). *October 1974 labour party manifesto—Britain will win with labour—foreward*. London: Labour Party.

Wood, B. (2000). *Patient Power?—The Politics of Patients' Associations in Briatin and America.* Buckingham: Open University Press.

# Chapter 7
# Germany

***Mit|be|stim|mung*** *• Substantiv, feminin • das Mitbestimmen, Teilhaben, Beteiligtsein an einem Entscheidungsprozess (besonders die Teilnahme der Arbeitnehmerinnen und Arbeitnehmer an Entscheidungsprozessen in der Wirtschaft)*[1]

***Selbst|ver|wal|tung*** *• Substantiv, feminin • unabhängige, eigenverantwortliche Verwaltung von etwas • **1** kommunale ~ • **2** die ~ der Universitäten*[2]

***Heimbeirat*** *• Der ~ ist das zentrale Mitwirkungsgremium und Interessenvertretung für die BewohnerInnen im Heim.*[3]

***Patientenbeteiligung*** *• Organisationen, die auf Bundesebene maßgeblich die Interessen von Patientinnen und Patienten und der Selbsthilfe chronisch kranker und behinderter Menschen in Deutschland vertreten, haben im G-BA entsprechend den Vorgaben des Fünften Sozialgesetzbuches (SGB V) ein Mitberatungs- und Antragsrecht, jedoch kein Stimmrecht.*[4]

## 7.1 Introduction

Germany with its 82,175,700 (as of 31 December 2015) inhabitants and its surface of 357,167 km$^2$ is the most populous country of our four case studies and the one with the second largest land surface (Statistische Ämter des Bundes und der Länder 2014; destatis 2016a). The huge variation in the population density between 69 inhabitants per square kilometre in Mecklenburg-Vorpommern and 3785 in Berlin (Statistische Ämter des Bundes und der Länder 2014; both as of 31 December 2012) tells something about the regional differences. Next to the geographical variety the federal structure also leaves its imprint on many formal structures.

[1] http://www.duden.de/rechtschreibung/Mitbestimmung; accessed on 12 February 2017.

[2] http://www.duden.de/rechtschreibung/Selbstverwaltung; accessed on 12 February 2017.

[3] http://www.heimbeirat.de/; accessed on 12 February 2017.

[4] https://www.g-ba.de/institution/struktur/patientenbeteiligung/; accessed on 12 February 2017.



A. Haarmann, *The Evolution and Everyday Practice of Collective Patient Involvement in Europe*, DOI 10.1007/978-3-319-64595-7_7

The country, which served as a role model for social insurances worldwide, is categorised as a counter-case, because it does not have any formal, collective patient involvement at the level of hospitals. However, there are other means of involvement in place: Next to the long tradition of self-governance, the country was, interestingly, first out in our sample with legislation regarding resident involvement in long-term care (Bundesgesetzblatt 1976). As will be shown below, its appraisal is much more critical than for its counterpart in the neighbouring Netherlands. In addition, it was never intended to be extended to the hospital sector.

This chapter will focus on the two formal, main pillars of patient involvement in Germany, namely the 'self-governance in sickness funds' (see Sect. 7.3.1 on page 195) and what can be perceived the self-governance of a self-administered health care system in the 'Joint Federal Committee' (*Gemeinsamer Bundesausschuss*; see Sect. 7.3.2 on page 199). The chapter will conclude by taking a glance at the involvement of residents in nursing homes (see Sect. 7.3.4 on page 206).

## *7.1.1 The Health Care System*

> The healthcare system we have, itself is good. For everyone. Even for the poorest man. Yet,. . . we should think about the funding. [. . . ] Since almost all hospitals—[. . . ] except for the state-run—operate in the red. And the privately run, of course, attempt to be in the black through savings in quality and personnel. (interview 28; author's translation)

Health insurance is mandatory in Germany. Up to a gross income of 4050 € citizens are obliged to be insured by one the of the statutory sickness funds (*Gesetzliche Krankenversicherung* (GKV); Bundesministerium für Gesundheit 2014b). Individuals with incomes above this ceiling can choose to either be voluntarily insured by one the statutory sickness funds or by one of the several private health insurances (*Private Krankenversicherung* (PKV)) with all its allegedly or actual advantages—such as long-going benefits and less waiting times—and disadvantages—such as higher contributions in old age and the lack of co-insurance for family members at no cost. Overall, 69.99 million beneficiaries (88.7% of the population) were insured via one of the sickness funds in 2014 and 8.95 million (11.3%) are via one of the private health insurance (statista 2014). As in the Netherlands, the number of sickness funds decreased considerably over the last decades: Of the 1815 sickness funds in the Federal Republic of Germany in 1970 and the 215 in late 2008 only 113 were left in 2017 (GKV-Spitzenverband 2017, 2014; cf. also Pressel 2010, p. 364). As Pressel (2010, pp. 361–364) points out, this is partly owing to competition between the funds as well as new insolvency legislation and subsequent mergers between sickness funds. The range extends from sickness funds with only several hundreds to and 9.4 millions (as of 2017; Barmer GEK 2017) and 10.6 millions (as of 2017; Techniker Krankenkasse 2017) beneficiaries for the two largest.

Health care is provided in 1956 hospitals (destatis 2016b) and by 144,769 physicians and 22,547 psychotherapists (Kassenärztliche Bundesvereinigung 2016), whereby practicing physicians are not included who solely treat patients insured by a private health insurance scheme or private patients.

As in the three other countries of this study, competences regarding (health-) care are distributed among several administrative levels. The ultimate responsibility for planning and providing long-term care lies with the federal states (*Länder* or *Bundesländer*; Busse & Riesberg 2005, pp. 132–133), which are also responsible for planning and providing the infrastructure for in-patient health care, i. e. the planning and building of hospitals (Busse & Blümel 2014, pp. 55–57, 60–61). Everyday operations for all kinds of (health-)care, in contrast, are funded by means of sickness funds and health insurances.[5] The larger framework legislation on funding, quality of provision, and the guide number of physicians is issued by the federal government (Busse & Riesberg 2005, pp. 58–60).

In accordance with the different responsibilities, a number of different mechanisms and instruments of steering actors can be discerned (Rosenbrock & Gerlinger 2006, pp. 274–289; cf. also Gerlinger & Schmucker 2009, pp. 5–6; Pressel 2010, p. 349). As Bandelow (2004, p. 95) highlights, 'negotiation' is one of the major forms (cf. also Pressel 2010, p. 349), among which also the self-governance of social insurances can be counted: To ease the administrative burden of the national state and the federal states, the whole health care system is run according to the concept of corporatist self-governance. This empowers various actors to administer and govern their own part of the health care system: Within the legislative and regulatory framework, the 'Associations of Statutory Health Insurance Physicians' (*Kassenärztliche Vereinigungen* (KVen)) and its counterpart the 'Associations of Statutory Health Insurance Dentists' (*Kassenzahnärztliche Vereinigungen* (KZVen)) negotiate the total remuneration with the 'State Associations of Sickness Funds' (*Krankenkassen Landesverbände*) at the level of the *Länder* (Busse & Riesberg 2005, pp. 35–43). Each association of statutory health insurance physicians redistributes the lump sum according to a previously defined ratio among their medical specialities.

The very concept of the corporatist self-governance permeates the health care system as other branches of the social insurances from what might be considered the base—the sickness funds—to the highest decision-making body—the 'Joint Federal Committee' (*Gemeinsamer Bundesausschuss* (G-BA or GemBA)). In sickness funds, representatives of employers and labour unions constitute the governing body, not only taking over official state competences but also representing the will of beneficiaries and, in consequence—according to the concept—the will of patients: According to the concept, beneficiaries get indirect influence via trade unions and employer organisations in the governance of sickness funds. The Joint Federal

[5]One peculiarity of the German welfare state is that it includes a large sector of cure and rehabilitation facilities (*Kur* and *Reha*) for citizens at all ages. These commonly 2- to 6-week long offers are traditionally provided away from home in a specialised facility, which is often situated in a specifically suited place. For employees, these provisions are usually not funded by the (statutory) health insurance, but by the pension funds (Busse & Blümel 2014, pp. 220–222).

Committee came into existence in 2004 and is comprised of representatives of five umbrella organisations of providers and sickness funds as well as several nonvoting representatives of patient organisations (Der Gemeinsame Bundesausschuss 2010; for more see Sects. 7.3.1 on page 195 and 7.3.2 on page 199).

Next to corporatism, elements of competition have been introduced over the last two decades, in particular in the 2000s. However, as Gerlinger (2002) and Rosenbrock and Gerlinger (2006) point out, they have not gained predominance over corporatism, but coexist side by side. The target of competition has changed over time: Were contributions the main focus, to which some minor differences in the benefit package could be added by the respective sickness funds (Gerlinger & Schmucker 2009, pp. 7–8), the focus has shifted to 'competition for quality' since the introduction of the Central Reallocation Funds (literally: health funds; *Gesundheitsfonds*) and a uniform contribution rate in 2009 (Bundesgesetzblatt 2007). The latest development with its fixed contribution rate for employers appears to rest upon the idea of stronger financial competition between sickness funds again, as sickness funds can levy additional contributions in case they do not manage to make ends meet with the centrally set contribution.

### 7.1.2 The Political System, Parties, and Trade Unions

Some part of the complex network of actors is owing to the federal constitution of the country, which is comprised of 16 federal states. Except for the few areas, for instance, culture and education—for which the federal states are responsible—or defence—for which the competences lie in the hands of the national state—most areas are divided into a directive national part and a (most often subordinate) part in the federal states. This is mirrored in authorities as well as in parastatal entities and public corporations and applies in equal measure to (health-)care as it does, e.g., to transport, inner security, environmental, or trade issues.

The national parliament is a bicameral one: The *Bundestag* with its 598 seats (plus overhang and levelling seats) is elected every fourth year according to the principle of 'proportional representation' with an election threshold of 5% (Ismayr 2009, p. 533). It is here, where the everyday legislative business takes place (Ismayr 2009). The election itself is a combination of voting for a direct mandate and a party's list. Since the latest national elections in 2013, a grand coalition of Christian and Social Democrats form the national government, two parties which are said to have converged in many ideas. The Christian Democrats (*Christlich Demokratische Union Deutschlands* (CDU); *Christlich Soziale Union* (CSU) in Bavaria) is the party, which formed the greatest number of governments in the history of the Federal Republic: In 13 out of 18 legislative periods the party formed the sole or major party of the government. The Social Democrats (*Sozialdemokratische Partei Deutschlands* (SPD)) stand for the remaining terms, always in combination with a coalition partner (see Table 7.1 on the facing page).

**Table 7.1** Overview and composition of German governments 1974–2015

| Period | Chancellor | Parties |
|---|---|---|
| 05/1974–09/1982 | Schmidt | SPD, FDP |
| 10/1982–10/1998 | Kohl | CDU, FDP |
| 10/1998–10/2005 | Schröder | SPD, Greens |
| 11/2005–10/2009 | Merkel | CDU, SPD |
| 10/2009–10/2013 | Merkel | CDU, FDP |
| Since 12/2013 | Merkel | CDU, SPD |

Source: own compilation

No matter which of the two big parties won the election, the Liberal Party (*Freie Demokratische Partei* (FDP)) was the coalition partner of choice until the first red-green government, except for a short period of grand coalition in the late 1960s. For the first time in their history, the party did not manage to pass the election threshold in the national elections 2013. The opposition is formed by 'The Left' (*Die Linke*) and the Green Party (*Bündnis 90/Die Grünen* (B90/Grüne)), both equally strong in the *Bundestag*. The two parties combined comprise only roughly 17% of the votes. Both parties constitute the coalition partner in several parliaments of the federal states (*Landtage*). In the realm of health care policies the history of reforms in Germany is a remarkable story of compromise between government and (the majority of) opposition parties. The only fundamental divide between the political parties is about how the health care of the future should be funded.[6]

The *Bundesrat*, in contrast, is comprised of delegates of the federal states' governments. Though much smaller with its 69 seats and holding only subordinate legislative competences, all legislation that touches upon competences of the federal states needs to be approved by the *Bundesrat* (Ismayr 2009). In consequence, this gives the federal states a strong veto position in many policy areas. In practice, this is of even more relevance, as the majority in the *Bundesrat* is often formed of the opposition parties of the *Bundestag*. In addition, during the election of the federal president (*Bundespräsident*; Ismayr 2009, p. 524), the formally highest post in the country, by the Federal Assembly (*Bundesversammlung*), both *Bundestag* and the *Länder* have the right to appoint an equal amount of electoral delegates (Ismayr 2009, p. 518).

Of the many interest organisations the 'Federal Association of German Industry' (*Bundesverband der Deutschen Industrie* (BDI)), the 'Chamber of Industry and Commerce' (*Deutscher Industrie- und Handelskammertag* (DIHK)), the 'Central Association of German Trades' (*Zentralverband des Deutschen Handwerks* (ZDH)), as well as the 'National Confederation of German Employers' Associations'

[6]The two concepts are the so-called citizen insurance (*Bürgerversicherung*), which is favoured by social democrats, greens, and the Left. The basic idea is to abandon the divide between mandatory sickness funds and private health insurances, while at the same time extending the basis for contributions to other kinds of income such as revenues from the capital market, real estate, and business. The alternative proposal by Christian democrats and liberals seeks to introduce lump-sum contributions.

(*Bundesvereinigung der Deutschen Arbeitgeberverbände* (BDA)) are the more important ones. The latter can be understood as the representative for matters of social insurances and pursues the aim 'to actively represent the interests of employers in the area of social policy' (Bundesvereinigung der Deutschen Arbeitgeberverbände 2014). On the employees' side the 'German Confederation of Trade Unions' (*Deutscher Gewerkschaftsbund* (DGB)) with its 6.05 million members is the most important actor (as of 2016; Deutscher Gewerkschaftsbund (DGB) 2016).

Patient organisations exist for almost any illness, but are not deeply rooted in public awareness. This might be owing to the fact, that an essential part of their aims lies in the provision of information, while political lobbying often happens behind closed doors. Another, more prominent role is played by the numerous welfare organisations, which mainly address social inequalities, poverty, long-term, and emergency care. With the ever increasing number of individuals in need of care and the rapid increase in providers of home care, the focus has somewhat extended to the quality of care in public perception, too.

The following chapters will, first, inform about the sources employed and explain the choice of federal states for a more detailed comparison. Thereafter, it will take a more detailed look at self-governance in general and the Joint Federal Committee in particular before heading on to involvement of persons in long-term care.

## 7.2 Sources

According to the study design, Germany constitutes the counter-case to the Netherlands. One of the main aims of this case study was to identify potential equivalents to collective patient involvement at the level of hospitals and find out about the reasons counteracting an implementation similar to England and the Netherlands. As will be discussed in more detail in the following chapter (see Sect. 7.3 on page 194), the emphasis in this book was put on the 'Joint Federal Committee' (*Gemeinsamer Bundesausschuss* (G-BA or GemBA)) and the decentralisation of involvement to nursing homes. This decision was taken since the topic of self-governance in Germany is sufficiently researched.

Regarding the decentralisation and reformation of involvement in nursing homes, it was opted for a most extreme cases design. Many federal states chose to adopt the previous federal law with rather small adaptations (for more details see Sect. 7.3.4 on page 206). Two groups stuck out from this general rule: A 'progressive' group, which tried to be very inclusive in terms of types of care, competences, and funding. And a group, that might be called 'conservative', which shelved legislation for as long as possible to eventually copy the previously federal legal text or even restrict involvement of those being cared for in comparison to the legislation previously in place.

The choice for the first group fell on Hamburg with 'Hamburg's Act on the Promotion of the Quality of Living and Care of Elderly and Impaired People and those Dependent on Care' (Hamburger Gesetz- und Verordnungsblatt 2009; for an overview of the respective federal states' acts see Appendix B.3.1 on page 346). The city with its 1.7 million inhabitants is the second largest in the country, *the* major one in the north, and one of the three so-called city states (*Stadtstaat*), i. e. federal states that consist of basically one major city. Situated at one of the largest natural ports, yet protected from the inclemencies of the North Sea the city with roots in the hanseatic league has been a major German port ever since. In combination with a high industrial production, it has developed into the cultural and economic commercial centre in northern Germany.

The latter group is represented by Saxony (*Sachsen*) and its 'Act on the Quality of Care and Living' (Sächsisches Gesetz- und Verordnungsblatt 2012). An additional aspect in favour of Sachsen (Saxony) was that legislation was under discussion during my field phase in Germany. This allowing to focus on one of the few laggards, while—e.g. in contrast to Thuringia (*Thüringen*—it was still possible to discuss the law's content to some extent. *Sachsen* with its four million inhabitants is situated in the south-eastern part of the country, bordering both the Czech Republic and Poland. Next to its two major cities Leipzig and Dresden it has a number of other important cities as well as industrial areas, and the second largest brown coal district in Germany. In contrast, in particular the southern rim of this federal state is an area for recreation, tourism, climbing, and hiking. Next to the adjacent federal state of Brandenburg the majority of the Sorbs live in Saxony, a Slavic people and one of Germany's two traditional ethnic minorities.

To complete the picture, an interview with the 'Mandatory of the Federal Government for the Concerns of the Patients' (*Beauftragter der Bundesregierung für die Belange der Patientinnen und Patienten*) would have been desirable. Unfortunately, the request was denied and only referred to brochures and the webpage.

As in the other countries, interview guidelines were sent out beforehand (see Appendix A.3 on page 337). Table 7.2 on the next page provides an overview of the interviews finally realised.[7]

As in the other countries, the transcripts were sent back to the interviewees in order to give them the opportunity to correct any statements that they would not support any longer, in case this had been agreed after the interview. Interviewees made use of this opportunity in only few cases and with more annotations than actual changes.

[7] A warm 'Thank you!' goes to Antonia Weinrich, who transcribed all German interviews!

All interviews in the entire study were conducted in an interested, well-wishing, and at times helpful atmosphere, characterised by the wish for mutual understanding. Interestingly, the only exemption was the last interview conducted in Germany. Even though it took almost 4 months and numerous attempts to get an appointment, the interviewee seemed completely unaware of the appointment and unprepared, though the interview guideline had been sent out one and a half weeks in advance. Audio-taping was denied, because I 'had not asked for it beforehand'. After only 9 minutes and several remarks accusing the author of being stupid and insolent, she told me that all had been said and ended the call, even though the questions were all the same as in Hamburg.

**Table 7.2** Overview of conducted interviews & talks in Germany

| No. of interview | Category of interview partner | Organisation and/or name | Date |
|---|---|---|---|
| 26 | Patient organisations | Federal Organisation of Care Users, national umbrella, 1 representative | July 2011 |
| 27 | | Federal Umbrella Organisation of Patient Consultation, 1 representative | July 2011[a] |
| 28 | | Senior Citizens' Advisory Board, Hamburg, 1 representative | December 2011 |
| 29 | | Senior Citizens' Advisory Council, Sachsen, 1 representative | May 2012[b] |
| 30 | Ministries & authorities | Federal Ministry of Family, Senior Citizens, Women, and Youth, 1 high-rank staff | July 2011 |
| 31 | | Federal Ministry of Health, 1 high-rank staff | July 2011 |
| 32 | | Authority for Health and Consumer Protection, Hamburg, 1 representative | November 2011 |
| 33 | | Representative of Saxonian Ministry of State Social Matters and Consumer Protection | January 2012[a,c] |
| 34 | Joint Federal Committee | Patients' bank, 1 member | November 2011 |
| 35 | | Patients' bank, 1 member | December 2011 |
| Total length of recorded interviews: 5 h 23 min | | | |

[a]The interview was conducted on the phone
[b]Answers were given in writing
[c]Audio-taping was denied

## 7.3 Involvement in the German Health Care System

As aforementioned, the main focus of this case study was to identify equivalents for collective patient involvement at hospitals. The self-governance of social insurances can, to some extent, be counted as one. A more immediate form of patient involvement is the centralisation of self-governance and inclusion of patients' advice in the joint federal committee. The patients mandatory can be viewed as to administer the patients' view as well. And finally the immediate involvement of residents in nursing homes, which bears a striking similarity with the Dutch WMCZ. As will be shown below, all of them contribute to a varying extent to the fact, that patient involvement in hospitals has not been introduced in Germany.

### 7.3.1 Self-Governance

> We have tried in the last reform, that we answered for in the grand coalition [...]: 'Can't we abolish the social elections?' I deem, I personally also deem them... I don't know... costly, and [...] only ritualised, and without actual bond. (interview 30; author's translation)
>
> It is a travesty. [...] The sickness funds still say it nowadays 'We are representatives of the residents'. That is not possible at all. That is window dressing and kidding oneself. They have completely different interests to represent than those of the residents. (interview 26; author's translation)

Shelfmetre after shelfmetre has been written about the self-governance within the German social insurances. This is not the place to add any seminal knowledge, as it has been done elsewhere better and in more depth than is feasible in this study (cf., e.g., Axer 2001; Berner 2009; Bogs 1977; Bogs & Ferber 1977; Braun & Buitkamp 2005; Braun & Klenk 2006; Braun, Greß, Lüdecke, Rothgang, & Wasem 2007; Döhler & Manow-Borgwardt 1992; Emde 1991; Heffter 1969; Hendler 1984; Klenk 2012; Paster 2010; Rudda 2000; Schnapp 2000; Schroeder 2008, 2009; Schuppert 1983; Tennstedt 1977; von Ferber 1977). However, in order to understand the logic of involvement in Germany, we need to dedicate some attention to it.

The self-governance in the German social insurances is corporatist in nature and the only form of involvement in this book that can be categorised under the heading of 'participation' in the sense of the definition given in Sect. 2.1 on page 23. Its basic concept is that representatives of employers and employees assume some of the state's responsibilities (cf., e.g., Braun, Klenk, Kluth, Nullmeier, & Welti 2009, p. 126; Braun, Klenk, Kluth, Nullmeier, & Welti 2008, pp. 132–138; Lehmbruch 1996; Schuppert 1983). The advantage for the state is that it does not need to burden or overload its administration with issues that the corporatist actors are said to be much more familiar with anyway, while at the same time corporatism bears the potential to pacify an adversarial policy field (cf., e.g., Emde 1991, pp. 5 et seq.). The disadvantage is that it needs regulation and supervision by the state, in order to prevent actors growing too strong.

Self-governance has been a vital part of the social insurances since their foundation in 1883. Ever since, criticism of the social insurances' self-governance has risen to a scale that questions its very existence. As in the other three countries, the ideal-typical traditional chain of legitimacy has always been an indirect one, yet different in its organisation: It always took the detour via an ideally work-based membership in sickness funds in which governing members have been thought to act as advocates for their members. Thereby, not only patients are represented in issues of health care provision but also the concerns of the net-payers. The assessment of self-governance has hardly changed over the last 35 years as the following quotation shows:

> Who nowadays tries to inform herself about the self-governance in the social insurances, will come across highly contradictory assessments. Opinions' range will go [...] from postulation of its reinforcement to the resigned notion to better abandon it. Whatever happens between these two poles is a more or less indifferent shrug: Either they know too little (or nothing at all) about it or it is perceived negligible whether or not such a thing exists. (Standfest 1978, p. VII; author's translation)

Though this has not changed, the perception of the situation has exacerbated: Despite several reforms of self-governance (cf. Braun et al. 2008; Nullmeier 2003; Rzesnik 2001), criticism has increased over the last four decades, which can mainly be traced back to three factors:

(a) According to the logic that social insurances provide work-related benefits, the governing board of most sickness funds is equally formed by representatives of employers and trade unions (Klenk 2012, p. 73).[8] This poses the inherent problem that a self-governance is only sufficiently legitimate as long as a larger majority of beneficiaries is or feels represented by the trade unions. Given the continuous increase of beneficiaries who do not participate in the workforce—owing to age, unemployment, or regulatory limitations such as for refugees and asylum seekers, for instance—as well as the general downturn of trade union membership from a peak in 1978 with 35.5% membership density down to 18.0% in 2011 (Visser 2013) we may cast doubts on to what extent trade unions actually do represent the 'common' beneficiary.

    Similar trends can be discerned on the employers' side (Silvia 2010) since a growing number of companies drop out of the wage agreement and pay different tariffs.

    Another factor decreasing the legitimacy of trade unions and employers as the sole representatives of patients are the increasing tax subsidies paid by the state (Gerlinger & Schmucker 2009, p. 13). Moreover, commencing with the 'Healthcare Modernisation Act' (Bundesgesetzblatt 2003; Busse & Blümel 2014, p. 38) the so-called additional contribution (*Zusatzbeitrag*) ended the parity funding between employers and employees (cf. also Schnapp 2005). The additional contribution can be levied by sickness funds which do not manage to make ends meet with the standard contributions centrally set by the national government and distributed by the 'Health Funds' (*Gesundheitsfonds*). It ranges from very few sickness funds with 0.3 or 0.4% to a major number with 1.1 to 1.3% and reach up to 1.8% (krankenkassen.de 2017). This trend is accentuated by the 'Sickness Fund Financial Structure and Quality Development Act' ('GKV-Finanzstruktur- und Qualitäts-Weiterentwicklungsgesetz (GKV-FQWG)', 2014), which became effective on 1 January 2015. It decreased the overall contribution rate and froze the employers' share at the same time to 7.3%. In essence, this means that all future increases will be borne by the insured themselves, no matter whether they are rooted in a higher contribution rate set by the government or additional contributions by the sickness funds.

[8]Given their historical legacy, there are several types of sickness funds, which have their peculiarities and form an exception to this general rule: The so-called substitute funds (*Ersatzkassen*) go back to the friendly societies as one of the predecessors of mandatory sickness funds. Owing to this development, the governing board is only comprised of representatives of the beneficiaries (Klenk 2012, p. 73). As the two largest single sickness funds are 'substitute funds' (TK and Barmer GEK), this exception affects a rather large number of beneficiaries. Governing boards of 'company sickness funds' (*Betriebskrankenkassen*), in contrast, are comprised of representatives of the employer and employees (Klenk 2012, p. 73). Not too large in terms of the number of members, they still constitute a larger number of funds.

However, whenever the question arises as to whether patients should solely be represented by trade unions and employer associations the uniform credo is that they do. Whenever the discussion gets tougher and this argument does not seem to entirely hold, quite to the contrary it is claimed that self-governance is not about interest representation of patients but of the common good. In that reading any other more straight-forward means of patient involvement would entail an unjustified and exaggerated consideration of patients' interests while net payers' interests would be jeopardised. Therefore, only self-governance in the existing form is able to balance out all interests so runs the argument (cf. Braun et al. 2008).

(b) The second issue are the elections to the governing boards. Voter turnout is usually around 30–35% for all social insurances combined, with estimates of the share of actual voters for the sickness funds alone even lower and ranging between 15.4% and 13.7% only for the period between 1986 and 1999 with decreasing tendency (Braun & Buitkamp 2005, p. 4). The democratic legitimacy provided through elections can, therefore, be questioned (cf. Braun et al. 2008, pp. 127, 153–159). Even more an issue are the widespread 'uncontested elections' (*Friedenswahlen*): If there are not more candidates than seats on the board, funds may abstain from elections completely, which potentially undermines legitimacy even more (Braun et al. 2008, pp. 155–159; Braun et al. 2009, p. 16; Schnapp 2000). This practice, though, must be seen as the rule for the huge majority of funds and elections since the Second World War (cf. Braun et al. 2009, pp. 72, 126–129): Out of the more than 130 sickness, funds only five ran elections in 2011 (Infobüro Sozialwahl 2011). The main reasons given for uncontested elections are the costs, which amounted to 0.92 € per eligible voter summarised over *all* branches of social insurance in the 2005 elections, which is widely portrayed in the media and by reputable actors like the tax payers' association (*Bund der Steuerzahler*; Braun et al. 2009, pp. 91, 110, 153–158). A second reason given is the difficulty to recruit volunteers to form a sufficient number of candidates to stand for actual elections (Braun et al. 2009, p. 157). Overall, this reinforces the power within the governance of social insurances. This can be contrasted with the external perception of the institution: For decades, the public awareness of the self-governing bodies lies relatively constantly around 30% of the general population (Braun et al. 2009, pp. 90, 210), which is to some extent understandable but not exactly the best argument in favour of this institution.

(c) A third issue is that the patients' and employers' representatives are shown to often pursue their own interests instead of the general good (Braun & Buitkamp 2005, p. 3; Wippler 1985). What is only too human, can be a serious challenge to interest representation and its legitimacy.

While the degree of familiarity is established at a rather low, yet constant level, other issues are not static and problems and criticism have increased over time. While Bogs and von Ferber (1977, p. 188) still drew the conclusion that some serious deficits need to be addressed but they, however, do not change the general legitimacy of the institution of self-governance (cf. also the positive image of a powerful actor drawn by Katzenstein 1987), 30 years later Braun et al. (2009), amongst others, conclude a much more fundamental problem:

> The normal evidence [of the justification of democratic legitimacy through elections] is by and large neglected with regard to the elections within the social insurances, since uncontested elections as a mechanism have been established as the rule. In its place is put a coordination system that relinquishes direct action of beneficiaries and [. . . ] employers and puts an only partly transparent action [. . . ] particularly of trade unions and employer associations in its place. (Braun, Klenk, Kluth, Nullmeier, & Welti 2009, p. 128; author's translation)

This is the point where we can contrast the development in Germany and the Netherlands, which has been similar to a large extent. In both countries the traditional chain of legitimacy between patients/users of health care services and corporatism in social insurances can be viewed as problematic, disrupted, or even broken. While this was *one* of the reasons to reform the relation between users, providers, state, and corporatism in the Netherlands, German politics formally still holds on to self-governance as the major means of involvement. This impression was strengthened when the previous government declared that its aim was

> 'the preservation and strengthening of the principle of self-governance through reinforcement of its legitimacy, acceptance, and effectiveness, as well as the representation of employers in governing boards of all sickness funds as well as the concentration of tasks of the Central Federal Association of Health Insurance Funds on fields, which need to be conducted jointly and uniformly'. (Pressel 2010, p. 347; author's translation)

However, despite a number of smaller reorganisations, some professionalisation (cf. Klenk 2012, pp. 84–87), and three 'Election Improvement Acts' (Braun, Klenk, Kluth, Nullmeier, & Welti 2008, pp. 73, 81), no fundamental changes have been made. The many proposals, which went further by envisaging how to adapt self-governance to make it more transparent, legitimate, responsive, and thereby transform it into an institution apt for today's necessities or criteria for legitimate representation and involvement have not been enacted (cf. Gerlinger and Schmucker 2009, p. 11; Klenk 2012; Pressel 2010, pp. 355–356; interview 30). The difficulty of fundamental change lies to some extent in the federal structure of the country with its divided competences. Even more so, however, does the multitude of often powerful actors affect and hamper sweeping political actions. This holds especially true for the powerful unions and employer associations, which are keen not to lose influence and power in the self-governance system. What is more, there are still objective, good reasons to keep the administration of sickness funds and decisions concerning the benefit catalogue a non-state task: On the one hand, there is good reason to assume that compromises negotiated between the actors concerned are more viable than any mediated or set standards by the government. On the other hand, blame avoidance can be a convenient step aside in difficult times, as we know from researchers like Weaver (1986, 10-12) and Pierson (1996). However, as it is very likely that the majority of the population does not exactly know the larger picture of responsibilities, whether the Ministry of Health, sickness funds, their physicians, the joint federal committee, or any other institution is responsible for specific decisions, this construct might—at least in part—prove to be a theoretical deception in this specific case. Thus, blame avoidance might play in into the perception of politicians and thereby have consequences in their actions (cf. Thomas & Thomas 1928, pp. 571–572), but should be less effective in more objective terms.

The most radical change is the centralisation introduced by the ‘Competition Reinforcement Act’ (*Wettbewerbstärkungsgesetz*; Bundesgesetzblatt 2007; Busse & Blümel 2014, p. 38; Jakubowski & Saltman 2013, p. 32). Owing to the historical multitude of sickness funds, their piecemeal evolution, and their legacy of in part estatist organisational principle (cf., e.g., Busse & Riesberg 2005, pp. 14 et seq.; Pressel 2010, p. 351), there had been seven different umbrella organisations of the respective types of sickness funds (Klenk 2012; Lehmbruch 1988; Pressel 2010, pp. 57,86). The centralisation into the *one* umbrella organisation ‘Central Federal Association of (the) Health Insurance Funds’ (*Spitzenverband Bund der Krankenkassen*, also called *GKV-Spitzenverband* (SpiBu)) can be interpreted as the legislator’s will to have one professionalised, more transparent, more effective, and more reliable counterpart for politics and providers (Pressel 2010, p. 359; Schroeder 2009). Furthermore, it can also be viewed as the attempt to disempower the existing organisations at meso-level by upholding and strengthening self-governance at the macro-level (Gerlinger & Schmucker 2009; Pressel 2010; Schroeder & Paquet 2009). The hope to legitimise self-governance by heaving it on a broader basis might have played in, too (Pressel 2010, p. 360). The precondition of this enforced unification was facilitated by reforms of the 1990s and 2000s, which changed the orientation from traditional sickness funds organised around the remnants of professional groups to regulated competition (cf., e.g., Busse & Riesberg 2005, pp. 219 et seq.; Gerlinger & Schmucker 2009; Pressel 2010, pp. 352, 354 et seq.).

The last step in this series of attempted reforms is the ‘Self-governance Reinforcement Act’ (*Selbstverwaltungsstärkungsgesetz*; Bundesgesetzblatt 2017), which passed parliament in spring 2017. The official line read that the government wanted to strengthen the functioning of self-governance by increasing transparency of it and by giving the ministry greater supervisory powers. Reading the act’s content it seems that the physicians’ associations opposition was not unprovoked as the main emphasis is not about empowering the self-governance’s actors but much more on tightening control on them and giving the ministry greater insight into the internal proceedings. This is in line with the trend to increase the potential interference by the state.

### *7.3.2 Joint Federal Committee: The ‘Little Legislator’*

> And, and the social self-governance from the sickness funds’ side cannot really claim to represent patients’ interests without blushing. It cannot. And folks like Franz Knieps, who was head of department in the ministry of health for long [. . . ] phrased it much bolder than I do it here, always told his members of the self-governance: ‘You are one brick short of a full load! What do you arrogate to yourself? You have overslept to modernise the social self-governance, you missed that boat, and now you are complaining that politics plonks something in front of you.’ That does not go together. (interview 34; author’s translation)

Of even more interest in the framework of this study, however, is the 'Joint Federal Committee' (*Gemeinsamer Bundesausschuss* (G-BA or GemBA)) established in its present form in 2004. Upon its foundation it is the highest and most powerful decision-making body within the self-governance (Jakubowski & Saltman 2013, p. 36; for an overview of the relations between the joint federal committee and the self-governance in the sickness funds see Fig. 7.1 on the next page). Its predecessor was founded in 1913 as the 'Central Committee' (*Centralausschuß*) in order to settle a conflict between sickness funds and the physicians' association, it was renamed to 'Imperial Committee of Physicians and Sickness Funds' (*Reichsausschuß der Ärzte und Krankenkassen*) in 1923, abolished under the fascist reign, only to be re-established as the 'Federal Committee of Physicians and Sickness Funds' (*Bundesausschuß der Ärzte und Krankenkassen*) in 1956 (Niebuhr, Rothgang, Wasem, & Greß 2004, pp. 17–18).

The competences of the G-BA and its predecessor have been extended successively since the late 1980s. The joint federal committee's overall, very broadly defined purpose is to 'determine, in order to safeguard the medical provision, the necessary guidelines about the warranty for a sufficient, appropriate, and economic provision for the beneficiaries' (Bundesgesetzblatt 1988, §92, I, 1; author's translation). To achieve this aim, the committee 'has been active with regard to defining the benefits package' since the early 1990s (Greß, Niebuhr, Rothgang & Wasem 2005, pp. 118, 129) and has assumed this task since the reform in 2004 even more so. Based on scientific evidence, the actors involved in the G-BA negotiate a solution, which in virtually all cases is accepted as the new standard to be followed. Since 1989, the committee's competences are comprised of the assessment of new technologies, which later on was extended to assess technologies already in use, too (Gerlinger & Schmucker 2009, p. 9; Greß et al. 2005, pp. 118–119). Since 1989 the setting of standards also includes the so-called substitute funds (*Ersatzkassen*), while in 2004 not only quality control within ambulatory but also for in-patient care was incorporated (Gerlinger & Schmucker 2009, p. 9). To this aim, the health care reform founded the 'Institute for Quality and Efficiency in Health Care' (*Institut für Qualität und Wirtschaftlichkeit im Gesundheitswesen* (IQWiG)), which undertakes the task of assessing pharmaceuticals and therapies (Gerlinger & Schmucker 2009, p. 10) on behalf of the G-BA. Thereby, it constitutes a step into the scientification of the assessment of therapies and pharmaceuticals and setting of the benefit catalogue. Though the Ministry of Health still holds supervisory powers and can rule the field by executive fiat if need arises, this plethora of competences and responsibility has led to the byname 'little legislator' (cf., e.g., Bronner 2009, p. 211; Heberlein 1998) and strengthened the role of the G-BA (Bronner 2009, p. 215; Gerlinger & Schmucker 2009, pp. 9–11). This shift in competences to the G-BA was far from clear from the outset and could not be taken as given: As Gerlinger and Schmucker (2009, p. 10) as well as Paquet (2009, p. 48) remind us, different options from curtailing the autonomy of the G-BA to making it a state authority subordinate to the ministry of health were under discussion during the legislation process in 2003.

After years of growth in terms of member size, which was in part owing to the incorporation of substitute funds (Plagemann 2005) and the merger of the committees

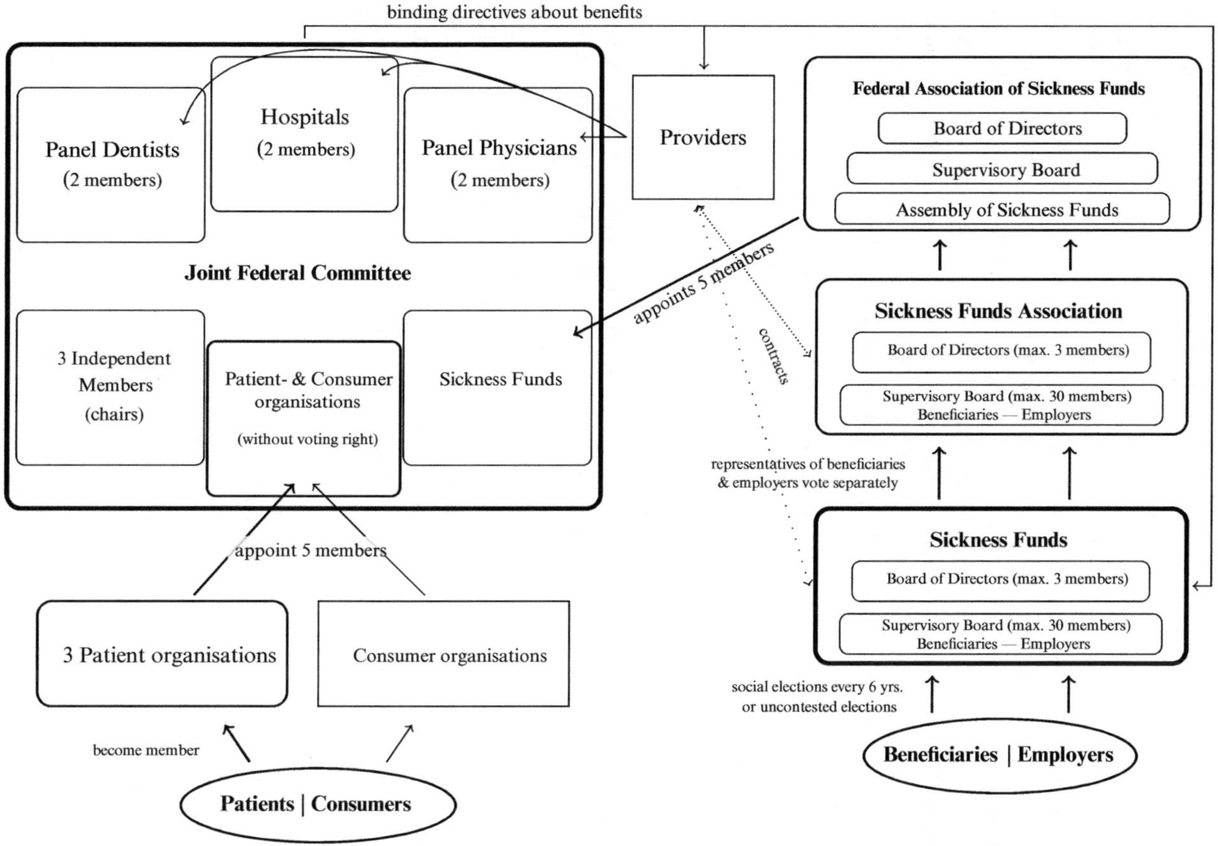


**Fig. 7.1** Schematic overview of the two pillars of self-governance in the German health care system. Source: adaptation of Klenk (2012, p. 85)

of physicians, hospitals, and coordination in 2004 (Schrinner 2005), the committee was reduced in size from 21 to 13 members with its reform in 2007 (Bronner 2009, pp. 217, 219). This was made possible since the subcommittees with only their sectoral competences within the G-BA had been abolished by then (Bronner 2009, p. 217). Nowadays, it is comprised of three independent members next to which there is a parity between providers and insurers: One representative of the 'Federal Association of Statutory Health Insurance Dentists' (*Kassenzahnärztliche Bundesvereinigung* (KZBV)), two each of the 'Federal Association of Statutory Health Insurance Physicians' (*Kassenärztliche Bundesvereinigung* (KBV)) and the 'German Hospital Society' (*Deutsche Krankenhausgesellschaft* (DKG)). Next to them, five members are appointed by the 'Central Federal Association of Health Insurance Funds' (*Spitzenverband Bund der Krankenkassen*, also called *GKV-Spitzenverband*; Bundesgesetzblatt 1988, §91, 2). Though some discussion around the legitimacy of the new composition of the G-BA unfolded, most commentators see it well founded (cf. Dierke 2005; Gerlinger & Schmucker 2009; Hase 2005; Hess 2009; Plagemann 2005).

Next to these actors, the composition of the committee was broadened. Of relevance in the context of this study is that one of the main aims of the 'Healthcare Modernisation Act' of 2004 was the reinforced orientation of the health care system towards the patients' needs (Etgeton 2009, p. 223). This can be understood as the political confession and insight that the self-governance within sickness funds is not and cannot be the sole representation of patients, beneficiaries, and people dependent on care. One of the means to meet this aim was to allow umbrella organisations to appoint a maximum of overall five representatives to the consultations in the G-BA in the interest of patients (Bundesministerium für Gesundheit 2003). With the 'German Handicapped Council' (*Deutscher Behindertenrat*), the 'Federal Working Consortium of Patients' Consultation' (*Bundesarbeitsgemeinschaft der PatientInnenstellen*), the 'Federal German Working Consortium of Self-help Groups' (*Deutsche Arbeitsgemeinschaft Selbsthilfegruppen*), and the 'Federal Consumer Association' (*Verbraucherzentrale Bundesverband*), now four organisations can agree on suitable candidates (Bundesministerium für Gesundheit 2003). Etgeton (2009, p. 222) points out that

> 'the status of patient representatives in the joint federal committee officially is not the one of 'members' [...], but they are involved in the meetings as 'knowledgeable individuals'. In that, they are—from a formal point of view—not part of the joint federal committee, but rather participant observers'. (author's translation)

The role of the patient representatives is, thus, solely advisory.

One of my interviewees described the reasoning during the legislation process by saying that

> it was the attempt to cut the Gordian knot, namely in answer to the question [sic!; ...] who is legitimised to be called patient representative? They [the government and secretaries; the author] said, 'I'm sick of hearing this. Now, we'll tell you!' It was a major effort. Why specifically those four, I do not know'. (interview 34; author's translation)

Though one might speculate that it was the political attempt to find a balanced mixture of more or less specific patient representatives, none of the interviews and documents was able to give an answer to the question, why just those umbrella organisations were chosen (interviews 30, 31, 34, and 35).

Despite this restriction, most commentators of and actors in the field acknowledge that the state tries to bring the several, at times antagonistic interests together.[9] It is then up to the actors concerned to find appropriate solutions (Hase 2005, p. 393). After some initial difficulties, there is agreement that patients' concerns are heard better than had previously been the case (interviews 34 and 35; Etgeton 2009, p. 214), a huge improvement compared to the previous mode of practice, which was viewed as opaque and not responding to patients' remarks and claims (Etgeton 2009, pp. 223–224; Ovey, Ley, Matuschke, & Schmutz 2011, pp. 29–32). The G-BA is very concerned about transparency in its decision-making process. All minutes are available to the public, easily accessible online. While one of my interviewees complained to have too small an amount of insight and that patients' concerns are not followed up to the same extent as by the other two 'banks' (interview 35), many sources agree that the patient bank is treated equally despite the formal difference (cf., e.g., Etgeton 2009, p. 224; interview 34). Overall, the influence of patients appears to have grown, even though their role within the committee is advisory only. One my interviewees illustrates this as follows:

> When patient representatives say: 'And we want that with the quality indicators for hygiene in hospitals the structural quality is documented, too, how many hospital hygienists there are' [...] that cannot simply be shoved aside, it will be intensely discussed. And it needs good reasons to state later on: 'Nope, we are only interested in the quality of the result. And how many hospital hygienists there are is none of our concerns.' I. e. they [the patient representatives; the author] sense exactly the blind spots and make it a topic. That is fundamentally new! And I think it is great. And I would even accept that there are whiners, who you would like to expel from from the room, but [...] they are everywhere, where interests are fought. (interview 30; author's translation)

On the one hand, it is maintained that it needs a certain degree of professionalism and time to permeate the often complex and intricate topics the G-BA is dealing with. This is why the three independent members have their full-time position as professionals (interview 34; Bronner 2009, p. 214). On the other hand, it is argued that the G-BA ideally shall be prevented from becoming a too professional body that its members shall maintain their linkage to their delegating groups and the population, which is why all other members are still volunteers. For the patients' side, this implies the problem of time (Etgeton 2009, p. 227): Though an attendance fee is paid, proper preparation can be time-consuming, in particular if lay-people at least to some extent want to keep pace with people dealing with the topics in question on a professional basis. In consequence, professionalisation among patient representatives occurs as in the three other countries of this study. This is in part

[9] For whatever reasons, in the context of the G-BA there is usually talk of three different 'banks': Providers, sickness funds, and patients. Patients' representatives are usually referred to as 'the third bank'.

a natural learning curve, in part owing to specialisation: According to one of my interviewees, there is a pool of 200 to 250 potential representatives with each of them specialised in a specific issue (interview 34). This way, patient organisations can draw on a number of people knowledgeable in the field under discussion, which to some extent offsets the professional advantage of the other groups.

Currently, a debate is going on as to whether or not the patients' side should be granted voting rights. Proponents argue that the voice of patients needs to be strengthened in order to be able to argue at eye level with providers and insurers. Opponents argue that patients are treated as one among equals already and that their neutrality and independence is at stake, in particular as they would be more prone to other actors' influence not least from the pharmaceutical industry. This is also the position taken by one of my interviewees:

> The fight that is now led and with open outcome, is whether they [the patient representatives; the author] should be given voting rights. And there are [...], of course, differing positions. I belong to those, who [...]– well, I advocate the assessment that it is a Greek gift to have voting rights as patient representatives, because it would rob the freedom [...] to really [...] bluntly add the patient perspective. (interview 34; author's translation; see also interview 35)

Despite the demise of self-governance in the sickness funds, self-governance in the joint federal committee has in many respects become more powerful than ever before. Overall, we can observe a centralisation of decision-making power in the world of sickness funds by bringing the different actors in the field of health care together. This is accompanied by a shift of power from sickness funds to the joint federal committee and a diversification to an extended range of actors, which gives patient and consumer umbrella organisations a say. In turn, this has initiated and to some extent re-legitimised a different concept of self-governance at the national level. In this, evidence seems to strengthen the position that patient representatives have a good opportunity to make patients' concerns heard and influence the discussion and decision in their favour.

## *7.3.3 Other Equivalents to Patient Involvement*

Next to these main opportunities to yield influence other potential ways can be discerned.

### 7.3.3.1 Patient Commissioner

Contemporaneously with the joint federal committee, the 'Federal Government's Commissioner for the Concerns of Patients' (*Beauftragter der Bundesregierung für die Belange der Patientinnen und Patienten*) was institutionalised by the 'Sickness Fund Modernisation Act' in 2004 (Der Beauftragte der Bundesregierung für die Belange der Patientinnen und Patienten (Patientenbeauftragter der Bundesregierung), 2010). According to the legal text of the social code, the

> [t]ask of the commissioned person is to work towards the end that concerns of patients, in particular regarding their rights to comprehensive and independent consultation and objective information by providers, funding side, and authorities in the healthcare system are considered as well as to the involvement in questions of safeguarding the medical provision. [...] The commissioned person shall compile the right of patients comprehensively and in generally intelligible language and keep it available for the information of the population. (Bundesgesetzblatt 1988, §140h, 2; author's translation)

Accordingly, several brochures have been published by the patient commissioner. Currently, Karl-Josef Laumann, undersecretary of state for health, is mandated to fulfil the tasks defined in the act.

It is difficult to assess to what degree the office is actually known to the general population and to what extent, in turn, it can have an effect on patient orientation. Outside the circle of newsletters published by patient organisations he is rarely mentioned in the general media.[10] Moreover, in contrast to its English counterpart, the German patient commissioner is not only passive in the sense that patients need to take action, but furthermore also passive in the sense that the office does not offer any active counselling, but relies mostly on published information. In conclusion, the patient commissioner in Germany can hardly be viewed as an equivalent to patient involvement at all.

#### 7.3.3.2 Patient Information and Rights

Next to patient organisations, the task of distributing relevant information and counselling patients about their rights is left to the 'Independent Patient Consultation' (*Unabhängige Patientenberatung Deutschland* (UPD)). It was founded in 2006 'with the aim to strengthen patient orientation in the healthcare system and to point out fields of problems in the healthcare system' (Bundesgesetzblatt 1988, §65b; author's translation). Via phone or in one of its 21 branches throughout the country, patients and beneficiaries can seek advice on specific illnesses, individual patient rights, and, in cases of disagreement between patient and physician and/or patient and sickness fund, on a mediation process. Independent patient consultation is run by a consortium of three charity and consumer organisations and report in a summarised manner on common issues to the patient commissioner (Unaghängige Patientenberatung Deutschland 2014).

---

[10]The commissioner's webpage provides rather sparse information (http://www.patientenbeauftragter.de/), while its thin content has slightly changed from a focus on acute to long-term care over time. In August 2014, for instance, visitors could download a brochure about the new 'Patient Rights Act', a brochure on adult autistics, read information on sickness funds threatened by insolvency, the 'new flu', co-payment regulations, additional provision that is not reimbursed by the sickness funds, and on the reimbursement of health care related travel costs. Brochures older than half a year, however, were taken off the webpage. Three out of the overall nine subpages provided information about the office of the patient commissioner, its legal foundation, and the biography of Mr. Laumann, while another one collected press releases and portrayed anniversaries of health care reforms of the past.

Next to these, a number of hospitals have introduced their local, independent patient commissioner(s)/ombudsman (*Patientenfürsprecher*) in order to mediate patients' complaints and make management and provision more responsive to criticism. In some federal states such as in Berlin, *Hessen*, and *Rheinland-Pfalz* (Rhineland-Palatinate) patient commissioners are institutionalised on a central level pursuant to acts in the respective state (Bundesministerium für Gesundheit 2014a).

To not only improve the information available for patients and those seeking advice but also make the legal situation more comprehensible, the 'Patient Rights Act' (*Patientenrechtegesetz* (PatRechteG)) became effective in early 2013. It attempts to strengthen and collect the scattered individual patient rights into one code. Therefore, strange enough, in comparison to other acts the 'patient rights act' seems not to be an act in its own right, but rather a list of changes in and links to other acts, that each contain one part of the rights. The act addresses the physicians duty to inform about different treatment options, to give the patient a say in what option eventually is chosen, gives the right of access to one's clinical records, and strengthens the rights towards health care providers in cases of dispute by shifting the burden of proof in specific cases. In addition, it clarifies the requirements for proper documentation of patient treatment and extends the involvement of patient organisations in the demand planning of the health care sector (Bundesgesetzblatt 2013).

Each of these—patient information, patient consultation, and a joint patient rights act—are important steps towards the informed patient; they can, however, not be compared to patient involvement.

### *7.3.4 Involvement in Nursing Homes*

> Homes or institutions, in-patient institutions have always been the working place of employees and not the dwelling place of people therein. And residents had always to adjust to the rhythm and the circumstances of the personnel—and not vice versa. And this is now put in question. (interview 26; author's translation)

Similar to the situation in the Netherlands, residents in long-term care homes and psychiatry as well as their relatives began to no longer take their nuisances and grievances related to conditions in care for granted. In the early 1970s a series of scandals involving ill-managed homes and neglect of dependents were revealed and received by a protesting public (Mußmann 2003). In consequence, politicians took action, and the government coalition consisting of social democrats and the liberal party passed a law to remedy the problem in 1974 as well as a corresponding decree in 1976 (Bundesgesetzblatt 2001, 1976). While the 'Home Act' (*Heimgesetz* (HeimG)) regulated administration, services, and providers of care, the 'Home Involvement Decree' (*Heimmitwirkungsverordnung* (HeimmwV)) established 'Home Advisory Boards' (*Heimbeirat*), which share a marked similarity with the 'Client Councils' found in the Netherlands. To them, four additional decrees were added in order to regulate the minimum requirements for home buildings, how to deal with the assets of the institution's residents, the minimum number and qualifications of the personnel, and administrative postulations (*Heimmindestbauverordnung, Heimsicherungsverordnung, Heimpersonalverordnung, Heimbuchführungsverordnung*; Mußmann 2003). Their overall task was to further and support residents in their everyday life and, therefore, take a mediating role between management and residents, which holds in particular true for the 'Home Involvement Decree'. In consequence and as in their Dutch counterparts, the boards do not deal with individual cases, but with issues that touch a larger number of residents if not all of them. The number of members of the board varied according to the size of the institution, and about one third of them could be recruited from outside the circle of residents (Bundesgesetzblatt 1976, 2002, §4). The decree regulated the election process, which usually took place every second year, the function of the supervisory authority, different functions within the board, and cost absorption by providers. In addition, it defined the board's competences, which were similar to the Dutch: Next to the organisation of the elections itself, the board's main competences were amongst other things to take measures to accident prevention, collaborate in improvement of the quality of care, in the setting of contributions, to advise regarding spare time activities, cases of mergers, reorganisations, and relevant changes in the character of provision (Bundesgesetzblatt 1976, 2002, §§29–32).

The so-called Reform of Federalism (*Föderalismusreform*), which clarified and in some cases reorganised competences between the federal states and the federal government, became effective in September 2006. Since then, the legislative responsibilities regarding involvement in long-term care have been devolved to the federal states. In the transition phase, the old act and decree were still valid as long as the federal states did not pass their own legislation. They, in turn, have made use of their newly acquired rights to various degrees and at a highly differing pace: *Baden-Württemberg* was first out in August 2008 while *Thüringen* followed as the last state first in July 2014 (for an overview of name and time of passage of the respective federal state acts see Appendix B.3.1 on page 347). Regarding the content of the new acts, basically three groups can be discerned: By and large, the first copied the federal predecessor with only minor or no changes at all. To this group can be counted, e.g., *Baden-Württemberg* and *Mecklenburg-Vorpommern*. A second group attempted to curtail competences for persons in care. In contrast, the third group extended their acts—to a varying degree at least—along one of the three following dimensions:

(a) In many cases an EXTENSION RUNS ALONG WIDENED AIMS. Here, not only 'appropriate involvement of residents' is the aim as previously stated but in some cases also the dignity of people in need of help or a meaningful spare-time are mentioned. In most federal states, however, the extension meant the inclusion of complaint management procedures by the new laws.

(b) A second dimension is the INCLUSION OF OTHER FORMS OF CARE: Care groups, certain forms of residential communities, or home care have been added. In all cases, hospitals remain implicitly or explicitly excluded.
(c) The third line of extension concerns the RIGHTS AND COMPETENCES ENTRUSTED TO RESIDENTS and other recipients of care.

The new acts of this last group are highly individual, some making only minor changes while others try to accomplish major ones. Thus, changes in comparison to their predecessor are not necessarily consistent among the federal states. In order to nevertheless get an idea of what the differences might look like, two extremes were sought to be compared. The federal acts for *Hamburg* and *Sachsen* (Saxony) were subsequently chosen. As hinted at in Appendix 7.2 on page 192, reasons for the choice of the first were the clear ambitions to involve residents of nursing or retirement homes and others in need of care more in decision-making processes and, at the same time, in social life beyond their institution or homes. The latter was chosen as it, coinciding with the German field study, was the one under parliamentary discussion. Here, the advantage was that questions could be dealt with concerning the relative lagging behind in comparison to the other federal states and the rather conservative content, which does not add too much to the previous federal act. In what follows, some of the key points will be taken up for both federal states.

#### 7.3.4.1 Hamburg

Regarding involvement, Hamburg pursues a twofold concept: *First*, 'Hamburg's Act on the Promotion of the Quality of Living and Care of Elderly and Impaired People, and those Dependent on Care/Support', which was passed under the coalition government of Christian democratic and Green party, expanded residents' competences of involvement to a larger population. One of the explicit goals of the act is to further recipients' self-determination (Hamburger Gesetz- und Verordnungsblatt 2009, (§§1 & 12)). It also regulates individual complaints, to some extent also the quality of care, qualification of the staff, procedures (Hamburger Gesetz- und Verordnungsblatt 2009, §§14–17), and the competences of the supervisory authority (Hamburger Gesetz- und Verordnungsblatt 2009, §§29–39; interview 32). It extends its range from nursing or retirement homes to residential communities, (home) nursing services, as well as short-term care. Moreover, it integrates the minimum requirements, for housing or qualification of staff, for instance, contained in several other acts into one. It regards residential communities as a voluntary arrangement, thus not stipulating any formal means of involvement (interview 32). The same applies to short-term care, where involvement is regarded less important compared to permanent residency (interview 32). Hospital care is explicitly excluded from the range of institutions (Hamburger Gesetz- und Verordnungsblatt 2009, §2, 10). According to my interviewee, this is justified by the differences in duration of stay and dependency on the (health-)care provider.

The boards possess more or less the same competences as granted in the previous national law as well as stronger rights in hiring support and expertise from outside the institution. Completely new is the option for residents and providers to jointly develop a model of involvement on their own:

> And the guideline is that if involvement... well, if they develop a model on their own, how to... well, to involve and to take their stand for the, for their own sake, if that works, if that is successful, they can compete with that model. Thus, that is an opening that we have said that within the work with the handicapped there are house communities, which have elected spokespersons, invent their own procedures, and they have control... We do not want anything more! (interview 32; author's translation)

In general, councils receive support in the form of volunteers who are specifically trained to go into institutions of long-term care and help where knowledge and/or support, e.g., in questions of strategy is needed. In cases where boards—e.g. owing to old age or mental impairment—would be difficult to set up, other means of involvement must be found (Hamburger Gesetz- und Verordnungsblatt 2009, §13, 4). One of the designated options is a residents' advocate or ombudsperson for the residents in a nursing or retirement home. Next to specific minimum requirements in qualification, they receive specific training by the city council to be able and be sensitised to fulfil their task (interviews 28 and 32).

The *second* pillar of Hamburg's concept is a 'Senior Citizens' Advisory Council' (*Seniorenbeirat*). The aim here is to get an overview of senior citizens' needs beyond (health-)care and to jointly work on finding solutions (Amtlicher Anzeiger 2011; interview 32 and 28). As the advisory boards are conceptualised to be the link between residents and the management in institutions of care, so is the advisory council between senior citizens and the municipality. It is comprised of overall 120 members (interviews 28 and 32), several sub-committees, and subject to election regulations.

#### 7.3.4.2 Sachsen

Given the brevity of the interview with the interviewee from the Saxonian Ministry of State (see footnote 7 on page 193), it is difficult to come to any more specific assessment about the situation in *Sachsen*. Regarding the range of the act itself, even the Saxonian parliament has chosen to opt for inclusion of the regulation of quality, flow of information, and tasks of the supervisory authority into one act, but, in contrast to its predecessor, to keep out contractual issues (Sächsisches Gesetz- und Verordnungsblatt 2012, §§3–7 & 9–19). The paragraph on residents' involvement is kept very brief and, thus, general (Sächsisches Gesetz- und Verordnungsblatt 2012, §8). Unfortunately, no answers at all were attempted regarding the difficulties, hot issues, and party political preferences. What *was* answered was that the stipulations of the act were carried over from its predecessor (interview 33). In comparison to the previously valid and much more detailed 'Home Involvement Decree' (Bundesgesetzblatt 2002); however, the act keeps a low profile. Beyond this, the interviewee told me that the late enactment was not owing to a conditioned backing by the political parties, but rather to complaints of very small, unspecified groups, which managed to leave short-term day and night care out of the scope of the act (interview 33; cf. Sächsisches Gesetz- und Verordnungsblatt 2012, §2, 2). It was claimed that the legislation process went as usual in politics, and no exceptional debate emerged (interview 33). In addition, the Christian-Democratic/Liberal Government had met the opposition of relatives, who, in particular for mental care, demanded to be involved instead of giving residents an extended say (interview 33).

However, it is no secret that years passed between the first draft of the bill and the enactment, in which virtually nothing happened. The coalition government consisting of Christian Democrats (CDU) and the Liberal Party (FDP) was confronted with a thin majority of 50.2% and a rather strong opposition (Landtag Sachsen 2009). Taking a cursory glance at the parliamentary minutes, the government appears to have wanted to push through the bill within a short period of time for no obvious reason. The coalition parties highlight the 'cautious development' of the previous national act without 'bossing around' recipients of care with superfluous regulation (Landtag Sachsen 2012). In essence, this meant that supervisory authorities received fewer powers and the target group was not extended as it was done in Hamburg. The opposition parties criticised in particular that no graded competences were introduced in order to include, for instance, residential communities and home services. Moreover, more control of providers was demanded in an almost unified way of the left party, the social democrats, and the greens (Landtag Sachsen 2012). It is also interesting to note that besides the common semi-public and sometimes even public discussion in the various federal states with a number of welfare organisations (*Der Paritätische* (DPWV), *Arbeitersamariterbund* (ASB), *Volkssolidarität*, and *Lebenshilfe* (a welfare organisation predominantly for handicapped people)) actors stepped into the debate which are interest organisations and providers of long-term care and day care themselves: They, like other initiatives supported by parents and relatives viewed the bill in conflict with the by then upcoming federal 'Care Reorientation Act' (*Pflege-Neuausrichtungs-Gesetz*), demanded the standardisation of definitions, the extension to residential communities, and clearer definitions of responsibilities between federal state and municipal authorities (Volkssolidarität Landesverband Sachsen e.V. 2012). The law was eventually passed with only minor changes.

In want of more information, we might speculate whether this development is a deliberate move to keep involvement open to individual solutions in the respective institutions or a lack of political emphasis on involvement. One of my interviewee's statements was that there would be a sufficient amount of 'window dressing laws' (*Schaufenstergesetze*) out there (interview 33), which might be interpreted as attempts to achieve an unambitious law, yet with aims that are unrealistic to achieve.

### 7.3.4.3 Appraisal of Involvement in Nursing Homes

> Well,... it is a kind of fig leaf, and many residents—and in particular the hale and hearty ones—conceive it as a blunt sword and are not willing to devote themselves—in quotation marks—and to squander their time. Since they can talk til they are blue in their face: If the institution does not want to, then it does not want to. (interview 26; author's translation)

Concluding from the interviews, there are some parallels of patient involvement in Germany to the one found in the other three countries: The situation varies from one institution to another, with a broad range from those with more than the stipulated rights for their residents to those where involvement appears to be mere embellishment.

A first similar observation is that—despite a general affirmation of the importance of involvement (e.g. interview 31; Braun, Klenk, Kluth, Nullmeier, & Welti 2008)—it is often difficult to recruit new volunteers, specifically in mental care (interviews 26–29). We can find a certain kind of professionalisation of involvement, be it by specific measures like trainings in Hamburg or the search for better qualified candidates in many institutions (interviews 26 and 28). At the same time, it depends on the viewpoint either commiserated or welcomed as a unique chance that welfare organisations are run as businesses with nothing left of the original idea of charity. This can entail immediate consequences for the quality of care and the qualification of carers (interviews 26 and 28).

A second point already known from the Netherlands is the description of a deep desire of harmony and gratitude for receiving care among the older generation (interviews 26 and 28). This, in turn, makes residents uncritical towards providers of care, constraining them from pursuing and enforcing their point of view. What is more, it adds to the information imbalance working to the disadvantage of residents (interviews 26 and 28).

One of the interviewees is a member of a senior citizens' advisory council and works as a voluntary 'advocate' for nursing homes in Hamburg, where no advisory board could be established. Regarding appraisal of the new act, he pays respect to the changes introduced by the new act and acknowledges the interest of several actors such as, Hamburg's transport services and the municipality. At the same time, he is rather pessimistic about the larger impact of involvement: Information would not be provided if residents and/or resident advocates do not ask for them and pick them up (interview 28). In his role as a residents' advocate he states that...

> [w]e are listened to. But the implementation... of the points that we raise, or, well, to put it this way that we can address– we frequently encounter rejection. First, because it is from the outside, second, because it costs. [...] Sometimes, pressure is applied to them [residents and members of the advisory board; the author]. If it is about new things or when they make proposals that cost some money, but ease the residents' life, it is blocked. 'Costs money and we do not have it'. Then we need to allocate it to the overheads, and they are high already. [...] Thus, they [the members of the advisory board; the author] are not popular, but they need to be there according to the law. (interview 28; author's translation)

Another interviewee works for the senior citizens' council in Sachsen. Even though the regulations in the bill as well as the residents competences are comparatively small in comparison to the situation in Hamburg, her conclusion highlights the greater transparency of decisions and a quota on the improved professional qualification of personnel compared to the previous situation (interview 29).[11] It is difficult to decide, whether the situation was even worse before, whether she wanted to keep a low profile towards the authorities, whether she wanted to look for the silver lining, or whether she actually viewed the situation as good.

However, what is clear that, in contrast to the suppositions of interviewee 29 and the interviews in the Netherlands, the assessment was divided between politicians and representatives of the authorities, on the one hand, and representatives of residents, on the other. The latter drew the picture of involvement as important, yet sometimes difficult to implement in practice, which was mainly attributed to financial issues, but also rooted in distinct interests of rather powerful actors. The first group mentioned few positive examples, but drew a rather critical overall picture of resident involvement in the federal states, that could be categorised as proactively encouraging collective involvement, and a clearly gloomy one for the others. It is important to note that this applied less to the formal competences than the factual influence and the providers' willingness to listen and spend even smaller amounts of money on involvement. Issues mentioned here were depiction of the supervisory authority for nursing homes (*Heimaufsicht*) as undermanned, in part toothless, and with reduced competences: Since it relies for the most part on reports on election results and the reports on the measures taken submitted by the nursing homes, so ran the argument, nursing homes could theoretically and in practice avoid abiding by the rules (interviews 26 and 28). In cases where competences were intended to be extended by the federal states' governments, they would have been whistled back by the federal government (interview 26 and 32), preventing supervisory authorities from taking an interventionist and mediating role between residents and providers in cases of conflict instead of a passive controlling one. For residents, this often only leaves the option to go to court with their case (interview 26 and 32), a most often unrealistic scenario given the age of residents, the financial situation, and their desire for harmony.[12]

[11]The character of the answers are strikingly different from the other interviews with patient organisations and representatives, not only in that the answers were given in writing but also in that the answers remain rather general and uncritical. Several of the questions were answered by the statement that it was not a patient organisation's task to make judgements about any political intentions. In connection with the somewhat strange interview with the Ministry of State for Sachsen, the impression left is that the atmosphere and discussion culture in Sachsen is somewhat harsher and differs from the other areas under research.

[12]'In such cases, the supervisory authority must go in and try to [? not comprehensible] by talking to them. Well, however, that is rejected by the Ministry for Families. They would not be responsible for this [it is claimed; the author]. [...] It is fought for keeping sinecures. [...] In Hessen it [the supervisory authority; the author] has dared to state, 'We want to check the contracts in order to see whether the minimum standards are satisfied'. An outcry from Berlin: 'You are not responsible for this!' Who else is to examine then? The courts. [...] No elderly person goes to court because of some 3.50 € paid too much, or claims them back, or poses questions regarding the investment costs,

Even in cases where action is taken—be it from residents' or the authorities' side—it is often a fruitless and imbalanced endeavour:

> And here, with our residents, [...] where do they have their chance? They are slower to express themselves, then they notice by their counterpart's posture that he absolutely does not have time and gets impatient, and that he practically already knows what he does that he only listens to the elderly for optical reasons that he could not care less, what the other spouts about. (interview 26; author's translation)

Overall, the assessment of resident involvement is not as positive as in the Netherlands, though Germany was actually one of the forerunners of a legal codification of residents' involvement and the formal competences are similar to the ones held by Dutch residents. This might, for one, be owing to a more negative attitude towards resident involvement per se while not used to the Dutch tradition of finding joint solutions; but it might, for another, also be rooted in a less supportive environment: Unanimous support and backing by politicians in terms of morale and financial support and training of the board members by non-sectoral patient organisations is lacking in Germany. The Dutch spirit 'Let's see what can be done!' seems to be subordinate to the primacy of measures free of charge, the full potential value of involvement is not recognised.

## 7.4 Summary

> [...] because these elections always induce excitement and disturbances in the institutions [of long-term care; the author]. That is, in turn, seen negatively. Instead of saying: That's better than pasting Santa Clauses, let them be somewhat excited. No, they did not want that... (interview 26; author's translation)

As was shown in this chapter, Germany still holds to its tradition of corporatist self-governance as the main means of involvement. This is the more interesting, as the situation in Germany in the 1980s and 1990s can be perceived roughly similar to the one in its contrasting and neighbouring country, the Netherlands: Similar governance arrangements, corporatism under criticism, and sickness funds' budget under (perceived) strain while expenditures were on the rise. In contrast to the Netherlands, not too much seems to have happened at first glance except for some parametric changes and the introduction of marketal elements to a small degree.

However, it is worth taking a second look so not to overlook two fundamental changes:

(a) Some key competences, such as, setting the contribution rate, had been withdrawn from sickness funds, oversight being tightened, while at the same time the various traditional sickness fund groups have been urged to form a joint association beyond the old particularistic boundaries between the sickness

or wonders whether it is justified to be relocated from A to B, though she has actually rented the room. [...] What person goes to court, what elderly person?' (interview 26; author's translation).

funds for different occupational groups. At the same time a certain degree of competition has been introduced into the health care system, though far from being as pronounced as in the Netherlands. Overall, this might be interpreted as a very slow, but steady process of de-corporatisation.

(b) To leave it with this conclusion, however, would be too narrow a perspective. With the Joint Federal Committee as the highest decision-making body within the self-governance of the health care system, corporatist rule is in some sense not only retained but also strengthened: The most important competences, determination of the benefit catalogue, falls even more clearly under the competences of the committee. Thus, while, on the one hand, a de-corporatisation at the level of sickness funds took place, a reverse movement of re-corporatisation occurs, on the other.

As Gerlinger and Schmucker (2009, p. 9) remind us, this it is not, however, simply a reorganisation of self-governance. By adding patient and consumer organisations as new actors, politics decreased the old corporatist groups' influence also here. This can also be observed in the scientification of decisions on therapies and pharmaceuticals by the foundation of the Institute for Quality and Efficiency in Health Care. In sum, it is more a reframing or recalibration of powers of corporatism and the governance within the field of health care than a simple reorganisation: In addition to a shift of competences to a centralised level and the incorporation of additional groups, policy seizes the powers to set the major contribution rate, supervise self-governance and determine its arrangements, and have the last word about the scope of self-governance.

This step-by-step repositioning of the actors among each other and towards politics matches the observation of incremental change in Germany in other policy areas (cf., e.g., Pierson 2003; Hinrichs 2001). Active, collective involvement of beneficiaries, patients, and residents in Germany mainly rests on the three pillars of self-governance in the respective sickness funds, the involvement of patient and consumer organisations in the joint federal committee, and the involvement in nursing homes. Given the unions' low membership rate, unions (also) pursuing their very own interests, and the huge share of uncontested elections, the actual influence of involvement in sickness funds can be questioned. Given the empirical evidence, patients and citizens have a considerably stronger position in the discussion of the benefit catalogue. The focus has, thereby, shifted from the administration of single sickness funds with an indirect influence on providers to the level of binding policy making.

Another barrier to fundamental change lies to some extent in the country's federal structures with its divided competences. The longstanding tradition of self-governance and its several powerful actors add to the challenges facing politicians as regards reform in the field. Another contributing factor might be that models oriented towards the free or open market were received by the realm of social security with a good pinch of scepticism (for the rather slow and pared-down reception of the New Public Management cf., e.g., Bäcker, Naegele, Bispinck, Hofemann, & Neubauer 2000; Borins & Gruning 1998; Budaus 1998; Nöthen,

Pichlbauer, & Eisenstecken 2004). Involvement of residents and their relatives in long-term care might play its part in the aforementioned reasoning: It can formally be maintained that both the health care and the care sector have their own and most appropriate type of involvement. Even though it is rhetorically applauded to the crucial moral and financial support necessary for successful implementation is missing: The well-informed patient, likewise patient involvement is seen as antagonistic to cost containment, which is the superior goal. Self-governance, on the other hand, portrays itself as the guarantor of cost containment through balancing antagonistic interests against each other, including those of net-payers.

The major hurdle to change, however, seems to be the perception of self-governance as the still convincing solution to the problem of legitimate interest representation by the political circle—given the existing context and constellations and despite decades of criticism and numerous suggested alternatives. The adherence to the principle of self-governance is all the more interesting as the situation during the 1980s until the late 1990s bears extraordinary similarities to the Netherlands, but the conclusions drawn are contrary: The assessment of corporatism as well as the concept of self-governance is seen more positively than in the Netherlands and still perceived a viable model. One reason for this can be found in the ascribed role of corporatism and the perceived consequences of too much patient involvement: Despite some scandals for which trade unions were responsible, for instance, the affair regarding Europe's biggest building and housing company '*Neue Heimat*' (New Home) owned mainly by trade unions (cf. Hoffmann 2014; Kunz 2002), corporatism is still held in high esteem and manages to maintain the reputation of a cost container. Thus, it has *not* received the reputation of an institution that caused the equivalent to the 'Dutch disease'. In contrast to the three other countries where the belief is held that patient involvement might cost some money, but that it bears the potential for cost savings, providers, politicians, and corporatist actors in Germany seem united in the assessment of patients: First, if they were too well informed and too much involved a costs spiral would be sparked as ever increasing demands for treatment would arise (cf. also the contribution by Dr. Frank Ulrich Montgomery (back then president of the medical council (*Ärztekammer*) of Hamburg cited in Badura 2000, p. 212; see interviews 28 and 26).

## References


Amtlicher Anzeiger. (2011, July 29). *Anordnung des Senatsüber die Einrichtung von Seniorenvertretungen.* Amtl. Anzeiger, 1753. Hamburg: Amtlicher Anzeiger.

Axer, P. (2001). Zur demokratischen Legitimation in der gemeinsamen Selbstverwaltung–dargestellt am Beispiel des Bundesausschusses der Ärzte und Krankenkassen: Tagungsband zum 8. Fachkolloquium des Instiuts für Sozialrecht am 28./29. Juni 2000 in Bochum. In F. E. Schnapp (Ed.), *Funktionale Selbstverwaltung und Demokratieprinzip – am Beispiel der Sozialversicherung* (Vol. 8, p. 115). Berlin: Bochumer Schriften zum Sozialrecht.

Bäcker, G., Naegele, G., Bispinck, R., Hofemann, K., & Neubauer, J. (2000). *Sozialpolitik und soziale Lage in Deutschland.* Wiesbaden: Westdeutscher Verlag.

Badura, B. (2000). Reform des Gesundheitswesens durch Aktivierung der Bürger, Versicherten und Patienten–eine Einführung. In H. Ettischer & K. Salice–Stephan (Eds.), *Bürgerbeteiligung im Gesundheitswesen–eine länderübergreifende Herausforderung–Ideen, Ansätze und internationale Erfahrungen*. Forschung und Praxis der Gesundheitsförderung. (Chap. 2.1, 10, pp. 34–39). Köln: Bundeszentrale für gesundheitliche Aufklärung (BZgA).

Bandelow, N. C. (2004). Governance im Gesundheitswesen: Systemintegration zwischen Verhandlung und hierarchischer Steuerung. In S. Lange & U. Schimank (Eds.), *Governance und gesellschaftliche Integration* (pp. 89–107). Wiesbaden: VS Verlag für Sozialwissenschaften.

Barmer GEK. (2017). Über das Unternehmen. Retrieved March 14, 2017, from https://www.barmer.de/ueberuns/barmer/unternehmen-26960

Berner, F. (2009). *Der hybride Sozialstaat: die Neuordnung von öffentlich und privat in der sozialen Sicherung*. Frankfurt a.M.: Campus.

Bogs, H. (1977). *Strukturprobleme der Selbstverwaltung einer modernen Sozialversicherung*. Bonn: Verlag der Ortskrankenkassen.

Bogs, H., & von Ferber, C. (1977). *Soziale Selbstverwaltung. Aufgaben und Funktion der Selbstverwaltung in der Sozialversicherung*. Bonn: Verlag der Ortskrankenkassen.

Borins, S., & Grüning, G. (1998). New Public Management–Theoretische Grundlagen und problematische Aspekte der Kritik. In D. Budäus, P. Conrad & G. Schreyögg (Eds.), *Managementforschung 8* (pp. 11–53). Berlin: deGruyter.

Braun, B., & Buitkamp, M. (2005). Zur Bekanntheit und Verankerung von Sozialwahlen und Selbstverwaltung in der GKV. *Soziale Sicherheit, 54*(3), 77–80.

Braun, B., Greß, S., Lüdecke, D., Rothgang, H., & Wasem, J. (2007). Funktionsfähigkeit und Perspektiven von Selbstverwaltung in der GKV: Ergebnisse von Umfragen bei Selbstverwaltern und Versicherern.

Braun, B., & Klenk, T. (2006). Soziale Selbstverwaltung: Traditionsreicher Steuerungsmechanismusmit welcher Zukunft? *Soziale Sicherheit, 55*(2), 54–58.

Braun, B., Klenk, T., Kluth, W., Nullmeier, F., & Welti, F. (2008). *Gutachten zur 'Geschichte und Modernisierung der Sozialversicherungswahlen'*. Baden-Baden: Nomos.

Braun, B., Klenk, T., Kluth, W., Nullmeier, F., & Welti, F. (2009). *Modernisierung der Sozialversicherungswahlen*. Baden-Baden: Nomos.

Bronner, D. (2009). Der Gemeinsame Bundesausschuss und die Gesundheitsreform 2007: Auch künftig Organ der Selbstverwaltung. In W. Schroeder & R. Paquet (Eds.), *Gesundheitsreform 2007. Nach der Reform ist vor der Reform* (pp. 211–221). Wiesbaden: VS Verlag.

Budäus, D. (1998). Von der bürokratischen Steuerung zum New Public Management–Eine Einführung. In D. Budäus, P. Conrad, & G. Schreyögg (Eds.), *Managementforschung 8* (10 et seq.). Berlin: deGruyter.

Bundesgesetzblatt. (1976, July 19). *Verordnung über die Mitwirkung der Bewohnerinnen und Bewohner in Angelegenheiten des Heimbetriebs (Heimmitwirkungsverordnung–HeimmwV)*. BGBl. I, S. 2896. Bundesgesetzblatt.

Bundesgesetzblatt. (1988, December 20). *Sozialgesetzbuch, Fünftes Buch*. Bundesgesetzblatt.

Bundesgesetzblatt. (2001). *Heimgesetz (HeimG)*. BGBl. I, S. 2970. BGBl.

Bundesgesetzblatt. (2002, July 31). *Verordnung über die Mitwirkung der Bewohnerinnen und Bewohner in Angelegenheiten des Heimbetriebes (Heimmitwirkungsverordnung–HeimmwV) in der Fassung der Bekanntmachung vom 25.07.2002*. BGBl. I Nr. 53. BGBl.

Bundesgesetzblatt. (2003, November 14). *Gesetz zur Modernisierung der gesetzlichen Krankenversicherung (GKV-Modernisierungsgesetz–GMG)*. Bundesgesetzblatt I, Nr. 55.

Bundesgesetzblatt. (2007, March 26). *Gesetz zur Stärkung des Wettbewerbs in der gesetzlichen Krankenversicherung*. Bundesgesetzblatt.

Bundesgesetzblatt. (2013, February 20). *Gesetz zur Verbesserung der Rechte von Patientinnen und Patienten (PatRechteG)*. BGBl., I, 277. Bundesgesetzblatt.

Bundesgesetzblatt. (2014, July 21). *Gesetz zur Weiterentwicklung der Finanzstruktur und der Qualität in der Gesetzlichen Krankenversicherung*. BGBl. I Nr. 33.

Bundesgesetzblatt. (2017, February 28). *Gesetz zur Verbesserung der Handlungsfähigkeit der Selbstverwaltung der Spitzenorganisationen in der gesetzlichen Krankenversicherung sowie zur Stärkung der über sie geführten Aufsicht.* BGBl. 2017, Teil I, Nr. 8.

Bundesministerium für Gesundheit. (2003, December 19). *Verordnung zur Beteiligung von Patientinnen und Patienten in der Gesetzlichen Krankenversicherung (Patientenbeteiligungsverordnung - PatBeteiligungsV).* Berlin: Bundesministerium der Justiz.

Bundesministerium für Gesundheit. (2014a, March 10). Patientenrechte–Informationsangebote für Patienten. Retrieved January 20, 2017, from http://www.bmg.bund.de/praevention/patientenrechte/informationsangebote-fuer-patienten.html

Bundesministerium für Gesundheit. (2014b). *Ratgeber zur gesetzlichen Krankenversicherung.* Berlin.

Bundesvereinigung der Deutschen Arbeitgeberverbände. (2014). Aufgaben der BDA. Retrieved January 20, 2017, from http://www.arbeitgeber.de/www/arbeitgeber.nsf/id/7B7AA8A7EF7D2988C1256DE70069F2DB

Busse, R., & Blümel, M. (2014). Germany–Health system review (Vols. 16). *Health systems in transition.* Copenhagen: WHO Regional Office for Europe.

Busse, R., & Riesberg, A. (2005). *Gesundheitssysteme im Wandel: Deutschland.* Kopenhagen: WHO Regionalbüro im Auftrag des Europäischen Oberservatoriums für Gesundheitssysteme und Gesundheitspolitik.

Der Beauftragte der Bundesregierung für die Belange der Patientinnen und Patienten (Patientenbeauftragter der Bundesregierung). (2010). Person und Amt. Retrieved January 20, 2017, from http://www.patientenbeauftragter.de/der-beauftragte/staatssekretaer-karl-josef-laumann

Der Gemeinsame Bundesausschuss. (2010). *Der Gemeinsame Bundesausschuss stellt sich vor.* Berlin.

destatis. (2016a). Bevölkerung auf Grundlage des Zensus 2011. Retrieved March 14, 2017, from https://www.destatis.de/DE/ZahlenFakten/GesellschaftStaat/Bevoelkerung/Bevoelkerungsstand/Tabellen/ZensusGeschlechtStaatsangehoerigkeit.html

destatis. (2016b). Einrichtungen, Betten und Patientenbewegung. Retrieved March 14, 2017, from https://www.destatis.de/DE/ZahlenFakten/GesellschaftStaat/Gesundheit/Krankenhaeuser/Tabellen/KrankenhaeuserJahreOhne100000.html

Deutscher Gewerkschaftsbund (DGB). (2016). DGB-Mitgliederzahlen ab 2010: Gesamtübersicht der Mitglieder der DGB-Gewerkschaften von 2010 bis einschließlich 2014. Retrieved March 14, 2017, from http://www.dgb.de/uber-uns/dgb-heute/mitgliederzahlen/2010

Dierke, S. (2005). 1 Jahr Patientenbebeteiligung im Gemeinsamen Bundesausschuss - Eine Zwischenbilanz. Retrieved January 20, 2017, from http://www.ewi-psy.fu-berlin.de/einrichtungen/arbeitsbereiche/ppg/service/newsletter/iPG-newsletterarchiv/iPG-NL-01-05/1JahrPatientenbeteiligung/index.html

Döhler, M., & Manow-Borgwardt, P. (1992). Korporatisierung als gesundheitspolitische Strategie. *Staatswissenschaften und Staatspraxis, 3*(1), 64–106.

Emde, E. T. (1991). *Die demokratische Legitimation der funktionalen Selbstverwaltung: Eine Verfassungsrechtliche Studie anhand der Kammern der Sozialversicherungsträger und der Bundesanstalt für Arbeit.* Berlin: Duncker & Humblot.

Etgeton, S. (2009). Patientenbeteiligung im Gemeinsamen Bundesausschuss. In W. Schroeder & R. Paquet (Eds.), *Gesundheitsreform 2007. Nach der Reform ist vor der Reform* (pp. 222–228). Wiesbaden: VS Verlag.

Gerlinger, T. (2002). *Zwischen Korporatismus und Wettbewerb: Gesundheitspolitische Steuerung im Wandel.* Berlin: WZB.

Gerlinger, T., & Schmucker, R. (2009). A long farewell to the bismarck system: Incremental change in the German health insurance system. *German Policy Studies, 5*(1), 3–20.

GKV-Spitzenverband. (2014). Alle gesetzlichen Krankenkassen. Retrieved August 28, 2016, from http://www.gkv-spitzenverband.de/krankenversicherung/krankenversicherunggrundprinzipien/allegesetzlichenkrankenkassen/allegesetzlichenkrankenkassen.jsp

GKV-Spitzenverband. (2017). Zahlen und Grafiken. Retrieved March 14, 2017, from https://www.gkv-spitzenverband.de/gkvspitzenverband/presse/zahlen_und_grafiken/zahlenundgrafiken.jsp

Greß, S., Niebuhr, D., Rothgang, H., & Wasem, J. (2005). Benefit decisions in German social health insurance: An international comparative study. In T. S. Jost (Ed.), *Healthcare coverage determinations* (Chap. 5, pp. 115–131). Maidenhead: McGraw-Hill.

Hamburger Gesetz- und Verordnungsblatt. (2009, December 15). *Hamburgisches Gesetz zur Förderung der Wohn- und Betreuungsqualität älterer, behinderter und auf Betreuung angewiesener Menschen (Hamburgisches Wohn- und Betreuungsqualitätsgesetz–HmbWBG)*. HmBGVBl. Nr. 56. Hamburger Gesetz- und Verordnungsblatt.

Hase, F. (2005). Verfassungsrechtliche Bewertung der Normsetzung durch den Gemeinsamen Bundesausschuss. *Medizinrecht, 23*(7), 391–397.

Heberlein, I. (1998). Der Bundesausschuss als "kleiner Gesetzgeber". *Recht und Politik im Gesundheitswesen, 4*, 143–153.

Heffter, H. (1969). *Die deutsche Selbstverwaltung im 19. Jahrhundert. Geschichte der Ideen und Institutionen* (2nd ed.). Stuttgart: K.F. Koehler.

Hendler, R. (1984). *Selbstverwaltung als Ordnungsprinzip. Zur politischen Willensbildung und Entscheidung im dynamischen Verfassungsstaat der Industriegesellschaft*. Köln u.a.: Carl Heymanns.

Hess, R. (2009). Herausforderungen an ein qualitätsorientiertes Gesundheitssystem–die Rolle des Gemeinsamen Bundesausschusses. In N. C. Bandelow, F. Eckert & R. Rüsenberg (Eds.), *Gesundheit 2030: Qualitätsorientierung im Fokus von Politik, Wirtschaft, Selbstverwaltung und Wissenschaft* (pp. 107–121). Wiesbaden: VS Verlag.

Hinrichs, K. (2001). Elephants on the move–patterns of public pension reform in OECD countries. In S. Leibfried (Ed.), *Welfare state futures* (pp. 77–102). Cambridge: Cambridge University Press.

Hoffmann, K. H. (2014, October). Die Neue Heimat. Retrieved January 20, 2017, from http://www.architekturarchiv-web.de/portraets/neue-heimat/index.html

Infobüro Sozialwahl. (2011). Mehr Wähler bei der Sozialwahl 2011: Fast 14,2 Millionen Versicherte und Rentner haben mitbestimmt. Retrieved August 16, 2014, from http://www.sozialwahl.de/ergebnisse-der-sozialwahl-2011.html

Ismayr, W. (2009). Das politische System Deutschlands. In W. Ismayr, S. Richter, & M. Söldner (Eds.), *Die politischen Systeme Westeuropas* (4th ed., pp. 515–566).Wiesbaden: VS, Verlag für Sozialwiss.

Jakubowski, E., & Saltman, R. B. (Eds.). (2013). *The changing national role in health system governance–a case-based study of 11 European countries and Australia*. Observatory Studies Series. Copenhagen: WHO Regional Office for Europe on behalf of the European Observatory on Health Systems and Policies.

Kassenärztliche Bundesvereinigung. (2016, March 17). Ärzte: Anstellung und Teilzeit liegen im Trend. Retrieved March 14, 2017, from http://www.kbv.de/html/201621535.php

Katzenstein, P. J. (1987). *Policy and politics in West Germany: The growth of a semi-sovereign state*. Philadelphia: Temple University Press.

Klenk, T. (2012). Deutschland: Korporatistische Selbstverwaltung zwischen Staat und Markt. In T. Klenk, P. Weyrauch, A. Haarmann, & F. Nullmeier (Eds.), *Abkehr vom Korporatismus?* (pp. 53–118). Frankfurt a.M.: Campus.

krankenkassen.de. (2017). Zusatzbeitrag: Liste der Krankenkassen nach Beitragssatz. Retrieved March 15, 2017, from http://www.krankenkassen.de/gesetzliche-krankenkassen/krankenkasse-beitrag/zusatzbeitrag/

Kunz, A. (2002). *Die Akte Neue Heimat. Krise und Abwicklung des größten Wohnungsbaukonzerns Europas 1982–1998*. Frankfurt: Campus.

Landtag Sachsen. (2009, August 31). Wahlergebnis 2009. Retrieved April 11, 2015, from http://www.landtag.sachsen.de/de/landtag/wahlengesetzgebung/148.aspx

Landtag Sachsen (Ed.). (2012, June 13). 2. Lesung des Entwurfs Gesetz zur Regelung der Betreuungs- und Wohnqualität im Alter, bei Behinderung und Pflegebedürftigkeit im Freistaat Sachsen (SächsBeWoG), Sächsischer Landtag, 5745–5762.

Lehmbruch, G. (1988). Der Neokorporatismus in der Bundesrepublik im internationalen Vergleich und die 'Konzertierte Aktion im Gesundheitswesen'. In G. Gäfgen (Ed.), *Neokorporatismus im Gesundheitswesen* (pp. 11–32). Baden-Baden: Nomos.

Lehmbruch, G. (1996). Die korporative Verhandlungsdemokratie in Westmitteleuropa. *Swiss Political Science Review, 2*(4), 1–41.

Mußmann, J. (2003). *Das Heimgesetz und die Heimmitwirkungsverordnung.*

Niebuhr, D., Rothgang, H., Wasem, J., & Greß, S. (2004). *Die Bestimmung des Leistungskataloges in der gesetzlichen Krankenversicherung: Verfahren und Kriterien zur Bestimmung des Leistungskatalogs in der Gesetzlichen Krankenversicherung vor dem Hintergrund internationaler Erfahrungen* (Vols. 108). Düsseldorf: edition der Hans Böckler Stiftung.

Nöthen, J., Pichlbauer, M., & Eisenstecken, E. (2004). New public management–Aufgaben, Erfahrungen und Grenzen der Verwaltungsmodernisierung in Deutschland. In M. Moldaschl, A. Hinz, & T.Wex (Eds.), *Reorganisation im Non-Profit-Sektor. Modernisierungsstrategien am Beispiel hochschulbezogener Dienstleistungen* (pp. 59–96). München: Rainer Hampp Verlag.

Nullmeier, F. (2003). Dauerreform ohne Reform: Paradoxien der Steuerungsstruktur des deutschen Gesundheitswesens. In J. Lang (Ed.), *Selbstverwaltung oder Selbstbedienung? Die Zukunft des Gesundheitssystems zwischen Korporatismus, Wettbewerb und staatlicher Regulierung* (pp. 19–29). Loccum: Evangelische Akademie Loccum.

Ovey, J.-D., Ley, S., Matuschke, M., & Schmutz, S. (2011, September 30). *Patienten- und Bürgerbeteiligung in Gesundheitssystemen: Gute Praxis in ausgewählten Gesundheitssystemen.* Basel: Prognos.

Paquet, R. (2009). Motor der Reform und Schaltzentrale: Die Rolle des Bundesministeriums für Gesundheit in der Gesundheitsreform 2007. In W. Schroeder & R. Paquet (Eds.), *Gesundheitsreform 2007. Nach der Reform ist vor der Reform* (pp. 32–49).Wiesbaden: VS Verlag.

Paster, T. (2010). Die Rolle der Arbeitgeber in der Sozialpolitik. In W. Schroeder & B. Weßels (Eds.), *Handbuch Arbeitgeber- und Wirtschaftsverbände in Deutschland: Die Rolle der Arbeitgeber in der Sozialpolitik* (pp. 342–362). Wiesbaden: VS Verlag.

Pierson, P. (1996, January). The new politics of the welfare state. *World Politics, 48*, 143–179.

Pierson, P. (2003). Big, slow-moving, and... invisible–macrosocial processes in the study of comparative politics. In J. Mahoney & D. Rueschemeyer (Eds.), Comparative historical analysis in the social sciences (Chap. 5, pp. 177–207). Cambridge: Cambridge University Press.

Plagemann, H. (2005). Der Gemeinsame Bundesausschuss–Auswirkungen auf den Leistungsanspruch der Patienten, dargestellt an ausgewählten Einzelfällen. *Medizinrecht, 23*(7), 401–409.

Pressel, H. (2010). Die Veränderung des Organisationsrechts der gesetzlichen Krankenkassen und ihrer Verbände durch die Große Koalition: Entstehung, Bestandsaufnahme und Ausblick. *Zeitschrift für Sozialreform, 56*(3), 347–372.

Rosenbrock, R., & Gerlinger, T. (2006). *Gesundheitspolitik: Eine systematische Einführung* (2nd ed.). Bern: Hans Huber.

Rudda, J. (2000). Die Selbstverwaltung–ein Garant für eine effiziente und soziale Führung des "Unternehmens Sozialversicherung". *Soziale Sicherheit*, (4), 366–373.

Rzesnik, N. (2001). Überlegungen zur Erhöhung der Akzeptanz der Selbstverwaltung. *Kompass. Zeitschrift für Sozialversicherung im Bergbau, 111*(5–6), 124–131.

Sächsisches Gesetz- und Verordnungsblatt. (2012). *Gesetz zur Regelung der Betreuungs- und Wohnqualität im Alter, bei Behinderung und Pflegebedürftigkeit im Freistaat Sachsen (Sächsisches Betreuungs- und Wohnqualitätsgesetz–SächsBeWoG).*

Schnapp, F. E. (2000). Friedenswahlen in der Sozialversicherung–vordemokratisches Relikt oder scheindemokratisches Etikett? In V. Epping, H. Fischer & W. H. Heinegg (Eds.), *Brücken bauen und begehen. Festschrift für Knut Ipsen* (pp. 807–828). München: C. H. Beck.

Schnapp, F. E. (2005). Die rechtliche Legitimation des Arbeitgeberanteils in der gesetzlichen Krankenversicherung. *SGb - Die Sozialgerichtsbarkeit, 52*(1), 1–8.

Schrinner, B. (2005). Normsetzung durch den Gemeinsamen Bundesausschuss aus Sicht der Krankenkassen. *Medizinrecht, 23*(7), 397–400.

Schroeder, W. (2008). *Zur Reform der sozialen Selbstverwaltung in der Gesetzlichen Krankenversicherung-Kasseler Konzept.* edition Hans Böckler Stiftung. Düsseldorf.

Schroeder, W. (2009). Soziale Selbstverwaltung: Von der klassischen Beteiligungs- zur professionalisierten Effizienzinstitution? In W. Schroeder & R. Paquet (Eds.), *Gesundheitsreform 2007. Nach der Reform ist vor der Reform* (pp. 188–197). Wiesbaden: VS Verlag.

Schroeder, W., & Paquet, R. (2009). *Gesundheitsreform 2007. Nach der Reform ist vor der Reform.* Wiesbaden: VS Verlag.

Schuppert, G. F. (1983). Selbstverwaltung als Beteiligung Privater an der Staatsverwaltung? Elemente zu einer Theorie der Selbstverwaltung. In A. von. Mutius (Ed.), *Selbstverwaltung im Staat der Industriegesellschaft, Festgabe zum 70. Geburtstag von Georg Christoph von Unruh* (pp. 183–205). Heidelberg: R. v. Decker's Verlag.

Silvia, S. J. (2010). Mitgliederentwicklung und Organisationsstärke der Arbeitgeberverbände, Wirtschaftsverbände und Industrie- und Handelskammern. In W. Schroeder & B. Weßels (Eds.), *Handbuch Arbeitgeber- und Wirtschaftsverbände in Deutschland* (pp. 169–182). Wiesbaden: VS Verlag.

Standfest, E. (1978). *Sozialpolitik und Selbstverwaltung. Zur Demokratisierung des Sozialstaates.* WSI-Studie. Köln.

statista. (2014). Anzahl der Mitglieder und Versicherten der gesetzlichen und privaten Krankenversicherung in den Jahren 2010 bis 2014 (in Millionen). Retrieved January 20, 2017, from http://de.statista.com/statistik/daten/studie/155823/umfrage/gkv-pkv-mitglieder-undversichertenzahl-im-vergleich/

Statistische Ämter des Bundes und der Länder. (2014). Gebiet und Bevölkerung–Fläche und Bevölkerung. Retrieved January 20, 2017, from http://www.statistik-portal.de/Statistik-Portal/dejb01jahrtab1.asp

Techniker Krankenkasse. (2017). Die TK auf einen Blick. Retrieved March 14, 2017, from https://www.tk.de/tk/unternehmen/unternehmensdaten/die-tk-auf-einen-blick/109214

Tennstedt, F. (1977). *Geschichte der Selbstverwaltung in der Krankenversicherung von der Mitte des 19. Jahrhunderts bis zur Gründung der Bundesrepublik Deutschland.* Bonn: Verlag der Ortskrankenkassen.

Thomas, W. I., & Thomas, D. S. (1928). *The child in America: Behavior problems and programs.* New York: Knopf.

Unaghängige Patientenberatung Deutschland. (2014, July). *Die UPD: Lotse, Wegweiser und Berater in Gesundheitsfragen.* Berlin.

Visser, J. (2013, April). ICTWSS: Database on Institutional Characteristics of Trade Unions, Wage Setting, State Intervention and Social Pacts in 34 Countries Between 1960 and 2007. Retrieved August 23, 2016, from http://www.uva-aias.net/208

Volkssolidarität Landesverband Sachsen e.V. (2012, June 1). Stopp zum Gesetzgebungsverfahren des Sächsischen Betreuungs- und Wohnqualitätsgesetzes. Volkssolidariät Landesverband Sachsen e.V.

von Ferber, C. (1977). *Soziale Selbstverwaltung–Fiktion oder Chance?* Bonn: Verlag der Ortskrankenkassen.

Weaver, R. K. (1986). The politics of blame avoidance. *Journal of Public Policy, 6*(4), 371–398.

Wippler, R. (1985). Die Entstehung oligarchischer Strukturen in demokratisch verfassten Organisationen. In G. Büschges & W. Raub (Eds.), *Soziale Bedingungen–Individuelles Handeln-Soziale Konsequenzen* (pp. 23–48). Frankfurt/Main: Lang.

# Chapter 8
# Sweden

***brukarråd*** • *ett organ för samråd och ömsesidig information mellan ansvariga för en verksamhet och brukare och närstående*[1]

***delaktighet*** SUBST. ~ en • ***1*** *aktiv medverkan:* ~ i barnens uppfostran*;* ***2*** SPEC. JUR. *medansvar:* ~ i mordet • ***3*** *†hafva delaktighet med (ngt), befatta sig med, hafva att göra med*[2]

***medverkan*** SUBST., BEST. F.=, N-GENUS • *det att medverka* □ SPEC. JUR.: ~ till brott

***samverkan*** SUBST., BEST. F.=, N-GENUS • *gemensamt handlande för visst syfte: samverkanslösning;* Här fordras en samverkan mellan alla berörda parter[3]

## 8.1 Introduction

Sweden is not only the country in our sample of four that has the largest surface but also the one with the smallest population: With a land surface of 531,794 km$^2$, its length of almost 1600 km, and only some 9.34 million inhabitants this amounts to an average of 21 inhabitants per square kilometre (Statistiska Centralbyrån 2011a, pp. 19, 94, 634), which makes it on average one tenth of the German and approximately 4% of the Dutch population density. It is also the country with the largest regional differences: While in particular the urban areas around Stockholm, the Mälar valley, Västra Götaland around Gothenburg, or the cities of Malmö and Lund are often reminiscent of typical continental population density and infrastructure, they grow smaller in the northern parts of the country, in particular off the coastline. One of the most extreme cases is the municipality of Kiruna in Lapland. Having the land surface of Wales, Saxony-Anhalt, or half of the Netherlands, it is the third largest municipality in the world. The average population density of 1.19 inhabitants per square kilometre is actually even smaller in practice,

[1] Socialstyrelsen 2001, p. 16.

[2] Auerbach 1922.

[3] Svenska Akademien (2012); Allén, Berg, Engdahl, Malmgren and Sjögren (1988).



A. Haarmann, *The Evolution and Everyday Practice of Collective Patient Involvement in Europe*, DOI 10.1007/978-3-319-64595-7_8

since some 60% of the population live in the city of Kiruna. In consequence, the closest hospital might be some 250 km away if living on the periphery of the municipality. This poses difficulties for the provision of health care and care and is in combination with the climate a potentially cost-increasing factor. This, however, does not seem to find expression in the financial figures. Given the vast distances especially in the northern parts of the country these rather abstract figures have serious implications for the everyday life of a smaller number of patients.

### 8.1.1 The Health Care System: An Overview

In Sweden it is citizen-status and not status of employment which entitles people to health care: Every person (prospectively) living in Sweden for at least 1 year is eligible for receiving (health-)care. The term usually used in Swedish to talk about the health care system, *hälso- och sjukvård* (fig.: health- and sickcare) does not necessarily differentiate between the county councils' responsibility for health care and the municipalities' for (long-term, mental, elderly, etc.) care. This points at the underlying encompassing approach. As, in addition, the short version *vården* in its most extensive meaning incorporates childcare, health care for children, care for the elderly, any kind of long-term care, health care, mental care, occupational medical care, medical checkups, prenatal exams, etc. both terms will be translated as a somewhat cumbersome '(health-)care' in the following, where sources do not indicate any clear-cut distinction—if not otherwise specified.

As in earlier days in the Netherlands and England, voluntary health insurances with some state subsidy were the main means of Sweden's health care funding until 1955, when the current system was implemented (Olsson 1993, pp. 117, 130–132, 165–170). To some extent, this development reflects the situation of Sweden as a late developer in terms of the welfare state. Yet, despite the fact that the largest part of the system is tax-funded, in contrast to England health care is not free at the point of delivery: On national average, 3.1%—or a median of 3.84%—of all health care expenditure was generated by out-of-pocket money in 2010 (Sveriges Kommuner och Landsting 2010b). With the exception of children and primary care in *Sörmland*, each patient usually has to pay an equivalent of between 11 € and 42 € per ordinary visit to a doctor in 2014 (Sveriges Kommuner och Landsting 2017). In order to keep health care affordable for everyone, there is a cap (*högkostnadsskydd*) of around 116 € per year applicable in the vast majority of counties, which is, however, unrelated to the individual income. (Glenngård & Anell 2012:1)[4]

---

[4]Pregnancy examinations as some other consultations—on, e.g., preventive care, contraception, abortion—are exempted from additional charges.

In order to direct more patients away from acute outpatient clinics (*akutvård* and *jourtid*) to the polyclinics (most common: *vårdcentral, hälsocentral, vårdmottagning*), prices are usually higher for outpatient clinics and specialist care (by factor 2 to 3; Sveriges Kommuner och Landsting

As in all four countries, the responsibility for care and health care is divided. The competences for framework legislation lie in the hands of the national government (Glenngård et al. 2005, pp. 1, 18–26; Socialstyrelsen 1998). It is also at the national level that quality and treatment guidelines are set by the authority in charge, the 'National Board of Health and Welfare' (*Socialstyrelsen*; Glenngård et al. 2005, p. 33), which at the same time is the supervisory authority. This is done in tight cooperation with other experts and authorities. In contrast, how and to what extent services are provided is to the largest extent left to the county councils (Glenngård et al. 2005, p. 33).

The country is divided into 21 *län* and regions, which are part of the national, political administration and can be understood as the representation of the state in the different parts of the country. They are administered by the *länsstyrelse*. In contrast to these tasks, the core of primary and secondary health care including the provision or commissioning of health care is the responsibility of the *landsting* (county councils) since 1963 (Olsson 1993, p. 114), most often with identical geographical borders as the *län*.[5] This is why they are most often officially

---

2011b). The same logic applies to the difference of referred vs. unreferred visits to specialists. A similar scheme is in place for pharmaceuticals, but with less expensive fees.

The mentioned out-of-pocket payments apply to seeing the doctor only. In comparison to many other countries, Sweden has implemented what in the literature is called 'advanced nursing' to some larger extent, i.e., handing over a number of competences to nurses, which have traditionally only been carried out by physicians (Arbetsförmedlingen 2011; Glenngård, Hjalte, Svensson, Anell & Bankauskaite 2005, pp. 79, 99, 111–112). Co-payments for visits to these specially trained 'district nurses' (*distriktsjuksköterska*) as well as other health care related professions such as physiotherapists or midwifes are usually lower and commence at 4.50 €.

Regarding caps for co-payments, there are several caps in place: As mentioned one for primary and secondary care, one for patient transportation services (155 €), therapeutic appliances (222 €), or (hospital) care per year each, and several discount steps with a maximum of overall 244 €. For dental care the patient will receive a minor subsidy for each treatment that exceeds 333 € (Vårdguiden 2012a,b; cf. also Söderholm Werkö 2008, p. 49; on the effects of out-of pocket payments cf. Bjöörn 2011; Haarmann & Wieseler 2006; Skriabikova, Pavlova & Groot 2010; Socialstyrelsen 2000:8; RAND Health 2006, p. 63).

[5]Regarding their size and competences *landsting* might as well be named provinces since this comes much closer to the Dutch *provincies* and in some respect to the German *Länder* than to the British county councils or German *Kreise*. By employing the translation 'county council' I follow the common usage by British and Swedish researchers in order to prevent terminological confusion. This is coherent with the legal status as a kind of 'secondary municipality' as they are sometimes called, still regulated by the Municipality Act (*Kommunallagen*; KL 2004:93).

In former times—and to add confusion to terminology—the emergence of *län* is tightly linked to early state involvement in health care: In 1698 the first regulation on the medical system was issued, in the early eighteenth century provincial physicians were employed in the newly established counties (Garpenby 1989, pp. 42–43). In 1773 the central government became responsible for the district medical organisation (Garpenby 1989, p. 43). Concerns about a population big and fit enough for the military service probably played its role at the time. With the re-introduction of *landsting* in 1862 the task was devolved to them before the nation state once again took over responsibility in the nineteenth century, only to return it in 1963.

With increased collaboration of county councils, the idea has formed to establish larger regions than the present 21 counties/regions. As the population size ranges from 126,500 for Jämtland's

called, e.g., *Västerbottens läns landsting*, which can be translated into 'the county (*landsting*) on the territory of the historical landscape (i.e. province, i.e. *län*) of Västerbotten'.

In consequence and strictly speaking, Sweden has a regional rather than a national health system. In contrast to the top-down perspective of *län*, the *landsting* established in 1862 (Olsson 1993, p. 108) represent the bottom-up perspective and constitute the democratically elected representation of the respective area (cf. also Jahn 2009, pp. 139–140). Elected politicians (*landstingsråd, fullmäktigeledamöter*, rarely: *landstingsfullmäktige*, i.e. members of the county councils' parliaments) constitute the highest decision-making body called (*landstings-*)*fullmäktige* (county council), which is the parliament of the county. MPs of the councils are elected every 4 years at the same time when also the national parliament, the *Riksdag*, and the city councils are elected, which ensures a high voter turnout amounting to 85.81% (Valmyndigheten 2014) in the last election in 2014. In contrast to many other countries, the overwhelming majority of politicians (90–98%) up to the level of county councils work as politicians alongside their regular jobs and are reimbursed for the committee meetings only. They form committees along topical lines, ensuring that decisions are implemented as intended. Most common are the health care committee (*Hälso- och sjukvårdsnämnden*) and the public transport committee (*kollektivtrafiksnämnden*). Within the limits set by the national government, county councils possess their own taxation and legislative rights in the areas of health care, culture, regional planning, and public transport. Financially, the largest single item, however, is primary and secondary health care, which amounted to 78% of the county councils' budgets in 2010 as the national average (with a median of 82% and a minimum of 68% and a maximum of 88%; Sveriges Kommuner och Landsting

---

to roughly 2.064 mio. for Stockholm's county the idea is to form more equally sized regions, for which it is easier to provide services. In 1999, a number of counties on the west coast and in the south formed the tentatively, the so-called regions *Västra Götaland* and *Skåne* (Scania), after which Halland followed in 2003 and the former municipality of *Gotland* in 2011. Since there are some rather contradictory ideas on how to organise the health care system of the future, this process has come to a halt for the moment. Nevertheless, there are at least proposals to make the existing regions permanent (interviews 38, 46–48, 50; cf., e.g., Prop. 2009).

Ethymologically, the word *landsting* emerges from the old Germanic word *ting* for meeting-site, tribe gathering, and also court (cf. also English or German *thing*, or the Icelandic *þing*). The juridical meaning also continues to live in the Swedish name of district courts, which are called *tingsrätt*.

2010b; own calculation).[6] An equivalent political organisation can be found within municipalities.

At a higher level, there are six health care regions for specialised care (*vård-regioner*), each specialising in a different medical area, so that there is one region specialised in, e.g., heart surgery, hip replacement, or treatment of rare sorts of cancer while the more common treatments are provided in each county (Glenngård et al. 2005, p. xiv, 1, 23, 34, 49, 59, 63, 81). At the same time, these regions are cooperations between different county councils using and funding regional hospitals to which regular public patient transport is undertaken.

It is the municipalities' task to provide long-term care. This was devolved to them through the so-called ÄDEL-reform in 1992 (Hjortsberg & Ghatnekar 2001, pp. 32, 49, 79–81; Söderholm Werkö 2008; on the general trend of decentralisation cf. also Jann 1983; Saltman, Bankauskaite & Vrangbæk 2007), which ended ill-defined responsibilities and the problem of high shares of hospital beds being occupied by recipients of long-term care.

### *8.1.2 The Political System, Parties, and Interest Groups*

As the United Kingdom and the Netherlands, Sweden is a constitutional monarchy. Though formally still head of state, the monarch has almost only representative rights since the constitutional reform of 1974, which was enacted shortly after the enthronement of the then new King Carl XVI Gustav, who, in contrast to the monarch in the Netherlands and Great Britain, no longer approves bills (Jahn 2009, p. 109). This change was promoted by the Social Democrats, whose party manifesto until recently still contained a passage calling for the abolition of the monarchy. A constitutional reform in 1970 converted the parliament, the *Riksdag*, founded in 1866, from a bi- to a unicameral system (SPRI 1993, p. 24; cf. also Henningsen 1986, pp. 288–289).

In the time before the previous government, only 14 years had not been governed by a social democratic government since autumn 1932 (for an overview of Swedish governments see Table 8.1 on the next page). Emerging from rather

[6]Municipalities' and county councils' income tax rates differ somewhat across the country (by roughly 6% points for municipalities and 1% point for counties (Statistiska Centralbyrån 2012)). Even though setting their specific tax rate is left to the respective county councils, competences of the national framework legislation allow the central government to set caps for raising tax rates. In consequence, limiting the taxation rate or pouring out additional money is one of the most important forms of steering county councils by the national state.

More important for consequences in health care, however, are population characteristics and differences in employment, which in combination entail quite different employing powers within health care between competitive county councils. This most often favours the industrialised and densely populated regions such as Stockholm, the valley of Mälar, Gothenburg, and Malmö and its surroundings, whereas the poorer county councils in the south-east and north experience difficulties in attracting staff (cf. Söderholm Werkö 2008, p. 46; Haarmann & Wieseler 2006, p. 69).

**Table 8.1** Overview and composition of Swedish governments 1936–2015

| Period | Minister of state | Party/parties | Annotations |
|---|---|---|---|
| 09/1936–10/1976 | Various | Continuously SAP | Rarely: in coalition with FP, *Högerparti*,[a] & *Bondeförbundet* |
| 10/1976–10/1979 | Various | | Various majorities & coalitions with C, FP, M |
| 10/1979–05/1981 | Fälldin | C, M, FP | |
| 05/1981–10/1982 | Fälldin | C, FP | |
| 10/1982–02/1986 | Palme | SAP | |
| 03/1986–10/1991 | Carlsson | SAP | |
| 10/1991–10/1994 | Bildt | M, C, FP, KD | |
| 10/1994–03/1996 | Carlsson | SAP | |
| 03/1996–10/2006 | Persson | SAP | |
| 10/2006–10/2014 | Reinfeldt | M, C, KD, FP | |
| Since 10/2014 | Löfven | SAP, MP | |

Source: own compilation
[a]*Högerparti*—Right-Party

poor circumstances, one of Sweden's peculiarities is that support for the '*Sveriges Socialdemokratiska Arbetarpartiet*' (SAP; Sweden's Social-Democratic Workers' Party) and the welfare state, in contrast to many western European countries, was always based on a relatively smaller group of industrial workers and backed by peasant labourers and a majority of farmers alike (cf., e.g., Olsson 1993, pp. 206–209; Sejersted 2011, pp. 82 et seq.). This even continues nowadays in that its strongest support is to be found in the sparsely populated north.

As Henningsen (1986, pp. 343–344) and more recently Jahn (2009, p. 123) rightly point out, one of the characteristics of Swedish politics is a clear distinction of parties along a leftist/rightist line: Whereas Social Democrats and the Left Party constitute the socialist block, the Moderates, People's Party, Centre Party, and Christian Democrats form the 'bourgeois' block. In the case of the latter, this block quite often coincides with the formation of government in various constellations. Even though it had never been part of any government before the formation of the government after the general elections in 2014, the Environmental Party supports a social democratic government in most decisions.

In the political arena, this meant that social democrats and the farmers' party collaborated from the early 1930s onwards and the first non-liberal government in history was a coalition between these two parties (cf. Olsson 1993, pp. 46, 48, 74–82, 109). The long-lasting success of the social democratic labour party over five decades stems to some extent from the incorporation of traditional values and a focus on the entire population including the rural parts. Inextricably linked with the Swedish *folkhemmet* (fig.: 'People's home'),[7]

Though it is not the place to go into depths of Swedish social democracy, a brief sketch of the history of Swedish social democracy might still be enlightening in order to better understand what implications social democracy and its thinking had for Sweden and its inhabitants. Whereas the Treaty of Saltsjöbaden of the 1930s was in line with a rather conservative and corporatist understanding of social democracy (Steinmo 1993, p. 88), it experienced a move to the left when the communists gained strength (Steinmo 1993, p. 123). The remainders of the old suffrage of estates, first abolished in 1971, implied some serious deficits in the legitimacy of bicameralism. Combined with the technocratic rule (Steinmo 1993, pp. 129–130, 125; SPRI 1993, p. 24; cf. also Wohlert 1996) applied in the 1950s, which bridged ideological deadlocks in order to raise employment but depoliticised politics, the very idea how different parties relate to each other did not always follow today's logic of democratically elected representatives. Until the mid-1970s even the 'bourgeois' parties would gain rather from cooperating than opposing the SAP (Steinmo 1993, p. 131). This led to a rather pale political profile of the parties in opposition and no noteworthy differences in the area of welfare politics in that both blocks supported the welfare state. It was only after the government lost in power that the opposition and claims from interest organisations grew stronger (Steinmo 1993, pp. 131–132; cf. also Hinrichs & Merkel 1987; Merkel 1996), leading to higher welfare demands. Interesting in this context is that the development was assessed differently from what it would be nowadays or what it would have been in the rest of Europe: After having had four decades with an absolute majority several minority governments were formed by the social democrats. After the first two elections, it was taken for granted that they would still form the government and set the agenda. The following headline of the major Swedish newspaper describes the obvious, yet, in the Swedish context of 1970 absurdly surprising fact that 'Government can be forced out by majority' (Malmström, 1970, quoted in Steinmo 1993, p. 133). Repercussions can be noticed even today. As one can the odd practice in *Riksdagen* considered that the budget drafts of minority governments should be accepted by the opposition. This unwritten rule was first broken in the parliamentary readings on the budget in late 2014.

[7] 'People's home' is the ideal of the Swedish welfare state, in which everyone would feel at home and taken care of, expedited mainly by the social democrat leader Per Albin Hansson (for more additional information on this cf., e.g., Berman 1998, pp. 156 et seq.; Henningsen 1986, pp. 312–317; Tilton 1990, pp. 126–140). In this context falls also Myrdal's 'art of social engineering'.

Consequently, there had been rather insignificant political (rhetorical) differences between the major two blocks for decades: For instance, the recipes to get out of the deep fiscal crisis emerging in Sweden of the early 1990s were still very similar between the two major political orientations, and both agreed to increase spending levels once the crisis is over. It can be noted that this has changed in part (cf. Starke, Kaasch & van Hooren 2013). Today, social democratic and bourgeois rhetoric is still much alike, taking a closer look at the content of policies. However, it becomes clear that welfare levels seem to have gone down especially for the most vulnerable and disadvantaged in society under the last bourgeois government in some political areas, whereas others experienced the extension of services. What increasingly differs between the two blocks is the view on the relation between society and the individual. Whereas, for instance, the 'bourgeois' aim is to create the preconditions for a sufficient number of jobs for everyone, the leftist side would rather highlight that the state needs to enable everyone to get into a job. One of the repercussions of the past is the long tradition of compromise between the different parties. With the increased self-consciousness of the bourgeois block since their second term in office between 2010 and 2014 this tradition is increasingly superseded by a rhetoric of competition and insurmountable block boundaries.

The Environmental Party—the Greens (*Miljöpartiet—de Gröna* (MP)) was formed in the early 1980s and is mainly backed in urban areas. Since the elections in autumn 2014, it for the first time forms a coalition government with the social democrats (see also Table 8.1 on page 226). The *Moderata Samlingspartiet* (most often abbreviated *Moderaterna* (M); Moderate Coalition Party) emerged as the second strongest party from the elections in 2010. The party's politics is a mixture of conservative and liberal viewpoints. Despite its liberal aspects, preserving the welfare state is high on the party's agenda, the main difference to the social democrats being the ways to achieve that goal. With regard to the health care system the party is one of the strongest proponents of private providers within a publicly funded system, which they demonstrated since the 1990s as the dominating party in Stockholm's county council and several attempts to privatise hospitals and polyclinics. Between 2006 and 2014, they formed part of the so-called (bourgeois) alliance (for Sweden) together with three smaller parties: The People's Party (*Folkpartiet* (FP)) is the party which can be perceived to represent the best example of a liberal party in Sweden. Earlier it was the strongest of the bourgeois parties for a long period of time. The Centre Party (*Centerpartiet* (C), formerly 'farmers' association, *bondeförbundet*) is traditionally the farmers' party. With the ongoing urbanisation since the 1940s, decentralisation of power and services became the main focus of the Centre Party. With a majority of voters in rural settings, environmental issues became prominent in the late 1970s. *Kristdemokraterna* (the Christian Democrats (KD)) are a relatively young social-liberal party, founded in the 1960s. It was first able in 1991 to enter into the national parliament and was, with only a few mandates, the smallest partner in the alliance which formed the government from 2006 to 2014.[8]

Trade unions are a rather influential actor in Sweden. With the strong umbrellas LO for workers (*Landsorganisationen i Sverige*; fig.: 'Country organisation in Sweden'), TCO for civil servants (*Tjänstemännens Centralorganisation*; 'Civil Servants' Central Organisation'), and SACO for academics including teachers (*Sveriges akademikers centralorganisation*; 'Sweden's academics central organisation') and an estimated organisational degree between 68 and 69% (EIRO 2009; Visser 2009; cf. also Jahn 2009, p. 131; Olsson 1993, pp. 209–212) they form a strong actor particularly in the area of labour-market policies. At least in the past, their strong position in society and their political influence was above all owing to two factors: The first one is the Gent system employed in Sweden—which in turn means that there was no separate unemployment insurance for non-members until the 1990s and unemployment benefits are still higher for members of trade unions.[9] The second reason can be regarded to root in the legislation process, in which all relevant parties are invited to leave their comments on any bill (*remissförfarandet*; Henningsen 1986, pp. 249, 251–252; Jahn 2009, p. 134), which also adds to the inclination to settle issues by joint agreement. Yet, unions play a considerably less important role when it comes to the health care system and regarding issues which go beyond concerns of the staff (Kjellberg 2006).

Sweden is often called 'association society' or 'society of the people's movement' (*föreningssamhälle* or *folkrörelsesamhälle*), which in the Swedish context, does not necessarily describe any social movement in its narrower sense, but simply the fact that almost everyone is member of an association (cf. also Henningsen 1986, pp. 230 et seq.; Söderholm Werkö 2008, p. 47): Though member size is in decline even in Sweden, some 90.2% of all Swedish inhabitants were a member in an association in the year 2000, 44.2% as active members (Vogel, Amnå, Munck & Häll 2003, p. 25; cf. also Petersson 2007) with labour unions, pensioner associations, and sports clubs as the three major designations in the survey (Vogel et al. 2003, p. 27). Interestingly in this context, however, Jahn (2009, p. 130) distinguishes

---

[8]Further parties on the national level are the 'Left Party' (*Vänsterpartiet* (V)), the position of which is somewhere in between a traditionally social democratic and communist party. Despite the programmatic closeness, it has never been part of a social democratic government, even though it signed treaties on cooperation during the Persson-era. In the elections in 2010 the Sweden Democrats (*Sverigedemokraterna* (SD)) got mandates for the *Riksdag* for the first time. The party was founded in 1988 and advocates national-conservative policies.

[9]The Gent system is one of the oldest arrangements of primarily unemployment insurances, less often also of occupational pensions. Its name stems from the fact that the system was first developed in Gent. It was later adopted by several other cities, regions, and countries. The main characteristic is that trade unions undertake the responsibility for the collection of contributions, their administration, and payment of benefits to its members (Bendz 2004; Henning 1974; Kjellberg 2006; Weyrauch 2012, pp. 194–197). For a long time this implied that employees needed to become member of their respective sectoral trade union in order to be eligible to join the unemployment insurance.

four different waves of association building over the last approximately 100 years. Interestingly, patient organisations are not mentioned in this context.

The following chapters will, first, provide an overview of the employed sources and a reasoning about the choice of county councils. It will then present potential equivalents to patient involvement in the Dutch and English sense before presenting the Swedish standard of involvement and how it emerged. Finally, an attempt to see and assess patient involvement through the eyes of the main actors is undertaken.

## 8.2 Sources

Having described the political and institutional background, the question arises as to what sources are most suitable to answer the main question of this study for the Swedish part. Taking into account the county councils' competences and responsibility for health care provision, it was clear that this level needed to be included in this book as well as the national level with its framework legislation rights. The potential diversity of the implementation throughout the country should be reflected in the diversity of the sample of sources and interviewees. Therefore, ideally the following requirements were set:

(a) The counties should in some way be TYPICAL FOR THE AVERAGE SWEDISH CITIZEN. In this sense, the two major cities Stockholm and Gothenburg should be excluded as they pose specific problems and advantages, which are not common to the majority of other county councils.
(b) Furthermore, the sample should also show some GEOGRAPHICAL VARIATION. This is in order to cover some variation in the population patterns and the distance from the political centre of the country. It is also to compensate for and track potential effects that might arise from closer networks or collaborations in individual areas, as well as the easier climate conditions and shorter distances in the south of the country.
(c) Next to these criteria, at least one of the chosen county councils should be one of the relatively NEWLY FORMED 'REGIONS' in order to check for potential implications for patient participation.
(d) As the degree of patient involvement might be subject to political majorities, some VARIATION IN THE POLITICAL TENDENCIES should be considered by opting for at least one county ruled by the 'bourgeois' block and a county ruled by the social democrats for a longer period of time.[10]

[10]Another criterion, that was particularly relevant during the 1990s, namely the introduction of a purchaser–provider split in some of Sweden's counties as well as the share of private providers, is no longer a meaningful separator, since all counties have some amount of contracted private providers within the publicly funded health care system. They, therefore, do not differ in any relevant sense from each other.

After a thorough look at the information provided by several authorities and the county councils on election results and what form of involvement takes place in the respective counties (to get an overview cf. Statistiska Centralbyrån 2011b; Sveriges Kommuner och Landsting 2011a,c) as well as several talks with researchers involved in the topic (interviews 36, 41, and 49), the three counties that matched the abovementioned criteria best were the region Skåne (Scania), the county of Östergötland,[11] and the county of Västerbotten.

The rather densely populated region SKÅNE was formed in 1999. With its major cities Malmö, Helsingborg, and Lund in the south it has been ruled by a conservative government for several years, but has been repeatedly shifting between the two major political blocks over time. Interestingly, the bourgeois block has formed a coalition government with the Environmental Party here. In recent years it has experienced an economic upswing in the sectors of agriculture and high-technology. VÄSTERBOTTEN in the north with Umeå as the only major town has a low population density in wider parts of its territory and has been governed by a social democratic government during the last decade. Beyond Umeå with its port and university it is mainly the woodworking industry, farming, and mining that is of importance. ÖSTERGÖTLAND, about halfway between Stockholm and Malmö, with its two major cities of Linköping and Norrköping has experienced a political change to a conservative majority after decades of a social democratic council. The county inherits a mixture of agricultural, industrial (with, e.g., SAAB Inc's headquarter), and high-technology sectors.

In order to approach the questions on the development and an assessment of patient involvement from both ends, the approach was to include a broad spectrum of patient organisations and those responsible for health care provision or commissioning in these three counties as well as on the national level. On the level of counties it was therefore decided to interview either politicians sitting on the respective health care committees, if possible those responsible for patient involvement, or civil servants who are responsible for this field.[12] On the side of patients, the best choice turned out to be the regional umbrella organisations of the patient organisations (see Sect. 8.3.1.3 on page 236).

In order to include the national perspective, these interviews were complemented by interviews with the Association of Sweden's Municipalities and Counties (*Sveriges Kommuner och Landsting* (SKL)), the newly established government authority health care analysis from a patient's and user's perspective (*Vårdanalys*), several patient umbrella organisations, and several research academics. Besides the interviews, the case study draws mainly on scientific literature and the 'State's

[11] In the meantime, the county Östergötland was renamed to 'region Östergötland' with effect as of 1 January 2015.

[12] In contrast to many continental countries, the role of the administration on municipal, county council, and national level is often essential, all the more since politicians up to the level of county counties most often do their job alongside their regular job. Depending on the topic, interviewing the civil servants responsible for specific fields might even be the better choice when it comes to a qualified overview.

**Table 8.2** Overview of conducted interviews & talks in Sweden

| Interview No. | Category of interview partner | Organisation and/or name | Date |
|---|---|---|---|
| 36 | Patient representatives | 1 representative, *Handikapporganisationernas sambarbetsorgan* (HSO), national umbrella | May 2011 |
| 37 | | Agneta Lindqvist, chairperson & Carola Eriksson, ombudsman, *Handikapporganisationernas samarbetsorgan* (HSO), branch Östergötland | September 2011 |
| 38 | | Lars Gustavsson, ombudsman, *Handikapporganisationernas samarbetsorgan* (HSO), branch Skåne | September 2011 |
| 39 | | 3 representatives, *Handikapporganisationernas samarbetsorgan* (HSO), branch Västerbotten | September 2011 |
| 40 | | Anki Sandberg, chairperson & NSPH, Kjell Broström, 'Attention' which collaborates with NSPH, the National Collaboration for Mental Health (*Nationell Samerkan för Psykisk Hälsa*) | September 2011 |
| 41 | Representatives of the County Councils | 1 civil servant, County council Östergötland | May 2001 |
| 42 | | 2 civil servants, County council Östergötland | September 2011 |
| 43 | | Christer Sörliden, Region of Skåne, politician for *Folkpartiet*, chairman of the Handicap committee | September 2011 |
| 44 | | Anders Åkesson, Region of Skåne, politician, responsible for health care and dentistry, group leader for the Green Party for the region of Skåne and chairman of the Green Party in county councils | September 2011[a] |
| 45 | | Karin Lundström, County council Västerbotten, politician for social democrats | September 2011 |
| 46 | Representatives at the state level | 1 senior employee, Sveriges kommuner och landsting (SKL) | September 2011 |
| 47 | | Fredrik Lennartsson, chairperson, State authority 'Myndigheten för vårdanalys' | September 2011 |
| 48 | | Toivo Heinsoo, Chief investigator for the previous government regarding patients' position and rights, nowadays Stockholm's county council's director | September 2011 |
| 49 | Researchers | Christina Fleetwood, Stockholms universitet | May 2011[b] |
| 50 | | Sophie Söderholm Werkö, Formerly Stockholms universitet, nowadays project manager at SBU | September 2011 |
| Total length of recorded interviews: 12 h | | | |

[a]This interview was conducted on the phone
[b]This interview was not audiotaped

Public Investigation Series' (*Statens offentliga utredningar* (SOU)). Table 8.2 on the preceding page gives an overview of the interviews finally conducted.[13]

## 8.3 Patient Involvement in the Swedish Health Care System

### *8.3.1 Equivalents to Patient Involvement*

> All citizens shall be given possibilities to participate in broad discussion also prior to decisions and between elections. (SOU 2000:1, p. 243; author's translation)

What potential equivalents for collective patient involvement at hospital level can be found in Sweden? The following portrays the work of patient organisations, the extent of individual patient rights, the ombudsmen's function as well as the Swedish form of collective patient involvement.

#### 8.3.1.1 Individual Patient Rights

Even though going beyond the British 'NHS constitution' in some respects, Sweden's individual patient rights are a relatively recent and still less marked phenomenon (cf., e.g., Glenngård et al. 2005, pp. 28 et seq.; cf. also Olofsson, Nilsson & Wahllöf 2010; Söderholm Werkö 2008, pp. 48, 49, 52; Trägårdh 1999, p. 17), which leads Trägårdh (1999, p. 13) to describe patient involvement prior to 1990 as 'a single white spot', at least as 'difficult terrain'. The main reason for weak patient rights is by many seen in the type of law that does not postulate what rights Sweden's citizens have, but rather clarifies the responsibility accruing to county councils (and municipalities) (*skyldighetslagstiftning* (fig.: legislation of obligations) versus *rättighetslagstiftning* (fig.: legislation of rights); more on this differentiation and its effects cf. Karlsson (2003).

Until the 1990s, citizens had to enrol at the polyclinic in the catchment area they lived in (Glenngård et al. 2005, pp. 52, 99; Haarmann & Wieseler 2006, p. 73; Hjortsberg & Ghatnekar 2001, p. 53; Olofsson et al. 2010; SOU 2008:37; cf. also Saltman 1994). Nowadays, they can choose any primary care provider, in most cases even outside their own counties (depending on the county called *vårdval* (fig.: choice of care) or *hälsoval* (fig.: choice of health)). However, this does not always work out as easy as it seems on paper (cf., e.g., Glenngård et al. 2005, p. 118; Söderholm Werkö 2008, p. 47). The individual right to be properly informed by the health care provider and take part in decision-making concerning treatment was decreed, too (Johnsson and Sahlin 2010; see Appendix B.4.1 on page 347). Besides

[13]A warm thank you goes to Ninni Mäki, who transcribed all the Swedish interviews!

these rights, all counties have introduced the national 'treatment guarantee',[14] the patient right to obtain a second opinion, to have access to one's own records, and for patients with a different mother tongue than Swedish to be assisted by a translator (Stockholms läns landsting 2004; Signäs 2009). These rights, though, are not enacted in the law. Another right, which patient organisations have long been striving for, is the right to be consulted by the same physician in primary care. However, this is impeded by limited capacities and the system of bookings appointments, so that patients often either need to wait several weeks or put up with a different physician.

Maybe it is not much of a surprise, then, that in such an environment almost any conversation and interview—with the exception of the patient organisations' umbrella organisations—heads towards the understanding of patient involvement as an *individual* involvement within the patient–physician dyad. Many equal the above-mentioned rights to patient involvement, which, of course, holds true in a certain sense, even though it is not the involvement under focus in this book.

Any further extension of individual patient rights is partly impeded by decentralisation (interview 48): At the national level the field of health care policies has become toothless as it lacks effective steering instruments. This is because county councils became more active in health care policies and began to reorganise their respective systems (cf., e.g., Jakubowski & Saltman 2013, pp. 60–61; Sahlin-Andersson 1999; on the attempt to re-centralise certain competences cf. Erlingsdóttir 1992; Glenngård et al. 2005, p. xv). As mentioned in several interviews, but specifically addressed by the representatives of the authority(-like) institutions at the national level (interviews 46–48): The treatment guarantee, the choice of provider in primary care, but also the health care act with its stipulation of involvement are examples of successful agreement between the national government and the county councils' governments. However, when the going gets rough, the central government can give whatever guarantee it wants in the field of health care, but if county councils decide not to comply there are no legally binding rules it could invoke. In order to compensate for the weak steering mechanisms, the central government is usually pouring out additional funding for the county councils' willing to comply, trying to regain some control over health care issues that way

[14] '*Vårdgarantin* (literally: care guarantee) aims at limiting waiting times in health care. It follows the so-called 0–7–90–90 maximum, which means that it must be possible to contact a primary health care provider on the very same day, get an appointment within 1 week, get an appointment with a specialist within 90 days after referral, and start the treatment within 90 days after a decision is reached, provided by another county council if need calls for it (Sveriges Kommuner och Landsting 2011d). The county councils Kalmar and Stockholm have somewhat lower guaranteed waiting times. Interesting enough, this is the third guarantee of its kind. The two previous ones were abandoned as soon as waiting lists fell below certain thresholds—and the additional funding poured out became too expensive—and re-introduced once waiting times were up again. Moreover, there is also another side of the guarantee as it yields unintended, negative consequences in that some surgeries are no longer solely determined by the medical urgency of treatment but rather by the aim not to trespass on the politically given waiting time limits (Nordin 2010; Sundelin 2011; Winblad & Andersson 2010:9).

(cf. also Haarmann & Wieseler 2006). This usually works out as some agreement is reached in the end, which very well fits into the traditional Swedish framework of consensual policy making (Jann 1983; North & Werkö 2002, p. 789).[15] The constellation shows how fragile the construction is.

#### 8.3.1.2 The System of Ombudsman

Interestingly, though Fallberg and MacKenny (2003) and Fallberg (2003) praise a well-functioning system of ombudsmen in Sweden, none of the people with whom I talked agreed. This ostensible contradiction, however, seems to be rooted in a slightly different terminology used: What was translated into 'ombudsman' is usually called *förtroendenämnd* ('Committee of Confidence').

Plans to introduce ombudsmen in the health care complaint boards dated back some decades (Karlsson 2003, pp. 175–201; cf. also Mot 1973/1190). Today, their aim is stated 'to further the contacts between the patients and the health care staff as well as to facilitate the help the circumstances demand' (1 § SFS 1992:563; author's translation). Even though parts of the competences—e.g. making contact to the citizens—have been transferred to other committees in some county councils, in practice one of the main tasks remains to serve as a kind of complaint committee (SOU 1997:154; cf. also Östman & Leijd-Tidbeck 1985, pp. 20–21). While the basic principle is ubiquitary, its specificities can vary from one county to the next.

'Committees of Confidence' exist in each county and in most municipalities and are, once again, usually composed of politicians (for a more general overview cf. Henningsen 1986, pp. 310–312). In contrast to England, where the Health Care Commissioner comes closest to an authority, or Germany, where the complaints office often is an association taking over this task or a council constituted of

[15]In this regard, context factors have completely shifted in comparison to the late 1980s, a time for which Immergut concludes the virtual lack of veto-points and rather unitary, national policies in Sweden (Immergut 1992, p. 228). This relates both to an absolutely different understanding of political opposition as the division of competences.

One of the interviewees summarised this point very well by saying, 'And that [...] can sometimes be experienced as a frustration by the state that it is difficult to steer with the [...] steering instruments it has to its disposal. And where, certainly, at the county council's level it is thought that the state steers too much. Concurrently, a lot of this has been developed by legislation in the first place, but [...] many a time [...] it was that from the side of the state and from the side of county councils they agreed about something and sealed an agreement about it first. Amongst other things the thing about the 'treatment guarantee' [...]. So, that is something which does not occur when the state says, 'And now this is what counts!', so to speak. But this is something which is developed in consensus between the state and the county councils.

But then, what one has found several times when it is agreed in an agreement it is not so clear for the patient what actually applies, what legal status [...] such an [...] agreement has. Now, most recently a 'waiting-milliard' [*kömiljard*; additional money paid by the national government in order to cut waiting times; the author], so they must achieve certain goals. But at the same time it is thought on the government's side that it is still unclear for the ordinary patient. What rights do I actually have?" (interview 47; author's translation).

different parties of professional representatives, the Confidence Committee in Sweden consists of politicians only. What might be perceived an odd set up within both the British and the German context can be understood as the expression of a far-reaching democratic spirit in Sweden and a strong confidence in politicians—with a pinch of intervention and criticism from the citizens' side—as interpretors of the law. According to this view, they strive for good solutions for the general public in their role as representatives and are actually able to achieve them.[16]

#### 8.3.1.3 Patient Organisations

> We have a mandate from the United Nations to monitor that a large part of the citizens—girls and boys, women and men with a handicap—are fully awarded their human rights. (Handikappförbunden 2011a; author's translation)
>
> In a way: What is going on is both centralisation and decentralisation. And we need to bring that together. (interview 45; author's translation)

As in other countries, many patient organisations were originally founded by physicians. The patient movement of the 1960s and 1970s added many others, mainly with the aim to improve the quality of information and knowledge about a specific disease and its everyday consequences, but at the same time work and lobby for better living conditions for those who suffer from this disease. Interestingly, the question of access debated in the Swedish context is usually not related to access to health care, but access to public buildings and integration of handicapped individuals into public life. In that context, especially the late 1990s and 2000s were the heyday of discussion and architectural implementation. Ramps, guiding patterns along the streets, sounds at pedestrian lights, etc. were some of the measures taken (for an overview cf. also Fleetwood 2005, p. 36; Jeppsson Grassman & Svedberg 2007, p. 51). The three associations with the highest number of members are the 'Rheumatics Association' with 51,200 members (Reumatikerförbundet 2010, p. 13), the 'National Association of Cardiacs and Lung Sick' with 43,400 (Hjärt- och Lungsjukas Riksförbund 2010, p. 31), and the 'Diabetes Association' with 25,000 members (Svenska Diabetesförbundet 2011). Parallel to these large organisations, there are others with overall only some 40, 50 members in the country. The power

[16]This is linked to a culture of attention to societal problems, which, in turn, creates an atmosphere of addressing and trying to solve them. This corresponds with the high levels of trust measured by many studies (cf., e.g., Delhey & Newton 2005; Niklasson 2012, pp. 254 et seq.; van der Meer 1999). Trust incorporates a plethora of different dimension and is different for the multitude of actors and institutions we can trust in. van der Schee, Braun, Calnan, Schnee and Groenewegen (2007) show that taking trust in health care and its professionals in the Netherlands, England and Wales, and Germany as an example, i.e. countries, that are rather similar from a global perspective, differs substantially. Trust in government has been shown to be highest in Sweden among the four countries of this study, followed with only a small margin by the Netherlands, while Germany ranks lowest at the same level as the United Kingdom (OECD 2014, pp. 25–37; cf. also OECD 2011; for trust in other institutions cf. Edelman 2013; OECD 2014). Even though the measurement might be perceived as rather crude, the difference of approximately 20% points is telling.

they are able to exert does not necessarily correlate with their number of members: One of the illustrations most often mentioned by my interviewees in this respect is the fact that diabetics are the only group of chronically ill that enjoys the benefit of free disease-specific medication (interviews 36–38, 40), which amongst other reasons leads several scholars to attribute the Diabetes Association a strong underlying power (cf. Söderholm Werkö 2008; Trägårdh 1999, pp. 31 et seq.). The outcome might, however, also be owing to medico-historical reasons and a good portion of lobbying rather than a conscious decision-making process fostering inequality among chronically ill.

Interestingly, while public authorities most often refer to patient organisations as 'user associations', most regional and even the national umbrella organisation often refer to themselves as 'disability association'. A more recent designation is 'patient and kinship organisation' (*patient- och anhörigorganisation*). Underlying this self-conception is the understanding that all members of the organisations experience some problems, barriers, and a negative impact on everyday life and are, thereby, handicapped in one way or another. In comparison to Great Britain, organisations are not as visible in public space, but seem nevertheless to be a much more natural part of society. This, in turn, seems to work specifically to the advantage of associations for the mentally ill: Whereas the interviews at foundation trust hospitals for mental care in England stated that it is considerably more difficult to attract new members for the Council of Governors compared to 'ordinary' hospitals, Swedish organisations have not referred to this as a problem when recruiting members (see especially interview 40). In their own words, their self-conception can be summarised as follows:

> We are bearer of the most important knowledge—the own experience [of the illness/disability and its consequences]. We use the expertise to constructively contribute to societal improvements.—We see society from a holistic perspective. Our task is to change society.—Our activity consists of politically influencing and developing forms of cooperation within the disability movement. (Handikappförbunden 2011a,b; author's translation)

However, despite the high share of the population that joins associations in general (see page 229), patient organisations do not benefit from this: The estimated 90% citizen share in all kinds of associations can be contrasted to estimates by the four interviewed patient umbrella organisations of a 20 to 35% membership rate of all diagnosed individuals (interviews 36–40, 50). Looking at the major designations of membership (Vogel et al. 2003, p. 27) it can be concluded that Swedes choose associations they can benefit from financially, in which they can organise their spare time, or socialise. Organisations with political, charitable, or societal aims in the wider sense including patient organisations seem to be less preferred.

Most often ponderously named 'Disability Organisations' Collaboration Body' (*Handikapporganisationernas Samarbetsorgan* (HSO)) Swedish patient organisations usually have some 20 to 50 voluntary member associations and a few staff at the level of counties and a respective umbrella at the national level (cf. Handikappförbundens samarbetsorgan 2008; on the diversity of these umbrellas cf. Hugemark & Roman 2007). What is different to the other three countries is that due to the definition of what is understood as a handicap, patient organisations cover a rather broad spectrum of chronically ill. This ensures, if you like, a broad representation—in that all kinds of disability associations are involved—within a rather narrowly defined group—in that not all patients, but only those who are 'disabled' and organised are involved (cf. also Hugemark & Roman 2007). Having most of these different associations under one umbrella, which then represents all the handicapped with one voice, resembles to some extent the model found in the Netherlands with its large umbrellas, and safeguards that a broad range of interests among regular users of health care services is voiced. Even though the basis of patient organisations is somewhat broader than in the other three countries, they constitute no real alternative to patient involvement as such. However, as the following chapter will show, they constitute a key actor in what can be understood as a real equivalent.

### *8.3.2 The Emergence of Collective Involvement*

> The people have the right and duty to participate individually and collectively in the planning and implementation of their healthcare.
> ('Declaration of Alma-Ata', 1978, Principle IV)

This heading might surprise the attentive reader, as Sweden was chosen as a counter-case to the English NHS. However, Sweden has found its own form of collective patient involvement, that has little to do with that found in the Netherlands and England, but can, nevertheless, be perceived as a full-grown equivalent to them.

When talking to representatives of the Swedish patient organisations, they unequivocally appealed to the United Nations' declaration of Alma-Ata. Their stance was that by signing the declaration Sweden as a state became obliged to give them far-reaching counselling and co-determination rights. The argument runs that this was strengthened by the 'Healthcare Act' enacted in 1982 (*Hälso- och Sjukvårdslagen* (HSL)): 'There is a legal obligation within health care to collaborate with different organisations of patients and relatives that are concerned. We have that since 1982' (interview 38; author's translation). Given the very general character of this kind of declaration and the gap between intent and implementation in many countries, the inhabitants of most other countries would merely take it as a loose statement of intent.

The very first collaboration between patient organisations was the 'Collaborative committee for those partially capable to work' (*Samarbetskommittén för partiellt arbetsföra*), an umbrella organisation founded in 1942. A collaboration was initiated by the government which led to the 'Committee for those partially capable to work' (*Kommittén för partiellt arbetsföra*) from 1943 onwards until it ceased to exist in 1949 (Fleetwood 2005, p. 33).

After a break of almost 20 years and similar to the development in the Netherlands, mental care was the first sector to experience some informal models to involve users from the late 1960s onwards. The handicap-commission suggested in its final report to form the so-called handicap councils (*handikappråd*; SOU 1970:64). Only 6 years later they could be found in most municipalities and in all the counties (Fleetwood 2005, p. 34). Already during preparations for a new health care act in the early 1980s, it was intended to codify patient involvement in the new act. In the government's proposition this reads as follows:

> The word co-operation intends to highlight that collaboration shall always be a question of mutual giving and taking. [...] It is therefore not in question to bring about an occasion to participate in, e.g., a certain proposal on expansion, but the intention is that she [the patient; the author] shall be given the possibility to influence the content of the proposal by commenting on it based on her knowledge and experience. (Prop. 1981; author's translation)

Consequently, patient organisations invoke the 'Healthcare Act' enacted in 1982 next to the charter of Alma-Ata (WHO 1978). The '*Hälso- och Sjukvårdslagen* (HSL)' includes some groundbreaking novelties, of which the most important in this context was the obligation to collaborate with relevant actors:

> 7 § The county council shall plan its healthcare with the starting point of people's need of such care. [...]
>
> 8 § In its planning and development of healthcare, the county council shall collaborate with relevant state authorities, organisations, and private healthcare providers (HSL 1982:763; SFS. 1995:835; SFS 2002:452; author's translation)[17]

A third pillar upon which, according to patient organisations, patient involvement rests are the recommendations of government commissions. The most obvious and unambiguous states that, '[a]ll citizens should be given possibilities to participate in broad discussions also prior to decisions and between general elections' (SOU 2000:1, p. 243; author's translation). This kind of 'promise' can be contrasted to the British Sect. 11 of the 'Health and Social Care 2001', which postulates the very same but is, however, interpreted much more indirect and less consequently. Even though no more specific claim or structure can be deduced, Swedish patient organisations take it, in absence of other rights, literally and perceive it as a kind of guarantee that they will be involved. Interestingly, the state, in turn, appears to be inclined to keep its promise.

### *8.3.3 Involvement via User Organisations*

In the time following the enactment of the 'Healthcare Act', there were some projects going on in several counties experimenting with different forms of involvement, the county councils of Västerbotten (Umeå), Östergötland (Linköping

[17] § 21 raises the same point with regard to municipalities and (long-term) care, §§ 1, 5, and 21a of the Social Services Act ('Socialtjänstlagen (SoL)'; SoL 2001:453-06) address the same point regarding social services, whereas § 6 of the Act on Support and Service for Certain Disabled ('Lag om stöd och service till vissa funktionshindrade (LSS)'; LSS 1993:387-05) aims at physically and mentally impaired.

and Norrköping), or Västra Götaland (Gothenburg) being pioneers in the field. Östergötland, for instance, had the so-called medical programme, which formed the basis for a broad societal and systematic discussion between politicians and citizens designed as a continuous feedback loop not only on health care related topics but also other topics related to democracy. This so-called citizen dialogue (*medborgardialog*), in turn, formed part of the 'Model for knowledge based (health-) care' (*model för kunskapsbaserad vård*; Broqvist 2002; Nyrén 1999). The role of being forerunners, however, seems to have less to do with population density or financial resources than above all the implementation of a purchaser–provider split and a debate about prioritising health care benefits as triggers in the first place. However, the picture that emerged over the time of my research showed that these forerunners rarely kept their position: As Östergötland, for instance, shows, project funding was eventually terminated as the 'citizen dialogue' was implemented in the regular routines. This did, however, not mean the continuation of the citizen dialogue but rather resulted in the change of administrative routines, which were viewed as a consequence of the dialogue. This was implemented just prior to elections to the county council and a generational change within administration, which exchanged a large portion of politicians and civil servants (interviews 41, 42; Garpenby 1997, 2002), brought Östergötland's leadership role in patient involvement to a halt, other counties caught up.[18]

The basic assumption in the early phase of my research in Sweden was that each county would—being influenced by party politics, by the dedication to models of a purchaser–provider split, by the financial power of the various county councils, or the population density—have developed and implemented its own form of patient involvement with its own specific degree of patient involvement. This could be the more assumed, because since the reorganisation of health care regions in 1995 it is up to each region to decide upon their own way to involve patients (for a more general overview cf. Fleetwood 2005, p. 36). Over time, however, one unitary model of collaboration between political committees and patient organisations emerged, which nowadays can basically be found in all counties with only minor variations. This main form of involvement called *samråd* (deliberation/consultation) is the regular discussion between representatives of the patient umbrella organisation and politicians at the county council level in charge of any topic relevant to chronic patients of the health care systems (interview 44; see Fig. 8.1 on the next page). Usually, there are one to two ordinary meetings per year between politicians, the county councils' administration, and patient representatives. Depending on the form of collaboration, a number of additional meetings with various topics and various compositions of those involved are convened, which predominantly occur in the

[18]It can be argued that the county council's organisation resembles the patient organisations in the sense that they are dependent on individuals to drive certain topics. If a concept, that has successfully been run for 10 years, comes to a halt because of a change in personnel, the routines do not seem to be rooted in the organisation, so that one can speak of a weak organisation. Credit for this observation as with many others regarding the relationship between politics and administration goes to Barbro Krevers.

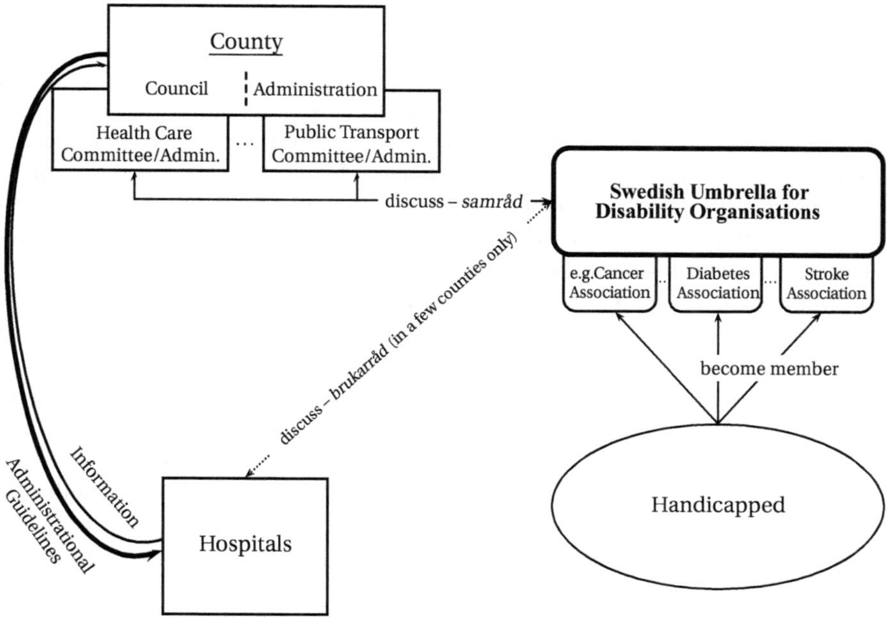


**Fig. 8.1** Common relations at the level of county councils. Source: own depiction

respective subcommittees. There is usually an equivalent at the municipal level to discuss matters of (long-term) care. At both levels, in particular, however, at the municipal level, youth and pensioner councils are incorporated in the discussion (cf. also SOU 1988:65).[19]

This main pillar of collective involvement is, at bottom, a kind of neo-corporatist and indirect setup, in a double sense. For the first, *representatives* of the patient organisations' umbrella are involved, for whom selection is applied all the way up: From all patients to only chronic patients, to only those who are organised in a sickness-specific patient organisation at the local level, to those who are also represented at the regional level, to only those whose patient organisations are members of the main umbrella in the respective county. It is, second, indirect with regard to health care provision in that the main form of collective involvement

[19]Keeping track of patient involvement within the different county councils is not an easy endeavour, as it is not a prominent issue in many of them. What adds to the difficulties of information gathering is that there is not one single word for involvement, neither in the scientific or political literature nor in everyday practice. The most usual terms are *samråd* (deliberation/consultation), *medverkan* (participation/involvement), *samverkan* (collaboration/cooperation), and *brukarråd* (board of users), but you will also find *folkstyre(lse)* (steering/governance by the people; somewhat dated), *inflytande* (influence), or *medborgardialogen* (citizens dialogue). All these terms imply slightly different connotations and are sometimes exclusively used in one specific context only. Overall, however, they all describe involvement of patients, recipients of care, or citizens.

does not occur with the respective hospital management, but politicians at the county council level acting as intermediaries. Among politicians responsible for health care issues there can be some responsible for a number of specific related areas in various subcommittees, which gives patient organisations the possibility to discuss difficulties and subpar solutions but also different needs for specific patient groups with politicians and exert influence. In that sense the Swedish form of involvement interestingly resembles the German 'Joint Federal Committee' (G-BA) in that the umbrella organisations of patient and consumer associations can discuss their concerns at decision-making level.

Owing to the often long-lasting contacts and the regular meetings between both sides a trusting work climate is not a rare phenomenon, which makes collaboration effective and appreciated by both sides (interviews 36–40, 43, and 44). The spectrum of topics varies immensely and ranges from improvements in access to public buildings for the handicapped, through the discussion on new vehicles or changed routes for public transport or ambulance services and inclusion of specific drugs or a specific therapy, to the organisation of treatment or better integration of health care run by the county council and care services run by municipalities.

From a more abstract point of view, a twofold development can be observed: While, on the one hand, competences for (health-)care are decentralised to the county councils and municipalities, as in the Netherlands a tendency to move away from lay-people to a more professionalised patient organisation can be discerned over the years, on the other. Hand in hand with this professionalisation goes a centralisation of patient organisations from the local to the county council level and, to some extent, also national level.

#### 8.3.3.1 A Change in Attitude Towards Involvement

> Previously, there was talk about the experience of users, but not about knowledge. (interview 40; author's translation)

So far, the question remains as to why the specific Swedish model of involvement evolved, what has led politicians to alter and amend an 'approved' and accepted chain of legitimacy, and why involvement emerged comparatively late? These questions can be answered by referring to a number of influencing factors.

#### 8.3.3.2 Historical Legacies

To sort things out, a short history of the Swedish welfare state might help to put things into perspective. At a more abstract level, a version could read as follows: At the beginning of the twentieth century, the Swedish welfare state was lagging behind in some parts, in others—as, e.g., health care—following an insurance model, which, however, in view of the low compensation levels is said to have been at the level of a 'social assistance state' (Sejersted 2011, p. 106). Besides the world's first national pension scheme (Olsson 1993, pp. 90–107, 216–221), the decision to subsidise unemployment funds and foster free collective bargaining between unions and employers—which was symbolically sealed by the historical 'Treaty of Saltsjöbaden' (*Saltsjöbadensavtalet*)—was one of the first and as of today still one of the most important steps in the emergence of the modern Swedish welfare state (Bendz 2004, pp. 117–119; SFS 1934:264). Whereas the pension system developed into a 'Bismarckian lite' insurance system (cf. Hinrichs 2007; Weaver 2004), the setup regarding wage bargaining has been revived and the way of paying unemployment benefits basically remains the same. Thus, pension and unemployment insurance can also be seen as one of the institutions reflecting the strong corporatist element in the Swedish welfare state (Pestoff 1992), which becomes the more relevant in this context as they can be interpreted as a self-governance in Sweden: In several documents and reports the Swedish version of the Gent model is presented as one of the democratic pillars of the Swedish welfare state (cf., e.g., SOU 1968:47, p. 71; cf. also Duffy 1989; Jahn 2009, p. 131; Sejersted 2011; for information on the Gent model see footnote 9 on page 229).

In contrast to these hitherto rather self-organised and -governed solutions, the rise of the Swedish social democrats beginning in the 1930s (Henningsen 1986, p. 153) gradually led to a different self-conception of the state: The concept of the solely enabling state changed to the role of the organising and providing guarantor of social rights and services. Concurrently, democratic rule became the primary new standard, which allowed corporatism to coexist as a special form compatible with democracy. Since then, it seems that the citizens' role has been confined to being the custodians of good practice while action is left to the well-meaning, patriarchal spirit of political bodies (cf. Söderholm Werkö 2008, p. 49).

#### 8.3.3.3 The Primacy of Democratically Elected Politicians

Given the circumstances and development described so far, a strong primacy of democratically elected politicians evolved over time. The underlying reasoning of the argument, which was also mentioned by some of my interviewees (interviews 45, 46, and 48), runs that patient involvement was not (perceived) necessary for a long period of time as the task was discharged by democratically elected politicians. This is explained by the logic of democratic elections as well as the closeness of local and regional politicians, who sometimes only represent several hundreds of inhabitants on the political bodies (Karlsson 2003, pp. 201–202; cf. also North & Werkö 2002, p. 782; Rothstein & Bergström 1999; Vienonen 2000, pp. 61–62). While some interview partners found some credibility of the argument regarding the local level, this leaves us with a somewhat more mixed image regarding county councils. On the one hand, '[c]ounty councils are nevertheless pretty large... In Sweden we have never found that there has been exceptionally much of a dialogue between the county councils' politicians and the population. The county councils' politics is pretty much unknown in Sweden.' (interview 37; author's translation) In this context, owing to the fact that the interest for elections at the level of county councils has never been particularly high they have even been called 'the forgotten elections' (Karlsson 2003, p. 92). Furthermore, Steinmo reminds us that social democrats worked hand in hand with large corporations in their early years in power in order to bring unemployment down. He also shows that they did not always follow the logic of democratically elected representatives of the people, either (see the section on technocratic ruling on page 227; Steinmo 1993, pp. 89, 125). On the other hand, taking Östergötland as an example with its almost 430,000 inhabitants and having 101 MPs in the county council (Landsting i Östergötland 2012), the likelihood that you know some of them is rather high compared to many other countries. Overall, as tricky as the argument is, it still gives a good idea of the view on the relation between state and citizen.

Getting back to the line of thought that democratically elected politicians safeguard the patients' interest, patient involvement is not of late emergence, but has always existed (in particular interview 46): Politicians were elected from the people, by the people, for the people, and knew what is good for the majority of the people. Moreover, with the ombudsmen and the 'National Board of Health and Welfare' (*Socialstyrelsen* (SoS)) there were even more actors who represented the patients' will (Karlsson 2003, p. 172). In that view and with such a bunch of actors and authorities acting in the name of the citizen, citizen or patient involvement was simply unnecessary. This is underlined by the following quotation by a representative of an umbrella of patient organisations. It shows that the acceptance of new actors next to politicians was difficult, whereas the existence of older corporatist actors was accepted:

> They say 'we cannot integrate you organisations, [...] then you are in and meddle in the citizens' power, which they have given to the politicians to decide. [...] And if [...] we would let you in [...] we would double the influence'. This actually holds true for all interest organisations, unions of all kinds, they are also subject to this double [influence; ...]. During the 1990s this political democracy was advocated [...]. And I know that we made references to other countries, I think Holland is an example, where you have user involvement legally codified. And we highlighted such examples in the debate. (interview 40; author's translation)[20]

However, if that was indeed the situation, how did change come into play?

[20]To some extent, the critical perspective on interest representation via patient organisations within the realm of politics sometimes still shines through contemporary rhetoric, even though formulated a bit differently: 'The patient movement, [...] they believe in any case...—but maybe it also is that way—I mean, do you have your own [political committee (*nämnd*)], so they have more access to meet them [the politicians]. And the questions are maybe prioritised in another form. However, by and large the whole healthcare system has a responsibility specifically for impaired and handicapped. And, I mean, it is often people who use healthcare pretty much, so that there are no clear-cut boundaries.' (interview 45; author's translation).

### Democratising Citizens

A first starting point in the change of the unmitigated primacy was a report commissioned by the government which made the underlying goal clear: To bring more democracy to the lowest administrative level, the municipalities, by devolving power to these lower administrative levels as well as by involving citizens (North & Werkö 2002, p. 782; SOU 1984:83; cf. also SOU 1984:84). In this view, the 'Healthcare Act' enacted in 1982 (HSL 1982:763) with its very broad claim to involve the groups relevant for health care pre-empted the general development to some extent. This changed view was partly inspired by the reform of the parliament in 1975 (cf. Sveriges Riksdag 2011, p. 16), which sought to democratice society . However, as it took another 10 to 15 years until patient involvement worth the name was practised in everyday life, it can be regarded an important piece in the jigsaw puzzle, but not the actual starting point or even a main reason.

### Purchaser–Provider Split, Prioritising, and the Spirit of Entrepreneurship

Having decades of the primacy of politicians as a baseline there were two catalysts in the field of health care that brought some change into what following Esping-Andersen might be called 'frozen landscape of involvement'. The first was the introduction of the treatment guarantee in combination with the introduction of the purchaser–provider split in a number of county councils in the mid-1990s.[21] As the second catalyst the discussion surrounding what is called 'open prioritising' health care treatment can be discerned.

Bringing in the perspective of competition (Michelsen 2002, pp. 177 et seq.; cf. also Bjuggren 1998; Calltorp, Persson, Holmström, Levin & Persson 1988)—even though in many cases only competition between public providers—was followed by legislation on quality in health care (Johnsson 2010; cf. also Krevers 2003, pp. 4 et seq.; on the difficulties of imperfect markets in this context cf., e.g., Cohn 1992:2). In combination with the first introduction of the treatment guarantee in 1992, county councils realised a less competitive position of their hospitals if quality and efficiency targets were not fully met and patient orientation less pronounced than in the case of private providers. This also gave rise to the insight that it is important to listen to and know what patients/users/clients think:

> It is possible that we have had a much more publicly steered healthcare, and that a perspective of competition in our (health-)care has been smaller, [...] that in the countries

---

[21] Or 'buy-sell' (*köpa-sälj*) as it is termed in some county councils, in order to avoid the ideologically laden terms of purchaser and provider (see interview 41). Even though the client- and user-terminology (see also Sect. 9.2 on page 288) was not as heavily employed as in England, a much stronger ideological distinction could be observed than nowadays between conservatives, who were generally in favour of a purchaser–provider split and even full privatisation to some extent, and social democrats who were only hesitantly positive.

where there is a greater [share of] private providers, it has been simply more relevant to find out about the user [preferences]. (interview 44; author's translation)

This development was paralleled by a change from saving costs as the main goal to maintaining spending levels and increasing quality at the same time.

The essential importance of this catalyst, however, was not primarily the formal reorganisation, but rather politicians' self-conception: With the first attempts to introduce a purchaser–provider split the ambivalent, dual role of politicians being in charge of deciding on the provision of health care services for the respective county council's citizens, on the one hand, and, at the same time, as the representatives of the very same citizens towards the provider—i.e. themselves—on the other, became more obvious and absurd (interview 41). Politicians decided to change their role and become the advocates of the citizens, rather than the commissioners of care. Owing to the shift of perspective, citizens were converted from a collective mass that is governed for its own best to individuals making their own decisions on 'shopping around' for high-quality care. The new relation between citizens and politicians became even more pointed in the term 'citizen politician' (*medborgarpolitiker*; North and Werkö 2002, p. 791), which a number of them applied to underline their understanding of their profession.

The second catalyst was the discussion on 'open prioritisations'—consciously chosen to mark the line to informal, opaque, unwanted prioritisations that are made unsystematically—which also gave rise to thinking about changed roles of politicians. The categorisation of health statuses and diseases into classes of necessity began in the late 1990s under the impression of austerity after the previous economic recession. The treatment classes lose in priority from top to bottom, whereby treatment, that falls into the lowest class is not funded by the public health system (for more information on prioritisation cf. Glenngård, Hjalte, Svensson, Anell & Bankauskaite 2005, pp. 36, 101–102; Hjortsberg & Ghatnekar 2001, pp. 27–28; Nyrén 1999; Rosén 2006; Söderholm Werkö 2008; SOU 2001:8).[22] With this trigger, a new process of rethinking the provision of health care was sparked in the internal circle of government, county councils, and their umbrella organisation 'County Councils' Association' (*Landstingsförbundet* (LF)), the predecessor of today's Swedish Association of Local Authorities and Regions (*Sveriges Kommuner och Landsting* (SKL)). Beyond this general framework, the

[22]To summarise the topic: Starting from the main assessment that health care related taxes should not be raised any further and funding was not sufficient for *all* kinds of treatments regardless of their necessity, a broader, philosophic-academic discussion was initiated, which resulted in the categorisation of four broad classes of treatment, which were subsequently considerably refined:

- 'care of life-threatening diseases, palliative care and care of people with chronic diseases and disabilities,
- preventive and rehabilitative services,
- care of patients with non-acute and non-chronic diseases, and
- care for reasons other than illness or injury' (Glenngård et al. 2005, pp. 26–27; SOU 2001:8; cf. also Socialstyrelsen 1999:16, p. 15; Twaddle 1999, pp. 9–11, 92 et seq., 212).

discussion was carried on in different contexts (Broqvist 2002; Garpenby 2002; SOU 2006:6) for the next 10 years. This is nicely summarised in one interview:

> But also this new view that has pressed in into public action. [...] The resources are, in relation to the need, not as large as they have been previously, but we rather have a stronger need to prioritise. And for this one want to have input on that we prioritise correctly. (interview 38; author's translation)

Overall, one consequence was that for the first time in decades, the state—in its wider sense, including the county councils—was not the only provider of health care. In combination with the discourse about prioritising services, this, in turn, partly changed the relation between politicians and citizens, who were now able to choose between providers and their quality of services.

#### 8.3.3.4 Zeitgeist, the Economy, and a New Generation of Politicians

> You met politicians, but I do not believe that you influenced [them]. It was rather that you sat there and exchanged information, in a way [...] that politicians came with almost adopted resolutions that now we are going to do it this way. Thus, it was rather that information was conveyed. However, this has changed into a form of dialogue. (interview 38; author's translation)

Via the detour of both of these developments and in combination with a generation change among politicians the perception of patients by civil servants and politicians has changed from that of being enervating whingers, always claiming more, always nit-picking, and criticising everything (interviews 43, 46) to eventually viewing them as contributors of valuable input, which can be summarised as follows:

> Previous generations of these politicians have not [...] been interested. Now we have had a huge age-shift within politics, and then it also matches the time we live in [...] to look at (health-)care in a different way. [...; M]any services are privatised, one is comparing oneself with the private sector. And there one goes with a different customer-thinking [...] and views patients more as a (health-)care customer. And there is basically no company that is not interested in 'what do the customers think about our products.' (interview 38; author's translation)

A first sign of this change in attitude was the memorandum *'Patienten har rätt'* (The patient is right; SOU 1997:154; cf. also Socialstyrelsen 2003b)—an attempt to dissolve the large psychiatric institutions and to accommodate the former patients out in the community. The final occasion that sparked action was a number of cases of malpractice and abuse in mental care—once again. In consequence, the government appointed a commission called 'psychiatry coordination' (*psykiatri-samordningen*), which worked from 2003 to 2007. In its final report, one of the major recommendations is to establish boards of users which incorporate all authorities concerned as well as relatives of users (Milton et al. 2006:100-11).

Many interviewees described patient involvement as something that needs to be done nowadays, which in other words might be described as a trend, a fashion, or following the zeitgeist. Next to a positive idea of democracy, the motivation for this development stems primarily from the hope to decrease relative costs for inefficient treatments, subpar workflows, and superfluous steps in the care chain:

> So, I think, if there is a focus on anything right now, it is precisely the one to involve patients [...] in the work in (health-)care. Thus, as a co-producer. The idea is to make (health-)care more effective by doing so. Thus, we get better results, it does not cost any money, it rather gets cheaper. [...] However, you never know how this will be in practice, but the idea [...] and the belief is that if the patient is more involved you will use [existing] resources more, you will obtain better results. [...] So, the vision and hope is in each case rather that it will make the use of resources more efficient. (interview 46; author's translation)

Patients are, in this view, another resource which can help with valuable knowledge that no other actor can provide. Thereby, patients are in a way also accepted as competent partners to discuss issues with:

> The thing we should not forget is that much knowledge is out there with the users, user organisations. And, thus, I believe that we must dare to let go [of the idea] that we are sitting here with all the right answers and have all knowledge ourselves. (interview 43; author's translation)
>
> I believe that a shift in perspective has happened, in the sense that it is realised that the patient has an unbelievably important knowledge surrounding her problems, her illnesses, and her sorrows, which [...] actually need to be considered in order to achieve good results. (interview 46; author's translation)

This meets the point of view of patient organisations and advocates of the patient perspective, who have a long time highlighted that not more resources per se will meet demands, but rather sometimes even small changes:

> We consider it very important not to become a creator of demand for more resources for (health-)care. We rather view it as our role to actually assist in making things more effective, not to become [...] someone who demands more resources for (health-)care, but rather who can contribute so that the existing resources can be utilised in a more effective fashion. (interview 47; author's translation)

At the same time, the aim of the dialogue to have more satisfied citizens can be discerned among both politicians and patient representatives alike. For this, the previously existing channels of (political) communication did not suffice, but new ones had to be invented. Today, *samråd* as the standard means of involvement described above (see Sect. 8.3.3 on page 240) is widely accepted and backed by government on all political levels and across all parties. Nevertheless, the abovementioned restrictions regarding legitimacy are not forgotten, thus, the search for a more encompassing involvement in one form or another goes on, be it 'citizens' dialogues' or founding authorities with a specific task:

> The tasks we have gotten from the government, they are to monitor and analyse (health-)care, dentistry, and the so-called interface between health care and care, but to do so from a patient, user, citizen perspective. And the explicit aim is partly to get more systematic and qualified monitoring of Swedish (health-)care. But also very clearly that [the government] want to see more of a monitoring and assessment, with a distinct patient perspective in order to contribute to strengthening the patient's position. (interview 47; author's translation)

No matter what form the dialogue between patients on the one and politicians and administration on the other hand take on, it serves at least two purposes simultaneously. It is easier to inform patients and to explain to them why certain cuts or changes have been decided on, which, ideally, in turn, is able to create understanding and trust between both parties, something that politicians themselves are conscious about: Talking about a new policy guideline on hearing aids, one of the interviewed politicians summarised:

> And [at this informational gathering] they could ask as many questions as they wanted, and I responded. And there I realised that if you had been critical in the beginning and you get knowledge about what shall happen, they also felt secure, even though they did not buy the whole reasoning there, either. [...] There were a lot of rumours, it is going to be like this, it is going to be like that. [...] And as it would not be this and that, they felt, well, this is not as my neighbour says, it is going to be all right. Thus, it is pedagogical to be out there [among the citizens]. I believe it is also about having the rewards for meeting up, not only to get viewpoints, but also to get the opportunity to explain. (interview 43; author's translation)

A second advantage is that special needs, which have been overlooked so far or were not judged to be of sufficient relevance by decision makers, can be addressed by the patient organisations and thereby awareness raised. Thus, in theory, patient involvement can be thought to serve several purposes and create a complete 'win-win situation'. In conclusion, it might be said that though it is no longer politicians who claim to automatically know what is best for the patients of their county, it is still them and the administration who weigh and translate problems into policy guidelines, which the interviewed representative of a patients' umbrella organisation puts it the following way,

> And there [...] is partly still something left over that one wants to inform, but it has proceeded more and more towards [...] that one wants to discuss the form [*utformningen*; of care], wants to have [feed-]back as a politician... Is there anything you think is not good, how do you experience (health-)care, and what can we do to make these things better? Thus, [...] there are more opportunities to influence. (interview 38; author's translation)

For politicians there lies an additional advantage in that the vote of a joint agreement weighs much more than simply their own word. Whether it is used strategically or not, it provides any proposal with additional legitimacy.

In that sense, neither has the previous primacy of politicians nor the view on patients simply been replaced, rather it has been complemented.

This has happened all within a timespan of about 10 years only, which makes involvement in (health-)care a rather new phenomenon. This can be observed in the academic literature, where, for instance, Liljeberg highlights the importance for health of being socially and politically involved and having the feeling of influence in society, while neither mentioning involvement in patient organisations nor in *samråd* or *brukarråd*. This is in line with the account on the changes over time of one of my interviewees me who began writing her PhD thesis on patient empowerment through involvement and knowledge transfer at the end of the 1990s and was met with reactions like,

> What is that? That is completely uninteresting! What do we need that for? [Nowadays, i]t is absolutely politically correct to speak about user involvement and to invite participants.

> And modern: Everyone wants to have a board of users. Then, however, what that actually comprises or means that can be something completely different. (interview 50; author's translation)

#### 8.3.3.5 Choice: Different Means to the Same End

> About choice and that like, it is really more of a political-ideological question, right? It has been believed that with greater competition it will become more effective, and that the quality will be raised, and things like this. But now, one is clearly not so sure about it. (interview 38; author's translation)

The turn towards collective patient involvement was preceded by the departure from reliance on choice as *the* credo in health care that will remedy most problems. Never a goal in itself and never as ideologically laden as in England, the departure was nevertheless a deliberate and pronounced one.

As mentioned earlier, the ideological differences between the two major political blocks had converged to a larger extent. Reasons for this diminished ideological toning might be the fact that there are more important issues to be solved or that rhetorics of choice and consumerism wore thin, were replaced by later developments, or were simply overtaken by the problems patients face. Another reason, however, might be that a social democratic Swedish government opposed plans of privatisation of hospitals proposed by conservative county council politicians for years in the 1990s and 2000s. In the end, neither type of health care provision—i.e. be it run by a county council or by a contracted hospitals—showing to be superior. This, as the latest reports on the issue show (cf., e.g., Hartman et al. 2011), has meant a serious blow for the idea of privatised health care provision. At the same time, the fear that the health care system would break down as soon as services are provided by non-state actors has not become reality, either.

The decline of ideological differences is in part also owing to a shift in the focus from the choice of provider to the choice of treatment across all political parties. The main concern, i.e., to raise quality and efficiency, still persists, only the recipe is exchanged (cf. Sveriges Kommuner och Landsting 2010a). What is more in the ascendance is the insight that not everyone has the resources to make active choices. Therefore, relying on patient choice will not work out for everyone. The interviewee at the association of municipalities and county councils (SKL) draws the parallel to the choice between different schools[23]:

> And there, I think, lies a responsibility to secure that all schools are good schools, and that they achieve some form of acceptable standard. It is the same in healthcare, too. You

[23] Interestingly, the way to the choice of provider took a similar pathway as in England, starting out from a promise of more quality through choice between schools, which over time has spread to the field of health care. According to the logic of improving democracy in general, involvement is—as in England—not confined to the field of health care, but it is striven for in other areas of society as well. More parents' involvement and competences in schools is one prominent area (SOU 2008:37, pp. 71–80), but far from being the only one.

> should not need to choose and be an active consumer [...] in order to be sure to receive good (health-)care, but you need to ensure...– There must be other systems in place. (interview 47; author's translation)

Hence, the latest idea is that, even though they are accompanied with their own intricacies, forms of patient involvement have the potential to fill this gap and ensure that everyone receives good (health-)care no matter what choice of provider and treatment is made.

### *8.3.4 Other Reasons for a Late Emergence of Patient Involvement*

Next to the main line of reasoning presented so far, other factors that might explain the late evolvement of patient involvement were mentioned by my interviewees. They could be perceived as alternative explanations. More convincing, however, is to see them as supplementary to the outlined story above.

#### 8.3.4.1 About Authoritarianism and Independence

One of these reasons, which was mentioned several times, perceived by patient organisations and politicians alike, was the a very hierarchical approach adopted by the medical profession in the past. The argument runs that physicians felt either independent enough, or primarily capable and skilled enough to know what is best for their patients:

> I think it is about culture, leadership that we maybe have had authoritarian people in the profession, who thought that 'I know things best', 'I do not need anyone who comes and tells me how I should do things to improve healthcare' [...]. I believe this is the major reason why we did not have user involvement earlier. (interview 43; author's translation)

As this was/is more or less the common attitude by physicians to be found in most western countries (until only rather recently) this speaks rather for a more marked change in Sweden than for a convincing reason particular to Sweden (cf. also Jespersen 1999). Another line of reasoning rather disproves this argument: It might well underline the emergence of *individual* shared decision making between physician and patient, but since physicians are usually not directly involved in most forms of collective patient involvement the argument is not really convincing for one single country.

Hierarchical behaviour is a point that does not necessarily contradict the above-mentioned observation of a democratic primacy. It has, of course, not only to do with a changed attitude on the side of politicians as well as patients, but also with some pivotal changes in the power relation between physicians and (many) patients, not only but to some degree owing to higher education, better self-management of chronic illnesses, and the rise of information technology.[24] Besides the sole statement on a change in the medical profession regarding hierarchy, one of the interview partners develops an interesting reasoning why each professional actor is sufficiently self-absorbed, yet somehow dependent on the other, the interplay between each other, and/or patients. Even though the argument is rather sketchy, it is definitively worth taking a second look at it, as it describes the actor network and its interdependencies very aptly:

> Previously, (health-)care was much more hierarchical so to speak. The consultant at a unit, he simply determines. Then, politicians could decide about certain overarching questions surrounding the budget and the like [...]. People agree much [...] when they are not in such a great need to take in considerations from the outside. Then, they thought, we know what is good for the patient. [...] All [actors] have in a way [...] a contradicting relationship to each other: Politicians think that people work against them from the bottom, and the medical profession, they think, so to speak, that they are exposed to permanent changes, permanent organisational reforms, and are not left alone to work in peace. And in between there is a broad layer of administrative clerks who want to present themselves as capable of acting. [...] And all of them seek partners for their [...] perspective in a way. We know that staff also get patients on their side who say, 'Stop, stop, this is not good!' [...] In that case [...] their position is naturally much stronger. [...] Politicians can also say [...] that the changes we propose now originally stem from patients. In that case [...] the position is much stronger. (interview 38; author's translation)

#### 8.3.4.2 Too Busy to...

A last supposition by an interviewee was that there were simply too many other reforms to the organisation of the welfare state in general and the health care system in particular, tasks that were perceived more urgent than listening to patients' needs directly:

> Previously, there were other problems absorbing all attention: Delivering the responsibility for (health-)care and the conversion of psychiatry. And many times, [...] patient organisations could only experience that municipalities and county councils were fully occupied with each other [...]. So, there was not that much time to listen to what patients, clients, or users [had to say]. (interview 40: author's translation)

[24]However, patriarchic and authoritative behaviour was embedded in society at large and not confined to the realm of medicine. In order to illustrate to what lengths a patriarchic-authoritarian spirit combined with the lack of service and customer orientation went (probably not only) in Sweden's mid-1970s, the following piece serves well: Karlsson (2003) recites the story of a journalist whose train was delayed by some hours after a journey of roughly 600 km and who claimed on the state-run railways to foot for the taxi bill for the last 60 km of his journey in order not to additionally add to the delay, as the next train would only depart in well over an hour. The Director General of the railways at the time referred to the terms of carriage (issued in 1925, still valid in the 1970s) denying any refund in cases of delay and added, 'Moreover, timetables have the purpose to show according to what plan railways are organised. They are, therefore, not intended to make a statement about departure or arrival times. [...] If SJ [*Statens Järnvägar*, Swedish Railways] needed to assume some kind of guarantee that trains run on schedule it might be that timetables are eliminated altogether.' (quoted in Karlsson 2003, pp. 9–10).

In my opinion, the argument is not convincing as such, as policy making is always a question of prioritisation and only to a smaller extent a question of limited attention. The arguments, however, lend some credibility if re-translated into a process orientation: Seen from an overarching perspective of the state the reforms implemented previously undoubtedly unlocked the greater potential for efficiency gains than patient involvement. In combination with the process to patient involvement outlined above, it was at least rational to implement other measures first. In addition, if the assumption holds true, it is another instance of the importance of perception as the selector of what topics are put on the agenda. In that sense, the question is not only whether the problem at hand is important, but it becomes a question of relative importance compared to other perceived problems.

### *8.3.5 Other Forms of Involvement*

> In the end, it counts that patients themselves think that they have power and influence. That is the final goal that is to be reached. [...] Most of what is written, said, and thought and organised is done from a provider's perspective, and that is completely untenable in the long run. Healthcare is there for the patients. (Vårdanalys (2012); author's translation)

No matter what kind of involvement is chosen in the four countries, representativeness and legitimacy is an issue in all of them. The aim is not just to pick anyone but to let individuals represent all patients acting not as individuals but as a fair representation of all concerned, even those who are 'net-payers' in the system. This seems less of a concern in Sweden, where patients with chronic illnesses and recipients of care are viewed as groups that do have some legitimate interest in how well the health care system operates and what is included in the benefits catalogue. In addition, supporting the ill is seen as a societal task. In that sense, the negative effects of illnesses are not individual, but societal issues, 'No-one should be left behind' (cf. LSS 1993:387-05; SoL 2001:453-06).

In addition to the general paradigm whereby politicians at all political levels are the true representatives of the entire population, some county councils have sought for—and some even implemented—additional measures of involvement. A rather rare approach is the so-called Citizens Dialogue' (*medborgardialogen*; in other areas also called 'Board of Citizens' (*medborgarråd*) or 'Citizens Panels' (*medborgarpenelen*). This is complemented by a pensioners council as an example for the attempt to come up with a universal approach to more citizens involvement (cf. Feltenius 2004; cf. also SOU 1988:65).

The county council of *Östergötland* experimented with this kind of involvement for several years, before the funding was withdrawn after a shift in government in 2002 (Garpenby 2001, 2002). The region *Skåne* has launched a similar programme on a permanent basis, which, however, is not limited to health care issues (Lidmark, Rosén and Skoog 2010–2011; Region Skåne 2009b, 2006; interviews 43, 44). The aims are manifold: Getting into contact with ordinary citizens is definitively one of them as is staying in touch with them and listening to their needs and concerns.

Furthering the relationship between the population and politicians by getting a much more direct feedback is definitively another. And, of course, even though all the politicians I talked to left at least the impression that they (also) hold a sincere belief in the added value of citizen and patient involvement, one might suspect that self-marketing plays also a role. Overall and lastly, citizens dialogue is specifically understood as an instrument to develop democracy (Nyrén 1999, cf.).

In addition to collective patient involvement *samråd*, a new form called *brukarråd* (council of users) was introduced. It resembles somewhat more the solution pursued in England and the Netherlands (cf., e.g., Regionstyrelsen Skåne 2011b; Region Skåne 2009a,b; cf. also Anbäcken 1985) and is in fact—with some modifications—fairly similar to the discussed alternative to the present system for Dutch hospitals, namely representation by patients' umbrella organisations. This form of involvement is the latest addition in user involvement in Sweden and only to be found in a few counties such as *Skåne*. Here representatives of the respective umbrella of patient organisations meet with representatives of the hospitals in the region in order to discuss issues they feel need to be addressed. It can be assumed that more provision related topics are raised during these talks, which can be decided without the involvement of the county council. Interestingly, whereas I got a detailed and vivid picture of *samråd*, little more was told about *brukarråd* other than that they exist and are of value, even in *Skåne*.

Meanwhile, the former *samråd* was abolished in Skåne in order to make way for a more encompassing collaboration: This is a merger of the former collaboration with patient organisations, the pensioners' representatives, and other actors relevant in the field of care and health care. It is intended to facilitate a more flexible platform for discussion and gather everyone around *one* table, which shall also extend discussion beyond the previous topics and, for instance, include questions related to the job market and health (interview 43).

Furthermore, the *brukarråd*, which were previously separated according to the respective group of users, were combined to form a joint so-called *brukarpanel* (user panel). The idea behind this new setup is to involve patient and pensioner organisations as well as groups of citizens concerned about certain topics and to form committees that suit the respective task at hand (interviews 43 and 44; Region Skåne 2011; Regionstyrelsen Skåne 2011a,b; Region Skåne 2009b). This might be facilitated by including only a subfraction of an interest organisation or by inviting all kinds of groups to have a joint discussion with all political and administrative committees of the county. Interestingly enough, the set-up of the *brukarpanel* once again resembles the practice applied for consultation within the 'federal joint committee' in Germany, where committees are formed from a larger pool of representatives according to topic and involving the particular group of experts (interviews 28 and 34). This is explained by one interviewee as follows:

> What we also have done is that we have gathered these Boards of Users to a user panel instead. And there are representatives from all of these [...] committees [*nämnder*]: healthcare committee, rehab committee, public transport committee. Representatives of our handicap organisations are also going to sit there. (interview 43; author's translation)

What politicians seek to accomplish is, thus, a broader base than just patient organisations, to get cross-topical groups around one table, and to jointly come up with solutions. Even though it remains to be seen to what extent these new instruments are successful, the development seems to go beyond *samråd* at least in some counties.

## 8.4 Appraisal of Patient Involvement by the Interviewees

> I would pose it this way: It is obvious that we are heading forward, but it is pretty slow. (interview 50; author's translation)
>
> We actually have very much legislation we can draw upon, but that does not play any role if no one cares what is in the law. (interview 37; author's translation)

In this chapter, an attempt at assessing patient involvement in Sweden from the actors' perspective is undertaken. One of the main differences to the Netherlands and England is that Swedish patients' umbrella organisations mention lobbying as one of their core activities much more often.

The following results on how patient organisations assess patient involvement in Sweden are all the more interesting as only few studies dealing with patient involvement exist, whereas the majority of studies on health care issues leave out the users' perspective completely (Fleetwood 2005, pp. 8, 10).

### *8.4.1 Topics Raised and the Way of Working Together*

> And also that it is a kind of individualisation. [...] The population is not viewed as a collective. (interview 44; author's translation)
>
> We use to say [...]—somewhat casually maybe, but—that the thing with user dialogue is a school [...] for our politicians to [...] understand that they are citizen representatives. (interview 42; author's translation)

Compared to interviews in the other three countries of this study, the focus mentioned by my interview partners was clearly not on collective patient involvement. Almost every single interview digressed towards issues of individual choice of treatment and the choice of provider (see also Sect. 8.3.3.5 on page 250), the age-old variant of 'exit and voice'. Patient organisations, naturally, highlighted the issues they had been dealing with. What concerned them most was what they were not satisfied with, and what they did to remedy those shortcomings. Representatives of the authorities and/or county councils' administration, naturally, raised topics of (health-)care organisation and quality (indicators). Moreover, what is remarkable is that besides these different emphases the assessment by politicians and civil servants, on the one hand, and patient organisations, on the other, coincide to a large extent.

An overall assessment of the discussion and collaboration with the county councils by patient organisations draws more or less the same conclusion as patients' umbrella organisations do in the Netherlands: Things are on track and doing fairly well, but there is still room for improvement. Moreover, the criticism levelled refers usually either to very specific decisions (e.g. the difference between 25 or 30 dB as a threshold for being granted a hearing-aid) or very broad trends within politics as, e.g. a perceived 'colder climate' in terms of social hardships under the 'bourgeois' government. The general framework of involvement, however, is hardly criticised at all. Representative for all other interview partners, the following quotation summarises the general perception by patient organisations fairly well:

> In my role as coordinator for NSPH ['National Collaboration for Mental Health'], especially the top level so to speak [...], we meet the authority's director of 'the National Board of Health and Welfare' or civil servants of the ministry of social affairs. They have a very good attitude towards us. (interview 40; author's translation)[25]

The answer from respondents who gave their assessment on who was the driving force behind more user involvement can be interpreted in such a way that of course it was the patient organisations' demand to increase patient and user involvement. However, it was not them who asked for the specific implementation to be found in contemporary Sweden. Rather, the final step was taken by politicians who found that more involvement was needed, a view which is not only supported by politicians themselves, but also backed by patient organisations:

> I do not really know whether one can say the patient organisations are behind these demands for greater involvement in care. I would rather like to say that it is rather the political parties which drive these questions. Rather. It is self-evident that patient organisations also do so. (interview 46; author's translation)

However, the following quotation illustrates two things: Firstly, it questions the politicians' role as the primarily driving force behind *collective* patient involvement. Secondly, and even more important, at least in the beginning there was a considerable difference in what is meant by 'patient involvement' between patient organisations, on the one hand, and politicians and civil servants, on the other: The possibility to influence policies appears to have been one of the differences of opinion in the past.

> That was what they [the authorities] wanted to accentuate, the individual level, while we wanted to highlight that we must get opportunities to be part and [...] influence how (health-)care is shaped altogether. (interview 40; author's translation)

Though patient organisations in some instances still wish to be involved at an earlier stage, they are taken with the fact that they are involved much earlier than

[25]One interviewee went as far as to say, 'I almost think that nowadays [...] it is almost easier for us to find a sympathetic ear among politicians and civil servants than it sometimes is to communicate internally, to get our own organisations started in the process, so [...] that inertia is almost stronger in our own world of members than... Concurrently, we have a pretty high average age.' (interview 38; author's translation).

in earlier days. No matter whom my interview partners represented, they agreed that meetings rather serve open-ended discussions whereby patients no longer primarily serve as a token only to legitimise political action without any further and more serious intention of involvement, which is not to say that using each other's statements in order to legitimise one's own action does no longer play in. Interestingly, even politicians seem to realise that a new openness, flexibility, and involvement worth the name is experienced very positively. One of my interviewees, who is in charge of introducing user involvement within the authority 'State's commission for medical assessment' (*Statens beredning för medicinsk utvärdering* (SBU)), spoke about her experiences with the users:

> There was a great gratitude from their [the patients; the author] side, because—they recounted that they are used to being invited to all kinds of public reviews and express their view. The common thing, however, is that when they are invited, they will get a ready-made proposal [. . . ], and they shall have some last-minute aspects on it. They were completely unused to being involved from the beginning when a project starts. So, they were very grateful that we invited them before our work had begun in the first place. (interview 50; author's translation)

The change of thought seems also to have influenced the way of dealing with each other. All interviewees agreed that most meetings take place in an atmosphere of open discussion among equals, when it comes to decisions on specific policy designs, designs of purpose-built buildings, or the regulation of organisation in health care. This new attitude towards recipients of care is described by two of my interviewees, politicians in *Skåne*:

> And this means that we jointly set the agenda and what questions shall be discussed, we set that jointly when we meet. [. . . ] And this is also the idea that the different boards of users—as where they meet the hospital's management—also have the opportunity to suggest ideas and thoughts, and first steps to the rather political level. (interview 44; author's translation)
>
> '[. . . ] I cannot promise that everything you think [is necessary] that it is [. . . ] what you will get, but I need to try to weigh in your aspects, look at other arguments [. . . ], and also try to have a holistic image of it all. [. . . ] [B]ut [it is important] to give an impression that you want to listen and that [. . . ] you do not involve the citizens, the patients when actually the decision has already been made. [. . . ] But you begin pretty early in that process, involve them, listen. 'What do you think? Yes, you think that way, yes, we have heard what you say, but maybe we still cannot go the whole way as you think. But what you said there, we think is good, we will take that along. We do not agree with that there, we do not take that along.' So that there is this honesty, you have an open dialogue.'
>
> For instance: 'I think there were 160 remarks in the beginning, when we were starting to build [the new hospital]. And while they were involved and they accompanied the process, so eventually we had succeeded in eliminating 150 of these 160 points. And here patient organisations, user organisations were allowed to be involved and influence the entire building process, from when it begun until it was completed.' (interview 43; author's translation)

One of the reasons for this surprisingly high appreciation of the model is probably the typically Swedish culture of negotiation, and the will to come to an agreement contributes considerably to a mutually positive perception of the other actors in the field. It should not be forgotten that despite all the will to achieve accepted compromises, patients are always voters, too. Another reason for the high appreciation of the model in Skåne might be the fact that patient organisations not only influence certain improvements on the local scale, as in the Netherlands and England, nor only can exert some influence on the benefit catalogue as some patient organisations can do in Germany, but have the opportunity to do both.

The overall positive evaluation does not, however, preclude negative assessment in some parts or specific aspects of user involvement, as the following quotation (and a number of points in the following sections) illustrate:

> Sometimes, I use to compare... psychiatry to, e.g., a restaurant. Psychiatry treats its 'guests' so to speak as if 'it is us who decide whether it is tasty or not...'. But that pub will not survive for long. 'Eat up, we only serve just this, and that is what you are going to get.' It is like: 'We do not have fish on the menu, take meat!' (interview 40; author's translation)

### 8.4.2 Development of Patient Organisations

> One of the big problems, we are always dealing with, is how we get from being an individual, who wants to have a say about her own (health-)care and her daily life, to becoming a representative for a larger group of people. (interview 40; author's translation)

It is not only the administrative or political side that has changed. Patient organisations notice a change also within their own ranks, away from acting as the independent actor only criticising what is wrong towards a more cooperative operation principle, collaborating where benefits are to be gained, offering opposition where things are perceived to be going in the completely wrong direction. As one of the representatives of a patients' umbrella organisation portrays,

> [p]reviously, patient organisations were, in a way, only a group [...] which came to the fore and complained about [...] the same thing. And 'We want'..., right? Nowadays, however, we are much, much more constructive than before. (interview 38; author's translation)

This is in line with the story told by one of the interviewees about the first meeting of their patients' umbrella organisation and politicians, when no one believed that they would agree on a joint solution and were all the more surprised how easily one was found in the end (interview 40). This capability apparently has come to the surprise of some of the actors involved in the process. Overall, the aim and the character of the organisation is thereby transformed from self-help to becoming more of a lobby organisation (interview 40). This is also owing to the luxury that in contrast, to their Dutch counterpart—whose main task it is to support the Board of Clients and to get politically and financially more independent from government support—and their English counterpart—who tries to achieve the same aim by fundraising—the Swedish patient organisations can simply focus on channeling their requests and discussions in order to influence politicians in their regular meetings. Even though Swedish patient organisations are just as keen to preserve their independence, they perceive their own work much more as a task for society as a whole, which is why governmental financial support is rather viewed as a necessary societal support.

Furthermore, without having any 'hard' proof for it, it seems there is some difference in what basically is meant by lobbying: In the Swedish context lobbying often means rather an open discussion and exchange of information and most often lacks the pressurising connotation found in many other countries. Respect for the rules of the representative democracy and the perception of pressuring other actors too much as something 'nasty' might be one explanation for the difference in the character of lobbying.

A similar process of professionalisation as in the Netherlands and in England can be discerned. This involves accumulating knowledge about illnesses, but also strategic ways on how to deal with the other actors in the field, what kind of claims is appropriate, and how to shape criticism constructively. This is self-critically summarised by one of the representatives of the patients' umbrella organisation:

> The first ten years, it maybe was not influencing. The formal premises were there, but the influence was not that strong, but it was disparities regarding knowledge and the like [...]. The patient representatives brought up too [...] trifling questions, which ultimately were no political but rather administrative questions. (interview 38; author's translation)

The development patient organisations are undergoing is generally regarded as something positive, i.e. assuming more responsibility, restructuring communications, and the relation between the leadership of an organisation and the ordinary members. Having an additional professional layer between lay-members and politicians, on the one hand, and the medical profession, on the other, comes, of course, at the expense of the risk to be detached from the member base:

> If you get the opportunity to influence, if you get influence and the like, [...] you often grow with that role. If you are a passive spectator and auditor of something only, you do not demand so much from yourself. But if you are allowed to ask questions and you realise that these questions are received, you [...] are forced to do different analyses, so to speak, than when you receive more passive information. You are maybe forced to have a different discussion with your members, be clearer, so it becomes an interplay which develops all the time in a way. (interview 38; author's translation)

### *8.4.3 Representativity and Legitimacy*

> It depends on how we– well, how these people are recruited for instance. Thus, we cannot speak of representativity. (interview 50; author's translation)

No matter how positively the collaboration between politicians and patient organisations is assessed, the question of representativity and legitimacy of the chosen organisations for *all* patients must be taken into consideration. One major difference to the interviews in the other countries was that patient organisations raised the issue themselves, thereby critically scrutinising their own role.

To begin with the very grassroots, one interviewee referred to the Swedish diabetes association with some 25,000 members in their ranks. Against that background,

> [t]he number of people suffering from diabetes is 350,000 [in Sweden]. So they still only have 10 % membership [sic!], so nine out of ten individuals choose to not join the association. From government's side, however, they still regard the diabetes association to represent the diabetics, they are considered to have a mandate despite the fact that they have no huge membership rate compared to the whole group at all. (interview 50; author's translation)

The same point is raised by one official during the interview:

> But we also think that it should be representatives of the 'ordinary' patient. And how do you proceed in order to identify representatives of ordinary patients? [...] But folks who more rarely make use of (health-)care services, who go to their primary care doctor several times a year and maybe end up in the casualty department for some emergency, they are not organised. So, how do you find them and give them a voice in (health-)care? (interview 47; author's translation)

To give justice to the Swedish Diabetes Association, it must be said that the general problem persists with all other patient organisation, too. My interviewees made the motivated guess that their organisation represented between 20 and 35% of the concerned population (interviews 36–40), thus better than the example mentioned, but far from being a share that would be an acceptable voter turnout in general elections, for instance. The patient organisations' point of view, in contrast, is that even though the membership rate is towards the low end, they do get in contact with a huge mass of concerned people, thus representing many more than just their own clientele:

> So, if you have 2,000 members you maybe meet 20,000 people, who you meet during your activities in the association. Thus, we often say that we represent a considerably larger group than those who are our members. (interview 40; author's translation)

Furthermore, one relatively widespread approach to enhance their legitimacy are study circles and the so-called dialogues (*dialogmöten*; North and Werkö 2002, p. 792; Söderholm Werkö 2008, p. 48). The initial aim is to structure the feedback process first and foremost within the organisation before reaching out, but also to extend it to other stakeholders. Usually, one topic is discussed per meeting, which quite often are held on a regular basis. It gives the organisations the opportunity to listen to their members, get to know newly arising issues, get to know the everyday practice with, for instance, new regulations, and get some feedback on their own programme and proposals. In turn, this creates a deeper legitimacy for talks with politicians and civil servants.

Nevertheless, the follow-up question to be posed is, then, who actually is represented, who becomes a member in one of the patient organisations? Part of the answer is that it is often parents of sick children, children for their parents in need of care, or people feeling the need for information, while the largest share is rather uninterested or 'freeriders' (Söderholm Werkö 2008; interview 50). One of the consequences is that even though it appears less of a problem to openly talk about mental illness in Sweden as compared to England, recruiting new, ideally capable members does not seem to be an easy task here, either (cf. also Östby, Norin & Andersson 2009):

> Sometimes, criticism is voiced [. . . ] when we shall represent in one [of] the projects [. . . ]. It is pretty prudent criticism, such as saying whether we cannot come up with some new and somewhat younger representatives [. . . ], understated that those who are sitting around, their experience is pretty old. [. . . ] And that criticism is valid. (interview 40; author's translation)

Thus, in conclusion, the same problem of recruiting members is prevalent in Sweden, too. A number of factors play in. One is, e.g., the interest by and the aim associated with joining a patient organisation, since what is held important and what function of an organisation is highlighted depends very much on the perspective: It can be argued that having a coffee together fulfils an enormously important function on the local level; if your aim is to lobby at the political level, however, strategies, hard facts, and sturdy members are rather what is needed (see also interview 50). Even if organisations manage to recruit highly motivated and capable members, wanting to achieve something for themselves is one thing, to achieve something on behalf of a larger group is another. Thus, it takes some training and experience to represent others in a suitable manner.

Another decisive factor, of course, is the available time, which naturally is higher for pensioners. In comparison to the other three countries under research, Sweden was the only country where it was not taken for granted that patient involvement should be seen as a kind of spare time activity, but that lay members of patient organisations participating should be paid more than a symbolic amount for their effort—the more in order to compensate for lost income. Even the fact that a reimbursement of 400 SEK per meeting (approximatelx 45 €) is paid (interview 44) does not completely offset the effort and time spent nor the difficulty to take a day off, runs the argument (cf. also Fleetwood 2005). In that context, one of my interviewees drew the comparison between patient involvement and the implementation of the act 'Co-determination on the Workplace' (*Medbestämmande i Arbeitslivet* (MBL)) in the mid-1970s. Indirectly, she criticises the comparative lack of financial and organisational support and adds stronger financial support as a remedy to boost recruitment:

> Nowadays, it has been written into policy documents that there should be user collaboration and user influence. That is beginning to get in. In contrast, it is not written into the economic parts. Thus, when you [. . . ] order [purchase] healthcare [. . . ] you formulate that you want to order this [service]. However, it is never mentioned in these orders that it will cost more money to have a good user influence. The clinic needs to do that for free. Everything else is specified, but not these things. [. . . ] There was an enactment on co-determination at the workplace [*Medbestämmande i Arbeitslivet* (MBL)] in Sweden in 1976. Then, the unions got money for training [. . . ] surely for six, seven years after [the enactment]. The copier ran hot from all the bills. And I met an owner of a training venue who said, 'Thank you, dear Lord, for MBL! We were close to bankruptcy before this act.' It was heavily invested in that the single union work council, the single representative, would understand the act. Meetings were organised, working hours were reimbursed depending on how many employees a firm or organisation had. [. . . ] The section of the 'Municipal Workers' Union' in Lund had 19 full time employees [for the emplementation of the act only]. (interview 40; author's translation)

In consequence, lacking a sufficiently large number of capable members, which in part is perceived to be caused by lack of funding, leads to the situation that patient organisations as health care providers feel unsupported. Regarding the recruitment of new members, only a fraction of all potential members joins the organisation, whereof only a fraction is capable and willing to assume responsibility and represent the organisation externally, and consequently only very few members bear the organisations' workload. This makes organisations dependent on enthusiasts driving issues, organising things, and carrying others along (see, e.g., interview 50; cf. also Fleetwood 2005, p. 35). This also leads to a situation in which not all invitations to discuss certain issues can be accepted as patient organisations simply cannot manage to attend all meetings. The proposal—again—is to raise the reimbursement:

> [Working with patient involvement, w]e have had people in the reference group who have said: 'We are a small organisation, we have one full-time employee, the others are doing this in their spare time so to speak. We cannot go everywhere where we are called to.' And from political the side one wants to say, 'Yes, we have taken in viewpoints bla-bla-bla', while if the only channel to find representatives is patient associations, maybe the public support or other contributions should be increased. (interview 50; author's translation)

With that in mind, opting for patient organisations as representatives for all patients is not seen as the ideal to strive for, but rather a pragmatic solution to an otherwise unsolvable intricacy:

> Then it is pretty difficult [...] If you ultimately maybe do not find that these professional representatives are ideal for patient organisations—yes, but it is very difficult to find other representatives, thus, most often it ends up in choosing patient associations. (interview 50; author's translation)

## 8.5 Summary

Sweden is an interesting case in that it was included in this study to represent a counter-case to the Netherlands and England. However, though no comprehensive involvement in hospitals exist, it could be shown that it has pursued its very own way to establish a genuinely Swedish type of patient involvement over time, which is relatively uniform across the Swedish counties. In more abstract terms, Sweden turned out to be more comparable to Germany than had been thought in the first place: The patient involvement in place can be classified as basically corporatist in kind and located at the county councils' committees. This involvement in the policy making arena can be compared to Germany's patient involvement in the 'Joint Federal Committee', the highest decision-making body.

Summarising the main threads could read as follows: Democratically elected politicians at the level of county councils were seen as the representatives of citizens even with regard to decisions within the health care system. On top of that, the introduction of a treatment guarantee and—in many county councils—a purchaser–provider split brought in a limited amount of competition. This, in turn, gave rise to an emerging 'customer' orientation, which gave patients a new role and position. At the same time, politicians found themselves in a double role between purchasers and sometimes providers of health care for the people and being their advocate. In the end, the self-definition as the advocate of the people was favoured over other political roles. Much more, however, than the discovery of the patient as a valuable 'customer', it seems, was the redefinition of what democracy implies: The understanding of democracy changed to one beyond the general right to elect politicians, to which the right to voice concerns and to exert influence in matters concerning major groups of citizens belong.

Next to democratisation, this development, however, has an additional, much more tangible facet: It is sparked by many incremental steps with efficiency-hunting as the golden thread. Be it the purchaser–provider split, be it prioritisation, choice of provider, choice of treatment, or patient involvement: Besides advantages for patients and users, the quest at the same time for higher quality or an extended provision of health care services costs always peeks around the corner.

Nevertheless, a characterisation of the environment in which patient involvement takes place can read as follows: Politicians of the county councils take the final decision and assume the role of intermediary between several actors, but aim at being the impartial advocate of the people. The very broad and non-specific legal basis leaves room for a wide range of interpretation, which to some extent could be observed in the various approaches and experiments throughout the country in the past. It also leaves room, however, for a continuing discourse on involvement in general, which—as the recent developments in Skåne show—is far from being finished in Sweden.

## 8.6 An Outlook

In the meantime, a number of scientific publications (Fleetwood 2005; Krevers 2003, 2008; Matscheck 2011; Nordén 2008; North & Werkö 2002; SPRI 1999; Wermeling 2011; Wigsell & Hansson 2003; Winblad 2011) as well as public sector publications (Nätverk Bohuslän 2010; Nätverk Måligan 2009; Regionstyrelsen Skåne 2011a,b; Socialstyrelsen 2003a; Vårdanalys 2014:11) appeared on the topic. One public sector publications was developed in close collaboration with patient organisations (SOU 2006:6), which highlights the good contact and collaboration between these actors.

The area with the most likely development in the years to come seems to be patient rights. Over the last decade, an extension of the choice of provider can be discerned: Was it first specifically a choice for those with specific elective surgeries and exceeding a certain waiting time limit, it was introduced in GP and secondary care in general a number of years ago. When it comes to patient/user involvement a plausible development is that shared decision-making on individual treatment will be strengthened. Regarding collective patient involvement a diversification with farther-reaching experiments will set in as it has begun in Skåne already, to go beyond the involvement of formal patient organisations.

Another project, announced almost 15 years ago, has not gotten anywhere so far: The basic idea was to convert the obligation for county councils to provide health care services into rights for patients and to merge them into one law (often called *patienträttighetslagen*, Act of Patient Rights; SoU (1998/99:3)). Despite the government's propositions (Prop. 1998, 1997), a government commission (*ansvarskommittén*—responsibility committee), numerous related parliamentary motions (cf., e.g., Mot 1998b,a, 2005a,b), and at least one official report of the Government's social committee (SoU 1998/99:3), the act itself has not arrived at the state of a proposed bill, and it is unlikely to pass parliament in the foreseeable future. This might also be seen against the background of the negative experience with implementation of the ''Lag om stöd och service till vissa funktionshindrade (LSS)'' (cf. also Lewin 2011).[26]

A territory reform of counties was already suggested many years ago, but has not gotten anywhere so far, since government and opposition disagree on how to proceed. There are numerous proposals ranging from devolving competences in health care to the municipalities—as they are closer to citizens—to merging several counties to form larger regions—in order to create a sound citizens and tax base. How ever the solution will turn out in the longer run, it will most probably have some larger impact on health care and patient involvement.

## References

Allén, S., Berg, S., Engdahl, B., Malmgren, S. -G., & Sjögren, C. (Eds.). (1988). *Norstedts Svenska Ordbok* (Specialversion för Åhle'ns). Stockholm: Norstedts.

Anbäcken, O. (1985, April). *Patientmedverkan och organisationsstruktur: en studie om patientens roll och funktion i vårdorganisationen* (Doctoral dissertation, Linköping University, Studies in Management and Economics, Linköping).

Arbetsförmedlingen. (2011, January 31). Distriktsköterska. Retrieved January 22, 2015, from http:www.arbetsformedlingen.se/For-arbetsgivare/Hitta-medarbetare/Rekryteringstips/Yrken-A-O.html?sv.url=12.6ce34027120299daa868000126146&url=1119789672/Yrken/YrkesBeskrivning.aspx?iYrkeId=70

Auerbach, C. (1922). *Svensk—Tysk Ordbok* (3:e stereotyperade upplagan). Stockholm: P. A. Norstedt & Söner.

Bendz, A. (2004). *I välfärdsstatens hägn—autonomi inom arbetslöshetsförsäkringen* (Doctoral dissertation, Statsvetenskapliga insitututionen, Göteborgs universitet, Göteborg). 297.

Berman, S. (1998). *The social democratic moment—Ideas and politics in the making of interwar Europe* (Doctoral dissertation, Cambridge, MA).

Bjöörn, I. (2011, September). En tredjedel av astmatikerna får svårt att betala sin medicin vid en höjning av högkostnadsskydd. Retrieved October 27, 2011, from www.astmaoallergiforbundet.se/pressrum/press.aspx?id=168

Bjuggren, P.-O. (1998). Competition for the market in the Swedish primary health care sector. *International Review of Law and Economics, 18*(4), 529–541.

Broqvist, M. (2002). *Medborgardialogen i Östergötland—ett utvecklingsarbete i landstinget.* Linköping: PrioriterincsCentrum—Nationellt kunskapscentrum för prioritering inom vård och omsorg.

[26]This act regulates services such as counselling, short-term care, and individual assistance for mentally challenged as well as mentally and physically handicapped. Responsibility for the administration and provision of services rests with the municipalities.

Calltorp, J., Persson, J., Holmström, S., Levin, L.-Å., & Persson, J. (1988). *Att beställa hälso- och sjukvård*. Göteborg: Beställarnätverket för landstingen i Sverige.
Cohn, D. (1992:2). *Reforming health care in Canada and Sweden*. Stockholm: University of Stockholm, International Graduate School of International Studies.
Delhey, J., & Newton, K. (2005, September). Predicting cross-national levels of social trust: Global pattern or nordic exceptionalism? *European Sociological Review, 21*(4), 311–327.
Department of Health. (2001). *Health and social care 2001*. London: Department of Health.
Duffy, D. M. (1989). The Effect of Sweden's corporatist structure on health policy and outcomes. *Scandinavian Studies, 61*(2/3), 128–145.
Edelman. (2013). *Edelman trust barometer executive summary*. New York: Edelman.
EIRO (Ed.). (2009). *Industrial relations profile*. Dublin: EIRO.
Erlingsdóttir, G. (1992). Kvalitetssäkringars översättning—recentralisering av kontroll. In E. Zeuthen Bentsen (Ed.), *Når styringsambitioner møder praksis* (pp. 57–85). København: Handelshøjskolens Forlag.
Esping-Andersen, G. (1990). *The Three Worlds of Welfare Capitalism*. Princeton: Princeton University Press.
Fallberg, L. (2003). Patients ombudsmen—a different approach to improve quality in health services. *European Journal of Health Law, 10* 339–342.
Fallberg, L., & MacKenny, S. (2003). Patient ombudsmen in seven European countries: An effective way to implement patients' rights? *European Journal of Health Law, 10*, 343–357.
Feltenius, D. (2004). *En pluralistisk maktordning?—Om pensionärsorganisationernas politiska inflytande* (Doctoral dissertation, Statsvetenskapliga institutionen Umeå universitet, Stockholm). Retrieved August 30, 2016, from http://urn.kb.se/resolve?urn=urn:nbn:se:umu:diva-421
Fleetwood, C. (2005). *Brukarsamverkan inom hälso- och sjukvård i Sverige och Storbritannien—Handikapporganisationernas delaktighet i planering och utveckling av vård* (Master of Public Health—MPH 2005:41, Nordiska högskolan för folkhälsovetenskap, Göteborg).
Garpenby, P. (1989). *The State and the Medical Profession—A cross-national comparison of the health policy arena in the United Kingdom and Sweden 1945–1985* (Doctoral dissertation, TEMA, Linköpings universitet, Linköping/Kungälv).
Garpenby, P. (1997). Implementing quality programmes in three Swedish county councils: The views of politicians, managers and doctors. *Health Policy, 39*(3), 195–206.
Garpenby, P. (2001). Informationen kan göra allmänheten oberoende, krävande eller kunnig—Treframtidsperspektiv på hälsoinformation. *Läkartidningen, 98*(23), 2812–2813.
Garpenby, P. (2002). *Samtalsdemokrati och prioritering — Utvärdering av ett försök med medborgarråd*. Linköping: PrioriteringsCentrum—Nationellt Kunskapscentrum för prioritering inom vård och omsorg.
Glenngård, A. H., & Anell, A. (2012:1). *Vad påverkar patientupplevd kvalitet i primärvården?*. Stockholm: Vårdanalys.
Glenngård, A., Hjalte, F., Svensson, M., Anell, A., & Bankauskaite, V. (2005). Sweden: Health system review. In V. Bankauskaite (Ed.), *Health systems in transition*. Copenhagen: WHO Regional Office for Europe on behalf of the European Observatory on Health Systems and Policies.
Haarmann, A., & Wieseler S. (2006). Gesundheitssysteme und Reformansätze im internationalen Vergleich (VII): Schweden. *Arbeitsmedizin, Sozialmedizin, Umweltmedizin*, (2), 62–75. Retrieved from http://www.asu-arbeitsmedizin.com/QUlEPTIwMTA1NyZNSUQ9MTA0Njkw.html?UID=4FB1D63713C3419BD9DB848D243C2DA0E6122AB009C5E6485F
Handikappförbunden. (2011a). om Handikappförbunden. Retrieved August 30, 2016, from www.hso.se/vi-ar-handikappforbunden/
Handikappförbunden. (2011b). Verksamhet. Retrieved August 30, 2016, from www.hso.se/verksamhet/
Handikappförbundens samarbetsorgan. (2008). *Handikappförbunden—43 organisationer i samverkan*. Sundbyberg: Handikappförbundens samarbetsorgan.

Hartman, L., Anell, A., Märk, E., Vlachos, J., Hanspers, K., Lundin, M., ... Wiklund, S. (2011, September). *Konkurrensens konsekvenser—Vad händer med svensk välfärd?*. Stockholm: SNS förlag.
Henning, H. (1974). Arbeitslosenversicherung vor 1914: Das Genter System und seine Übernahme in Deutschland. In H. Kellenbenz (Ed.), *Wirtschaftspolitik und Arbeitsmarkt* (pp. 271–287). München: Oldenbourg.
Henningsen, B. (1986). *Der Wohlfahrtsstaat Schweden* (1. Aufl.). Nordeuropäische Studien. Baden-Baden: Nomos-Verlag-Gesellschaft.
Hinrichs, K. (2007). Enlarging freedom of choice: Pension reforms in the Nordic countries and Germany. In B. Hvinden & H. Johansson (Eds.), *Citizenship in Nordic welfare states: Dynamics of choice duties and participation in a changing Europe* (Chap. 14, pp. 200–215). Milton Park, Abingdon: Routledge Chapman & Hall.
Hinrichs, K., & Merkel, W. (1987). Der Wolhfahrtsstaat Schweden: Was bleibt vom Modell? *Aus Politik und Zeitgeschichte, B51*, 23–38.
Hjärt- och Lungsjukas Riksförbund. (2010). *Verksamhetsberättelse och Årsredovisning 2010*. Stockholm: Hjärt- och Lungsjukas Riksförbund.
Hjortsberg, C., & Ghatnekar, O. (2001). Health care systems in transition: Sweden. In A. Rico, W. Wisbaum & T. Cetani, (Eds.), *Healthcare systems in transition*. Copenhagen: European Observatory on Health Systems and Policies.
HSL. (1982:763). *Hälso- och Sjukvårdslagen (HSL)*. SFS1982:763. Stockholm: Socialdepartmentet.
Hugemark, A., & Roman, C. (2007). Diversity and divisions in the Swedish disability movement: Disability, gender, and social justice. *Scandinavian Journal of Disability Research, 9*(1), 26–45.
Immergut, E. M. (1992). *Health politics: Interests and institutions in Western Europe*. Cambridge: Cambridge University Press.
Jahn, D. (2009). Das politische System Schwedens. In W. Ismayr, S. Richter & M. Söldner (Eds.), *Die politischen Systeme Westeuropas* (4th ed., pp. 107–150). Wiesbaden: VS, Verlag für Sozialwiss.
Jakubowski, E., & Saltman, R. B. (Eds.). (2013). *The changing national role in health system governance—A case-based study of 11 European countries and Australia*. Observatory Studies Series. Copenhagen: WHO Regional Office for Europe on behalf of the European Observatory on Health Systems and Policies.
Jann, W (1983). *Staatliche Programme und 'Verwaltungskultur'*. Opladen: Westdeutscher Verlag.
Jeppsson Grassman, E., & Svedberg, L. (2007). Civic participation in a Scandinavian welfare state: Patterns in contemporary Sweden. In L. Trägårdh (Ed.), *State and civil society in Northern Europe—The Swedish model reconsidered*. European Civil Society (Chap. 4, Vol. 3, pp. 126–164). New York: Berghahn.
Jespersen, P. K. (1999). New Public Management reformers betydning for den administrative og lægefaglige profession i sygehusorganisationen. In E. Zeuthen Bentsen (Ed.), *Når styrings-ambitioner møder praksis* (pp. 143–169). København: Handelshøjskolens Forlag.
Johnsson, L.-Å. (2010). *Den nya patientsäkerhetslagen och patientens rättigheter: handbok för ombud och vårdpersonal* ([2., omarb. och utök. uppl.]). Stockholm: Thomson Reuters Professional.
Johnsson, L.-Å., & Sahlin, J. (2010). *Hälso- och sjukvårdslagen: med kommentarer* (8., [rev.] uppl.). Stockholm: Norstedts juridik.
Karlsson, L. (2003). *Konflikt eller harmoni? Individuella rättigheter och ansvarsutkrävande i svensk och brittisk sjukvård*. Göteborg: Cefos.
Kjellberg, A. (2006, April). The Swedish unemployment insurance—will the Ghent system survive? *Transfer—European Review of Labour and Research, 1*, 87–98.
KL. (2004:93). *Kommunallag (KL)*. SFS2004:93. Finansdepartementet.
Krevers, B. (2003, February). *Patient and relative perspectives regarding quality in hospital care for older people—Theory and methods* (Doctoral dissertation, Linköpings universitet Faculty of Health Sciences, Department of Health and Society, Division of Physiotherapy, Linköping).

Krevers, B. (2008, March). *Patient- och närståendeperspektivet i Socialstyrelsens Nationella Riktlinjer—En arbetsmodell utvecklad inom riktlinjerna för depression och ångestsjukdom.* Stockholm/Linköping: Socialstyrelsen/Linköpings universitet.

Landsting i Östergötland. (2012, December). Landstingsfullmäktige. Retrieved December 11, 2012, from www.lio.se/Politik-och-paverkan/Fortroendemannaorgan/Landstingsfullmaktige

Lewin, B. (2011). *För din skull, för min skull eller för skams skull: om LSS och bemötande* (1st ed.). Lund: Studentlitteratur.

Lidmark, J., Rosén, P., & Skoog, K. (2010–2011). *Det kloka samtalet.* In Enheten för demokratiutveckling (Ed.), Malmö: Region Skåne.

Liljeberg, K. (2005). *Hur påverkas hälsan av delaktighet och inflytande i samhället? En litteratursammanställning.* Östersund: Statens Folkhälsoinstitut.

LSS. (1993:387-05). *Lag om stöd och service till vissa funktionshindrade (LSS).* SFS1993:387. Socialdepartmentet.

Matscheck, D. (2011). *Att skapa former och arenor—Lokal samverkan inom psykiatri/socialpsykiatri.* (Masteruppsats, Stockholms universitet—Institutionen för socialt arbete).

Merkel, W. (1996). Vergangenheit, Gegenwart und Zukunft der Sozialdemokratie. In J. Borchert, L. Golsch, U. Jun, & P. Lösche (Eds.), *Das sozialdemokratische Modell.* Europa-und Nordamerika Studien (Vol. 2, pp. 81–103). Opladen: Leske + Budrich.

Michelsen, K. (2002). *Gesundheitswesen und Wohlfahrtsstaat in Schweden—Gesundheitspolitik im Wandel des sozialdemokratischen Wohlfahrtsstaatsregimes* (Doctoral dissertation, Universität Frankfurt, Frankfurt).

Milton, A., Wieselgren, I.-M., Delisle, K., Evelius, K., Fredriksson, E., Hagström, . Tjernberg, A. (2006:100–11). *Ambition och ansvar—Nationell strategi för utveckling av samhällets insatser till personer med psykiska sjukdomar och funktionshinder.* Statens offentliga utredningar. Stockholm: Socialdepartmentet.

Mot. (1973/1190). *Om översyn av medicinalväsendets ansvarsnämnds verksamhet.* Riksdag.

Mot. (1998a, October 20). *Motion med anledning av prop. 1997/98:189 Patientens ställning.* Riksdag.

Mot. (1998b, October 22). *Patientens rättigheter och ställning—Motion till riksdagen.* Riks.

Mot. (2005a, September 27). *Patientens ställning inom hälso- och sjukvården—Motion till riksdagen.* Riksdag. Motion 2005/06:So352

Mot. (2005b, September 27). *Patientens ställning inom hälso- och sjukvården—Motion till riksdagen.* Motion 2005/06:So330

Nätverk Bohuslän. (2010, December). *Lag om Stöd och Service till vissa funktionshindrade (LSS)—En jämförelse av kommunerna ur ett medborgarperspektiv* Jämförelseprojektet—Ett samarbete mellan SKL, RKA och Finansdepartementet. Stockholm. Retrieved October 4, 2012, from www.jamforelse.se

Nätverk Måligan. (2009, December). *Lag om Stöd och Service till vissa funktionshindrade (LSS)—En jämförelse av kommunens Handikappomsorg ur ett medborgarperspektiv.* Jämförelseprojektet— Ett samarbete mellan SKL, RKA och Finansdepartementet. Stockholm. Retrieved October 4, 2012, from www.jamforelse.se

Niklasson, B. (2012). Sweden. In K. Verhoest, S. Thiel, G. Bouckaert, & P. Lægrid (Eds.), *Government agencies: Practices and lessons from 30 countries* (Chap. 23). Public Sector Organizations. Houndmills, Basingstoke: Palgrave Macmillan.

Nordén, H. (2008). *Kunskap att hämta—brukarmedverkan för en bättre psykiatri,* Stockholm: Gothia Förlag.

Nordin, E. (2010, December). Vårdgarantin ett politiskt jippo. *Sjukhusläkaren.se.*

North, N., & Werkö, S. (2002). Widening the debate? Consultation and participation in local health care planning in the English and Swedish health services. *International Journal of Health Services, 32*(4), 781–798.

Nyrén, G. (Ed.). (1999). *Modell för kunskapsbaserad prioritering och resursfördelning.* Medicinska program i Östergötland. Linköping: Landstingets kansli.

OECD. (2011). Social Cohesion Indicators—Trust. Retrieved January 20, 2017, from http://dx.doi.org/10.1787/888932382064

OECD. (2014). *Government at a glance*. Paris: OECD publishing.
Olofsson, C., Nilsson, A., & Wahllöf, U. (2010). *Patientens val—en bok om primärvård och vårdval*. Lund: Studentlitteratur.
Olsson, S. E. (1993). *Social policy and the welfare state in Sweden*. Lund studies in social welfare (2nd, enlarged ed.). Lund: Arkiv förlag.
Östby C., Norin, J., & Andersson, U. (2009). *Stolthet & Fördom—möte med psykiatrin idag*. In C. Östby (Ed.), Skellefteå: Psykiatriska kliniken i Skellefteå.
Östman, L., & Leijd-Tidbeck, K. (1985). *Får vi vara med?—Om patientupplevelser och förtroendenämnder*. Stockholm: Brevskolan.
Pestoff, V. A. (1992). *Towards a new Swedish model: From neo-corporatist to neo-liberal priorities for the welfare state*. Warzawa/Krakow: Friedrich Ebert Stiftung/Academy of Economics.
Petersson, O. (2007). *Svensk politik* (7:e uppl.). Stockholm: Norstedts Juridik.
Prop. (1981). *Förarbete till Hälso- och sjukvårdslagen*. Stockholm.
Prop. (1997). *Patientens ställning—Regeringens proposition*. Riksdag.
Prop. (1998). *Stärkt patientinflytande—Regeringens proposition*. Riksdag.
Prop. (2009). *Regeringens proposition—Regionalt utvecklingsansvar i vissa län*. Regeringen.
RAND Health (Ed.). (2006). The health insurance experiment—a classic RAND study speaks to the current health care reform debate. Santa Monica: RAND Corporation
Region Skåne. (2006, October). *medborgardialog—Handbok för Region Skånes förtroendevalda*.
Region Skåne. (2009a). *dialog*.
Region Skåne. (2009b, January 8). *Översyn av Region Skånes brukarsamverkan*. Koncernkontoret— Regionkansliet. Malmö
Region Skåne. (2011, May 12) *Beslutförslag—Samverkan mellan Region Skåne och Brukargrupper 2011—2014* (No. 6.4). Regionstyrelsen. Malmö
Regionstyrelsen Skåne. (2011a, January). Ny modell för brukarsamverkan i Region Skåne—beslutsförslag.
Regionstyrelsen Skåne. (2011b, January). Samverkan mellan Region Skåne och Brukargrupper.
Reumatikerförbundet. (2010). *Verksamhetsberättelse med Årsredovisning 2010*. Stockholm: Reumatikerförbundet.
Rosén, P (2006). Public dialogue on healthcare prioritisation. *Health Policy, 79*, 107–116.
Rothstein, B., & Bergström, J. (1999). *Korporatismens fall—och den svenska modellens kris*. Stockholm: SNS Förlag.
Sahlin-Andersson, K. (1999). I mötet mellan reform och praktik. In E. Zeuthen Bentsen (Ed.), *Når styringsambitioner møder praksis* (pp. 293–311). København: Handelshøjskolens Forlag.
Saltman, R. B. (1994). Patient choice and patient empowerment in Northern European health systems: A conceptual framework. *International Journal of Health Services, 14*, 201–229.
Saltman, R. B., Bankauskaite, V., & Vrangbæk, K. (Eds.). (2007). *Decentralization in health care—Strategies and outcomes*. New York/Maidenhead: McGraw Hill/Open University Press.
Sejersted, F. (2011). *The age of social democracy—Norway and Sweden in the twentieth century*. Princeton: Princeton University Press.
SFS. (2002:452). *Lag om ändring i hälso- och sjukvårdslagen*. Socialdepartmentet.
SFS. (1934:264). *Kungl: Maj:ts förordning om erkända arbetslöshetskassor*
SFS. (1992:563). *Lag om förtroendenämndverksamhet inom hälso- och sjukvården, m.m.* Socialdepartmentet.
SFS. (1995:835). *Lag om ändring i hälso- och sjukvårdslagen*. Socialdepartmentet.
Signäs, G. (2009, April). Dina rättigheter i vården. Retrieved January 20, 2017, from www.vardguiden.se/Safunkardet/Lagar--rattigheter/
Skriabikova, O., Pavlova, M., & Groot, W (2010, June 23). Review: Empirical models of demand for out-patient physician services and their relevance to the assessment of patient payment policies: A critical review of the literature. *International Journal of Environmental Research and Public Health, 7*(6), 2708–2725.
Socialstyrelsen. (2000:8). *Patientavgifter och vårdefterfrågan—en kunskapsöversikt*. Socialstyrelsen (SoS).

Socialstyrelsen. (1999:16). *Prioriteringar i sjukvården* SoS-rapport. Stockholm: Socialstyrelsen (SoS).
Socialstyrelsen. (1998). *Sjukvården i Sverige*. Stockholm: Socialstyrelsen (SoS).
Socialstyrelsen. (2001). *Brukarråd och brukarrevisioner inom verksamheter för personer med psykiska funktionshinder* Stockholm: Socialstyrelsen (SoS).
Socialstyrelsen. (2003a). *Brukarmedverkan i socialtjänstens kunskapsutveckling*. Socialstyrelsen (SoS).
Socialstyrelsen (Ed.). (2003b). *Patientens rätt till information och delaktighet och medinflytande—Läget efter lagändringarna 1 januari 1999* (Vols. 2003-103-5).
Söderholm Werkö, S. (2008). *Patient Patients? Achieving Patient Empowerment Through Active Participation, Increased Knowledge and Organisation* (Doctoral dissertation, Stockholm University School of Business Administration, Stockholm).
SoL. (2001:453-06). *Socialtjänstlagen (SoL)*. SFS2001:453. Socialdepartmentet.
SoU. (1998/99:3). *Socialutskottets betänkande—Stärkt patientinflytande m.m.* Socialutskottets betänkande.
SOU. (2000:1). *En uthållig demokrati!—Politik för folkstyrelse på 2000-talet—Demokratiutredningens betänkande*. Fritzes kundservice.
SOU. (2001:8). *Prioriteringar i vården—perspektiv för politiker profession och medborgare. Slutbetänkande från Prioriteringsdelegationen* Stockholm: Fritzes offentliga publikationer.
SOU. (2006:6). *Så vill vi ha det – Patient-, brukar- och anhörignätverkets krav på framtida vård, stöd och behandling inom psykiatriområdet – rapport från Nationell psykiatrisamordning*. Stockholm.
SOU. (2008:37). *Vårdval i Sverige : delbetänkande av Utredningen om patientens rätt*. Stockholm: Fritze.
SOU. (1970:64). *Bättre socialtjänst för handikappade : förslag från Handikapputredningen om bättre färdmöjligheter för handikappade och bättre samordning i handikappfrågor*. Stockholm.
SOU. (1984:83). *Folkstyret i kommunerna — medverkan—delaktighet—ansvar — diskussionsbetänkande från 1983 års demokratiberedning*. Stockholm: Liber/Allmänna förl.
SOU. (1984:84). *Lokalt folkstyre genom brukarmedverkan—Exempel och erfarenheter — Betänkande från 1983 års demokratiberedning*
SOU. (1968:47). *Förvaltning och folkstyre—betänkande av länsdemokratiutredningen*. Statens offentliga utredningar Stockholm.
SOU. (1988:65). *Pensionärerna—inflytande och medbestämmande*. In K. E. Persson, & M. Albertsson (Eds.), Statens offentliga utredningar. Stockholm: Allmänna Förlaget.
SOU. (1997:154). *Patienten har rätt*.
SPRI. (1993). *The reform of health care in Sweden*, Stockholm 339.
SPRI. (1999). *Missnöjda patienter: vad vill de påverka?—en studie i samverkan med hälften av landets patientnämnder*. In M. Thorngren Hansson (Ed.), SPRI rapport. Stockholm: SPRI.
Starke, P., Kaasch, A., & van Hooren, F. (Eds.). (2013). *The welfare state as a crisis manager: Explaining the diversity of policy responses to economic crisis*. Houndsmill: Palgrave Mcmillan.
Statistiska Centralbyrån. (2011a). *Statistisk årsbok för Sverige*. Stockholm: Statistiska Centralbyrån (SCB).
Statistiska Centralbyrån. (2011b). Valstatistik 1871–1999. Retrieved January 20, 2017, from www.scb.se/Pages/List_292050.aspx
Statistiska Centralbyrån. (2012, December). Skattesatser 2016 i kommuner län och hela riket. Retrieved August 30, 2016, from www.scb.se/Pages/TableAndChart_67873.aspx
Steinmo, S. (1993). *Taxation and democracy—Swedish, British and American approaches to financing the modern state*. New Haven: Yale University Press.
Stockholms läns landsting. (2004, June). *Att stärka patientens ställning—vägledningn för patienter och personal*. Stockholm.
Sundelin, C. (2011, March 5). Vårdgaranti med biverkningar. *Upsala Nya Tidning*.
Svenska Akademien. (2012). Svenska Akademiens Ordbok. Retrieved January 20, 2017, from http://g3.spraakdata.gu.se/saob/

Svenska Diabetesförbundet. (2011). Svenska Diabetesförbundet. Retrieved January 20, 2017, from http://www.diabetes.se/sv/Om-oss/

Sveriges Kommuner och Landsting. (2010a). *Patient- och brukarmedverkan — Positionspapper— för ökad kvalitet och effektivitet i hälso- och sjukvården*. Stockholm.

Sveriges Kommuner och Landsting. (2010b). *Statistik om hälso- och sjukvård samt regional utveckling 2010—Verksamhet och ekonomi i landsting och regioner*. Stockholm: Sveriges Kommuner och Landsting (SKL).

Sveriges Kommuner och Landsting. (2011a, December 20). Adresser till landstingen och regionerna. Retrieved January 20, 2017, from http://sklse/tjanster/kommunerlandsting/adressuppgifterlandstingregioner.1247.html

Sveriges Kommuner och Landsting. (2011b, January). *Patientavgifter fr. o. m. den 1 januari 2011. Sveriges Kommuner och Landsting (SKL). Stockholm.*

Sveriges Kommuner och Landsting. (2011c, November 18). Politisk majoritet i landstingen. Retrieved November 14, 2012, from www.skl.se/kommuner_och_landsting/om_landsting_och_regioner/politisk_majoritet_i_landstingen

Sveriges Kommuner och Landsting. (2011d). Väntetider i vården—tillgänglig vård — Vad är vårdgarantin? Retrieved January 20, 2017, from www.vantetider.se/vad-aer-vaardgarantin

Sveriges Kommuner och Landsting. (2017, January 11). Patientavgifter fr.o.m. den 1 januari 2017. Retrieved March 17, 2017, from http://sok.sklse/click/searchskl/?ua=f2c0cec7476d6689abeed88fcc91d90c&num=4&url=https%3A%2F%2Fskl.se%2Fdownload%2F18.4dccf2b515940748fbfe6295%2F1485270114485%2Favgift_%25C3%25B6ppenv%25C3%25A5rd_inkl.missiv_slutenavg17_final_24jan.pdf&resid=1268126901

Sveriges Riksdag. (2011). *Sveriges grundlagar och riksdagsordningen*. Stockholm: Riksdagens Interntryckeri.

Tilton, T. (1990). *The political theory of Swedish social democracy—Through the welfare state to socialism*. Oxford: Clarendon.

Trägårdh, L. (1999). *Patientmakt i Sverige USA och Holland—Individuella kontra sociala rättigheter*. Spri förmedlar. Stockholm/Lund: SPRI/Institutet för hälso- och sjukvårdsekonomi.

Twaddle, A. C. (1999). *Health care reforms in Sweden, 1980–1994*. Westport, CT: Auburn House.

Valmyndigheten. (2014, September 19). Val till riksdagen—Röster. Retrieved March 17, 2017, from http://www.val.se/val/val2014/slutresultat/R/rike/index.html

van der Meer, T. (2010). In what we trust? A multi-level study into trust in parliament as an evaluation of state characteristics. *International Review of Administrative Sciences, 76*(3), 517–536.

van der Schee, E., Braun, B., Calnan, M., Schnee, M., & Groenewegen, P. P. (2007). Public trust in health care: A comparison of Germany, The Netherlands, and England and Wales. *Health Policy, 81* 56–67.

Vårdanalys. (2014:11). *Vården ur patienternas perspektiv: jämförelser mellan Sverige och 10 andra länder* [Resultat från the commonwelath fund 2014 international health policy survey]. Vårdanalyse. Stockholm.

Vårdanalys. (2012). Om Vårdanalys. Retrieved January 20, 2017, from http://www.vardanalys.se/Om-Vardanalys/

Vårdguiden. (2012a, January). Högkostnadsskydd för läkemedel. Retrieved January 20, 2017, from www.vardguiden.se/Sjukdomar-och-rad/Om-lakemedel/Hogkostnadsskydd/

Vårdguiden. (2012b, January). Högkostnadsskydd för patientavgifter. Retrieved January 20, 2017, from www.vardguiden.se/Sa-funkar-det/Lagar--rattigheter/Hogkostnadsskydd/

Vienonen, M. A. (2000). Von einer Ethik der Ignoranz hin zur Bürgerbeteiligung. In H. Ettischer & K. Salice-Stephan (Eds.), *Bürgerbeteiligung im Gesundheitswesen—eine länderübergreifende Herausforderung—Ideen, Ansätze und internationale Erfahrungen*. Forschung und Praxis der Gesundheitsförderung (Chap. 3.1, 10, pp. 58–64). Köln: Bundeszentrale für gesundheitliche Aufklärung (BZgA).

Visser, J. (2009, January). Die ICTWSS-Datenbank: Datensammlung über institutionelle Besonderheiten von Gewerkschaften, Lohnfestsetzung, staatliche Intervention und Sozialpakte. Retrieved August 23, 2016, from http://www.uvaaias.net/208

Vogel, J., Amnå, E., Munck, I., & Häll, L. (2003). *Föreningslivet i Sverige—Välfärd—Socialt kapital—Demokratiskola*. Levnadsförhållanden. Statistiska Centralbyrån.

Weaver, R. K. (2004). Public Pension Regimes in an A]ge of Austerity In M. A. Levin & M. Shapiro (Eds.), *Transatlantic policymaking in an age of austerity: Diversity and drift*. Washington: Georgetown University Press.

Wermeling, E. (2011). *Brukarmedverkan: ett nytt sätt att arbeta*. Stockholm: SKL Kommentus Media.

Weyrauch, P. (2012). Belgien: Auf dem Weg zu einer tripartistischen Selbstverwaltung. In T. Klenk, P. Weyrauch, A. Haarmann, & F. Nullmeier (Eds.), *Abkehr vom Korporatismus?* (pp. 179–240). Frankfurt a.M.: Campus.

WHO. (1978). *Declaration of Alma-Ata*. WHO. Copenhagen.

Wigsell, K., & Hansson, J. (2003). *Brukarmedverkan i socialtjänstens kunskapsutveckling* (Socialstyrelsen, Ed.). Stockholm: Socialstyrelsen.

Winblad, U. (2011). Hur kan patienter och medborgare påverka och styra hälso- och sjukvården?—Diskussionsunderlag inför workshop 10 maj 2011. Institutionen för folkhälso- och vårdvetenskap, Universitet Uppsalas.

Winblad, U., & Andersson, C. (2010:9). *Kåren och köerna—En ESO-rapport om den medicinska professionens roll i styrningen av svensk hälso- och sjukvård*. Rapport till Expertgruppen för studier i offentlig ekonomi. Regeringskansliet—Fritzes.

Wohlert, C. (1996). Paradigmenwechsel in der schwedischen Wirtschaft. In B. Henningsen & B. Ståth (Eds.), *Deutschland, Schweden und die Ostsee-Region* (pp. 78–99). Baden-Baden: NOMOS.

# Part III
# Conclusions from the Empirical Evidence of Four Countries and Linking Back to Theory

# Chapter 9
# Comparison: Bringing Four Cases Together

*Up to now we have walked around the sociologist's supermarket. [Now, let's draw some conclusions.] (Boudon 1981, p. 134)*

## 9.1 Empirical Findings and Commonalities

Arriving at a comprehensive explanatory framework for countries of such heterogeneous background, evolution of patient and public involvement is not an easy task. Most generally, what can be stated is that like other typical fields of the welfare state, formal patient/citizen involvement in health care might bring memories from Esping-Andersen's 'frozen landscapes' for several decades after the Second World War (1996; cf. also Palier & Martin 2007) at first sight. However, small changes have occurred, sometimes hidden under the surface. In some countries this has led to the 'elephant on the move' (cf. Hinrichs 2001), while others continue to resemble lively water in a pond, which boundaries have not changed at all. Yet others rather resemble a liberating, once in a lifetime frog or grasshopper leap. This chapter revisits the major findings of the previous chapters and reflects on congruences and discrepancies between theory and reality in order to highlight the most interesting bits of development as well as improve the theoretical approaches used.

### *9.1.1 Emerging Forms of Involvement and Commonalities*

#### 9.1.1.1 Individual Paths

First of all, it is important to note what all countries have in common: They followed *their* individual path to find their answer, to offer at least one option of patient involvement. All four have had their individual reasons for why they enacted collective patient involvement in hospitals or relied on traditional or newly invented equivalents. This is the main reason, why in this chapter, although the commonalities



A. Haarmann, *The Evolution and Everyday Practice of Collective Patient Involvement in Europe*, DOI 10.1007/978-3-319-64595-7_9

are in the focus, the pathway of all four case studies is presented separately. Despite the existence of single factors of commonalities, no coherent pattern could be found on a more concrete level.

#### 9.1.1.2 Legitimacy and the Relocation of Powers

Regarding commonalities, all countries share that policy changes—at least to some extent—can be seen as a political answer: Patient/citizen involvement in all four countries is viewed as a contribution to more legitimacy and higher quality of care. This is particularly prevalent in England, the Netherlands, and Sweden, less pronounced, however, in Germany. The countries' pathways, however, differ: While the Netherlands, England, and Sweden chose to decentralise their level of involvement to make it more locally accountable, Germany opted to centralise one of the main means of involvement from the various sickness funds to the national level. All the solutions found can thereby to some extent be regarded functional equivalents of patient involvement at the level of hospitals that was in the focus of this study even though their mechanisms, their focus, their implications, and potential to be achieved differ. Furthermore, it is interesting to note that regardless of the form of involvement it is understood as a part of the endeavour to not only make (health-)care more responsive but also more effective in all countries.

#### 9.1.1.3 Extension of the Groups Involved and Advice

What they also share is that no matter how patient involvement is implemented throughout the four countries, it is *advisory* in nature, leaving the last word of decision making to providers, politicians, and/or corporatist actors—and thereby to the actors that have hitherto been the decision maker, anyway. However, by enlarging the range of actors involved in the decision-making process by patients, citizens, residents, or their respective interest organisations incorporates new perspectives and aspects and sometimes alters the decision-making processes as such. Despite the solely advisory competences of the new actors, they constitute a vital part in the process since the ones finally deciding on the issues are often inclined to take ordinary patients' voice into account or to follow it right away to a high degree.

#### 9.1.1.4 Difficult Recruitment and Professionalisation

Yet another point holds true for all countries: Interviewees in all countries report about difficulties to recruit young, educated, and capable volunteers for the often time-consuming and thematically demanding work in the patient or citizen councils or patient organisations. This is paralleled by a professionalisation of the members of the various lay-boards and lay-committees in all four countries, which, in turn, makes recruitment even more difficult. As professionalisation finding the respective roles, the topics you would like to make an issue, the best way to talk with each other and the best way to talk for a collective seems to take an average of ten to 15 years at least. In some instances like Germany's involvement in long-term care, the 'right' mode seems to not have been found after more than four decades, yet—if we assume that the search is still on.

In this context, there is something that can be read between the lines of (almost) all interviews, most pronounced however in the Netherlands. Interestingly, it does not matter to what category of interviewee the interview belongs; the perspective differed, but the phenomenon described was the same: Professionalisation creates a new problem between the two extremes 'lay' and 'expert'. At the one extreme, recipients of care are not accepted as discussion partners for the management, because they are too amateurish, cannot think figures, strategy plans, and are much too much centred around small everyday problems. At the other extreme, they are not accepted as discussion partners for the management, because they are too professional (cf. also Trappenburg 2008, p. 163; van Egmond, Heerings, & Munnichs 2014, chap. 6): They lack authenticity, are too distant from their co-clients, and lack their pure knowledge. Therefore, in conclusion there is relatively little room for acceptance of patients, which might be called 'window of acceptance' (see Fig. 9.1).

What professionalisation and the narrow room for acceptance have in common, is that obviously it is not plain patient knowledge that is sought after, but a specific kind of 'expert knowledge', which on the other hand must neither be too specific nor too advanced. What it also shows is that despite all progress, bridging the two lifeworlds remains still intricate and that patient organisations and client councils—for various reasons—are not as naturally established in the minds of providers and politicians. Despite the otherwise rather successful implementation in the Netherlands, one interviewee summarised this in the following statement: '[A] real third party, I think, they have not become in the Netherlands so far'. (interview 11; author's translation)

Overall, the two preferences of professionalisation and a narrow window of acceptance contradict each other: Whereas the patient/citizen boards are glad to have experts in their ranks—which to some extent is still owing to the misunderstanding that they need to follow the formally given rights instead of prioritising what *they* think is important—the management would like to have somewhat less professional members on the client councils , in order to not have an additional professional body next to the executive and supervisory board.

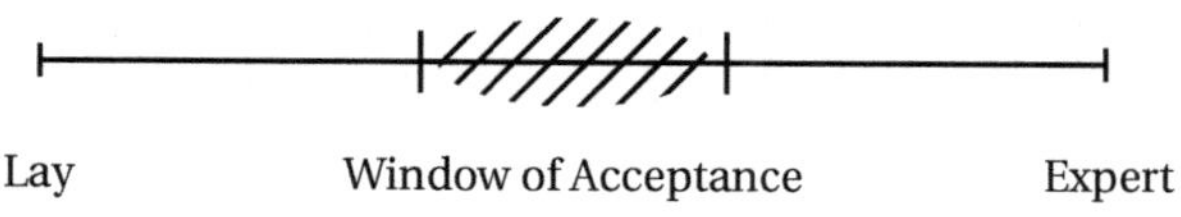


**Fig. 9.1** Schematic lay—expert continuum. Source: own depiction

### 9.1.2 *More Commonalities: The Market, NPM, and Patients as Customers as Precondition*

At first sight, for marketisation or related governance reforms as the general driving force, no support could be found. This is fully in line with the general assumption that external pressure leading in one or another way to marketisation cannot be regarded as one of the main reasons for a formal change in governance and involvement (see Chap. 1, Sect. 1.2 on page 10). Though the transition to a 'marketised' health insurance in the Netherlands became one of the main drivers over time and managerial autonomy for foundation trust hospitals in England could be understood as a form of market-like governance in the widest sense, this does not seem to have any major impact in general: Sweden was one of the earliest implementors and strongest proponents of NPM and the purchaser–provider split, while even Germany had its time of competition for prices between sickness funds and—though rather late—its national variant of NPM (cf. Borins & Grüning 1998; Calltorp, Persson, Holmström, Levin, & Persson 1988, p. 16; Naschold 1996, pp. 37, 47–51, 130; Schedler & Proeller 2000, pp. 5, 35, 56–62). Marketisation and related governance reforms are, thus, not restricted to the two first-mentioned countries and can be found with their various expressions in all four countries to a varying degree.

However, while the role NPM, competition, and market elements play in the respective countries did not give rise to any specific measure regarding patient/citizen involvement without additional factors, it can be perceived as the initial catalyst that sparked the awareness about the patient/citizen as someone, whose appraisal about the provision of health care should be taken into consideration in one way or another. Even though the value of patient/citizen involvement was understood in a rather mechanistic way, what can be stated is that the incorporation of some form of market elements can be viewed as *one* necessary precondition for seeing patients as 'clients' with immediate demands to the provider. The combination with other factors in the respective countries will be discussed in the following chapters.

### 9.1.3 *Actor Relations*

In what follows, the attempt is made to arrive at a comparative understanding of the actors and the institutions involved. According to the actor-centred institutionalist perspective, the relation between different actors is at the centre of any analysis (Mayntz & Scharpf 1995, p. 52; Scharpf 1997, p. 43). In this sample of countries, politicians were a or the major actor in the legislation process regarding involvement, which makes the focus on their relations an important aspect. This may sound self-evident, as legislation is done by politicians. However, though other actors played in, even pre-empted the result in the Netherlands already on a voluntary basis, and urged politicians to take legislative action, politicians took the lead and were the main driver and decision makers against all kinds of opposition in the

Netherlands, England, but also in Sweden in the end. In England, the Netherlands, and Germany scandals about malpractice in mental care fostered a situation that the public opinion and politicians could not ignore. Having said that, the direction of action differed: While it was a pure top-down approach in England and to a larger extent in Germany, it was rather bottom-up in the Netherlands by drawing on the voluntary agreements in place. In Sweden the development can be described as a joint search for the best solution.

What both the Netherlands and England have in common is that the success of the reforms depended to a larger extent on the two strong personalities and commitment of the ministers in charge, Els Borst for the Netherlands and Alan Milburn for England, without whose effort the bill maybe would not have passed parliament. While Els Borst advocated the bill and put greater lengths into consensus building, Alan Milburn was busy dissipating concerns and—maybe even more important—strategically thinking how the bill could be enacted despite the strong opposition. In this sense, it can be observed that the policy process parallels the implementation process, for which all four countries have shown that individual enthusiasts on the ground are vital for the implementation's success.

One group that could be expected to emerge in the discussion and did not in three of the four countries is the medical profession. When asked, why they thought there was no lobbying or protest, my interviewees replied that the medical profession took a neutral stance as the new acts did not touch upon their everyday work. This is plausible to some extent, in particular in a relative perspective compared to a nursing home's or hospital's management. However, my interviews show a number of cases where the flow of care or specific therapies were changed. Working for the patient's or resident's best, another, more convincing explanation might be that it was less of importance for them in terms of cost and autonomy. The only exception, where the medical profession was opposed to the bill, is England: Here, the Labour government saw itself confronted by a massive protest of professionals within the NHS. This opposition, however, not only applies to this specific act, but is part of a tradition of the English medical profession and management against patient involvement at large. As in the political field, the government utilised its unitary position of a strong majority in parliament and defied the opposition.

#### 9.1.3.1 Complex Actors

In the English case, the vast differences in opinion within the government party cannot be overlooked at whatever stage in the decision-making process. It is a rather rare occurrence that it was not about any gradual preferences, but that even at the time of voting in favour or against the bill a great part of the government party voted against. The reasons mentioned were not only political but also arguments put supported by interest groups such as the medical profession.

Even though a specific case, this raises the question how to deal with and analyse empirical, heterogeneous 'complex actors' theoretically and in practice (see also Sect. 3.1.3). Scharpf suggests to take them *pars pro toto* or as their 'average', while at the same time highlighting that it is harder for complex actors to achieve their goals, whereas majority ruling and hierarchic decisions eases decision-making processes (Scharpf 1997, pp. 58–60). Scharpf, thereby, to some extent acknowledges the intricacies of his own approach to treat them as a unitary actor. Taking the latter perspective, however, he deals with 'complex actors' from an *internal situation for complex actors* like organisations or political parties only, still treating them as more or less unitary actors. This can analytically be at best risky, at worst completely misleading, both in what actor(s) stand for and in the consequences. As long as diversity does not exceed a certain extent, we might strive for the 'average' of a complex actor's opinion and perception, even here potentially underestimating strong positions. Where it exceeds, however, it is all the more important to not only acknowledge the actor's 'official' point of view, but also to widen the perspective to at least capture the extremes if not the grades in between, too (see Sect. 4.4.1). We can assume, however, that the underlying logic of intra-actor relations and negotiations is similar to the ones for the *intra-political* and *extra-political* negotiations as they translate into higher costs if major actors oppose reforms (Mayntz & Scharpf 1995, p. 58; Scharpf 1997, p. 59).

In order to incorporate all the diversity that can be observed between different fractions and single politicians into the analysis a new sub-layer for complex actors is suggested in this book, treating it as any other group of actors. In doing so, three nested layers or spheres of actor relations can be identified in the policy field of health care in this analysis, which also illustrate that no matter how strong actors might be, they are always interwoven in a network of relations with a varying degree of dependence (see Fig. 9.2):

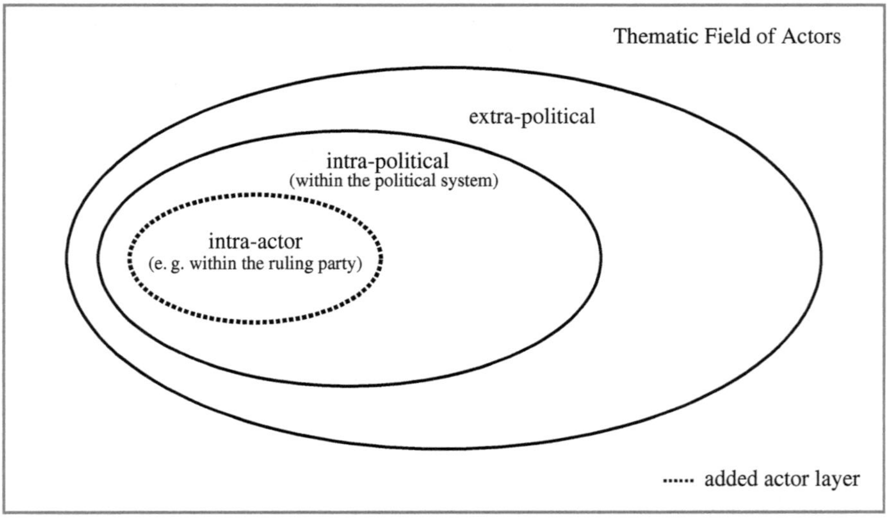


**Fig. 9.2** Schematic overview of levels of actors' relation in the field of health care. Source: own depiction

(a) The RELATION AMONG THE MEMBERS OF THE RULING PARTY/PARTIES, a 'complex actor' in Scharpf's (1997) terminology.
(b) INTERACTIONS WITHIN PARLIAMENT AND BETWEEN THE DIFFERENT CHAMBERS OF PARLIAMENT and finally
(c) BETWEEN POLITICAL AND OTHER ACTORS IN THE FIELD as, e.g. providers, associations, health insurance, or social partners.

What role diverse stances within complex actors play is also a matter of timing: Starting the analysis at a later point of the legislation process, for instance, when discussions have led to a joined result already, is likely to yield in different results. In many of these instances this level might not play in to the same extent as it does in this analysis.

While disagreement in the intra-political field is common, the cases of England, Germany, and Sweden do show some peculiarities: England in that it overrode a vote by the House of Lords and thereby sailed close to the wind, Germany and Sweden in that there were hardly any party political differences. Germany has a tradition of the extremes of seeking compromise in basic questions regarding the health care system, on the one hand, or stalemate, on the other. Sweden, in contrast, was politically completely undivided regarding patient involvement. In the Netherlands, the objections raised by the different parties clearly reflected the stances of various patient and provider organisations pretty well. What unites at least the Netherlands, England, and Germany is that the politicians' role has changed to become a 'manager of authority' (*Herrschaftsmanager*) over time (cf. Rothgang, Schmid, & Schneider 2012, p. 178). In this sense, the creation of patients boards in the Netherlands and England as well as in particular the 'Joint Federal Committee' can be regarded as instances of this changed role.

Interests in the extra-political field and between the political and extra-political field are the hardest to distinguish in this study, if not mentioned implicitly or explicitly in the sources, since interest groups may exert subtle pressure on MPs directly or via other interest organisations. However, the various concerns can in most cases easily be discerned as they are represented well in the political arena. This applies, for instance, to the concern of patients', residents', and relatives' organisations in the Netherlands that the new regulation would fall behind the competences accomplished on a voluntary basis. Furthermore, providers of care feared additional costs and a takeover of governance by patients. These concerns could be solved over the run of the legislation process. The pressure of patients' and relatives' organisations was also present in Germany, where they demanded more influence in order to remedy the shortcomings in the care sector and to prevent further scandals. Overall, it can be observed that providers' and patient organisations' concerns were drawn into the intra-political level and not left to the extra-political realm. In the observed cases it can be concluded that interest representation worked very well.

#### 9.1.3.2 Negotiation Costs vs. Veto-Points

In more theoretical terms, there are several ways to arrive at an agreement between different actors or, to phrase it in more theoretical language, to deal with additional costs:

(a) Differing claims might be ignored or accepted if an actor is willing to pay the potential price.
(b) Another option is to start negotiations with actors of different stances in order to reduce costs. As the cases of England and the Netherlands show, the duration of the entirety of the legislation process can last from a few months to a few decades, which is immediately related to arising costs. Next to the immediate costs, it needs to be kept in mind that the longer the time span stretches the more not only changes in content need to be considered but also potentially shifting power balances between the actors. This might open up the situation and facilitate a solution or achieve the contrary.

Taking the new perspective of treating complex actors analytically as any other group of actors bears the potential of negotiation costs that most often precede negotiations with any other actor. They thereby constitute an equivalent to what Korpi (1983) and historic institutionalism term veto-power (cf. also Korpi & Palme 2003). In that sense, understanding the rules that both complex actors and institutions follow makes the dividing line to historical institutionalism fade. In consequence, rather than being disparate, the divide between actor-centred and historical institutionalism is rather a question of perspective adding some details to the respective other one.

Regarding negotiation costs, the difficulty arises how to interpret situations like the one found in England: As the Netherlands, England is—with regard to health care policy—a unitary state. What is noticeable, though, is that although the Labour government in England met fierce opposition from the political opposition, the House of Lords, and its own members, they were able to push the reform through. Theory postulates high costs for actors in such a context with voting the Labour government out of office as the ultimate one. This thread, however, did not prevent the Labour government from proceeding with the bill. Apparently, this leaves us with two options—and any mixture of them—which are likely to varying degrees depending on the respective circumstances. In this case, it may very well be a combination of both as both options lend some credibility

(a) One possibility is that the perception of a situation is not always right (more on this see Sect. 9.3 on page 290). In the English case, e.g. the Labour government might have overestimated the support by its own MPs and the voters in the medium term, thereby underestimating the real costs of enacting yet another health care reform against a strong opposition.
(b) Another option is that governments are sometimes less concerned about the costs falling back on them as long as they firmly believe in doing the right thing. In that sense, this case might show that though Scharpf's (1997, p. 40)

postulation might be right, empirical examples show that even the risk of losing office is not always perceived too high a cost.

In contrast, opposition to the proposal was never that fundamental in the Netherlands, which might for a large part be owing to the fact that coalition governments are common. Despite a government majority and only suspending powers of the 'First Chamber', they sought compromise, which took the country almost 20 years and can in part be attributed to the often larger number of small parties in coalition governments.[1] Evidence from all four case studies suggests that there is no coherent pattern of political constellations in parliament, political systems, or health care system type that eases the process of institutional reform. Translating negotiation costs from an actor-centred perspective as *potential* veto-points with each of their individual, context-sensitive, and actor-specific potentials for conflict, consensus, and negotiation costs appears to come much closer to reality than any broad-brush addition of veto-points.

### 9.1.4 Historical Institutionalism

> Political decisions that can be tied to social inequalities, [...; are] much more difficult to justify than those mediated by the market. (Borchert 1996, p. 57; author's translation)

The process in the Netherlands and England can be described as a departure from the institutional path hitherto pursued: Corporatist influence was repressed and completely new ways of involvement were enacted in the Netherlands. Also in England, traditional means of involvement were left behind and new ways found. Reforms in Germany, in contrast, can be perceived as changes within the system, pursuing the same path: Though new actors were incorporated and decision-making centralised, changes occurred within the corporatist logic.

Sweden is a most interesting example in that formally, only one half-sentence was added to the health care act without any specification of which and how 'relevant actors' should be involved. Therefore, strictly speaking, change neither of path nor formal organisation has occurred. Nevertheless, both politicians as patient representatives expect a favourable return on their part in this rather informal relationship—be it actually the case or not. In the meanwhile, the relation has perpetuated and institutionalised itself and thereby lost its informal character. The most important conclusion is that despite its (initial) informality, new actors get involved and receive an almost obligatory say.

[1] Authors like van Waarden (1992, 1993, 2002) tend to explain differences with different cultural heritages. Though, in my opinion, there should be more to an explanation than cultural differences, it may well able to explain certain cultural traditions as one element in a process like, for instance, the custom of consensus seeking, which can make all the difference in otherwise similar circumstances.

'Blame avoidance', as one of the most often phrases made use of in the context of historical institutionalism, scores with a divided result: In principal, patient/citizen involvement per se can both be perceived to be (ab-)used for blame avoiding purposes. In one respect, the devolution of power to the social partners constitutes an essential part of the concept of corporatism, yet with an explicitly positive notion of blame avoidance. Maintaining to implement the wishes of patients/citizens provides politicians and managers in the four countries with a strong position to spend money—e.g. vis-à-vis the political opposition. Less often in the context of health care, however, it is about the classic example of cutting expenditures. Thinkable scenarios, in which patients are involved concerning their preferences regarding cuts, might develop in the short or long run, but have not evolved so far: With managers and politicians having the final word in the Netherlands, England, and Sweden the classic blame avoidance only works in the German case to its full extent. Hence, patient and public involvement can only to a very small extent be perceived as a device of blame avoidance.

#### 9.1.4.1 Theoretical Conclusions

It could be shown that low interaction-costs in negotiations or less veto-points do not automatically result in change—just as little as high costs preclude actors from taking action which potentially hurts themselves—as long as any majority can be found for this policy. In this sense, veto-points or costs of opposition should not be reinterpreted as absolute obstacles but rather as relative likelihoods. In this reading, the embeddedness in a wider field of actors comes indeed closer to what historical as well actor-centred institutionalism suggests: Powerful corporatist and professional actors as well as the federal division in Germany make radical institutional change more unlikely than in the Netherlands or England.

The same as for Germany applies to Sweden: Here the devolution of responsibility for health care to the county councils has a restraining effect on the national politics in that field. As was mentioned above, neither of the process descriptions offered by Streeck and Thelen is applicable to the Swedish case. Therefore, the new category 'Enhancement' is suggested. It describes a situation which does not change the formal institutional processes, while changing the informal (in this case: decision making) procedures. Thus, while formally neither organisation nor competences are changed, the institution is 'enhanced' regarding, e.g. its circle of members, its competences, its internal processes or the like.

Furthermore, Dutch multi-party governments can be juxtaposed to England with its 'first-past-the-post' election system and the rarely resulting need to form a coalition. It provides an additional answer to why the Dutch government negotiated while the British passed the bill with its own majority. However, to what extent the observation that both England and the Netherlands are unitary states—the decision-making power, thus, in one hand and not scattered over several regional levels—actually is decisive depends on the relative power of other actors and the relative costs to change other context variables. What unites both countries, however, is the centralised legal responsibility for health care, which gives government greater freedom to enact their ideas. In both Sweden and Germany greater negotiation skills would be needed than in particular in England.

### *9.1.5 Ideas*

As another commonality, all countries share—at least to some extent—the idea, to involve patients in order to contribute to improved quality and/or efficiency, a quest that is particularly pronounced in the two NHS countries. This is strongly interwoven with the underlying idea to decentralise and devolve power in the Netherlands, England, and Sweden. Only Germany sticks out in that respect on the political level, probably owing to the fact that responsibilities are dispersed among many different actors anyway. Moreover, in both the Netherlands and in Sweden democratisation was the explicit aim of involvement.

At second sight, we can detect an interdependency between accepting the idea of some kind of 'marketisation' and what role is intended for patients: In the Netherlands, they are perceived to be clients or consumers and therefore to 'purchase' not only their health insurance policy with the best cost-benefit ratio but also to monitor the quality of the providers. In England, they are perceived the 'owners' and thereby stakeholder and governors of FTs, having in common that even they should monitor the provision. Thus, in both countries we have the individual bond between competing providers and the patient/citizen. In contrast, Sweden's competition is confined to county councils purchasing health care provision whereby patients can choose between different providers and can thereby indirectly influence the quality of services. Though the overall function of the patient is similar, the role of patients in Sweden is rather that of reporting shortcomings to the supervisory authorities. First and foremost, however, this is the professionals' task (cf. SFS 2010:659, Chaps. 3 & 6, §4). In Germany, the choice of provider is rather seen as a traditional patient right, which is not necessarily associated with quality. The latter, in turn, is traditionally (thought to be) influenced by the sickness funds. According to official reading, after competition for clients by means of different insurance fees for several years, there was the somewhat absurd notion of 'competition via means of quality' between sickness funds for some years. Only recently (autumn 2014) was competition based on prices reintroduced on a comparatively small scale. The rather newly obtained advisory rights in the Joint Federal Committee follow the tradition of self-governance. This combines a devolution to actors who ideally are more competent in the field than politics, a devolution that relieves the state from some of its tasks. Though the image drawn is very sketchy, it can be stated that reforms in both the Netherlands and England have given patients a very immediate and to some extent controlling role, while in Germany and Sweden this is mediated via other institutions.

As postulated by most theorists, ideas can linger without receiving much attention for a long time or even throughout their entire life (see page 43; Kingdon 2003, pp. 116 et seq., 127 et seq., 139, 179). In the Netherlands, England, and regarding long-term care also Germany, it was drawn on (partly) existing organisational models, which then were adapted: In the Netherlands, the already existing client councils in long-term care were made the general norm for all in-patient (health-)care. The German equivalent, the *Heimbeirat*, followed the same path. Taking evidence from these two countries only, it might be concluded that it is easier to get accustomed and apply ideas whose practical capability has already been proven. England, in contrast, took the organisation of Spanish Foundation Trusts as a role model, which then was intertwined with citizen/patient involvement. In that, it can be counted as policy learning in the widest sense, but should more precisely be called 'institution learning' (cf. also Leiber, Greß, & Manouguian 2010) or 'ideational learning', since England did not borrow from the very Spanish policy but adapted one institution and partly its underlying idea. Beyond that, in contrast to the Netherlands, the implementation of citizen involvement in England is a top-down approach, not previously rooted in society (cf. also Barnes 1999). Moreover, as the 'institutional learning' only applies to the organisation side of Foundation Trust hospitals, but not involvement, this contradicts the assumption made from the Dutch and German cases, as apparently radical change can be based on completely new and untested, even immature ideas. In both Sweden and England there is, however, also the internal cross-field case of policy/institutional learning in that in both countries involvement in schools played its role when arguing for patient/resident involvement.

What else can be observed is that the Labour government also tried a ruse by highlighting that health care is the genuine field of Labour policies and thereby depicting the Labour character of the reform. This was done by both alluding to Foundation Trust hospitals as in line with the tradition of cooperatives and by making use of the terminology of 'people owning their hospital'.

Another artifice of strategic action is the 'coupling of ideas' (see page 45 in Sect. 3.2.1; Kingdon 2003, p. 173), for which the Netherlands and in particular England provide interesting examples. In *the Netherlands*, the proposal to introduce patient involvement in hospitals was coupled to the much longer existent proposal of resident involvement in long-term care settings. The coupling was not present in the two predecessors of the WMCZ, but first introduced with the bill for the WMCZ. Clearly, the main desire of MPs and patient organisations to implement involvement lay in the field of long-term care, while—just as clearly—major concerns of both MPs and providers related to patient involvement in hospitals. Beyond the fact that hospital treatment took longer than nowadays and that the zeitgeist was different, none of my interviewees could give a plausible answer to where this coupling stemmed from.

The *Labour government's* coupling was much more obvious, but not less successful: Longstanding demands for amongst other things higher funding, better dental, primary, and paediatric health care, and more local, managerial independence were coupled with a new specific hospital organisation, including patient involvement, a two-tiered system of funding and supervision, and competition for funding and patients. While an overwhelming majority of MPs, managers, and health care personnel would endorse increased funding and improvements, opposition of all actors against the specific form of Foundation Trust hospitals was fierce.

In *Sweden and Germany* in contrast, the ideas lay much closer at hand to the previous institutions and were, thereby, less conflicting with the already existing structures. At an abstract level it was sought for ideas that yielded change without leaving 'known territories': Both the extension of the joint federal committee and the Swedish health care committees can be interpreted in that way, as decision-making power remains with self-governance or politicians. Even though it does not tell anything about the impact this change has for patients, it suits the observation of politicians' endeavour to deal with opposition by institutions and actors made above.

In addition, in Germany we can find what Kingdon (2003, pp. 190 et seq.) terms 'spill-over effects': Creating the Joint Federal Committee (G-BA) with its central and vital position for the benefit catalogue in Germany and including new actors that had not been part of the corporatist governance leaves the corporatist actors, that had hitherto been unchallenged in the health care field, with less backing. Over time, this might considerably change the power balance between the actors to the disadvantage of the 'old' corporatist actors, in favour of the voice of patients and in favour of politicians.

#### 9.1.5.1 Theoretical Conclusions

Reflecting on congruences and discrepancies between theory and reality, the case of England is of particular interest. Contrasting the empirical evidence from the Netherlands and Germany that ideas can exist for years without being acted upon, the development in England shows that new ideas can be and actually are born and generated in an ad hoc fashion: Spanish Foundation Trust hospitals completely lacked the component of citizen involvement. Though difficult to impossible to prove, given the short amount of time between the first mention of involvement in FTs and the eventual enactment of the bill, the opposition from providers, as well as its immature clarity for implementation it is fair to assume that a concrete idea about citizen involvement in the organisation of hospitals was widely non-existent as late as 1 year before Alan Milburn's and Tony Blair's visit to Spain—if existent at all even at that point in time. Therefore, ideas might linger in a reservoir of ideas until needed or outdated, it might even be the rule for the majority of them; this should, however, not mislead us into believing that ideas cannot pop out of nowhere.

With regard to the Netherlands, we might conclude that ideas that have already been implemented and tested in everyday life have a higher chance to be adopted. However, as hinted at before, the example of England shows that even spontaneously developed ideas with a lower level of maturity have the chance to be implemented, given that other circumstances are favourable.

Furthermore, the abovementioned observation of feigned arguments in an attempt to convince opposing MPs of the Labour party to vote in favour of the bill can be described from different theoretical angles: As described above, it suits Scharpf's theoretical reflection (1997, pp. 108–109) of strategic actors, lobbying, and the importance of actors' relations. However, it can equally well be described by Maier's 'ideas on hooks', which consists of rephrasing or mitigating the original or underlying idea in order to make it more appealing or acceptable (Maier 2003, pp. 47, 48; cf. also Béland 2005, pp. 10–11). Interesting enough, once again the case of England challenges the theoretical assumptions: Maier (2003, p. 47) points out that 'ideas on hooks' only make sense for actors to be used if there is a sufficiently large group that 'buys' the hooks as realistic options. Though a number of MPs fell for these 'hooks' (cf. House of Commons 2003a,b,c,d), the majority did *not* buy them. Yet, this shows either the level of desperation of the Labour government or underlines the importance of perceptions and assumptions: If actors perceive the likelihood to be successful with their hook sufficiently large, they will give it a try, no matter what the actual outcome might be (see also Sect. 9.3 on page 290).

## 9.2 On Patients, Users, Consumers, and Customers

One thing that definitively differs between the four countries is the use of terminology to describe recipients of (health-)care in everyday professional language. Germany is clearly the country with the most traditional/conservative use of terminology—conservative regarding its literal sense, not referring to the usually negative connotation. The Netherlands is the forerunner in terms of reshaping terminology: In none of the other countries included in this study has the terms 'client', 'customer', and 'consumer' such a self-evidently exposed position as in the Netherlands, and that regardless of whether it is a paper by the official authorities, providers, or patient organisations. England, where a frequent use of words like client and customer for their patients and recipients of care can be observed, follows on its heels. Here applies what holds true for the terminology applied regarding policy reforms as well, a larger share of mere rhetoric is accompanied in England.

The mere use of different terminology would not be something to pay attention to. However, the use also reflects the view on patients and the relation between state, providers, and patients: In England it shows how politicians and the NHS would like the NHS to be. In the Netherlands it rather reflects the transition to a privatised health care insurance. In Sweden, the use is a mirror of recent changes while core principles and values of the health care system are retained at the same time, to which, for instance, the competences for politicians and public authorities can be counted. And even in Germany, the relative continuity is reflected astonishingly well (Table 9.1).

Except in Germany, interviewees were very well able to reflect upon the use and the connotation they want to bring across. Most of them differentiated between

**Table 9.1** Overview of the main terminology used

| | Acute health care | Health care for chronically ill | Long-term care |
|---|---|---|---|
| The Netherlands | Patient | User/consumer/customer | Client/customer/resident |
| England | Patient | Patient/user | User/care receiver |
| Germany | Patient | Patient | Resident |
| Sweden | Patient | Consumer | Care receiver |

Source: own compilation

customers in retail trade and health care. This is expressed by a Dutch interviewee, when he refers to the providers:

> Where they view it a bit more sceptically is that they are forced to create a market by politics. And if you apply a market function, you should listen well to your customers. And that needs an Albert Heijn [large supermarket chain in the Netherlands; the author] usually, too, because if the butter sold by Albert Heijn is not good then no customer will drop by. That is a different story regarding (health-)care. And that's what the secretary of state thinks [...], I absolutely do not want the comparison in this field about a pack of butter and (health-)care, because (health-)care is common property, is also something we stand for as a welfare state [...]. Thus, hospital care is also something [delivered] by society. And in that a customer is different from the supermarket or whatever. (interview 4; author's translation)

Basically, the point made by the English interviewees is similar. Here, the turn to high quality standards, good performance, and the underlying competition between foundation trusts and hospitals is seen as contributing to a change in the use of terminology:

> I think the move to Foundation Trusts means that patients are seen more as customers. It is the whole thing about choice, the customer is always right. Although people do not like to think like that—because as soon as you start to say customers you start to see the organisation as such as a business. Well, it is a business: We turn over 170 million a year, we have got 2,500 staff. It is a business. [...] You know, satanically they are customers. We do not call them customers. In mental care we say 'service users', in acute hospitals they are patients. It completely depends on where you are in the NHS, because mental health users did not like to be called patients, because not all of them are patients. Some of them are based in the community. [...] They are users of the service. (interview 17)
>
> We do use this [word customer; the author] in the NHS. This has crept in a lot now [...]. It is jargon, isn't it? I am a customer of Marks & Spencer. I buy things from them. I expect a certain standard in what they deliver to me for the product they give me. That is how I see a customer. I am a customer of British Gas, I expect them to supply me with gas. Now, am I a customer in healthcare? Well, yeah, I guess I am, because I pay for it through my taxes. But it does not seem quite the same as being a patient. I think, [...] you are a customer, you are receiving a service, a healthcare service, which is indirectly or directly paid for through taxation. (interview 18)

Though there is some academic discussion occurring around terms like customer, choice, 'the modern patient' (cf. e.g. Anell & Rosén 1996; Borgenhammar & Fallberg 1997; Lian 2011; Olofsson, Nilsson, & Wahllöf 2010; cf. also Anell 2005; SOU 1999:149), rhetorics of market and subsequently of clients and customers, the terminology has not become equally established in Sweden. Even those counties where the wave of New Public Management and the purchaser–provider split was most prominent have returned to a rather traditional terminology: There is talk of 'patients' again in most contexts, whereas chronically ill and those receiving (long-term) care are most often referred to as 'users'.[2]

> Are you a patient, consumer, user, member, relative, close to someone—all of these definitions are extremely important. And there were quite a lot of people suffering from diabetes who absolutely did not want to be called consumer, who felt, 'Damn, I have not chosen to go and buy a fridge, I have gotten an illness, I do not want to have. I do not want to be a consumer.' [...] If you are consumer, you can choose: 'Oh, I want to have a pink or a blue fridge, or a combination of fridge and freezer. But I cannot choose whether I want to take an insulin injection.' (interview 50; author's translation)
>
> We are cautious. At least when we talk with our own ranks, we do not talk about clients, but we use rather the term '(health-)care consumer'. We consume (health-)care, because a consumer is still active and makes active choices, but you are not in a purchasing situation, as often is associated with [the term] customer. There are different discussions, but that depends on what mental image you have of the respective [terms]. (interview 38; author's translation)

Another aspect of the relation between state, providers, and patients touches the question which group of lay-people is supposed to be a counterbalancing force in order to prevent that too much power is agglomerated or, seen from a different perspective, help authorities that each actor acts as she is supposed to. In the Netherlands the political view is that patients in collaboration with their health insurance are to act against too powerful providers. In Germany, this would be the role of the corporatist actors, i.e. according to the logic the beneficiaries of sickness funds. The focus here, however, is more on the profligacy of providers and patients alike. In the two NHS countries, the counterbalancing role is traditionally assigned to politicians—or, in a broader view, the whole electorate. In this view, lay-people have started to support politicians since these countries changed the involvement of citizens.

## 9.3 Perception: The Undervalued Factor

> If men define situations as real, they are real in their consequences.
>
> (Thomas & Thomas 1928)
>
> Decisive is the aspect of legitimisation. No institution can successfully establish one's position or being sanctioned, if it is not supported by the interpretative patterns of the actors.
>
> (Münnich 2011, p. 493; author's translation)

[2]The National Board of Health and Welfare (SoS) tries to diminish stigmatisation among patients. The path, however, is not approved by everyone as the following quotation suggests: 'The National Board of Health and Welfare keeps another time whingeing about this term [user; ...], to only talk about individuals, but that is also going to be... With the stubbornness of a mule, I try [...; to bring home] that it is the relation you need to know about. Whether you are a bus driver or passenger... Yes, everyone is an individual so to speak, we exist as a fuzzy collective, [...] who then is responsible for anything?' (interview 40; author's translation).

In the previous chapters the importance of perceptions was mentioned already. As addressed in the section on 'complex actors' (see Sect. 9.1.3.1 on page 279), talking about *the* actor's perception is difficult. What, therefore, is referred to here is what can be concluded from the final action taken. Since politicians were among or *the* leading actors for change in all countries and, of course, the final ones to pick different ideas for enactment, decisions are, in their turn, obviously led by a mixture of necessities, the limiting factors such as already existing institutions, the power of convincing arguments and lobbying, the context, and the perceivable best.

This is exactly where perception comes into play, which is best demonstrated by the following example: On the surface, the Netherlands and Germany were fairly comparable in the 1980s and 1990s in terms of a degree of corporatism, the system of sickness funds and their potential underfunding, the degree of organisation in these funds, and, thus, the context of the situation, problems, and a lack of legitimacy of health care. However, while the Netherlands withdrew power from the corporatist actors and turned to a market logic, Germany clung to its self-governance in sickness funds. Thus, though the situation was comparable in both countries, the perception of what steps were to be reformed necessarily differed considerably. In consequence, the perception of a problem must be comparatively more severe in the Dutch case to still propose more radical changes and to counterbalance the well-known and already mentioned hampering factors. Thus, overall, there is as much topical as perceptual reasoning for or against continuing with a corporatist rule.[3]

Though actor-centred institutionalism explicitly mentions 'perception' as one factor in decision-making processes (cf. Scharpf 1997, pp. 39–42), it remains vague and does not receive much attention. Nevertheless, it must be assumed that it comes to the foreground and can play a or even *the* decisive role, when it comes to legislation. What Kingdon (2003, pp. 111–112) already hinted at when pointing out the importance of framing a problem, manifests itself even more pronounced empirically, for instance, when analysing the four different pathways. Notwithstanding, the point to be made here is not whether the assessment is right or wrong, but that perception and the assessment of a situation building upon it plays in. Drawing on conclusions from the English case study, what is important to note here is that even the projected costs for one actor need to be understood through the lens of the actor's perception in question at the time of the assessment. There is, for instance, no reason to assume that the Labour government did not act rationally: It can be assumed that leaving a Labour imprint on the NHS, making hospitals more efficient, and preventing a competitive market after a potential change in government, outweighed the perceived costs. It can, however, be doubted whether

[3]Of course, this is a rather sketchy image of a decision-making process, since many more factors can play in. One of the keys lacking in Germany was the experience of the 'Dutch disease' and its handling by the corporatist actors that helped to unite politicians to act and to delegitimise corporatism to some extent. However, the abrupt turn from a situation in which competences for corporatist actors should be extended to one in which support had decreased considerably within such a short amount of time shows the latitude politicians have even towards powerful actors, when the opportunity is seized.

the action taken would have been the same if Labour's party leaders had known the devastating election result beforehand. Furthermore, the situation of holding a comfortable majority in parliament might have led it to believe that the government was not at stake. Therefore, it is the assessment of the government itself at the time of decision making, not the perception of others, or the actual loss afterwards, that needs to be taken into account when analysing policy changes.

Depending on the context, this can make politicians' perception of problems the key to understanding policy change. Overall, this makes it a very relative concept, which beyond subjective preferences has at least two different layers. First, the focus on perception might also explain why countries with an aligned development but different development levels sometimes have the same analysis of a problem: Owing to the perception of the actors, the *relative* differences—e.g. between the present situation and the desirable or between the previous and the present one—can be more important than the absolute difference. Second, regarding the given explanation that other things were more relevant to be solved first, this means that a problem—even in the perception of politicians—can be pressing, however, in comparison with other problems it is not on high priority.

## 9.4 Policy Paradigms and Path Breaks: Fuzzy Assumptions and a Vague Relation

Now that we have reasoned out the most important common factors as well as the most obvious peculiarities for each country, the questions still remains, what sparked the idea, what made the Netherlands and England depart from their path, and why at the point in time they actually did? Applying the concept of 'political paradigms' gives an initial, broad answer. Despite being rather vague (see footnote 8, p. 47) and though the concept essentially does not add completely new facts, it can be employed as a focus on critical junctures and the context around the threshold to new paradigms. It includes the underlying concept of ideas, highlights what previous elements were no longer found convincing, and what paradigm replaced the former one. The default is set on continuity, which is maintained as long as the guiding principle is convincing to the actors in question and solutions to emerging problems can still be fitted under the old paradigm. If both are no longer possible, a new paradigm needs to be found. It thereby is able to define the turning point, a potential transitional period of time, and explain the abstract reasons for more extensive change. Overall, it can be said that the approach achieves a better description in cases with more radical changes.

The Netherlands is a good example for a shift, while England can be viewed as an ambivalent case. Corporatism had served as the major mode of governance for the Dutch welfare state until the early 1990s. When corporatist actors were blamed for inefficiency, beneficial payments instead of reintegration of workers, and misappropriations of funds, many politicians felt that corporatism had failed and could not be trusted any longer, all previous reforms seemed to have been in vain (Borghi & van Berkel 2007, pp. 89, 95; Roebroek & Hertogh 1998, pp. 418, 421 et seq.; Trampusch 2000, pp. 263–265, 311; Visser & Hemerijck 1998, pp. 198 et seq.) and did no longer seem to provide convincing solutions any longer. In the field of health care, corporatist involvement had been watered down to some extent, previously. Nevertheless, the guiding principle politics had clung to for decades was phased out in a relatively short amount of time. The empty room needed to be filled by some alternative concept of governance. Some years earlier, the so-called Dekker commission (Commissie 'Structuur en Financiering Gezondheidszorg' (Dekker) 1987) had issued its report with a strong plea to let competition between health insurances and other measures make the health care system more efficient. The (regulated) market as the main mode of steering superseded the corporatist paradigm. Overall, this development builds on a similar change from a purely top-down approach between providers of care and receivers of care to resident/relative involvement in long-term care.

The story for England could read similarly: The belief in an effective, governance centralised led from Whitehead faded, while variants of the internal market had its downsides and were—at least rhetorically—unacceptable to many. Therefore, a new guiding principle was sought for. This means that, on a more abstract level, the common denominator between the Netherlands and England was not the market in itself, but can be seen in the search for a new guiding principle according to which the health care system could be steered. These observations are in line with Hall's (1993, pp. 288–289) and Kingdon's (2003, p. 125) postulation that policies often do not materialise through the pressure of interest groups but ideas that are able to fill gaps. These gaps have either not been perceived before or, if seen in combination with the approach on paradigm shifts, need to be re-filled as the solutions hitherto employed no longer seem to be adequate or convincing, just as old-age poverty of the 1980s and onwards or 'new social risks' can be seen as further examples for such gaps to be filled.

Overall, it can also be asked what constituted the 'aim' that was pursued in light of the new ideas? In the Netherlands, the wish to democratise health care and give patients a voice is clearly a new aim. In England, two competing aims can be identified: A new goal of strengthening the local influence on health care provision can be contrasted to the continuous one of achieving good quality and efficient use of resources. The answer to the question, which of them is the more important, depends on the perspective but given that the main emphasis was on performance of hospitals and strengthening managerial leeway as well as PPI can rather be perceived as a means of goal achievement, there are good reasons to argue that it is more about improvements in health care provision and less about patients' voice, and, thus, rather a second order change, but no shift of the political paradigm (see Sect. 3.2.2).

At the same time, there is good reason to also reinterpret institutionalism's path dependency and its institutions into the relative importance of its *dominant* institution: Even though institutions can exist in a pure form, they are often comprised of several subinstitutions. When corporatism in the Netherlands, for

**Table 9.2** Overview of elements of change regarding formal involvement

| | Formal change of... | | | | |
|---|---|---|---|---|---|
| | Goals | Instruments | Settings | Paradigm shift | Path break |
| The Netherlands | ✗ | ✗ | ✗ | ✗ | ✗ |
| England | | ✗ | ✗ | | ✗ |
| Germany | | | ✗ | | |
| Sweden | ✗ | | | | (✗) |
| 1st order change | | either | or | | |
| 2nd order change | | | | | |
| 3rd order change/shift | | | | | |

Source: own compilation

instance, was the main way of involving citizens and patients in policies, other elements of competition and the market were added. After the Dutch path break and the turn to private health insurances, staying within the budgetary limit remains as difficult as it always has been. Though not codified and of the same significance as previously, politics has started to involve corporatist actors next to the new mechanisms in place.[4] What has changed is the *dominant* institution and the relative importance of the market and corporatism, but neither have market elements come out of nowhere nor has corporatism completely dissolved. In that sense, the postulation of an 'irreversible' path break is more about relative weighting and the length of the considered time span: Even though a return to exactly the same institutions is highly unlikely, a future return with different elements and relative importance is not.

Even though a shift of political paradigms can in some cases be translated into the notion of historical institutionalist 'path breaks', the overview in Table 9.2 shows that both concepts take a different angle and do not necessarily coincide: Instead of simply stating a break in the path hitherto pursued, the concept of policy paradigms directs the focus to an abstract level of why a paradigm continues or is changed. In addition, even though Streeck and Thelen's (2005) descriptions of change include information on whether we are dealing with first, second, or third order changes, this does not lead to a systematic assessment of path dependency or break. In that sense, there is a path break in England, since the institution of hospital governance underwent considerable change when involvement was brought in. Though debatable, this can be contrasted to the conclusion drawn by the approach of policy paradigms, which states that FTs are just another means to somehow involve the public the underlying goal, however, did not change. Based on the reasoning that perpetuation of informal settings institutionalises them, it might even be argued that Sweden has experienced a form of path break. Given the fuzzyness of both approaches, describing changes simply as first, second, or third order changes perhaps still gives the most accurate description.

[4]Credit for this observation goes to Peter Groenewegen.

## 9.5 Towards a Revised Model of Policy Processes

As was demonstrated above, the core analysis needs to focus on the level of actors: It is here that decisions are taken, policies can be shaped, and lobbying occurs. The factor most underrated by actor-centred and historical institutional approaches was shown to be the perception of limiting as well as enabling factors and the problem definition by key actors interlinked with this perception. We could see that historical institutionalism could not answer the question 'Who acted why?' and lacked discriminatory power between completely distinct pathways and the capacity to qualitatively describe these. The processes in both the Netherlands and Germany could be described as change by 'layering'. At the same time, however, historical institutionalism would describe the German case as path continuity while the Dutch qualifies for a path break. Nevertheless, the institutional legacy clearly left its traces and impeded radical changes in some countries.

Overall, we could identify four main factors influencing the decision-making processes of politicians in this policy field: Framing of a problem as the flipside of perception,[5] institutional settings, as well as the cost for compromising with other actors in the political realm and beyond. This leaves us with a dynamic and relative concept of decision making.

As a (theoretical) model we may think of a given surface, onto which flexible cubes—i.e. variable in size—are laid, illustrating the different relevant factors identified for the legislation process and each taking their part of this surface (illustrated in Fig. 9.3 for an equilibrated situation of factors). If factors are of more importance in the decision-making process, they repress cubes/factors and occupy a relatively larger area of the surface. As an extreme, this can lead to a situation in which one cube occupies the entire surface, i.e. one factor constitutes the only decisive factor for action—a relation that can easily be rephrased in more technical/mathematical terms.

This set of factors is at the heart of a wider and longer decision-making process. Starting out from the first model developed above (see Fig. 3.1) and concluding from the analysis we can start to revise the process. Ideal-typically, the process starts out with a once in a while repeated check whether or not the status quo is still convincing, which in most cases will be positively answered. The decision itself will, in turn, be influenced by the known and preliminarily assessed alternatives and the perceived context in the field of actors, i.e. to what extent amongst others actors and institutions support or oppose change. At this stage a preliminary decision about the degree of change will be undertaken: Most often depending on the context factors in the wider policy arena at large it will be decided whether the planned change will be framed within the guiding principle hitherto applied or whether

[5]The framing of a problem as the problem definition of politicians includes its perceived severity and character. For the theoretical model it was opted for the term 'framing' over 'perception' because it is easier and closer at hand to observe, while the perception usually can only be inferred.

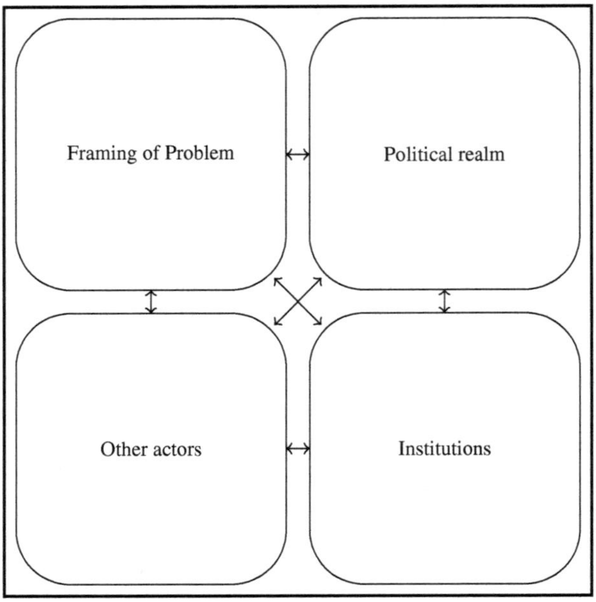


**Fig. 9.3** Schematic visualisation of equilibrated factors of influence. Source: own depiction

the situation is no longer convincing at a higher level. In the latter case a new guiding principle needs to be established, which requires a new idea to be picked or developed. This is usually done in the topical discourse, which is tightly interwoven with the thematic field of actors. Here, a smaller selection of potential ideas is discussed. As described above, the outcome depends amongst other things mainly on the constellation of actors, their relation, the framing of the problem, existing institutions, lobbying, and the perception of actors. The complete revised model is depicted in Fig. 9.4. Even though this linear model cannot give justice to reality's complexity for analytic purposes and the sake of simplicity it will suffice (Figs. 9.5, 9.6, 9.7, 9.8).

## 9.6 Four Countries Revisited

In what follows, the main threads for each of the four countries will be summarised to a condensed line of argument. The summaries will be structured according to the four main factors in the thematic field of actors. They will, where necessary, be complemented by other factors of the policy process. To allow for an easier overview and comparability, Fig. 9.9 on page 302 will assemble the key dates of each country. Moreover, Table 9.3 summarises the influencing factors found in the four countries in the form of theses. To some extent they can be understood as relative likelihoods for the success of enactment of collective patient involvement in the four countries.

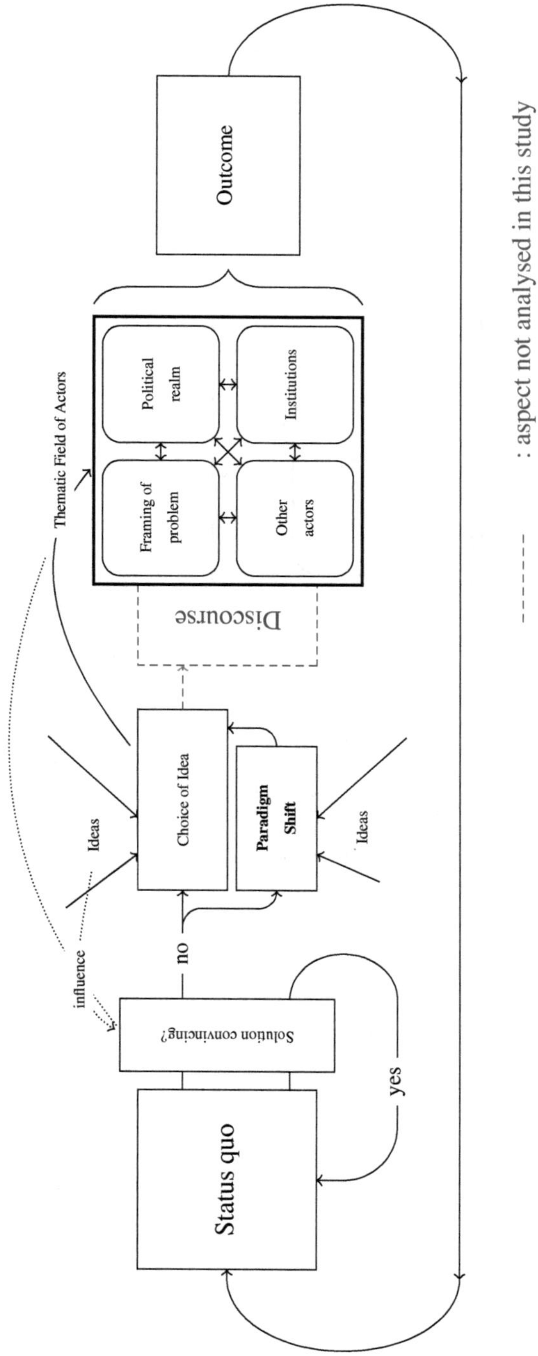


**Fig. 9.4** Revised schematic model of policy processes. Source: own depiction

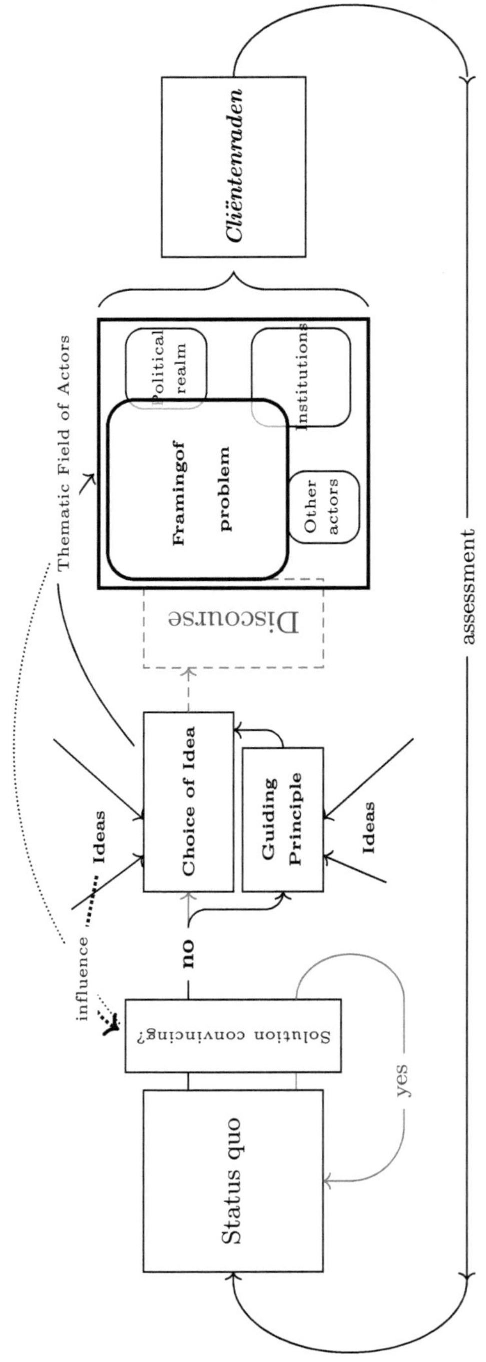


**Fig. 9.5** Visualisation of the policy process in the Netherlands. Source: own depiction

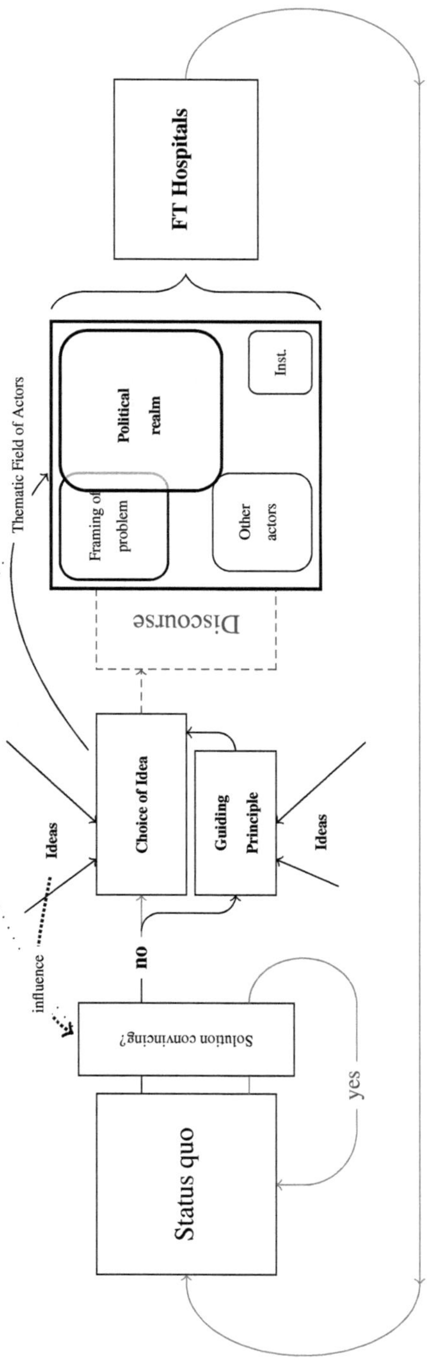


**Fig. 9.6** Visualisation of the policy process in England. Source: own depiction

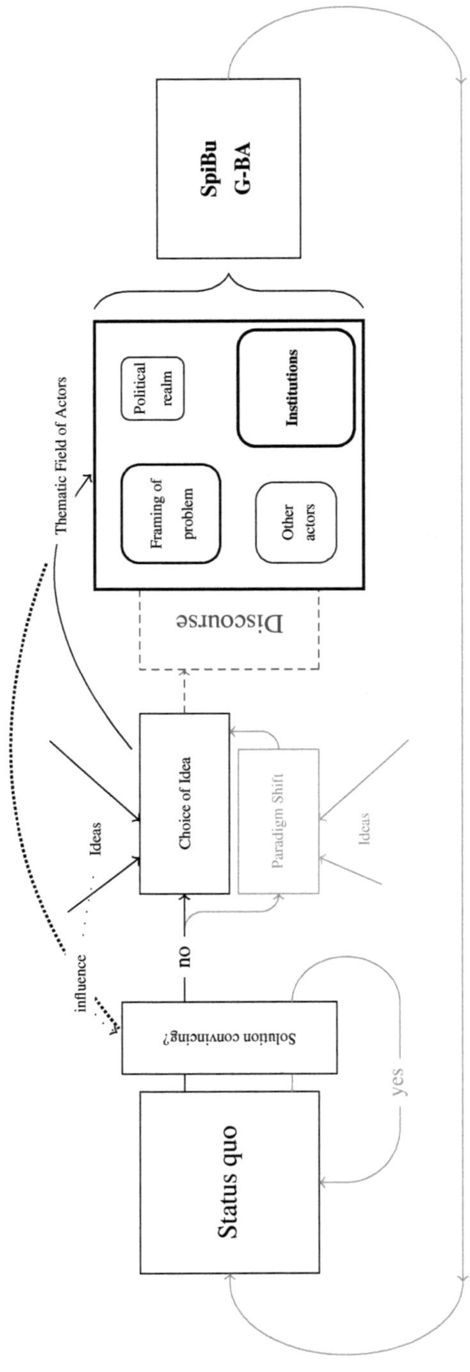


**Fig. 9.7** Visualisation of the policy process in Germany. Source: own depiction

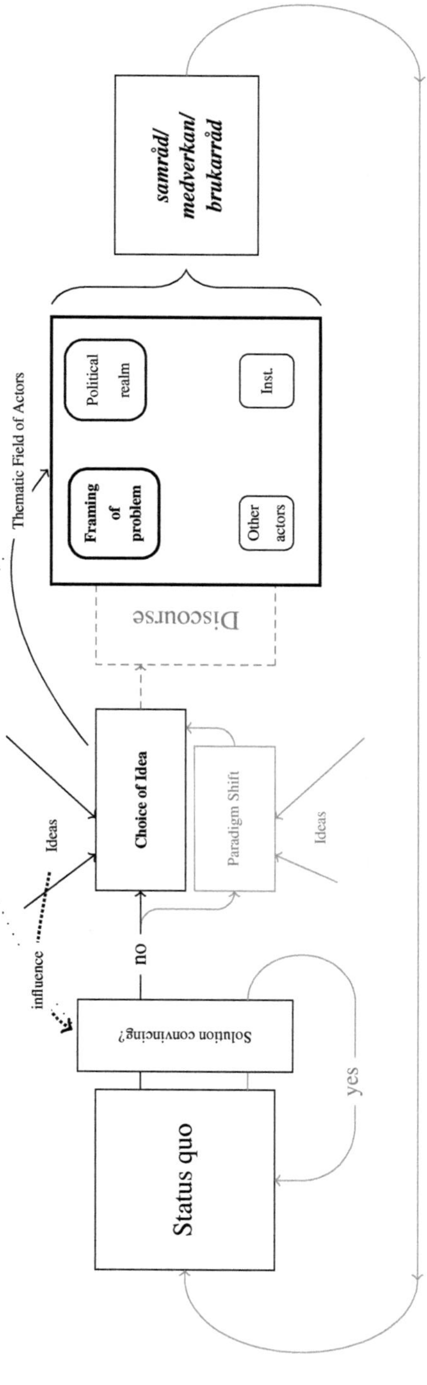


**Fig. 9.8** Visualisation of the policy process in Sweden. Source: own depiction

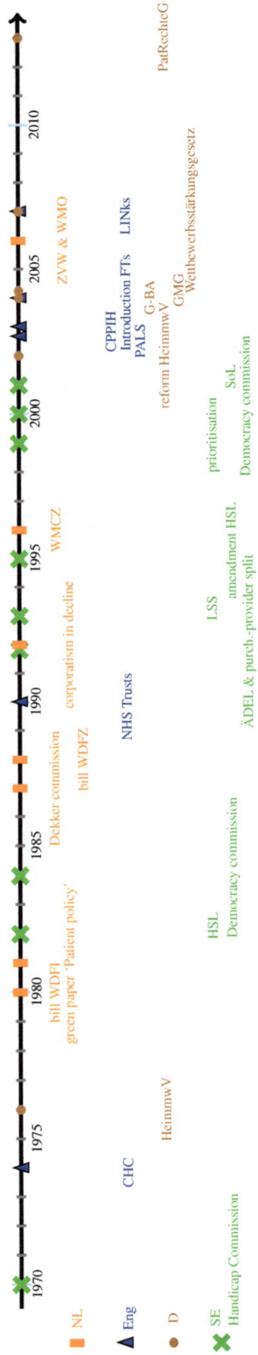


**Fig. 9.9** Overview of important landmarks—timeline. Source: own depiction

**Table 9.3** Overview of influencing factors found in the study to contribute to the introduction of formal involvement

| | Effect |
|---|---|
| Centralised responsibility for health care | + |
| Determination to change by (single politicians in) government | ++ |
| Existing examples of successful informal involvement | + |
| Framing of lack of involvement as severe problem | ++ |
| Successful 'ideas on hooks' and/or 'coupling of ides' | + |
| Lack of alternatives/equivalents of involvement | + |
| Multi-party governments as the rule | – |
| Public awareness of deficits (e.g. through scandals) | + |
| Recent reason for delegitimation of previous guiding principle | + |
| Rhetoric of the market | + |
| Search for new guiding principle | + |
| (Semi-)autonomous entities responsible for health care | – |
| Strong actors in the field not promoting change | – |
| Strong government | + |
| Tradition of and/or willingness to negotiate agreement in particular in intra-actor & intra-political field | + |
| Weak/modest effect on spending levels & limitations on managements' & politicians' scope of action | + |

Source: own compilation

## 9.6.1 *The Netherlands*

### 9.6.1.1 The Idea

The idea for collective patient involvement was rooted in a more general attempt to democratise the health care system with its public funding commencing in the late 1960s. As there were existing examples of voluntary family and user participation in long-term care in place, politics took up the organisational idea.

Though this underlying goal never completely disappeared, greater emphasis was laid on the position of the 'customer' in a 'privatised' health insurance market all the more clearly when preparations for the conversion from statutory health insurances to private health insurances proceeded (cf. also Okma 2008): To protect them from too strong market forces, their position should be strengthened where the state's position alone was perceived not far-reaching enough or the patient's position *per se* should be strengthened. Though we can portray the legislation process as one process towards patient involvement, we must actually distinguish *three* steps: First was the fading out of corporatism, which was no longer perceived to provide satisfactory solutions to the problems at hand. Second, the decision to turn to a marketised health insurance system bears strong traits of economic and management ideas of the time and was perceived to lead to greater efficiency and quality. Patient involvement as the final step followed in part as the *consequence* of the second.

However, the idea to democratise health care was never completely relinquished and shines through, for instance, when patient involvement at hospital level was coupled to resident involvement in long-term care.

Accordingly, we also need to distinguish three different ideas: Chronologically first, we have the idea to involve those being cared for. Its emergence was pushed by relatives and users of care in cooperation with providers and was aimed to improve the quality of care and life for the users of care. Second, we have the market as a steering instrument that ranks as the new paradigm to supersede the principle of corporatism. The idea to democratise health care and, third, to strengthen the clients' position was a political one, though it drew on organisational ideas long proved.

#### 9.6.1.2 The Actors

In the beginning, relatives of receivers of care and their newly founded patient organisations were the ones to urge politicians to enact legislation about some kind of involvement for long-term care which was paralleled by voluntary agreements between service providers and receivers of care or their relatives. From the early 1980s onwards, politicians took the lead and were the main driver behind the legislation process. Though the conservative and liberal parties liked the idea of a privatised health insurance system they were not too enthusiastic about the idea of involvement. Nevertheless, most of them agreed in the end, so that the final bill was passed with a large parliamentary majority. The perception that the patients' position needed to be strengthened—thereby accepting the underlying tale of market efficiency—outweighed the assumed burden for providers of care and the existing constitutional objections. The legislation process was very much oriented towards the practical feasibility in everyday life, much more so than in any other country of this study. This orientation as well as the promise to assess the outcome after 1 year also helped to overcome the concerns of relatives and residents alike that the 'minimum legislation' might fall behind the involvement already negotiated between relatives/recipients of care and providers on a voluntary basis. The government's confidence that (health-)care providers would seize the opportunity and adapt involvement to the institution's individual needs and go beyond the minimum stipulations, however, proved ungrounded in the majority of cases.

#### 9.6.1.3 The Institutional Level

Never as strong as in Germany anyway, the declined support of corporatist solutions has further decreased the involvement of the insured in sickness funds, though not ceased it to exist completely. Other advisory boards with lay participation were partly turned into expert boards. To these, a new institutional layer was added at the level of health care providers. Taking up Streeck and Thelen's (2005) suggestion for a classification of institutional change, 'layering' describes the processes in the

Netherlands best. To shut out corporatist actors to such a degree as done in the Netherlands not only qualifies for the description as a path break, the new goal of democratisation meets also the criterion of a paradigm shift. Among the four countries, it is probably the case with the deepest implications, not only because it applies to all institutions of long-term (health-)care but even more because so many other related institutions changed. Patient involvement is enacted in the wake of this paradigm shift or path break as a solution to close the gap arising after the decline of corporatism. This break from the path was, in turn, only possible under three conditions:

(a) The intra-political differences could be settled over the 16 years between the first attempt to pass a bill on involvement of users of care and the final act. This can also be ascribed to the so-called politics of no regret, the Dutch variant of incremental changes, which, taken separately, did hardly change anything. Overall, however, they irreversibly pointed the way from a corporatist sickness fund system to a privatised health insurance (cf. Groenewegen 1998).
(b) The extra-political context held favourable circumstances in that other actors opposed the basic matter to involve residents and patients only moderately while no institutions known as veto-points opposed the legislation.
(c) All parties backed the idea to diminish the hold of corporatism. Despite the multi-party governments that are common for the Netherlands and which constitute a restricting factor for change, the capability to negotiate and agree sets this downside off. The centralised responsibility for health care worked in favour of change.

As all of these conditions neatly fit together in a very favourable way, we could speak of a 'window of opportunity' (Kingdon 2003, pp. 166–169). Though no precondition for the enactment, as one of the contributing factors to the relative success of involvement must be counted the foundation and funding of non-sectoral patient organisations to support the client councils. This not only supported client councils in their search for a way to debate with providers in the initially unfamiliar situation, but also underlined the political will to foster involvement.

A summary of the process could read: 'Solidary funding needs a greater say; the market is the most efficient steering mechanism, therefore, the clients' voice needs to be strengthened!'

## *9.6.2 England*

### 9.6.2.1 The Idea

In England, the idea of the 'internal market' always played in: Against the background of its failure, it served as a negative definition, a counter-idea to the desirable. While this counter-idea was all too clear-cut, the positive idea was rather blurred, which, in turn, might be owing to the fact that actually politicians sought for an improved version of the internal market without labelling it as such. The origin for involvement drew on two unrelated strands: The idea for the organisational side, which strove for more managerial freedom to foster more efficiency and higher quality, was directly copied from Spanish Foundation Trust hospitals. Hence, here as in the Netherlands and Sweden, increasing quality and/or efficiency was explicitly mentioned as an aim of involvement. The idea for patient involvement itself stemmed from the longstanding political desire to close the perceived gap of legitimacy within the NHS, thereby refreshing the original idea of NHS Trusts. On a more abstract level, it can be concluded that the Netherlands and England were united in the search for a new guiding principle regarding governance and legitimacy of the health care system. At the same time, having 'learned' from community health councils and their 'interference', England tried to prevent too powerful forms of involvement. In the end, however, it was an ad-hoc measure to combine patient involvement and the new form of hospital, untested, opposed, and not thought through. In an attempt to convince MPs within the own ranks, this measure was linked to the rhetoric of 'owning one's hospital' and to cooperatives, though this lacked any deeper meaning and intention.

#### 9.6.2.2 The Actors

The main driver for change was the Labour Government led by Tony Blair. It was not asked for by patient organisations, while to the contrary it was—at least in part—opposed by the medical profession and consultants in the NHS. Furthermore, it met fierce opposition from the opposition parties as well as from within the Labour party in the short legislation process. Although the House of Lords advocated a larger number of changes to the bill, the government ignored 'the other house's' right. After only three rather brief readings in parliament, the bill was passed by the House of Commons with a thin margin of 17 only, which is the more telling as the government held a comfortable majority of 167 seats.

According to the negative definition of the idea and an only vague positive idea, on the one hand, and owing to the comparatively short legislation process, on the other, it is noticeable that the legal text contains a high degree of detail regarding amongst other things the aims of foundation trust hospitals, the managerial freedoms, and the election rules. In contrast to the Netherlands and despite the opposition, which gave good reasons to discuss the issues and boil them down to a less abstract level, the legal text itself is of rather normative character, but not oriented towards a pragmatic implementation. This leads to ill-defined roles of governors and the council as well as, in turn, a very heterogeneous implementation.

#### 9.6.2.3 The Institutional Level

England seems to be the country with the fewest institutional obstacles: Patient organisations busy enough raising funds to finance research and thus too busy to interfere, no federalism, no corporatism, and a second parliamentary chamber, the vote of which apparently can be ignored as long as the government's majority allows. Most decisive in this case, however, is an elective franchise that favours strong parties and governments, adding to a centralised responsibility for health care. Two conclusions can be drawn: First, in order to be able to push through a radical reform like the one in question against all opposition it needs an electoral system like the British resulting in strong majorities and an institutional environment like the British that does not 'burden' government with too influential veto-powers nor with too strong other actors. Second, it can be concluded that as long as a government is willing to risk losing an election or perceives the decision to not have any wider effects on their staying in power *and* holds a sufficiently strong majority, it has more freedom than any other government in this sample of countries.

At the same time, and in comparison to the other three countries, England is also an interesting case in that only the hospital sector and therein only a specific type of hospital is concerned. This entails far-reaching consequences, as not only a new form of hospital has been introduced but also this specific type of patient involvement was explicitly tied to this organisation, which is accompanied by new actors in terms of supervisory authorities and admission boards, with altered relations between citizens, medical staff, management, and politicians. It is probably also the country with the busiest history of reforms. What Streeck and Thelen (2005) term 'conversion' probably describes the process in England best.

A summary could read as follows: 'Local, economic decision making is most effective, so let's do something contrary to what we have done over the past 40 years and give latitude to local managers. Ah, and, by the way, can we somehow link that to public involvement?'

## *9.6.3 Germany*

Interestingly, Germany was first out regulating resident involvement in long-term care (Bundesgesetzblatt 1976), even prior to the Netherlands' first attempt on legislation in the field. The trigger here was—as in its neighbouring country—a number of scandals in long-term care. However, this has not translated into involvement in curative care and is not likely to do so in the foreseeable future.

### 9.6.3.1 The Idea

In adhering to the tradition of self-governance in curative care, the idea to represent the general interest through corporatist actors is formally maintained. The devolution of decision-making power to other actors than politicians and their subordinate authorities follows the logic that their knowledge delivers the best results in terms of quality. Efficiency is not only directly addressed by the actors of self-governance, who claim to be its best custodian of the general interest. Next to this, the quest for efficiency penetrates the decision about reforming the governance of the health care system, since politics seeks to implement a solution that is reconcilable with the goal of an overall cost-effective health care system. This follows the view that reform might be necessary, however, that the overall performance of the health care system's governance is either working well and/or the actors involved too powerful to be challenged. Thus, if change is unavoidable, the foundations of the governance of the welfare state should still be left intact. One reason for this stance is that it can rightfully be argued that with resident involvement in long-term care, i.e. the sector where involvement at the level of service provision is really meaningful, an additional means of involvement is (formally) in place so that involvement in the health care sector via self-governance is sufficient.

#### 9.6.3.2 The Actors

The tradition of self-governance of sickness funds and the medical profession results in strong actors in the field that are opposed to too much change. Health care policy is most often the field in politics where government and (at least the main) opposition parties manage to back a joint compromise. No matter what party constituted the major part of a government, almost all of them identified major problems with the self-governance of the social insurances. However, they unanimously tried to only moderately reform self-governance and supported its underlying major principle.

The enforced merger to form the 'Central Federal Association of (the) Health Insurance Funds' (*Spitzenverband Bund der Krankenkassen*) tried to achieve both the continuity of the self-governance and to remedy the fragmentation between several umbrella organisations of sickness funds and a disunited communication between these organisations and politics. This makes it easier for politicians to address and check. In addition, it can be assumed that the incorporation of patients in the 'Joint Federal Committee' was not only an end in itself but might also have been a means to end the stalemate that sometimes prevailed in the old federal committee.

It is difficult to tell whether politicians were actually convinced that self-governance is still the best way to represent the beneficiaries' interests or whether they perceived change too costly. Overall, the problem was not framed prominently enough to transcend the threshold to win over the institutional heritage. Therefore, though the situation in Germany was similar to the one in the Netherlands in many respects the framing of the problem at hand as well as the perception of the context led to a different pathway.

The creation of the 'Joint Federal Committee' in 2004 (cf. Bundesgesetzblatt 2003) was in line with this step: The idea of self-governance is kept alive by adapting it to a changed context. It not only resulted in a shift and concentration of responsibility, but also brought in new actors, thereby weakening the previous actors' position, who have hitherto been in the field. Today, the social partners in sickness funds are to represent the general patients' interest as do consumer and patient organisations in the joint federal committee. It remains unclear, however, why specifically these consumer and patient organisations have been chosen to represent the general interest of patients and contribution payers. Politicians seem to see their own role rather as enabler and supervisor and, thus, remain weak as creators of change in comparison to other countries. However, it should be noted that though these changes constitute minor steps, they might, however, incrementally change power constellations in the long run.

#### 9.6.3.3 The Institutional Level

Owing to strong actors, the federal division, and the devolution of tasks to several associations and professions in the field, the scope of government is more limited than in other countries. As mentioned above, the creation of the Joint Federal Committee in 2004 with its introduction of new actors into the field can be regarded a *de facto* loss of power for the institution of self-governance, though *formally* its primate is maintained. It is difficult to maintain sufficient discriminatory power between 'complex actors' and 'institutions', which in the case of Germany becomes blurred. Basically, in this case it is just a different angle on the same scene, drawing almost identical conclusions. The process in Germany contains elements of Streeck and Thelen's (2005) 'drift', primarily, however, 'layering'.

The appraisal of resident involvement by patient organisations and representatives in Germany is rather negative. Comparing involvement of recipients of long-term care in Germany and the Netherlands, the so-called non-sectoral patient organisations play a vital role for the relative success in the Netherlands: For one, in the beginning heavily funded by the government, they are a political symbol of political and financial support by the Hague, which is not the case in Germany. Another point is the immediate support in the everyday business of the client councils through strategic and legal help as well as schooling.

The political view in Germany could read: 'Let the actors in the field start quarrelling with each other about the best solution—and let politics not bother them too much; and vice versa.'

### *9.6.4 Sweden*

What we can see in the Swedish case study is somewhat of a contradiction: Though it is classified as one of the countries *without* patient involvement at hospital level, it has nevertheless taken considerable lengths to close the gap of legitimacy and to reform representation of the sick. In this attempt, the country has found its unique way to ensure that the experience and opinion of the chronically ill are heard in the political decision-making process, which is the more essential in a (partly) state-run health care system.

#### 9.6.4.1 The Idea

As in Germany, there was no grand idea to be implemented in Sweden. Showing some similarities with the Dutch case, the development can be described as a process, in which several evolutionary steps built upon each other. The linking element of all of these steps was the underlying desire to democratise society in several areas, to create transparency, and to get people involved beyond elections following the logic that society—and health care as an essential part of it—is *by* and *for* the people. This was rather to be a right to be implemented than a problem to be solved. Later on, the attempt to make the health care system more effective is added to the aim of democratisation.

While democratisation was on the agenda already, the role of politicians changed as an indirect consequence of the idea that competition between health care providers—even the public ones—leads to more cost-effective care. The double role of politicians being purchasers of care while at the same time being the citizens' representatives led to the decision to strengthen the role of advocates for citizens and source out the technicalities of the purchaser–provider split to the provinces' administration.

#### 9.6.4.2 The Actors

Politicians on the national and regional level were the main actors in the process. Negotiation partners were the main Swedish patient umbrella organisations. As finding compromises in order to suit as large a majority as possible is as important a goal as in the Netherlands, the process is described as fairly egalitarian by both the patients' and the politicians' side. Involvement serves to strengthen claiming credit as well as the legitimacy of decisions.

#### 9.6.4.3 The Institutional Level

Regarding institutions, Sweden offers another peculiarity: Except for two tiny, extremely unspecific sentences in the Healthcare Act (HSL 1982:763, §§ 7–8) neither laws nor institutions have been changed, and no regulations added. Nevertheless, Sweden has found a highly functioning equivalent to patient involvement in hospitals: Previously existing institutions and competences are retained, while being complemented by widely accepted but—in its strict sense—unofficial and unregulated patient advisory meetings. Owing to the county councils' responsibilities for health care the national state is rather toothless when proposing new policies and need to find compromises. Overall, none of Streeck and Thelen's (2005) ideal-typical types of process really fits the Swedish case. 'Conversion' would come closest, though even that does not really match empirical evidence. For the observed policy process in Sweden an additional type 'enhancement' is suggested here. Alternatively, it might be argued that the perpetuation of an informal setting institutionalises it.

The short summary for Sweden could read: 'Politicians should be the impartial advocates of the people to jointly find solutions to our problems with patients' representatives. Specific regulation is unnecessary for this.'

## 9.7 Four Countries, Two Types of Involvement, and Beyond

Having revisited and summarised the four countries of this study, the main aim of this chapter is to systematise the forms of involvement found in this study and, at the same time, go beyond them by theorising about potential additional forms. The underlying theoretical assumption based on health care state typology postulates that these types will organise their funding, governance, and provision in a uniform manner for each type. One of the main conclusions to be drawn from this study is that apparently there is considerable variation (of development and/or characteristics) within each of the types. If we do not want to reject the overall idea of health care state types—and there are good reasons not to do so—evidence suggests that countries characterised as belonging to one of the types do not necessarily need to change to a different type to change certain aspects of their health care systems. The type of health care system seems to suggest a crude direction of change. Somewhat oversimplified it can be said that NHS countries tend to incorporate more choice and competition, whereas Bismarckian countries reorganise the relation of actors to safeguard more state influence. The development regarding patient involvement, in contrast, is too individual and at times arbitrary and overall too crude to leave much scope for any system type influence to become apparent.

In contrast, in the four case studies two different main types of involvement can be discerned, which run transversely to those to be assumed according to health care state typology (for an overview see upper part of Table 9.4). There is no theoretical reason to believe that these two types cannot coincide with any of the types of health care states (see Table 1.1 on page 5).

**Table 9.4** Overview of different empirical forms of involvement in hospitals & institutions of long-term care

| | The Netherlands | England | Sweden | Germany |
|---|---|---|---|---|
| Patient involvement—provision level | X | H | g | |
| Patient involvement—policy level | | | X | X |
| Resident involvement | X | | x | X |
| Self-governance in sickness funds | x | | | X |
| Patient advocacy | | x | | X |
| Others | | X | x | |

X—present; x—present, but restricted; g—geographically confined to some parts of the country; H—in a specific type of hospital
Source: own compilation

(a) On the one hand, we have the FORMAL PATIENT INVOLVEMENT AS ADVISORY COUNCILS TO (HEALTH-) CARE PROVIDERS as exemplified in the Netherlands and England. The most immediate collective form of involvement is to some extent based on a notion of patients as clients choosing services and demanding high quality.
(b) On the other hand, Germany and Sweden exemplify a type of PATIENT INVOLVEMENT AS AN ADVISORY PARTNER TO DECISION MAKERS ON HEALTH CARE POLICIES, even though the mechanisms of influence vary widely. As Germany and Sweden show, there is no common underlying view on patients and citizens: While in Germany decision-making power remains devolved to the actors in the field, in Sweden the political primacy is retained.

In general, these two types can be considered the most immediate—and, therefore, in many constellations probably also the most effective—types. Next to these two main forms, more indirect forms of involvement have been mentioned already and even more can be thought of, which were not present in our sample of case studies. The following extension of the list is, therefore, to be understood in the sense of ideal types (cf. Weber 1968; 1991 (1904), p. 73) and does not preclude the possibility of mixed types with predominant forms of involvement alongside subordinate others.

(c) Other countries put more emphasis on INVOLVEMENT VIA THE (CORPORATIST) REPRESENTATION OF THE INSURED. Austria constitutes the ideal-typical example for this type of involvement, but even in Germany this form still plays a major role.
(d) Other forms such as ADVISORY COMMITTEES can be named. They can be part of diverse institutions and do not necessarily take any official form. Committees can, for instance, be found for the major part of health care institutions in the UK.
(e) PATIENT ADVOCACY most often serves as some kind of complaint office, while possibilities to actively influence providers or policies are less immediate. Therefore, depending on the respective setup the line between involvement (and self-representation), on the one hand, and third-party representation, on the other, is transgressed. Advocacy can be found in many welfare states such as the UK, Germany, Austria, or the Netherlands.
(f) REGULAR AND SYSTEMATIC SURVEYS can be regarded as another, albeit unidirectional way to involve patients and residents of care.
(g) Finally, examples can be thought of where NO FORM OF INVOLVEMENT whatsoever is in place.

These types do not need to follow any pattern, either, and can, basically, be combined with one another, as they can coexist with different types of health care states. In that sense, it is not only conceivable but empirically evident that several parallel forms of involvement can exist in one country. The rather crude categorisation of involvement is a first approach and deliberately chosen for two reasons: First, it reflects the narrow data base of only four case studies, which can be

**Table 9.5** Overview of influencing factors found in the study to contribute to the successful implementation of involvement

| | Effect |
|---|---|
| Clear role definition | + |
| (Considerably) increased spending levels owing to user involvement | – |
| (Continuous) support (idealistic & monetary) & training | + |
| Flexibility to adapt framework to local needs | + |
| Political will & support | + |
| Short-term orientation | – |
| User involvement fitting into or tying in with existing structures | + |

Source: own compilation

extended by future studies. Second, despite the disadvantage of being less precise it is advantageous over more detailed forms of the Arnstein-type in that it can be applied without any strong normative background and does not require too detailed knowledge of the practice (Table 9.5).

In order to get an idea where this might be heading, Table 9.6 was compiled. It is mainly based on information provided by the chapter 'patient empowerment' of the respective reports of the 'Health Systems in Transition' series.[6] It gives an overview of different forms of involvement within the health care systems of Europe. The forms reported in the table could be translated into both Arnstein's rungs and the abovementioned forms. However, future and more refined research would for several reasons require considerable efforts: For one, some of the reports are dated and the information on patient/citizen involvement was included beginning only at a later stage. Promising sub-national trials or even established regional forms of involvement (such as the '*Regionale Gesundheitskonferenz NRW*' and '*Kommunale Gesundheitskonferenzen NRW*' (Regional and Municipal Health Conferences Northrhine-Westphalia); Borchart 2004; Landeszentrum Gesundheit Nordrhein-Westfalen, 2014 or the ones in Sweden) are not mentioned at all. For another, the inconsistent definitions of involvement constitute a major obstacle for a quick compilation.

[6]The information on Austria, the Czech Republic, France, England, the Netherlands, Norway, and Sweden was completed by additional sources mentioned in the list below.

As a side note, it is also interesting that despite many differences in detail, Israel has independently opted for a very similar solution of self-governance in sickness funds and patient involvement in its 'National Health Council' as Germany (Chinitz 2000, pp. 67–69; Rosen & Samuel 2009).

## 9.8 Lessons to Be Learnt from Implementing Patient Involvement

Before heading on to some more general implications, some conclusions for the implementation of patient involvement shall be drawn. This section is mainly based on the assessment of implementation by the interviewees and the conclusions drawn from our own analyses (see Sects. 5.6, 6.5, 7.3.4.3, and 8.4). The main points are summarised in Table 9.5.

The greatest commonality impressively shown by the case studies in all four countries is that PATIENT INVOLVEMENT TAKES TIME TO BE IMPLEMENTED. As in particular the Dutch and the English interviewees point out, the two different life worlds of subjective, often short-term perspective of patients and receivers of care, on the one hand, and the strategic planning and efficiency orientation of management, on the other, need to be bridged. Experience gained in the two countries indicates that building a mutual understanding between patients/residents and management based on a common language takes some 10 to 15 years. This includes the learning curve to understand that patients/residents actually can contribute something to successful management of a (health-)care institution from the management's side while, on the other hand, you can criticise plans and decisions of the management and do not need to show gratitude from the patients'/residents' side.

One precondition to successfully implement involvement is that a minimum FOLLOW-UP AND CONTINUOUS SUPPORT IS SAFEGUARDED at least throughout the first couple of years after enactment. As could be demonstrated above, the Dutch version of resident involvement and the German one are in many points almost identical in terms of stipulated rights and the process to establish the council, for instance. However, while in Germany it was assumed that residents and providers would find their way to cooperate and the overall process should not cost anything on top of the usual expenditure, their Dutch counterpart was supported by a regular political follow-up as well as training by umbrella organisations. This, in turn, requires the political will and some funding. Thus, it is a delusion to assume that patient/resident involvement will be successful just because of legal stipulations.

Another precondition to be met for a successful implementation of user involvement seems to be a WELL-BALANCED RELATION BETWEEN NECESSARY FLEXIBILITY AND CLEAR-CUT ROLE DEFINITIONS. The ways pursued in England and the Netherlands regarding these two points are nicely contrasting each other. While England attempted to legally standardise procedures regarding, for instance, member elections and the application of uniform standards of representativity while disregarding the local context the Netherlands kept the framework sufficiently flexible to locally adapt it to varying needs. The possibility to adapt concept and management according to local preconditions and the patients'/residents' wishes raised the acceptance for regulation both on the part of providers and receivers. While setting some minimum standards, as done in the Netherlands, is absolutely desirable, the case also shows that most often not too much will be accomplished beyond the minimum standard.

While England attempted to legally define different constituencies the Netherlands left this to be defined in an evolutionary process. Here, the same applies as regards the previous point: a mixture of minimum requirements and specific stipulations is a good start; however, they rarely suffice. First, despite defining different types of constituencies the English legislator overlooked to properly define the roles governors should assume in the governance of the new hospitals. Consequently, governors were struggling to fill the role with life for months. Second, the definition of membership was changed later on, while membership numbers have been increased to sometimes absurdly unrealistic levels. This combination of repeated half-baked legal demands and fuzzy definitions that need to be interpreted, circumvented, or changed later on has not proven fruitful in this sample of countries.

Flexibility in adaptation is one of the cornerstones to create acceptance among key actors involved, in particular providers. Even though it needs to be emphasised that user involvement is not about 'taking over' the governance of (health-)care providers—or other institutions—we should also bear in mind that reaching consensus on issues brought up by providers and users alike is a key to successful and sustainable work on involvement.

There have been CRITICAL VOICES ABOUT REPRESENTATIVITY, COSTS FOR INVOLVEMENT, AND THE FORM OF INVOLVEMENT. First, one issue to be solved is whether the members of the council or even the electorate need to be representative for the catchment area or even whole region or country. Even here, the balance between clear-cut stipulations and flexibility is, therefore, delicate, which makes them all the more important to be realistic and further local implementation: a general claim for representativity along lines of age, sex, and ethnicity in a deprived, mixed-ethnic neighbourhood, for example, is futile knowing that *all* interviewees witnessed difficulties in recruiting members for the lay-council the likelihood to get patients involved decreases with lower formal education and having a migration background (on this cf. also Dalton et al. 2016, 3; Martin 2008, 1). While this is exacerbated regarding council members in mental health, the willingness to volunteer is also culturally mediated. This may require different solutions in different countries. Overall, there are good reasons to argue that both the members of the council and the electorate should be somehow representative for the dominant users of care and services—even though this is subject to limitations for the very old aged and, to some extent, the low-educated—as long as the general interest is safeguarded. This is not only the stance from a democratic theoretical perspective, but follows both the tradition of involvement in many health care systems and other kinds of citizen involvement. Many local or regional providers of public transport, for instance, have established a client council to better respond to clients' needs and to improve quality. Even though skyrocketing spending levels need to be preempted, it is predominantly daily commuters comprising the councils and not the relatively low rider share of the whole population. The question is whether this could be applied as a guiding principle and what it needs to safeguard the general interest.

Second, given that funding should primarily be spent on receivers of care, the direct and indirect costs of involvement should be kept as low as possible. User involvement is in the first place not about higher funding, but about reshuffling resources to pay services that match users' needs and wishes. Keeping costs low also increases chances of a successful implementation. Given the high costs of an estimated average of 265,000 € per hospital in England maintaining a formal membership register for election purposes alone seems to be exaggerated an exercise. If, however, costs increase owing to a general perception of too low quality of food or the provision of care (see, e.g., Sect. 5.6.3.3), this might be a different case. Too formal definitions, however, do not help to achieve the main aim of user involvement, which is to give them a say in matters immediately affecting them in order to prevent too low quality and give users a dignified quality of life. User councils are a means to achieve that goal by enabling a bi-directional culture to discuss serious matters based on mutual reliance and trust.

Third, it is about the form of involvement. It has correctly been argued that patient involvement in short-term in-patient hospitals nowadays rarely makes sense. In contrast, user influence in long-term relations with in- or out-patient (health-)care services is highly desirable. The described forms of involvement may in large parts be viewed as good practice examples.[7] In that sense, and given that forms of involvement that tie in with existing structures in a region or country are more likely to be successful, they can serve as a source of inspiration: It does, however, not necessarily mean that a specific type should be employed. The Netherlands as well as Sweden are currently experimenting with different, more flexible forms of user involvement including out-patients managing chronic conditions. It should be borne in mind that though survey forms are often perceived the preferred, cost-cutting alternative by service providers, this can be a complementing uni-directional measure, but cannot replace the benefits of immediate explanation and discussion of the abovementioned forms of involvement.

Hence, overall, the question is more about a meaningful involvement in a given context than a specific form of involvement. The same applies to other sectors of (health-)care (for an overview on involvement in primary care cf. for instance Groenewegen, Kroneman, van Erp, Broeren, & van Birgelen 2016).

## 9.9 General Implications: Involvement and Beyond

As more general conclusions for the health care system or policy processes at large, a number of different points can be concluded. Asking whether the findings will become new ingredients of the recipe book for policy analysis, the answer

[7]Underlying the choice of terminology of 'good practices' compared to the formerly commonly used 'best practice' is the observation that there is rarely 'one fits all' solution, but a number of good examples that may serve as a source of inspiration for other regions.

In addition, the term 'best practice' suggests that this one practice cannot be improved anymore. However, despite a successful implementation of well evaluated practice, there will always be elements that can be improved. In that sense, it is more about a competition of good ideas to be shared than about a competition of implementation sites, which is another reason away from the use of terminology of 'best practices'.

must be a cautioning yes *and* no. Yes, there are a number of aspects—particularly those mentioned in the paragraphs captioned with 'theoretical considerations'—that alter some of the postulations and views of the theories employed, adding new theoretical facets and implying a recalibration of existing aspects. In the sense of theory building rooted in empirical studies (cf. e.g. George & Bennett 2005) these aspects should be taken into account and be addressed in consecutive studies. They might eventually serve to improve theories.

However, there is also the potential 'no' in the answer: Patient/citizen participation might be a specific field in which politicians do not have too much to gain or lose—right in contrast to fields such as pension policies, decisions on health care spending or tax levels—that are usually linked to greater budgetary resources, they are much more polarising in the general population, and accommodate long-going vested interests. In consequence, the behaviour, rationale, and the power balance in this study might differ from what decisions would be in other policy fields.

Speculating about linkages beyond the abovementioned influencing factors, we might think of less prominent ones. It can, for instance, be assumed that the interest of politicians to introduce collective patient involvement in purely marketised health care systems as the United States is rather low. The very concept of a paying purchaser and a provider establishes a dyad, where interference by framework regulation has no place. In the unlikely event, HMOs seem the most likely institution to think of.

As mentioned above, concepts mediated via market elements can play in: As mediators this can be the patients, whose role needs to be strengthened, it can be the new role of patients as clients/customers, who need to be listened to better than previously and/or who need more choice, often in an attempt to circumvent problems of access—as in the UK and the Netherlands. This orientation towards market rhetoric—no matter whether it is primarily rhetoric only—is more likely to think of collective involvement at the level of providers if new ways of involvement are sought. On the one hand, it fits the idea of the responsible customer, on the other, it fits the new role of the state as an enabler rather than the immediately responsible provider and supervisor. Having patients as an additional watchdog for quality control seems to neatly match the image. An educated guess might be that countries where choice has been rooted for a longer time already and/or where a more traditional role of the patient is assumed, are not as prone to change. Thus, the emphasis on client–provider relationships in otherwise solidary health care systems might give rise to involvement at the level of providers.

Another strand takes a closer look at the type of health care system. It can be hypothesised that politicians in countries in which the health care system is centrally organised—for instance, in England and the Netherlands—have no interest to establish powerful institutions that either interfere into their business and/or have the potential to yield in powerful, competing actors. Traditional corporatism at a national scale, for instance, is, therefore, rather unlikely to emerge. Furthermore, what often is missing is an intermediate layer of institutions that is closer to citizens, that citizens are aware of and has some credibility and practical relevance. It can be said that this, for instance, rules out, for instance, the Dutch provinces, since the mid-1990s also corporatism in the Netherlands or the regional health authorities in England as potential institutions for involvement. Taking these two suppositions together, the conclusion might be drawn that centrally organised health care systems with no or no pronounced intermediate layer of political involvement or legitimate administration are more likely to implement involvement at the provider level, if they are seeking for a change.

Regarding decentralised systems it can be differentiated between NHS countries and other health care systems. If nothing unforeseen gets in the way, the latter can be assumed to be as (dis-)interested in collective patient involvement as market-based health care systems, since politicians do not have too much to gain, when they do not immediately answer for health care services anyway.

While centralised NHS countries are covered in the previous paragraph already, it is fair to say that once again it seems existing typologies are not able to catch the essential peculiarities of regional health care systems fully. As could be shown for Sweden, also Norway, and Denmark as regional health care systems have established some form of exchange of patients with politicians at the decision-making level—i.e. the health care regions—that is able to influence policy making. Though more diverse, the same applies for the local health care system in Finland. There are several factors playing in: On the one hand, the often immediate proximity is given, while, on the other, it is here that the immediate responsibility for health care lies. This results in a stronger legitimatory position of politicians, as the chain of legitimacy is not too long, and the capability to immediately change things, both in policies and benefits and often regarding health care services as well. At the same time, politicians can be assumed to value involvement at the policy level more than by politicians in countries, where they are more distanced. As long as involvement is not understood as interference in political decision making, the discussion about health care topics, feedback about planned policies and measures as well as the patients' backing when arguing for a specific policy comes as extra support for political decisions. Overall, we might state that regional health care systems are more likely to opt for involvement at the policy level if new ways of involvement are sought. Italy and Spain might be candidates for this direction, Austria with its federal states (*Länder*) might be another, in case the archetypical corporatism would not represent such a strong persisting factor. This reasoning may find its limits in geographically larger entities like Canadian provinces, but for the rather confined European distances this should not be of too much relevance. Moreover, the stronger the framing of user rights derived from citizen rights—in contrast to user rights derived from competition and choice—the more likely it seems that institutions like in Sweden will be sought, if change is planned. Thus, overall we might hypothesise that regional health care systems are closer to involvement influencing the policy process.

Having said this, one of the most difficult factors to weigh in is publicity. In particular negative publicity and scandals over malpractice and low quality might eventually urge politicians to react. One might speculate that publicity about quality issues is more likely to yield influence on the providers. In contrast, scandals over a greater number of deaths resulting from restrictions on certain treatment options

**Table 9.6** Entries for respective category of 'patient empowerment' in country's HiT

| | Patient participation | | | | | | Primary care choice | | Patient rights | | | |
|---|---|---|---|---|---|---|---|---|---|---|---|---|
| | Lobbying patient as-sociations | Via patient associations | Via patient advocacy | Via health board | Advisory board | Via sickness funds | GP | Listed at GP | Complaint procedures | Access to individual records | Mediation | Ombudsperson |
| **A**ustria | | | x | | | x | g | | | | | x |
| **B**elgium | | | | | | i | x | | x | x | | |
| Bulgaria | | | | | | x | x | | x | | | |
| **C**roatia* | | | | | | | | x | | | | |
| Cyprus | x | | | | | | x | | x | | | |
| Czech Republic | | | | | | r | x | | | | | |
| **D**enmark | x | | | | | | | ca | x | x | | x |
| **E**ngland | | | | FT | | | | | ca | x | | |
| **F**inland | x | | | | | | ca | | x | x | | x |
| France | | | | | | csf | x | | x | x | | |
| **G**ermany | | | x | | | x | x | | | x | | |
| Greece | | | | | | | x | | x | | | |
| **H**ungary | | x | x | | | | x | | x | x | | |
| **I**reland | | | | | x | | x | | x | x | | |
| Italy | | g | | | | | x | | | | g | g |
| **L**ithuania | | | x | | | | x | | x | x | | |
| **M**alta* | x | i | | | | | ca | | | | | |
| **N**etherlands, the | | | | | | x | | | x | | | |
| Northern Ireland | | | | | | | | x | | | | |
| Norway | | | | x | | | | x | x | x | | x |
| **P**oland | | | x | | | | x | | x | x | | x |

(continued)

**Table 9.6** (continued)

| | Patient participation | | | | | | Primary care choice | | Patient rights | | | |
|---|---|---|---|---|---|---|---|---|---|---|---|---|
| | Lobbying patient associations | Via patient associations | Via patient advocacy | Via health board | Advisory board | Via sickness funds | GP | Listed at GP | Complaint procedures | Access to individual records | Mediation | Ombudsperson |
| Portugal | x | | | | | | | ca | | x | | |
| Romania | | x | | | | | | x | x | | | |
| Scotland | | | | x | | | | x | x | x | | x |
| Slovakia | | x | | | | | | x | x | | | |
| Slovenia | x | | i | | | | x | | x | | | x |
| Spain | | | | | | | x | ca | x | x | | |
| Sweden* | | i | | g, i | | | x | | x | | | x |
| Switzerland* | | | | | | | x | | | | | |

*keys*: ca—confined to catchment area; csf—involvement in complimentary sickness funds; FT—Foundation Trust Hospitals only; g—geographically confined to certain regions; i—informally; r—involvement via sickness funds in a restricted number of funds; x—applies; *—section 'patient empowerment' not available in respective HiT report

Sources: Albreht et al. (2009, pp. 31–35), Barros, Machado, and de Almeida Simões (2011, pp. 46–50), 22–26, Boyle (2011, 44–68), Bryndová, Pavloková, Roubal, Rokosová, and Gaskins (2009); Busse and Blümel (2014), Chevreul, Durand-Zaleski, Bahrami, Hernández-Quevedo, and Mladovsky (2010, pp. 37–42), Dimova et al. (2012, pp. 38–42), Economou (2010, pp. 40–45), European Observatory on Health Care Systems (1999, 2000) Gaál, Szigeti, Csere, Gaskins, and Panteli (2011, pp. 52–57), García-Armesto, Abadía-Taira, Durán, Hernández-Quevedo and Bernal-Delgado (2010), Gerkens and Merkur (2010, pp. 65–78), Glenngård, Hjalte, Svensson, Anell, and Bankauskaite (2005), Haarmann (2012a,b), Hofmarcher (2013, pp. 66–73), Klenk (2012), Lægrid, Opedal and Stigen (2005), Longley, Riley, Davies and Hernández-Quevedo (2012, pp. 17–20), Matthes (2012b,a), McDaid, Wiley, Maresso, and Mossialos (2009, pp. 38–49), Murauskiene, Janoniene, Veniute, van Ginneken, and Karanikolos (2013, pp. 39–41), O'Neill, McGregor, and Merkur (2012, pp. 20–21), Olejaz, Juul Nielsen, Rudkjøbing, Okkels Birs, Krasnik, and Hernández-Quevedo (2012, pp. 45–51), Ringard, Sagan, Sperre Saunes, and Lindahl (2013, pp. 41–48), Sagan, Panteli, Borkowski, Dmowski, Czyżewski and Busse (pp. 35–41 2011, pp. 43–53), Scalzo, Donatini, Orzella, Cicchetti, Profili, and Maresso (2009, pp. 31–38); Schäfer, Kroneman, Boerma, van den Berg, Westert, Devillé, and van Ginneken (2010, pp. 36–51), Steel and Cylus (2012), Szalay, Pažitný, Szalayová, Frisová, Morvay, Petrovič, and Ginneken (2011, pp. 44–56), Theodorou, Charalambous, Petrou, and Cylus (2012, pp. 29–33), Trondheim Kommune (2005), Vlădescu, Scîntee, and Olsavszky (2008, pp. 33–38), Voncina, Jemiai, Merkur, Golna, Maeda, Chao, and Dzakula (2006), Vuorenkoski (2008, pp. 38–42), Weyrauch (2012a,b)

might rather result in involvement in the policy process. However, other measures like increasing transparency, as well as showing that the government and providers really care, i.e. the traditional way of reactions, might be tried first.

## 9.10 Overall Conclusions

This study took a thorough look at collective patient involvement in hospitals in the Netherlands and England. The analysis included Germany and Sweden as counter-cases and attempted to answer the question, what factors can be identified as having contributed to or hampered the implementation of collective patient involvement in hospitals. What ideally can be gained from any more serious form of involvement is a higher legitimacy of the health care system, services that are adapted better to the actual needs of the population, a better quality and optimised flow of (health-)care, and a better understanding of citizens' needs on the part of politicians and managers. Speaking of 'countervailing power', it might be argued that patient and user involvement compensates for the in part massive lobbying by the pharmaceutical and medical devices industry as well as the established negotiation partners in the field.

It could be concluded that though all countries have pursued their individual paths, they all offer patient/citizen involvement. Two different types of involvement could be identified among the four countries of this study: Involvement in the policy process can be found in Germany via the corporatist self-governance and patient and consumer representatives in the joint federal committee as well as in Sweden via *samråd*, a regular meeting between representatives of the patients' umbrella organisation and the politicians in charge for health care. The other type is involvement at the level of (health-)care providers as present in the Netherlands and England. In essence, a number of assumptions of ideational, institutionalist literature, and actor-centred institutionalism could be discovered, others played a less pronounced role or none at all, while yet others need to be rephrased or refined. Though marketisation was not an immediate cause for the enactment of collective involvement, it could be perceived as a less obvious, underlying precondition in the Netherlands as well as in England for patients to be regarded as clients/customers. What sparked and reinforced the policy process, however, was (a) the framing of the problem as serious or important as well as (b) the assessment that the problem cannot be convincingly solved by instruments in the traditional government toolbox. At the same time, the government were *the* or at least a major actor in the framing of the problem and drawing on existing or new ideas in all four countries. The framing of the problem as well as the perception of the relative strength of the various actors by the government throughout the whole process is the key to understanding action in each country.

Once it is decided that the old policy solution hitherto pursued is no longer convincing, four different factors could be identified to be of major importance: (a) The framing of the problem coincides with the perception of a problem. It is at this stage that potential equivalents are assessed against new proposals. The severity in the framing of the problem is decisive to what degree the new solution will finally be new wine in old wineskins and what kind of solution is favoured. Furthermore, the other three factors are vital for the success of the attempted change, too: (b) Actors and institutions within the political realm, (c) other actors outside of it, and (d) different institutions that might impede or foster change. It is here that institutionalist factors like the central responsibility for health care in England and the Netherlands, the strong Labour government in England, and the capability to negotiate in a multi-party government in the Netherlands plays in as well as actor specific, strategic, and subjective intentions. The overall policy process was schematically visualised in Fig. 9.4. If transaction costs to reach a compromise appear to high, the process might be terminated or not begun at all. An abstract version of the influencing factors that were found to be of relevance in the four countries of this study were summarised in Table 9.3.

Regarding the relation between actors, it could be shown that 'complex actors' need to be treated in more detail or as several entities within this type at times, as the hitherto suggested handling is not convincing. Furthermore, the role of the few individuals who work as enthusiasts and thereby advance a whole project has so far received rather unsystematic attention. What is more, patient involvement can be used for blame avoiding purposes, but is, put positively, rather used as strengthening legitimacy for certain policies when they are backed by patients. Institutions were found to be restricting the speed and/or scope of reform at times—like, for instance, in Germany—at other times it did not seem to play any major role—as, e.g. in England—whereby windows of opportunity supported the process—as in the Netherlands. Predecessors based on voluntary agreements between providers and receivers of care played their role to further the idea of involvement in two countries.

Concerning the often posed question about convergence of different types of welfare and health care also this study's countries showed *some* convergence at a higher level of abstraction: All countries have undertaken at least some move away from the traditional means of involvement and thereby altered or complemented the chain of legitimacy. The two traditionally rather corporatist countries have reframed or limited the influence of corporatist actors, while the two NHS countries have mainly introduced an element of competition. An obvious, broader extent of convergence, however, is difficult to distinguish.

This applies also to the relation between health care system type and the kind of involvement. Even though the existing typologies might cover the mode of funding, provision, and to some extent governance, the types of involvement in this study run right across them. Beyond some hypotheses about more refined factors that are not covered by today's health care state typologies (see Sect. 9.9 on page 316), a clear relationship between health care system type and type of involvement cannot be established. Overall, it can be concluded that within each health care type much more diversity might be hidden than has hitherto been assumed.

A lesson for politicians to learn from the examples of the Netherlands and England is that policies can be actively and radically shaped. This is not to advocate the political style of the lone government pushing through their very idea of how things need to be done regardless of all meaningful opposition, which is also something that can be learned from the English case. The Netherlands, in contrast, and Sweden to some extent show that over time the same or much more can be achieved by agreement between different actors, which, in turn, however, require a long-term vision. This makes it difficult to pursue such endeavours in today's political landscape. However, both examples are impressive evidence that, contrasting the impression left by politicians in many countries that they are all too cautious to confront opposition of influential and powerful actors, they actually *are* capable of making a difference and bringing about considerable change—if only will and/or skill is present. Politicians should be aware of this scope of action and be encouraged to responsibly use it instead of being discouraged by *any* kind of headwind.

Another lesson to be learned is that it is not about either voice or choice, when exit is no feasible option. In that, they are just as little rivalling concepts as one does not forego the right to vote for politicians in general elections after having had a discussion with them in person. In that sense, the involvement landscape found in Germany looks perfect at first sight: The country offers several types of involvement including a say in both the policy process and the provision in long-term care, while patient advocacy and a wide choice of service providers exists, too. What, based on the literature and the answers of my interviewees, can be concluded, however, is that lay-involvement in long-term care is not really working, while pretty effective in the joint federal committee. Thus, choice and voice do not preclude each other but should ideally complement one another.

Contrasting formal means and practical implementation reveals a larger discrepancy, which questions the actual impact of patients' influence or, vice versa, the value of legal forms of involvement. This is because it can also be concluded that legal stipulations are not necessarily what counts, but the communication culture and the will of providers and recipients of care to jointly achieve something for the better. The Netherlands' pre-legal, voluntary state of involvement in nursing and old-age homes provides the best example for this. Finally, the Netherlands also show very strikingly that it needs public, financial, and/or political support to mount patient/citizen/resident involvement, some jump start over the first 10 or 15 years to get things going. The country with its non-sectoral patient organisations providing support for the client councils is definitively *one* key for the relative success compared to its counterpart England.

What is clear, however, that involvement of the type as in the Netherlands and England comes at a price. Estimating the costs for the approximately 800 institutions of long-term care in the Netherlands and the approximately 130 hospitals we end up at 27.9 € million per year if we assume a very cautious estimate of 30,000 € per institution and year. Projecting the approximate number of 156 Foundation Trust hospitals in England and the average costs of £ 200,000 per hospital and year we arrive at some 35 € million and have not even theoretically covered all hospitals or patients throughout England. The corporatist self-governance in the social insurances in Germany with remunerations for attendance and the usually roughly 40 € million also comes at a price. In light of the huge budget for the health care system, this does not carry too much weight, but nevertheless needs to be counterfinanced somehow. The costs, however, are not an external factor, but rather part of the framing of the situation: The likelihood of (financial) support for involvement is higher when receivers of care and patients are framed as the weak client, who needs help in order to make her voice heard, as in the Netherlands, or as an attempt to compensate for the disadvantage of being ill as a societal task, as in Sweden. Highlighting the necessity to contain patients demands in order to protect the vast majority that does not utilise health care services, as in Germany, or the introduction of involvement without a clear aim and vision for involvement as such, as in England, rather decreases the willingness to spend additional money on the support of lay-people and management to adjust to their new roles. On the positive side, the experience from the Netherlands and Sweden suggests, there is reason to believe that in the medium term involvement also creates a better understanding for costs and adherence. This, in turn, could, over time, not only result in better quality of care, but also a more responsible utilisation by providers and patients/residents alike and a potentially better individual health status. In the end, it remains a normative question of how much value a society attributes to collective involvement and what vision it has for the relation between its citizens and the state.

However, the question should also be raised as to what kind of involvement and what kind of competences are meaningful. While involvement in long-term care owing to its dependency, its lack of 'exit', and longevity can improve the quality of life, there is good reason to argue that involvement in the way it is done in most Dutch hospitals and in English Foundation Trust hospitals are probably not the ideal form. The alternative forms found in the Dutch and Swedish context in combination with regular patient surveys seem more appropriate here (for other attempts to involve citizens cf. also Nanz & Fritsche 2012; Schicktanz & Naumann 2013; Stadt Bielefeld 2014; Stumpf & Raspe 2012). Even though it seems difficult to keep people interested in less specific contexts (cf. regional health conferences in Germany; cf. Borchart 2004; Landeszentrum Gesundheit Nordrhein-Westfalen, 2014), completely new, maybe wider compositions might be considered including, e.g. GPs (for an overview on involvement in primary care cf. for instance Groenewegen et al. 2016), patients, transport services (for patients who do not need an ambulance), sickness funds or the administration purchasing or administering health care as well as specialists for cancer treatment, dialysis, HIV treatment, etc. Open, regular meetings of everyone interested and with changing committee compositions once or twice a year at each hospital with long-term specialist care or any larger group practice for chronically ill will probably serve similar functions as a client council/board of governors, achieve more than a patient commissioner, while coming a lower price than a standing council.

Another question is whether it really makes sense to comprise the core competences of issues such as the annual budget that are hardly understood by anyone on the council that owing to framework conditions such as a global budget are difficult to influence anyway, and that sidetrack from other issues that are much closer to the patient/resident? Therefore, the question should be posed anew as to which rights are necessary in order to strengthen the position vis-à-vis amongst others providers, health insurances, and politicians, and which competences can be even misleading, distracting, or useless despite best intentions? A report with the somewhat provocative title '*Warning: Too Much Information Can Harm.*' (Better Regulation Executive & National Consumer Council 2007) suggests that not information *per se* but the right dose of information at the right level of abstraction and linking to the life world of consumers is what is needed in order to make policies successful. Thus, it is probably a good idea to give patients/residents the right to have insight into the budget, but it might be more important to focus their advice on more immediate things ,for instance, housing, food, treatment, and their contribution to strategy. This would to some extent also prevent the necessity of lay-professionals who, in turn, exclude 'Joe Bloggs' from the councils. Furthermore, to be successful, involvement obviously needs to take patients and users of care seriously, it needs a topic people can identify with, feel rewarded by and, thus, at best is pretty specific. And, of course, it needs the potential to actually change something as well as some financial and political support. This shows that the questions whom to involve in what form and with what competences can only temporally be solved and need to be posed again once in a while.

Thus, overall patient/resident/public involvement has a great potential in terms of quality and optimisation of (health-)care, democratic legitimacy and support, making their voice heard, and (health-)care more responsive to offer. In order to make it a meaningful tool and make it succeed it needs good will on both patient and provider side, a good concept as of what shall be achieved, some resources, thorough implementation, and patience.

## References


Albreht, T., Turk, E., Toth, M., Ceglar, J., Marn, S., Pribaković Brinovec, R., & Schäfer, M. (2009). Slovenia: Health system review. In M. Schäfer, O. Avdeeva & E. Ginneken (Eds.), *Health systems in transition*. Copenhagen: WHO Regional Office for Europe on behalf of the European Observatory on Health Systems and Policies.

Anell, A. (2005). Swedish healthcare under pressure. *Health Economics, 14*, S237–S254.

Anell, A., & Rosén, P. (1996). *Valfrihet och jämlikhet i vården* (1:e uppl.). Stockholm: SNS (Studieförb. Näringsliv och samhälle).

Barnes, M. (1999, March). Users as citizens: Collective action and the local governance of welfare. *Social Policy & Administration, 33*(1), 73–90.

Barros, P. P., Machado, S. R., & de Almeida Simões, J. (2011). Spain: Health system review. *Health systems in transition*. Copenhagen: WHO Regional Office for Europe on behalf of the European Observatory on Health Systems and Policies.

Béland, D. (2005). Ideas and social policy: An institutionalist perspective. *Social Policy and Administration, 39*(1), 1–18.

Better Regulation Executive & National Consumer Council. (2007, November). *Warning: Too much information can harm*. London: Better Regulation Executive and National Consumer Council.

Borchart, D. (2004). *Prävention und Gesundheitsförderung in NRW*. Positionspapier der ASG NRW.

Borchert, J. (1996). Alte Träume und neue Realitäten: Das Ende der Sozialdemokratie: Organisationsstrukturen und Politikinhalte im Wandel. In J. Borchert, L. Golsch, U. Jun & P. Lösche (Eds.), *Das sozialdemokratische Modell*. Europa- und Nordamerika-Studien. Opladen: Leske + Budrich.

Borgenhammar, E., & Fallberg, L. H. (1997). *Våga vara vårdkonsument–vägar till medvetenhet* (1:e uppl.). Stockholm: SNS (Studieförb. Näringsliv och samhälle).

Borghi, V., & van Berkel, R. (2007). New modes of governance in Italy and the Netherlands. The case of activation policies. *Public Administration, 85*(1), 83–101.

Borins, S., & Grüning, G. (1998). New Public Management–Theoretische Grundlagen und problematische Aspekte der Kritik. In D. Budäus, P. Conrad & G. Schreyögg (Eds.), *Managementforschung 8* (pp. 11–53). Berlin: de Gruyter.

Boudon, R. (1981). *The logic of social action–An introduction to sociological analysis.* London: Routledge & Kegan Paul.

Boyle, S. (2011). United Kingdom (England): Health system review. *Health systems in transition.* Copenhagen: WHO Regional Office for Europe on behalf of the European Observatory on Health Systems and Policies.

Bryndová, L., Pavloková, K., Roubal, T., Rokosová, M., & Gaskins, M. (2009). Czech Republic: Health system review. In M. Gaskins & E. Ginneken (Eds.), *Health systems in transition.* Copenhagen: WHO Regional Office for Europe on behalf of the European Observatory on Health Systems and Policies.

Bundesgesetzblatt. (1976, July 19). *Verordnung über die Mitwirkung der Bewohnerinnen und Bewohner in Angelegenheiten des Heimbetriebs (Heimmitwirkungsverordnung–HeimmwV).* BGBl. I, S. 2896. Bundesgesetzblatt.

Bundesgesetzblatt. (2003, November 14). *Gesetz zur Modernisierung der gesetzlichen Krankenversicherung (GKV-Modernisierungsgesetz–GMG).* Bundesgesetzblatt I, Nr. 55.

Busse, R., & Blümel, M. (2014). Germany–Health system review. *Health systems in transition* (Vol. 16). Copenhagen: WHO Regional Office for Europe.

Calltorp, J., Persson, J., Holmström, S., Levin, L.-Å., & Persson, J. (1988). *Att beställa hälsoochsjukvård.* Göteborg: Beställarnätverket för landstingen i Sverige.

Chevreul, K., Durand-Zaleski, I., Bahrami, S., Hernández-Quevedo, C., & Mladovsky, P. (2010). France: Health system review. *Health systems in transition.* Copenhagen: WHO Regional Office for Europe on behalf of the European Observatory on Health Systems and Policies.

Chinitz, D. (2000). Regulierter Wettbewerb und Bürgerbeteiligung–Lektionen aus Israel. In H. Ettischer & K. Salice-Stephan (Eds.), *Bürgerbeteiligung im Gesundheitswesen–eine länderübergreifende Herausforderung–Ideen, Ansätze und internationale Erfahrungen.* Forschung und Praxis der Gesundheitsförderung (Chap. 3.2, 10, pp. 64–72). Köln: Bundeszentrale für gesundheitliche Aufklärung (BZgA).

Commissie 'Structuur en Financiering Gezondheidszorg' (Dekker). (1987). *Bereidheid tot verandering.* 's Gravenhage: Distributiecentrum Overheidspublikaties (DOP).

Dalton, J., Chambers, D., Harden, M., Street, A., Partker, G., & Eastwood, A. (2016). Service user engagement in health service reconfiguration: A rapid evidence synthesis. *Journal of Health Services Research & Policy,* (21), 195–205.

Dimova, A., Rohova, M., Moutafova, E., Atanasova, E., Koeva, S., Panteli, D., & van Ginneke, E. (2012). Bulgaria: Health system review. *Health systems in transition.* Copenhagen: WHO Regional Office for Europe on behalf of the European Observatory on Health Systems and Policies.

Economou, C. (2010). Greece: Health system review. *Health systems in transition.* Copenhagen: WHO Regional Office for Europe on behalf of the European Observatory on Health Systems and Policies.

Esping-Andersen, G. (1996). After the golden age? welfare state dilemmas in a global economy. In G. Esping-Andersen (Ed.), *Welfare states in transition* (pp. 1–31). London: SAGE.

European Observatory on Health Care Systems. (1999). Malta. *Health systems in transition.* Copenhagen: WHO Regional Office for Europe.

European Observatory on Health Care Systems. (2000). Switzerland. *Health systems in transition*. Copenhagen: WHO Regional Office for Europe.
Gaál, P., Szigeti, S., Csere, M., Gaskins, M., & Panteli, D. (2011). Hungary: Health system review. *Health systems in transition*. Copenhagen: WHO Regional Office for Europe on behalf of the European Observatory on Health Systems and Policies.
García-Armesto, S., Abadía-Taira, M. B., Durán, A., Hernández-Quevedo, C., & Bernal-Delgado, E. (2010). Spain: Health system review. *Health systems in transition*. Copenhagen: WHO Regional Office for Europe on behalf of the European Observatory on Health Systems and Policies.
George, A. L., & Bennett, A. (2005). *Case studies and theory development in the social sciences*. Cambridge, MA: MIT press.
Gerkens, S., & Merkur, S. (2010). Belgium. *Health systems in transition*. WHO Regional Office for Europe on behalf of the European Observatory on Health Systems and Policies.
Gesundheitskonferenzen. (2014). Retrieved January 22, 2015, from www.lzg.gc.nrw.de/themen/Gesundheitplanen/konf
Glenngård, A., Hjalte, F., Svensson, M., Anell, A., & Bankauskaite, V. (2005). Sweden: Health system review. In V. Bankauskaite (Ed.), *Health systems in transition*. Copenhagen: WHO Regional Office for Europe on behalf of the European Observatory on Health Systems and Policies.
Groenewegen, P. P. (1998). Besluitvorming in de gezondheidszorg op macroniveau. In C. W. Aakster & J. W. Groothoff (Eds.), *Medische sociologie–Sociologische perpectieven op ziekte en zorg* (5th ed., Chap. 2, pp. 295–302). Groningen: Wolters-Noordhoff.
Groenewegen, P., Kroneman, M., van Erp, K., Broeren, R., & van Birgelen, C. (2016). *Kennissynthese: Patiëntenparticipatie in de eerste lijn*. Utrecht: Nivel & Zorgbelang Brabant.
Haarmann, A. (2012a). Niederlande: Soziale Sicherung zwischen staatlicher Grundsicherung und For-Profit-Versicherern. In T. Klenk, P. Weyrauch, A. Haarmann & F. Nullmeier (Eds.), *Abkehr vom Korporatismus?* (pp. 367–438). Frankfurt a.M.: Campus.
Haarmann, A. (2012b). Österreich: Verfestigung des Selbstverwaltungskorporatismus. In T. Klenk, P. Weyrauch, A. Haarmann & F. Nullmeier (Eds.), *Abkehr vom Korporatismus?* (pp. 121–180). Frankfurt a.M.: Campus.
Hall, P. A. (1993, April). Policy paradigms, social learning, and the state–the case of economic policymaking in britain. *Comparative Politics, 25*(3), 275–296.
Hinrichs, K. (2001). Elephants on the move–patterns of public pension reform in OECD countries. In S. Leibfried (Ed.), *Welfare state futures* (pp. 77–102). Cambridge: Cambridge University Press.
Hofmarcher, M. M. (2013). Austria. In W. Quentin (Ed.), *Health systems in transition*. WHO Regional Office for Europe on behalf of the European Observatory on Health Systems and Policies.
House of Commons. (2003a, November). House of commons hansard debates on the health and social care (Community Health and Standards) Act 2003, 19 November, London.
House of Commons. (2003b, May). House of commons hansard debates on the health and social care (Community Health and Standards) Act 2003, 7 May, London.
House of Commons. (2003c, July). House of commons hansard debates on the health and social care (Community Health and Standards) Act 2003, 8 July, London.
House of Commons. (2003d, May). House of commons hansard debates on the health and social care (Community Health and Standards) Act 2003, 8 May, London.
HSL. (1982:763). *Hälso- och Sjukvårdslagen (HSL)*. SFS1982:763. Stockholm: Socialdepartmentet.
Kingdon, J. W. (2003). *Agendas, alternatives, and public policies* (2nd ed.). New York: Longman.
Klenk, T. (2012). Deutschland: Korporatistische Selbstverwaltung zwischen Staat und Markt. In T. Klenk, P. Weyrauch, A. Haarmann & F. Nullmeier (Eds.), *Abkehr vom Korporatismus?* (pp. 53–118). Frankfurt a.M.: Campus.
Korpi, W. (1983). *The democratic class struggle*. London: Routledge and Kegan Paul.

Korpi, W., & Palme, J. (2003, August). New politics and class politics in the context of austerity and globalization: Welfare state regress in 18 countries, 1975–95. *American Political Science Review, 97*(3), 425–446.

Lægrid, P., Opedal, S., & Stigen, I. (2005). The Norwegian hospital reform: Balancing political control and enterprise autonomy. *Journal of Health Politics, Policy and Law, 30*(6), 1027–1064.

Leiber, S., Greß, S., & Manouguian, M. -S. (2010, August). Healthcare system change and the cross-border transfer of ideas: Influence of the Dutch model on the German health reform 2007. *Journal of Health Politics, Policy and Law, 35*(4), 539–568.

Lian, O. S. (2011). Patienten som kund. In A. Tjora (Ed.), *Den moderna patienten* (Chap. 2, pp. 43–68). Lund: Studentlitteratur.

Longley, M., Riley, N., Davies, P., & Hernández-Quevedo, C. (2012). United Kingdom (Wales): Health system review. *Health systems in transition*. Copenhagen: WHO Regional Office for Europe on behalf of the European Oberservatory on Health Systems and Policies.

Maier, M. L. (2003). Wissens- und ideenorientierte Anätze in der Politikwissenschaft: Versuch einer systematischen Übersicht. In M. L. Maier, F. Nullmeier, T. Pritzlaff & A. Wiesner (Eds.), *Politik als Lernprozess–Wissenszentrierte Ansätze der Politikanalyse* (pp. 25–77). Opladen: Leske + Budrich.

Martin, R. G. (2008). 'Ordinary people only': Knowledge, representativeness, and the publics of public participation in healthcare. *Sociology of Health & Illness, 30*, 35–54.

Matthes, C. (2012a). Tschechische Republik: Unvollständige Wiedereinführung korporatistischer Selbstverwaltung. In T. Klenk, P. Weyrauch, A. Haarmann & F. Nullmeier (Eds.), *Abkehr vom Korporatismus?* Frankfurt a.M.: Campus.

Matthes, C. (2012b). Ungarn: (Selbst-)Verwaltung zwischen Tripartismus und Etatismus. In T. Klenk, P. Weyrauch, A. Haarmann & F. Nullmeier (Eds.), *Abkehr vom Korporatismus?* Frankfurt a.M.: Campus.

Mayntz, R., & Scharpf, F. W. (1995). Der Ansatz des akteurzentrierten Institutionalismus. In R. Mayntz & F. W. Scharpf (Eds.), *Gesellschaftliche Selbstregelung und politische Steuerung* (Chap. 2, pp. 39–72). Frankfurt am Main: Campus.

McDaid, D.,Wiley, M., Maresso, A., & Mossialos, E. (2009). Ireland: Health system review. *Health system in transition*. Copenhagen: WHO Regional Office for Europe on behalf of the European Oberservatory on Health Systems and Policies.

Münnich, S. (2011). Wie weit reicht der Einfluß von Ideen?–Herausforderungen und Grenzen ideen- und diskursorientierter Wohlfahrtsforschung. *Zeitschrift für Sozialreform, 57*(4), 487–498.

Murauskiene, L., Janoniene, R., Veniute, M., van Ginneken, E., & Karanikolos, M. (2013). *Lithuania: Health system review.* Health Systems in Transition. Copenhagen: WHO Regional Office for Europe on behalf of the European Oberservatory on Health Systems and Policies.

Nanz, P., & Fritsche, M. (2012). *Handbuch Bürgerbeteiligung–Verfahren und Akteure, Chancen und Grenzen*. Schriftenreihe. Bonn: Bundeszentrale für politische Bildung.

Naschold, F. (1996). *New frontiers in public sector management*. Berlin: de Gruyter.

Okma, K. (2008, January). Recent changes in Dutch health insurance: Individual mandate or social insurance? Paper Commissioned by the National Academy of Social Insurance.

Olejaz, M., Juul Nielsen, A., Rudkjøbing, A., Okkels Birs, H., Krasnik, A., & Hernández-Quevedo, C. (2012). Denmark: Health system review. *Health systems in transition*. Copenhagen: WHO Regional Office for Europe on behalf of the European Oberservatory on Health Systems and Policies.

Olofsson, C., Nilsson, A., & Wahllöf, U. (2010). *Patientens val–en bok om primärvård och vårdval.* Lund: Studentlitteratur.

O'Neill, C., McGregor, P., & Merkur, S. (2012). United Kingdom (Northern Ireland): Health system review. *Health systems in transition*. Copenhagen: WHO Regional Office for Europe on behalf of the European Oberservatory on Health Systems and Policies.

Palier, B., & Martin, C. (2007, December). From "a frozen landscape" to structural reforms: The sequential transformation of Bismarckian welfare systems. *Social Policy & Administration, 41*(6), 535–554.

Ringard, Å., Sagan, A., Sperre Saunes, I., & Lindahl, A. K. (2013). Norway: Health system review. *Health systems in transition*. Copenhagen: WHO Regional Office for Europe on behalf of the European Observatory on Health Systems and Policies.

Roebroek, J. M., & Hertogh, M. (1998). *De beschavende invloed des tijds*. 's Gravenhage: VUGA Uitgeverij.

Rosen, B., & Samuel, H. (2009). Israel–Health system review. In S. Merkur (Ed.), *Health Systems in Transition*. Copenhagen: European Observatory on Health Systems and Policies.

Rothgang, H., Schmid, A., & Schneider, S. (2012). Transformationen des Interventionsstaates und ihre Erklärung: Das Beispiel nationaler Gesundheitssysteme. In M. Bach (Ed.), *Der entmachtete Leviathan: Löst sich der souveräne Staat auf?* (Vol. Sonderband 5, pp. 175–196). Baden-Baden: Nomos.

Sagan, A., Panteli, D., Borkowski, W., Dmowski, M., F., D., Czyżewski, M., ... Busse, R. (2011). *Poland: Health system review*. Health Systems in Transition. Copenhagen: WHO Regional Office for Europe on behalf of the European Oberservatory on Health Systems and Policies.

Scalzo, A. L., Donatini, A., Orzella, L., Cicchetti, A., Profili, S., & Maresso, A. (2009). *Italy: Health system review*. Health Systems in Transition. Copenhagen: WHO Regional Office for Europe on behalf of the European Oberservatory on Health Systems and Policies.

Schäfer, W., Kroneman, M., Boerma, W., van den Berg, M., Westert, G., Devillé, W., & van Ginneken, E. (2010). The Netherlands: Health system review. In E. van. Ginneken & R. Busse (Eds.), *Health systems in transition*. Copenhagen: WHO Regional Office for Europe on behalf of the European Observatory on Health Systems and Policies.

Scharpf, F. W. (1997). *Games real actors play–actor-centered institutionalism in policy research*. Boulder, CO: Westview Press.

Schedler, K., & Proeller, I. (2000). *New public management*. Bern: Haupt/ UTB.

Schicktanz, S., & Naumann, J. (Eds.). (2013). *Bürgerkonferenz: Streitfall Gendiagnostik* [Ein Modellprojekt der Bürgerbeteiligung am bioethischen Diskurs]. Heidelberg: Springer.

SFS. (2010:659). *Patientsäkerhetslag*. SFS 2010:659. Stockholm: Socialdepartmentet.

SOU. (1999:149). *Upphandling av hälso- och sjukvårdstjänster*. Stockholm: Socialdepartmentet.

Stadt Bielefeld. (2014). Zukunft Mobielefeld. Retrieved from http://www.zukunftmobielefeld.de/

Steel, D., & Cylus, J. (2012). United Kingdom (Scotland): Health system review. *Health systems in transition*. Copenhagen: WHO Regional Office for Europe on behalf of the European Observatory on Health Systems and Policies.

Streeck, W., & Thelen, K. (2005). Introduction: Institutional change in advanced political economies. In W. Streek & K. Thelen (Eds.), *Institutional change in advanced political economies* (pp. 3–39). New York: Oxford University Press.

Stumpf, S., & Raspe, H. (2012). Deliberative Bürgerbeteiligung in der Priorisierungsdebatte: Welchen Beitrag können Bürger leisten? *Zeitschrift für Evidenz, Fortbildung und Qualitätim Gesundheitswesen, 106*(6), 418–425.

Szalay, T., Pažitný, P., Szalayová, A., Frisová, S., Morvay, K., Petrovič, M., & Ginneken, E. van.(2011). Slovakia: Health system review. *Health systems in transition*. Copenhagen: WHO Regional Office for Europe on behalf of the European Observatory on Health Systems and Policies.

Theodorou, M., Charalambous, C., Petrou, C., & Cylus, J. (2012). Greece: Health system review. *Health systems in transition*. Copenhagen: WHO Regional Office for Europe on behalf of the European Observatory on Health Systems and Policies.

Thomas, W. I., & Thomas, D. S. (1928). *The child in America: Behavior problems and programs*. New York: Knopf.

Trampusch, C. (2000). *Arbeitsmarktpolitik, Gewerkschaften und Arbeitgeber. Ein Vergleich der Entstehung und Transformation der öffentlichen Arbeitsverwaltungen in Deutschland, Großbritannien und den Niederlanden zwischen 1909 und 1999*. Göttingen: Georg-August-Universität.

Trappenburg, M. (2008). *Genoeg is genoeg*. Amsterdam: Amsterdam University Press.

Trondheim Kommune. (2005). *Brukerråd, hva da?*

van Egmond, S., Heerings, M., & Munnichs, G. (2014, March 26). *Sterke verhalen uit het ziekenhuis: Leren van patiëntenervaringen voor goede zorg*. Den Haag: Rathenau Instituut.

van Waarden, F. (1992). The historical institutionalization of typical national patterns in policy networks between state and industry. *European Journal of Political Research, 21*(1–2), 131–162.

van Waarden, F. (1993). Über die Beständigkeit nationaler Politikstile und Politiknetzwerke. Eine Studie zur Genese ihrer institutionellen Verankerung. In R. Czada & M. G. Schmidt (Eds.), *Verhandlungsdemokratie, Interessenvermittlung, Regierbarkeit* (pp. 191–212). Opladen: Westdeutscher Verlag.

van Waarden, F. (2002). Dutch consociationalism and corporatism: A case of institutional persistence. *Acta politica–International Journal of Political science, 37*(1–2), 44–67.

Visser, J., & Hemerijck, A. (1998). *Ein holländisches Wunder?* Frankfurt: Campus.

Vlădescu, C., Scîntee, G., & Olsavszky, V. (2008). Romania: Health system review. In S. Allin & P. Mladovsky (Eds.), *Health systems in transition*. Copenhagen: WHO Regional Office for Europe on behalf of the European Observatory on Health Systems and Policies.

Voncina, L., Jemiai, N., Merkur, S., Golna, C., Maeda, A., Chao, S., & Dzakula, A. (2006). *Croatia: Health system review*. In S. Merkur, N. Jemiai & E. Mossialos (Eds.), *Health systems in transition*. Copenhagen: WHO Regional Office for Europe on behalf of the European Observatory on Health Systems and Policies.

Vuorenkoski, L. (2008). Finland: Health system review. In P. Mladovsky & E. Mossialos (Eds.), *Health systems in transition*. Copenhagen: WHO Regional Office for Europe on behalf of the European Oberservatory on Health Systems and Policies.

Weber, M. (1991 (1904)). Die Objektivität sozialwissenschaftlicher und sozialpolitischer Erkenntnis. In *Schriften zur Wissenschaftslehre* (pp. 21–101). Reclam.

Weber, M. (1968). *Die Protestantische Ethik II. Kritiken und Antikritiken.* Hamburg: Siebenstern.

Weyrauch, P. (2012a). Belgien: Auf dem Weg zu einer tripartistischen Selbstverwaltung. In T. Klenk, P. Weyrauch, A. Haarmann & F. Nullmeier (Eds.), *Abkehr vom Korporatismus?* (pp. 179–240). Frankfurt a.M.: Campus.

Weyrauch, P. (2012b). Frankreich: Von der sozialen Demokratie zum Regulierungsstaat. In T. Klenk, P. Weyrauch, A. Haarmann & F. Nullmeier (Eds.), *Abkehr vom Korporatismus?* (pp. 287–364). Frankfurt a.M.: Campus.

# Part IV
# Appendix

# Appendix A
# Appendix: Interview Guidelines

## A.1 The Netherlands

### *A.1.1 Interview Guideline: Client Councils*

- Hoe ziet de WMCZ in de praktijk op instellingsniveau uit?
  - Hoe is de cliëntenraad samengesteld en hoe werven jullie nieuwe leden (b. v. via advertenties, verkiezingen)?
  - Hoe ziet het werk van de cliëntenraad in de instelling uit? Wat waren b. v. onderwerpen gedurende het afgelopen jaar over die de cliëntenraad geadviseerd heeft? Heeft de raad ook ongevraagd advies uitgebracht? Was er genoeg tijd om advies uit te bringen, genoeg overleg met het bestuur?
  - Zijn er rechten die de cliëntenraad boven de wettelijk bepaalde minimumrechten worden toegestaan? Zijn er rechten van die de cliëntenraad afstaat?
  - In hoever kunnen patiënten daadwerkelijk invloed uitoefenen in een instelling? Zijn gewone patiënten in de positie met een professioneel instellingsmanagement overleg te houden? In hoeverworden gehandicapte patiënten serieus genomen?
  - Was er ooit een situatie waarin een ernstig verschill van mening tussen bestuur en cliëntenraad bestond? Hoe werdt deze situatie opgelost?
  - Hoe goed zijn de soms iets ingewikkelde regels en het recht om op te stappen? Hoe wordt U de positie van cliënten in het vierkant van artsen, bestuur en verzekeraar gewaar?
- Hoe zou U cliënt van patiënt en medezeggenschap van participatie differentiëren?



A. Haarmann, *The Evolution and Everyday Practice of Collective Patient Involvement in Europe*, DOI 10.1007/978-3-319-64595-7

### *A.1.2 Interview Guideline: Patient Organisations and Politicians*

- Wat waren de hoofdredenen voor het wetsvoorstel en de aanvarding van de WMCZ?
- Wat maakte de WMCZ meer aanvaardbaar dan de WDFI of de WDFZ?
  - Waarom werdt voor de WMCZ gepleit alhoewel een hogere aantal punten van kritiek nog steeds onopgelost waren?
  - Wat leidde tot de uitbreiding van de werkingssfeer van langdurige zorgverlening—zoals in verpleeghuizen- en bejaardenoorden of in de GGZ—tot alle intramurale instellingen zoals ook gewone ziekenhuisen?
  - Welke rol speelde de toekering naar een nieuw zorgstelsel op lange termijn? Kan de wet in die zin als alleen een verdere nieuwe cliëntenrecht worden verstaan? Stonden er sinds 1974 misschien al weer andere 'ideologische' redenen voorop (b. v.: niet zozeer democratisering maar patiënten als countervailing power)?
  - In hoever speelde decentralisatie en deregulering als gedachte een rol?
  - Welke bijdrage had de Nederlandse ontzuiling voor het onstaan van een patiëntenbeweging?
- Welke aktoren waren er bij het wetgevingsproces betrokken?
  - Wie was de drijvende motor van het project?
  - Kunnen er verschillende standpunten langs de politieke lijnen worden onderscheiden?
  - Wat waren inzonderheid de redenen voor de politiek?
  - Hoe was toen de reactie van aanbieders en medici?

---

- Hoe tevreden bent U met de implementatie van de WMCZ in de praktijk op instellingsniveau?
  - Denkt U dat aanbieders hebben begrepen dat het een minimumwet is?
  - Hoe goed zijn de soms iets ingewikkelde regels en klachtrechten?
  - Hoe verhoudt zich de WMCZ tot andere cliëntenrechten zoals de WKCZ of WGBO?
  - In hoever verschild de praktijk tussen zorginstellingen voor langdurige en kortdurende zorg?
  - In hoever kunnen patiënten daadwerkelijk invloed uitoefenen in een instelling? Zijn gewone patiënten in de positie met een professioneel instellingsmanagement inspraak/ overleg te houden?
- Hoe ziet de WMCZ in de praktijk op instellingsniveau uit?
  - Hoe goed zijn de soms iets ingewikkelde regels en klachtrechten?

- In hoever verschild deze tussen zorginstellingen voor langdurige en kortdurende zorg?
- Wat is goed en wat kan beter?

- In de literatuur kan men de positie aantreffen dat patiëntenorganisaties en/ of hun koepels door de overheid te belast zijn door steeds nieuwe taken van toezicht en raadpleging.
- Hoe ziet U op de financiering van de raden? Is het een problem dat ze door de instelling zelf kan worden vastgezet? Hoe ziet U op overheidssubsidies voor projecten?
- Hoe ziet U op het wetsvoorstel van de "Wet cliëntenrechten zorg"?

## A.2 England

### *A.2.1 Interview Guideline: Hospitals*

- *How does public involvement look like in everyday life?*
  - How are new members recruited for the Council of Governors? Is it difficult to attract qualified volunteers?
  - How is the Council comprised in your Foundation Trust Hospital when it comes to the number of members, age, gender, expertise, or illnesses? To what degree can it be regarded representative for the patients and citizens in the service area of the hospital?
  - How is the contact to constituents guaranteed? What ways of communication are there?
- *How does the work of the Council of Governors in the hospital look like?*
  - What were the issues discussed during the last year? How often have the Board of Directors and the Council of Governors met?
  - Is there any cooperation between the Council of Governors and non-executive directors taking place?
  - To what extent can the public actually exert influence on the management's policies? To what extent is the average patient/citizen in state to advise and supervise a hospital's management?
  - In what ways does the Foundation Trust Governors' Association support your local Council of Governors?
- How do you view the interplay between complaint procedures (e.g. through PALS), public involvement (e.g. through LINks), and involvement at the level of healthcare provision (through the Council of Governors)? Are they complementary or rather mutually exclusive? Does not the current framework establish redundancies without fostering cooperation between social services, acute healthcare, primary healthcare, and commissioning?

- According to your opinion: What role does patient, respectively, public involvement play in improving healthcare? Cannot patient involvement be substituted by a stronger emphasis on choice and/ or surveys about patient satisfaction?
- How would you define the following terms and their differences with regard to the healthcare sector: citizen, public, patient, customer?
- What do you think: Is patient involvement in an institution like hospitals with a high patient turnover a feasible thing or would it rather suit services in long-term care?
- What has changed compared to NHS Trust status?
  - Since 20 years there has been said a lot about giving more power into local hands. To what extent has this been fulfilled according to your experience?
  - There has been equally much said about stronger accountability in healthcare. What is your experience?
  - As how independent do you actually experience Foundation Trusts from Whitehall and/or Monitor?
  - To what extent do you think official ratings and risk ratings are helpful for patients and the governance of the hospital? Do they depict your hospital's reality?

### *A.2.2 Interview Guideline: MPs*

- *What were the main reasons for the change of hospitals from NHS Trusts into Foundation Trusts and for involving patients in the Board of Governors?*
- To what extent can the reform be seen in line with...
  - the debate around choice,
  - higher accountability, or
  - the attempt to raise quality or lower costs within the NHS?
  - On what grounds were previous ways of patient involvement viewed unsuccessful?
- *What actors were involved in the legislation process?*
  - Who was the driving force behind the project?
  - As far as I understand, there were no clearly distinguished political lines in the parliamentary debates, but even Labour MPs were opposing the idea. What did/do you personally think about it?
  - What were the reactions of the medical profession and managers within the NHS upon the bill?
  - How satisfied are you with the outcomes so far?
- Would not public and patient involvement on the commissioning side, i.e. in Primary Care Trusts or a joint board/council for primary, acute and social care in the community be even more important than on the provision side?

- What do you think does the NHS and public involvement within the NHS of the future look like?

## A.3 Germany

### *A.3.1 Interview Guideline: Ministerial Staff*

- Vergleicht man Soziale Selbstverwaltung, individuelle Patientenrechte, Mitspracheregeln in Pflege- und Versorgungsheimen und die Patientenbeteiligung über den Gemeinsamen Bundesausschuss:
  - Sind Ihrer Meinung nach alle gleich wichtig oder gibt es zwischen ihnen Unterschiede in der Wichtigkeit?
  - Haben sie im Alltag die Bedeutung, die ihnen Ihrer Meinung nach zukommen sollte?
- Was meinen Sie: Wie sieht die Patientenbeteiligung der Zukunft in Deutschland aus?

---

- Was waren die Gründe, die Kompetenzen für Äquivalente zur Heimmitwirkungsverordnung den Ländern zu übertragen?
  - Welche Resonanz hatte die vom Bundesfamilienministerium in Auftrag gegebene "Evaluation der Heimmitwirkung" (2007)?
  - Gab es irgendwann (z. B. im Verlauf der Überlegungen zur Kompetenzübertragung oder im Rahmen der Neufassung der HeimmwV 2002) Überlegungen, Mitwirkung auf nicht-stationäre (z. B. Pflegedienste) oder andere stationäre Einrichtungen auszuweiten (z. B. Krankenhäuser)?

---

### *A.3.2 Gemeinsamer Bundesausschuss*

- Welche Idee stand hinter der Einführung des Gemeinsamen Bundesausschusses?
  - Wer war die treibende Kraft dabei?
- Was war die Motivation, die Patientenbeteiligungsverordnung zu stiften?
  - Geschah dies in Zusammenarbeit oder auf Druck von Patientenorganisationen? Warum hat man sich nicht auf Vertreter von GKV, Ärzteschaft und Krankenhäusern beschränkt?

- Konnte man parteipolitische Schwerpunkte in der Debatte ausmachen?
- Wie kam es zu just dieser Auswahl "anerkannter Organisationen"?
- Wie sieht die Zusammenarbeit zwischen Patientenorganisationen und professionellen Mitgliedern des Ausschusses aus?
- In welchem Maße können Patienten tatsächlich Einfluss auf Beschlüsse des Ausschusses ausüben? Wie ernst werden sie genommen?

• Seit Jahrzehnten gibt es Kritik an der Sozialen Selbstverwaltung. Warum wurde Patientenbeteiligung auf nationaler Ebene eingeführt? Wäre es nicht konsequent gewesen, direkte Patientenbeteiligung auch auf Kassenebene einzuführen?

### *A.3.3 Interview Guideline: Nursing Homes*

• Wie erleben Sie die Mitsprache von Patienten und Gepflegten in Einrichtungen in der Praxis?

  - Wie ist der Heimbeirat i.d.R. zusammengestellt? Wie werden neue Mitglieder gewonnen?
  - Wird der Heimbeirat i.d.R. automatisch mit in Planungen einbezogen oder hat er immer noch Akzeptanzprobleme?
  - Gibt es vielleicht auch Fälle, in denen sich der Träger weigert, ihm Mitsprache einzuräumen? Oder in denen das Personal auf eine Zusammensetzung hinwirkt, die für den Träger "pflegeleicht" ist?
  - Gibt es Beispiele, in denen ihm mehr als die gesetzlich festgelegten Rechte eingeräumt werden? Wie häufig kommt es vor, dass er von den ihm gesetzlich zugestandenen Rechten keinen Gebrauch macht?
  - Inwiefern sind Heimbeiräte in der Lage, Einfluss auszuüben? Sind "normale" Bewohner in der Position, mit einem professionellen Management zu sprechen? Inwiefern werden behinderte oder demente Bewohner hier ernst genommen?

• Wie nehmen Sie die Position von Bewohnern im Viereck zwischen Trägern, Ärzten, Pflegern und Kostenträgern wahr?
• (Wie) Hat sich die Situation seit Einführung der Länderäquivalente zum Heimgesetz verändert?
• Was denken Sie: Würde es Ihrer Meinung nach Sinn machen, Mitwirkung etwa auf mobile Pflegedienste oder die Behandlung chronisch Kranker auszuweiten?

## A.4 Sweden

### *A.4.1 Interview Guideline: Politicians/Civil Servants at County Councils and Researchers*

- *För att få en ungefärlig överblick av hur sjukvården ser ut i region's/county council's name or Sweden:*
  - *Hur många sjukhus, läkarmottagninar och läkare finns i regionen? Hur många av dem är landstingsanställda, hur många kontrakterade läkare?*
  - *Om du jämför hälso- och sjukvården i Skåne med andra landsting: Vad skulle du säga är det mest specifika här? Vad framstår som största problem? Och vad anser du fungera bättre än i andra landsting?*[1]
- Vilka möjligheter att medverka och/eller utöva inflytande finns inom vården i landstinget (vård ska förstås här i bred betydelse: främst hälso- och sjukvård men även t. ex. äldrevård eller psykvård (även om jag vet att det egentligen är kommunernas ansvarsområde))?
- Vilka aktörer är inblandade? Har det förekommit krav från medborgarnas eller patientorganisationernas sida på större inflytande inom vården?
- Vad tycker du vilken mening karakteriserar brukarmedverkan bäst: Det...
  - ...är en bra möjlighet att informera medborgarna om vad som försiggår inom hälso- och sjukvården och vilka förändringar planeras.
  - ...är bra för att diskutera sjukvårdsrelaterade ämnen mellan politiker och medborgar.
  - ...ger medborgarna inflytande över hur vården utformas.
- Om man ser på t. ex. individuell valfrihet och inflytande på vårdgivare så är patientinflytande och brukarmedverkan en förhållandevis sen företeelse i Sverige. Vad tror du är anledningen till detta?
- Vad har förändrats under tiden att man ansåg att nya former är nödvändiga? Vem var den drivande kraften bakom förändringarna?

---

For the region Skåne some additional questions were put at this point (within horizontal lines):

- I Skåne fanns det så kallade Centrala patient- och handikapprådet, dessförinnan brukarrådet.
  - Vilka befogenheter hade de?
  - Hur var deras rol tänkt?

[1]The lines in italics were omitted for the interviewed researchers and were printed in normal in the respective guideline.

  - Vilka teman var det som främst blev diskuterade?
  - Vad var anledningen till att avskaffa och ersätta dem med nya organ?

- Vilken rol spelade medborgardialogen inom hälso- och sjukvårdsområdet?

---

- Hur bra fungerar samverkan mellan den landstingsdrivna vården och kommunal/närvården? Hur bidrar patienter/brukare faktiskt till en förbättring? Hur stor potential ser du här?
- Hur skulle du förstå de följande begreppen i sammanhang med vården: Kund, konsument, patient, brukare och medborgare?
- Även om det finns exempel på medverkan från allmänheten—såsom t. ex. medborgarråd, medborgarjurys, samråd—förefaller tyngdpunkten ligga på brukarnas synpunkter.

  I flera länder anses brukarmedverkan ensidigt gynna vårdens brukarna medan intressena av de bidrags-/skattebetalarna som är nettobetalare inte tillräckligt tillgodoses. Detta kan—så låter argumentet—leda till ett uppblåst hälso- och sjukvårdssystem därför att medicinska tjänster levereras som inte kan rättfärdigas på enbart samhällspolitiska/ekonomiska grunder. Hur ser du på detta?
- Vid sidan om individuella patienträttigheter och vid sidan om en generell medverkan har såväl Nederländerna som England infört medverkan av såväl brukare av vård och medborgare på vårdutförarnivå, dvs. t. ex. i sjukhus och vårdhem. Här handlar det inte om stora beslut utan om rent praktiska, men för patienterna/brukarna viktiga vardagsangelägenheter såsom en bättre bussförbindelse, mat, inredning, upprustning eller nedskärning av avdelningar osv. Det är framför allt råd av lokala patienter/brukare eller deras anhöriga som har samråd med sjukhusets eller hemmets ledning.

  Skulle det kunna fungera i Sverige?
- Hur ser framtidens brukarmedverkan ut i Östergötland?

### *A.4.2 Interview Guideline: Patient Organisations*

- För att få en bättre förståelse: Kan du berätta lite om *organisation's name*?
- Vilka möjligheter att medverka och/eller utöva inflytande finns inom vården i landstinget (vård ska förstås här i bred betydelse: främst hälso- och sjukvård men även t. ex. äldrevård eller psykvård (även om jag vet att det egentligen är kommunernas ansvarsområde))?
- Vilka aktörer är inblandade? Har det förekommit krav från medborgarnas eller patientorganisationernas sida på större inflytande inom vården?
- Vad tycker du vilken mening karakteriserar brukarmedverkan bäst: Det...

  - ...är en bra möjlighet att informera medborgarna om vad som försiggår inom hälso- och sjukvården och vilka förändringar planeras.

  - ... är bra för att diskutera sjukvårdsrelaterade ämnen mellan politiker och medborgar.
  - ... ger medborgarna inflytande över hur vården utformas.

- Om man ser på t. ex. individuell valfrihet och inflytande på vårdgivare så är patientinflytande och brukarmedverkan en förhållandevis sen företeelse i Sverige. Vad tror du är anledningen till detta?
- Vad har förändrats under tiden att man ansåg att nya former är nödvändiga? Vem var den drivande kraften bakom förändringarna?

---

For the region Skåne some additional questions were put at this point (within horizontal lines):

- I Skåne fanns det så kallade Centrala patient- och handikapprådet, dessförinnan brukarrådet.
  - Vilka befogenheter hade de?
  - Hur var deras rol tänkt?
  - Vilka teman var det som främst blev diskuterade?
  - Vad var anledningen till att avskaffa och ersätta dem med nya organ?
- Vilken rol spelade medborgardialogen inom hälso- och sjukvårdsområdet?

---

- Hur bra fungerar samverkan mellan den landstingsdrivna vården och kommunal/närvården? Hur bidrar patienter/brukare faktiskt till en förbättring? Hur stor potential ser du här?
- Hur skulle du förstå de följande begreppen i sammanhang med vården: Kund, konsument, patient, brukare och medborgare?
- Även om det finns exempel på medverkan från allmänheten—såsom t. ex. medborgarråd, medborgarjurys, samråd—förefaller tyngdpunkten ligga på brukarnas synpunkter.

  I flera länder anses brukarmedverkan ensidigt gynna vårdens brukarna medan intressena av de bidrags-/skattebetalarna som är nettobetalare inte tillräckligt tillgodoses. Detta kan—så låter argumentet—leda till ett uppblåst hälso- och sjukvårdssystem därför att medicinska tjänster levereras som inte kan rättfärdigas på enbart samhällspolitiska/ekonomiska grunder. Hur ser du på detta?
- Vid sidan om individuella patienträttigheter och vid sidan om en generell medverkan har såväl Nederländerna som England infört medverkan av såväl brukare av vård och medborgare på vårdutförarnivå, dvs. t. ex. i sjukhus och vårdhem. Här handlar det inte om stora beslut utan om rent praktiska, men för patienterna/brukarna viktiga vardagsangelägenheter såsom en bättre bussförbindelse, mat, inredning, upprustning eller nedskärning av avdelningar osv. Det är framför allt råd av lokala patienter/brukare eller deras anhöriga som har samråd med sjukhusets eller hemmets ledning.

  Skulle det kunna fungera i Sverige?
- Om du hade tre önskemål: Hur skulle framtidens brukarmedverkan i Skåne se ut?

# Appendix B
# Appendix: Additional Material

## B.1 The Netherlands

### *B.1.1 Topics Under Discussion During the Legislation Process of the WMCZ*

The following points are an attempt to summarise the essence under discussion during the parliamentary debate of the WMCZ (based on Tweede Kamer der Staten-Generaal 1992—1993, 1994a,b,c; 'Wet medezeggenschap cliënten zorginstellingen' 1996; for a more encompassing description cf. van der Voet 2005).

CLIENT COUNCILS VS. PATIENT PLATFORMS—This point raised the question whether a council staffed by patient organisations would not be the better option for specific institutions such as hospitals. This was sometimes intermingled with the question as to whether or not a central council of clients could yield better results and would be more practical in governance terms than the proposed council per (health-)care unit and perhaps central one on top.

COSTS—Members of several parties doubted whether the necessary costs would actually be as insignificant as suggested by the government. The argument was employed against the bill by many rather conservative parties—additional costs should be avoided and therefore the bill should not pass—or in order to demand higher financial support for involvement from the government by the more leftist and social liberal actors.

DOUBTS ABOUT THE NECESSITY OF THE ACT—Doubts were raised concerning whether legal regulation would still be necessary as so many councils of clients/residents had already been established on a voluntary basis. As the act was planned as a minimum act in order to fit all (health-)care sectors, it was feared that for many institutions the act would constitute a regress. The position was shared by a number of parties. In addition, the understanding of the role of the state had changed towards propagating a considerably less prominent role, which



A. Haarmann, *The Evolution and Everyday Practice of Collective Patient Involvement in Europe*, DOI 10.1007/978-3-319-64595-7

is officially expressed in the green paper 'Legislation' (Nota Zicht op wetgeving; Tweede Kamer der Staten-Generaal 1991; cf. also Groenewegen 1998, p. 295; van der Voet 2005, pp. 30–32, 170).

EVALUATION OF THE WMCZ—Several parties suggested an evaluation of the WMCZ in order to assess whether it actually yields the effect it was intended to have. The idea was immediately taken up by the minister.

INCLUSION OF EXTRAMURAL HEALTHCARE—As with its predecessors, it was questioned whether institutions of long-term care and short-term care should be treated equally. The argument was specifically targeted at hospitals and social care (*maatschappelijke opvang*) such as care of homeless and drug addicts, to some minor extent also to home care. As only the treatment, but not the quality of the inner environment of the respective institutions per se influence the everyday quality of life, it was (a) questioned whether the establishment was justified and (b) doubted whether a functioning council could be established.

LIAISON COMMISSION—The task of this commission (*Commissie van vertrouwenslieden*) is to mediate and rule on cases of dissent between the advice of the council of clients and the provider's management. The line of argumentation regarding this commission was similar of the aforementioned point: Would not a sectorwise, central, or provincial mediating commission make more sense than one commission per provider?

LOCAL VERSUS CENTRAL COUNCIL OF CLIENTS—The act stipulates a local council in all provider's units. If the council wishes to delegate certain competences to a central council it is free to do so. The more conservative parties argued that this would impose too great a burden upon care providers and one central council of clients would suffice, whereas the Social Democrats wanted to discuss whether a central council would not be more meaningful depending on the character of the institution.

PROPOSAL OF HEAD OF DEPARTMENT AND ONE MEMBER OF THE SUPERVISORY BOARD—The act stipulates the right of the council of clients to bindingly propose the heads of the care department(s) and one member of the supervisory board of the institutions. This was one of the most heatedly debated points. Whereas PvdA, VVD, and D66 wanted to extend the right to a larger number for the supervisory board and even the board of directors, other parties viewed this too great an interference in the internal affairs of the providers.

RELATION OF THE COUNCIL OF CLIENTS TO WORKS COUNCILS—The relation between the two councils is not clear-cut in the legal text as there is some overlap of competences. It was feared that this situation might give rise to playing off the residents against members of staff. Another strand of argument wondered, why competences and legal enforcement was dealt with so differently, i.e. why the more far-reaching competences laid down in the 'Act on works councils' ('Wet op de ondernemingsraden (WOR)' 1971) should not serve as the rule, though both acts regulate the involvement of a specific group.

RIGHT OF CONSENT—This was the second heatedly discussed point. The act distinguishes between advice that is asked for by the provider and such that is not (*gevraagd en ongevraagd adviesrecht*). This is contrasted to the right of consent (*verzwaard adviesrecht*) on a number of topics. D66, VVD, and GroenLinks pleaded for the extension of topics to be classified under the right of consent, while other parties at the conservative spectrum perceived the list in the bill as too extensive.

WMCZ STRIDES AGAINST THE CONSTITUTION—One of the most severe concerns against the WMCZ was that the obligation of publishing minutes and the binding proposal of a member of the supervisory board were unconstitutional: As most (health-)care providers in the Netherlands are private legal entities, any government interference in their governance would only be acceptable in exceptional cases, for instance, when the public order was endangered. As the public order was not threatened, so ran the argument, the act would be unconstitutional.

### *B.1.2 Extended Right of Consent in the WMCZ*

"§ 3, 1 In any case, the provider of care gives the client council the opportunity to advise on each taken decision that concerns the institution in the following matters:

a. an alteration of the objective or the fundamental values;
b. the devolution of participation or merger or the initiation or discontinuation of a long-term collaboration with another institution;
c. the complete or partial abolition of the institution, relocation, or substantial conversion;
d. a substantial alteration in the organisation;
e. a substantial diminution, extension, or other change of the services;
f. the appointment of personnel, who immediately shall exert the decisive power in leading the work of the institution;
g. the budget and the annual report;
h. the general policy regarding the admission of clients and the termination of provision of care for clients;
i. matters of food of general kind and the general policy in the field of security, health or hygiene, and spiritual provision [religious services], societal support and spare time, and recreational activities for clients;
j. the systematic monitoring, surveillance, and improvement of the quality of the care provided to clients;
k. the issuing or alteration of a regulation concerning the handling of clients' complaints and the instruction of personnel, who are entrusted with the handling of such complaints;

   [...]

m. entrusting personnel with leading a section of the institution where care is provided for clients by day, who as a general rule remain in the institution on a long-term basis."

('Wet medezeggenschap cliënten zorginstellingen' 1996; author's translation)

## B.2 England

### *B.2.1 Main Points of the NHS Constitution*

- Access
- Quality of care and environment
- Nationally approved treatments, drugs, and programmes
- Respect, consent, and confidentiality
- Informed choice
- Involvement in your healthcare and in the NHS

  "You have the right to be involved in discussions and decisions about your healthcare, and to be given information to enable you to do this." (Department of Health 2010a, section 2a; cf. also Department of Health 2010b, p. 54)
- Complaint and redress

(Department of Health 2010b)

## B.3 Germany

### *B.3.1 Federal State Acts on User Involvement Within Long-Term Care*

| Federal state | Name of act | Effective since |
|---|---|---|
| Baden-Württemberg | Landesheimgesetz für Baden-Württemberg | July 2008 |
| Bayern | Gesetz zur Regelung der Pflege-, Betreuungs- und Wohnqualität im Alter und bei Behinderung (PfleWoqG) | August 2008 |
| Berlin | Gesetz über Selbstbestimmung und Teilhabe in betreuten gemeinschaftlichen Wohnformen (WTG) | July 2010 |
| Brandenburg | Gesetz über das Wohnen mit Pflege und Betreuung des Landes Brandenburg (BbgPBWoG) | January 2010 |
| Bremen | Bremisches Wohn- und Betreuungsgesetz (BremWoBeG) | October 2010 |
| Hamburg | Hamburgisches Gesetz zur Förderung der Wohn- und Betreuungsqualität älterer, behinderter und auf Betreuung angewiesener Menschen (HmbWBG) | January 2010 |
| Hessen | Hessisches Gesetz über Betreuungs- und Pflegeleistungen (HGBP) | March 2012 |
| Niedersachsen | Niedersächsisches Heimgesetz | July 2011 |

(continued)

| Federal State | Name of Act | effective since |
|---|---|---|
| Mecklenburg-Vorpommern | Gesetz zur Förderung der Qualität in Einrichtungen für Pflegebedürftige und Menschen mit Behinderung sowie zur Stärkung ihrer Selbstbestimmung und Teilhabe—Einrichtungenqualitätsgesetz | May 2010 |
| Nordrhein-Westfalen | Gesetz zur Umsetzung der Föderalismusreform auf dem Gebiet des Heimrechts und zur Änderung von Landesrecht/Wohn- und Teilhabegesetz<br>including: Gesetz über das Wohnen mit Assistenz und Pflege in Einrichtungen (Wohn- und Teilhabegesetz—WTG) | December 2008 |
| Rheinland-Pfalz | Landesgesetz über Wohnformen und Teilhabe | January 2010 |
| Saarland | Landesheimgesetz Saarland (LHeimGS) | June 2009 |
| Sachsen | Betreuungs- und Wohnqualitätsgesetz | July 2012 |
| Sachsen-Anhalt | Gesetz über Wohnformen und Teilhabe des Landes Sachsen-Anhalt (WTG LSA) | February 2011 |
| Schleswig-Holstein | Gesetz zur Stärkung von Selbstbestimmung und Schutz von Menschen mit Pflegebedarf oder Behinderung (SbStG) | August 2009 |
| Thüringen | Thüringer Gesetz über betreute Wohnformen und Teilhabe | July 2014 |

Source: own compilation

# B.4 Sweden

## *B.4.1 Individual Patient Rights*

"2 a § Healthcare shall be driven in a way that it accomplishes the requirement of good care. That means that it shall particularly

(a) be of good quality with good hygienic standard and satisfy the patient's need of safety in care and treatment,
(b) be easily accessible,
(c) be based on respect for the patient's self-determination and integrity,
(d) further good contacts between the patient and healthcare staff,
(e) satisfy the patient's need of continuity and safety in healthcare.

The healthcare system and treatment shall as much as possible be shaped and driven in consultation with the patient. Different measures shall be coordinated in an expedient manner.

2 b § The patient shall be given individually adjusted information about

(a) her health condition,
(b) the existing methods for examination, care and treatment,

(c) her possibilities to choose a healthcare provider [“*vårdgivare och utförare*”] within the publicly funded healthcare, as well as
(d) the treatment guarantee [*vårdgarantin*]

6 § [. . . ] The individual patient shall be given influence and co-determination on measures taken to greatest possible extent.” (HSL 1982:763; SFS 1985:560, 1992:567, 1998:1660, 2006:493, 2009:430, 2010:243, 2010:662; author’s translation)

## References

Amtlicher Anzeiger (2011, July 29). *Anordnung des Senats über die Einrichtung von Seniorenvertretungen* Amtl. Anzeiger 1753. Hamburg: Amtlicher Anzeiger.

Bayrischer Landtag (2008, July 3). *Gesetz zur Regelung der Pflege-, Betreuungs- und Wohnqualität im Alter und bei Behinderung (Pflege- und Wohnqualitätgesetz—PfleWoqG)*, Drucksache 15/10997. Bayrischer Landtag.

Bremer Bürgerschaft (2010, October 21). *Gesetz zur Sicherstellung der Rechte von Menschen mit Unterstützungs-, Pflege- und Betreuungsbedarf in unterstützenden Wohnformen (Bremisches Wohn- und Betreuungsgesetz—BremWoBeG)*. Die Senatorin für Arbeit, Frauen, Gesundheit, Jugend und Soziales. Freie Hansestadt Bremen

Department of Health. (2010a, March). *The NHS constitution—the NHS belongs to us all*. London: Department of Health

Department of Health. (2010b, March). *The NHS handbook to the NHS constitution for England*. London: Department of Health

Gesetz- und Verordnungsblatt Berlin. (2010, June 3). *Gesetz über Selbstbestimmung und Teilhabe in betreuten gemeinschaftlichen Wohnformen (Wohnteilhabegesetz—WTG)*. GVBl. S. 285. Gesetz- und Verordnungsblatt Berlin.

Gesetz- und Verordnungsblatt Brandenburg. (2009, July 8). *Gesetz über das Wohnen mit Pflege und Betreuung des Landes Brandenburg (Brandenburgisches Pflege- und Betreuungswohngesetz—BbgPBWoG*. GVBl. I/09, [Nr. 13] S. 298. Gesetz- und Verordnungsblatt.

Gesetz- und Verordnungsblatt für das Land Rheinland-Pfalz. (2009, December 22). *Landesgesetz über Wohnformen und Teilhabe (LWTG)*. Gesetz- und Verordnungsblatt für das Land Rheinland-Pfalz, Nr. 20. Gesetz- und Verordnungsblatt für das Land Rheinland-Pfalz.

Gesetz- und Verordnungsblatt Mecklenburg-Vorpommern. (2010, May 17). *Gesetz zur Förderung der Qualität in Einrichtungen für Pflegebedürftige und Menschen mit Behinderung sowie zur Stärkung ihrer Selbstbestimmung und Teilhabe (Einrichtungenqualitätsgesetz—EQG M-V* GVOBl. M-V 2010, S. 241. GVOBl. M-V 2010, S. 241.

Gesetz- und Verordnungsblatt Sachsen-Anhalt. (2011, February 17). *Gesetz über Wohnformen und Teilhabe des Landes Sachsen-Anhalt (Wohn- und Teilhabegesetz—WTG LSA)*. GVBl. LSA 2011, 136. GVBl. LSA 2011, 136.

Gesetzblatt Baden-Württemberg. (2008, June 10). *Heimgesetz für Baden-Württemberg (Landesheimgesetz—LHeimG*. GBl. S. 404. Gesetzblatt.

Gesetzblatt Baden-Württemberg. (2010, March 30). *Verordnung des Ministeriums für Arbeit und Sozialordnung Familien und Senioren über die Mitwirkung der Bewohner in Angelegenheiten des Heimbetriebs in Baden-Württemberg (Landesheimmitwirkungsverordnung—LHeimMitVO)*. GBl. S. 169. Gesetzblatt.

Gesetzessammlung Mecklenburg-Vorpommern. (2010, November 10). *Verordnung über die Mitwirkung von Menschen mit Pflege- und Betreuungsbedarf in Einrichtungen bei der Gestal- tung der ihnen angebotenen Leistungen (Einrichtungenmitwirkungsverordnung—EMitwVO MV)*. GS Meckl.-Vorp. Gl. Nr. 860 - 13 - 3. GS Meckl.-Vorp. Gl. Nr. 860 - 13 - 3.

Groenewegen, P. P. (1998). Besluitvorming in de gezondheidszorg op macroniveau. In C. W. Aakster & J. W. Groothoff (Eds.), *Medische sociologie—Sociologische perpectieven op ziekte en zorg* (5th ed., Chap. 2, pp. 295–302). Groningen: Wolters-Noordhoff.
Hamburger Gesetz- und Verordnungsblatt. (2009, December 15). *Hamburgisches Gesetz zur Förderung der Wohn- und Betreuungsqualität älterer behinderter und auf Betreuung angewiesener Menschen (Hamburgisches Wohn- und Betreuungsqualitätsgesetz—HmbWBG)* HmBGVBl. Nr. 56. Hamburger Gesetz- und Verordnungsblatt.
Hessisches Gesetz- und Verordnungsblatt. (2012, March 7). *Hessisches Gesetz über Betreuungs und Pflegeleistungen (HGBP)*. GVBl. 2012, 34. Gesetzes- und Verordnungsblatt.
HSL. (1982:763). *Hälso- och Sjukvårdslagen (HSL)*. SFS1982:763. Stockholm: Socialdepartmentet.
Landtag NRW. (2008, November 18). *Gesetz über das Wohnen mit Assistenz und Pflege in Einrichtungen (Wohn- und Teilhabegesetz—WTG, NRW)*. Landtag NRW.
Ministerin für Soziales, Gesundheit, Familie, Jugend und Senioren Schleswig-Holstein. (2009, July 17). *Gesetz zur Stärkung von Selbstbestimmung und Schutz von Menschen mit Pflegebedarf oder Behinderung (Selbstbestimmungsstärkungsgesetz—SbStG)*. Ministerin für Soziales, Gesundheit, Familie, Jugend und Senioren Schleswig-Holstein.
Niedersächsisches Gesetz- und Verordnungsblatt. (2011, June 29). *Niedersächsisches Heimgesetz (NHeimG)*. Nds. GVBl. 2011, 196. Nds. GVBl. 2011, 196.
Saarländisches Amtsblatt. (2009, May 6). *Saarländisches Gesetz zur Sicherung der Wohn-, Betreuungs- und Pflegequalität für ältere Menschen sowie pflegebedürftige und behinderte Volljährige (Landesheimgesetz Saarland—LHeimGS)*. Amtsblatt 2009, S. 906. Amtsblatt 2009, S. 906.
Sächsisches Gesetz- und Verordnungsblatt. (2012). *Gesetz zur Regelung der Betreuungs- und Wohnqualität im Alter bei Behinderung und Pflegebedürftigkeit im Freistaat Sachsen (Sächsisches Betreuungs- und Wohnqualitätsgesetz—SächsBeWoG)*.
SFS. (2010:243). *Lag om ändring i hälso- och sjukvårdslagen*. Socialdepartmentet.
SFS. (2010:662). *Lag om ändring i hälso- och sjukvårdslagen*. Socialdepartmentet.
SFS. (2009:430). *Lag om ändring i hälso- och sjukvårdslagen*. Socialdepartmentet.
SFS. (2006:493). *Lag om ändring i hälso- och sjukvårdslagen*. Socialdepartmentet.
SFS. (1985:560). *Lag om ändring i hälso- och sjukvårdslagen*. SFS1985:560. Socialdepartmentet.
SFS. (1992:567). *Lag om ändring i hälso- och sjukvårdslagen*. SFS1985:560. Socialdepartmentet.
SFS. (1998:1660). *Lag om ändring i hälso- och sjukvårdslagen*. Socialdepartmentet.
Thüringer Gesetz- und Verordnungsblatt. (2014, June 10). *Thüringer Gesetz über betreute Wohnformen und Teilhabe Thüringer Wohn- und Teilhabegesetz—ThürWTG)*. GVBl. 2014, 161. Gesetz- und Verordnungsblatt.
Tweede Kamer der Staten-Generaal. (1992—1993). In H. Ancona & H. Simons (Eds.) *Wetsvoorstel van Regels ter bevordering van de medezeggenschap van de cliënten van uit collectieve middelen gefinancierde instellingen op het terrein van de maatschappelijke zorg en gezondheidszorg (Wet medezeggenschap cliënten zorginstellingen)—Oorspronkelijke tekst van het voorstel van wet en van de memorie van toelichting zoals voorgelegd aan de Raad van Staate en voor zover nadien gewijzigd*
Tweede Kamer der Staten-Generaal. (1991). *Nota—Zicht op wetgeving*. 's Gravenhage: SDU Uitgeverij.
Tweede Kamer der Staten-Generaal. (1994a, September 6). *Notulen Tweede Kamer der Staten-Generaal—88ste vergadering 6 september 1994, Aanvang 14.00 uur*. 's Gravenhage.
Tweede Kamer der Staten-Generaal. (1994b, September 7). *Notulen Tweede Kamer der Staten-Generaal—89ste vergadering 7 september 1994, Aanvang 13.00 uur*. 's Gravenhage.
Tweede Kamer der Staten-Generaal. (1994c, January 6). In H. Ancona & H. Simons (Eds.), *Regels ter bevordering van de medezeggenschap van clieänten vanuit collectieve middelen gefinancierde zorgaanbieders op het terrein van de maatschappelijke zorg en gezondheidszorg (Wet medezeggenschap cliënten zorginstellingen)—Memorie van antwoord*. 's Gravenhage
van der Voet, G. W. (2005). *De kwaliteit van de WMCZ als medezeggenschapswet* (Doctoral dissertation, Rotterdam, PhD-Thesis).

Wet op de ondernemingsraden (WOR). (1971, February 18). *Ministerie van Justitie.*

Wet medezeggenschap cliënten zorginstellingen. (1996). *Wet van 29 februari 1996, houdende regels ter bevordering van de medezeggenschap van de cliënten van uit collectieve middelen gefinancierde zorgaanbieders op het terrein van de maatschappelijke zorg en gezondheidszorg (Wet medezeggenschap cliënten zorginstellingen).* 's Gravenhage

MIX
Papier aus verantwortungsvollen Quellen
Paper from responsible sources
FSC® C105338

If you have any concerns about our products,
you can contact us on
**ProductSafety@springernature.com**

In case Publisher is established outside the EU,
the EU authorized representative is:
**Springer Nature Customer Service Center GmbH**
**Europaplatz 3, 69115 Heidelberg, Germany**

Printed by Libri Plureos GmbH
in Hamburg, Germany